# Contents

**Coffee and cakes**
colour section
following p.272

**The Secession**
colour section
following p.112

Michaeler-
kirche
SCHAUFLER-
PLATZ        **Colour maps**
             following p.368
Hofburg

◀◀ View over Michaelerplatz ◀ Neues Rathaus

## Introduction to

# Vienna

**Most people visit Vienna with a vivid image of the city in their minds: a monumental vision of Habsburg palaces, trotting white horses, old ladies in fur coats and mountains of fat cream cakes. And they're unlikely to be disappointed. Vienna positively feeds off imperial nostalgia – High Baroque churches and aristocratic piles pepper the old town, or Innere Stadt, monumental projects from the late nineteenth century line the Ringstrasse, and postcards of the Emperor Franz-Josef and his beautiful wife "Sisi" still sell by the sackful.**

Just as compelling as the old Habsburg stand-bys are the wonderful Jugendstil and early modernist buildings, products of fin-de-siècle Vienna, when the city emerged as one of Europe's great cultural centres. This was the era of Freud, Klimt, Schiele, Mahler and Schönberg, when the city's famous coffeehouses were filled with intellectuals from every corner of the empire. In a sense, this was Vienna's golden age, after which all has been in decline: with the end of the empire in 1918, the city was reduced from a metropolis of over two million, capital of a vast empire of fifty million, to one of barely more than one and a half million, federal capital of a small country of just eight million souls.

Given the city's twentieth-century history, it's hardly surprising that the Viennese are as keen as anyone to continue plugging the good old days. This is a place, not unlike Berlin, which has had the misfortune of serving as a weather vane of European history. Modern anti-Semitism as a politically viable force was invented here, in front of Hitler's very eyes, in the first decade of the century. It was the assassination of an arrogant Austrian archduke

The **Rough Guide** to

# Vienna

| Bath & North East Somerset | |
|---|---|
| 1 9 0021547   6 | |
| Askews | 21-Apr-2009 |
| 914.361 | £12.99 |
| | |

written and researched by

## Rob Humphreys

that started World War I, while the battles between Left and Right fought out in the streets of Vienna mirrored those in Berlin in the 1930s. The weekend Hitler enjoyed his greatest electoral victory in the Reichstag was the day the Austrians themselves

▲ MuseumsQuartier

invented Austro-fascism. In 1938, the country became the first "victim" of Nazi expansion, greeting the Führer with delirious enthusiasm. And after the war, for a decade, Vienna was divided, like Berlin, into French, American, British and Soviet sectors.

The visual scars from this turbulent history are few and far between – even Hitler's sinister concrete Flaktürme are confined to the suburbs – but the destruction of the city's once enormous Jewish community is a wound that has proved harder to heal. Vienna's Jewish intellectuals and capitalists were the driving force behind much of the city's fin-de-siècle culture. Little surprise then, that the city has since struggled to live up to its glorious past achievements. After the war Vienna lost its cosmopolitan character and found itself stuck in a monocultural straightjacket. Since the end of the Cold War, however, this has begun to change, with the arrival

▲ Majolikahaus

▼ Marble Hall, Kunsthistorisches Museum

of a second wave of immigrants from the former provinces of the old empire. How Vienna will learn to accept its new, multicultural identity remains to be seen.

For all its problems, Vienna is still an inspiring city to visit, with one of the world's greatest art collections in the Kunsthistorisches Museum, world-class orchestras, and a superb architectural heritage. It's also an eminently civilized

▲ Mozart monument

place, clean, safe (for the most part) and peopled by a courteous population who do their best to live up to their reputation for *Gemütlichkeit* or "cosiness". And despite its ageing population, it's also a city with a small, but lively, nightlife of cool cafés, clubs and drinking holes. Even Vienna's traditional restaurants, long famous for quantity over quality, have begun to overhaul their methods of cooking and presentation, although these are supplemented by a wonderful residue of reassuringly old-fashioned *Kaffeehäuser*, where the fin-de-siècle city is lovingly preserved in aspic.

# What to see

For all its grandiosity, Vienna is a surprisingly compact city: the centre is just a kilometre across at its broadest point, and you can travel from one side of the city to the other by public transport in less than thirty minutes. This means you can get to see a lot of the city in a relatively short space of time.

The most obvious place to start is in Vienna's central district, the old medieval town or **Innere Stadt** (literally the "inner town"). Retaining much of its labyrinthine street layout, it remains the city's main commercial district, packed with shops, cafés and restaurants. The chief sight here is Stephansdom, Vienna's landmark cathedral and its finest Gothic edifice, standing at the district's pedestrianized centre. Tucked into the southwest corner of the Innere Stadt is the **Hofburg**, the former imperial palace and seat of the Habsburgs, now home to a whole host of museums.

When the old fortifications surrounding the Innere Stadt were torn down in 1857, they were gradually replaced by a showpiece boulevard called the **Ringstrasse**. It is this irregular pentagon-shaped thoroughfare that, along with the Danube Canal, encloses the Innere Stadt. Nowadays the Ringstrasse is used and abused by traffic as a ring road, though it's still punctuated with the most grandiose public buildings of late-imperial Vienna: the parliament, town hall, opera house and university and several museums, including the city's fabulous new arts complex, the MuseumsQuartier, and the Kunsthistorisches Museum, home to one of the world's finest art collections.

Beyond the Ringstrasse lie Vienna's seven inner suburbs, the **Vorstädte**, whose outer boundary

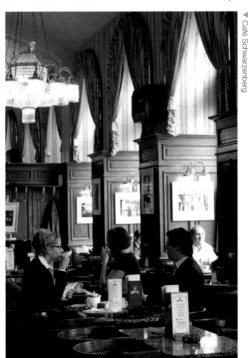

▼ Café Schwarzenberg

## Public transport

If there's one thing every visitor would like to take home with them from Vienna, it's the public transport system, which is one of the most efficient in the world. The U-Bahn is clean and constantly expanding, the trams are silent and smooth, and, even more remarkably, the buses run on schedule, to a timetable. Imagine: you go to a bus stop, look up the time of the next bus, and it arrives when it says it will. Simple, you might think, but just a dream for many of the world's urban commuters. The funkiest of the **U-Bahn** lines is the spanking new U3; the most aesthetically pleasing is the U6, which has lots of original Jugendstil stations designed by Otto Wagner. On the **trams**, take the #1 or #2 for a (clockwise or anticlockwise) free tour of the Ringstrasse. Best of all, though, is **bus** #2a, which winds its way through the impossibly narrow streets of the Innere Stadt and finally through the courtyards of the Hofburg itself. For the privilege of using this system, the Viennese pay just €14 a week, less than half of what commuters in London have to spend. And the whole system runs on trust. At least once a month, you're likely to be stopped by an inspector, and with the fines high and the ticket prices low, you'd be a fool to get caught.

is comprised of the traffic-clogged *Gürtel* (literally "belt") or ring road. If you're travelling on any kind of budget, you're likely to find yourself staying somewhere out in the Vorstädte. The highlight here is the **Belvedere**, to the south of the Innere Stadt, where you can see a wealth of paintings by Austria's trio of modern artists, Egon Schiele, Gustav Klimt and Oskar Kokoschka.

Although the Danube is crucial to Vienna's identity, most visitors see very little of the river, whose main arm flows through the outer suburbs

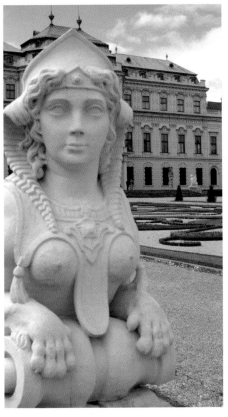

to the northeast of the city centre. In fact, east of the Danube Canal, only the **Prater**, with its famous Ferris wheel and funfair, is essential viewing.

There's little reason, either, to venture beyond the *Gürtel* into the outer suburbs, except to visit **Schönbrunn**, the Habsburgs' former summer residence, a masterpiece of Rococo excess and an absolute must if only for the wonderful gardens. The hilly woodland paths of the **Wienerwald**, on the northwestern edge of the city, have been a popular rural retreat for the Viennese since the days of Beethoven and Schubert, who gained inspiration from their vine-backed slopes. Both composers now lie – along with thousands of other Viennese – at the opposite end of the city, in the far southeast corner, in the city's fascinating **Zentralfriedhof** (Central Cemetery).

When it comes to **day-trips**, there's scope for further excursions into the Wienerwald, to the old imperial spa town of Baden, or to the court of the Esterházys at Eisenstadt; or up the Danube to the spectacular monasteries of Klosterneuburg and Melk, to Tulln, the birthplace of Egon Schiele, or to the medieval, wine-producing town of Krems. All the above can be easily reached from Vienna within an hour by public transport.

Immervoll beisl ►

▼ Shoppers at Kohlmarkt

# When to go

ying at the centre of Europe, Vienna experiences the extremes of temperature typical of a continental climate, with hot summers and correspondingly cold winters. In terms of weather, therefore, late spring and early autumn are by far the best times to visit. There are other reasons, too, for avoiding July and August in particular, as this is when many of the city's theatres and concert halls close down. Sure, there's enough cultural activity to keep the tourists amused, but the Viennese tend to get the hell out. In contrast, Christmas and New Year are peak season in Vienna. Not only does the city look great in the snow – and you can be sure that the Viennese are very efficient about keeping the paths clear – but also the ball season, known as *Fasching*, gets under way, along with the glittering Christmas markets and, of course, the world-famous New Year's Day concert.

# 20

## things not to miss

*It's not possible to see everything that Vienna has to offer on a short trip – and we don't suggest you try. What follows is therefore a subjective selection of the city's highlights, from the showpiece museums and churches to its relaxed cafés, tranquil parks and appealing day-trip destinations – all arranged in five colour-coded categories to help you find the very best things to see, do and experience. All entries have a page reference to take you straight into the guide, where you can find out more.*

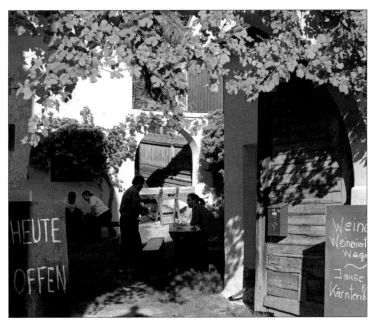

**01** **Heurigen** Page **277** • Sitting in an orchard surrounded by vineyards, overlooking the city, sipping the local wine, is one of the pleasures of a Viennese summer.

**02** **Prater** Page **180** • With its iconic Ferris wheel and old-fashioned funfair, the Prater is probably the best reason to venture east of the Danube Canal.

**03** **Kirche am Steinhof**
Page **211** • Otto Wagner's Jugendstil masterpiece is a magnificent domed church built for the inmates of the local psychiatric hospital.

**04** **The Third Man** Page **123** • This classic black-and-white film was shot amidst the rubble of postwar Vienna – it's shown every weekend in one of the city's cinemas, guided tours take place weekly and there's even a museum.

**05** **Karlskirche** Page **121** • Quite simply the most spectacular Baroque church in the capital, inside and out.

**06 Schönbrunn** Page **191** • By far the most magnificent of the Habsburgs' many palaces, Schönbrunn also boasts the most wonderful gardens, woods, fountains, mazes, hothouses and zoo.

**08 Trześniewski** Page **263** • Minimalist snack bar, presided over by formidable assistants, serving tiny *Brötchen* washed down with a *Pfiff* – a city institution.

**07 Stephansdom** Page **42** • The undisputed heart of Vienna, the city's cathedral features some superb medieval craftsmanship, extensive catacombs and a couple of great viewpoints from its twin towers.

**09 Opera** Page **286** • Vienna boasts one of the world's top opera houses, and also one of its most democratic, with standing-room tickets for as little as €2.

**10 Kunsthistorisches Museum** Page **132** • A spectacular late nineteenth-century building housing one of the world's greatest art collections, famous above all for its Breughels.

**12 Zentralfriedhof** Page **222** • One of the world's most awesome municipal cemeteries, with over two and a half million corpses, including Beethoven, Schubert, Brahms, Schönberg and the entire Strauss family.

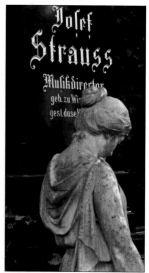

**11 Fiakers** Page **26** • In a place so steeped in nostalgia, it would be churlish not to have a ride in a Fiaker.

**13 Schatzkammer** Page **83** •
The imperial family may have gone, but their hoard of crown jewels is full of absolute gems.

**15 MuseumsQuartier** Page **111** • Vienna's newest arts complex houses an orgy of works by Schiele, the city's chief modern art museum, and a host of funky cafés and bars.

**14 Belvedere** Page **152** • Twin Baroque palaces separated by formal gardens and a great collection of works by Klimt, Schiele and Kokoschka.

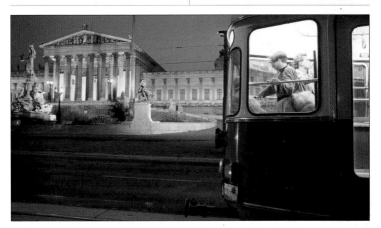

**16 Tram round the Ringstrasse** Page **103** • For a free sightseeing tour of the Ringstrasse, just hop on tram #1 or #2 and start reading Chapter 3.

**17 Naschmarkt** Page 123 • Genuinely multiethnic outdoor food market, with a great flea market on Saturdays.

**19 Melk** Page 245 • Perched on a woody bluff overlooking the Danube, Melk's Baroque monastery is one of the country's most rewarding to visit.

**18 Secession** Page 119 • This remarkable Jugendstil art gallery still puts on contemporary art shows, as well as preserving Klimt's original fresco from the 1902 exhibition.

**20 Kaffeehäuser** Page 261 and *Coffee and cakes colour section* • With their tuxedoed waiters, calorific cakes, copious newspapers and unhurried air, Vienna's *Kaffeehäuser* are the city's most important and enduring social institutions.

# Basics

# Basics

# Getting there

Unless you're coming from a neighbouring European country, the quickest way to get to Vienna is by plane. There are direct flights from just about every European capital city, with flight time from London just over two hours. There are also one or two nonstop flights from North America, though you'll get a much wider choice – and often lower fares – if you fly via London or another European gateway.

How much you pay to fly to Vienna depends on the season, with the highest fares charged from Easter to October, and around Christmas and New Year. Alternatively, with budget airlines, the earlier you book, the cheaper the prices. Most people now book their flights online, and good deals can often be found through discount or auction sites, as well as through the airlines' own websites.

Another option, if you're travelling from Britain or elsewhere in Europe, is to go by train, bus or car – this will take considerably longer than the plane and may not work out that much cheaper, but it's an eminently civilized way of travelling and is undoubtedly better for the environment. For more details, see p.20.

## Flights from Britain and Ireland

You can fly to Vienna direct from London and Dublin. The most competitive fares are with the budget airlines, though the national airlines, British Airways (BA) and Austrian Airlines, have had to slash their prices accordingly. If you book far enough in advance or can be flexible about your dates, you can get return fares from London to Vienna for as little as £50 (taxes included). From Ireland, return airfares start at around €90 return from Dublin. Of course, if you don't book early, prices can skyrocket. If you can't find a cheap fare to Vienna, it's worth considering flying to **Bratislava**, the Slovak capital, which is less than 50km east of the city (and linked via a shuttle bus), and is served by a wider range of budget flights. Since routes can change – and airlines can go under – with little notice, it's best to check the airport websites for the latest.

## Flights from the US and Canada

Austrian Airlines and Air Transat offer nonstop flights from North America to Vienna. You'll get a much wider choice of flights and ticket prices, though, if you opt for an indirect flight and one or two changes of plane, allowing you to depart from any number of North American cities and travel via one of the major gateways.

Flying time from the east coast to Vienna is about nine hours. **Fares** depend very much on the flexibility of the ticket and on availability, with a New York–Vienna return costing $700 and upwards, and a Toronto–Vienna return costing C$800 and upwards.

## Flights from Australia and New Zealand

Flight time from **Australia and New Zealand** to Vienna is more than twenty hours, depending on routes and transfer times. There's a wide variety of routes, with those touching down in Southeast Asia the quickest and cheapest on average. Given the length of the journey involved, you might be better off including a night's stopover in your itinerary, and indeed some airlines include one in the price of the flight.

The cheapest direct scheduled flights to London are usually to be found on one of the Asian airlines. Average return **fares** (including taxes) from eastern gateways to London are A$1500–2000 in low season, A$2000–2500 in high season. Fares from Perth or Darwin cost around A$200 less. You'll then need to add A$100–200 onto all these for the connecting flight to Vienna. Return fares from Auckland to London range between NZ$2000 and NZ$3000 depending on the season, route and carrier.

## Fly less – stay longer! Travel and climate change

Climate change is the single biggest issue facing our planet. It is caused by a build-up in the atmosphere of carbon dioxide and other greenhouse gases, which are emitted by many sources – including planes. Already, flights account for around 3–4 percent of human-induced global warming: that figure may sound small, but it is rising year on year and threatens to counteract the progress made by reducing greenhouse emissions in other areas.

Rough Guides regard travel, overall, as a global benefit, and feel strongly that the advantages to developing economies are important, as are the opportunities for greater contact and awareness among peoples. But we all have a responsibility to limit our personal "carbon footprint". That means giving thought to how often we fly and what we can do to redress the harm our trips create.

### Flying and climate change

Pretty much every form of motorized travel generates $CO_2$, but planes are particularly bad offenders, releasing large volumes of greenhouse gases at altitudes where their impact is far more harmful. Flying also allows us to travel much further than we would contemplate doing by road or rail, so the emissions attributable to each passenger become truly shocking. For example, one person taking a return flight between Europe and California produces the equivalent impact of 2.5 tonnes of $CO_2$ – similar to the yearly output of the average UK car.

Less harmful planes may evolve but it will be decades before they replace the current fleet – which could be too late for avoiding climate chaos. In the meantime, there are limited options for concerned travellers: to reduce the amount we travel by air (take fewer trips, stay longer!), to avoid night flights (when plane contrails trap heat from Earth but can't reflect sunlight back to space), and to make the trips we do take "climate neutral" via a carbon offset scheme.

### Carbon offset schemes

Offset schemes run by **climatecare.org**, **carbonneutral.com** and others allow you to "neutralize" the greenhouse gases you are responsible for releasing. Their websites have simple calculators that let you work out the impact of any flight. Once that's done, you can pay to fund projects that will reduce future carbon emissions by an equivalent amount (such as the distribution of low-energy light bulbs and cooking stoves in developing countries). Please take the time to visit our website and make your trip climate neutral.

ⓦ**www.roughguides.com/climatechange**

## Trains

Travelling **by train** is a pleasantly old-fashioned and extremely leisurely way to reach Vienna. You can travel from London overnight in around twenty hours. Fares start at around £200 return but depend on the route you take and how far in advance you book your ticket.

There are three possible routes from London to Vienna, all of which require two changes. The cheapest is **via Brussels and Cologne**, with a change in both, and an overnight service from Cologne (Köln) to Vienna. The other two routes are via Paris, changing either in Strasbourg or Munich.

Although you can simply crash out on the seats on the overnight service from Köln to Vienna, it makes sense to pay the extra (which can be as little as £7) for a **couchette**. Couchettes are mixed-sex and allow little privacy; for a little more comfort, you can book a bed in a single-sex two-berth **sleeper** for around £25 extra one way.

**Fares** for continental rail travel are much more flexible than they used to be, so it's worth shopping around for the best deal, rather than taking the first offer you get. Tickets are usually valid for two months and allow as many stopovers as you want on the specified route. If you're travelling with one or more companions, you may be eligible for a further discount.

The cheapest way to book tickets is usually **online**, but you may have to use more than one website – alternatively, you can phone one of the agents listed on p.22.

## Buses

One of the cheapest ways to get to Vienna is **by bus**. Eurolines run a direct service from London's Victoria Coach Station more or less daily. Coaches tend to set off in the morning, arriving in Wien-Mitte/Landstrasse roughly 22 hours later. The trip is bearable (just about), but only really worth it if you absolutely can't find the extra cash for the cheap flight. Fares start at around £75 return, though under-26s and over-60s can get a further discount.

## Driving

With two or more passengers, **driving to Vienna** can work out relatively inexpensive. However, it is not the most relaxing option, unless you enjoy pounding along the motorway systems of Europe for the best part of a day and a night.

**Eurotunnel** operates a 24-hour train service carrying vehicles and their passengers from Folkestone to Calais. At peak times, services run every ten minutes, with the journey lasting 35 minutes. Off-peak fares in the high season start at £150 return (passengers included). The alternative is to catch one of the **ferries** between Dover and Calais, Boulogne or Dunkirk. Prices vary enormously but if you book in advance, summer fares can be as little as £70 return per carload. Journey times are usually around ninety minutes. If you're travelling from north of London, however, it might be worth taking one of the longer ferry journeys from Rosyth, Newcastle, Hull or Harwich. To find out the cheapest fares across the Channel, check out ⓦ www.ferrysmart.co.uk.

Once you've made it onto the continent, you've got something in the region of **1200km of driving** ahead of you. For Vienna, the most direct route from Ostend or Calais is via Brussels, Liège (Luik), Cologne (Köln), Frankfurt and Nuremberg (Nürnberg). It costs nothing to drive on motorways in Belgium and Germany, but to go on an Austrian autobahn, you must buy and display a sticker or *Vignette* (available at border crossings and petrol stations); the cheapest version is valid for ten days and costs €7.60. If you're travelling by car you'll need proof of ownership or a letter from the owner giving you permission to drive the vehicle. You also need a country identification sticker, a red warning triangle in case you break down, a first-aid kit (all these are compulsory in Austria), and a "Green Card" for third-party insurance cover at the very least.

## Airlines, agents and operators

### Online booking

ⓦ **www.airfaresflights.com.au** (in Australia)
ⓦ **www.cheapflights.co.uk** (in UK) ⓦ **www .cheapflights.ie** (in Ireland) ⓦ **www .cheapflights.com** (in US) ⓦ **www.cheapflights .ca** (in Canada)
ⓦ **www.cheapo.com** (in UK)
ⓦ **www.expedia.co.uk** (in UK) ⓦ **www.expedia .com** (in US) ⓦ **www.expedia.ca** (in Canada)
ⓦ **www.lastminute.com** (in UK)
ⓦ **www.opodo.co.uk** (in UK)
ⓦ **www.orbitz.com** (in US)
ⓦ **www.travelocity.co.uk** (in UK) ⓦ **www .travelocity.com** (in US) ⓦ **www.travelocity .ca** (in Canada)
ⓦ **www.zuji.com.au** (in Australia) ⓦ **www.zuji .co.nz** (in New Zealand)

### Airports

**Bratislava** ⓦ www.airportbratislava.sk
**Vienna** ⓦ www.viennaairport.com

### Airlines

**Aer Lingus** ☏ 0818/365 000; ⓦ www.aerlingus.com
**Air Canada** Canada ☏ 1-888/247-2262; ⓦ www .aircanada.com
**Air New Zealand** NZ ☏ 0800/737000, Australia ☏ 0800/132 476, Canada ☏ 1-800-663/5494, UK ☏ 0800/028 4149, USA ☏ 1-800-262/1234; ⓦ www.airnz.co.nz
**Air Transat** Canada ☏ 1-866/847-1112; ⓦ www .airtransat.com
**American Airlines** US ☏ 1-800/433-7300; ⓦ www.aa.com
**Asiana Airlines** Australia ☏ 02/9767 4343; ⓦ www.flyasiana.com

**Austrian Airlines** Australia ☏ 1800/642 438 or 02/9251 6155, Canada ☏ 1-888-8174/444, Ireland ☏ 1800/509 142, UK ☏ 0870/124 2625, US ☏ 1-800/843-0002; ☻ www.aua.com
**British Airways** UK ☏ 0870/850 9850, Australia ☏ 1300/767 177, Ireland ☏ 1890/626 747, New Zealand ☏ 09/966 9777, South Africa ☏ 114/418 600, US and Canada ☏ 1-800/AIRWAYS; ☻ www.ba.com
**Cathay Pacific** Australia ☏ 13 17 47, New Zealand ☏ 09/379 0861; ☻ www.cathaypacific.com
**Delta** US and Canada ☏ 1-800/221-1212; ☻ www.delta.com
**easyJet** UK ☏ 0905/821 0905; ☻ www .easyjet.com
**Malaysia Airlines** Australia ☏ 13 26 27, New Zealand ☏ 0800/777 747; ☻ www .malaysia-airlines.com
**Niki** UK ☏ 0870/738 8880; ☻ www.flyniki.com.
**Qantas Airways** Australia ☏ 13 13 13, New Zealand ☏ 0800/808 767 or 09/357 8900; ☻ www.qantas.com
**Ryanair** Ireland ☏ 0818/303 030, UK ☏ 0871/ 246 0000; ☻ www.ryanair.com.
**Singapore Airlines** Australia ☏ 13 10 11, New Zealand ☏ 0800/808 909; ☻ www .singaporeair.com
**SkyEurope** UK ☏ 0905/722 2747; ☻ www .skyeurope.com
**Virgin Atlantic** US ☏ 1-800/821-5438; ☻ www .virgin-atlantic.com

## Agents and operators

**North South Travel** UK ☏ 01245/608 291, ☻ www.northsouthtravel.co.uk. Friendly, competitive travel agency, offering discounted fares worldwide. Profits are used to support projects in the developing world, especially the promotion of sustainable tourism.
**STA Travel** UK ☏ 0870/1630 026, US ☏ 1-800/ 781-4040, Canada ☏ 1-888/427-5639, Australia ☏ 1300/733 035, New Zealand ☏ 0508/782 872, South Africa ☏ 0861/781 781; ☻ www.statravel .com. Worldwide specialists in independent travel; also student IDs, travel insurance, car rental, rail passes, and more. Good discounts for students and under-26s.
**Trailfinders** UK ☏ 0845/058 5858, Ireland ☏ 01/677 7888, Australia ☏ 1300/780 212; ☻ www.trailfinders.com. One of the best-informed and most efficient agents for independent travellers.

## Rail contacts

**Deutsche Bahn** ☏ 0871/880 8066 (Mon–Fri 9am–5pm), ☻ www.bahn.co.uk. Competitive discounted fares for any journey from London across Europe, with very reasonable prices for journeys passing through Germany.
**European Rail** ☏ 020/7387 0444 (Mon–Fri 9am–5pm), ☻ www.europeanrail.com. Rail specialist consistently offering competitive prices on international rail tickets from anywhere in the UK.
**Eurostar** ☏ 08705/186 186 (Mon–Fri 8am–9pm, Sat 8am–8pm & Sun 9am–5pm), ☻ www.eurostar .com. Latest fares and youth discounts (plus online booking) on the Eurostar service, plus competitive add-on fares from the rest of the UK.
**Man in Seat 61** ☻ www.seat61.com. The world's finest train website, full of incredibly useful tips and links for rail travel anywhere in the world.
**National Rail** ☏ 0845/748 4950 (24hr), ☻ www .nationalrail.co.uk. First stop for details of all train travel within the UK – fares, passes, train times and delays due to engineering works.
**Rail Europe** ☏ 08705/848 848 (Mon–Fri 8am–9pm, Sat 9am–6pm & Sun 10am–5pm), ☻ www.raileurope.co.uk. SNCF-owned information and ticket agent for all European passes and journeys from London. They also have an office at 179 Piccadilly, London W1 (Mon–Fri 10am–6pm, Sat 10am–5pm).
**TrainsEurope** ☏ 0871/700 7722 (Mon–Fri 9am–5pm), ☻ www.trainseurope.co.uk. Agent specializing in discounted international rail travel.

## Bus contacts

**Eurolines** UK ☏ 0871/781 8181, ☻ www .eurolines.co.uk; Ireland ☏ 01/836 6111, ☻ www .eurolines.ie. Tickets can also be purchased from any National Express or Bus Éireann agent.

## Ferry contacts

**DFDS Seaways** ☏ 0871/522 9955, ☻ www .dfds.co.uk. Newcastle to Amsterdam.
**Eurotunnel** ☏ 08705/35 35 35, ☻ www .eurotunnel.com. Folkestone to Calais through the tunnel.
**Norfolk Line** ☏ 0870/870 1020, ☻ www .norfolkline-ferries.co.uk. Dover to Dunkirk.
**P&O Stena Line** ☏ 0870/598 0333, ☻ www .poferries.com. Dover to Calais and Hull to Rotterdam and Zeebrugge.
**Sea France** ☏ 0870/571 1711, ☻ www.seafrance .com. Dover to Calais.
**Stena Line** ☏ 0870/570 7070, ☻ www.stenaline .co.uk. Harwich to the Hook of Holland.
**Superfast Ferries** ☏ 0870/234 0870, ☻ www.superfast.com. Rosyth (near Edinburgh) to Zeebrugge.

# Arrival

Vienna is a surprisingly compact city, with a population of just one and a half million, and its airport lies just over 20km southeast of the city centre, with fast connections to get you into town. The international train stations and the main bus terminal are linked to the centre by the fast and efficient U-Bahn (metro) system.

## By air

**Flughafen Wien-Schwechat** (☎7007, ⓦwww.viennaairport.com) is clean and efficient, has a supermarket open daily until late, and a half-decent selection of bars and restaurants. It's connected to the centre by the City Airport Train or **CAT** (daily 5.30am–11.30pm; ⓦwww.cityairporttrain .com); tickets cost €8 and trains leave every thirty minutes, taking sixteen minutes to reach the City Air Terminal at Wien-Mitte (U-Bahn Landstrasse/Wien Mitte). Alternatively, you can catch **S-Bahn** line S7 (daily 4.30am–10pm); trains leave every thirty minutes, taking thirty minutes to reach Wien-Mitte and terminating at Wien-Nord (U-Bahn Praterstern). This is the cheapest way of getting into town, costing €3 one way; however, if you plan to do a bit of travelling when you first arrive, you'll save some money if you ask for a travel pass (*Netzkarte*) for the central zone (see p.24) at the same time. **Vienna Airport Lines buses** from the airport to Schwedenplatz are even more frequent, leaving every twenty minutes (daily 6.20am–midnight); they take around twenty minutes to reach the city centre, and cost €6. There are also buses every thirty minutes to the Südbahnhof and Westbahnhof (see opposite). If you're taking a **taxi** to the centre, opt for an airport taxi rather than a standard one; if you go to C&K Airport Service (☎444 44), for example, they will charge around €28 one way.

## By train and bus

Arriving in Vienna by train from the west, you'll end up at the **Westbahnhof**, five U-Bahn stops west of Stephansplatz in the city centre on the U3 line. Trains from the east, Italy and the Balkans terminate at the **Südbahnhof**, to the south of the city centre; you can either walk five minutes west to U-Bahn Südtiroler Platz, or hop on tram #D, which will take you to the Ringstrasse. Of Vienna's other stations, **Franz-Josefs-Bahnhof**, in the northern suburb of Alsergrund, serves as an arrival point for services from Lower Austria and the odd train from Prague (take tram #D into town), while **Wien-Nord** (U-Bahn Praterstern), in Leopoldstadt, is used exclusively by local and regional trains, including the S-Bahn to the airport. For more on Vienna's international train connections, see p.20.

Since Vienna has no main bus station, your arrival point will depend on which company you're travelling with. Eurolines long-distance buses currently arrive at Erdberg U-Bahn, on the southeastern edge of the city centre. In the unlikely event of your arriving on one of the **DDSG boat services** (ⓦwww.ddsg-blue -danube.at) from Bratislava, you disembark near the city centre by Schwedenplatz. From further up the Danube, or from Budapest, you'll find yourself disembarking at the Schiffahrtszentrum by the Reichsbrücke, some way northeast of the city centre; the nearest station (U-Bahn Vorgartenstrasse) is five minutes' walk away, one block west of Mexikoplatz.

## Arriving in Bratislava

If you're flying to **Bratislava** with one of the budget airlines, a SkyShuttle Bus service (April–Oct) will take you to U-Bahn Erdberg in around eighty minutes; tickets cost €10 one way. There's also a year-round Eurolines coach service, which takes around two hours to reach U-Bahn Südtiroler Platz; tickets cost €11 one way.

# City transport

Vienna's city centre is best explored on foot, but for covering larger distances, you'll need to use the extremely efficient city transport system, known as the *Wiener Linien* (ⓦ www.wienerlinien.at). The trams and buses are punctual and the rapidly expanding U-Bahn (metro) is clean and very quick, and very reasonably priced too.

## Tickets and passes

A single-journey **ticket** (*Fahrschein*), standard for all forms of public transport, costs €1.70 from machines and ticket booths (*Vorverkauf*) at major tram junctions and U-Bahn stations, and also from tobacconists (*Tabak-Trafik*). When you enter the U-Bahn, or board a tram or bus, you must punch (*entwerten*) your ticket in one of the blue machines. You can then make one journey, during which you can change buses, trams or U-Bahn lines as many times as you like, as long as you proceed in a logical direction without any "breaks". If you don't get it together to buy a ticket before boarding a tram or bus, you can buy one for €2.20 from the machines beside the driver – these need not be punched. Tickets for kids aged 6 to 15 cost €0.90; under-6s travel free and under-16s travel free on Sundays, public holidays and during school holidays (you can pick up a calendar at a *Wiener Linien* information office).

If you're planning on making more than two journeys a day, you should invest in a **travel pass** or *Netzkarte*, which allows travel on all trams, buses, U- and S-Bahn trains within the city limits. You can buy a 24-hour ticket (€5.70) or a 72-hour ticket (€13.60) from machines and booths at all U-Bahn stations; when buying your ticket from a machine, select the central zone or *Kernzone* (*Zone 100*), which covers all of Vienna. You must punch your single *Netzkarte* at the

beginning of your first journey – your 24 or 72 hours starts from that point. The Vienna Card/*Wien-Karte* (€18.50) gives various discounts at local attractions as well as being a 72-hour *Netzkarte* (see opposite for more details). The *Wiener Einkaufskarte* (€4.60) is a daily travel pass valid between 8am and 8pm, aimed at shoppers and not available on a Sunday.

Another option is a four-journey **strip ticket** or *Streifenkarte* (€6.80). The card can be used by one or more people – simply punch one strip on the card for each person in the group. To do this you must fold the card over before inserting it in the blue machines, starting with strip 1. Even more useful is the **8-day ticket**, or *8-Tage-Karte* (€27.20), which works like the strip ticket, but is valid for eight (not necessarily consecutive) days' travel, calculated in 24-hour periods from the hour of purchase. It can be used by one person for eight days, two people for four, and so on.

If you're staying in Vienna longer than three days, it might be worth buying a **weekly card** or *Wochenkarte* (€14), available only from coded ticket machines or ticket offices at U-Bahn stations. The pass runs from 9am Monday to 9am the following Monday so there's no need to punch the ticket, and it is transferable (in other words it may be passed on to another person for them to use, but two people travelling

## Travel information offices

There are *Wiener Linien* **information offices** at the following U-Bahn stations: Stephansplatz, Karlsplatz and Westbahnhof (all Mon–Fri 6.30am–6.30pm, Sat & Sun 8.30am–4pm); Erdberg, Floridsdorf, Praterstern, Philadelphiabrücke, Schottentor and Landstrasse (all Mon–Fri 6.30am–6.30pm).

## Vienna Card (Wien-Karte)

The much-touted **Vienna Card** (*Wien-Karte*) costs €18.50, lasts for 72 hours and is perfect if you're on a flying visit to the city. Not only does it give you free travel on the city transport system (worth €13.60 in itself), it also gives you discounts of around 10–20 percent (occasionally more) on most of the city's sights, opera tickets, shops and even taxis. For more information, visit ⓦ www.wienkarte.at.

together need two separate tickets). The **monthly ticket** or *Monatskarte* (€49.50), which runs for a calendar month, works in much the same way.

The Viennese being a law-abiding bunch, there are few **ticket inspectors**, but if you are caught without a valid ticket or pass – known by the politically incorrect term *Schwarzfahren* (black travelling) – you'll be handed an on-the-spot fine of €70 (plus €2.20 for a ticket).

### U-Bahn

Vienna's **U-Bahn**, which opened in 1978, boasts five lines (U1–4 and U6), and is by far the fastest way of getting around the city, with trains running from between 5 and 6am to between midnight and 1am (the times of the first and last trains are posted up at each station). Not all U-Bahn lines are underground: the U4 and U6 lines run partly on the old overground Stadtbahn created in the 1890s, and both lines retain some of their original stations and bridges designed by Otto Wagner. Each line is colour-coded (U1 is purple, U2 red and so on); to figure out which platform you want, look out for the name of the end station in the direction you wish to travel. A U2 extension, from Stadion in the Prater to Aspernstrasse, should be up and running by 2010.

### Trams and buses

Vienna has one of the largest **tram** systems in the world, with more than thirty routes crisscrossing the capital. Electric trams – Strassenbahn or *Bim* (after the noise of the bell) as they're known locally – were introduced in 1897 and most still sport the traditional white-and-red livery. After the U-Bahn, trams are the fastest and most efficient way of getting around, running every five to ten minutes, depending on the time of day. They're pretty punctual, though some

lines don't run on weekends or late at night, so be sure to check the timetables posted at every stop (*Haltestelle*). The final destination of the tram is also indicated by a small sign above the timetable itself.

**Buses** (*Autobusse*) tend to ply the narrow backstreets and the outer suburbs, and despite having to battle with the traffic, are equally punctual. In the heart of the Innere Stadt, where there are no trams and only two U-Bahn stations, there are several very **useful bus services** (Mon–Sat only): #1A, which winds its way from Schottentor to Stubentor; #2A from Schwedenplatz through the Hofburg to U-Bahn Neubaugasse; and #3A from Schottenring to Schwarzenbergplatz. Bus #13A is another useful route as it wends its way through the fourth to the eighth districts of the Vorstädte.

### S-Bahn and Regionalbahn

The **S-Bahn**, or *Schnellbahn* to give it its full name, is of most use to Viennese commuters. It's also the cheapest way of getting to and from the airport, and is useful for day-trips to places like Klosterneuburg, Tulln and Krems. S-Bahn trains are less frequent than U-Bahn trains – running every fifteen to thirty minutes – and are strictly timetabled. The double-decker rolling stock, known as the *Wiesel* (weasel), is air conditioned and a pleasure to ride on. You're even less likely to have to use the suburban railway system or **Regionalbahn**, unless you're heading out to Melk or Eisenstadt; trains leave from the mainline stations.

### Taxis, faxis and night buses

**Taxis** are plentiful and fairly reliable, with the minimum charge around €2, plus €1 if you've gone to a taxi rank and €2 if you've called one up by phone, followed by an extra €1 or so per kilometre or couple of minutes. You can't flag down a taxi, but you can catch a cab at one of the taxi ranks around town, or phone ☎31 300, 40 100 or 60 160. If you want a woman driver, call Ladytaxi (☎60160, ⓦwww.ladytaxi.at). You can, however, hail a bicycle taxi, known as a faxi (☎0699/120 05 624, ⓦwww.faxi,at), which costs €2.50 per kilometre.

The only other way of getting home in the small hours is to catch one of the NightLine **night buses**, which run every thirty minutes from 12.30am to 5am; all 22 routes pass through Schwedenplatz at some point. Tickets are the same as for all other forms of transport and travel passes are valid.

## Bicycles, cars and Fiaker

Despite the fact that **cycling** isn't very popular in Vienna, the city has introduced a system of free bike rental called Citybike (ⓦwww .citybikewien.at). Equipped with a credit card, you can pick up (or drop off) one of the bikes (*Fahrräder*) from fifty different street locations across the city. The bikes are free for the first hour, €1 for the second hour, another €2 for the third and so on. Note that the bike stations are closed in the winter when the weather's bad. You can also rent state-owned bicycles cheaply enough (€10–15 a day) between April and October from Westbahnhof, Südbahnhof, Wien-Nord and Floridsdorf train stations and can return the bikes to a different station. For other bike rental firms,

---

### Guided tours and walks

Vienna Sightseeing Tours (ⓦwww.viennasightseeingtours.com) run a variety of **bus tours** around the city and surrounding districts. The standard city tour (daily: April–Oct 9.45am, 10.45am & 2.45pm; Nov–March 9.45am & 2pm; €35) takes around three and a half hours, though only the summer 10.30am tour and winter 2pm tours have English commentary. They also run a **hop-on hop-off bus** (daily; hourly 9.30am–4.30pm), with running commentary in English and German; tickets cost €20 for a day-ticket.

Alternatively, you can save yourself the commentary by hopping on **tram** #1 or #2, which circumnavigate the Ringstrasse clockwise and anticlockwise respectively. You can also take an hour-long ride on a 1920s tram known as the Oldtimer-Tramway (May–Sept Sat 11.30am & 1.30pm, Sun 9.30am, 11.30am & 1.30pm; €15). Trams leave from beside the Otto Wagner pavilions on Karlsplatz; tickets are available from Karlsplatz U-Bahn.

Most appealing are the **walking tours** organized by Vienna's official tourist guides – you'll find details, such as whether the tours are in German or English, in the monthly *Wiener Spaziergänge* leaflet from the tourist office (ⓦwww.wienguide .at). These cover a relatively small area in much greater detail, mixing historical facts with juicy anecdotes in the company of a local specialist. Subjects covered range from Jugendstil (Art Nouveau) architecture to Jewish Vienna, and the twice-weekly Third Man tour (see p.123). With the exception of the latter, tours cost around €12 and last between one and a half and two hours. Simply turn up at the meeting point specified.

The main company running **boat trips** on the Danube is the DDSG (ⓦwww .ddsg-blue-danube.at). Its **Grosse Donaurundfahrt** (April–Sept 2–5 daily) departs from the Danube Canal beside Schwedenplatz, goes through a lock and calls at the Reichsbrücke on the Danube itself, so you can embark and disembark at either stop. A one-way ticket between the two points costs €16, a return costs €18. Vienna doesn't look its best from the canal or the river, but you will get to see Hundertwasser's Fernwärme or paper incinerator, Otto Wagner's weir and lock at Nussdorf, the Millenniumstower, and, on the way back, the Prater and the Buddhist temple. There's even a Hundertwasser-designed boat, MS *Vinobona*, which sets off for a round-trip cruise (Fri–Sun 2 daily; €12) from the Reichsbrücke (U-Bahn Vorgartenstrasse).

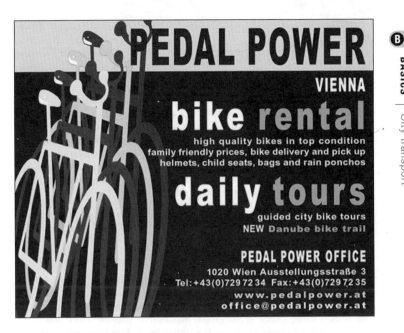
see ⓦwww.wien.gv.at/english. Bicycles can be taken on the U- and S-Bahn from Monday to Friday between 9am and 3pm and after 6.30pm, and on Saturdays and Sundays from 9am. You must buy a half-price ticket for your bike. If you're thinking of taking a day-trip out of Vienna, it's useful to know that you can rent bikes from Klosterneuburg, Tulln, Melk, Krems and Eisenstadt stations for between €10 and €15 a day.

**Cars** are really not necessary for getting around Vienna. If, however, you arrive in the city by car and need to park, it's as well to know the **parking restrictions** in the blue zones (*Blauzonen*), also called short-term parking zones (*Kurzparkzonen*). In general, the maximum length of stay in the first district (Altstadt or Innere Stadt) is ninety minutes (Mon–Fri 9am–7pm, Sat as indicated on sign); in the second to ninth districts (inner suburbs or Vorstädte),

and in the twentieth district, you can park for up to two hours (Mon–Fri 9am–8pm, Sat as indicated on sign). On Sundays it's a free-for-all. However, check the signs before parking, as exact restrictions do vary. If there's no pay-and-display machine, you'll need to buy a 30-, 60- or 90-minute parking voucher (*Parkscheine*) from a tobacconist or post office, and fill it in before displaying it.

An expensive Viennese indulgence is a ride in a soft-top horse-drawn carriage or **Fiaker**, driven by bowler-hatted, multilingual coachmen who will happily give you a guided tour; there are *Fiaker* ranks at Stephansplatz, Heldenplatz, Michaelerplatz and Albertinaplatz. It's best to settle on the price and duration of your ride beforehand; the going rate is €50 for twenty minutes, or €70 for forty minutes, but it's worth haggling.

# The media

You'll find the full range of foreign newspapers at kiosks dotted around the city centre. They're generally a day old, though one that you can buy on the day of issue is the European edition of *The Guardian*, printed in Frankfurt. Similarly, the *International Herald Tribune* is widely available the same day, and contains a useful distilled English version of the *Frankfurter Allgemeine Zeitung*. The weekly English-language newspaper *Austria Today* is available at most newsstands, and gives a fairly dull rundown of Austrian news, plus a few listings. *Ether* is a slick monthly magazine for English-speaking expats.

## Newspapers and magazines

Heavily subsidized by the state, the **Austrian press** is for the most part conservative and pretty uninspiring. Nearly half the (adult) population reads the populist *Kronen Zeitung* tabloid, commonly known as the Krone, while plenty of the rest read another right-wing tabloid, *Kurier*. Of the qualities, the liberal *Der Standard*, printed on pink paper, tends to support the Social Democrats (SPÖ) while the rather straight-laced *Die Presse* backs the conservative People's Party (ÖVP). One peculiarly Austrian phenomenon is the bags of newspapers you'll find hung from lampposts. Law-abiding citizens take one and put their money in the slot provided.

Vienna boasts a good weekly **listings** tabloid, *Falter* (⊛www.falter.at), which is lively, politicized and critical, and comes out on Wednesday. Even if your German isn't great, you should be able to decipher the pull-out *Wienprogramm & Lexicon* section, which contains the week's listings. Most of the headings are self-explanatory, but it's just as well to know that Musik-E covers classical music, while Musik-U is for pop, jazz and folk. The national dailies also have limited listings of what's on in Vienna.

Nearly all cafés and bars, and, in particular, the traditional Viennese coffeehouses, have a wide selection of newspapers and magazines for patrons to browse through, occasionally even English-language ones.

## Television and radio

Austrian **television** is unlikely to win any international awards for cutting-edge programming or presentation. There are just two state-run channels: ORF 1 and ORF 2 (which has regional programmes), with only one really dreadful commercial channel, ATV, for competition. As a result, Austrians tend to tune into German channels such as ARD and ZDF for a bit of variety. Many hotels and pensions have satellite TV, bringing the joys of CNN and MTV straight to your room.

The state-run **radio** channels all feature a lot of chattering, though Ö1 (87.8/92FM) offers some decent classical music, in addition to news in English at 8am, followed shortly after by news in French. FM4 (103.8FM) broadcasts in English until 2pm, plays indie/dance music, with hourly news and weather in English during the day. The **BBC World Service** (⊛www.bbc.co.uk/worldservice) broadcasts in English on 100.8FM in Vienna, though you can also receive it on short wave. Also available on short wave is Radio Austria International, which broadcasts Austrian news in English, Spanish and Russian.

# Festivals

Vienna has such a vast number of festivals and events throughout the year that it's hard to turn up without coinciding with at least one. Below are some of the highlights.

**New Year's Day Concert (Neujahrskonzert)**
The Vienna Philharmonic's world-famous, schmaltzy Strauss-fest is broadcast live around the world from the Musikverein (and beamed live onto a large screen on the front of the Rathaus). Ⓦ www .wienerphilharmoniker.at

**Fasching ends** Vienna's ball season reaches its climax during the Carnival season, with the most famous ball of the lot, the Opernball, taking place on the **Thursday before Ash Wednesday** and the **beginning of Lent**. Ⓦ www.ballkalender.info

**International Accordion Festival** This vibrant festival pulls in groups from the US to the Balkans and is held over the course of **four weeks from late February to mid-March**. Ⓦ www .akkordeonfestival.at

**Osterklang** This **Easter** music festival, held at the Theater-an-der-Wien, is devoted to ecclesiastical music from Baroque to contemporary. Ⓦ www.festwochen.or.at

**Vienna City Marathon** On a Sunday in **late April/ early May**, the Vienna Marathon starts at the Reichsbrücke by the UNO City and finishes with a circuit of the Ring. Ⓦ www.vienna-marathon.com

**Wiener Festwochen** The city's main cultural festival runs from **early May until mid-June** and features opera, music and theatre from all over the world. It kicks off with a free concert in front of the Rathaus. Ⓦ www.festwochen.or.at

**Klangbogen** While the main opera houses go on summer vacation, Klangbogen brings a wide range of opera to the Theater-an-der-Wien from **mid-July to early September**. Ⓦ www.klangbogen.at

**Jazz Fest Wien** The two-week jazz festival takes place across the city's jazz clubs and other live-music venues in **late June/early July**. Ⓦ www.viennajazz.org

**ImPulsTanz** International dance festival in **July and August** showcasing every genre of contemporary dance. Ⓦ www.impulstanz.com

**Donauinselfest** The Donauinselfest is a free pop festival held on the Donauinsel on a weekend in **August** and sponsored by the Social Democrats (SPÖ). Ⓦ www.donauinselfest.at

**Viennale** The city's film festival, the Viennale, takes place over two weeks at the **end of October**. Ⓦ www.viennale.or.at

**All Saints' Day (Allerheiligen)** On All Saints' Day (**November 1**) huge numbers of Viennese head for the city's cemeteries, in particular the Zentralfriedhof, to pay their respects to the dead.

**Wien Modern** A festival of contemporary classical music held in **November** at the Konzerthaus. Ⓦ www.wienmodern.at

**Ball season November 11** marks the official beginning of the ball season, which lasts **until Ash Wednesday**, though the balls don't really get going until after New Year. Ⓦ www .ballkalender.info

**Christkindlmarkt** From the end of **November to Christmas Eve**, there's a Christkindlmarkt, selling Glühwein (mulled wine) and lots of tacky Christmas gifts, in front of the Rathaus. Smaller versions are laid out in Spittelberg, Freyung, Schön-brunn and a few other venues across the city. Ⓦ www .christkindlmarkt.at

# Travel essentials

## Addresses

When writing **addresses**, the Viennese write the number of the district first, followed by the name of the street, and then the house number; most residential addresses also include an apartment number, separated from the house number by a slash. For example: 9, Löblichgasse 11/14, denotes Flat 14 at no. 11 Löblichgasse in the ninth district. We have used this system throughout the book. Sometimes you'll find addresses preceded by the postal code rather than the district, often with an "A" (for Austria) hyphenated to the beginning. However, it's easy enough to decipher the postal district from the code; for example: A-1010 Wien denotes the first district, A-1020 the second, and so on. Lastly, there are a few common abbreviations to be aware of, including: –str. for –strasse, –g. for –gasse, and –pl. for –platz.

## Children

**Children** are generally neither seen nor heard in Vienna. You won't see too many of them in the cafés and restaurants around town; hotels and pensions tend to be slightly more accommodating. For those with kids, Schönbrunn (see p.191) is a must, as it harbours the Tiergarten (Zoo),

Palmenhaus (Palm House), Wüstenhaus (Desert House) and Irrgarten (Maze). Closer to the centre there's the Schmetterling-haus (Butterfly House) in the Hofburg (see p.73) and the aviary and aquarium of Haus des Meeres (see p.167). The Prater (see p.180) can also be fun, and most children love to ride on the trams. Museums that might appeal to small kids include the Strassenbahnmuseum (Tram Museum) described on p.163, the Kindermuseum in the MuseumsQuartier (see p.111); older kids might get more from the Technisches Museum (see p.210), the militaria at the Heeresgeschichtliches Museum (see p.160), the brilliant hands-on Haus der Musik (see p.54) or – at a stretch – the Theatermuseum (see p.92).

## Costs

Although Vienna is by no means a budget destination, it is not quite as **expensive** as people imagine. It's true that coffee and cake at a traditional coffeehouse will cost you dear, but restaurants on the whole are moderately priced, as are rooms in the city's pensions and hotels. That said, Austria is one of the wealthiest countries in the world, and if you have the money, Vienna has plenty of luxury shops, hotels

**POSTAL DISTRICTS**

N

| LEGEND | |
|---|---|
| 1. Innere Stadt | 13. Hietzing |
| 2. Leopoldstadt | 14. Penzing |
| 3. Landstrasse | 15. Rudolfsheim-Fünfhaus |
| 4. Wieden | |
| 5. Margareten | 16. Ottakring |
| 6. Mariahilf | 17. Hernals |
| 7. Neubau | 18. Währing |
| 8. Josefstadt | 19. Döbling |
| 9. Alsergrund | 20. Brigittenau |
| 10. Favoriten | 21. Floridsdorf |
| 11. Simmering | 22. Donaustadt |
| 12. Meidling | 23. Liesing |

0          5 km

and restaurants ready to relieve you of it. After you've paid for your own room, count on a minimum of €30 a day, which will buy you breakfast, a takeaway lunch, a budget dinner and a beer or coffee, but not much else. Eating sit-down meals twice a day, visiting museums and drinking more beer and coffee (especially coffee) will cost you more like €60 a day; if you want to go to the opera or a club, then you could easily double that figure.

## Crime and personal safety

Vienna comes across as pretty **safe** compared to many capital cities. The Viennese themselves are a law-abiding lot, almost obsessively so. Old ladies can be seen walking their dogs in the city's parks late at night, and no one jaywalks. That said, crime does, of course, exist in Vienna as elsewhere and is on the rise, so it's as well to take the usual precautions.

Large sections of the Gürtel ring road double as a red-light district, and as such are best avoided. The Karlsplatz underpass and the Stadtpark both have dubious reputations, as do the major train stations, in particular the Südbahnhof, after dark. Even so, none of these places are, strictly speaking, no-go areas.

Almost all problems encountered by tourists in Vienna are to do with petty crime. Reporting thefts to the police is straightforward enough, though it takes some time to wade through the bureaucracy. The Austrian **police** (*Polizei*) – distinguishable by their dark blue uniforms and white peaked caps, with a red-and-gold band – are armed, and are usually civil. It's important to carry ID with you at all times, ideally your passport, or at the least a driving licence. Making photocopies of your passport and tickets is a very sensible precaution.

The main central police station (*Polizei-inspektionen*) can be found at 1, Deutsch-meisterplatz 3 (U-Bahn Schottenring).

## Disabled travellers

Like most EU countries, there are regulations in force in Austria that mean that all public buildings must be wheelchair-friendly (*Rollstuhlfreundlich*). As a result Vienna is becoming gradually more **accessible** for travellers with special needs.

Wheelchair access to hotels is by no means universal, however, and is more likely in upmarket establishments than in inexpensive places. Access to the country's public transport system is improving and hassle-free if you plan your trip and contact the relevant train station several days in advance.

Access to urban transport in Vienna is patchy, with only the new U3 and U6 subway lines fully equipped with lifts, escalators and a guidance system for the blind. The old trams are not at all wheelchair-friendly, but new ones are entirely low-floor, and buses in Vienna "kneel" to let people on and off, and have retractable ramps for wheelchair users. For a clearer picture, get a copy of the English-language leaflet *Vienna for Visitors with Disabilities* from the Vienna tourist board (see p.36) before you set off. This describes the level of access to U-Bahn stations, hotels and many tourist sights, and contains lots of other useful pieces of information.

## Discounts

Most sights and some cinemas and theatres in Vienna offer **concessions** for senior citizens, the unemployed, full-time students and children under 16, with under-5s being admitted free almost everywhere – proof of eligibility will be required in most cases. Once obtained, **youth/ student ID cards** soon pay for themselves in savings. Full-time students are eligible for the International Student Identity Card or ISIC (Ⓦwww.isiccard.com), which entitles the bearer to special air, rail and bus fares, and discounts at museums, theatres and other attractions. The card costs £7 in the UK, €13 in the Republic of Ireland, $22 in the US; C$16 in Canada, A$18 in Australia, and NZ$20 in New Zealand. If you're not a student, but you are 25 or younger, you can get an International Youth Travel Card, or IYTC, which costs the same as the ISIC and carries the same benefits.

## Electricity

**Electricity** is continental 220 volts AC; standard, round two-pin plugs are used. Equip yourself with an adapter/transformer before leaving home if you want to use your hairdryer, laptop etc, while travelling.

## Embassies and consulates

**Australia** 4, Mattiellistrasse 2–4 ☏506 74-0; U-Bahn Karlsplatz; ⓦwww.australian-embassy.at

**Canada** 1, Laurenzerberg 2 ☏531-38-3000; U-Bahn Schwedenplatz; ⓦwww.kanada.at

**Ireland** 1, Fifth Floor, Rotenturmstrasse 16–18 ☏715 4246; U-Bahn Schwedenplatz

**UK** 3, Jaurèsgasse 10 ☏71613-5333; tram #71; ⓦwww.britishembassy.at

**US** 9, Boltzmanngasse 16 ☏31339-0; tram #5, #33, #37, #38, #40, #41 or #42; ⓦwww.usembassy.at

## Emergencies

**Fire** ☏122
**Police** ☏133
**Ambulance** ☏144

## Entry requirements

Citizens of the US, Canada, Australia, New Zealand and all European countries (except Albania, Belarus, Bosnia, Macedonia, Montenegro, Russia, Serbia and Ukraine) do not require an **entry visa** for Austria. EU citizens need only a national identity card and can stay for as long as they want, but if they're planning on staying permanently they should register with the local police. Citizens of the US, Canada, New Zealand and Australia require a passport, and can stay up to three months. Visa requirements do change, however, and it is always advisable to check the current situation before leaving home.

## Health

EU **health care privileges** apply in Austria, so on production of a passport you are entitled to free emergency hospital treatment. The main A&E department (*Unfall* is an "accident") is in the gargantuan Allgemeines Krankenhaus (AKH), 9, Währinger Gürtel 18–20 (☏40400, ⓦwww.akhwien .at; U-Bahn Michelbeuern-AKH). If it's a child that's ill, though, it's best to head for Sankt Anna Kinderspital 9, Kinderspitalgasse 6 (☏40170, ⓦwww.stanna.at; U-Bahn Alser Strasse). On production of a European Health Insurance Card (EHIC), you can

also visit the doctor free of charge – phone ☏513 95 95 to find an English-speaking doctor. Most pharmacies (*Apotheken*) are open Monday to Friday 8am to noon and 2pm to 6pm, Saturdays 8am to noon; all of them should have directions to the nearest 24-hour pharmacy posted in the window.

## Insurance

Even though EU health care privileges apply, it's as well to take out a travel **insurance policy** to cover against theft, loss and illness or injury. For non-EU citizens, it's worth checking whether you are already covered before you buy a new policy.

If you need to take out insurance, you might want to consider the travel insurance offered by Rough Guides. Rough Guides has teamed up with Columbus Direct to offer insurance policies that can be tailored to suit your needs. Products include a low-cost backpacker option for long stays; a short break option for city getaways; a typical holiday package option; and others. There are also annual multi-trip policies for those who travel regularly. Different sports and activities (trekking, skiing, and so on) can usually be covered if required. See ⓦwww.roughguidesinsurance.com for eligibility and purchasing options. Alternatively, call the following numbers: UK ☏0870/033 9988; Australia ☏1300/669 999; New Zealand ☏0800/55 9911. If you live outside these three countries, call ☏+44 870/890 2843.

## Internet

The Viennese are keen Internet users and most cafés, restaurants, hotels, shops and museums have websites. With any luck the hotel or hostel you're staying at will have **Internet access**. Otherwise, you can get online at numerous cafés and bars in Vienna – some even have Wi-Fi, known locally as WLAN – including the Bignet Internet café, 1, Hoher Markt 8–9 (daily 9am–11pm; ⓦwww .bignet.at), as well as at congenial cafés such as *Café Stein* (see p.269) and *Das Möbel* (see p.268). For details of how to get your laptop online when abroad, check out the useful website ⓦwww.kropla.com.

## Laundry

There are no coin-operated **launderettes** in the Innere Stadt; the nearest one is at 9, Nussdorferstrasse 80 (U-Bahn Nussdorfer Strasse). Alternatively, you can do a service wash at one of the city's central dry-cleaners such as Gisela-Putzerei, 1, Rauhensteingasse 1 (U-Bahn Stephansplatz).

## Left luggage

The main train stations all have €2 coin-operated **lockers** (*Schliessfächer*); the airport and smaller stations have a left-luggage counter (*Gepäckaufbewahrung*).

## Lost property

The city's chief **lost property** office is the Zentrales Fundamt, 18, Bastiengasse 22 (☎4000-8091). If the item was lost on public transport phone ☎79 09 43-500; if it was lost on Austrian Railways phone ☎58 00 22-222.

## Mail

Vienna's main **post office** (*Hauptpostamt*) is at Fleischmarkt 19, A-1010, just off Schwedenplatz (daily 6am–10pm; ☎0810 010 100). The post offices in the Westbahnhof (Mon–Fri 7am–10pm, Sat & Sun 9am–8pm), Südbahnhof (Mon–Fri 7am–8pm, Sat & Sun 9am–2pm) and Franz-Josef-Bahnhof (Mon–Fri 7am–8pm, Sat & Sun 9am–2pm) are all open late. All other post offices – identified by a yellow sign saying *Postamt* – have regular opening hours (Mon–Fri 8am–noon & 2–6pm), with the main ones eschewing their lunch break and opening on Saturdays, 8am to 10am.

**Air mail** (*Flugpost*) between Austria and the UK usually takes three or four days, about five days to reach the US, and a week to ten days to Australia and New Zealand. Stamps (*Briefmarken*) for postcards within the EU are obtainable from tobacconists (*Tabak*), though for anything more complicated or further afield, you'll probably have to go to a post office, where they like to weigh everything.

**Poste restante** (*Postlagernd*) letters can be sent to any post office, if you know the address. At the main post office (see above) go to the counter marked *Postlagernde Sendungen*. Mail should be addressed using this term rather than "poste restante"; it will be held for thirty days (remember to take your passport when going to collect it).

## Maps

The maps in this guide, together with the untold number of **free city plans** you'll pick up from tourist offices and hotels, should be sufficient to help you find your way around. For something more durable, the best maps are by Freytag & Berndt, who produce a whole variety of plans of the city, marked with bus and tram routes. The 1:20,000 spiral-bound *Buchplan Wien* map is the most comprehensive. Alternatively, Falkplan produces an attractive fold-out map, with a good large-scale section of the Innere Stadt.

## Money

Austria's currency is the **euro** (€). The euro is split into 100 cents. There are seven euro notes – in denominations of 500, 200, 100, 50, 20, 10 and 5 euros, each a different colour and size – and eight different coin denominations, including 2 and 1 euros, then 50, 20, 10, 5, 2 and 1 cents. Euro coins feature a common EU design on one face, but different country-specific designs on the other. No matter what the design, all euro coins and notes can be used in the following EU states: Austria, Belgium, Finland, France, Germany, Greece, Ireland, Italy, Luxembourg, Portugal, Slovenia, Spain and the Netherlands.

There are **ATMs** all over Vienna, from which you should be able to take out cash using either a debit or credit card. Banks tend to give the best rates and charge the lowest commission when it comes to changing money and traveller's cheques; most are open Monday to Friday 8am to 12.30pm and 1.30 to 3pm, with late closing on Thursdays at 5.30pm.

## Opening hours

Shops are allowed to open Monday to Friday 6am to 7.30pm, Saturday 6am to 6pm, with late shopping usually on Thursdays. Some still close at lunchtimes and on Saturday afternoons, and all are shut on Sundays. The only exceptions to this rule, apart from pharmacists and a few bakeries, are the shops in the main train stations and the airport, which are open late and at weekends. Those in search of cigarettes after hours will find cigarette machines outside most state-run tobacconists (*Tabak*). Cafés, bars and restaurants tend to be open for much longer. The traditional coffeehouses in particular often open as early as 7am and continue until or after 11pm, and the trendier cafés stay open until 2am and later. Formal restaurants tend to open at lunch and dinner, but close in between. Most places where you can drink and eat have a weekly closing day or *Ruhetag*.

## Phones

Austrian **phone booths** are easy enough to spot and to use, with instructions in four languages (including English). The dialling tone is a short pulse followed by a long one; the ringing tone is long and regular; engaged is short and rapid. At the time of going to press the minimum charge is 20 cents, but you're likely to need much more to make even a **local call**, since telephone calls are still quite expensive despite the recent deregulation.

Viennese **telephone numbers** within the city vary in length. One further peculiarity is those numbers that include a hyphen. It's not always necessary to dial the numbers after the hyphen, especially if it's a zero, which simply signals the system has **direct dial extension numbers** (*Durchwahlen*). If you know the extension you want, or it's given as part of the number, then you may dial it immediately after the main number.

You can make an **international call** from any phone, though it's easier to do so with a **phone card** (*Telefonkarte*) rather than from a coin-operated phone. Best value are pre-paid phone cards, which will give you much longer call time and can be used from any public or private phone. Simply call the toll-free access number and then punch in the PIN given on the card.

If you're taking your **mobile/cell phone** (known as a *Handy* in German) with you, check with your service provider whether your phone will work abroad and what the call charges will be. Mobiles bought for use in Europe, Australia and New Zealand should work fine, though a mobile bought for use in the US is unlikely to work unless it's a tri-band phone.

---

## Useful telephone numbers

### Phoning Vienna from abroad

**From Australia and New Zealand** ☏ 0011 + 43 + 1
**From Britain and Ireland** ☏ 00 + 43 + 1
**From North America** ☏ 011 + 43 + 1

Note that although the Vienna city code is 1 when phoning from abroad, it's 0222 when phoning from elsewhere in Austria.

### Phoning abroad from Vienna

Note that the initial zero is omitted from the area code when dialling the UK, Ireland, Australia and New Zealand from abroad.

**Australia** ☏ 00 + 61 + city code
**New Zealand** ☏ 00 + 64 + city code
**Republic of Ireland** ☏ 00 + 353 + city code
**UK** ☏ 00 + 44 + city code
**US and Canada** ☏ 00 + 1 + area code

### Information

**Directory enquiries & operator** ☏ 11 88 77

You can also view the Vienna telephone directory and Yellow Pages online at ⓦ www.herold.at

## Public holidays

On the national **public holidays** listed below, banks and shops will be closed all day. Museums and galleries will, somewhat confusingly, either be closed or open for free. Note, too, that all the city's museums are always free on May 17 (International Museum Day) and October 26 (National Day). During the school summer holidays – July and August – you'll find Vienna quieter than usual, with many theatres and other businesses closed for all or some of the period.

**January 1** (Neues Jahr)
**January 6** (Epiphany/Dreikönigsfest)
**Easter Monday** (Ostermontag)
**May 1** (Labour Day/Tag des Arbeit)
**Ascension Day** (6th Thurs after Easter/ Christi Himmelfahrt)
**Whit Monday** (6th Mon after Easter/ Pfingstmontag)
**Corpus Christi** (2nd Thurs after Whitsuntide/ Fronleichnam)
**August 15** (Assumption Day/Maria Himmelfahrt)
**October 26** (National Day/Nationalfeiertag)
**November 1** (All Saints' Day/Allerheiligen)
**December 8** (Immaculate Conception/ Maria Empfängnis)
**December 25** (Weihnachtstag)
**December 26** (Zweite Weihnachtsfeiertag)

## Soccer

Vienna's top **soccer** (*Fussball*) **teams** are SK Rapid Wien (Ⓦwww.skrapid.at), who play at the 20,000-capacity Gerhard Hanappi Stadion on Keisslergasse in Hütteldorf (U-Bahn Hütteldorf), and FK Austria Wien (Ⓦwww.fk-austria.at), their main rivals, who play at the 12,000-capacity Franz-Horr-Stadion on Fischhofgasse in Favoriten (tram #67 two stops from U-Bahn Reumannplatz); big international games are played at the 50,000-plus-capacity Ernst-Happel-Stadion in the Prater (U-Bahn Stadion), for more on which see p.184.

## Swimming pools

The Amalienbad, 10, Reumannplatz 23 (U-Bahn Reumannplatz), has a wonderful Art Deco interior, particularly the sauna. The Angelibad, 21, An der oberen Alten Donau (U-Bahn Neue Donau), is an open-air riverside swimming place. Jörgerbad, 17,

Jörgerstrasse 42–44 (tram #43), is also very beautiful inside, while Krapfenwaldbad, 19, Krapfenwaldlgasse 65–73 (bus #38A), is a swish, stylish 1920s outdoor pool up in the foothills of the Wienerwald (May–Sept) with great views; so too the Schafbergbad, 18, Josef-Redl-Gasse 2 (bus #42B).

## Time

Austria is normally one hour ahead of the UK and Ireland, six hours ahead of EST and nine hours ahead of PST, with the clocks going forward in spring and back again some time in autumn – the exact date changes from year to year.

## Tipping

**Tipping** is expected in the more upmarket hotels, taxis, and in most cafés, bars and restaurants, usually up to the nearest euro depending on how much you've spent and how good the service was. In more expensive restaurants, you'll find the bill arrives with a fifteen-percent service charge already tacked on to the total.

## Tourist information

The main **tourist office** of the Vienna Tourist Board or *Wien Tourismus* is behind the opera house on Albertinaplatz at the corner of Maysedergasse (daily 9am–7pm; ☏24 555, Ⓦwww.vienna.info). The staff should be able to answer most enquiries, and will happily hand out a free map of the city, with all the bus routes, tram lines and metro stations marked on, plus all the opening times of the various museums and galleries.

It's also worth asking for the tourist board's monthly *Programm* for opera, concert and theatre schedules, upcoming exhibitions, and the monthly goings-on at the state museums. Those under 26 might prefer to try the youth-oriented tourist office, *WienXtra*, at 1, Babenbergerstrasse 1 (Mon–Sat noon–7pm; Ⓦwww.wienxtra.at), on the corner of the Ringstrasse. There are also **information desks** at the airport (daily 8.30am–9pm) and at the Westbahnhof (daily 7am–10pm).

For the most comprehensive and critical **listings**, you need the weekly tabloid *Falter* (see p.28).

## Websites

**Austria – general information** Ⓦ www .tiscover.com. Tourist site for booking accommodation, including self-catering and campsites, flights and car rental online. Updated regularly so it can tell you what's happening in the next few weeks/months in Vienna.

**Austrian Encyclopaedia** Ⓦ www.aeiou.at. Website based on the Austrian Encyclopaedia, so should give the answer to any Austrian query you have. You can navigate in English, though occasionally source material is in German only. Exhaustive links.

**Austrian Search Engine** Ⓦ www.austrosearch.at. The best Austrian-specific English/German search engine on the net. Not only can you get three-day weather forecasts and up-to-date Austrian news, you can join chat groups, and find links for all sorts of Austro-nonsense.

**Ex-pat Vienna** Ⓦ www.virtualvienna.net. Generally quite fun (largely US) expat website packed full of news, features, culture and listings.

**Vienna City Hall** Ⓦ www.wien.gv.at. The city-council website has lots of information in German, but it also has a very useful search engine that will find any address in the city for you on a map – click on *Stadtplan-Suche* and write in the street name.

**Vienna Life** Ⓦ www.veinna-life.com. Light-hearted website about all things Viennese, from the Ultravox song to the Congress, plus an online guide of hotels, bars, shops, museums and galleries, with reviews.

**Vienna Tourist Board** Ⓦ www.wien.info. The official Vienna tourist board's English/German website, with information on everything from secondhand bookshops to late-night eating options and art exhibitions. You can also book hotel accommodation online.

**Wiener Zeitung** Ⓦ www.wienerzeitung.at. Website of the official Vienna city authorities' newspaper. The English version gives you lots of news and tourist information and has plenty of useful links.

# The City

# The City

# The Innere Stadt

V ienna's first district – the **Innere Stadt** (Inner City) or Altstadt (Old City) – has been the very heart of the place since the Romans founded Vindobona here on the banks of the Danube in 15 BC. It was here, too, that the Babenberg dukes built their power base in the twelfth century, and from 1533, the Habsburgs established the Hofburg as their primary imperial residence (covered separately in Chapter Two). Consequently, unlike the older quarters in many European cities, the Innere Stadt remained the chief place of residence for the city's aristocracy throughout the Baroque period and beyond, and its narrow, cobbled lanes remained the unlikely addresses of dukes and duchesses, princes and ambassadors. In fact, the city occupied pretty much the same space from the thirteenth century until the zigzag fortifications, which had protected the city on two occasions against the Turks, were finally taken down in the mid-nineteenth century.

The focus of the Innere Stadt – and the one thing on all tourists' itineraries – is the city's magnificent Gothic cathedral, **Stephansdom**, whose single soaring spire also acts as a useful geographical landmark. Close by are the chief pedestrianized shopping streets of **Kärntnerstrasse**, **Graben** and **Kohlmarkt**, which get progressively more exclusive the nearer you get to the Hofburg. There's a steady ebb and flow of folk along these streets at most times of the day, but the **Kaisergruft**, the last resting place of the Habsburgs, just off Kärntnerstrasse, is the only other sight that gets clogged up with tour groups. Head off into the rest of the Innere Stadt with its baffling medieval lanes, hidden courtyards and passageways, and you'll soon lose the crowds. For although most of the city's finest Baroque churches and palaces are to be found here, the dearth of premier-league sights puts many off the scent.

## Stephansplatz

The geographical heart of the Innere Stadt is **Stephansplatz**, a lively, pedestrianized square overlooked by the hoary Gothic bulk of the city cathedral. The square hasn't always been so central – the first church built here lay outside the medieval city walls, and the square itself was a graveyard until 1732. Nowadays, though, it's one of the best places for watching Vienna's streetlife, from the benign young slackers who lounge around on the benches by the U-Bahn, to the beleaguered folk in eighteenth-century costumes, wearily flogging tickets for classical concerts. The other whiff of heritage is the smell of horse dung that wafts across the square from the *Fiaker* lined up along the north wall of the cathedral.

**RESTAURANTS**

| | |
|---|---|
| Achilleus | 28 |
| Augustinerkeller | 52 |
| Beim Czaak | 21 |
| Bio Bar | 5 |
| Brezlg'wölb | 6 |
| Culinarium Österreich | 47 |
| Do & Co | 34 |
| Esterházykeller | 17 |
| Expedit | 12 |
| Figlmüller | 29 |
| Gigerl | 45 |
| Gösser Bierklinik | 13 |
| Göttweiger Stiftskeller | 42 |
| Griechenbeisl | 10 |
| Gulaschmuseum | 40 |
| Hollmann Salon | 15 |
| Hotel Riviera | 25 |
| Ilona-Stüberl | 33 |
| Immervoll | 48 |
| Kornat | 4 |
| Limes | 8 |
| Meinl am Graben | 28 |
| Melker Stiftskeller | 3 |
| Ofenloch | 9 |
| Palatschinkenkuchl | 19 |
| Pfudl | 35 |
| Plachutta | 41 |
| Regina Margherita | 23 |
| Reinthaler | 50 |
| Toko-Ri | 2 |
| Zum Finsteren Stern | 7 |
| Zwölf-Apostelkeller | 22 |

**CAFÉS**

| | |
|---|---|
| Aera | 1 |
| Aida | 37 |
| Alt Wien | 27 |
| Bizi | 24 |
| Bräunerhof | 43 |
| Central | 14 |
| Demel | 30 |
| Diglas | 31 |
| Engländer | 38 |
| Frauenhuber | 49 |
| Griensteidl | 32 |
| Hawelka | 36 |
| Kleines Café | 44 |
| Korb | 16 |
| Krugerhof | 53 |
| Markusplatz | 11 |
| Meinl am Graben | 26 |
| Tirolerhof | 51 |
| Trześniewski | 39 |
| Wrenkh Natürlich | 46 |
| Zanoni & Zanoni | 20 |
| Zum schwarzen Kameel | 18 |

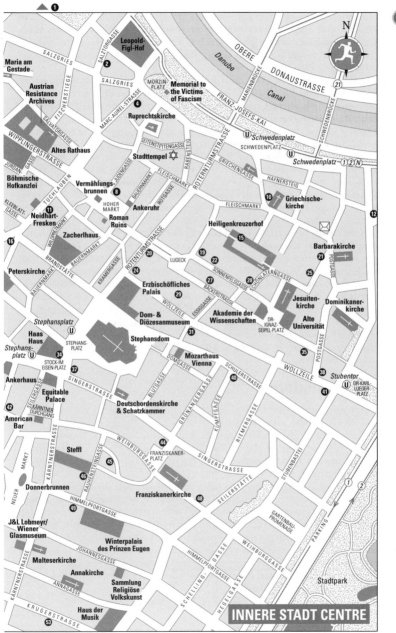

INNERE STADT CENTRE

Apart from the cathedral, the most dominant feature of the square is the tinted glass-and-polished-stone carbuncle of the **Haas Haus**, which, understandably, caused something of a furore when it was unveiled in 1990. The architect, Hans Hollein, also designed several equally uncompromising jewellery stores along Graben and Kohlmarkt, each of which is a minor masterpiece. Here, though, the effect is simply brash, and to cap it all, the interior is an unimaginative mini-shopping mall.

Despite appearances, Haas Haus isn't in fact on Stephansplatz at all, it's on **Stock-im-Eisen-Platz**, a little-known geographical entity which covers the no-man's-land between Graben, Stephansplatz and Kärntnerstrasse. The square takes its name – literally "stick-in-iron" – from the nail-studded, sixteenth-century slice of larch tree that stands in a glass-protected niche set into the grandiose **Equitable Palace** on the corner of Kärntnerstrasse. According to Viennese tradition, apprentice locksmiths and blacksmiths would hammer a nail into the trunk for good luck. The Equitable building itself is well worth exploring: built in the 1890s, the ornate vestibule (originally designed to be a metro entrance) is a superb example of the Ringstrasse style of the period, with lashings of marble and wrought iron, and a glass-roofed courtyard faced in majolica tiles.

In the paving between the Haas Haus and the cathedral, the ground plan of the **Magdalenenkapelle**, a charnel house that burnt to the ground in 1781, is marked out in red sandstone. Almost immediately below it is another church building, the Romanesque **Virgilkapelle**, which was discovered during the construction of the U-Bahn in the 1970s, and is now preserved in the Stephansplatz station itself. The thirteenth-century chapel – at one time the family crypt of the Chrannests, one of whom was finance minister to the Habsburgs – is little visited, though the strangeness of its location and the simple beauty of its recesses, decorated with red wheel crosses, make it an intriguing sight. If the chapel is closed, you can satisfy your curiosity by looking down from the metro's viewing platform by the information office.

# Stephansdom

The **Stephansdom** (ⓦwww.stephanskirche.at) still towers above the Innere Stadt and dominates the Viennese skyline as it has done for centuries. An obvious military target, it has endured two Turkish sieges, Napoleonic bombardment, and in the latter stages of World War II the attentions of American bombers and Russian artillery. That it survived at all is a miracle, and has ensured it a special place in the hearts of the Viennese.

Work began on the current building in 1304, though the cathedral's chief founder and patron is considered to be Rudolf IV, who modelled his designs for the greatly expanded nave on St Vitus Cathedral in Prague, which was being built at the time by his rival, Emperor Charles IV. Poor old Rudolf, however, could only secure collegiate status for his church, under the bishopric of Passau. In the end, it took more than a hundred years before an independent bishopric was established, yet another century before the final touches were added to the exterior, and it wasn't until the early twentieth century that the choir and several of the chapels were completed.

## The exterior

The cathedral's most magnificent **exterior** feature is the sublime south tower or Südturm – ironically nicknamed "**Steffl**" (Little Stephen) by the locals – which soars to a height of 137m. The planned north tower (Nordtürm), or Eagle

STEPHANSDOM

High Altar

Wiener Neustädter Altar

Capistrano Pulpit

Donor's Tomb

Tomb of Friedrich III

Choir

Steffl Entrance

Barbara-kapelle

Katherinen-kapelle

Nordturm (Adlerturm)

To the Catacombs

Zahnwehherrgott

Südturm or Steffl (Hochturm)

Pilgram Organ Case

Lift to the Pummerin

Nave

Pulpit

Shop

Pötscher Madonna

Kreuz-kapelle

Heidenturm

Heidenturm

Riesentor (Main Entrance)

0          10 m

Tower (Adlerturm), was to have been built along similar lines, but fell victim to cost-cutting during the build-up to the first Turkish siege of 1529, its half-built stump eventually receiving a diminutive copper cupola in 1556. You can take the lift up the north tower to see the cathedral's great bell known as the **Pummerin** or "Boomer" (daily: April–Oct 8.30am–5.30pm; July & Aug 8.30am–6pm; Nov–March 8.30am–5pm; €4), accessible from inside the cathedral, though the **Südturm** (daily 9am–5.30pm; €3), a blind scramble up 343 steps, accessible from the outside, has better views. The current bell is a postwar rehash of the twenty-ton original, which was cast from a Turkish cannon captured during the 1683 siege.

The cathedral's steeply pitched **roof** has been decorated with multicoloured tiles forming giant chevrons since 1490, and is said to be modelled on a Saracen carpet; on the south side is a double-headed imperial eagle, dating from 1831, while on the north are the emblems of the City of Vienna and the Second Republic and the date 1950, when the roof was retiled.

The main entrance to the cathedral is via the **Riesentor** (Giants' Gates), a rare survivor from the present building's twelfth-century predecessor. Flanking the Riesentor are two robust Romanesque towers, known as the **Heidentürme** (Pagans' Towers), which are peppered with crockets. Before you enter the cathedral, it's also worth noting the O5 inscription, the symbol of the Austrian resistance (for more on which, see p.67) to the left of the main door. The thirteenth-century sculpted figures around the main portal are also worth pausing at, though the iron railings and the ebb and flow of visitors make it hard to appreciate them. Christ Pantocrator is depicted in the tympanum; more interesting, however, are the devilish creatures situated to the left, below the apostles.

### The interior

The first thing that strikes you as you enter the gloomy, high-vaulted interior of the cathedral is that, despite the tourists, Stephansdom is still very much a place of worship. At peak times, it can be difficult to get a seat in the area immediately to your right, facing the **Pötscher Madonna** painting, which sits below a delicate late-Gothic baldachin. Legend has it that the Madonna, an object of great veneration, even today, wept tears from her unusually large eyes during the Battle of Zenta against the Turks in 1697, and in so doing miraculously secured victory against the infidels.

The leader of the imperial troops at Zenta, Prince Eugène of Savoy, is buried in the **Kreuzkapelle**, on the other side of the cathedral, off the north aisle – all of him, that is, but his heart, which, it is thought, was transported to Turin, the city he liberated in 1706. Sadly, the chapel is usually shut behind heavy iron gates, which prevent even the slightest glimpse of the prince's tomb on the south wall. What you can see, though, is a fifteenth-century crucifix, whose statue of Christ sports a shaggy black beard of human hair, which, according to legend, is still growing. Close by, in the north aisle itself, another ornate Gothic baldachin shelters a Sacred Heart picture, in which Christ reveals his flaming, bleeding heart as if showing off a new T-shirt.

The highlight of the cathedral, though, is without doubt the early sixteenth-century carved stone **pulpit**, with portraits of the four fathers of the Christian Church (saints Augustine, Gregory, Jerome and Ambrose), naturalistically sculpted by an unknown artist (until recently believed to be the Moravian Anton Pilgram), who "signed" his work by showing himself peering from a window below the pulpit stairs. The filigree work above and below the staircase is masterly, as are the salamanders and toads (sadly now under protective perspex), symbolizing good and evil, pursuing one another up the banister and culminating in a barking dog who keeps them all at bay. Pilgram himself can be spotted on the wall of the north aisle, in polychrome, peeping out below the (now defunct) organ case he designed. The organ itself originally sat above the last of the cathedral's late-Gothic baldachins, whose lovely, lacy filigree work can be seen on the opposite side of the nave.

If you want to escape the crowds, head for the twin chapels at either end of the transepts. Though shut off behind wrought-iron railings, the **Katharinenkapelle**, to the south, boasts a beautiful baptismal font, made in 1481; the marble base features the four apostles, the niches of the basin are decorated with the twelve disciples, Christ and St Stephan, while the wooden lid is shaped like a church spire and smothered with sculpted scenes. Up above, there's a wonderful ceiling boss of St Catherine with her wheel and sword, on the end of a drooping pendant. To the north, the **Barbarakapelle** also features hanging pendants, this time stamped with heraldic bosses. The chapel is dedicated to all those killed in concentration camps, and the small triangle in the crucifix below Christ's feet contains ashes from Auschwitz. On the wall opposite, as you leave the chapel, look out for a half-torso of Christ in suffering, known as the **Zahnwehherrgott** (Our Lord of the Toothache). According to Viennese legend, the three students who coined the nickname were immediately struck down with toothache, which no barber-surgeon could cure, until the young men had fallen prostrate before the statue and prayed for forgiveness.

The **choir**, beyond the transepts, is roped off, and only strictly visitable on a guided tour (see box opposite). At the far end of the Women's Choir (to the north), however, you should just be able to make out the winged **Wiener Neustädter Altar**, a richly gilded masterpiece of late-Gothic art which dates from the mid-fifteenth century but was brought to the cathedral in 1883. If the altar's wings are closed only four rows of saints will be depicted; when the wings are opened they reveal up to 72 saints. At the centre of the altar are the Madonna and Child, the Birth of Christ, the Adoration of the Magi, the Coronation of Mary and the latter's death, all sculpted in high relief out of wood. Below the altar to the left lies the **Donor's Tomb**, adorned with sandstone effigies of Rudolf IV and his wife, Catherine of Bohemia (they're actually buried in the catacombs), which would originally have been richly gilded and peppered with precious stones. In the Apostles' Choir to the south stands the glorious red marble **Tomb of Emperor Friedrich III**. In among the 240 statues, 32 coats of arms and numer-ous scaly creatures which decorate the tomb is the emperor's mysterious acronym, AEIOU, composed of the vowels of the Roman alphabet, which has prompted numerous interpretations, ranging from the obvious A*ustria* E*rit* I*n* O*rbe* U*ltima* ("Austria will be the last in the world"), to the ingenious A*quila* E*lecta* I*ovis* O*mnia* V*incit* ("The chosen eagle conquers all things"). Friedrich himself revealed the German version to be A*lles* E*rdreich* I*st* Ö*sterreich* U*ntertan* ("The whole world is subject to Austria"), though some wags put forward the more appropriate A*ller* E*rst* I*st* Ö*sterreich* V*erloren* ("In the first place, Austria is lost"), since Friedrich had great difficulty keeping hold of Upper and Lower Austria and was in fact driven out of Vienna by the Hungarian king Matthias Corvinus in 1485.

## The catacombs

A stairway in the north transept leads down into the **catacombs** or *Katakomben* (guided tours only: every 30min Mon–Sat 10–11.30am & 1.30–4.30pm, Sun 1.30–4.30pm; €4), which, initially at least, are a bit disappointing, having been over-restored in the 1960s. It's here that Rudolf IV and his wife are actually buried, along with other early Habsburg rulers, plus sundry priests, bishops and archbishops who served in the cathedral. Rudolf himself died aged 26, though during his seven-year reign he managed to found both the cathedral and the university; he died in Milan in 1365 and was carried back to Vienna sewn into a cowhide to preserve his body. Last of all, there's a small chamber lined with cages filled with bronze caskets containing the entrails of the later Habsburgs. The bodies of the later Habsburgs are buried in the Kaisergruft (see p.50); their hearts are buried in the Augustinerkirche (see p.92).

From the bottom of the stairs you enter the damp, dimly lit labyrinth of eighteenth-century catacombs, which were closed in 1783 after the stench became too overpowering, and have been left more or less untouched by the city's otherwise overzealous restorers. Around 16,000 locals are buried here, their bones piled high in more than thirty rooms, and in the final chamber, there's a particularly macabre pile left over from a medieval plague pit. You exit from the catacombs via a secret staircase that deposits you outside the cathedral, by the place where Mozart's body was blessed before being buried in St Marxer Friedhof (see p.162). At the very northeastern corner of the cathedral, near the exit from the catacombs, is the **Capistrano Pulpit**, originally the cathedral's main pulpit, placed outside after its replacement by the present version. It was from here that the Venetian priest, St Johannes of Capistrano, preached his sermons against the Turks during the fifteenth century; the extravagant sunburst and statue of St Francis trampling on a Turk are Baroque additions.

# Around Stephansplatz

Badly bombed in the war, few of the buildings on Stephansplatz itself are worthy of mention. Even those that survived the bombs lack a little something – you'd hardly suspect that the unassuming two-storey building on the north side of Stephansplatz is in fact the seventeenth-century **Erzbischöfliches Palais** (Archbishops' Palace). Next door is the equally nondescript **Zwettlhof**, originally an abbey founded by Cistercians from Zwettl in Lower Austria, but bought by Rudolf IV for use as the cathedral priory.

The Zwettlhof now houses the **Dom- und Diözesanmuseum** (Tues–Sat 10am–5pm; €7; @www.dommuseum.at) on its first floor (access through the passageway at Stephansplatz 6). This is basically the dumping ground for a mishmash of the cathedral's most valuable treasures and artwork. There are, however, some arresting medieval sculptures in wood – St Dionysius (aka Denis) carrying his severed head to his place of burial (in 3D relief), St Aegydius (aka Giles) looking rather sadly at the arrow stuck through his hand – and some High Baroque, not to say high kitsch, pieces, like the shrine of the Madonna, whose cloak opens up to reveal God (forming the main part of her body) with a host of worshippers' faces tucked inside her cloak. The highlight, though, is the fourteenth-century stained-glass window of an angel from the Stephansdom. The dimly lit treasury is stuffed with monstrances and macabre reliquaries, including St Leopold's hipbone, a piece of the Virgin Mary's belt and a smidgen of holy blood.

## Schatzkammer and Deutschordenskirche

An even more bizarre ecclesiastical treasure-trove, belonging to the Teutonic Knights, can be seen at the **Schatzkammer des Deutschen Ordens** (May–Oct Tues, Thurs & Sat 10am–noon, Wed & Fri 3–5pm; €4; @www.deutscher-orden .at), spread over five rooms on the second floor of the Deutschordenshaus; enter from Singerstrasse 7, one block south of Stephansplatz, and be sure to ask for the information booklet in English. The Teutonic Knights were one of the three main military-religious orders to emerge during the Crusades in the twelfth century and for many centuries had their base in Marienburg (in what is now Poland). When the Order split along religious lines in the sixteenth century, those still loyal to Catholicism moved their headquarters to Mergentheim in Bavaria, until they were disbanded by order of Napoleon in 1809. Thirty years or so later the Order was reconstituted in Vienna, where it remains active as a charitable body.

The treasury's varied collection, assembled by seven centuries of **Grand Masters** (*Hochmeister*), ranges from the mundane – seals, coins and crosses in room 1 – to the peculiar, particularly well represented in room 2. Note the red coral salt-cellar tree hung with fossilized sharks' teeth – which were thought to be adders' tongues and therefore able to detect poisoned food – and a whole series of vessels made from coconut shells. One Goan specimen has silver mountings, complete with tiger-shell spoons sporting wonky silver handles, while another in chinoiserie style has a wonderful "swizzle stick". Also in this room is the most amazing table clock, smothered in a garland of silver-gilded leaves studded with garnets and turquoise. There are more bizarre exhibits from the Kunstkammer, collected by the Grand Master Archduke Maximilian III, in room 3, like the three bezoars – "a concretion found in the stomach of Persian wild goats" – to which the Persians attributed great healing powers, and a coral pendant depicting Jonah reclining on the tongue of a diminutive whale. The Order's military past is represented by a collection of exotic arms and armour, including a wiggly sixteenth-century Sumatran dagger with a handle carved out of rhino horn into the shape of the Buddha, with sapphire eyes and ruby eyebrows.

Before you leave, be sure to pop inside the **sala terrena** (which looks like a gazebo) on the ground floor, at the bottom of the staircase, to admire the Baroque trompe l'oeil murals of flowers, birds, statues and carousing gods; the room is now used for touristy concerts of Mozart by performers clad in period garb. The building's misshapen cobbled **courtyard** is an almost pastorally peaceful spot festooned with ivy and flower boxes. Brahms spent the best part of two years here in 1863–65, but inevitably it's Mozart who gets the plaque for his brief sojourn here in the spring of 1781. After the likes of the *sala terrena*, the Order's church, the **Deutschordenskirche**, on street level, appears relatively modest. Incorporated into the Order's buildings in the fourteenth century, the church has retained its Gothic origins (despite remodelling in later centuries), is decorated with the Order's numerous coats of arms, and features a superb sixteenth-century Flemish winged altarpiece depicting the Passion.

## Mozarthaus Vienna

The **Mozarthaus Vienna** (daily 10am–8pm; €9; Ⓦwww.mozarthausvienna.at) lies immediately east of the cathedral (to get there, pass through the *Durchhaus* at Stephansplatz 5a and enter at Domgasse 5). Here, on the first floor, Mozart, Constanze and their son, Karl Thomas, lived for three years, during which the composer enjoyed his greatest success. It was Mozart's swankiest accommodation in Vienna, where he even had his own billiards room and space for visitors. The composer Johann Nepomuk Hummel stayed here as Mozart's live-in pupil for two and a half years; Josef Haydn was a regular visitor, opining that Mozart was "the greatest composer that I know in person or by name".

Sadly, however, despite a lavish makeover, video installations and an audioguide, the museum is a bit disappointing. A lift whisks you to the third floor, so that you have to wade through two floors of manuscript facsimiles and portraits before you reach the apartment itself. The highlight is probably the animated version of *Die Zauberflöte* on the second floor. Only one of Mozart's rooms actually retains the original decor

## Mozart in Vienna

**Wolfgang Amadeus Mozart** (1756–91) moved to Vienna in March 1781, after a summons from his employer, the irascible Archbishop of Salzburg, Count Colloredo, who was visiting his sick father in the city. Within three months Mozart had resigned from his post as court organist to the archbishop or "arch-oaf" (*Erzlimmel*) as he called him, causing a rift with his overbearing father, who was assistant *Kapellmeister* in Salzburg. The relationship was further strained when Mozart, against his father's wishes, moved in with the all-female Weber family, and grew particularly attached to one of the daughters, **Constanze**. In August 1782, Mozart eventually married the 19-year-old Constanze in the Stephansdom. Their union appears to have been happy, despite most biographers' misogynist attacks on Constanze as unworthy of his genius. Mozart himself hated to be parted from her, if his letters – "I kiss and squeeze you 1,095,060,437,082 times" – and the fact that he rarely left her side, are anything to go by.

After giving many concerts as conductor and pianist, Mozart turned his hand to **opera**, enjoying his greatest success in July 1782 with what is now his least-known operatic work, *Die Entführung aus dem Serail* (The Escape from the Harem). It was after hearing *Die Entführung* for the first time that the Emperor Josef II is alleged to have said: "Too beautiful for our ears, and an awful lot of notes, dear Mozart", to which Mozart replied, "No more notes than necessary, Your Majesty!" Such tales have led to a popular belief that Mozart and Josef were constantly feuding over artistic debates: in his letters, however, Mozart's criticisms of the notoriously stingy emperor were on purely financial matters.

Mozart's next opera, *Le Nozze di Figaro* (The Marriage of Figaro), was premiered in May 1786 to a decidedly mixed reception, running for just nine performances. This was partly because its subject matter, in which a lecherous count is prevented from seducing a servant girl by an alliance between the serving classes and his own long-suffering wife, was controversial – as a play it had already been banned in Paris and Vienna. Josef II obviously liked it, however, inviting the cast to give a special performance at his summer residence at Laxenburg. And *Figaro*'s subversive overtones went down a storm in Prague, where Mozart premiered two later operas, *Don Giovanni* and *La Clemenza di Tito* (The Clemency of Tito), both of which were written in Vienna.

Mozart's **final work** was his *Requiem*, which was commissioned anonymously by an "unknown messenger" in the last year of the composer's life. Only after Mozart's death did the patron's identity become known: it was the recently widowed Count Franz Walsegg-Stuppach, who wished to pass the composition off as his own. In the end it became Mozart's own requiem, since it was still unfinished when he died during the night of December 4–5, 1791, after suffering rheumatic fever for two weeks. Few biographers have forgiven Constanze for not attending the **funeral service** at Stephansdom; some, however, assert that she was too distraught to show up. She has also been criticized for having the *Requiem* completed by one of Mozart's pupils, Sussmayr, so as to get the final payment – though this seems fair enough for a widow left with their two remaining children to raise (and apparently Mozart had suggested this course of action on his deathbed).

Yet more anecdotes surround the generally accepted rivalry with the *Kapellmeister* Antonio Salieri, though this, too, has been overplayed. Salieri was exclusively an opera composer, while Mozart, at least until 1786, was known chiefly as an instrumental composer and virtuoso pianist. Some went as far as to suggest that Salieri himself poisoned Mozart, an allegation strenuously denied by Salieri on his deathbed years later, but to no avail: Alexander Pushkin dramatized it, Nicolai Rimsky-Korsakov made it into an opera, and most famously *Amadeus*, Peter Shaffer's play on the subject, was made into an Oscar-winning film by Miloš Forman. For the story of how Mozart ended up in a pauper's grave, see p.163.

of marble and stucco (the Camesina family, who owned the property, were stucco artists) and there are none of Mozart's personal effects and precious little atmosphere. Nevertheless, it's worth a visit if only for the building's lovely courtyard, the views along Blutgasse, and the chance to hear some of Mozart's music.

# Kärntnerstrasse

As its name suggests, **Kärntnerstrasse** lies along the old road from Vienna to the southern Austrian province of Carinthia (Kärntner), and beyond to the Adriatic. Widened in the nineteenth century, badly bombed in World War II and pedestrianized in the 1970s, it retains only a few reminders of the days when it was home to the city's luxury retail trade. Nevertheless, it's still a favourite street for promenading and for window-shopping. As a whole the street has gone downmarket but one exception is **J. & L. Lobmeyr** (Ⓦwww.lobmeyr.at), at no. 26, which, as well as flogging expensive glass and crystal, also houses the **Wiener Glasmuseum** (Mon–Fri 10am–7pm, Sat 10am–6pm; free). The assistants are quite happy for you to wander through to the back of the shop, where you'll find the stairs that lead to the second-floor balcony. The wonderful, mostly antique, exhibits here include an incredible range of chandeliers, culminating, in both senses of the word, in a copy of the 1960s chandelier which graces the New York Metropolitan Opera House. Downstairs, in the shop itself, you'll see glassware sets still made to designs by Adolf Loos and Josef Hoffmann for the Wiener Werkstätte (see p.129).

The only other buildings of any architectural merit are no. 16, opposite the Steffl department store, which sports quasi-medieval frescoes, and the **Malteserkirche**, directly opposite Lobmeyr. The church is difficult to miss thanks to its imposing Neoclassical entrance, a misleading introduction to what is basically a simple, single-nave Gothic church. Inside is a splendid Neoclassical monument to Jean de la Valette, Grand Master of the Knights of Malta, who in 1565, as depicted in the monument's frieze, defended the island from the Turks – two of whose moustachioed brethren hold up the monument. Beyond, on the corner of Annagasse, is the street's oldest secular building, the modest three-storey Palais Esterházy, now a casino. Kärntnerstrasse continues south past the Staatsoper (see p.114), across the Ringstrasse to Karlsplatz (see p.118).

## Neuer Markt and Kaisergruft

Just west of Kärntnerstrasse lies the **Neuer Markt**, formerly the city's medieval flour market, now rather shamefully used as a car park. The centrepiece of the square is the Baroque Providentia fountain, better known as the **Donnerbrunnen**, after its sculptor Georg Raphael Donner. The nudity of the figures perched on the edge of the fountain – they represent the four Austrian tributaries of the Danube: the Enns, March, Ybbs and Traun – was deemed too risqué by the Empress Maria Theresia, who had the lead statues removed in 1770 to be melted down and made into cannons. They were returned unharmed in 1801, and in 1873 replaced by bronze copies: the young male figure of Traun, in particular, depicted on the point of catching a fish with his trident, clearly showed rather too much buttock for contemporary tastes, hence the judiciously placed fig leaf.

The buildings that surround the square are as undistinguished as those on Kärntnerstrasse itself – and that goes, too, for the **Kapuzinerkirche**. Yet this grim-looking church is one of the premier sights in Vienna, for since 1633, its

▲ J. & L. Lobmeyr

crypt – the **Kaisergruft** (daily 10am–6pm; €4) – has been the unlikely resting place of the Habsburgs (with just a few notable exceptions). They chose the lowly, mendicant Order of the Capuchins as a gesture of modesty; to underscore the point, an elaborate ceremony was enacted at each Habsburg funeral. As the funeral cortege approached the church, the prior would ask "Who seeks entry here?"

The grand master of the court would reply "I am His Majesty the Emperor of Austria, King of Hungary." The prior would then maintain "I know him not, who seeks entry?" "I am the Emperor, Apostolic King of Hungary, King of Bohemia, Dalmatia, Croatia, Slavonia, Galicia, Lodomeria, Illyria, Jerusalem, Archduke of Austria, Grand-Prince of Transylvania, Grand Duke of Tuscany and Krakow, Duke of Lorraine, Salzburg, Styria, Carinthia and Carniola." The prior would insist "I know him not, who seeks entry here?" At this the grand master would kneel, saying "A humble sinner, who begs God's mercy" – only then would the coffin be allowed in.

The Kaisergruft itself is entered from a doorway to the left of the church. Notices demand a respectful *Silentium!* – but don't let them kid you, this place is a tourist attraction above all else. Inside, though the crypt is neither gloomy nor Gothic in any sense of the word, it is, nevertheless, an intriguing insight into the Habsburgs' fascination with death.

To follow the tombs in chronological order, turn right immediately as you enter the crypt, and head for the small **Founders' Vault** on the right at the far end; here you'll find Matthias and his wife, Anna, who founded the Kaisergruft, and whose bodies were transferred here in 1633 (a decade or so after their deaths). The tombs that line the vault along which you've just walked are mostly fairly modest seventeenth-century works, though when you consider that twelve of the incumbents are children, these are clearly pretty big coffins. Bigger still are the final four monster Baroque pewter sarcophagi by the main entrance. Those of Leopold I and Josef I were both designed by Johann Lucas von Hildebrandt, the latter sporting ghoulish skulls in full armour below, and with bat wings above. Those of Karl VI and his wife are utterly "his'n'hers" designs carried out by Rococo artist **Balthasar Ferdinand Moll**: his sits on lions, with toothy skulls sporting crowns at each corner; hers sits on eagles, with women in mourning veils at each corner.

The main focus and highlight of the crypt is the nearby **Maria Theresia Vault**, almost entirely taken up with Moll's obscenely large double tomb for the empress and her husband, Franz Stephan. Over three metres high and wide, six metres long, and smothered in Rococo decorations, the imperial couple are depicted sitting up in bed, as if indignantly accusing one another of snoring. Immediately below their feet lies the simple copper coffin of their son, Josef II, to whom such pomposity was anathema. It was he who instigated the idea of a reusable coffin, and issued a decree enforcing its use in all funerals – not surprisingly, given the Viennese obsession with elaborate send-offs, the emperor was eventually forced to back down. Several more of Maria Theresia's sixteen children lie in the shadow of

## Meissl und Schadn

Emperor Franz-Josef was famous for eating *Tafelspitz* (boiled rump of beef) for lunch every day. His courtiers, naturally, followed suit and one of the best places to sample the dish was at the legendary **Meissl und Schadn** restaurant on Neuer Markt, which regularly offered more than 25 varieties of *Tafelspitz*. The restaurant was also the scene of imperial Vienna's most famous **political assassination**. On October 21, 1916, Prime Minister Count Karl von Stürgkh was shot dead, while enjoying his after-dinner cigar, by fellow diner Friedrich Adler. The assassin, son of the leader of the Social Democrats, Viktor Adler, was appalled by the slaughter of the war, and incensed by Stürgkh's refusal to reconvene parliament. Adler was sentenced to life imprisonment, but later released in an act of clemency by Emperor Karl I, and went on to outlive *Meissl und Schadn* itself, which was destroyed in the air raids of World War II.

## On Mozart's trail

It's almost as difficult to avoid images of Mozart in Vienna – on chocolate boxes, on liqueur bottles, on tourist brochures, on flyers for concerts – as it is in his home town of Salzburg. For it was in Vienna that Mozart spent the last decade of his life, during which he composed almost all of his most famous works. He moved thirteen times, for a variety of reasons, not least because he never managed to secure a permanent full-time posting, which meant that he was always on the point of leaving the city. Today the streets of the Innere Stadt are littered with plaques marking his various addresses, though in fact, only one – the Mozarthaus – still stands, and is now a museum to the composer. The following is a chronological list of all his known Viennese residences:

**Singerstrasse 7**. On his arrival in March 1781, Mozart stayed here with the Archbishop of Salzburg in the House of the Teutonic Knights.

**Petersplatz 11**. In May, Mozart rented a room from the Weber family, but had to move out in early September, due to rumours about his liaison with one of the daughters, Constanze.

**Graben 17**. After leaving the Webers, he moved round the corner to lodge with the Arnsteins, the city's most privileged Jewish family.

**Wipplingerstrasse 19**. Following the success of his opera Die Entführung aus dem Serail, Mozart moved here in July 1782, to be joined, after their marriage in August, by Constanze.

**Wipplingerstrasse 14**. In December 1782, the Mozarts moved down the street to a house belonging to a wealthy, converted Jew, Baron Wetzlar, where they lived in two rooms on the fourth floor.

**Kohlmarkt 7**. Three months later, in February 1783, Mozart moved again, as a favour to Wetzlar, who needed the rooms. Wetzlar waived the back rent, paid for the move, and paid for the Kohlmarkt lodgings.

**Judenplatz 3**. In April 1783, Mozart moved into "good accommodations", where his first child, Raimund Leopold, was born (his wife's cries during labour are alluded to in the second movement of his D minor String Quartet).

**Graben 29**. In January 1784, the Mozarts moved to the Trattnerhof, one of the most famous addresses in all Vienna at the time, owned by the wealthy publisher, Johann Thomas von Trattner, whose second wife, Maria Theresia, was one of Mozart's first pupils.

**Schulerstrasse 8**. In September 1784, the Mozarts moved into the Camesina House, behind Stephansdom (now the Mozarthaus; see p.47).

**Landstrasse Hauptstrasse 75–77**. In April 1787, the Mozarts moved out of the Innere Stadt into a garden apartment in the third district of Landstrasse – here he composed Eine kleine Nachtmusik.

**Tuchlauben 27**. In December 1787, landlord problems forced them to move to the corner of Schultergasse and Tuchlauben.

**Währingerstrasse 26**. In June 1788, due to financial difficulties, the Mozarts moved again. Mozart's financial crisis was partly precipitated by the Turkish threat – 1788 was known as the Türkenjahr – and compounded by the French Revolution.

**Judenplatz 4**. They kept this address from January 1789 for almost two years. It was here that their fifth child died and Constanze's illness began – an ulcerated leg with fears of infection, which brought further financial worries, as she had to move temporarily to Baden to take the cure.

**Rauhensteingasse 8**. Mozart's last move – his thirteenth address – took place in September 1791, when it appears that he had largely overcome his money problems. During their time here the couple's sixth child, Franz Xaver, was born, Mozart wrote La Clemenza di Tito and Die Zauberflöte, and spent his last days working on his Requiem. The plot is now occupied by the Steffl department store, whose ground floor contains a memorial/shop dedicated to the composer (daily 9.30am–7pm; free).

their mother, in ornate Rococo coffins, as does the only non-Habsburg among the crypt's 143 coffins, Karoline Fuchs-Mollard, the empress's governess.

After the Maria Theresa Vault it's all downhill architecturally. The **Franz II Vault** contains only the fairly plain tombs of the emperor and his four wives. Ferdinand I and his wife share the **Ferdinand Vault** with 37 others, though they're all buried in niches in the wall. At the far end of the crypt is the gloomy postwar bunker of the **New Vault**, which features jazzy, concrete, zigzag vaulting. Star corpses here include Maximilian I, Emperor of Mexico, who was assassinated in 1867, and Marie Louise, Napoleon's second wife. Their son, the Duke of Reichstadt or "L'Aiglon" (see p.201), who died of consumption at the age of 21, was also buried here until 1940, when Hitler had his remains transferred to Paris as a gesture of goodwill.

Finally, there's the **Franz-Josef Vault**, the emperor's sarcophagus, permanently strewn with fresh flowers. Even more revered, though, is his wife, Empress Elisabeth, who was assassinated in 1898, her tomb draped in Hungarian wreaths and colours. On the other side of the emperor is the coffin of their eldest son, Crown Prince Rudolf, who committed suicide in 1889 (see p.231).

The **Chapel** beyond contains the Kaisergruft's most recent arrival, the Empress Zita, who died in 1989 in exile in Switzerland, and was buried here with imperial pomp and circumstance. In the corner is a bust of her dashing, bemedalled husband, the Emperor Karl I, who was deposed in 1918, and is buried on the island of Madeira, where he died of pneumonia in 1922.

# East of Kärntnerstrasse

The Kaisergruft may be the main tourist attraction off Kärntnerstrasse, but there are a couple of other sights a short stroll east of the street. The most obvious is **Franziskanerplatz**, a pretty little square halfway along Weihburggasse, centred on a statue of Moses, and dominated by the Renaissance facade of the **Franziskanerkirche**, with its distinctive volute gable adorned with miniature obelisks. The interior, though, is High Baroque, with a high cherub count on just about every altar and ledge, and an incredible slab of sculpted drapery falling down in folds from the ceiling, on the left as you walk in. The St John of Nepomuk monument employs a similar theatrical effect – this time it's sculpted water flowing over the side – while the high altar features a huge Gothic Madonna set against a giant sunburst.

One block south, at Himmelpfortgasse 8, is the former **Winterpalais des Prinzen Eugen** (Mon–Thurs 8am–4pm, Fri 8am–3.30pm; free), a typically mighty Baroque palace strung out along a narrow street. Designed by Fischer von Erlach and extended by Hildebrandt, the palace now houses the Ministry of Finance; the only part visible to members of the public is the staircase, executed in grandiose style despite the restricted space. Four writhing Atlantes flank the stairs, and a figure of Hercules stands in the niche above the landing; the ceiling painting of Apollo is by Louis Dorigny. To reach the staircase, pass through the main entrance and take the last door on the right before the Rococo courtyard. To view the equally splendid state rooms, where the prince received foreign dignitaries, you must make a prior appointment by calling ☏51433.

Another block south at Johannesgasse 8 is the **Sammlung religiöse Volkskunst** (March–Dec Wed 10am–5pm; €3; Ⓦwww.volkskundemuseum.at), a department of the Folk Art Museum, housed in the city's former Ursuline convent (now the Academy of Music). Among the small collection of eighteenth-century folk paintings, travelling altars, and simple drawings illustrating the roads to heaven and hell, the highlight is, without doubt, the Baroque convent apothecary, built in 1747 and still in situ, with its pots and bottles arrayed in tall glass-fronted dressers.

One final block south is the pretty little pedestrianized street of Annagasse, lined with Baroque houses and named after its church, the **Annakirche**, an oasis of calm disturbed only by the odd snatch of muffled music coming from the nearby conservatoire. Built in the seventeenth century, the church was given a Baroque going-over in the following century by the Jesuits, who employed David Gran to paint a series of superb ceiling frescoes, and the high altar painting of the Holy Family.

### Haus der Musik

Signposts on Kärntnerstrasse point east to the **Haus der Musik** (daily 10am–10pm; €10; Ⓦwww.hdm.at), a hugely enjoyable interactive museum down Annagasse in the headquarters of the Wiener Philharmoniker (Ⓦwww.wienerphilharmoniker.at). On the first floor is a museum dedicated to this world-famous orchestra, which only allowed women to join its ranks in 1996. It comes as something of a surprise then, to find on the second floor a startling, state-of-the-art exhibition on the nature of sound, filled with high-tech installations.

To get you into the mood, the walls of the first, bare room you enter vibrate with prenatal synthesized sound. After a brief rundown on the biology of the ear, you enter the "laboratory of perception", where a bank of beautifully designed touch-screen computers explore human responses to frequency, volume and so on. Elsewhere on this floor, you can watch and stretch the sound waves created by your own voice, play around with prerecorded sounds in the dimly lit "sea of voices" room, and stick your head into sound bowls to hear everyday noises from around the world.

On the third floor, the subject is more conventional, with a room on each of the big three classical composers – Haydn, Mozart and Beethoven – as well as one each dedicated to Schubert, Strauss, Mahler and Schönberg's modernist posse. The displays are still a whole lot more imaginative than all the city's other musical memorials put together. There's plenty of hands-on fun and games: you can isolate each of the parts to Mozart's *Eine kleine Nachtmusik*, take a virtual tour of musically significant parts of Vienna, and do some virtual conducting.

There's yet more musical tomfoolery upstairs in the Brain Opera, where you can create your own music on the Gesture Wall, come over all percussive at the Rhythm Tree, and feed musical chips into a sophisticated computer-bank of sounds at the end.

# Graben and Kohlmarkt

The prime shopping streets of **Graben** and **Kohlmarkt** retain an air of exclusivity that Kärntnerstrasse has lost. Their shops, many of which are preserved in aspic as if the Empire lives on, advertise long-defunct branches in places such as Karlsbad, Leipzig and Prag. Others still sport the "K. K." or "k.u.k." emblem – *kaiserlich und königlich* (Imperial and Royal) – the Austrian equivalent of the "By Appointment to Her Majesty the Queen" flaunted by the shops of upper-crust London. In between these old-fashioned stores are several Art Nouveau edifices, and trendy designer jewellers produced by the doyen of modern Austrian architecture, **Hans Hollein**.

## Graben

**Graben** – its name translates as "ditch" – was once a moat that lay outside the Roman camp. It was filled in sometime in the thirteenth century, and, like Kärntnerstrasse,

## Designer shops

The shops at street level on Graben and neighbouring Kohlmarkt are by no means all stuck in the Habsburg era; in fact, several are minor masterpieces of twentieth-century design. First off, there's the **Knize** tailors at Graben no. 11, whose luxuriant black marble facade was designed by Adolf Loos in 1910. It's a typical example of Loos's work, which combines a love of rich materials with a strict aversion to unnecessary ornamentation. The sales room on the ground floor is tiny, but upstairs there's a much larger wood-panelled fitting room, unchanged since Loos's day. Another characteristic Loos facade can be seen at Kohlmarkt 16, designed in 1912 for the bookshop **Manz**. Despite his name (and rumours to the contrary), Loos did not design the underground toilets on Graben, which are the work of Wilhelm Beetz.

After World War II, Hans Hollein, of Haas Haus infamy (see p.42), continued where Loos had left off. The first real shot across the bows of the city's dour postwar architecture was his **Retti** candle shop (now a jewellers) at Kohlmarkt 8–10, designed in the 1960s, the doorway of its smooth aluminium facade shaped like a giant keyhole. Then, in the early 1970s, he gave the **Schullin** (now Caesars) jewellers, Graben 26, a polished marble facade spliced by a seam of mercurial gold that trickles down into the door frame. The jewellers were clearly enamoured, and commissioned Hollein to design another Schullin branch at Kohlmarkt 7 in the 1980s; this time, he chose a more subtle interplay of shapes and materials rather than a single arresting image: slender wooden columns support a gilded, industrial sheet-metal pediment, while portholes serve as showcases, and brass snakes as door handles.

was widened at the beginning of the nineteenth century, from which era most of its buildings date. The most conspicuous monument on Graben is Fischer von Erlach's **Pestsäule** (Plague Column), or Dreifaltigkeitssäule (Trinity Column) to give its full title, a towering, amorphous mass of swirling clouds, saints and cherubs, gilded crowns and shields, all covered in a cobweb of netting to keep the pigeons off. On the south side of the column, below the kneeling Emperor Leopold I, Faith and a cherub can be seen gleefully plunging a flaming torch into the guts of an old hag (Plague). Ostensibly erected to commemorate the end of the 1679 plague, similar monuments were raised throughout the Empire on the initiative of the Jesuits, as much to celebrate deliverance from the Protestant or Turkish "plague". As such, they became symbols of the Counter-Reformation.

The Pestsäule, and the Hildebrandt-designed **Bartolotti-Partenfeld Palace** at no. 11 on the corner of Dorotheergasse, are the only survivors of the Baroque era on Graben. The two most imposing buildings on the street are early works by Otto Wagner, best known for his later Jugendstil architecture: the 1895 **Ankerhaus**, at no. 10, which forms the block between Spiegelgasse and Dorotheergasse, and the much earlier **Grabenhof**, whose red marble loggia forms the most eye-catching ensemble. If you look up at the roof of the Ankerhaus, you'll see a wrought-iron-and-glass superstructure, originally intended as Wagner's own purpose-built studio.

The **Sparkasse** at the far end on the right, is a classic post-Napoleonic, or Biedermeier, building, both in its function, as a savings bank for the burgeoning bourgeoisie (note the busy-bee symbol on the facade), and in its severe, unadorned Neoclassicism. The latter became the officially sanctioned style of the Metternich era, its lack of ornament acting as a visual symbol of the latter's repressive, reactionary politics. The cluster of naked caryatids – the Graben nymphs – at the far end of the street are an unintentional reminder of the area's one-time associations as a red-light district, which stretch back to the Josephine era. The caryatids flank the entrance to the flagship store of **Julius Meinl** (Ⓦwww.meinl.com), Vienna's equivalent of Harrod's food hall.

# Peterskirche

Set back slightly from Graben, occupying a little square of its own, is the **Peterskirche**, more or less completed by Hildebrandt in 1708, and without doubt the finest Baroque church in the Innere Stadt. The confines of space within which he had to design the building mean that the twin-towered church is somewhat overwhelmed by its great green oval dome, both outside and in. Within, the dome's fresco of *The Assumption of the Virgin Mary* by Johann Michael Rottmayr is difficult to discern, but still adds immeasurably to the overall sense of theatrics, created by the lashings of ochre and gold stucco employed throughout. The High Baroque main altar and the fabulous cupola painting in the choir are the work of the Galli-Bibiena theatrical designers, a group of early eighteenth-century artists from Bologna who specialized in trompe l'oeil. The lavish gilded pulpit is, likewise, truly magnificent, but the most dramatic work of art is the silver and gold monument, designed by Lorenzo Mattielli, opposite, depicting St John of Nepomuk being thrown off Prague's Charles Bridge by some nasty-looking Czech bully-boys, with Václav IV in Roman garb directing the proceedings. Also worth noting are the church's fabulously ornate pew ends, which sprout a trio of cherubic heads, and the bejewelled and fully clothed skeletons from the catacombs in Rome, which lie in glass coffins in the Michaelskapelle and the Kapelle der Heilige Familie. The latter also boasts a portrait of the founder of the Opus Dei movement, José Maria Escrivá, whose Viennese base is here in the Peterskirche.

# Dorotheergasse

Of all the streets that fan out from Graben, the most rewarding is **Dorotheergasse**, home of several famous Viennese institutions. The first two face each other at the bottom of the street: the bohemian, nicotine-stained *Café Hawelka* (see p.264), and the ultimate stand-up sandwich bar, *Trzesniewski*, opposite (see p.263). Further up on the left is the *Hotel Graben*, where, from 1914 until his death in 1919, the poet Peter Altenberg was a permanent guest.

### Jüdisches Museum

Further up Dorotheergasse is the city's intriguing **Jüdisches Museum** (daily except Sat 10am–6pm, Thurs until 9pm; €6.50; ⑩www.jmw.at), halfway up in the Palais Eskeles at no. 11. Vienna was home to the first Jewish Museum in the world, founded in 1896 but forcibly closed by the Nazis in 1938; it wasn't until 1989 that it was finally re-established. Lavishly refurbished, the museum boasts an excellent bookshop and the *Teitelbaum Café*.

On the **ground floor**, pick up an audioguide and head for the covered courtyard (now a lecture hall), dominated by a giant glass cabinet display of Judaica by artist Nancy Spero. The prophetic nature of its etched quotations from the Torah and other sources is revealed on the walls, which are peppered with photographic images from Jewish culture and history. On the whole, though, the curators have rejected the usual static display cabinets and newsreel photos of past atrocities. Instead, the emphasis of the museum's excellent temporary exhibitions on the first floor is on celebrating Viennese Jewish life and culture, past and present. It's a bold and provocative approach, which succeeds in challenging the viewer's prejudices.

Special exhibitions also occupy part of the **second floor**, which contains the museum's permanent displays. Taking the Marxist Jewish critic Walter Benjamin's contention that "the past can only be seized as an image which flashes up at the instant when it can be recognized and is never seen again", the museum employs a series of free-standing glass panels imprinted with holograms – ranging from the knob of Theodor Herzl's walking stick, to a short clip capturing an everyday instance of anti-Semitism from 1911. These ghostly images, accompanied by judiciously selected soundbites (in German and English) on Zionism, assimilation and other key issues, pithily trace the history of Vienna's Jewry, juxtaposing the enormous achievements of the city's Jews – from Gustav Mahler to Billy Wilder – with its justified reputation as a hotbed of anti-Semitism.

Taking something of a different tack, the **third floor** contains the museum's *Schaudepot* or storage depot. The displays of Hanukkah candelabra and other ritual objects, located in large moveable glass cabinets, are deliberately haphazard – they constitute all that is left of the pre-1938 Jewish Museum and the community it served, and include many items literally pulled from the burnt embers of the city's synagogues, torched during *Kristallnacht* (see p.317).

### Dorotheum

Further on, beyond the Jüdisches Museum, stands the institution from which the street gets its name. The **Dorotheum** (Mon–Fri 9am–6pm; Ⓦwww.dorotheum .com) is the city's premier auction house, founded in 1707 by the Emperor Josef I as a pawnshop for the rich – the euphemism for those who had fallen on hard times was "going to visit Aunt Dorothy". Nowadays auctions take place daily, and you'll find almost anything up for sale from second-rate artworks, which go for a song, to Jugendstil furniture and minor works by the likes of Klimt and Schiele, for which you need to take out a mortgage.

Don't, however, be intimidated by the plush interior – anyone can walk in and view the goods free of charge. In the Glashof, on the ground floor, there are even fixed-priced goods for sale over the counter, everything from Hoffmann chairs to utter tat. The grandest of the showrooms is the main auction hall on the first floor with its high ceiling and second-floor balcony. There's another fixed-price shop for fine art on the second floor, along with an excellent café.

# Kohlmarkt

The line of the old Roman moat continues down the narrow street of Naglergasse, but most shoppers and strollers turn left at the end of Graben up **Kohlmarkt**, site of the old wood and charcoal market. The most striking aspect of the street is the perfectly framed vista of the Michaelertor, its green dome marking the main entrance to the Hofburg from the Innere Stadt. Before you head up Kohlmarkt, though, be sure to look up at the roof of the building on the corner, whose copper cupola is topped by a splendid Hussar, once used to advertise a shop.

Even more than Graben, Kohlmarkt is the city's last bastion of luxury retailing, perhaps best expressed by **Demel**, a very "k.u.k." establishment, which still advertises itself as the imperial and royal confectioners. Established in 1786 as *Zuckerbäckerei* to the Habsburgs, its very famous and opulent *Kaffee-Konditorei*, dating from 1888, is at no. 14 (see p.264). Another Viennese institution is the **Artaria Haus**, a Jugendstil building set back from the street at no. 9, and faced in marble by Max Fabiani in 1901, the bolted slabs on the first floor anticipating Wagner's Postsparkasse (see p.130). The bookshop of the master mapmakers, Freytag & Berndt, occupies the ground floor, while Artaria & Co itself, publishers of musical tracts by the likes of Haydn, Mozart and Beethoven, is situated on the first floor.

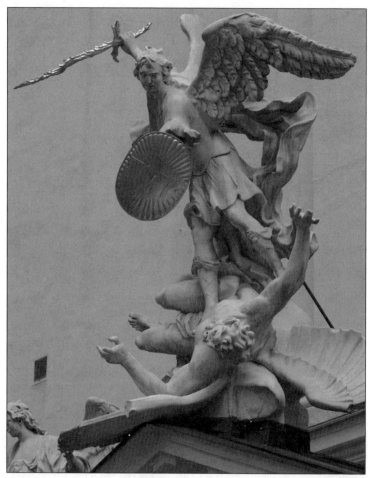

▲ Michaelerkirche

# Michaelerplatz to the Mölker Bastei

**Michaelerplatz**, the square at the top of Kohlmarkt, is the Hofburg's backdoor, and, like nearby **Herrengasse** ("Lords' Lane") and **Minoritenplatz**, has long been a high-prestige address due to its proximity to the royal court. Once upon a time, every single house here was the town palace of some aristocratic family or another; these now serve as ministries and embassies for the most part, making this something of a lifeless quarter, especially at the weekend. Nevertheless, both Michaelerplatz and Minoritenplatz are showpiece squares, and Herrengasse is worth exploring, if only for the Palais Ferstel, which houses the famous *Café Central* (see p.264) and Vienna's most opulent nineteenth-century shopping arcade, which brings you out onto the triangular square of **Freyung**, home to some of the city's finest exhibition galleries.

# Michaelerplatz

**Michaelerplatz** is dominated on one side by the exuberant arc of the neo-Baroque Michaelertrakt, begun in the 1720s by Fischer von Erlach's son, but only completed in the 1890s. Its curving balustrade is peppered with a lively parade of eagles, giant urns and trophies, while the gate's archways are framed by gargantuan statues of Hercules, and, at either end, fountains overburdened with yet more ungainly statuary: to the right, imperial land power; to the left, imperial naval power – though both were in short supply at the time the works were erected in 1897. The centre of the square is now occupied by a collection of archeological remains that lie exposed in a designer concrete trench (another of Hollein's works); most of what you see, however, are heating ducts dating only from the nineteenth century – hardly heart-stopping stuff.

Much more intriguing is the **Loos Haus**, on the corner of Kohlmarkt and Herrengasse, which caused an uproar when it was built in 1909–11 by Adolf Loos. Franz-Josef despised this "house without eyebrows" – in other words without the customary sculpted pediments which sit above the windows of most Viennese buildings. Work on the building was temporarily halted due to the protests, and only allowed to continue after Loos had acquiesced to adding bronze flower-boxes (to be filled with flora all year round). Today, it's difficult to see what all the fuss was about. The rippling green marble columns that frame the main entrance look inoffensive enough, but the building's lack of ornamental dressing, particularly in the upper storeys, was shocking at the time. The original occupants, Loos's own tailors, Goldman & Salatsch, went bankrupt in 1925, but the current owners, Raiffeisenbank, have their name displayed in simple gilt letters across the upper facade, just as Loos originally instructed Goldman & Salatsch. The bank holds regular exhibitions on the first floor of the building, so feel free to walk in.

The next block along from the Loos Haus is taken up by the altogether more conventional late-nineteenth-century Palais Herberstein, erected on the site of the **Café Griensteidl**, which was demolished in 1897. Reconstructed and reopened on the ground floor in 1990 to cash in on the nostalgia for fin-de-siècle Vienna, the *Griensteidl* was, in its day, the preferred meeting place of the *Jung-Wien* (Young Vienna) literary circle, most notably Arthur Schnitzler, Hermann Bahr and Hugo von Hofmannsthal. The journalist Karl Kraus, another regular, wrote his most famous diatribe, *The Demolished Literature*, against the *Jung-Wien* circle, shortly after the destruction of the café, suggesting that the movement "would soon expire for lack of a foyer". Instead, the *Jung-Wien* posse simply moved down Herrengasse to the *Café Central* (see opposite), much to the annoyance of Kraus himself, who was a regular there, too.

The oldest building on Michaelerplatz, and the source of its name, is the **Michaelerkirche** (daily 7am–10pm; free; ⓦwww.michaelerkirche.at), first built in the thirteenth century, though the Neoclassical facade, added in 1792, somewhat obscures this fact. Inside, the church retains its plain Gothic origins, but it's the later additions that are of more interest, in particular the *Fall of Angels*, a Rococo cloudburst of cherubs and angels rendered in alabaster, tumbling from the ceiling above the high altar. The gilded organ – the largest Baroque organ in Vienna – is very fine, and there are regular recitals.

# Herrengasse

**Herrengasse** was the preferred address of the nobility from the time the Habsburgs moved into the Hofburg until the fall of the dynasty in 1918. Its name dates from the sixteenth century, when the Diet of Lower Austria (*Niederösterreich*) built its regional headquarters or **Landhaus,** which still stands at no. 13. As well as being a federal Land in its own right since 1922, Vienna was for centuries also the capital of Lower Austria – the region that surrounds the city – until 1986, when St Pölten became the new capital. It was here at the Landhaus that the Viennese **1848 revolution** began on March 13. A large crowd of students, artisans and workers gathered outside the building demanding, among other things, freedom of the press and the resignation of the arch-conservative Prince Metternich. At one o'clock in the afternoon, soldiers fired into the crowd, killing several people and

## The Redl affair

Without doubt the greatest scandal to hit the Habsburgs in their twilight years was the infamous affair of **Colonel Alfred Redl,** who committed suicide in the early hours of May 25, 1913. Not only had the head of counterespionage in the imperial army been uncovered as a Russian secret agent, but he had been blackmailed into it because of his homosexuality, and had been in the pay of the Russians for the past seven years.

For some time, the Austrian military had been concerned about the leaking of classified information to the Russians. Then, early in April 1913, a letter was discovered to one "Nikon Nizetas", containing a considerable sum of money and the names and addresses of several Russian spies. It had been sent to the main post office in Vienna, but had remained unclaimed. Austrian counterespionage decided to stake out the post office and wait for someone to pick up the incriminating letter. For six weeks, two agents sat in the building opposite waiting for a clerk in the post office to ring the bell that had been specially installed to warn them of the arrival of "Nikon Nizetas".

When the bell finally rang at 5.55pm on May 24, one agent was having a pee, and the other was in the canteen. By the time they reached the street, they had missed their man, though they managed to take down the cab number. As the two men stood around considering their next move, the self-same cab miraculously reappeared outside the post office. Fortuitously for them, they discovered that "Nizetas" had left the felt sheath for his dagger in the back of the cab. They eventually retraced "Nizetas" to the *Hotel Klomser,* in the Palais Battyány, Bankgasse 2. The agents were shocked to find that the man who answered to Nizetas's description was one of their own superiors, Colonel Redl, who had just returned to the hotel. The agents handed the sheath to the concierge and waited to see if Redl would reclaim it. Caught off-guard as he left the hotel, Redl accepted the sheath from the receptionist, and then realizing what he had done, took flight. After a brief chase through the Innere Stadt, Redl gave himself up. He was handed a loaded revolver and told to go to his hotel room and do the honourable thing.

The whole affair would have been successfully hushed up – suicide among the upper echelons was very common – if it hadn't been for the locksmith who was called in to break into Redl's Prague flat. The place was decked out like a camp boudoir with pink whips on the wall and women's dresses in the cupboard. Unfortunately for the authorities, the locksmith in question was supposed to be playing football with the investigative journalist, Egon Erwin Kisch. When he told Kisch why he had been unable to turn up, Kisch immediately sent the story to a Berlin newspaper, and on May 29, the War Ministry was forced to admit the real reasons behind Redl's suicide. Redl's lover, Lieutenant Stefan Hromodka, on whom he had spent a small fortune, was sentenced to three months' hard labour (he later married, had several children and lived for another fifty years). Kisch became a popular hero overnight, with the best table in the *Café Central* reserved for him on all his visits to Vienna. The Redl affair later served as the plot for John Osborne's 1965 play *A Patriot for Me* and the subject of the 1985 film *Colonel Redl* by István Szabó.

sparking off a mass uprising in the city. Metternich resigned and fled the city the next day, disguised, so the story goes, as a washerwoman. The Emperor Ferdinand was another political casualty, abdicating in favour of Franz-Josef, but the revolt was eventually crushed on October 31.

Two doors up from the Landhaus, at no. 9, is the **Palais Mollard**, a Baroque palace which now houses two museums run by the Nationalbibliothek: the Globenmuseum and the Esperantomuseum (see p.90). Opposite the Landhaus is the grandiose Italianate **Palais Ferstel**, built in the Ringstrasse style by Heinrich Ferstel in 1860 for the Austro-Hungarian National Bank (it also housed the Stock Exchange until 1877). More importantly, the palace has long been home to Vienna's most famous *Kaffeehaus*, **Café Central**, restored in 1986 primarily as a tourist attraction, though admittedly a very beautiful one. At the turn of the century, the café's distinctively decorated Gothic vaults were *the* meeting place of the city's intellectuals, harbouring not only the literary lights of the *Jung-Wien* movement, but also the first generation of Austrian Socialists: Karl Renner, Viktor Adler and Otto Bauer. The latter were occasional chess adversaries of Leon Trotsky, who whiled away several years here before World War I. At the entrance to the café is a life-sized papier-mâché model of the moustachioed poet Peter Altenberg, another of the café's fin-de-siècle regulars.

Further up Herrengasse, past the café, is the entrance to the **Freyung Passage** – built in the 1860s as part of the Palais Ferstel – an eminently civilized, lovingly restored shopping arcade, which links Herrengasse with Freyung (see p.62). The focus of this elegant marble passage is a glass-roofed, hexagonal atrium, with a fountain crowned by a statue of the *Donaunixen* (Danube Mermaid), whose trickling water echoes down the arcade.

# Minoritenplatz

On the opposite side of Herrengasse, hidden away round the back of the Hofburg, is **Minoritenplatz**, a peaceful, cobbled square entirely surrounded by the Baroque former palaces of the nobility, now transformed into ministries and embassies.

At its centre is the fourteenth-century **Minoritenkirche**, whose stunted octagonal tower is one of the landmarks of the Innere Stadt (the top was knocked off by the Turks during the 1529 siege). The main entrance boasts probably the best-preserved Gothic portal in Vienna, with a tripartite tympanum depicting the Crucifixion. Inside, the church is impressively lofty, but it's the tacky copy of Leonardo da Vinci's *Last Supper*, on the north wall, which steals the show – only close inspection reveals it to be a mosaic, so minuscule are the polished mosaic pieces. The work was actually commissioned in 1806 by Napoleon, who planned to substitute it for the original in Milan, taking the latter back to Paris. By the time it was finished, however, Napoleon had fallen from power and the Emperor Franz I bought it instead, though it wasn't until 1847 that the Austrians managed to bring it back to Vienna.

On the south side of the square is a magnificent palace built for the Emperor Karl VI by Hildebrandt as the Court Chancery, and now the **Bundeskanzler-amt** (Federal Chancery), home of the Austrian Chancellor and the Foreign Ministry, whose main entrance opens onto Ballhausplatz. It was in this palace that Prince Metternich presided over the numerous meetings of the Congress of Vienna in 1814–15 (see p.62), and here, in the Chancellor's office, that the Austro-fascist leader, Engelbert Dollfuss, was assassinated during the abortive Nazi putsch of July 25, 1934. On that day, 154 members of the outlawed SS entered the building, and in the mêlée, Dollfuss was shot; his demands for a

## The Congress of Vienna

The one time that Vienna truly occupied centre stage in European history was during the **Congress of Vienna**. In October 1814, two emperors, three kings, eleven princes, ninety ambassadors and fifty-three uninvited representatives congregated in Vienna under the chairmanship of Prince Metternich, to try and thrash out a balance of power following the collapse of the Napoleonic Empire. In addition to the Big Four of Austria, Prussia, Britain and Russia, there were innumerable smaller delegations, including 32 minor German royals, with their wives, mistresses and secretaries of state – there was even an unofficial deputation from the Jews of Frankfurt. Lord Castlereagh, Britain's chief emissary, thought the Congress would last four weeks at the most – in the end, it dragged on for nearly nine months. The Final Act of the Congress wasn't signed until June 1815, long after Napoleon's escape from Elba – "The Congress is dissolved," he announced on landing at Cannes – and just twelve days before the final showdown at Waterloo.

The Congress has gone down in history as the largest and longest party the city has ever seen, encapsulated in the famous quote by the Prince de Ligne*: "Le congrès danse, mais il ne marche pas" ("The Congress dances, but it doesn't work"). Empress Maria Ludovica, Franz I's wife, said the Congress cost her ten years of her life – and indeed she died within a year of its conclusion.

In order to distract the lesser participants from the futility of the Congress, a vast programme of entertainment had to be organized. Ironically, the Austrian Emperor Franz I, who ultimately footed the bill, was no great party animal himself. Nevertheless, every night dinner was served in the Hofburg at forty tables; 1400 horses were required to transport the royal guests to the palace. There were tombolas, fireworks, tournaments, ballooning, theatre performances, sleighing expeditions in the Wienerwald, concerts – including the premiere of Fidelio conducted by Beethoven himself – and lots of dancing.

The Tsar, it was said, danced forty nights on the trot, his amorous adventures compounding his political rivalry with Metternich; the Russian Princess Bagration, nicknamed "the naked angel" for her habit of displaying her décolletage publicly, was voted the most beautiful; and Lord Castlereagh was deemed the most ridiculous. He was later joined by the Duke of Wellington, who hated the whole charade: "The hot rooms here have almost killed me," he wrote home. At one ball in the palace's Redoutensaal, 6000 guests turned up instead of the 3000 invited, as the imperial bouncers re-sold the tickets, and there was a brisk trade in the uneaten food from the tables of the Hofburg. Appropriately enough, the Congress's most lasting contribution to posterity was the popularization of the waltz. It was also during the Congress that Brie de Meaux was officially declared "le roi des fromages" by the Prince de Talleyrand during a cheese competition.

* The prince, who was in his eighties at the time, actually coined the epigram even before the Congress had begun, repeating it on every possible occasion until his death in December, brought on by a cold contracted while waiting outside his house for his latest mistress.

doctor and a priest fell on deaf ears, and, after two and a half hours, he died from his wounds.

# Freyung

The aforementioned Freyung Passage from Herrengasse brings you out onto **Freyung** itself, a misshapen square centred on the Austria-Brunnen, unveiled in 1846 with bronze nymphs representing Austria and the key rivers in the Habsburg Empire at the time: the Danube, Po, Elbe and Vistula. In medieval times Freyung was a popular spot for public executions, and during the annual

Christkindl Markt, held here in the eighteenth and nineteenth centuries, there were open-air theatre performances. Freyung boasts a **market** once more, this time selling organic produce (Fri & Sat), and in the run-up to Christmas, there's even a small Christkindlmarkt.

## Schottenstift

Freyung – meaning "Sanctuary" – derives its name from the **Schottenstift** (Monastery of the Scots), which dominates the north side of the square, and where fugitives could claim asylum in medieval times. The monastery was founded in 1155 by the Babenberg Duke Heinrich Jasomirgott, though the Benedictine monks invited over were, most probably, Irish and not Scottish. They were eventually expelled, after having shocked Viennese society by "trading in furs, initiating wild dances and starting games of ball". The monastery's glory days may be over, but its highly respected grammar school, the Schottengymnasium, founded in 1807, remains one of the most prestigious boys' schools in the country. Beyond the ornate Baroque plasterwork and faux marble, the **Schottenkirche** retains just a few reminders of its Romanesque origins in its southern choir chapel.

To view the former monastery's impressive art collection, in the **Museum im Schottenstift** (Thurs–Sat 11am–5pm; €5; Ⓦwww.schottenstift.at), you must first buy a ticket from the *Klosterladen* (monastery shop) beside the church, and take the stairs to the first floor. The walls are covered with mostly seventeenth- and eighteenth-century Dutch and German still lifes and landscapes. The prize exhibit, though, is the fifteenth-century winged altarpiece, which used to reside in the Schottenkirche. Thirteen out of the original sixteen panels survive: one side depicts scenes from the life of the Virgin; the reverse side (originally shown only at Easter) tells the story of the Passion. The vivid use of colour, the plasticity of the faces, and the daring stab at perspective mark this out as a masterpiece of late-Gothic art. Interestingly, the story is given a local setting: the Visitation of the Virgin Mary to Elizabeth takes place in Spiegelgasse, the town of Krems is portrayed in the picture of Christ carrying the cross, while medieval Vienna forms the backdrop for the Flight to Egypt.

# Mölker Bastei

The **Mölker Bastei**, one of the few remaining sections of the old zigzag fortifications that once surrounded the Innere Stadt, can be found up Schreyvogelgasse, to the west of Freyung. The sloping cobbled lane of Schreyvogelgasse should be familiar to fans of the movie *The Third Man*, for it's in the doorway of no. 8 that Harry Lime (played by Orson Welles) appears for the first time.

High up on the Mölker Bastei itself, at no. 8, is the **Pasqualatihaus** (Tues–Sun 10am–1pm & 2–6pm; Tues–Sat €2; Sun free; Ⓦwww.wienmuseum.at), where Beethoven lived on and off from 1804 onwards (he stayed at more than thirty addresses during his 35 years in Vienna). Herr Pasqualati wisely left the flat below empty so Beethoven could make as much noise as he wanted. The composer's apartment is now a museum (one of three museums dedicated to Beethoven in Vienna), though as usual, there's no indication of how the place might have looked at the time he lived there. Perhaps this is just as well – according to one visitor it was "the darkest, most disorderly place imaginable... under the piano (I do not exaggerate) an unemptied chamber pot... chairs... covered with plates bearing the remains of last night's supper". Instead, you're left to admire Ludwig's gilded salt and pepper pots and battered tin sugar container, or sit down and listen to some of his music.

# Am Hof to Hoher Markt

The area of the Innere Stadt that lies between **Am Hof** and **Hoher Markt** is where Vienna began. It was here that the Roman camp of Vindobona lay, with Hoher Markt, roughly speaking, as its main forum; later, the Babenbergs established their royal court at Am Hof, with the city's medieval Jewish ghetto close by. Few reminders of those days remain – above ground at least – although Marc-Aurel-Strasse (which commemorates the philosopher Emperor Marcus Aurelius, who died here in 180 AD), like neighbouring Wipplinger Strasse and Tuchlauben, is an old Roman road. Several of the city's most beguiling alleyways are hidden deep within this part of the Innere Stadt, as is Rachel Whiteread's controversial **Holocaust memorial** and one of the city's finest Gothic churches, **Maria am Gestade**.

## Am Hof

**Am Hof** is the largest square in the Innere Stadt, an attractive, tranquil spot, marred only by the surface protrusions of its underground car park. The name – *Hof* means both "royal court" and "courtyard" – dates from medieval times, when this was the headquarters of the Babenbergs, who lorded it over Vienna until the Habsburgs took over the reins in 1273. The jousting tournaments, religious plays and public executions have long gone, and the centrepiece is now the rather forbidding, matt black **Mariensäule** (Marian Column), erected by the Emperor Ferdinand III as a thank you to the Virgin for deliverance from the Protestant Swedish forces in the Thirty Years' War. At the base of the column, blackened cherubic angels in full armour wrestle with a dragon, lion, serpent and basilisk, representing hunger, war, heresy and the plague.

Dominating the square is the **Kirche am Hof**, from whose balcony the end of the Holy Roman Empire was declared in 1806, on the orders of Napoleon. The church's vast Baroque facade, topped by a host of angels, belies the fact that this is, for the most part, a fourteenth-century Gothic structure. Inside, it's quite frankly a stylistic mess, with the old Gothic Carmelite church struggling to get out from under some very crude later additions, dating from the period when the place was handed over to the Jesuits: Corinthian capitals are glued onto the main pillars, and the aisles have been turned into a series of side chapels, with stuck-on stucco porticos – only the coved and coffered ceiling of the choir works at all well. The adjoining former Jesuit seminary became the imperial war ministry, and as such was a prime target during the 1848 revolution. On October 6, the mob stormed the building, dragged out the War Minister, Count Latour, and promptly strung him up from a nearby lamppost. Three railway workers were later hanged for the offence.

Opposite the church is another architectural illusion, for behind the palatial facade of no. 7–9 is the city's **Feuerwehr Zentrale** (Central Fire Station); the engines are hidden behind the series of double doors. The firemen originally kept their equipment next door at no. 10 in the former **Bürgerliches Zeughaus** (Civic Armoury), suitably decorated with a panoply, several trophies and a double-headed eagle, and crowned by a spectacular cluster of figures holding up a gilded globe.

### Off Am Hof

If you pass under the archway by the Kirche am Hof, and head down Schulhof, you can see the church's Gothic origins clearly in its tall lancet windows and buttresses. Watchmakers continue to ply their trade from tiny lock-ups in between the buttresses at the back of the church, while opposite stands the Baroque Obizzi Palace, home to the city's **Uhrenmuseum** (Tues–Sun 10am–6pm; €4; ⓦwww .wienmuseum.at), ranged over three floors of Schulhof 2. Founded in 1917, this is the world's oldest clock museum, though the conservative displays fail to bring the collection alive. Nevertheless, you'll find every kind of time-measuring device, from sophisticated seventeenth-century grandfather clocks to pocket sundials. Other unusual exhibits include the smallest pendulum clock in the world, which fits inside a thimble, and a wide selection of eighteenth-century *Zwiebeluhren*, literally "onion clocks", set within cases shaped like fruit, musical instruments and the like.

## Judenplatz

Taking either of the two alleyways that lead north from Schulhof brings you to **Judenplatz**, one of the prettiest little squares in Vienna, now totally dominated by a bleak concrete mausoleum designed by British sculptor Rachel Whiteread as a **Holocaust-Mahnmal** (Holocaust Memorial) and unveiled in 2000. Smothered in row upon row of concrete casts of books like an inside-out library, the bunker-like memorial deliberately jars with its surroundings; a chilling A to Z of Nazi death camps is inscribed into its low plinth.

As the name suggests, Judenplatz was originally the site of the city's medieval Jewish ghetto, dating as far back as the twelfth century, and during the building of the Holocaust memorial, excavations revealed the smoke-blackened remains of the ghetto's chief synagogue, which was burnt to the ground in 1421. The foundations, and a few modest finds, can now be viewed in the **Museum Judenplatz** (Mon–Thurs & Sun 10am–6pm, Sat 10am–2pm; €4; ⓦwww.jmw.at), whose entrance is at no. 8. In addition, there's a short video with an English audioguide, and an interactive multimedia exhibition, both on medieval Jewish life in Vienna.

Ironically, Judenplatz already has a much older memorial commemorating the pogrom of 1421, known as the Wiener Geserah, and clearly visible on the oldest house on the square, **Zum grossen Jordan** (The Great Jordan), at no. 2. However, in this case, the inscription, beside a sixteenth-century relief of the Baptism of

▲ Rachel Whiteread's Holocaust-Mahnmal

## Jews in Vienna

Nine tenths of what the world celebrated as Viennese culture of the nineteenth century was a culture promoted, nurtured or in some cases even created by Viennese Jewry.

Stefan Zweig, *The World of Yesterday*, 1942

Most Jews have mixed feelings about Vienna: the city that nurtured the talents of Jewish geniuses such as Sigmund Freud, Gustav Mahler and Ludwig Wittgenstein also has a justifiable reputation as a hotbed of **anti-Semitism**. The city where the father of Zionism, Theodor Herzl, spent much of his adult life (see p.215) is also seen by many as the cradle of the Holocaust, where Hitler spent five years honing his hatred; where in 1986, Kurt Waldheim was elected president, despite (or more likely thanks to) rumours that he had participated in Nazi atrocities in the Balkans; and where, in 2000, the extreme right-wing FPÖ, led by Jörg Haider, helped form a coalition government.

Jews have lived in Vienna on and off for something like a thousand years, yet like most of the diaspora, they have been tolerated only when it suited the powers that be. They have been formally **expelled** twice, firstly in 1420, when the community was accused of supporting the Czech Hussite heretics (the real incentive for the expulsion was to boost the royal coffers by appropriating the Jews' property). The following year, those that remained – around 200 of them – were burned at the stake. Apart from a few individual exceptions, Jewish resettlement only took off again at the beginning of the seventeenth century, when Ferdinand II established a walled **ghetto** east of the Danube (now Leopoldstadt; see p.178). For around fifty years Jewish life flourished in the ghetto, but as the Counter-Reformation gathered pace, there was increasing pressure from Catholics to banish the Jews altogether. Finally, in 1670, Emperor Leopold I once more expelled the community.

The city suffered financially from the expulsion, and with the Turks at the gates of the city, a small number of Jewish financiers and merchants, hastily granted the status of *Hofjuden* or **"Court Jews"**, were permitted to resettle. The most famous of the Court Jews was Samuel Oppenheimer, who was appointed chief supplier to the imperial army by Leopold I in 1677. Despite the elevated status of the Court Jews, their position was precarious, and it wasn't until Josef II's 1781 **Toleranzpatent** that

Christ, celebrates the slaughter, when the Jews were driven out of Vienna. Those Jews lucky enough to escape fled to Hungary; the rest were burned at the stake, or – to avoid that fate – killed by the chief rabbi, who then committed suicide himself. The Latin inscription reads: "By baptism in the River Jordan bodies are cleansed from disease and evil, so all secret sinfulness takes flight. Thus the flame rising furiously through the whole city in 1421 purged the terrible crimes of the Hebrew dogs. As the world was once purged by the flood, so this time it was purged by fire."

The square's Jewish associations are also recalled by the statue of the writer **Gotthold Ephraim Lessing** (1729–81), striding forward in a great trench coat. Lessing, himself a theology graduate, was a key figure in the eighteenth-century German Enlightenment, who pleaded for tolerance to be shown towards the Jews. Erected in 1935, the statue proved too much for the Nazis, who had it destroyed; after the war, the sculptor Siegfried Charoux made a new model, but it wasn't returned to its original spot until 1982.

The most elaborate building on the square is the former **Böhmische Hofkanzlei** (Bohemian Court Chancery), designed by Fischer von Erlach and so monumental its Baroque facade continues halfway down Jordangasse. What you see on Judenplatz they were allowed to take up posts in the civil service and other professions and to build their own synagogue. At the same time, the *Toleranzpatent* began the process of assimilation, compelling Jews to take German names and restricting the use of Yiddish and Hebrew.

After the **1848 revolution**, all official restrictions on Jews were finally abolished. At this point there were only around 2000 Jews living in Vienna. In the next sixty years, thousands arrived in the city from the Habsburg provinces of Bohemia, Moravia and Galicia, the majority of them settling, initially at least, in **Leopolds-tadt**. By 1910, there were approximately 180,000 Jews in the city – almost ten percent of the total population and more than in any other German-speaking city. Though the majority of them were far from well-off, a visible minority formed a disproportionately large contingent in high-profile professions like banking, medicine, journalism and the arts. The Rothschilds were one of the richest families in the empire; virtually the entire staff on the liberal newspapers *Neue Freie Presse* and the *Wiener Tagblatt* were Jewish; the majority of the city's doctors were Jews, as were most of the **leading figures** in the Austrian Socialist Party. Other prominent Viennese Jews were the writers Arthur Schnitzler, Robert Musil, Stefan Zweig and Josef Roth, and the composers Arnold Schönberg, Alban Berg and the Strauss family.

Those Gentiles who found themselves sinking into poverty after the stock market crash of 1873 desperately needed a scapegoat. They eagerly latched onto anti-Semitism, which began to be promoted by the Christian Social Party under Karl Lueger, the city's populist mayor from 1897 to 1910. Perversely, this virulent anti-Semitism helped to save more Jews from the Nazis than in other more tolerant places, since thousands had already fled the country before the 1938 **Anschluss**. Initial humiliations instigated by the Nazis, such as making Jews clean toilets with prayer shawls, or forcing them to chew the grass of the Prater like cows, which were enjoyed by voyeuristic locals, meant that by 1941 a total of 120,000 Viennese Jews had escaped. Those that remained, however, were trapped, and some 65,000 died in the **Holocaust**. Right now, the community of around 9000 – many of them immigrants from eastern Europe – is enjoying something of a **renaissance**, much of it centred once again in Leopoldstadt, maintaining a dozen synagogues and several schools across the city.

is only the side of the building, whose lavish main portal actually looks out onto Wipplingerstrasse. It was from here that the Austrians ruled over the Czechs from 1627 to 1918; the building now houses the country's supreme Constitutional and Administrative courts.

## Altes Rathaus

On the other side of busy Wipplingerstrasse from the Böhmische Hofkanzlei is the **Altes Rathaus** (Old Town Hall), a dour-looking Baroque palace that served as the city's town hall until 1885 (when the huge Ringstrasse Rathaus was finished; see p.105). The main courtyard is undistinguished but for Donner's wonderful **Andromeda Brunnen** from 1741, which depicts the Greek myth in lead relief. Andromeda is sculpted in full relief, left at the mercy of a sea monster to appease the gods, and looks unfeasibly calm as Perseus, in very low relief, descends from afar on a winged horse to do away with the beast, which meanwhile spouts water noisily from its mouth into the basin below.

The Altes Rathaus now houses, among other things, the highly informative **Archives of the Austrian Resistance** (Mon, Wed & Fri 9am–5pm, Thurs 9am–7pm;

free; ⓦwww.doew.at), situated on the ground floor, with a permanent exhibition on the Austrian antifascist resistance, accompanied by German and English labelling throughout. The bulk of the displays cover resistance to the Nazi regime, but there's also a brief summary of the political upheavals of the interwar republic, including a detailed section on the rise of Austro-fascism in the 1930s. Despite the high level of popular support for the Nazis, the Austrian resistance remained extremely active throughout the war, as a result of which 2700 of its members were executed and thousands more were murdered by the Gestapo.

No one knows where the city's original town hall stood, but by the fourteenth century there was one located close to what is now the oldest part of the Altes Rathaus. The **Salvatorkapelle**, a Gothic chapel founded as the town hall chapel, is today hidden away at the opposite end of the courtyard from the fountain. It's a strange little building, much altered over the centuries, whose most handsome feature is its ornate Renaissance portal, flanked by richly carved columns, and visible only from Salvatorgasse.

# Maria am Gestade

A more compelling ecclesiastical edifice by far is the Gothic church of **Maria am Gestade**, up Salvatorgasse, which is topped by an elaborate filigree spire prickling with crockets and pinnacles, symbolizing the Virgin's heavenly crown – a stunning sight after dark when lit from within. With its drooping, beast-infested pendants and gilded mosaics, the stone canopy of the tall, slender west facade is also worth admiring, best viewed from the steps that lead up from Tiefergraben. The unusual interior – the nave is darker and narrower than the choir and set slightly askew – is a product of the church's cramped site, lying as it does on the very edge of the old medieval town. Much of what you see, it has to be said, both inside and out, is the result of nineteenth-century over-restoration, as the church caught fire in 1809 when it was used by the Napoleonic forces as an arms depot.

In one of the side chapels, the remains of the city's little-known patron saint, **Klemens Maria Hofbauer** (1751–1820), can be seen in a gilded reliquary, set within a jazzy, modern marble table beneath some rare medieval stained glass. As well as reviving the Marian cult, being a trained baker, and kick-starting Catholicism after the reforms of Josef II, Hofbauer was also made responsible for the welfare of the city's Czech community, which at its peak numbered over 100,000, and which the church has served since 1812. Incidentally, the church's name "am Gestade" means "by the riverbank" – the steep drop from the west door, which now goes down to Tiefergraben, used to be a minor tributary of the Danube, and the church was originally founded as a church for bargees.

# Hoher Markt and around

It's difficult to believe that the **Hoher Markt**, an unremarkable square surrounded by dour, postwar buildings and packed with parked cars, is Vienna's oldest square – yet this was the heart of the Roman camp, Vindobona. The **Roman ruins** (Tues–Sun 9am–1pm & 2–6pm; Tues–Sat €2, Sun free; ⓦwww.wienmuseum .at) of two large houses, with under-floor and wall heating, can be viewed beneath the shopping arcade on the south side of the square. In medieval times, Hoher Markt became a popular spot for public humiliations, the victims being displayed in a cage (later replaced by a pillory and gallows). That particular spot is now occupied by the square's centrepiece, Fischer von Erlach's **Vermählungsbrunnen** (Marriage Fountain), depicting the marriage of Mary and Joseph by the High Priest, for which there is no biblical evidence and few iconographical precedents.

Even more remarkable is the ornate bronze baldachin and gilded sunburst, held aloft by Corinthian columns with matching rams'-head urns (which light up at night), under which the trio shelter.

The real reason folk crowd into Hoher Markt, however, is to see the glorious Jugendstil **Ankeruhr**, a heavily gilded clock designed by Franz Matsch in 1914, which spans two buildings owned by Der Anker insurance company on the north side of the square. Each hour, a gilded cut-out figure, representing a key player in Vienna's history, shuffles across the dial of the clock, and at noon tour groups gather to watch the entire set of twelve figures slowly stagger across to a ten-minute medley of slightly mournful organ music (the identities of the figures, which range from Marcus Aurelius to Josef Haydn, are revealed on the clock's street-level plaque). Before you leave, check out the giant sculpted brackets on the underside of the clock bridge, which feature Adam, Eve, the Devil and an angel.

There are a couple of other sights worth seeking out in the streets around Hoher Markt, in particular the secular medieval **Neidhart-Fresken** (Tues 10am–1pm & 2–6pm, Fri–Sun & public hols 2–6pm; Tues, Fri & Sat €2, Sun free; Ⓦwww .wienmuseum.at), discovered in 1979 at Tuchlauben 19 during rebuilding works there. Executed around 1400, the wall paintings are patchy but jolly, some of them illustrating the stories of the *Minnesinger* (aristocratic minstrel) Neidhart von Reuenthal, others depicting a snowball fight, a ball game, dancing and general medieval merriment.

Round the corner in Brandstätte is a rather more recent architectural highlight, the **Zacherlhaus**, a residential block with business premises on the ground floor, built by the Slovene Josip Plečnik in 1905. The exterior is all grim, grey granite, relieved only by the ranks of Atlantes holding up the cornice and by the winged figure of the Archangel Michael above the ground floor, but it's the building's lens-shaped stairwell, hidden away at no. 2–4 Wildpretmarkt, that makes its way into the coffee-table books and postcards. Once you've made it down the black marble corridor, and sneaked past the janitor, you can admire the weird and wonderful lamps whose twisted bronze stands topped by lighted globes punctuate each floor of the wood-panelled stairwell.

# Around the Ruprechtskirche

In the 1980s the area around Ruprechtskirche became known as the "Bermuda Dreieck" or **Bermuda Triangle**, the idea being that there are so many bars in these few narrow streets that you could get lost forever. There are still a staggering number of bars hereabouts, particularly along Seitenstettengasse and Rabensteig, but you'd have to do some serious drinking to actually lose your way. During the day, the atmosphere is pretty muted, disturbed only by the few tourists who've come to appreciate the area's narrow cobbled streets and the two main sights: the Ruprechtskirche, the city's oldest church, and the Stadttempel, the only synagogue to survive *Kristallnacht*.

## Stadttempel (Synagogue)

Ironically, it was the building restrictions in force at the time the **Stadttempel** (Mon–Thurs guided tours 11.30am & 2pm; €3; bring your passport) was built, in 1826, that enabled it to be the only synagogue (out of 24) to survive *Kristallnacht* in 1938. According to the laws enacted under Josef II, synagogues had to be concealed from the street – hence you get no hint of what lies behind 2–4 Seitenstettengasse from the outside. Despite its hidden location, it did suffer some damage in 1938, since the area was predominantly Jewish and the surrounding buildings were torched, though it has since been lavishly restored. Designed from top to bottom by Biedermeier architect Josef Kornhäusel, it's a perfect example of the restrained architecture of the period, its top-lit, sky-blue oval dome dotted with golden stars and supported by yellow Ionic pillars which frame the surrounding two-tiered gallery. The slightly sinister presence of police with dogs and machine guns outside on Seitenstettengasse is a sad consequence of the terrorist attack on the Stadttempel which killed three people in 1983, the continuing vandalism of Jewish property that takes place in Austria and, of course, the controversial policies of the Israeli government.

## Ruprechtskirche and around

Round the corner from the Stadttempel on Ruprechtsplatz stands the ivy-covered **Ruprechtskirche**, its plain, stout architecture attesting to its venerable age. Originally built as long ago as the eighth century, the current building dates partly from the twelfth century, though it has been much altered and expanded since. Inside, the vivid reds and blues of the modern stained glass are a bit overwhelming, detracting from the church's uniquely intimate ambience. Mass is still said here, and the space is also frequently used for art exhibitions.

Steps lead down from beside the Ruprechtskirche to **Morzinplatz** by the Danube Canal, a notorious address during the Nazi period. On the west side of the square stood the *Hotel Metropol*, erected by a rich Jewish family to cope with the influx of visitors to the city's 1873 exhibition, but in 1938 taken over by the Gestapo, and used as their headquarters. Thousands were tortured here before the building was razed to the ground towards the end of the war. The plot is now occupied by the Leopold-Figl-Hof, named after the country's postwar Foreign Minister, who passed through the *Metropol* en route to Dachau. A **Monument to the Victims of Fascism** showing a prisoner surrounded by granite boulders from Mauthausen concentration camp was erected in front of the apartments in 1985. There's also a permanent **Memorial to the Victims in the Austrian Resistance Movement** (Mon 2–5pm, Thurs & Fri 9am–noon & 2–5pm; free) around the back of the building, on Salztorgasse, where detainees were bundled in for interrogation.

# East of Rotenturmstrasse

**East of Rotenturmstrasse**, which stretches from Stephansplatz to Schwedenplatz, Vienna's intricate, medieval streetplan continues. It's this, more than any specific sight, which makes a wander in this quarter rewarding, though four churches, varying in styles from High Baroque to neo-Byzantine, provide a focus. Incidentally, the red tower which gave Rotenturmstrasse its name – it was actually a red-and-white chequered city gate – has long since disappeared.

## Fleischmarkt and Postgasse

**Fleischmarkt**, the old meat market, straddles Rotenturmstrasse east as far as Postgasse. Greek merchants settled here in the eighteenth century and, following the 1781 "Toleranzpatent" (see p.305), built their own Greek Orthodox church on Griechengasse. The only inkling you get that there's a church there is from the cupola and pediment, which face onto Hafnersteig. On Fleischmarkt itself, though, there's another more imposing stripy, red-brick **Griechische Kirche**, redesigned in mock-Byzantine style in 1861 by Ringstrasse architect Theophil Hansen, its decorative castellations glistening with gilt. Opening hours are erratic, and you may not be able to get past the gloomy, arcaded vestibule – the best time to try is on a Sunday – to see the candle-lit interior, pungent with incense and richly decorated with icons, gilded frescoes and a giant iconostasis. Next door to the church, at no. 11, is the popular inn, *Griechenbeisl* (see p.272), a Viennese institution for more than five centuries; patronized by the Greeks, by textile merchants from Reichenberg (Liberec) in Bohemia, and by the likes of Beethoven, Brahms, Schubert and Strauss – inevitably, it milks the connections.

At the end of Fleischmarkt, turn right into Postgasse and you'll come to another neo-Byzantine edifice, the Ukrainian Greek-Catholic **Barbarakirche**, a much lighter concoction, with a pistachio-and-apricot-coloured facade. It's worth peeking inside at the pale-pink-and-blue nave to see this Greek-Catholic church's Rococo iconostasis studded with medallion-style icons. Far more imposing, though, is the Italianate facade of the **Dominikanerkirche**, further south along Postgasse; the vast interior is an orgy of early Baroque stucco and frescoes, rebuilt from scratch in the 1630s after being damaged in the first Turkish siege.

# Dr-Ignaz-Seipel-Platz and Heiligenkreuzerhof

One block west of Postgasse along Bäckerstrasse lies **Dr-Ignaz-Seipel-Platz**, named after the leader of the Christian Socials, who became the country's chancellor in 1922. Son of a cab driver, a trained priest, and, ironically, one-time professor of moral theology, Seipel was one of the city's most vociferous anti-Semites, who openly flirted with the idea of re-ghettoizing the Jews. Given the eventual fate of Austria's Jews, this rather attractive little square might have been better left as Universitäts Platz, since its east side is still taken up by the **Alte Universität** (Old University), founded by Rudolf IV in 1365, and thus the second oldest (after Prague's) in the German-speaking world. The current barracks-like building dates from the seventeenth century when, along with many of the country's leading educational institutions, it was handed over to the Jesuits.

By the eighteenth century, the university had outgrown its original premises and a more fanciful Baroque extension – now the **Akademie der Wissenschaften** (Academy of Sciences) – was built on the opposite side of the square. The building's barrel-vaulted Freskenraum, decorated with frescoes by Franz Maulbertsch, is occasionally open to the public during the summer vacation for exhibitions (Mon–Fri 10.30am–5.30pm). Josef Haydn made his last public appearance here when he attended the premiere of his oratorio *Die Schöpfung* on his seventy-sixth birthday in 1808. It was at this concert that Haydn – commonly known, even during his lifetime, as "Papa Joe" – is alleged to have laid his hands on the kneeling Beethoven, saying "What I have started, you shall finish."

Next door to the university is the **Jesuitenkirche** (also known as the Universitätskirche), whose rigidly flat facade rises up in two giant tiers that tower over the square. Begun in 1627 at the peak of the Jesuits' power, the church smacks of the Counter-Reformation and is one of the most awesome Baroque churches in Vienna. Inside, the most striking features are the gargantuan red-and-green barley-sugar spiral columns, the exquisitely carved inlaid pews, the richly gilded pulpit and Andrea Pozzo's clever trompe l'oeil dome – the illusion only works from the back of the church; walk towards the altar and the "dome" is revealed as a sham.

Behind the Jesuitenkirche runs the picturesque, cobbled lane of **Schönlaterngasse** (Beautiful Lantern Lane); a copy of the ornate lamp, immortalized in the street's name, juts out of the wall of no. 6. Opposite, at no. 9, the **Alte Schmiede** (Ⓦwww.alte-schmiede.at), now home to an arts club, houses an old smithy in the basement. Next door, at no. 7, stands the **Basilikenhaus**, where the dreaded basilisk – the half-toad, half-cock king of the serpents – was allegedly discovered in 1212 at the bottom of a well. The canny baker's apprentice, who volunteered to go down and capture the beast, took a mirror with him, and the basilisk, seeing its own reflection, turned to stone – you can view a sculpture of the creature in a niche on the facade.

Next door is a gateway into one of Vienna's hidden gems, the **Heiligenkreuzerhof**, the secret inner courtyard belonging to the Cistercian abbey of Heiligenkreuz, southwest of Vienna. A perfectly preserved slice of eighteenth-century Vienna, the courtyard is used for a weekly craft market on Sunday mornings. To visit the courtyard's winsome Bernardikapelle – a favourite venue for posh weddings – you must ring the bell of the *Hauswart* (caretaker) and ask permission, or phone ⓉT512 58 96.

# The Hofburg

His gaze wandered up high walls and he saw an island – gray, self-contained, and armed – lying there while the city's speed rushed blindly past it.

Robert Musil, A Man without Qualities

Enmeshed in the southwest corner of the Innere Stadt, the **Hofburg** (Court Palace) is a real hotchpotch of a place, with no natural centre, no symmetry and no obvious main entrance. Its name is synonymous with the Habsburgs, the dynasty that, at one time, ruled a vast multinational empire, stretching the length and breadth of Europe. Nowadays, apart from the tiny proportion that has been retained as the seat of the Austrian president, the palace has been taken over by various state organizations, museums and, even more prosaically, a conference centre.

Seven centuries of architecture lie within the sprawling complex, much of it hidden behind anodyne, Baroque facades. Part of the reason for the palace's complicated ground plan was the unwritten rule among the Habsburgs that no ruler should use the rooms of his or her predecessor. Oddly enough, the most attention-grabbing wing of the palace, the vast Neue Burg, is a white elephant, only completed in 1913, and never, in fact, occupied by the Habsburgs.

Despite its plummet in status, two of Vienna's most famous attractions keep the Hofburg at the top of visitors' agendas: the **Wiener Sängerknaben** (Vienna Boys' Choir), who perform regularly in the Hofburgkapelle, and the **Spanische Reitschule** (Spanish Riding School), who trot their stuff in the Winterreitschule. The real reason to visit the Hofburg, though, is the **Schatzkammer** (Imperial Treasury), with its superb collection of crown jewels, and the **Prunksaal**, Fischer von Erlach's richly decorated Baroque library. Also here are the **Kaiserappartements**, where the Emperor Franz-Josef I (1848–1916) and his wife Elisabeth lived and worked – her life is the subject of the palace's popular **Sisi Museum**. The palace also boasts several excellent museums and galleries: the **Albertina**, home to one of the world's great graphics collections, several departments of the Kunsthistorisches Museum, housed within the Neue Burg – the **Hofjagd- und Rüstkammer** (Court Hunting and Arms Collection), the **Sammlung alter Musikinstrumente** (Collection of Early Musical Instruments) and the **Ephesos Museum** (Ephesus Museum) – the **Museum für Völkerkunde** (Museum of Ethnology), and the **Schmetterlinghaus** (Butterfly House), part of the Burggarten.

## The Hofburg in history

The first fortress to be built on the site of the Hofburg was erected around 1275 by the Bohemian king Otakar II, who was also Duke of Austria. Three years later, the first of the Habsburgs, **Rudolf I** (1273–91), defeated and killed Otakar in battle, and set about

THE HOFBURG

**CAFÉS**

| | |
|---|---|
| Bräunerhof | 2 |
| Demel | 1 |
| Do & Co Albertina | 6 |
| Griensteidl | 3 |
| Palmenhaus | 8 |
| Soho | 7 |
| Tirolerhof | 4 |

**RESTAURANTS**

| | |
|---|---|
| Augustinerkeller | 5 |

NEUER MARKT

SPIEGELGASSE

DOROTHEERGASSE

STALLBURGGASSE

KOHLMARKT

HERRENGASSE

Palais Lobkowitz (Theatermuseum)

Augustinerkirche

Palais Pallavicini

Stallburg

Lipizzaner Museum

JOSEFSPLATZ

Josef II

Prunksaal

Redoutensäle

Winterreitschule

Schatzkammer

Hofburgkapelle

Alte Burg

SCHWEIZER HOF

Schweizertor

Franz I (II) IN DER BURG

Kaisertor

Kaiserappartements

Leopoldischinertrakt

Silberkammer

Reichskanzleitrakt

Michaelertor

MICHAELERPLATZ

Palais Mollard (Globenmuseum/ Esperantomuseum)

Amalienburg

MINORITENPLATZ

BALLHAUSPLATZ

Monument against War and Fascism

ALBERTINAPLATZ

Albertina

HANUSGASSE

GOETHEGASSE

Burggarten

Franz-Josef (I)

Mozart Denkmal

Schmetterlinghaus

Sammlung alter Musikinstrumente

Ephesosmuseum

Neue Burg

Hofjagd- und Rüstkammer

Museum für Völkerkunde

Prince Eugene of Savoy

HELDENPLATZ

Archduke Karl

Burgtor

BURGRING

Theseus-Tempel

Volksgarten

Grillparzer Monument

DR-KARL-RENNER-RING

Empress Elisabeth

BANKGASSE

LÖWELSTRASSE

▼ Volkstheater U-Bahn

▼ Babenbergerstrasse U-Bahn

OPERNRING

TEGETTOFFSTRASSE

AUGUSTINERSTRASSE

HABSBURGERGASSE

REITSCHULGASSE

SCHAUFELGASSE

Passageway

0   50 m

THE HOFBURG

expanding and strengthening the place. Rudolf's successor, Albrecht I (1291–1308), added a chapel to the palace, but it wasn't until **Ferdinand I** (1556–64) decided to make Vienna the Habsburgs' main base that the Hofburg became established more or less permanently as the chief dynastic seat.

Although the palace was protected by the city walls until 1857, the Habsburgs left nothing to chance after **Friedrich III** (1440–93) and his family were besieged in 1462 by the angry Viennese, and later by the Hungarian king Mathias Corvinus, during which they were forced to eat the pets – and the vultures who landed on the roof – in order to survive. Subsequent generations usually quit the palace (taking the imperial treasury with them) long before the enemy arrived. In 1683, with the Turks at the gates of Vienna, **Leopold I** (1657–1705) left in such haste, one eye-witness reported "the doors of the palace were left wide open". The same happened in 1805 and 1809, when Napoleon and his troops passed through, and in 1848, when the court fled, leaving the revolutionaries free to convene in the Winterreitschule.

**Court life** at the Hofburg reached its dramatic climax under Leopold I, who built a huge wooden theatre onto the palace fortifications, its three tiers of galleries seating up to 1500 under a trompe l'oeil painting of a Baroque church vault. Here, Leopold's own musical compositions were performed, along with numerous theatrical productions, in which the emperor himself often took the lead role. Inside the palace, courtiers had to wear the elaborate dress and abide by the complex etiquette of the Spanish court, described by one former courtier as "a strange medley of Olympian revelry, of Spanish monastic severity, and the rigorous discipline of a barrack". To get away from such formalities, the emperor was as keen as the rest of the court to spend much of the year in the more informal atmosphere of the family's various country retreats.

Though the Hofburg remained the Habsburgs' official winter residence, neglect of the complex became something of a recurring pattern with subsequent generations. Even under **Karl VI** (1711–40), who was responsible for building the incredible library and riding school, the palace remained lifeless for much of the year. **Maria Theresia** (1740–80) preferred the summer palace at Schönbrunn, even in winter, and after the death of her husband, Franz Stephan, in 1765, stayed there more often than not. The rooms they shared in the Hofburg were turned into empty shrines, while on the rare occasions when Maria Theresia did stay here, she used rooms on the third floor, draped with funereal black silk. Under the large-scale reforms of Emperor **Josef II** (1780–90), Spanish court ceremonial was abolished, much of the palace lay unused, and the palace guard reduced to a mere ninety men, considerably fewer than today. By 1792, one English visitor found the place "much out of repair, and so abominably dirty that its appearance is (if possible) more shabby and contemptible than that of our St James's".

During the **Congress of Vienna** in 1815 (see p.62), court life came back to the Hofburg for a hectic nine-month period. Tsar Alexander II of Russia had his own suite of rooms in one wing, while the Austrian emperor Franz I (1792–1835), as the Congress's chief host, was obliged to serve dinner for forty tables of foreign dignitaries on a nightly basis. Even **Franz-Josef I** (1848–1916), whose austere personal tastes are those most visible in the imperial apartments of the Hofburg, actually preferred to stay at Schönbrunn, not least because he could drop in on his mistress for breakfast there. His unhappy wife, Elisabeth, spent as little time as possible in the Hofburg (or Schönbrunn), to escape from the strictures of court life.

After the downfall of the Habsburgs, the palace became more or less a state-run concern, though the imperial apartments and the court silver and porcelain collection are now run by a private company. Only one wing, the Leopoldischinertrakt, is retained for affairs of state, and since 1946 has been home to the **Bundespräsident** (Ⓦwww.hofburg.at). Otherwise, the Hofburg is a relaxing place to wander round, mercifully free of officious types telling you to refrain from sitting on the steps and the like, and you can walk through the courtyards at any time of the day or night – there's even a bus service (#2a) that runs right through the palace.

## Approaching the Hofburg

The following account is divided into four main sections: In der Burg, the Alte Burg, Josefsplatz and the Neue Burg. If time is limited, the two most rewarding sights are the imperial **Schatzkammer** and the **Nationalbibliothek's Prunksaal**. The Spanish Riding School and Vienna Boys' Choir are the top tourist attractions, though getting to see either of them takes considerable forward planning, time and money, which you might be better off spending elsewhere. The tourist office leaflet, *Spanische Reitschule/Wiener Sängerknaben*, explains the intricate schedules of both institutions.

With an amorphous mass like the Hofburg, it's difficult to know how to go about attacking the place. There are two main **approaches**: from the Ringstrasse (trams #1 and #2, or U-Bahn Volksoper or Museumsquartier) or from Michaelerplatz in the Innere Stadt (U-Bahn Herrengasse). Bus #2a passes right through the complex,

---

### Hofburg opening times

The **opening times** of the various sights in and around the Hofburg are fiend-ishly complex; note especially that many are closed on Tuesdays. Though there's a charge for just about each attraction, there are several money-saving Kombi-Tickets available and most **entrance fees** are waived on May 18 and October 26; in addition, the collections in the Neue Burg are free on November 2, December 24 and December 31.

**Albertina** daily 10am–6pm, Wed till 9pm; €9.50; Ⓦ www.albertina.at; see p.93.

**Ephesos Museum** daily except Tues 10am–6pm; €8; Ⓦ www.khm.at; see p.96.

**Esperantomuseum** Mon–Wed, Fri & Sat 10am–2pm, Thurs 3–7pm; €2; Ⓦ www.onb.ac.at; see p.90.

**Globenmuseum** Mon–Wed, Fri & Sat 10am–2pm, Thurs 3–7pm; €3; Ⓦ www.onb.ac.at; see p.91.

**Hofburgkapelle** Jan–June & mid-Sept to Dec Mon–Thurs 11am–3pm, Fri 11am–1pm; €1.50; Mass mid-Sept to June Sun 9.15am; Ⓦ www.wsk.at; see p.86.

**Hofjagd- und Rüstkammer** daily except Tues 10am–6pm; €8; Ⓦ www.khm.at; see p.95.

**Kaiserappartements, Sisi Museum & Silberkammer** daily 9am–5pm; July & Aug until 5.30pm; €9.90; Ⓦ www.hofburg-wien.at; see p.77.

**Lipizzaner Museum** daily 9am–6pm; €5; Ⓦ www.lipizzaner.at; see p.88.

**Museum für Völkerkunde** daily except Tues 10am–6pm; €10; Ⓦ www.ethno-museum.ac.at; see p.97.

**Papyrusmuseum** Mon & Wed–Fri: July–Sept 10am–4pm; Oct–June 10am–5pm; €3; Ⓦ www.onb.ac.at; see p.92.

**Prunksaal** Tues–Sun 10am–6pm, Thurs until 9pm; €5; Ⓦ www.onb.ac.at; see p.89.

**Sammlung alter Musikinstrumente** daily except Tues 10am–6pm; €8; Ⓦ www.khm.at; see p.96.

**Schatzkammer** daily except Tues 10am–6pm; €10; Ⓦ www.khm.at; see p.83.

**Schmetterlinghaus** April–Oct Mon–Fri 10am–5pm, Sat & Sun 10am–6.30pm; Nov–March daily 10am–4pm; €5; Ⓦ www.schmetterlinghaus.at; see p.98.

**Spanische Reitschule** training Tues–Sat 10am–noon; €12; Ⓦ www.srs.at; see p.89.

**Theatermuseum** Tues–Sun 10am–6pm; €4.50; Ⓦ www.theatermuseum.at; see p.92.

to and from the Michaelertor, through In der Burg, across Heldenplatz, underneath the Burgtor, and on to U-Bahn Neubaugasse.

# In der Burg

**In der Burg** is the largest of the Hofburg's enclosed courtyards, and the one that sees the most human traffic – mostly tourists and passengers alighting from bus #2a. It was once a much livelier place, the venue for the daily changing of the guard under the Habsburgs, and, in the Middle Ages, the scene of tournaments, military parades and executions. The courtyard's seemingly uniform Baroque facades are the result of a century of ad hoc imperial extensions and not some grand plan. At the centre is an overblown monument to the **Emperor Franz**, dressed, appropriately enough, in a Roman toga, since as well as being (as Franz I, after 1804) the first Austrian emperor, he was (as Franz II, until 1806) the last Holy Roman Emperor (see p.306). Erected in the 1840s, the monument was a culmination of the patriotic cult of "Franz the Good", victor over Napoleon and host of the Congress of Vienna. Franz fever took off as soon as the emperor breathed his last in 1835, when aristocratic ladies fought over the feathers from the pillow on his deathbed.

The south side of the courtyard is occupied by the vast range of the **Leopoldischinertrakt** (Leopold Wing), with its lime green pilasters. Built by, and named after, Leopold I, and later occupied by the Empress Maria Theresia, it is now part of the president's official residence and is closed to the public. Opposite, the **Reichskanzleitrakt** (State Chancellery Wing), a giant, cream-coloured, Baroque confection, was built by a combination of Hildebrandt and the Fischer von Erlachs. Taking its name from the bureaucrats of the Holy Roman Empire, who resided here until 1806, it now houses the Kaiserappartements of Franz-Josef. The two wings are joined at the west end by the **Amalienburg**, built in the sixteenth century for Emperor Rudolf II, though he preferred Prague to Vienna. It takes its present name from Amalia, the widow of Josef I, who lived here until her death in 1742. Though essentially a Renaissance building, it sports a dinky little Baroque bell tower and weather vane, not to mention a sundial, a clock and a gilded globe that shows the current phase of the moon. Several subsequent emperors resided here, but the rooms now open to the public date from the time of Empress Elisabeth, who died in 1898, and Emperor Karl I (1916–18).

## Kaiserappartements

The **Kaiserappartements** (daily 9am–5pm; July & Aug until 5.30pm; €9.90; Ⓦwww.hofburg-wien.at) have always been a bit disappointing. Unlike Schönbrunn, virtually every room is decorated in the same style – dowdy, creamy-white walls and ceilings with gilded detailing, parquet flooring and red furnishings. The decor is a legacy of their last full-time imperial occupant, the **Emperor Franz-Josef**, who, though a stickler for pomp and protocol at official functions, was notoriously frugal in his daily life. For opulence, you need to see Maria Theresia's apartments at Schönbrunn (see p.191).

In an effort to spice up the proceedings, the palace has installed the crowd-pulling **Sisi Museum**, a hagiographical exhibition on Franz-Josef's wife, the empress Elisabeth, whose cosseted life was pretty miserable, whose demise was violent and unexpected, and who has long had an almost cultish following among

## Empress Elisabeth (1837–98)

**Empress Elisabeth** – or Sisi as she was, and still is, affectionately known – was born into the eccentric Wittelsbach dynasty that produced the likes of "Mad" King Ludwig II of Bavaria, one of Elisabeth's cousins. She enjoyed a carefree, sheltered upbringing, only to find herself engaged to the Habsburg emperor **Franz-Josef I** – another cousin – at the age of just 15, after an entirely public, two-day courtship. Franz-Josef was undoubtedly devoted to his new bride, but he was also in thrall to his mother, the Archduchess Sophie, who was a control freak obsessed with court ceremonial. She prevented Elisabeth from fulfilling her role either as empress or mother to her children, by hand-picking her ladies-in-waiting, and having the children removed from her care as soon as they were born. Later, Elisabeth advised her daughter, "Marriage is an absurd institution. At the age of fifteen you are sold, you make a vow you do not understand, and you regret for thirty years or more that you cannot break it."

By 1860, having dutifully produced a male heir, Elisabeth developed a pathological aversion to the Viennese court, abandoning her children and husband and fleeing to Madeira for six months. She spent much of the rest of her lonely life travelling around Europe, under the pseudonym of **Countess Hohenembs**. She crisscrossed the continent, never staying in one place for long, and went on interminable cruises (she had an anchor tattooed on her shoulder), alarming her companions by asking to be tied down on deck during storms. She sought solace in fencing, hiking and riding – she was reckoned to be one of the finest horsewomen in Europe – in the preservation of her beauty, and in writing poetry. When her cousin, King Ludwig, and then her only son, Rudolf, committed suicide within a few years of each other, she became convinced that she too was mentally unstable. From then on, she dressed only in black, and carried a black fan which she used to hide the wrinkles that were beginning to appear on her face. As she herself put it, "When we cannot be happy in the way that we desire there is nothing for it but to fall in love with our sorrows."

The similarities between Elisabeth's life and that of Britain's Princess Diana are difficult to ignore. Her marriage to Franz-Josef was the wedding of the century. The

her former subjects. The labelling is in German and English throughout, and there's a free audioguide in English available.

### Sisi Museum

Before you reach the Kaiserappartements, you must pass through the **Sisi Museum**. The exhibition purports to examine the myth and reality of Elisabeth's life, though, to be honest, the curators are too busy hyping up the myth and hamming up the reality to be bothered with any serious analysis. The melodramatic displays begin with the empress's death mask and mourning fan, the latter painted by her daughter, Marie Valerie. Next is a corridor filled with Sisi memorabilia, photos of the numerous monuments to Elisabeth that were erected throughout the empire, and – best of all – film clips of the various celluloid incarnations of Sisi. A copy of one of Elisabeth's fantastic ball gowns dominates the next room, but the highlight has to be the kitsch collection of half-life-sized plaster statues of the imperial couple through the decades – like a complete set of imperial garden gnomes.

Room 5 boasts Franz Xavier Winterhalter's famous portrait of the empress, aged 28, décolletée, dressed in her star gown, with jewelled stars in her hair, plus replicas of those very stars and several other sets of the empress's jewellery, plus an unbelievable three-quarter-size gilded statue of Elisabeth. Also displayed here is Sisi's famous "duck squeezer" – she was an enthusiastic consumer of raw meat juice – as well as the weighing machine with which she was obsessed in later life, emperor was marrying a virginal, "fairy-tale princess", whom he hardly knew, and, despite public appearances, the marriage was a disaster. The issue of Franz-Josef and Elisabeth, like that of Charles and Diana, divided folk then, as it does historians and biographers now. Either Franz-Josef was a boorish, unimaginative prig, who visited brothels during their honeymoon, or Elisabeth was a frigid, neurotic, narcissistic brat, obsessed with her looks. Like Diana, Elisabeth won people's hearts with her beauty. Yet at the time many Viennese resented her frequent absences from the capital, and were appalled at her **pro-Hungarian** sentiments. She was fluent in Hungarian – she even wrote letters to the rest of the family in Hungarian – and was instrumental in the political compromise with Hungary in 1867. After a brief reconciliation between the imperial couple, which resulted in the birth of Marie Valerie, the only child Elisabeth was ever close to, Sisi and Franz-Josef remained irrevocably estranged. She even encouraged Franz-Josef to get a mistress, introducing him to the actress Katharina Schratt, "very much as a woman might put flowers into a room she felt to be dreary", as biographer Rebecca West put it.

By 1897, Elisabeth's health began to deteriorate rapidly to the extent that she could barely walk. Despite her poor health, and her obsession with madness and death, few would have predicted her final demise. On September 10, 1898, the empress was assassinated by an Italian anarchist, **Luigi Luccheni**, on Lake Geneva. A local newspaper had unwisely announced the arrival of the empress, who was attempting to travel incognito. As she was about to board a steamer to go to tea with Baroness Rothschild, Luccheni rushed up and stabbed her in the heart with a sharpened file. Like the empress, Luccheni had also been wandering aimlessly around Europe, in his case looking for someone famous to kill. He was fixed on assassinating the Duke of Orléans, but when he failed to turn up in Geneva as planned, resolved to attack the Austrian empress instead. Naturally enough, thousands turned out for Sisi's funeral in Vienna; however unpopular she may have been, few would have wished her such a violent end. Over the years, her martyrdom has ensured that the myth and mystery around her life remain as compelling as ever.

and a reconstruction of her opulent personal railway carriage saloon. Her apotheosis, though, occurs in the shrine-like room, where a Sisi mannequin stands bathed in dark-green light surrounded by the sound of seagulls and the repeated line from one of her poems "*Eine Möwe bin ich von keinen Land*" (I am a seagull from no land). In the final room, still sporting its original forensic label from the trial in Geneva, is the **murder weapon**: a three-sided metal file with a wooden handle.

### Franz-Josef's apartments

Following the Sisi Museum, you enter **Franz-Josef's apartments**. Despite being a field marshal, the emperor almost invariably dressed in a simple lieutenant's uniform. His eating habits were equally spartan: a breakfast of coffee, *Semmel* (bread roll) and a slice of ham (except during Lent) was followed by a lunch of *Tafelspitz* (boiled rump). He distrusted telephones, cars and electricity, and his only concession to modern life was his use of the telegraph. The second room you come to is the **Waiting Room to the Audience Chamber**, which is crowded with costumed wax figures, from peasants to soldiers, waiting for an audience with the emperor. On the walls formulaic Neoclassical frescoes glorify the emperor Franz I, executed by Johann Peter Krafft, a pupil of Jacques-Louis David, and commissioned by the emperor's fourth wife, Caroline of Bavaria. Once granted an audience, the supplicant was ushered forward into the adjacent **Audience Room**, where the emperor would stand twice a week behind the high desk to receive

▲ Empress Elisabeth

the hoi polloi – the *Audienz-Liste* from January 3, 1910, can be seen on the desk. According to court etiquette, visitors had to bow three times at the beginning and at the end of the audience, backing out of the room so as not to display their derrières to the emperor. Of the imperial portraits in the room, the most familiar – reproduced on countless postcards across the city – is the easel painting of the octogenarian Franz-Josef, sporting his trademark bushy sideburns and slumped slightly in his chair, the year before his death.

Passing swiftly through the pale turquoise Conference Room, where the emperor used to consult his ministers, you come to the **Emperor Franz-Josef's Study**. Here, the emperor would sit at his rosewood desk, poring over official paperwork and giving each document, however trivial, his close attention before signing it, thus earning himself the nickname, "the first bureaucrat of the empire". Pride of place over the emperor's desk was always given to Winterhalter's portrait of the Empress Elisabeth, décolletée, hair down and ready for bed, though the version you see here is, in fact, a copy. A hidden door leads into a cramped room that was occupied by the emperor's personal valets. Franz-Josef went through valets "like candles", literally wearing them out with his early-morning routine.

The **Emperor's Bedroom** features the simple iron bedstead in which he would sleep under a camelskin cover. The delights of a modern washbasin were alien to the ascetic emperor, hence the foldaway toilet set. It was only at the insistence of Elisabeth that Franz-Josef agreed to install lavatories in the Hofburg; he himself preferred to use a bedpan. Moving through the Large Salon, you reach the **Small Salon**, now a memorial room to Franz-Josef's ill-fated brother, Maximilian, Emperor of Mexico, and his wife, Charlotte, daughter of the king of the Belgians, whose portraits hang here. The bust is of the Austrian naval hero, Tegethoff, who defeated the Italians at the Battle of Lissa in 1866,

## Emperor Franz-Josef I (1848–1916)

**Emperor Franz-Josef I** was Europe's longest-serving monarch, and Austria's most popular. His 68-year reign was the most sustained period of relative stability the country had ever known, and a stark contrast with what followed. Like his grandfather, Franz I – "Franz the Good" (see p.77) – he was a legend in his own lifetime, and, thanks to the Viennese love of nostalgia, the myth continues today. As historian William Johnston wrote, "Franz-Josef I symbolized more than he achieved." His aversion to innovation was legendary, epitomized by his addiction to the Spanish court ceremonial. At dinner, guests could only begin to eat when the emperor did, and had to cease eating at the moment the emperor finished each course. Since Franz-Josef was a very fast eater, his guests rarely enjoyed more than a few mouthfuls. Such dinners were also very silent, as no one was permitted to speak unless spoken to by the emperor – and he was more intent on eating. On his sickbed, during a particularly severe illness, though he could barely speak, he is said to have reprimanded the doctor who had been hastily summoned: "Go home and dress correctly." "Lord, this court is stuffy," remarked Edward VII, when in Vienna while Prince of Wales.

Despite the pomp and protocol that surrounded him, Franz-Josef was a simple man. When the first official census was conducted in Austria, he famously wrote down his occupation as "self-employed civil servant". Indeed, his dedication to his job was legendary: he woke at 4am (occasionally 3.30am), washed in cold water and would be at his desk by 5am. Twice a week he would give general audience to any of his citizens who wished to see him – as many as one hundred in a morning (the supplicants were, of course, vetted first). After finishing work around 5.30pm, he would tidy his desk and, towards the end of his life, be in bed by 8.30pm. He had no great love of the arts – "I go to the opera as a sacrifice to my country," he once wrote to his mistress. His only passions were hunting and mountain climbing, and his annual holiday was invariably taken in Bad Ischl, in the Salzkammergut.

Franz-Josef's personal life was something of a disaster. He was in awe of his powerful mother, the Archduchess Sophie, who arranged and then proceeded to sabotage his marriage to Elisabeth, one of his cousins (see p.78). Despite his estrangement from Elisabeth – she spent as little time as possible in his company – Franz-Josef remained dedicated to her all his life. Meanwhile, for over thirty years, he conducted an affair with the Burgtheater actress **Katharina Schratt**. Matters outside the bedroom were no better. His brother Maximilian was executed in Mexico in 1867, his only son Rudolf committed suicide in 1887, and his wife was assassinated in 1898.

On the morning of November 20, 1916, at the age of 86, Franz-Josef rose at 3.30am for the very last time. His last words to his valet that night were: "Tomorrow morning, half past three".

and was later entrusted with bringing back Maximilian's body to Vienna from Mexico, after his assassination in 1867.

## ② Elisabeth's apartments

The empress's suite of rooms in the Amalienburg adjoins the Small Salon, beginning with the **Empress's Living Room and Bedroom**. Originally kitted out for the imperial newlyweds in 1854, these rooms were used exclusively by Elisabeth after the couple's estrangement – if Franz-Josef wanted to enter, he had to ring the bell behind the curtains in the Small Salon. Even so, the empress considered the Hofburg "a prison fortress", and spent as little time as possible here. Any feminine touches there might have been have long since disappeared – in any case, the empress slept on a simple fold-away iron bed (painted to imitate walnut), which was removed to another room during the day.

Significantly, the paintings in the **Empress's Dressing and Exercise Room** are not of the imperial family – most of whom she despised – but of her own family and of her beloved horses and dogs. Here you get to see some of the gymnastic equipment on which the empress exercised daily, a practice considered highly unorthodox at the time. She even had wooden rings screwed into the gilded panelling above the doorway. Elisabeth was obsessed with her beauty, whose maintenance became a full-time job as she entered her middle age. She was in the habit of rising at 5am, plunging into a cold bath, after which she would have a massage and then do some gym. Elisabeth took as long as three hours to dress, and in order to maintain the inch-perfect waistline demanded of nineteenth-century women – she boasted a 50cm waistline until the day she died – the empress would lace herself so tightly she was frequently short of breath. Her hair, which reached down to her heels, often took another three hours to prepare; washing it in cognac and egg took up an entire day.

## Alexander's apartments

Lastly, you come to the handful of rooms named after the Russian tsar who stayed in the Hofburg for the best part of a year during the Congress of Vienna in 1815. The decor, as usual, is almost identical to the rooms in the rest of the palace, and there are no reminders of Alexander's time here. Passing quickly through the Anteroom and the Red Salon, hung with Gobelin tapestries, you come to the **Dining Room**, laid out as it would have been in the time of Franz-Josef, with silver and gold cutlery placed to the right of the plate, in compliance with the Spanish court ceremonial, and napkins folded according to a secret court formula. The strictures of eating with the emperor are described on p.81; Elisabeth herself detested formal dinners, and on the few occasions when she did appear, refused to touch the food.

## Silberkammer

On the ground floor, seven rooms are devoted to the **Silberkammer** (Imperial Silver Collection) – not to be confused with the Schatzkammer (see opposite), which is where the crown jewels are displayed. The latter has universal appeal, whereas the Silberkammer is something of an acquired taste. Among the numerous cake and jelly moulds, kitchen utensils, bed linen, crockery, candelabra and Sèvres, Minton and Meissen porcelain, the star exhibit is the early nineteenth-century monster Milanese table-centrepiece in gilded bronze, which stretches for more than ten metres in a covered courtyard along a table strewn with classical figures and gilded bronze-and-crystal urns. Also on display are the chests for moving all this gear around from palace to palace, several original imperial menus and napkins folded (to a secret formula) to look like birds. More unusual still is the silverware used by Empress Elisabeth on her many sea voyages, the dolphin service made for the empress's villa in Corfu and the Hungarian earthenware service made for her private dairy at Schönbrunn. Finally, don't miss the stone jugs and salvers, with which the emperor and empress washed the feet of 24 ordinary men and women every year on Maundy Thursday – there are pictures close by depicting the event, though the Empress Elisabeth, who only had to wash the feet of the oldest woman, usually opted out altogether (which meant all the women missed out on the ceremony).

# Alte Burg

The **Alte Burg** (Old Palace) lies at the very heart of the Hofburg, occupying roughly the same space as the first fortress built here in 1275, and gradually enlarged over the centuries by successive Habsburgs. A small section of the old moat, and the original drawbridge mechanism, can still be seen by the main entrance to the Alte Burg, known as the **Schweizertor** (Swiss Gate) after the Swiss mercenaries who were employed to guard it under Maria Theresia. The gateway itself, with its maroon-and-grey-banded columns and gilded relief, was erected in 1552 under Ferdinand I, whose innumerable kingdoms are listed in the gilded inscription above the gateway, ending with the glorious "ZC", meaning "etc". Passing through the Schweizertor, you enter the inner courtyard of the Alte Burg, or **Schweizerhof** (Swiss Courtyard), given a unified, rather dull facade by Maria Theresia's court architect, Nicolo Pacassi. The stairs on the right lead up to the Hofburgkapelle, where the Vienna Boys' Choir performs Mass every Sunday (see p.86). Below is the entrance to the world-famous Schatzkammer, where the Habsburgs' most precious treasures reside.

## Schatzkammer

Of all the museums in the Hofburg, the imperial **Schatzkammer** (daily except Tues 10am–6pm; €10; Ⓦwww.khm.at) is by far and away the most rewarding. Here you can see some of the finest medieval craftsmanship and jewellery in Europe, including the imperial regalia and relics of the Holy Roman Empire, not to mention the Habsburgs' own crown jewels, countless reliquaries and robes, goldwork and silverware. Much of it was collected by Ferdinand I for his *Kunstkammer*, and from his reign onwards, the collection became a sort of unofficial safety-deposit box for the Habsburgs. In the reign of Karl VI, the treasury was gathered together and stored on the ground floor of the Alte Burg; the original iron door displayed at the entrance is dated 1712. You can wander at will around the twenty or so dimly lit rooms, though since the labelling is in German only, you might wish to avail yourself of the English-language audioguide (€3).

### Insignia and mementoes of the Habsburgs

From the fifteenth century onwards, with only a brief caesura, the Habsburgs ruled as Holy Roman Emperors. In 1804, Franz II pre-empted the dissolution of the Holy Roman Empire by two years, declaring himself Franz I, Emperor of Austria, and using the stunning golden **Crown of Rudolf II**, studded with diamonds, rubies, pearls and, at the very top, a huge sapphire, as the Austrian imperial crown. The crown now forms the centrepiece of room 2, and, like the accompanying orb and a sceptre carved from a narwhal's tusk, it was made in Prague at the beginning of the seventeenth century. There's a bronze bust of the moody, broody Rudolf by his court architect, Adriaen de Vries, displayed here too. For Franz I's coronation as King of Hungary in 1830, he commissioned for himself a glorious gold-embroidered burgundy cloak, with an ermine collar and a long train, now displayed in room 3 alongside some lovely velvet hats for knights, sporting huge ostrich feathers.

The sequence of rooms goes slightly awry at this point, so pass quickly through room 9, and turn left into room 5, where the mother of all cots resides: an overwrought, silver-gilt cradle with silk and velvet trimmings, made in 1811 by the City of Paris for Napoleon's son – known variously as the **Duke of Reichstadt** or "King of Rome" – by his second wife, Marie Louise, daughter of the emperor Franz I. The poor boy must have had nightmares from the golden eagle that hovers over the cot, and it comes as no surprise that this sickly, sensitive child died of tuberculosis at the age of just 21 (see p.201). Also displayed here are mementoes of Franz-Josef's ill-fated brother, Emperor Maximilian of Mexico, including his Mexican gold sceptre and chain of state.

Passing swiftly through the beautiful baptismal robes and vessels in room 6, some of which were embroidered by Maria Theresia herself for her grandchildren, you enter room 7, which contains the remnants of the **Habsburgs' private jewellery** (most of it was spirited out of the country on the orders of Emperor Karl I in the last few weeks of World War I). There are some serious stones on display here, including the largest cut emerald in the world, the 2680-carat Colombian emerald the size of a fist, which was carved into a salt cellar in Prague in 1641 and stands centre stage, and the huge garnet, "La Bella", which forms the centre of a double-headed eagle, along with an amethyst and an opal set in enamel (both considered to be as valuable as diamonds at the time). Another notable treasure is the solid gold Turkish crown of the rebel King of Hungary, István Bocskai, from 1605, inlaid with pearls and precious stones. More difficult to spot are the few pieces of the Empress Elisabeth's jewellery, looking a bit upstaged among such illustrious company. Finally, before you leave, don't miss the golden rosebush presented by the pope to Franz I's wife, a traditional papal gift on the fourth Sunday in Lent to "the most worthy person".

Room 8 contains the so-called **"inalienable heirlooms"**, two pieces collected by Ferdinand I, which the Habsburgs were very keen to hold onto: a giant fourth-century agate dish, stolen from Constantinople in 1204 and thought at the time to be the Holy Grail, and a 2.43m-long narwhal's tusk, which was originally believed to have come from a unicorn and therefore to be a sacred symbol of Christ.

## Geistliche Schatzkammer

At this point, you come to the five rooms (I–V) devoted to the **Geistliche Schatzkammer** (Sacred Treasury), which kicks off with a long corridor of ecclesiastical robes, a vast seventeenth-century amber altar from Prussia, plus a super-kitsch silver-gilt, gem-encrusted miniature of the Mariensäule on Am Hof (see p.64). Elsewhere there are a bewildering number of golden goblets, crystal crosses, jade candlesticks, huge monstrances, and best of all, reliquaries. In room IV, the star reliquary is the one purporting to contain the nail that pierced the right hand of Christ, though there's also a monstrance boasting a fragment of the cross, and one of only three pieces of St Veronica's *sudarium* or veil to be authenticated by the Vatican. One of room IV's most macabre items is the small seventeenth-century ebony-framed glass cabinet, filled with miniature skeletons partying round the glittering red-and-gold tomb of Ferdinand III, commissioned by his son, Leopold I.

## Insignia of the Holy Roman Empire

Continuing a thematic tour through the Schatzkammer entails backtracking through the Sacred Treasury, followed by rooms 6 and 5, to return to room 9. Here, you'll find the late medieval **crown jewels and regalia of the Electoral Prince of Bohemia**, including matching gold lamé cloak, gloves and hat. Since the Holy Roman Emperor was automatically also King of Bohemia from the fourteenth century onwards, someone had to stand in for the latter during the imperial coronation. There are still more ancient royal insignia in room 10, which found their way into Habsburg hands via the Hohenstaufen dynasty. Among the most striking items have got to be the snazzy red silk stockings of William II of Normandy, and the red silk mantle decorated with Kufic inscriptions worn by Roger II when he was crowned King of Sicily in the twelfth century.

The highlight of the whole collection is the **crown jewels of the Holy Roman Empire** in room 11, the majority of which were traditionally kept in Nuremberg, but were brought to Vienna in 1796 and retained by the Habsburgs after the abolition of the empire in 1806. The Nazis brought them back to Nuremberg in 1938, but the Americans made sure they were returned to the Austrians in 1945. The centrepiece is the octagonal **imperial crown** itself, a superb piece of Byzantine jewellery, smothered with pearls, large precious stones and enamel plaques. Legend has it that the crown was used in the coronation of Charlemagne in 800, but it now seems likely that it dates back only to that of Otto I in 962. Similarly encrusted with jewels are the eleventh-century imperial cross, the twelfth-century imperial orb, and the very venerable ninth-century **Purse of St Stephen**, which belonged to Charlemagne himself and, so the story goes, contained earth soaked in the blood of the first Christian martyr.

Also on display in room 11 is a relic of the **Holy Cross**, with a hole said to have been made by one of the nails and therefore soaked in Christ's blood. In the same glass cabinet is the legendary **Holy Lance**, with which the Roman soldier pierced the side of Christ whilst he was on the cross. The lance, which actually dates from the eighth century, was long considered to be the most important imperial relic, and alleged to have magic powers – whoever possessed it held the destiny of the world in their hands. It was in front of this exhibit that the young Hitler is supposed to have had a mystical revelation, which changed the course of his life (and therefore of twentieth-century history), though the story is probably apocryphal.

Room 12 is given over to the **imperial relics**, many of them donated to the treasury by Emperor Karl IV, who was a serious relic freak. What you see is a mere *soupçon* of the original collection – he is thought to have gathered together more than two hundred relics (he apparently even stole one from the pope). There's a tooth from John the Baptist, a bit of the tablecloth from the Last Supper, a bone from the arm of St Anne, a chip of wood from Christ's manger, and even a small piece of his bib.

## The Burgundian treasures

The last four rooms (13–16) of the Schatzkammer contain the substantial dowry that came into Habsburg hands in 1477, when the emperor Maximilian I married the only daughter and heiress of the Duke of Burgundy. By so doing, Maximilian also became Grand Master of the **Order of the Golden Fleece**, the exclusive Burgundian order of chivalry founded in 1430, whose insignia are displayed here: heavy mantles embroidered with gold thread, a collar of golden links from which the "fleece" would hang, and the ram emblem, worn by the 24 knights of the order at all times. The Grand Master was responsible for replacing any collars that were lost in battle; to his financial embarrassment, Maximilian had to pay for four golden collars that vanished in hand-to-hand fighting during the Battle of Guinegate in

1479. After Maximilian, the Habsburgs became more or less hereditary sovereign Grand Masters of the Order, which still exists, albeit in a debased form, today. The final room contains an amazing collection of fifteenth-century gold-embroidered Mass robes covered in portraits of saints.

## Hofburgkapelle

The **Hofburgkapelle** (Jan–June & mid-Sept to Dec Mon–Thurs 11am–3pm, Fri 11am–1pm; €1.50), up the stairs above the entrance to the Schatzkammer, was built in the late 1440s by the emperor Friedrich III. Despite numerous alterations over the centuries, the interior retains its Gothic vaulting, its carved ceiling pendants, and much of its fifteenth-century wooden statuary protected by richly carved baldachins. The chapel is a favourite venue for society weddings, but for the public the real point of visiting it is to hear Mass performed by the Hofmusikkapelle, made up of members of the Wiener Sängerknaben, or **Vienna Boys' Choir** (Ⓦwww.wsk.at), accompanied by musicians from the Staatsoper.

Founded back in 1498 by Emperor Maximilian I, the choir was closely linked to the imperial family, for whom they used to perform; famous Sängerknaben have included Schubert and Haydn. In 1918, the choir went under with the dynasty, but was revived in 1924 and, dressed in ludicrous sailors' uniforms and caps (fashionable in the 1920s), has since become a major Austrian export. There are, in fact, four choirs, who rotate jobs, the most important of which is to tour the world. The easiest way to hear them in Vienna is to go to Mass at the Hofburgkapelle on Sunday mornings (and on religious holidays) at 9.15am (Jan–June & mid-Sept to Dec). **Tickets** can be bought in person (Fri 11am–1pm & 3–5pm, Sun 8.15–8.45am), or booked in advance by fax or email (Ⓕ533 99 27-75, Ⓔhmk @aon.at). The boys remain just about out of sight up in the organ loft for the whole of the Mass, and the only time you get a proper look at them is when they get their photos taken next to the congregation after the service.

# Josefsplatz and around

**Josefsplatz** is without doubt one of the most imposing squares in Vienna, lined on three sides by the blank, brilliant-white Baroque facades of the Hofburg. The square started out as the churchyard of the **Augustinerkirche** (now masked by the south wing of the Augustinertrakt), and later served as the training ground for the **Spanische Reitschule** (now housed to the north). It's appropriate then, that the central spot is occupied by an equestrian statue of the emperor Josef II – rather surprisingly, the first-ever public statue of a Habsburg when it was unveiled in 1807. It's Josef who lends his name to the square, which he opened to the public by tearing down the wall that enclosed it within the Hofburg.

The facades of the north and south wings, by Nicolo Pacassi, are typically severe and unadorned, but the middle wing – which houses the **Prunksaal** of the Nationalbibliothek (see p.89) – is a much earlier, more exuberant work by Johann Bernhard Fischer von Erlach, completed in 1735 by his son, Josef Emanuel. The attic storey bristles with marble statuary and urns, the central sculptural group above the main entrance features Minerva, goddess of wisdom, trampling Ignorance and Hunger with her four-horse chariot; on either side Atlantes struggle to contain a cluster of scientific instruments and two giant gilded globes from tumbling onto the cobbles below.

If any Habsburg embodied the spirit of the Enlightenment it was **Emperor Josef II**. Born in 1741, the eldest son of Empress Maria Theresia, Josef was groomed for his role from an early age. After the death of his father, Franz Stephan, in 1765, his mother appointed him co-regent with her, and from 1780 he ruled in his own right. Though his reforming zeal surpassed that of all his predecessors put together – it's estimated that he published 6000 decrees and 11,000 new laws – he was in many ways only continuing and furthering the work his mother had begun.

Josef's most famous reform was the 1781 **Toleranzpatent**, which allowed freedom of worship for non-Catholics, and, significantly, lifted many restrictions on Jews. In addition, he expelled the Jesuit order, and dissolved and sold off four hundred contemplative or "idle" monasteries. Though his policies incurred the wrath of the established church (including Pope Pius VI), Josef himself was a devout Catholic – his intention was to reduce the power of the Church in secular life, thereby giving him and his officials a much freer hand. Other decrees had more altruistic motives: aristocratic privilege before the law was abolished, with miscreant counts made to sweep the streets as punishment in the same way as commoners had for centuries. Among his most popular measures was the opening of the royal gardens of the Prater and Augarten in Vienna to the public, and of the court opera house to non-aristocratic patrons.

Josef's decrees didn't end with the general populace. During his reign, the royal household was stripped of its former grandeur, and court ceremony virtually disappeared. One of his first acts as co-regent was to abolish the imperial birthdays and gala-days, forty of which were observed annually. He wore simple, almost bourgeois clothing, drove through the streets in a two-seater carriage and was often seen on foot with the people. On becoming regent, he handed over his personal inheritance to the state treasury and demanded that his brother Leopold do the same, much to the latter's disgust. He lived for most of the time in a small outbuilding in the **Augarten** (see p.187), boarding up much of the Hofburg and Schönbrunn to avoid the expense of having to guard them.

Despite his liberal policies, Josef was something of a despot – "everything for the people, and nothing through the people" was his catchphrase – who listened to no advice, and whose invasions of his subjects' privacy did not endear him to them. He forbade the wearing of corsets, on health grounds, the superstitious practice of ringing of church bells to ward off lightning, the dressing of saintly images in real clothes, and even the baking of honeycakes (which he considered bad for the digestion). Most famously, he banned the use of coffins, because of a shortage of wood, insisting corpses should be taken to the cemetery in reusable coffins, and buried in linen sacks to hasten decomposition, again on health grounds. In the end, he issued so many decrees that few of them could be effectively executed, and many were rescinded as soon as his reign was over.

"As a man he has the greatest merit and talent; as a prince he will have continual erections and never be satisfied. His reign will be a continual Priapism." Despite the Prince de Ligne's predictions, it was the emperor's wives who ended up dissatisfied. Though Josef clearly loved his first wife, **Isabella of Parma**, she had eyes only for his sister, Maria Christina. Isabella died of smallpox in 1763, having given birth to two daughters, neither of whom survived to adulthood. Josef's second marriage, to **Maria Josepha of Bavaria**, was no love match. "Her figure is short, thick-set, and without a vestige of charm. Her face is covered with spots and pimples. Her teeth are horrible," he confided to a friend on first setting eyes on her. He treated her abysmally, and it was a release for her when she too died of smallpox in 1767. The emperor failed to attend the funeral, never remarried, took no mistresses, and lived as a bachelor until his death of tuberculosis at the age of just 48 in 1790.

The north wing on Josefsplatz houses the **Redoutensäle**, originally the court theatre, but remodelled in the 1740s as a ballroom and banqueting hall. Mozart and Beethoven both conducted performances of their own works here, and the rooms became the traditional venue for the annual Hofball, held in February under the Habsburgs at the high point of the *Fasching* (carnival or ball season). Anthony Trollope's mother, Fanny, who attended a masked ball here in 1836 at which over four thousand were said to be present, thought "the press was almost intolerable, and the dust raised by it such as quite to destroy the beauty and effect of this very magnificent room".

Josefsplatz features heavily in the film *The Third Man* – it's here that Harry Lime is alleged to have been run over by a truck. The Baroque **Palais Pallavicini**, at no. 5, with its distinctive caryatids flanking the entrance, was used as Harry's apartment.

# Winterreitschule and Stallburg

Performances of the Spanische Reitschule (see below) take place regularly in the splendid Baroque **Winterreitschule** (Winter Riding School) on the west side of Reitschulgasse. Purpose-built by Josef Emanuel Fischer von Erlach in 1735, the 55m-long Reitsaal is surrounded by a two-tiered spectators' gallery (with notoriously bad sightlines) held up by 46 Composite columns. Situated at one end of the Reitsaal, the former imperial box features an equestrian portrait of the emperor Karl VI, to which all the riders raise their hats on entering, in thanks for the wonderful arena he bequeathed them. It was in these unlikely surroundings that Austria's first democratically elected assembly met in July 1848 and voted to abolish serfdom (the court having fled to Innsbruck).

## Visiting the Winterreitschule

Access to the Winterreitschule is usually from the north side of Josefsplatz, outside which the riding school's complicated public schedule of training sessions and performances is posted up. There are one or two **performances** (*Vorführungen*) a week (usually Sun 11am) from March to June and from September to December, though for at least a month of the latter period, the school is usually on tour. Seats **cost** €24–165, and standing room is €18–28. Even at those prices, the performances are booked solid months in advance, so you need to plan ahead (@www.srs.at). The alternative is to buy direct through a ticket agency in Vienna, who will charge you a heavy commission.

From February to June and from late August until December, the school also holds **training sessions** (*Morgenarbeit mit Musik* or *Leichtes Bewegen*; Tues–Sat 10am–noon); seats cost €12 and are sold at the Josefsplatz-entrance box office or the Lipizzaner Museum (see below). If you want a good seat, it's best to get to the box office when it opens at 9am; if you don't want to queue, turn up after 11am, when it's usually easy enough to get in as folk soon get bored.

## Stallburg: Lipizzaner Museum

Sixty-five horses are kept in the **Stallburg** (stables), an arcaded Renaissance palace, on the other side of Reitschulgasse, conceived in 1559 by Ferdinand I as a private residence for his son, Maximilian. Lack of finance delayed the project, and when Maximilian became emperor, he converted the building into the imperial stables. You can glimpse the horses as they are taken over to (and brought back from) the Winterreitschule for their morning exercise, but for a closer look at the nags, you need either to watch a training session (see above), or visit the **Lipizzaner Museum** (daily 9am–6pm; €5; @www.lipizzaner.at), which is now housed in part of the

The Habsburgs' world-famous **Spanische Reitschule** (Spanish Riding School) has its origins with the Archduke Karl, brother of Maximilian II, who established several studs at Lipizza, northeast of Trieste (now the Slovene town of Lipica), in the 1570s. By cross-breeding Spanish, Arab and Berber horses, the studs created the Lipizzaner strain, which subsequently supplied the Habsburgs with all their cavalry and show horses. However, it was only properly expanded by the Spanish-bred Emperor Karl VI, who gave the riding school a permanent home in the Hofburg. After World War I, the stud was moved to Piber near Graz, though the horses are now bred at both places.

Since an imperial decree in the early nineteenth century, only silver-white stallions have been used, though when they're born Lipizzaner foals can be any shade of brown to grey, their coats turning white when they are at least four years old. They begin to learn the dressage steps from the age of seven, gradually progressing to the aerial exercises for which they are famous, and can live to the ripe old age of 32. The highlight of the dressage is the Kapriole, where the horse leaps into the air and tucks up all four of its legs. In deference to tradition (and with an eye to their tourist appeal) the riders wear period costume: black boots which reach above the knee, white buckskin jodhpurs, double-breasted brown tail coats, white gloves and a black bicorn hat.

The Spanish Riding School is such an intrinsic part of Vienna's Habsburg heritage industry, it's difficult not to feel a certain revulsion for the whole charade. That said, to witness the Lipizzaners' equestrian ballet is an unforgettable, if faintly ridiculous, experience; certainly those with any interest in horses will feel compelled to see at least a rehearsal. As Edward Crankshaw famously remarked more than half a century ago:

"The cabrioling of the pure white Lipizzaners is, by all our standards, the absolute of uselessness. The horses, fine, beautiful, and strong, are utterly divorced from all natural movement, living their lives in an atmosphere of unreality with every step laid down for them and no chance whatsoever of a moment's deviation. And so it was with the nineteenth-century Habsburgs."

Stallburg. Along with various equestrian bits (literally) and bobs, you can watch videos of the various set-pieces of equestrian ballet, look at the horses snoozing in their stables through a two-way mirror, and catch a clip from the Disney film of the riding school's liberation by the US Army under General Patton in 1945.

# Nationalbibliothek

Spread out across the Hofburg, the **Nationalbibliothek** (Ⓦwww.onb.ac.at) is first and foremost the country's largest working library, home to millions of books. Although the main reading room (in the Neue Burg) is open to the public, most visitors only ever see the library's Baroque Prunksaal on Josefsplatz, which, despite its 200,000 venerable volumes, is primarily an architectural tourist attraction. You can also visit the library's various offshoots, the Globenmuseum, Esperantomuseum, Papyrusmuseum and Theatermuseum.

## Prunksaal

If the Karlskirche (see p.121) is Johann Bernhard Fischer von Erlach's sacred masterpiece, then the **Prunksaal** (Tues–Sun 10am–6pm, Thurs until 9pm; €5) is his most stunning secular work. The library was begun in 1723, the year of his death, and, like so many of his projects, had to be finished off by his son,

Josef Emanuel. It's by far the largest Baroque library in Europe, stretching the full length of the first floor of the central wing on Josefsplatz. Access to the Prunksaal is via the monumental staircase in the southwest corner of the square.

The first thing that strikes you on entering the library is its sheer size: nearly 80m in length and 30m in height at its peak. Not an architect to be accused of understatement, Fischer von Erlach achieves his desired effect by an overdose of elements: massive marble pillars and pilasters, topped by gilded capitals, gilded wood-panelled bookcases, carved balconies accessed by spiral staircases, and from floor to ceiling, thousands of leather-bound books, including the 15,000-volume personal library of Prince Eugène of Savoy.

▲ Prunksaal

The space is divided into two quasi-transepts by a transverse oval dome, underneath which stands a statue of the emperor Karl VI, just one of sixteen marble statues of Spanish and Austrian Habsburg rulers executed by the unlikely-named Strudel brothers, Peter and Paul. Directly above you (and Karl) is Daniel Gran's magnificent, colourful fresco, with the winged figure of Fame holding a rather misshapen pyramid. The emperor himself appears on a medallion just below Fame, flanked by Hercules and Apollo. Among the other celestial groups, there's a model of the library heading Karl's way – in case you miss it, the woman depicted as Austrian magnanimity is pointing to it. At the lowest level, Gran has painted trompe l'oeil balconies, on which groups of figures hold scholarly discussions. If you're really keen to work out what's going on, there's an inexpensive guide to the dome fresco available at the ticket desk.

## Esperantomuseum

Several of the Nationalbibliothek's collections have been moved to the **Palais Mollard**, a short stroll away from Hofburg at Herrengasse 9. Here, on the ground floor, you'll find the **Esperantomuseum** (Mon–Wed, Fri & Sat 10am–2pm, Thurs 3–7pm; €2), along with the Sammlung für Plansprachen (Collection of Planned Languages). It's a fascinating and totally unexpected little exhibition with captions in German, Esperanto and English.

Dr Esperanto (meaning "Hopeful One") was the pseudonym used by Polish optician **Dr Ludvik Zamenhof** when he invented his artificial language in 1887 – you can hear the man himself reading a passage in Esperanto. Zamenhof was a Jew who hailed from Bialystok, where Polish, Russian, Yiddish and German were all spoken. He saw Esperanto as an easy-to-learn, worldwide *lingua franca*. Esperanto certainly carries less ideological baggage than English, but it's still a deeply Eurocentric language. Its roots come almost exclusively from Latin-based Romance languages, making it plain sailing for an Italian, but virtually impenetrable at first sight for, say, an Egyptian. Despite the fact that it never caught on in the way its creator originally hoped, there are now more than 100,000 Esperanto-speakers worldwide.

As well as giving you a quick rundown on how Esperanto works, the museum also contains sections on other **planned languages** such as Interlingua (a kind of grammarless Latin), neo-Slavic, designed to replace the seven or so Slav languages that plagued the Austro-Hungarian Empire, and Solresol, a musical language. There's even a chance to hear Hamlet's famous "To be or not to be" soliloquy spoken in Klingon.

## Globenmuseum

The first floor of Palais Mollard, Herrengasse 9, is occupied by the state-of-the-art **Globenmuseum** (Mon–Wed, Fri & Sat 10am–2pm, Thurs 3–7pm; €3), the largest of its kind in the world, originally founded in the 1940s by Robert Haardt, the man who invented the rolling globe without a fixed axis. The collection begins with a copy of the world's oldest terrestrial globe, a depiction of the European's pre-Columbus world from 1492 by Martin Behaim of Nuremberg (where the original is kept). There are two beautifully executed giant globes from late seventeenth-century Venice, one terrestrial and one celestial, the latter covered in the most wonderful pictorial representations of the constellations. Other highlights include a globe pair by Mercator, the first to depict rhumb lines crossing the meridians at the same angle. Look out, too, for the giant early inflatable globe from 1831 and the unusual planetary globes of Venus and Mars.

## Palais Lobkowitz (Theatermuseum)

The **Theatermuseum** (Tues–Sun 10am–6pm; €4.50; Ⓦwww.theatermuseum
.at) – part of the Nationalbibliothek's collection – is also just a short distance from
Josefsplatz. To get there, head up Augustinerstrasse and take the second street on
your left (Spiegelgasse). Here, on the corner, overlooking Lobkowitzplatz, stands
the splendid, silver-white, early Baroque **Palais Lobkowitz**, originally designed
by Giovanni Tencala for Count Dietrichstein, but later acquired by the powerful
Lobkowitz family. The museum is worth visiting for its architecture alone, though
it's also fun to visit for nonspecialists and even those with little or no German.

From the main courtyard, which centres on a Hercules fountain, you
ascend a grandiose stuccoed staircase to reach the magnificent marble-decked
**Eroicasaal**, decorated with the most wonderful trompe l'oeil ceiling fresco, on
which are superimposed strikingly colourful allegorical portraits of the arts.
This former banqueting hall, where both Haydn and Mozart gave concerts,
gets its name from Beethoven's third symphony, which was premiered here for
the composer's patron, Count Lobkowitz, in 1804, followed three years later
by his fourth symphony.

The various rooms off the Eroicasaal feature tricksy displays on the history of
Austrian theatre: in one you have to hold up a mirror to read the text the right
way round; another has a giant "swing of thought" in the middle; to view the set
designs, you open the door to a theatre box. In the Figurentheater, visitors can
make up their own puppet performance, and admire Richard Techner's finely
carved rod puppets and his Golden Shrine stage from 1912; check the current
programme for details of up-and-coming **puppet shows**. In the manuscript
room, you'll find copies of Richard Strauss's notes on *Elektra*, Max Reinhardt's
Hollywood diary and Mahler's farewell note to Vienna's opera house (see p.114).
Look out for Picasso's costumes for the Ballets Russes's *The Three Cornered Hat*
in among the costume display, and for Gustav Klimt's *Nuda Veritas*, which was
bequeathed to the museum by the critic Hermann Bahr.

### Papyrusmuseum

The Nationalbibliothek's **Papyrusmuseum** (Mon & Wed–Fri: July–Sept 10am–4pm;
Oct–June 10am–5pm; €3) is located near the main reading room in the Neue Burg
(see p.94); to get there turn left as you approach the library turnstiles and descend
to the basement. What you see is but a minuscule selection of the 100,000 or more
papyri in the collection. The labelling is mostly in German, but there is some English
scattered about. There are sample texts in numerous ancient tongues from Hebrew
to Aramaic, among them receipts, snippets of literature, aphorisms, magic spells, lists
and tax accounts. Among the quirkier items are a fourth-century BC Greek recipe
for toothpaste, Arabic advice from the ninth century on how to mix up a laxative,
and the marriage and divorce contracts of a couple who tied the knot and went
their separate ways all in the space of a year (158 AD). The oldest written papyrus is
the vast Book of the Dead in the end cabinet, executed in 1500 BC and smothered
in hieroglyphics.

# Augustinerkirche

Masked by Pacassi's bland facade, the **Augustinerkirche** (Ⓦwww.augustinerkirche
.at), to the south of Josefsplatz, is one of the oldest parts of the Hofburg, dating
back as far as the 1330s. The church was originally built for the monks of the adjacent Augustinian monastery, but was gradually swallowed up by the encroaching
Hofburg, which adopted it as the court parish church in 1634. It was the scene of
several notable Habsburg weddings, including those of Maria Theresia and Franz

Stephan, Franz-Josef and Elisabeth, Crown Prince Rudolf and Stephanie, and the proxy marriage of the Archduchess Maria Louisa to Napoleon in 1810 (his stand-in was the Archduke Karl who had been defeated by the French emperor at Deutsch-Wagram the previous year).

Inside, the church has clearly taken a beating over the years, though it retains its lofty quadripartite Gothic vaulting. The chief attraction is Antonio Canova's Neoclassical **Christinendenkmal** in the right-hand aisle, a lavish memorial to Maria Christina, favourite daughter of Maria Theresia, erected in 1805 by her husband, Albert, Duke of Saxony-Teschen. A motley procession of marble mourners heads up the steps for the open door of the pyramidal tomb, while a winged spirit and a sad lion embrace on the other side, and another winged genius holds aloft the Duchess's medallion. They'd be disappointed if they ever got inside, though, for she's actually buried in the Kaisergruft. Canova's pupils were so taken with the mausoleum that they adapted the design for Canova's own mausoleum in Venice's Frari church.

Several more monumental tombs can be found in the **Georgskapelle**, a self-contained, two-aisled chapel, built in the fourteenth century to the right of the chancel (and only open on Sundays after Mass or by appointment; ℡533 7099; €2). In the centre of the chapel lies the empty marble tomb of the emperor Leopold II, whose brief reign of less than two years ended in 1792. Balthasar Ferdinand Moll's gilded wall tomb for Count Leopold Daun, on the far wall, is significantly more extravagant, and includes a relief of the 1757 Battle of Kolín in which Daun trounced the Prussians. Also buried here is Maria Theresia's faithful physician, Gerhard van Swieten, who saw her successfully through fifteen pregnancies.

To get to the Georgskapelle, you must pass through the Lorettokapelle, at the far end of which lies the **Herzgruft** (Heart Crypt), where, arranged neatly on two semicircular shelves, are 54 silver urns containing the hearts of the later Habsburgs. The two tiny grilles in the wrought-iron door are usually kept shut, so if you want to have a peek, you must make an appointment with the monks (Mon–Fri 11am & 3pm; ℡533 70 99; free). Before you leave, take time to admire the richly gilded Rococo organ, on which Anton Bruckner composed and gave the premiere of his *Mass no. 3 in F minor* in 1872. The church still has a strong musical tradition, and a full orchestra accompanies Sunday morning Mass.

## Albertina

At the far end of Augustinerstrasse, beyond the Augustinerkirche, the newly refurbished **Albertina** (daily 10am–6pm, Wed till 9pm; €9.50; ⓦwww.albertina.at) is a mishmash of a building, incorporating parts of the former Augustinian monastery, the late eighteenth-century Tarouca Palace, and the southernmost bastion of the Hofburg. The entrance is from the vast raised terrace, which overlooks the back of the Staatsoper and is surmounted by a grand equestrian statue of the Archduke Albrecht, who vanquished the Italians at the Battle of Custozza, one of the few bright moments in the otherwise disastrous Austro-Prussian War of 1866.

Founded in 1768 by Albert, Duke of Saxony-Teschen (after whom the gallery is named), the Albertina boasts one of the largest collections of **graphic arts** in the world, with approximately 50,000 drawings, etchings and watercolours, and more than a million and a half printed works. Within its catalogue, it has some 43 drawings by Raphael, 70 by Rembrandt, 145 by Dürer – more than any other gallery in the world – and 150 by Schiele, plus many more by the likes of Leonardo da Vinci, Michelangelo, Rubens, Bosch, Bruegel, Cézanne, Picasso, Matisse, Klimt and Kokoschka.

With such a vast archive, the gallery can only hope to show a tiny fraction at any one time, and in any case, graphics are notoriously sensitive to light. As a result, the Albertina only ever stages temporary exhibitions, devoted to one artist, period or theme: whatever the exhibition, however, it'll be worth a look. The Albertina is also home to the **Filmmuseum** – not, in fact, a museum, but a cinema, which shows a wide range of documentaries and full-length features drawn from its extensive archives (see p.289).

As well as the temporary exhibition galleries, the Albertina has a few fancy **Prunkräume**, palatial Neoclassical rooms designed by Josef Kornhäusel, which feature lashings of gilding, quality parquet flooring, top-notch chandeliers and colourful silk-lined walls. Only a couple of rooms, like the Goldkabinett and the Marmorsaal, stand out – more interesting is the selection of works displayed in the rooms, from Michelangelo to Klimt, which give an idea of the depth and range of the collection. If you're flagging, the *Do & Co Albertina* **café** is a great place to stop, with a lovely summer terrace overlooking the Palmenhaus and Burggarten (see p.97).

# Neue Burg

The last wing of the Hofburg to be built – completed in 1913 – was the **Neue Burg**, a piece of pure bombast crafted in heavy neo-Renaissance style by Gottfried Semper and Karl von Haseauer. Semper originally planned to create a vast *Kaiserforum* by enclosing Heldenplatz with another new palatial wing mirroring the Neue Burg, and by linking both wings to the nearby *Hofmuseen* via a pair of triumphal arches spanning the Ringstrasse. In the end, only the southern arc of the Neue Burg got built; the exterior was completed in 1913, but the interior was still being given the finishing touches in 1926, long after the Habsburgs had departed.

**Heldenplatz** (Heroes' Square) thus remains a wide, slightly meaningless, expanse, which nonetheless affords a great view across to the Rathaus and Parlament buildings on the Ringstrasse (see p.107). The square takes its name from Anton Fernkorn's two nineteenth-century equestrian statues, whose generals appear to be marshalling the surrounding parked cars into battle. The more technically remarkable of the two is the earlier one of the Archduke Karl, who defeated Napoleon at Aspern in 1809 (and then lost to him at Deutsch-Wagram shortly afterwards) and whose horse is cleverly balanced on its hind legs. Fernkorn failed to pull off this unique trick with the statue of Prince Eugène of Savoy, and had to resort to using the horse's tail for extra stability; he died insane the following year.

The Neue Burg itself is now home to the Nationalbibliothek's main reading room, the Papyrusmuseum (see p.92), an offshoot of the Naturhistorisches Museum, and three departments of the Kunsthistorisches Museum. For the Viennese, though, it's forever etched in the memory as the scene of Hitler's victorious return to Vienna on March 15, 1938, when thousands gathered here to celebrate the Anschluss. "To say that the crowds which greeted him… were delirious with joy is an understatement," observed eye-witness George Clare before he fled the country. Hitler appeared on the central balcony of the Neue Burg and declared: "As Führer and Chancellor of the German nation and the German Reich I hereby announce to German history that my homeland has entered the German Reich."

To the west of Heldenplatz, the **Burgtor** cuts something of a pathetic figure as the official entrance to the Hofburg. Built into the walls in the 1820s – to commemorate the Battle of Leipzig in 1813, when the Austrians defeated Napoleon

– it is the city's only surviving gateway. However, stripped of its accompanying walls, its classical lines and modest scale are at odds with everything around it. It was converted by the Austro-fascists in the 1930s to serve as Vienna's chief memorial to the fallen soldiers of World War I.

# Neue Burg museums

Access to the **museums** within the Neue Burg is via the main entrance. A single ticket (daily except Tues 10am–6pm; €8; ⓦwww.khm.at) covers all three departments run by the Kunsthistorisches Museum: the Hofjagd- und Rüstkammer (Court Hunting and Arms Collection), the Sammlung alter Musikinstrumente (Collection of Early Musical Instruments), and the Ephesos (Ephesus) Museum. There's no English information provided for the above museums, so if you're keen, it's a good idea to pick up a free audioguide. The Museum für Völkerkunde (Museum of Ethnology) has its own separate entrance and requires a separate ticket (see p.97).

## Hofjagd- und Rüstkammer

The **Hofjagd- und Rüstkammer** or Waffensammlung (Weaponry Collection) boasts one of the world's finest assemblages of armour. Most items date from the fifteenth to the seventeenth century; for the arms and armour of the later imperial army, you must go to the Arsenal (see p.160). Before you get to the first room, as you mount the stairs, admire the Albanian helmet from 1460, which sports a golden goat's head, and the fourteenth-century crested funereal helmet, which, weighing 7kg, was too heavy to be used for anything except tournaments. Also on the stairs are two dog-snout-shaped visors – devised to replace the closed helmet, in which it was extraordinarily difficult to breathe – which probably came from the estate of Duke Ernst of Austria (1377–1424), who was responsible for starting the weaponry collection.

To the right of Saal I, there's a splendid array of **jousting equipment** made for the knights of Emperor Maximilian I (1493–1519). To try and minimize the death rate among competitors, whose necks were particularly vulnerable, the helmets were attached to the armour. The High Renaissance **costume armour** in Saal III was meant only for show, its design deliberately imitating the fashionable clothes of the time: puffy sleeves, decorative bands inlaid with gilded silver, and slightly comical pleated skirts. It's difficult to imagine getting married in the wedding suit made for Albrecht of Brandenburg in 1526, with its huge pleated skirt, beetle-crusher shoes and grotesque helmet with wings and a beak.

There's some fabulous sixteenth-century **Milanese armour** crafted by Filippo Negroli in Saal IV, including numerous shields depicting heroic exploits, and a suit of armour with a cap complete with naturalistic ears and curly hair. The museum's other great weaponry freak was the manic collector Archduke Ferdinand of Tyrol (1525–95), who ordered the bank-breaking **Adlergarnitur** (Eagle Armour) in Saal V, with its exquisite gilded garniture. Equally resplendent is the blue-gold suit of armour made for Emperor Maximilian II (1564–76), with vertical gold bands in imitation of contemporary Spanish court dress. The **gold rapier** in this room, with its gilded cast-iron hilt, was a gift to Ferdinand from his brother, Maximilian II, and is one of the finest works in the entire collection. Check out, too, the ghoulish Turkish masks in the side gallery, ordered for a jousting tournament in the 1550s.

Saal VI features some great Ottoman arms and armour – sabres, jewel-studded daggers, horse plumes and the like – taken as spoils during the sixteenth-century wars against the Turks. Yet more richly decorated suits of armour fill Saal VII, including the **Rosenblattgarnitur** (rose-petal armour) ordered by Maximilian II for the tournament held in Vienna in 1571 to celebrate his brother Karl's wedding; equally fancy suits, known as the **Flechtbandgarnitur** (interwoven armour), were created for his two sons, Rudolf and Ernst. There's more Milanese craftsmanship in Saal VIII, including a rapier whose hilt features numerous Moors' heads.

## Sammlung alter Musikinstrumente

If you've absolutely no interest in instruments of death, however beautifully crafted, you can skip the entire collection, and head straight for the **early musical instruments**. The Archduke Ferdinand of Tyrol is again responsible for many of the rare pieces, which were designed to be admired for their artistry rather than the sound they produced. You can hear some of the instruments on the audioguide, and are free to actually play those replicas marked with a green dot.

You enter the collection at Saal XI, where you'll find a vertically strung **clavicytherium** richly inlaid with ivory, ebony, tortoiseshell and mother-of-pearl – it was played by Emperor Leopold I himself, who was a musician and composer in his own right. The unique set of six sixteenth-century **dragon-shaped shawms**, in Saal X, is from Ferdinand's *Kunstkammer*. Also on display are the set of miniature instruments he had made up as toys for his kids, and an ivory-backed lute from 1580, which Ferdinand himself used to play. Saal XII is loosely based around Josef Haydn, featuring instruments from his day, plus a quadruple music stand for a string quartet; the extraordinarily lifelike beeswax bust of the composer sports a wig of real human hair.

The **tortoiseshell violin**, decorated with gold and ivory, in Saal XIII, was bought by Maria Theresia for the imperial Schatzkammer, and, like many such showpieces, is totally unsuitable for playing. Also in this room is a wooden composing table made for the elderly empress after she became blind, and a set of six ornate silver and gold trumpets used in the Hofmusikkapelle until the end of the nineteenth century. If you're itching to hear what kind of sound any of these instruments makes, look out for the room's reproduction clavichord, marked with a green spot. In the far corner, you'll find an early nineteenth-century **glass harmonica** of the variety invented by the American statesman Benjamin Franklin.

Next door the ornate **Marble Hall** (Saal XIV) is still occasionally used as a concert venue and features a "piano of complete harmony", with six rows of keys, and played at one time or another by Haydn and Beethoven. Eye-catching exhibits in Saal XV include a crystal flute, and a string instrument that doubled as a walking stick, both from the time of Schubert. In the final room there's a Wiener Werkstätte piano designed by Josef Hoffmann, a harmonium designed to play Schönberg's twelve half-tones, and a self-portrait of the artist-composer.

## Ephesos Museum

From 1866 until a ban on the export of antiquities from Turkey stopped the flow early last century, Austrian archeologists made off with a lot of first-class relics from the ancient city of Ephesus, on the coast of Asia Minor. It wasn't until 1978 that the loot was finally publicly displayed in the **Ephesos Museum**, occupying one half of the Neue Burg's monumental staircase.

The most significant find of the lot is the impressive forty-metre-long **Parthian Frieze**, sculpted in high relief around the second century AD, shortly after the Roman victory in the Parthian Wars. The relief formed the outer walls of a pantheon in honour of the commander of the Roman forces, Lucius Verus, who was joint emperor of the Roman Empire, along with his adoptive brother, Marcus Aurelius. The adoption of the two brothers by Antoninus Pius (himself adopted by the emperor Hadrian), is depicted at the end of the corridor on the right, followed by battle scenes from the campaign, and finally Lucius Verus's apotheosis on the far left of the corridor (he was deified on his death in 169 AD).

Other notable finds include one side of the Octagon, a burial chamber with Corinthian columns, an Amazon from the Temple of Artemis – one of the Seven Wonders of the Ancient World – and a Roman bronze copy of a classical Greek sculpture depicting an athlete cleaning sand from his hands with a scraping iron. You can also see a vast wooden model of Ephesus (and lots of text in German on the excavations), and a model of the Temple of Artemis. Finally, there's a selection of minor finds from the Sanctuary of the Great Gods on the Aegean island of Samothrace, excavated in the 1870s by Austrian archeologists.

### Museum für Völkerkunde

In the section of the Neue Burg nearest the Ring, the **Museum für Völkerkunde** (daily except Tues 10am–6pm; €10; Ⓦwww.ethno-museum.ac.at), which should have reopened by 2009, houses a bewildering array of secular and religious artefacts from around the world. The highlights of the museum's collections include artefacts from **Polynesia**, many of them brought back from Captain Cook's expeditions, and then snapped up at auction in 1806 by the emperor Franz I – who could resist the Hawaiian firelighter shaped like a giant penis? The single most prized item is undoubtedly the stunning sixteenth-century gilded **Aztec feather headdress**, believed for many years to have belonged to Emperor Moctezuma II (Montezuma), and later given by Hernán Cortés, the Spanish imperialist, to Emperor Karl V.

## Volksgarten

The **Volksgarten** (daily: April–Oct 8am–10pm; Nov–March 8am–8pm; free), which forms a large triangular wedge to the northwest of Heldenplatz, was opened in 1820 on the site of the old Burgbastei (palace bastions), blown up by Napoleon's troops in 1809. Appropriately enough, given its origins, it was laid out as a formal French garden, and quickly became a favourite resort of the nobility – especially the "Aristocratic Corner", for which an entry fee had to be paid. When the rest of the fortifications were torn down in 1857, the garden was extended, and it remained an upper-crust haunt long after that.

The focal point today is the Doric **Theseus-Tempel** – a replica of the Theseion in Athens – erected in the 1820s. Originally commissioned by Napoleon to house *Theseus and the Minotaur* by Antonio Canova, it's been more or less permanently closed since the statue was transferred to the staircase of the newly opened Kunsthistorisches Museum in 1890. Plans in the 1930s by Carl Moll and Josef Hoffmann to turn the temple into a pantheon of Austria's musicians sadly came to nothing and the building remains unused for the most part. In the far northern corner of the garden, a seated statue of **Empress Elisabeth** presides over a melancholic sunken garden of remembrance. The opposite corner of the Volksgarten shelters an equally imposing monument to **Franz Grillparzer** (1791–1872), the poet and playwright, seated before a marble backdrop with reliefs illustrating his plays.

## Burggarten and Schmetterlinghaus

The **Burggarten** (daily: April–Oct 6am–10pm; Nov–March 6.30am–7pm; free), like the Volksgarten, came into being fortuitously after Napoleon blew up the bastions around the Hofburg. Unlike the Volksgarten, however, it was landscaped in the informal English style, and retained as a private garden for the Habsburgs until 1918. It now lies hidden behind the giant Neue Burg, though its entrance off the Ringstrasse is announced grandly enough by the marble **Mozart Denkmal** by Viktor Tilgner. Unveiled on Augustinerplatz in 1896 and moved to its present site in 1953, the plinth features frolicking cherubs, two reliefs from *Don Giovanni*, as well as representations of the composer's father and sister, with whom he used to tour Europe as a *Wunderkind*.

Elsewhere, in the shrubbery, there's an equestrian statue by Balthasar Ferdinand Moll of Franz Stephan, Maria Theresia's husband, which has come down in the world since the bastion it used to adorn was blown up, and a rather downcast statue of **Franz-Josef** in his customary military garb. Incredibly, despite the omnipresence of the latter's image during his long reign – the emperor's portrait hung in millions of households across the empire – and the great trade in memorabilia since then, there was no public statue of Franz-Josef in Vienna until this one was erected by private individuals in 1957.

On the far side of the garden is the elegant glass **Palmenhaus**, designed by Friedrich Ohmann in Jugendstil around 1900. The left-hand section provides a suitably steamy environment for the colourful tropical butterflies, moths, birds and bats of the **Schmetterlinghaus** (April–Oct Mon–Fri 10am–5pm, Sat & Sun 10am–6.30pm; Nov–March daily 10am–4pm; €5; Ⓦwww.schmetterlinghaus.at) – such is the heat that you'll do well to take more than half an hour. The much larger, middle section of the Palmenhaus has been converted into a very swish, palmy **café** (see p.266).

# 3

# The Ringstrasse

From morning until late at night, I ran from one object of interest to another, but it was always the buildings that held my primary interest. For hours I could stand in front of the Opera, for hours I could gaze at the Parliament; the whole Ringstrasse seemed to me like an enchantment out of The Thousand and One Nights.

Adolf Hitler, Mein Kampf

On Christmas Eve 1857, the emperor Franz-Josef I announced the demolition of the zigzag fortifications around the old town and the building of a **Ringstrasse**, a horseshoe of imperial boulevards to be laid out on the former *glacis* (the sloping open ground between the walls and the suburbs). Vienna had been confined within its medieval walls since the last Turkish siege of 1683 – now, with the Ottoman threat receding, the Habsburgs could create a boulevard befitting an imperial capital. Twelve major public buildings were set down along its course between 1860 and 1890 – among them a court opera house and theatre, two court museums, a parliament building, a university and a town hall – all at no cost to the taxpayer. By the end of World War I, though, the Habsburgs were no more: as Edward Crankshaw wrote, "[the Ringstrasse] was designed as the crown of the Empire, but it turned out to be a tomb".

Today Vienna's Ringstrasse looks pretty much as it did in the last days of the Habsburgs, studded with key landmarks. The monumental public institutions remain the chief sights: heading anticlockwise, they include the **Börse**, **Votivkirche**, **Rathaus**, **Burgtheater**, and **Parlament** buildings, the two monster museums – the **Naturhistorisches** and **Kunsthistorisches** (covered in Chapter Four) – and the **Staatsoper**. Countless other cultural institutions occupy prime positions on the Ring and on neighbouring Karlsplatz, most notably the **Musikverein**, the city's premier concert venue, the glorious Jugendstil **Secession** building, the city's new cultural complex, the **MuseumsQuartier**, and three more excellent museums: the **Akademie der bildenden Künste**, the **Wien Museum**, and the **MAK** (Museum of Applied Art). Last, but not least, Karlsplatz also boasts Vienna's most imposing Baroque church, the **Karlskirche**.

## Ringstrasse architecture and history

Unlike the rest of Vienna, the Ringstrasse was built on an epic scale, its width partly designed to facilitate the mobilization of cannons in the event of rebellions from the proletarian districts beyond. Memories of 1848 were still fresh in the minds of Franz-Josef's military advisers, and it's no coincidence that among the first buildings to be completed were the two **barracks** strategically placed at either end of the Ring. The speed with which the Ringstrasse was constructed was unprecedented: by the time of the stock market crash of 1873, which

**THE RINGSTRASSE**

brought the building programme to a brief halt, almost half of the total real estate had been developed.

However, within a decade of the imperial decree of 1857, Austria's political make-up had changed from an undiluted autocracy to a constitutional monarchy. As a result, the emphasis of the Ringstrasse shifted, too, from an imperial showpiece to more of an expression of liberal values, with a **town hall** among its landmarks.

| CAFÉS | |
|---|---|
| Am Heumarkt | 23 |
| Bendl | 8 |
| Do & Co Albertina | 15 |
| Drechsler | 27 |
| Eiles | 9 |
| Halle | 20 |
| Imperial | 24 |
| Landtmann | 5 |
| Leopold | 21 |
| Ministerium | 6 |
| Museum | 25 |
| Österreicher im MAK | 11 |
| Palmenhaus | 12 |
| Prückel | 10 |
| Sacher | 16 |
| Savoy | 28 |
| Schottenring | 1 |
| Schwarzenberg | 22 |
| Una | 17 |
| Urania | 4 |

While the nobility, ensconced in Baroque palaces in the old town, tended to look down on the Ringstrasse as a place of residence, the wealthy **bourgeoisie** were happy to snap up buildings, which, designed to ape the aristocratic *palais*, were in reality little more than glorified apartment blocks or *Zinspalais* (rented palaces). It was a popular deceit, as even the modernist architect Adolf Loos, who dubbed Ringstrasse Vienna's "Potemkinstadt", had to admit: "Viennese landlords were

101

RINGSTRASSE:
BEFORE AND AFTER

*Glacis*

Schottentor

*Danube Canal*

Stephansdom

Hofburg

Stubentor

*River Wien*

Burgtor

Kärntnertor

*Glacis*

N

0    500 m

**1857**

**1887**

Barracks

*Danube Canal*

Votivkirche

Börse

SCHOTTENRING

FRANZ-JOSEFS-KAI

Universität

Rathaus

FRANZENSRING

Barracks

Parlament

Stephansdom

Justizpalast

BURGRING

Burgtor

Hofburg

PARKRING

River Wien

Hofmuseen

OPERNRING

Staatsoper

Kursalon

KÄRNTNER RING

Akademie
der bildenden
Künste

N

0    500 m

delighted with the idea of owning a mansion and the tenants were equally pleased to be able to live in one."

From its earliest days, the Ring was a **fashionable** place to hang out, particularly around the new opera house, where every stratum of society would take part in the daily afternoon promenade. In April 1879, at the emperor's **silver wedding** celebrations, several hundred thousand Viennese, including the imperial family, watched as tens of thousands took part in a choreographed and costumed procession. Hans Makart, the society artist, led the ensemble, dressed as Rubens in black velvet, and mounted on a white horse.

Later, it became a popular spot for **demonstrations**, the largest of which took place in November 1905, when 250,000 workers marched silently along the Ring to demand universal suffrage. Similar crowds lined the Ring to greet Hitler on his triumphal entry into the city after the Anschluss of April 1938 – and again when Karl Renner appeared at the Rathaus to proclaim the restoration of the Austrian Republic. Unfortunately, with the advent of the motor car, the Ring has become little more than a public racing track. The great institutions remain, along with their attendant cafés, but in between, airline offices, fast-food outlets and travel agents predominate. It's still a favourite spot for political demonstrations, but the only mass gathering that regularly takes place here is for the last lap of the annual Vienna marathon.

# Schottenring

If you take the tram along any part of the Ring, it should be the northernmost section, **Schottenring**, which stretches from the Danube Canal to the Votivkirche. This is the least interesting portion to walk along, since none of the buildings can be visited, and all of them can be viewed well enough from the tram window.

## The Rossauer-Kaserne and the Börse

The **Ringturm**, erected in 1955 at the very northern apex of the Ring, is one of the few high-rise buildings in central Vienna, acting as a marker (or so its architects like to think) for the start of the Ringstrasse. A more distinguished building, on the opposite side of the Ring, is the **Rossauer-Kaserne**, a fanciful, red-brick barracks (currently used by the police), built in the late 1860s. One of the first constructions on the Ring, occupying three blocks, it formed a strategic and architectural pendant to the former imperial barracks on Stubenring, where the

Postsparkasse now stands (see p.130). Only the crenellated central block, with its mock-Gothic turrets and machicolations, is actually visible from the Ring, across **Deustchmeisterplatz**, which features a giant militaristic monument, topped by a flag-wielding bronze soldier.

The key public building on Schottenring is the former **Börse** (Stock Exchange), designed in the 1870s by the Danish architect Theophil Hansen, one of the pioneers of the historicist architecture that characterizes the Ringstrasse. In his design of the Börse, exactly halfway along Schottenring, Hansen chose to ape the Italian Renaissance – viz the arches, rooftop battlements and corner towers – a style popularized with the construction of the opera house a decade earlier. The main hall was partially destroyed by fire in 1956, so you're not missing anything by viewing the building from the tram, though it's not clear from the building's solid exterior that much of its vast ground plan is in fact taken up with a large central, open courtyard.

## Votivkirche

The first public building on the Ringstrasse – begun in 1854 even before the emperor had ordered the demolition of the city ramparts – was the **Votivkirche** (Tues–Sat 9am–1pm & 4–6.30pm, Sun 9am–1.30pm; free; Ⓦwww.votivkirche .at), a monumental church built by the Vienna-born architect Heinrich Ferstel in the style of the great Gothic cathedrals of Cologne and Chartres. Erected opposite the spot where a Hungarian tailor, János Libényi, had tried to stab the emperor Franz-Josef the previous year – he was thwarted only by the emperor's collar and cap – the church was to be "a monument of patriotism and of devotion of the people to the Imperial House". Forever associated with the old order – the Church and the Crown – the Votivkirche differed from the later Ringstrasse buildings, which derived much of their inspiration from the liberal ideology of the newly ascendant middle class.

For all its size, there is something spiritually lacking in the Votivkirche. Built partly to serve the large influx of soldiers to the capital following the 1848 revolution, the church has no natural parishioners, and the interior, badly damaged in World War II, is gloomy, and remains underused and little visited. The one monument worth a look is the sixteenth-century marble tomb of Count Salm, who commanded Vienna during the Turkish siege of 1529. It's also worthwhile visiting the church's **museum** (Tues–Fri 4–6pm, Sun 10am–1pm; €2.90), which contains the Antwerp Altar, a superb full-relief, polychrome depiction of the Passion, from 1460.

# Rathausplatz

**Rathausplatz** is the Ringstrasse's showpiece square, framed by no fewer than four monumental public buildings – the Rathaus, the Burgtheater, Parlament and the Universität – all completed in the 1880s. The architectural style of each building was carefully chosen to allude to its function: Flemish Gothic for the Rathaus, conjuring up municipal wealth and independence; hybrid Baroque for the Burgtheater, recalling the era in which theatre first flourished in Vienna; Neoclassicism for the Parliament building, in honour of the birthplace of democracy, Ancient Greece; and Italian Renaissance for the University, that bastion of secular scholarship.

# Rathaus

The most imposing building of the four is the cathedralesque **Rathaus** (City Hall) – strictly speaking the Neues Rathaus – a powerful symbol of the city's late nineteenth-century political clout. Designed by the German architect Friedrich Schmidt in imitation of Brussels' Gothic Hôtel de Ville, the Rathaus opened for business in 1884, though one can only feel sympathy for the city bureaucrats who had to work in its gloomy neo-Gothic chambers before the advent of electricity. The central tower, which soars to a height of more than 100m, is topped by a copper statue of a medieval knight in full armour, known affectionately as the *Rathausmann*; you can inspect a replica of him at close quarters in the Rathauspark below.

You're free to walk through the town hall's seven courtyards, but to get a look at the ornate interior, home to the *Bürgermeister* (mayor) and the *Gemeinderat* (city council), you must join a 45-minute **guided tour** in German (Mon, Wed & Fri 1pm except during council sessions or holidays; free; ⓦwww.wien.gv.at); call ⓣ525 50 to confirm, and assemble at the information office in the Schmidthalle. Concerts are occasionally held in the main Arkadenhof, and in July and August, free opera and classical concerts are beamed onto a giant screen on the town hall's main facade. Restaurants set up stalls selling food and beer, though these are as nothing compared to the number of stalls that fill the Rathauspark in the month leading up to Christmas, when the famous **Christkindlmarkt** takes place (mid-Nov to Christmas; ⓦwww.christkindlmarkt.at). During this period, the area in front of the Rathaus is crowded with stalls selling candy, decorations, traditional wooden toys, and just

## Karl Lueger (1844–1910)

**Karl Lueger**, mayor from 1897 to 1910, is by far the most famous of Vienna's *Bürgermeister* – the section of the Ring that crosses Rathausplatz is named after him, and his statue occupies a prime site at the beginning of Stubenring. Brought up by his widowed mother, who ran a tobacco shop, Karl made it to the city's most prestigious private school, the Theresianum, as a day scholar, subsequently becoming a lawyer before entering politics as a left-wing Democrat in 1870.

His elegant appearance, impeccable manners and skilful oratory earned him the nickname "*der schöne Karl*" (handsome Karl), but his reputation will always be clouded by the **anti-Semitic rhetoric** he adopted during the 1880s. In 1890, he made a speech in the Reichsrat suggesting that the city's Jews should be put on a ship, sent out to sea and sunk. By 1893, he had formed the **Christian Social Party** (Christlichsoziale Partei), whose blend of municipal socialism, Catholicism and anti-Semitism proved irresistible to the Viennese petite bourgeoisie, in which Lueger had his roots. However, his election as mayor in 1895 was followed by two years of deadlock as Emperor Franz-Josef refused to ratify his taking office, wary of his popularity and his crude anti-Semitism. Once in power, Lueger toned down his anti-Semitism, resorting to it when he needed to maintain his popular appeal, and dropping it when he needed the cooperation of the city's wealthy Jewish financiers – hence his catchphrase, "*Wer a Jud is bestimm' i*" ("I decide who is a Jew").

In his thirteen years as mayor, Lueger succeeded in laying the foundations for the municipal socialism that was greatly extended by the Social Democratic Workers' Party (SDAP) in the 1920s. He was responsible for much of the infrastructure the Viennese enjoy today: he piped in water from Styria, built gas works, established a green belt around the city, made provisions for cheap burials, built schools and old people's homes, enlarged the parks, and electrified the tram and subway network. His funeral in 1910 was the largest the city had ever seen, with more than 200,000 lining the streets, among them one of Lueger's biggest fans, the young, out-of-work artist, Adolf Hitler.

about every kitsch Christmas present you can think of. Families come to admire the luminous tree decorations, play on the rides, and participate in the workshops for kids within the town hall, while even more folk flock here after work to drink hot *Glühwein* and *Punsch* to ward off the cold. For the New Year, the area in front of the Rathaus is turned into a giant outdoor ice-skating rink (daily noon–11pm).

## Burgtheater

Directly opposite the Rathaus, the **Burgtheater** (Ⓦwww.burgtheater.at) seems modest by comparison – until you realize that the sole function of the theatre's two vast wings is to house monumental staircases leading to the grand boxes. In practical terms, though, the design by Gottfried Semper and Karl Hasenauer was none too successful. Less than a decade after the opening night in 1888 the theatre had to close in order to revamp the acoustics, which were dreadful, and to modify the seating, some of which allowed no view of the stage at all. The auditorium was badly gutted by fire during the liberation of Vienna in April 1945, and has since been totally modernized. Thankfully, the staircase wings survived, and still boast their sumptuous decor, including ceiling paintings by Franz Matsch and Gustav Klimt. To see these, you need to go on one of the theatre's fifty-minute **guided tours** (July & Aug daily 2 & 3pm; Sept–June Mon–Sat 3pm, Sun 11am & 3pm; €5.50); tours in English are available from Friday to Sunday.

When the Burgtheater opened, it was, of course, known as the k.u.k. Hofburg-theater (Imperial and Royal Palace Theatre), as the lettering on the facade still proclaims. The royals had their own entrance, so they could slip in from the Hofburg. Nowadays, the theatre devotes itself solely to spoken drama, but the original Burgtheater, which stood on Michaelerplatz in the Innere Stadt, also functioned as the chief ballet and opera house. It was there that Mozart's *Die Entführung aus dem Serail*, *Figaro* and *Cosi fan tutte* were premiered, as well as Gluck's *Orfeo*, *Alceste*, and *Paris and Helen*, and Beethoven's second piano concerto and his first symphony. It was also where the emperor Franz-Josef first clapped eyes on the actress Katharina Schratt, who was to be his mistress for more than forty years.

## Universität

The **Universität** (Ⓦwww.univie.ac.at) – strictly speaking the Neue Universität – is the most unassuming of the four public buildings on Rathausplatz. It's also the one that had to campaign longest to secure a prominent Ringstrasse site, owing to its radical past. Vienna's students had been among the most enthusiastic supporters of the 1848 revolution, forming their own Academic Legion, manning the barricades and dying in their hundreds. Finally in 1873, Heinrich Ferstel was commissioned to design new premises for the Law and Philosophy faculties in the ubiquitous neo-Renaissance style. More famously, in 1894, the painter Gustav Klimt was commissioned, along with Franz Matsch, to paint murals for the university's Aula or **Grosser Festsaal** (Great Hall).

Sadly, it's no longer possible to view the paintings, which caused possibly the biggest scandal in the institution's history. Klimt and Matsch had already completed murals for the Burgtheater (1886–88) and the Kunsthistorisches Museum (1891), and the university no doubt expected more of the same. However, by the time the first picture, *Philosophy*, was unveiled in March 1900, Klimt had broken with Vienna's main independent artists' association and helped found the rebellious Secession – more importantly, he had moved a long way from the university's original proposal for a painting to illustrate the triumph of light over darkness. It was this, as much as anything else, which caused 87 professors to sign a petition of protest. The painting's tangled mass of naked, confused humanity – "a victory of darkness over all" in the words of one critic – was certainly not what the Ministry of Culture and Education had had in mind.

The scandal drew 34,000 onlookers to see the painting in just two months. Unperturbed, Klimt exhibited the second of the murals, *Medicine*, the following year, its naked and diseased figures provoking further abuse. Questions were asked in parliament, where the artist was accused of "pornography" and "perverted excess". Eventually in 1905, having completed the last, but by no means least controversial, of the trio, *Jurisprudence*, Klimt resigned the commission. The Ministry tried to insist that it still owned the paintings, and were only persuaded otherwise when Klimt threatened the removal men with a gun. The fee was returned with the help of the industrialist August Lederer who received *Philosophy* in return. Klimt's friend and fellow artist Kolo Moser, co-founder of the Secession, purchased the other two in 1911. All three were placed in Schloss Immendorf in the Salzkammergut for safe-keeping during World War II, but were destroyed in a fire started by retreating SS troops on May 5, 1945.

## Parlament

On the south side of Rathausplatz stands the Neoclassical **Parlament** (ⓌWww .parlament.gv.at), one of five major Ringstrasse buildings by the Danish architect Theophil Hansen. From street level, it's difficult to see past the giant Corinthian portico and its accompanying wings and pavilions. Stand back, though, and it becomes clear that the huge main body of the building – home to the *Bundesrat* (Federal Council) and *Nationalrat* (National Council) of the Austrian parliament – is mostly hidden behind the projecting facade. The interior, with its atrium of fluted columns, is well worth a visit and there are **guided tours** in German and English (mid-July to mid-Sept Mon–Sat hourly 11am–4pm; mid-Sept to mid-July Mon & Tues 11am & hourly 2–4pm, Fri 11am & hourly 1–4pm, Sat hourly 11am–4pm; €4), except when parliament is in session.

Even if you don't go on a guided tour, it's worth admiring the building's **sculptural decoration**. The main pediment frieze shows the emperor Franz-Josef I granting the seventeen peoples of the empire a deeply undemocratic constitution, but for the most part, Hansen plumped for classical antiquity, with Roman horse-tamers and seated historians punctuating the two ramps. Between the ramps stands a gargantuan **statue of Athene**, goddess of wisdom, sporting a natty gilded plume in her helmet and presiding over a fountain served by four writhing mermen, representing the Danube, Inn, Elbe and Moldau. The attic of the main building, meanwhile, is peppered with 76 classical statues, 66 reliefs and four bronze chariot groups – these are best viewed from the sides of the building, where you'll find porticos held up by **caryatids** modelled on the Erechtheion on the Acropolis.

The Austrian parliament has had a chequered history since it moved into its new premises in 1883. Initially, it served as the *Reichsrat* (Imperial Council) for the Austrian half of the empire, a body deadlocked by nationalist factions of Croats, Czechs, Poles, Romanians, Slovenes and Germans. The nadir came in 1897 when the Polish count Kasimir **Badeni** attempted to introduce his language ordinances, which would put Czech on an equal footing with German in the Czech Lands. Conservatives and German-Nationals organized an "Obstruction Concert", with whistles, sleigh bells, harmonicas, cowbells, gongs, toy trumpets, hunting horns and snare drums. During the din, one member delivered a twelve-hour filibuster that ended at 8.45am the next morning. Following the Badeni debacle, the emperor bypassed parliament and ruled through the bureaucracy, until the introduction of universal male suffrage in 1907. Parliament was again prorogued shortly before World War I and didn't reconvene until after Franz-Josef's death.

On November 12, 1918, the *Reichsrat* held its last session, during which the Austrian republic – known officially as **Deutsch-Österreich** (German-Austria) – was declared from the ramps before parliament. The Babenberg colours of the new Austria, red-white-red, were hoisted on the tall masts either side of Athene; also present were the Pan-German nationalist students with their black-red-gold banners, and the Communist-dominated 41st battalion of the *Volkswehr* known as

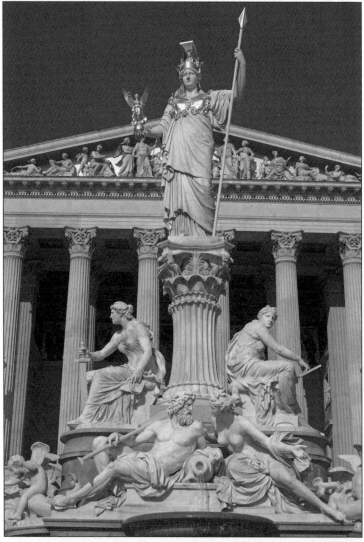

▲ Parlament

## The burning of the Justizpalast

Set back slightly from the Ring, behind the Monument of the Republic, lies the **Justizpalast**, an impressive neo-Renaissance monster of a building that holds a special place in Austrian history. On July 15, 1927, the day after three right-wing activists were acquitted of murdering a Socialist man and boy, a spontaneous demonstration of several thousand workers descended on and set fire to the Justizpalast. Chaos ensued, with mounted, armed police charging the crowd, and police reinforcements shooting live ammunition, leaving eighty-odd people dead, and up to one thousand wounded. The Socialists promptly called a general strike, which was deftly crushed by the heavily armed *Heimwehr*, the right-wing militia, who acted as strike breakers, and civil war was put off for a few more years.

the *Rote Garde* (Red Guard). The latter tore up the Pan-German banners, and also removed the white from the Austrian banners, leaving red rags flying. Shots were fired, the *Rote Garde* tried to storm the parliament building; two people were killed and 45 injured. Five months later, there were more revolutionary rumblings as a posse of Communists, spurred on by the Soviet republics in Bavaria and Hungary, broke in and set fire to the parliament building. In the street fighting that followed, five policemen and a woman were killed.

On the Ides of March, 1934, democracy was put on hold indefinitely as the Austro-fascists ordered police to block the entrance to the building to prevent parliamentary members from assembling. On seizing power, one of the Austro-fascists' first acts was to remove the **Monument of the Republic**, erected to the south of the parliament building after World War I, and featuring the busts of the Socialist politicians Jakob Reumann, Viktor Adler and Ferdinand Hanusch. Strangely, the monument wasn't destroyed, but simply put into storage (rather like Austrian democracy itself), and returned to its rightful place after World War II.

# Burgring

On the other side of **Burgring** from the Hofburg stand the two so-called *Hofmuseen* (court museums), which were opened to the public in the late nineteenth century. The **Kunsthistorisches Museum** (History of Art Museum), which houses one of the world's top art collections, is covered in detail in Chapter Four; the **Naturhistorisches Museum** (Natural History Museum) is described below. Designed in pompous neo-Renaissance style, with giant copper-domed cupolas and colossal wings, they are both the work of Karl Hasenauer, and as such, virtual mirror images of each other. The overall plan was thought up by the great Dresden architect, Gottfried Semper, who envisaged a monumental *Kaiserforum*, linking the museums to the Neue Burg via a pair of triumphal arches spanning the Ringstrasse. The project was interrupted by World War I, and then binned altogether after the fall of the Habsburgs.

Today, the museums remain cut off from the Hofburg by the traffic roaring round the Ring. They stare blankly at one another across **Maria-Theresien-Platz**, a formal garden peppered with topiary and centred on a gargantuan monument to Empress Maria Theresia who presides over four of her generals (on horseback), and three of her advisers, plus her doctor (standing). If you stand between the two big museums with your back to the Hofburg, you will find yourself looking at the **MuseumsQuartier** or **MQ**, Vienna's newest cultural complex, more or less hidden away in the former Messepalast (Trade Fair Palace), originally the imperial stables, built in the eighteenth century by Johann Bernhard Fischer von Erlach.

## ③ Naturhistorisches Museum

In many ways very little has changed at the **Naturhistorisches Museum** (daily except Tues 9am–6.30pm, Wed until 9pm; €8; ⓦwww.nhm-wien.ac.at) since it opened in 1889. Whereas most European cities have tried to pep up their natural history collections with automated dinosaurs, ecological concerns and the like, the hard sell has pretty much passed Vienna by. Many of the display cabinets are more than a century old, the dim panes of glass almost pre-industrial, and the stuffed animals within having succumbed to a uniform, musty, grey hue. Even now places as distant as Illyria (the eastern Adriatic coast) and Galicia (part of present-day Poland and Ukraine) are described as part of Austria. It's really only as a museum of museums that the Naturhistorisches continues to be of any interest – though, of course, it goes without saying that the building itself is a visual feast.

One of the most successful innovations of recent years has been the **Vivarium**, immediately to your left as you enter the building, a tropical aquarium, vivarium and aviary featuring everything from clown fish and snakes to terrapins and Australian goldfinches. The upper ground floor (or *Hochparterre* as it's called) kicks off with five rooms of **minerals** (I–V) in the east wing, among them some impressive slabs of green malachite, a giant fluorescent red ammonite and a huge chunk of transparent quartz. Polished marble tiles are accompanied by the names of buildings within the old Empire that feature the materials. The penultimate room (IV) contains various objects made from precious and semiprecious stones – perhaps the most interesting section for the nonspecialist – including a bouquet made with 761 semiprecious stones and 2102 diamonds, given as a (morning-after) wedding gift by Maria Theresia to Franz Stephan. The final room contains Franz Stephan's very own orrery and several **meteorites**, the biggest of which is a 909kg monster found in Australia in 1884.

The paleontology section (VII–X) starts in room X – a huge hall decorated with caryatids struggling with weird, evolutionary beasts – where you can find the skeleton of a diplodocus, complete with fossilized dino-poo. Many of the **fossils** in room IX originate from the ocean floor of the Miocene Sea (which is where Vienna was fifteen million years ago). Look out for the beautiful giant palm-leaf fossils, the giant skeleton of a "small" deinothere (a kind of prehistoric elephant) and, in room VII, the fossil of a Megarachne, the world's largest-ever spider, which grew to 50cm in diameter in the high-oxygen carboniferous tropical swamps of 320 million years ago. The prehistoric section begins in room XI with the **Venus of Willendorf**, by far the most famous exhibit in the entire museum, with its own darkened display chamber. This fertility symbol – a stout, limestone figure with drooping breasts – stands just 11cm high, but is something like 25,000 years old, and as such is an object of some fascination.

The west wing includes finds from the prehistoric Beaker folk and various implements, jewellery and arms from Iron Age burial tombs at **Hallstatt** in the Salzkammergut. There's some impressive Thracian silver jewellery, a reconstructed gilded funereal chariot from the Iron Age, and a staggering collection of human skulls. The Kindersaal, beyond, is the museum's one concession to modernization, though this tired playroom, built in the 1970s, isn't going to impress kids brought up on interactive, hands-on displays.

Zoology occupies the top floor, with the exception of the first room (XXI), which contains the **Mikrotheater** (Sat 1.30, 3 & 4.15pm, Sun 11am, 1.30,

3 & 4.15pm; €2), where images from under the microscope are projected onto a screen, and a 3D **panopticon** through which you can take a peek at natural wonders of the world (including bits of the museum itself). The exhaustive **zoology** displays progress from starfish, corals and seashells in the east wing, through butterflies, spiders and frogs, to a bevy of bears, big cats and monkeys in the west. Some may find the pickled fish and lizards, the jars of snakes and reptiles, and the dissected frog, more than they can stomach, but young kids will undoubtedly enjoy it. There's a little light, historical relief in room XXIX, where you can see two stuffed eagles caught by Crown Prince Rudolf, just nine days before his suicide.

# MuseumsQuartier

Vienna's dynamic new **MuseumsQuartier** (Ⓦwww.mqw.at) is almost entirely hidden behind the plain but vast facade of the former imperial stables. Opened in 2001, the MQ is home to a bewildering array of galleries and museums, performance and arts spaces, as well as some great cafés, restaurants and shops. The paler of the two cubes that dominate the MQ's central courtyard or *Haupthof* houses the **Leopold Museum**, probably the most universally popular attraction here, containing, among other things, the world's largest collection of works by Egon Schiele. Less successful has been **MUMOK**, the darker cube, which provides a home for Vienna's permanent collection of modern art. Overall, however, the MQ has succeeded in carving out a respectably trendy niche for itself on Vienna's crowded cultural map.

The two (more or less) permanent displays are described in detail below, but there are various temporary exhibition spaces also worth exploring. The central former winter riding school is now used by **Kunsthalle Wien** (daily 10am–7pm, Thurs until 10pm; €11.50; Ⓦwww.kunsthallewien.at), the city's top contemporary art gallery, as well as providing a modern dance performance space for **Tanzquartier Wien** (Ⓦwww .tqw.at). Over in two wings of the westernmost courtyard (Hof 7), the **Architekturzentrum Wien** (daily 10am–7pm; €5; Ⓦwww .azw.at), or Az W, houses a permanent exhibition on twentieth-century Austrian architecture, and hosts temporary exhibitions that are always worth a look. Adjacent to the Az W is the **designforumMQ** (Mon–Fri 10am–6pm, Sat & Sun 11am–6pm; €4; Ⓦwww .designforum.at), which puts on exhibitions on product design and advertising.

Last, but not least, there's the **ZOOM Kindermuseum** (Mon–Fri 8.30am–5pm, Sat & Sun 10am–5.30pm; children €5, adults €3.50; ☏524 79 08, Ⓦwww.kindermuseum .at), a real hands-on treat for kids in Hof 2. The introductory section is an enjoyable interactive exhibition for kids aged 6 to 12 exploring everything from sculpture to astronomy; in the ZOOM Studio, children can get stuck into some serious artistic endeavours. Those with younger kids should head straight for ZOOM Ocean, which is basically an indoor marine-themed play area, while older kids from 8 to 14 can try their hand at animation and music making in ZOOM Lab. The staff all speak English so language shouldn't be an issue, but you really need to book a few days in advance – numbers are restricted and visits are timed.

If you've got kids, it's as well to know about the nearby **Kinderinfo** office (Tues–Thurs 2–7pm, Fri–Sun 10am–5pm), which has an indoor play area with a slide and free Internet access for older children. Also in this courtyard is **Dschungel Wien** (Ⓦwww.dschungelwien.at), which puts on theatre performances and workshops for young people.

### Leopold Museum

The light limestone cube of the **Leopold Museum** (daily 10am–7pm, Fri until 9pm; €9; Ⓦwww.leopoldmuseum.org) houses the private collection of Rudolf Leopold, an ophthalmologist by training, who later became an obsessive art collector. Leopold was particularly keen on the works of **Egon Schiele**, which he picked up for next to nothing in the 1950s, but which eventually got him so heavily in debt that he had to strike a deal with the Austrian state: they wrote off his tax bill and built a museum, and he allowed his remarkable collection to be shown to the public.

With so many works, both major and minor, on display, spread over five floors, it's as well to focus your energies on just one or two highlights in the permanent collection, and perhaps the current temporary exhibition exhibited in the basement (U2). As good a place as any to start is on the ground floor (EG), where you'll find several works by **Gustav Klimt** (1862–1918), ranging from early superrealistic canvases such as *Blind Man* to the dreamy, square-framed landscapes that Klimt knocked off in his summer holidays on the Attersee. The most important work in the collection, however, is *Death and Life* from 1916, in which the colourful jumble of humanity seems oblivious to Death with his little red cudgel. There are also several canvases by the little-known **Richard Gerstl** (1883–1908), whose works were never exhibited during his brief life. His nude self-portrait from the year of his suicide is as uncompromising and honest as his almost Christ-like *Self-Portrait Against a Blue Background*, from a few years earlier, is striking and unusual. Alongside these are works by contemporaries Kolo Moser, Carl Moll and Adolf Loos – everything from oil paintings to stained-glass designs, furniture and glasswork.

Next, you should head for the top floor (O3), where the chief works by **Egon Schiele** (1890–1918) are displayed. The Leopold Museum owns some superb canvases (though not all will necessarily be shown at any one time), including Schiele's famous (and much reproduced) *Reclining Woman*. The hypocritical Habsburg

# The Secession

In 1897, a number of artists broke away from the Künstlerhaus, Austria's leading independent artists' association, and set up their own organization, which they named the Secession. The second half of the nineteenth century had seen the ossification of the arts in Vienna, exemplified in architecture by the heavy-handed historicism of the Ringstrasse, and epitomized in painting by the flattery of Hans Makart (1840–84). Broadly speaking, the aims of the new group were to regenerate the arts in Vienna, and to promote "art for art's sake", in particular the latest style, Art Nouveau, known in German as Jugendstil (literally "Youth-style").

Wiener Werkstätte vases ▲

Beethoven Frieze ▼

Secession building ▼

# Klimt and his followers

The first president of the Secession was the artist **Gustav Klimt** (1862–1918), who became the group's driving force over the next eight years. Klimt had begun his career as a promising young master of the old ideology. In the movement's striking, purpose-built headquarters, however, in full view of the Künstlerhaus, he now helped put on a series of exhibitions of new work. Initially, the reception among the Viennese critics and public was good; the emperor himself visited, and several of the Secessionists went on to receive faculty appointments at the Arts and Crafts School. However, the movement ran into trouble when Klimt exhibited *Medicine* here, part of his controversial mural intended for the University. The ensuing public scandal (see p.107) and the mixed reception given to the group's fourteenth exhibition in 1902, for which Klimt painted the *Beethoven Frieze*, eventually prompted Klimt, along with a number of his followers, to leave the Secession and retreat from public life for several years.

Between 1898 and 1903, the Secession group also published *Ver Sacrum*, a successful arts journal employing lavish Jugendstil typography and layout. Instrumental in its production and design were two of the Secession's co-founders, **Josef Hoffmann** (1870–1955) and **Kolo Moser** (1868–1918). Hoffmann and Moser went on to pursue their interest in applied art, forming the craft-based Wiener Werkstätte in 1902 (see p.129), and eventually leaving the Secession in 1905 along with Klimt. All three later worked together to organize the **Kunstschau** exhibitions of 1908 and 1909 (see p.126), which rejected the decorative art of the Secession in favour of Expressionism.

# Wagner and Loos

As Hermann Bahr wrote, "without Wagner, there would be no Secession, no Klimt group, no applied art". Though only a peripheral character in the Secessionist organization, the architect **Otto Wagner** (1841–1918) was a seminal figure in the Viennese art world throughout the period. Wagner not only completed more buildings than any other Secession architect, he also designed the entire Stadtbahn system from 1894 to 1901, including all the stations and bridges, many of which are extant on the U4 and U6 metro lines. Though he remains the highest-profile exponent of the Secession style, his works in fact range from nineteenth-century historicism to twentieth-century modernism. He started out as a Ringstrasse architect, and had become an establishment figure by the time he joined the Secession in 1899. In the next decade he executed some of his finest work, initially opting for ornate curvilinear motifs derived from nature, but later moving towards more rectilinear, abstract forms. Wagner's shift towards minimalism and his enthusiastic adoption of new materials such as concrete and aluminium – best seen in his Postsparkasse (see p.130) – make him a key figure in the emergence of modernism. It's also worth mentioning **Adolf Loos** (1870–1933), who published two articles in *Ver Sacrum*, one of which was a stinging attack on Ringstrasse architecture. Loos's relationship with the Secession was brief, however, and in 1908 he published a thinly veiled criticism of the movement in an article entitled *Ornament is Crime*. As an architect, Loos went on to design some of Europe's first, truly modernist buildings, most notably the Loos Haus (see p.59) and his villas in Hietzing (see p.208).

▲ Karlsplatz station

▲ Ver Sacrum cover

▼ Wiener Werkstätte museum

Linke Wienzeile 38, Otto Wagner ▲
Kunstschau poster ▼

# A Jugendstil hitlist

## Otto Wagner

**Döblergasse 4**, Spittelberg p.168. Wagner's apartment and studio in town is now a museum.

**Hofpavillon Hietzing**, Hietzing p.206. Wagner's most ornate U-Bahn station, built outside Schönbrunn for the imperial family.

**Kirche am Steinhof**, Baumgarte Höhe p.211. The world's most beautiful psychiatric hospital church.

**Majolikahaus**, Naschmarkt, Ringstrasse p.124. Ceramic-clad apartment block sporting a lively floral motif, overlooking the Naschmarkt.

**Nussdorfer Wehr- und Schleusenanlage**, Nussdorf p.220. Never have municipal weirs and locks looked so good.

**Postsparkasse**, Stubenring, Ringstrasse p.130. The architect's iconic modernist building.

**Rennweg**, Landstrasse, Vorstädte p.151. A trio of early Wagner houses.

**Schützenhaus**, Donaukanal, Leopoldstadt p.185. A dinky little lock-keeper's house, soon to be a museum and café.

**Pavillon Karlsplatz**, Resselpark, Ringstrasse p.120. Two preserved ornate U-Bahn stations.

**Wagner Villas I & II**, Hütteldorf p.211. Two country villas built at either end of his career.

## Others

**Artaria Haus**, Kohlmarkt, Innere Stadt p.57. Max Fabiani's marble-faced precursor to the Postsparkasse.

**Portois & Fix**, Landstrasse, Vorstädte p.150. Fabiani's ceramic-clad exterior looks like digital art.

**Secession**, Karlsplatz, Ringstrasse p.119. The movement's landmark headquarters, popularly known as the "Gilded Cabbage".

**Zacherlhaus**, Hoher Markt, Innere Stadt p.69. Josip Plečnik's remarkably eclectic inner-city apartment block.

establishment that had imprisoned him for "immorality" and "seduction" is the target in *Cardinal and Nun* and *The Hermits*, a double-portrait of Schiele and Klimt dressed in monks' habits from around the same period. There are several autumnal townscapes inspired by Schiele's brief sojourn in his mother's Bohemian hometown, Český Krumlov (Krumau), and several frankly disturbing, morbid depictions of motherhood: *Blind Mother*, *Dead Mother* and *Mother with Two Children II*. Look out, too, on the top floor, for the emerald-green, fairy-tale-like *Dolomite Landscape* (1913) by **Oskar Kokoschka** and his self-portrait from the end of World War I.

The other two floors are of more specialist interest. On the second floor (O2), you'll find several rooms of Austrian interwar and postwar art. Probably the most intriguing artist here is **Albin Egger-Lienz** (1868–1926), who, after a brief flirtation with the Secession, rejected it – and Vienna – in favour of his Tyrolean homeland. His depictions of the hardships of peasant life are heartfelt, and the effect of World War I on his work is marked, particularly in his didactic *Dance of Death*, but also more subtly in his three versions of *The Reapers* from 1907, 1918 and 1922. On the first level of the basement (O1), there's also a vast range of **nineteenth-century art**, from folk art, alpine watercolours and Biedermeier genre paintings to works by Austrian artists such as Emil Jakob Schindler, Hans Makart, Anton Romako, plus a couple of token Courbet landscapes.

## MUMOK

Built to house the city's chief permanent collection of modern art, the dark grey basalt cube of the **Museum Moderner Kunst Stiftung Ludwig Wien**, better known as **MUMOK** (Tues–Sun 10am–6pm, Thurs until 9pm; €8; ⓦwww .mumok.at), is an intimidating building from the outside. Inside, things don't get much better: the layout is confusing – you enter at level 4 – and the lack of natural light depressing. Still, if you like your art conceptual, MUMOK owns some great stuff, and though much of it remains hidden in the vaults, enough is put on show to keep you amused. The entrance fee lets you look at the (more or less) permanent displays described below, plus the three or four temporary exhibitions staged by the gallery.

To start with, head off down to the basement (level 1), where the **Wiener Aktionismus** archive tells the story of the city's very own extremely violent performance-art movement that spilled blood and guts (literally) all over Vienna in the 1960s. Next, head for level 3 where you'll find much more familiar stuff: **Pop Art** by Warhol and Lichtenstein, one of César's ubiquitous crushed cars, a Klein blue painting, a small wrapped object from Christo's early years, plus works by the likes of Nam June Paik, Robert Rauschenberg's "neo-dada" cardboard collages, and John Chamberlain's anti-consumerist scrap-metal sculptures, to name but a few. And don't miss **Yoko Ono**'s *Painting to Hammer a Nail*, which the artist exhibited in London in 1966. It was at the opening that Yoko first met John Lennon. She asked him for five shillings to hammer an imaginary nail into the painting; he said he'd give her an imaginary five shillings for the imaginary nail. Instant Karma.

# Around Oper

The human congestion around **Oper** – the city's opera house or Staatsoper – makes this the busiest section of the Ringstrasse. It's here that the shoppers of Kärntner-strasse cross the Ring, or rather descend into the seedy Opernpassage, which stretches south as far as Karlsplatz (see p.118). In the late nineteenth century, this crossroads became known as the "Sirk Ecke", after the then-fashionable *Sirk Café* on the corner of Kärntnerstrasse and Kärntner Ring. The latter, which runs down to Schwarzenbergplatz, quickly became the Viennese Corso, where, according to one contemporary French visitor, "every branch of society from the great world, to the *demi-monde*, to the 'quarter world', as well as the world of diplomacy and the court" promenaded in the afternoon. Nowadays most people prefer to stroll along Kärntnerstrasse rather than battle with the roaring Ringstrasse traffic.

## Staatsoper

That the **Staatsoper** (State Opera House; ⓦwww.wiener-staatsoper.at) was the first public building to be completed on the Ringstrasse – opening in May 1869 with a performance of Mozart's *Don Giovanni* – is an indication of its importance in Viennese society. Designed in heavy Italian Renaissance style – even the Austrians deferred to Italy as the home of opera – it has a suitably grandiose exterior, with a fine loggia beneath which the audience could draw up in their carriages. However, compared with the other monumental edifices on the Ringstrasse the opera house sits low. This was the most common criticism of the building when it was completed, and when Emperor Franz-Josef was heard to concur with his aides on this issue, one of the architects, Eduard van der Nüll, hanged himself. Van der Nüll's grief-stricken friend and collaborator on the project, August Siccardsburg, died two months later of a heart attack; neither architect lived to witness the first night. Thereafter Franz-Josef always chose the safe riposte "*Es war sehr schön, es hat*

### Gustav Mahler (1860–1911)

Mahler's symphonies are now firmly established in the concert repertoire, but it wasn't that long ago that his music was only rarely performed. In his lifetime Mahler was much better known as a conductor. Born to a Jewish family in provincial Bohemia, he studied at the **Vienna Conservatory** before spending the best part of a decade as a jobbing *Kapellmeister* at various provincial theatres in the Prussian and Habsburg empires. At the age of just 28, the ambitious Mahler got his big break when he landed the job at the Royal Hungarian Opera in Budapest. Ten years later, in 1897, following a judicious (and entirely mercenary) conversion to Roman Catholicism, he reached his "final goal" and became director of the **Hofoper**, Vienna's imperial opera house (now the Staatsoper).

Mahler's ten years in charge of the Oper (including a couple as chief conductor of the Vienna Philharmonic as well), were stormy to say the least. He instituted a totally new regime in the house, banning claques (opera stars' paid supporters), insisting that the lights of the auditorium be dimmed during performances, and allowing latecomers entry only after the overture or between acts. In his behaviour towards performers he was something of a tyrant, hiring and firing with abandon and earning himself the nickname of *Korporal vom Tag* (Duty Corporal) for his demanding work schedules and his bluntness. "Is music meant to be so serious?" the emperor is alleged to have said when hearing of these innovations, "I thought it was meant to make people happy."

The music critics were evenly divided, many praising his painstaking attention to detail, others lambasting him for constantly reworking other composers' scores. Needless to say, the anti-Semitic press had a field day, subjecting Mahler to racist jibes, objecting to his "Jew-boy antics on the podium", and caricaturing his eccentric appearance. The gossip columnists were also kept busy, especially when, in 1902, Mahler married **Alma Schindler**, the strikingly beautiful stepdaughter of Carl Moll, the Secession artist, and, at 22, a woman almost half his age. Mahler's views on marriage *mir sehr gefreut*" (It was very beautiful, I enjoyed it very much) whenever he was asked his official opinion.

The Staatsoper has always had a special place in the hearts of the Viennese, besotted with their musical heritage, so it was a particularly cruel blow when the building caught fire during an air raid on March 12, 1945. The main auditorium was rebuilt in a much plainer style, and is now pretty undistinguished. Prestigious past directors include Gustav Mahler, Richard Strauss, Herbert von Karajan and Claudio Abbado, though each one had notoriously difficult relationships with the opera house.

As the name suggests, the Staatsoper still receives massive state subsidy, and hundreds of cheap *Stehplätze* (standing-room tickets) are sold each day on a first-come-first-served basis (see p.329). This is probably the best way to visit the opera house, but you can also go on a 35-minute **guided tour** in English (times posted up on east side; €5). For the truly obsessed only, there's the **Staatsopernmuseum** (Tues–Sun 10am–6pm; €3), round the corner at Goethegasse 1. One large round room contains a photo gallery of the stars who've graced the opera's stage since it reopened in 1955.

## Behind Oper

Vienna's top three hotels – the *Sacher*, the *Bristol* and the *Imperial* – are all within a stone's throw of the opera house. The most famous of the trio, directly behind the Staatsoper, is the **Hotel Sacher**, built in the 1870s on the site of the old

were rigidly bourgeois: she was to give up her music, despite the fact that she was a fledgling composer in her own right. "You must become 'what I need' if we are to be happy together, ie my wife, not my colleague," he wrote to her. Not surprisingly, the marriage was to prove an extremely difficult one for both parties.

Ten years at the helm of the Oper took its toll: "Other theatre directors look after themselves and wear out the theatre. I look after the theatre and wear out myself," he wrote to a friend. Towards the end of 1907, Mahler pinned a farewell note to the opera house notice board, saying "I meant well, I aimed high … In the heat of the moment, neither you nor I have been spared wounds, or errors." The previous summer, at the Mahlers' private villa by the Wörthersee in Carinthia, their elder daughter, Maria (Putzi), had died of scarlet fever, and Mahler himself had been diagnosed as having a heart valve defect. It was time to move on. By signing up with the **New York Metropolitan Opera**, Mahler simultaneously doubled his income and drastically reduced his workload. However, the increased travelling and the strain it imposed on his marriage and health proved too much.

By 1910, Alma was more or less openly conducting an affair with the modernist architect Walter Gropius, and Mahler, in desperation, travelled all the way to Holland to consult Freud. Mahler blamed himself (probably rightly so) for selfishness, and attempted to make amends, showering Alma with affection and encouraging her to compose again. As it turned out, though, Mahler didn't have long to live. In New York he was diagnosed as having subacute bacterial endocarditis, and the family travelled back to Vienna for the last time. Crowds gathered outside the sanatorium, the press issued daily bulletins from the bedside of "der Mahler". He died during a thunderstorm (just like Beethoven), and his last word is alleged to have been "Mozart!" According to his wishes, his tombstone in **Grinzinger Friedhof**, designed by Josef Hoffmann, has nothing but "Mahler" written on it. "Any who come to look for me will know who I was", he explained, "and the rest do not need to know".

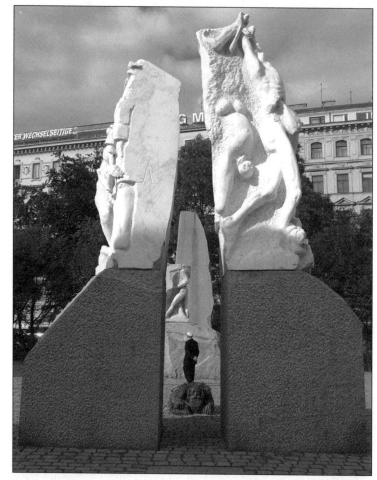

▲ Monument against War and Fascism

Kärntnertor Theater, where Beethoven's ninth symphony premiered in 1824. Founded by Eduard Sacher, the hotel became the aristocrats' favourite knocking shop, particularly after 1892 when it was run by Eduard's widow, the legendary, cigar-smoking Anna Sacher, until her death in 1930. Without doubt, the most famous incident that took place here was when Archduke Franz Ferdinand's younger brother, the flamboyant Archduke Otto, appeared in the hotel lobby naked except for his sword and the Order of the Golden Fleece around his neck. The *Sacher*'s continuing popularity, though, rests on its famous *Sachertorte* invented by Eduard's father, Franz, who was Prince Metternich's chef. The cake is, of course, available all over Vienna, but the *Sacher* claims that no one else has the true recipe.

The Philipphof, a typically ornate Ringstrasse-style building which was home to the exclusive Jockey Club, originally stood to the north of the *Sacher*. However, during the air raid of March 12, 1945, the building received two direct hits, killing several hundred people sheltering in the basement. The lot remained vacant until the 1980s, when the city council commissioned Alfred Hrdlicka to erect a **Monument against War and Fascism** – a controversial move given the site's history and its extreme prominence. Hrdlicka's final design makes no direct mention of the Holocaust, but includes instead a crouching Jew scrubbing the pavement, recalling the days following the Anschluss, when some of the city's Jews were forced to clean up anti-Nazi slogans with scrubbing brushes dipped in acid. Many Jews, however, have found the image degrading, among them Simon Wiesenthal, who successfully campaigned for a Holocaust memorial to be erected in Judenplatz (see p.65).

## Akademie der bildenden Künste

Set back from the Ring, the **Akademie der bildenden Künste** (Tues–Sun 10am–6pm; €5; ⓦwww.akademiegalerie.at) – Academy of Fine Arts – occupies an imposing neo-Renaissance building by Theophil Hansen on Schillerplatz,

### Hitler in Vienna

Although he was born and grew up in Upper Austria, **Adolf Hitler** (1890–1945) spent five and a half formative years in Vienna. He arrived in the city aged just 17, hoping to enrol at the Academy of Fine Arts. However, though he passed the entrance exam, his portfolio, mostly architectural sketches of Linz, was rejected as "inadequate". Saying nothing about his failure to his family, he stayed in Vienna for a whole year, living fairly comfortably off his father's inheritance and, following the death of his mother, his orphan's pension. In September 1908, Hitler tried once more to get into the Academy: this time he failed the entrance exam. These two rejections hit hard, and still rankled two years on, as he wrote to a friend, "Do you know – without any arrogance – I still believe that the world lost a great deal by my not being able to go to the academy and learn the craft of painting. Or did fate reserve me to some other purpose?"

Very little is known about the rest of Hitler's time in Vienna, though he spent a good three years in a men's hostel in the eastern district of Brigittenau, abutting Leopold-stadt, where he sold his mediocre paintings mostly to Jewish frame dealers. The evidence is scanty, but Hitler appears to have worked for brief periods as a snow shoveller at the Westbahnhof (and elsewhere), and as a painter and decorator at the Kunsthistorisches Museum; he even auditioned for a part in the chorus at the Theater-an-der-Wien, but was rejected when he couldn't produce the right clothes for the part.

Though there is no proof to back up the rumour that Hitler contracted syphilis from a Jewish prostitute while in the city, it is possible that he may have contracted some minor sexually transmitted ailment, hence his obsession with syphilis and prostitu-tion – both of which he rails against at length in *Mein Kampf*. Other accounts portray Hitler as some kind of proto-hippy, with beard and long hair, practising yoga and tripping on mescaline. Again, there's no concrete evidence, though Hitler certainly experienced a period of homelessness in the winter of 1909, after which he became increasingly unkempt, wearing his beard and hair long.

For much of his stay in Vienna, Hitler was a draft evader – something he neglects to mention in *Mein Kampf* – since he should have signed up in 1909. By the end of 1912 he was liable to a year in prison and a large fine; it was this which eventually led him to flee to Germany in 1913. After a 25-year gap, Hitler returned to Vienna under rather different circumstances in March 1938, following the Anschluss. He stayed at the *Hotel Imperial* on the Ringstrasse, gave a speech to the multitude from the Neue Burg on Heldenplatz and, within 24 hours, was on a plane back to Germany.

to the southwest of the Staatsoper. The Academy was founded in 1692, and its main purpose continues to be teaching, but the school also houses a small, much-overlooked study collection. To see the paintings, follow the signs to the **Gemäldegalerie**: turn right after the porter's lodge, up four flights of stairs to the first floor, then right again to the end of the corridor. The **Aula** – straight ahead as you pass through the main entrance – is also worth a glimpse, both for its decor and for the regular, wacky student installations.

The Academy's collection is tiny, and extremely patchy, compared with the Kunsthistorisches Museum. Nevertheless, it does have one or two superb works, and one star attraction: *The Last Judgement* triptych by **Hieronymus Bosch** (c.1450–1516), the only Bosch triptych outside Spain. The action in the left panel, *Paradise*, is a taster for the central panel, the *Last Judgement* itself, most of which is taken up with strange half-animal devil figures busy torturing sinners in imaginatively horrible ways; the right panel, *Hell*, looks even less fun. Overall, the possibility of salvation seems painfully slim, with only a lucky few having made it to the small corner of the painting given over to heaven.

Displayed in the same room as the Bosch are two works by Lucas Cranach the Elder: *Lucretia*, a classic Cranach nude, and his moralistic-erotic *Ill-Matched Couple*. The Academy's Italian works are fairly disappointing, with the exception of **Botticelli**'s *Madonna Tondo*, and Titian's *Tarquin and Lucretia*, a late work replete with loose brushwork and brooding, autumnal colours. In the same room as the last two, look out for Murillo's sentimental *Two Boys Playing Dice*.

It's Flemish and Dutch paintings that make up the core of the Academy's collection, however, with an early **Rembrandt** portrait of a young woman in a black dress, a self-portrait by Van Dyck aged just 14, preparatory studies for the Jesuit church frescoes in Antwerp (and lots of nudes) by Rubens, plus works by Jordaens, Ruisdael, Hoogstraten and David Teniers the Younger. After Bosch, though, the other outstanding masterpiece is the *Family Group in a Courtyard* by **Pieter de Hooch** (1629–84), with its sublime tranquillity and clever play on perspective.

Also on display are several Venetian views by Guardi, Biedermeier paintings by Waldmüller (who taught at the Academy), and a much-reproduced portrait of Maria Theresia by her official court painter, Martin van Meytens. In the final room, there's a brief selection of twentieth-century Austrian art, including works by Friedensrich Hundertwasser, Fritz Wotruba and Herbert Boeckl.

# Karlsplatz

Overlooked by the city's most awesome Baroque church, several key Ringstrasse institutions, the gilded Secession building and Otto Wagner's wonderful Art Nouveau pavilions, **Karlsplatz** should be one of Vienna's showpiece squares. Instead, the western half is little more than a vast traffic interchange, with pedestrians relegated to a set of seedy subways that stretch north as far as Oper. The problem is that there's never been any grand, overall plan at Karlsplatz – the Naschmarkt was held here until the 1890s, and when it moved to the nearby Wienzeile, the heart was ripped out of the square. The city council provided a site for the Secession, but the avenue that should have connected it with the Karlskirche never materialized. As a result, it's actually impossible to stand back and admire the Secession building without seriously endangering your life.

KARLSPLATZ & NASCHMARKT

| RESTAURANTS | | CAFÉS | |
|---|---|---|---|
| Aux Gazelles | 1 | Amacord | 7 |
| Ra'mien | 3 | Anzengruber | 9 |
| Silberwirt | 11 | Cuadro | 10 |
| Tancredi | 12 | Drechsler | 6 |
| Umar | 5 | Museum | 2 |
| | | Savoy | 8 |
| | | Sperl | 4 |

## Secession

In 1898, Joseph Maria Olbrich completed one of the most original Jugendstil works of art in Vienna, the headquarters for the art movement known as the **Secession** (Tues–Sun 10am–6pm, Thurs until 8pm; €6; ⓦwww.secession.at). The dome of gilded bronze laurel leaves is obviously the most startling feature – the Viennese dubbed it the "golden cabbage" – though all the building's decorative details are worth closer inspection. On the side, three wise owls suddenly emerge from the rendering, while the main entrance is adorned with a trio of gorgons, a pair of salamanders and copious gilded foliage; above is the group's credo, "For every age its art; for art its freedom", replaced after being removed by the Nazis. Don't miss the tortoises at the feet of the ornamental bowls, Georg Klimt's bronze doors with snake handles, and Arthur Strasser's bronze statue of an overweight Mark Anthony on a chariot drawn by panthers (originally displayed at the group's fourth exhibition in 1899).

The main hall upstairs continues to stage contemporary art installations, while downstairs in the basement Gustav Klimt's **Beethoven Frieze** is on permanent display. The frieze was intended to last only for the duration of the fourteenth exhibition held in 1902 – in the end it was preserved, but not shown to the public again until 1986. The centrepiece of the exhibition was a heroic nude statue of Beethoven by the German sculptor Max Klinger (now in the entrance of Leipzig's Neues Gewandhaus, with an incomplete copy in the Wien Museum). For the opening of the exhibition, Gustav Mahler conducted his own orchestration of the fourth movement of Beethoven's ninth symphony. Auguste Rodin deemed Klimt's frieze "tragic and divine", but most visitors were appalled by the whole exhibition, with its bare concrete chambers designed by Josef Hoffmann, and it proved a financial disaster.

With much of the mural consisting of huge blank spaces framed by floating maidens, Klimt's frieze looks strangely half finished. In between are three heavily painted sections: *Longing for Happiness*, where the weak, represented by three naked emaciated figures, appeal to a knight in golden armour; *Hostile Forces*, featuring a slightly comical giant ape with a serpent's tail and wings, and his three daughters, the gorgons, backed up by the figures of Disease, Madness and Death, and surrounded by decorative sperm and ovaries; and finally *Ode to Joy*, which culminates in an embracing couple, offering, in Schiller's words, *Diesen Kuss der ganzen Welt!* (this kiss to all the world). An excellent leaflet in English (available from the ticket desk) explains in greater detail the symbolism behind the frieze; also on display are Klimt's preparatory sketches.

## Resselpark

The central, traffic-free section of Karlsplatz is the leafy **Resselpark**, named for Josef Ressel, Czech inventor of the screw propellor. Despite thinking up the device some ten years before John Ericsson, Ressel was prevented from experimenting with it by the Habsburg bureaucracy, and was thus confined to relative historical obscurity. Ressel's statue stands close to that of another hapless innovator, the tailor Josef Madersperger, who invented a sewing machine in 1815, but died penniless because no Austrian would market it. Johannes Brahms, who died in 1897 at Karlgasse 4, now part of the nearby Technische Universität, is also represented.

Resselpark is chiefly remarkable, however, for Otto Wagner's **Pavillon Karlsplatz**, a duo of entrances erected in 1899 on either side of nearby Akademiestrasse to access the Stadtbahn, and moved here in the 1960s. Wagner broke with his usual design here, partly in deference to the presence of the nearby Karlskirche, adding gold trimmings and a sunflower motif. The green, wrought-iron framework, which was a feature of all his Stadtbahn stations, forms an essential part of the overall design, framing a series of thin marble slabs and creating a lovely, curving, central canopy. Today, one of the pavilions is put into use as a **café** during the summer months, while the other holds exhibition space for the **Wien Museum** (April–Oct Tues–Sun 10–6pm; €2); both have retained some of their original interior decor.

From the terrace between the pavilions, you can also admire two key institutions on the north side of Karlsplatz, both executed in Ringstrasse style. The neo-Baroque **Künstlerhaus** (daily 10am–6pm, Thurs until 9pm; €12; Ⓦwww.k-haus .at) was built in 1881 as the exhibition hall of Austria's Society of Artists (from which the Secession group split in 1897), whose members continue to exhibit their contemporary works on the second floor.

Next door stands the **Musikverein** (Ⓦwww.musikverein.at), Vienna's number one concert hall, designed by the ubiquitous Theophil Hansen in the 1860s. The classical terracotta exterior apes the opera house with its front loggia, but you really need to attend a concert in the Grosser Saal to appreciate the unbeatable acoustics and the sumptuous decor with its parade of gilded caryatids. Home to the world-famous **Vienna Philharmonic** (Ⓦwww.wienerphilharmoniker.at), the Musikverein's most prestigious event is the annual schmaltzy Neujahrskonzert on New Year's Day, a tradition started under the Nazis in 1939, and one which is now transmitted live around the world to an estimated 1.3 billion viewers (it's also beamed live onto a large screen on the front of the Rathaus).

The concert hall itself also has a rich musical history as the place where the composer **Arnold Schönberg** and his followers unleashed atonal music – Schönberg preferred to call it "the emancipation of dissonance" – on an unsuspecting and unready Viennese public. The worst disturbance took place on March 31, 1913, at a concert conducted by Schönberg, during which two of Alban Berg's

*Altenberg Lieder*, songs based on the *bon mots* scribbled on the back of postcards by poet Peter Altenberg, were premiered. Programmes were used as missiles, blows were exchanged and the concert had to be abandoned after an ambulance was sent for. Schönberg, of all people, later complained that Berg's *Altenberg Lieder* were "so brief as to exclude the possibility of extended thematic development". Berg was mortified and the *Lieder* remained unheard and unpublished until seventeen years after his death in 1935.

# Karlskirche

Rising majestically above everything around it, the **Karlskirche** (Mon–Sat 9–12.30am & 1–6pm, Sun 1–5.45pm; €6; Ⓦwww.karlskirche.at) is, without doubt, the city's finest Baroque church. A huge Italianate dome with a Neoclassical portico, flanked by two giant pillars modelled on Trajan's Column, and, just for good measure, a couple of hefty Baroque side towers, it's an eclectic and rather self-conscious mixture of styles, built to impress. Even surrounded by the mess that is now Karlsplatz, the church is an awesome sight – particularly at night when it is bathed in blue light and reflected in the lake – and must have been even more so when there was nothing between it and the Hofburg except the open space of the *glacis*.

The story goes that the **emperor Karl VI** vowed to build a church during the plague of 1713. Architect Johann Bernhard Fischer von Erlach won the competition to design the building; his son, Johann Michael, completed the job in 1737. The church is actually dedicated to the sixteenth-century saint, **Carlo Borromeo**, canonized for his ministrations during the famine and plague in Milan. However, the fact that the emperor and saint shared the same name no doubt played a part in Karl VI's choice, conveniently glorifying both of them at the same time. The Karlskirche's dual nature – votive and imperial – is nowhere more evident than with the columns: imperial symbols, whose reliefs, rather than portraying Emperor Trajan's campaigns (as on the originals), illustrate the life of Borromeo. As if to emphasize the point, the columns are topped by giant gilded Habsburg eagles, and, above the lanterns, the imperial crown.

Your entry fee includes an English audioguide, which can be useful for orientating yourself. Thanks to the windows and lantern in the oval dome, the interior is surprisingly sparse and light, allowing a much better appreciation of **Johann Michael Rottmayr**'s vast fresco than you get of the artist's work in the Peterskirche (see p.56). The subject is the apotheosis of Carlo Borromeo, along with a bit of Counter-Reformation Luther-bashing – note the angel setting fire to the German's Bible and the depiction of Luther in cahoots with the devil. Everything else in the church finds it rather hard to compete with the sublime beauty of the dome, though Fischer von Erlach's sunburst above the main altar is definitely worth a closer look. Interwoven with the golden rays are stucco clouds and cherubs accompanying St Carlo as he ascends into heaven. The small **Museo Borromeo** upstairs contains the saint's vestments, including a terrific cardinal's hat and golden mitre.

# Wien Museum Karlsplatz

Housed in an unprepossessing modernist block to the side of the Karlskirche, the **Wien Museum** (Tues–Sun 9am–6pm; €4; Ⓦwwwwienmuseum.at) is foolishly overlooked by many visitors. The permanent collection may be uneven and the English labelling only sporadic, but it does contain, among other things, a pretty good fin-de-siècle section, which alone more than justifies a visit: there are paintings by Gustav Klimt, Egon Schiele, Carl Moll and Richard Gerstl, an interior by Adolf Loos, and several cabinets of Wiener Werkstätte pieces. In addition, excellent temporary exhibitions on the city's social and political history are held on the ground floor.

## The ground and first floors

The permanent display begins on the ground floor with the **Roman and Gothic** section – like much of the museum rather a ragbag assortment. The largest of the Roman remains is the tomb of a cavalryman who died in Vindobona (Vienna) in 96 AD. There's a fifteenth-century gilded leather helmet – one of several hung on the wall – topped with a female figure whose arms are in the process of being swallowed by a giant fish, and the Albertinischer Plan, the oldest map of the city, from 1421. The most interesting pieces here, though, are the stained-glass windows and sandstone statues salvaged from the Stephansdom after the bomb damage of World War II, and the wonderfully beastly gargoyles from the Minoritenkirche.

The museum also owns a welter of paintings, including minor works by the key artists of the **Baroque** period. On the first floor, there are several representative works, though no masterpieces, by the three artists whose frescoes adorn so many churches in the former empire – Paul Troger, Johann Michael Rottmayr and Franz Anton Maulbertsch – and a fine portrait of a dapper young art collector by Angelika Kaufmann. You can also view a smattering of spoils from the city's two Turkish sieges in 1529 and 1683: a vast red silk banner, Turkish horse plumes sporting crescent moons, several swashbuckling sabres, and an ornate tent lantern. Before you head upstairs be sure to take a look at the model of Vienna, which shows the city shortly before the old zigzag fortifications were torn down in 1857.

## The second floor

To continue viewing the exhibits chronologically, ignore the tempting fin-de-siècle stuff ahead and to your right at the top of the stairs, and instead turn left into the section devoted to the **Biedermeier** era (1815–48), which marked a return to simple, bourgeois values after the excesses of the Baroque period. There's an entire room decorated in "Pompeii style" from a now demolished old town palace where, in the early nineteenth century, the wealthy Geymüller family entertained a coterie of artists. Among the guests was the Austrian poet and playwright Franz Grillparzer, whose musty living quarters are lovingly preserved further on. Surrounding Grill-parzer's room are more than enough mawkish Biedermeier paintings for most people, epitomized by Ferdinand Georg Waldmüller's sentimental depictions of rural folk and flattering portraits of the bourgeoisie.

Moving on through the modest collection of 1848 revolutionary memorabilia, you come to two paintings by **Hans Makart**, who was lionized by the Viennese in his day, but has since been eclipsed by his more famous pupil, **Gustav Klimt**. Don't miss, either, the wonderful mother-of-pearl studded chair, designed by **Otto Wagner**, and presented to the Mayor of Vienna, Karl Lueger, in 1904, on his sixtieth birthday, nor Josef Engelhart's emblematic *Im Sophiensaal*, which captures perfectly the loose sexuality of Viennese café life.

The centrepiece of this section, though, is another model of Vienna, this time from after the construction of the great Ringstrasse buildings of the late nineteenth century, accompanied by before and after photos. To the side is an entire living/dining room designed in 1903 by the modernist architect **Adolf Loos** for his first marital home on nearby Bösendorferstrasse. Despite his diatribes against ornament of any kind, Loos loved rich materials – marble, mahogany and brass – and created for himself a typically plush *gemütlich* interior.

Beyond Loos's room are various works of art from Vienna's artistic golden age, including Max Klinger's nude statue of Beethoven, which formed the centrepiece of the Secession exhibition of 1902 (see p.119), albeit without its coloured marble drapery and seat. Max Kurzweil's striking portrait of a *Woman in Yellow*, lounging luxuriantly on a sofa, is a classic fin-de-siècle painting. Several of **Gustav Klimt**'s works can be found here, too, including his *Pallas Athene* from 1898, marking his first extensive use of gold, which was to become a hallmark of his work, and, elsewhere, the portrait of his lover, Emilie Flöge, in a dress of her own design.

The museum also owns a handful of excellent works by **Egon Schiele**, several of which should be on display. Among them an idiosyncratically distraught study of sunflowers from 1909 and the harrowing *Blind Mother II* hang beside a fondly painted view of the artist's bedroom in Neulengbach, a clear homage to Van Gogh, executed shortly before his brief imprisonment on a charge of "displaying an erotic drawing in a room open to children". The characteristically angular portraits of the art critic and collector Arthur Roessler and his wife Ida – loyal friends and patrons throughout Schiele's life – are among the artist's earliest commissioned portrait oils. Also of note are **Richard Gerstl**'s nervous self-portrait from 1905 and his portrait of Arnold Schönberg, with whose wife Gerstl had a disastrous affair. Schönberg's own portrayal of fellow composer Alban Berg hangs close by, as does his portrait of his daughter.

## Naschmarkt and around

The River Wien, which used to wend its way across Karlsplatz, was, by all accounts, an unsavoury stretch of water: "This black and vilely-smelling ditch is a foul blot upon the beauty and neatness of this lovely city, and must certainly produce a miasma extremely prejudicial to health," noted Anthony Trollope's mother, Fanny, in the early nineteenth century. So it was no doubt with some relief that it was eventually paved over in the 1890s, allowing the **Naschmarkt** (Mon–Sat 9am–6pm) to move from the square to its present site over the old course of the river, between the Linke and Rechte Wienzeile. The market – its name

### The Third Man

Filmed on location during the postwar period when Vienna was divided (like Berlin) between the four Allied powers, **The Third Man** (directed by Carol Reed in 1949) is without a doubt the city's most famous contribution to cinematic history. The stark, black-and-white, expressionist cinematography, the haunting theme tune and seedy bombed-out locations perfectly captured the fatigued, defeated atmosphere of the city at the beginning of the Cold War.

Since the early 1980s, *The Third Man* has been shown every Friday and Saturday night at the Burgkino, Opernring 19, and the film's continuing popularity has spawned a mini tourist industry all of its own. You can visit several key locations off your own bat – Josefsplatz, the Zentralfriedhof, the Prater – but if you want to check out the sewers, you should join one of the regular **Third Man Tours** (Mon & Fri 4pm; 2hr 30min; €17; @www.viennawalks.com), which are conducted in German and English. Film buffs should also head for the **Third Man Museum** (Sat 2–6pm; €6; @www.3mpc.net), a couple of blocks south of the Naschmarkt at Pressgasse 25. This private collection includes photos and news clippings from the period, as well as posters, stills and reviews of the film, plus you get to see a two-minute clip from an old 1930s projector to whet your appetite. There's even a mock-up of the Gartenhaus from the Heuriger, run by Anton Karas (who wrote and performed the film's zither theme tune), and the chance to hear more than 300 different versions of the tune.

translates literally as "nibble market" – is now the city's premier source of fruit and vegetables, and is one of the few places where you get a real sense of the city's multicultural make-up: Turkish, Arab, Slav and Chinese stallholders vie for customers all the way to the Kettenbrückengasse U-Bahn. It's a great place to eat on the hoof, and on Saturdays, the market extends even further west as the weekly flea market joins in. The Linke and Rechte Wienzeile, on either side of the market, now function as a six-lane motorway. There are, however, a couple of sights along the Linke Wienzeile which make a stroll through the market doubly rewarding.

## Theater-an-der-Wien

First off, at no.6, there's the **Theater-an-der-Wien**, which opened in 1801 under the directorship of Emanuel Schikaneder, depicted above the main portico as the feathered bird-catcher Papageno – a role he played in the première of Mozart's *Die Zauberflöte* (Magic Flute). Schikaneder, who also wrote the libretto for Mozart's opera, was instrumental in supporting Beethoven, putting the theatre at his disposal, and even allowing him to live there on and off. Beethoven's opera *Fidelio* premiered here on November 20, 1805, exactly a week after the French had marched into Vienna. Under such extreme conditions – French soldiers made up much of the audience – it's hardly surprising that the opera flopped, running for just three performances. The theatre is also intimately connected with many other Austrian classics: Franz Grillparzer's *Ahnfrau*, almost all of Johann Nestroy's farces, Johann Strauss's *Die Fledermaus* and Franz Lehár's *Die lustige Witwe* (The Merry Widow), were all first performed here. After World War II, while the Staatsoper was being repaired, the theatre once more staged operas, though it now concentrates on popular musicals.

## Otto Wagner

A good 500m further west on the same side are two of Otto Wagner's most appealing Secession buildings from 1899, the apartment blocks of **Linke Wienzeile 38** and **40**, next to each other overlooking the market. Wagner's ultimate aim was to transform the Wienzeile – which leads eventually to Schönbrunn – into a new Ringstrasse, though stylistically both buildings signal a break with the Ringstrasse style. Eschewing any pretensions to resemble a palace, the separation between the commercial ground floor and the residential apartments above is deliberately emphasized. The right-hand building (no. 38) is richly embossed with gold palm fronds and medallions – the latter designed by Kolo Moser – and even features an elaborate top-floor loggia with Art Nouveau swags, urns and a couple of figures. The left-hand building (no. 40) is more unusual, its pollution-resistant cladding of majolica tiles giving rise to the nickname, **Majolikahaus**. To contemporary eyes, the facade looks highly decorative, but what mattered to the Viennese was that – as with the Looshaus – there was virtually no sculptural decoration, and no mouldings or pediments above the windows. Instead, Wagner weaves an elaborate floral motif – a giant, spreading rose tree or a vine of sunflowers – on the tiles themselves.

# From Schwarzenbergplatz to Stubenring

The last stretch of the Ringstrasse – Schubertring, Parkring and Stubenring respectively – runs more or less in a straight line from Schwarzenbergplatz to the Donaukanal (Danube Canal). Although it has slightly fewer landmark buildings than the rest of the Ringstrasse, it does, nevertheless, boast the city's most congenial central green space, **Stadtpark**, Vienna's superb applied arts museum, the **MAK**, and Otto Wagner's seminal exercise in modernism, the **Postsparkasse**.

# Schwarzenbergplatz

Bombarded by the din of cars and trams whizzing across its cobbles, it's difficult to believe that the large, rectangular traffic intersection of **Schwarzenbergplatz** was once a fashionable address. The aristocracy, though they owned up to a third of the property on the Ring, usually turned their noses up at actually living there – but with Schwarzenbergplatz they made an exception. The square became the nobility's own personal enclave, centred on an equestrian statue of one of their own, Prince Karl von Schwarzenberg, a member of one of the most powerful Austrian families, commander-in-chief (and victor) at the Battle of Leipzig in 1813.

At the southern end of the square, dramatically floodlit at night and spurting water high into the air, stands the **Hochstrahlbrunnen** (High Jet Fountain), erected in 1873 as a celebration of the city's nascent modern water-supply system. Once the focal point of the square, it is now thoroughly upstaged by the bombastic **Russen Heldendenkmal** (Russian Heroes' Monument), which rises up behind the jet of water. A giant curving colonnade acts as the backdrop to the central column, crowned by the Unknown (Soviet) Soldier in heroic stance, flag aloft, sporting a gilded shield and helmet; on the red granite plinth are the names of the fallen and a quote from Stalin (after whom the square was briefly renamed in 1945). For the Viennese, though, it's more a grim reminder of the brutality of the liberators and the privations suffered by those in the city's postwar Russian zones. No doubt aware of their unpopularity, the Soviets made sure that a clause ensuring the proper upkeep of the monument was written into the 1955 Austrian State Treaty.

Before the erection of the Soviet war memorial, the backdrop to the fountain was the **Palais Schwarzenberg**, Lucas von Hildebrandt's grandiose Baroque palace, built for Count Mansfeld-Fondi in 1704 and now hidden behind foliage. It was bought by the Schwarzenbergs who employed Hildebrandt's arch rival, Fischer von Erlach, to further embellish it in 1716. A bomb lopped off the central dome in World War II, and destroyed most of the frescoes by Daniel Gran, but the palace is otherwise well preserved. The Schwarzenbergs still live here, though they've turned the best rooms into a hotel and restaurant, and rented out one of the outbuildings to the Swiss Embassy. Sadly, the palace and its extensive gardens are closed except to hotel and restaurant guests, or embassy staff.

More accessible, though rather more specialist, is the **Arnold Schönberg Center** (Mon–Fri 10am–5pm; €3; ⓦwww.schoenberg.at), situated in the Palais Fanto, to the east of the Soviet war memorial, on the corner of Zaunergasse and Daffingerstrasse. The centre holds vast archives, and puts on talks, concerts and temporary exhibitions about the composer, which are held on the second floor of the building (the entrance is on Zaunergasse). Schönberg is considered the father of atonal music, and was the leading figure in what has become known as the Second Viennese School. He was an accomplished artist, too, and one or two of his drawings are usually on display as part of the exhibitions – most people find that his artwork is a lot easier on the eye than his atonal works are on the ear. There's also a reconstruction of Schönberg's study in Los Angeles (to which he fled in the 1930s), containing original furniture and objects, many of which he himself designed from recycled materials. Whatever you do, don't forget to ask about Schönberg's greatest invention: chess for four players.

## Kunstschau

Shortly before the Konzerthaus was built, Klimt and his followers, who had left the Secession in 1905, staged their own exhibition, **Kunstschau Wien 1908**, on the empty site. Josef Hoffmann designed the pavilion and formal garden as a sort of stripped-down summerhouse, Oskar Kokoschka designed the poster, the Wiener Werkstätte took part and the centrepiece was a retrospective of Klimt's work hung in a room designed by Kolo Moser. The show was an outstanding success, and even before the exhibition closed, the Austrian state had purchased Klimt's *The Kiss* (now in the Belvedere; see p.156).

The next year, with Klimt's blessing, Egon Schiele exhibited his work for the first time at the **Kunstschau Wien 1909**. Klimt expected the exhibition to cause a scandal, but it was actually Kokoschka's brutal, sexually aggressive play, *Mörder, Hoffnung der Frauen* (Murderer, Hope of Women), premiered in the Kunstschau's garden theatre, which proved the most controversial. Some imperial army soldiers from Bosnia in the audience took exception to the play and started a riot. The archduke Franz Ferdinand, reading the newspaper reports the next day, memorably opined, "Every bone in that young man's body should be broken." Though Kokoschka avoided that particular fate, his art school stipend was withdrawn at the instigation of the Ministry of Culture.

The most illustrious concert venue in Vienna after the Musikverein (see p.120) is the **Konzerthaus**, just east of Schwarzenbergplatz on Lothringerstrasse, home to the Wiener Symphoniker (Ⓦwww.wiener-symphoniker.at), three concert halls, the Akademietheater and a studio theatre. Built in late Secession style in 1913 by the great Austrian theatre-building firm, Helmer and Fellner, it boasts a lovely, illuminated wrought-iron-and-glass canopy, surmounted by octagons and a half-moon gable.

## Stadtpark

Straddling the canalized River Wien much as the *glacis* once did, the **Stadtpark** is the largest of the Ringstrasse parks. Opened in 1862 as the city council's first public park, it's best known for Edmund Hellmer's eye-catching, over-the-top **Strauss Monument** from 1925, with its statue of the "Waltz King", Johann Strauss Junior, violin in hand. Gilded from head to toe and dramatically floodlit at night, the composer stands framed by a stone arch of naked, swirling naiads. Tour groups turn up at regular intervals to admire the monument, while the benches close by are a favourite spot for Vienna's elderly population. Vienna's younger generation also like to hang out here, too, in the summer, smoking and drinking on the grass; the authorities occasionally move the scene on a few hundred metres or so, but without any great enthusiasm.

Several other artistic types are honoured with statues in this park, but none deserves much attention. You're better off heading for the much-diminished River Wien itself, where the **Wienflussportal** – a series of rather wonderful Jugendstil pavilions and quaysides – was constructed in 1905 by Friedrich Ohmann, nicely complementing Otto Wagner's adjacent Stadtbahn station, which survives as the Stadtpark U-Bahn. The other architectural landmark is the **Kursalon**, built in neo-Renaissance style at the same time as the park, daubed in soft *Kaisergelb* (imperial yellow) and still a prime venue for waltzing. Another possible focus for your wanderings is the state mint or **Münze**, built in the 1830s on the eastern edge of the Stadtpark. Somewhat surprisingly, the Münze puts on excellent temporary exhibitions (Mon–Fri 10am–4pm, Wed until 6pm), often with only a very vague numismatic bent.

# MAK

North of the Stadtpark, the **Österreichisches Museum für angewandte Kunst** (Austrian Museum of Applied Art) – better known simply as the **MAK** (Tues 10am–midnight, Wed–Sun 10am–6pm; €7.90, free on Sat; ⓦwww.mak.at) – is one of the most enjoyable and relaxed museums in Vienna. The highlights of its superlative, highly eclectic selection of *objets d'art*, stretching from the Romanesque period to the twentieth century, are **Gustav Klimt**'s *Stoclet Frieze* and the unrivalled collection of **Wiener Werkstätte** products. But what really sets it apart is the museum's interior design; the MAK gave some of Austria's leading designers free rein to create a unique series of rooms.

The MAK was founded as the Museum für Kunst und Industrie in the 1860s by Rudolf von Eitelberger, who was inspired by a visit to what is now London's Victoria and Albert Museum. Designed by **Heinrich Ferstel** in a richly decorative neo-Renaissance style in 1872, the building was later extended to house the Kunstgewerbeschule (Arts and Crafts School), where Kokoschka and Klimt both trained. At the turn of the century the school became a stronghold of the Secession movement, handing out faculty positions to Josef Hoffmann and Kolo Moser, and promoting the work of the Wiener Werkstätte.

At the **ticket office**, you'll be given a plan of the museum in German and English and offered a ludicrously heavy *MAK-Guide* (for an extra €2), which you should decline, and an audioguide (also €2), which might be worth considering. Each room features a slightly pretentious, bilingual introduction by the designer, and a leaflet in English cataloguing and explaining each exhibit. Temporary exhibitions are held, for the most part, in the museum's Ausstellungshalle, whose main entrance is on Weiskirchnerstrasse; the café is excellent (see p.266).

## Romanesque to Rococo

To follow the collection chronologically, you should begin with the **Romanik, Gotik, Renaissance** room, on the ground floor, off the beautiful, glass-roofed courtyard, with its wacky sofas and double-decker loggia. The minimalist display cabinets in this room are beautifully offset by deep cobalt-blue walls. The curators have deliberately restricted the number of items on show, allowing you to pay detailed attention to each exhibit, though inevitably you also end up with a slightly staccato history of the applied arts. Aside from a few pieces of beautifully inlaid sixteenth-century furniture and some very early thirteenth-century canonical garments, most of the exhibits are items of Italian sixteenth-century majolica, decorated with richly coloured mythological scenes and grotesque faces.

The main focus of the next-door room – **Barock, Rokoko, Klassizismus** – is a room within a room. Acquired by the museum in 1912, the mid-eighteenth-century Porcelain Room was removed piece by piece from the Palais Dubsky in Brno and reassembled here. It derives its name from the ceramics that have been used to decorate everything right down to the wall panelling, candelabra, chandeliers and table-tops. Outside the Porcelain Room exhibits include two huge eighteenth-century maple and walnut marquetry panels, an unusually large section of Chinese wallpaper from the same period, portraying an idealized landscape, and a pair of pink, gilded double doors salvaged from the Palais Paar in the Innere Stadt in 1938.

## Renaissance to Art Deco and the Orient

As you cross the courtyard to the next set of rooms, the designers begin to impose themselves more emphatically. **Barock, Rokoko** consists of two long, central glass cabinets displaying Bohemian, Silesian and Venetian glass, with examples of Italian, French and Flemish lacework set against a black background all along the walls. The **Empire, Biedermeier** room is much quirkier. A parade of early nineteenth-century Viennese chairs, arranged as if for a game of musical chairs, occupies the central space, while, up above, the cornice is broken by fast-moving, polemical, multilingual LED text on the social history of the era. To take it all in, sit down on the aluminium version of one of the Biedermeier sofas on display.

The museum's *pièce de résistance*, though, in terms of design, comes in the **Historismus, Jugendstil** room. Two parallel shadow screens, running the length of the room, create a corridor down which you can stroll while admiring the changing geometry of chair design over the last hundred years in silhouette. If you want a 3D look at the chairs, you can simply go round the back of the screens. The exhibits include modernist designs by the likes of Josef Hoffmann, Otto Wagner and Adolf Loos, and, of course, the bentwood Thonet chair that became an inexpensive design classic, selling millions around the world.

The final ground-floor room is devoted to tiles and carpets from the **Orient**, laid on the walls and floors, creating a mosque-like atmosphere. The carpets, mostly from the sixteenth and seventeenth centuries, were avidly collected by the Habsburgs – look out for the silk *Jagdteppich*, which belonged to Emperor Leopold I and is decorated with hunting scenes.

## The twentieth century and beyond

Three rooms on the first floor are given over to the permanent collection. One room is devoted to the **Wiener Werkstätte** (see opposite), whose archives were donated to the museum in 1955. The range and scope of the WW is staggering, and just about every field in which they were active is represented here, from jewellery and metalwork, primarily by Peche and Hoffmann, to the WW's prolific fashion offshoot. One of the finest works is Kolo Moser's wood-inlaid writing desk, which includes a retractable armchair that can be slotted into place to make the whole thing appear like a chest of drawers.

The **Jugendstil, Art Deco** room is dominated by Gustav Klimt's working designs for his *Stoclet Frieze*, a series of mosaics commissioned in 1904 for the dining room of the Palais Stoclet in Brussels. Predominantly gold, with Byzantine and Egyptian overtones, the frieze marks the climax of Klimt's highly ornamental phase (the finished product was inlaid with semiprecious stones). The tree of life is the central motif, the birds of prey in its branches symbolizing death, and the figures beneath it representing paradise. Close by the Klimt hangs a frieze by Margaret Macdonald, executed for Fritz Wärndorfer, and clearly inspired by Klimt's own *Beethoven Frieze*. Also on show is furniture by the likes of Otto Wagner and Kolo Moser, Charles Rennie Mackintosh, and an amazing selection of Bohemian glass – from the Lötz factory's iridescent, plant-like Art Nouveau vases to monochrome, geometric bowls from Haida (Nový Bor) – displayed in a glass cabinet suspended from the ceiling. A staircase leads up to **Gegenwartskunst**, an entire room of contemporary art.

Finally, there's a **20/21 Jahrhundert Architektur** room, filled with models of realized and unrealized architectural works ranging from Frank O. Gehry's Santa Monica residence from 1978 to Daniel Libeskind's recently completed Jüdisches Museum in Berlin.

## Studiensammlung

If you've got the time and energy, head off down to the museum's **Studiensammlung** (Study Collection), hidden away in the basement. The rooms here are as crowded as those in the permanent collection are sparse. The first room, **Ostasien**, displays a

After the Secession, probably the most important Austrian art movement was the **Wiener Werkstätte** (Vienna Workshop), founded in 1903 by the architect Josef Hoffmann, the designer Kolo Moser and the rich Jewish textile merchant, Fritz Wärndorfer. Hoffmann and Moser, both founder-members of the Secession, were initially inspired by William Morris and the English Arts and Crafts Movement. As with Morris & Co, the idea was to grant designers and craftsmen equal status – all Wiener Werkstätte produce bears the WW monogram, and the name of both the artist and craftsman. The other parallel with Morris & Co was the sheer range and breadth of the WW, whose work encompassed furniture, glassware, metalwork, porcelain, fashion, children's toys, postcards and even wrapping paper.

Artistically, the WW drew on a wide range of talents, including the likes of Oskar Kokoschka, Egon Schiele and Gustav Klimt. However, the strongest influences on Hoffmann and Moser were the Glaswegians Charles Rennie Mackintosh and his wife, Margaret Macdonald, who exhibited at the Secession in 1900 – their rectilinear, geo-metrical style became the hallmark of the WW in their first decade. In 1907, the WW made a big splash in Vienna with the opening of the legendary *Cabaret Fledermaus* on Kärntnerstrasse, all of which they had designed, from the toilets to the cutlery. However, despite winning numerous international prizes, and opening shops as far afield as New York and Zürich, the WW proved less successful financially. Unlike Morris & Co or Bauhaus, their works were not meant for mass production, and they remained attached to the old-fashioned idea of the single, unrepeatable object, designed for rich patrons, the majority of whom recoiled from such avant-garde designs. Though from 1915 onwards, Dagobert Peche's softer, more decoratively playful style, dubbed *spitzbarok* (spiky Baroque), significantly widened the appeal of the WW, the company eventually folded in 1932.

The most complete WW work – the 1905 Palais Stoclet designed by Hoffmann (in collaboration with Klimt) – is actually in Brussels, but the room devoted to the WW in the MAK is the next best thing. There are also exhibits in the Wiener Glasmuseum (see p.49). Another good place to head for is the Backhausen interior-design shop, just off the Ringstrasse at Schwarzenbergstrasse 10, which not only still produces WW pieces, but also has a charming **Wiener Werkstätte Textilmuseum** (Mon–Fri 9.30am–6.30pm, Sat 9.30am–5pm; free; ⓦ www.backhausen.com) in the basement. Beautifully laid out, it explains the history of the shop's connection with the WW, and exhibits a mixture of original textiles, reproductions, design sketches and samples.

whole variety of stuff from the Far East, from wood, stone and bronze Buddhas to Chinese ceramic beasts, nephrite vases, porcelain bowls, rhino-horn beakers, and wooden boxes inlaid with mother-of-pearl. Top marks, though, go to the two rooms devoted to **Sitzmöbel** (Furniture), with their truly democratic displays: a Baroque settee shares space with bean bags, De Stijl chairs, classic Wiener Werkstätte works and the director's daybed from the Postsparkasse by Otto Wagner.

The two **Keramik, Glas** rooms boast a collection ranging from Meissen porcelain figures to Jugendstil and Wiener Werkstätte produce; the glass, which kicks off with medieval stained-glass windows, ends with another incredible display of Jugendstil and Art Nouveau glassware similar to that in the permanent collection, with works from Gallé, Tiffany and Lobmeyr as well as contemporary pieces. In the **Metall** room, a watering can from Wolverhampton sits happily among gold goblets, silver chalices, Art Nouveau candelabra and a collection of teapots. Finally, there's a partial reconstruction of the utopian **Frankfurter Küche**, a fitted kitchen designed in 1926 by Margarete Schütte-Lihotsky, and replete with funky aluminium pull-out drawers and a fold-down ironing board.

## Postsparkasse and around

The final segment of the Ringstrasse, **Stubenring**, was the last to be laid out, erected mostly in the decade before World War I. The two biggest public buildings built here were the new Kriegsministerium (War Ministry) and the central office of the Postsparkasse or **PSK** (Postal Savings Bank). The latter was a state-funded attempt to counteract the perceived threat of Jewish capital, in particular that of the Rothschilds. With this duo in place, the Ringstrasse had, in many ways, come full circle: having begun with a barracks and a church – the Votivkirche – in the 1850s, it was to end with another reassertion of the army and Catholicism.

Despite the reactionary politics behind the **Postsparkasse** (Mon–Fri 8am–3pm, Thurs until 5.30pm), the design with which Otto Wagner won the competition for its construction was strikingly modern. The building is by no means entirely devoid of ornament – this is, after all, a prime Ringstrasse site. For a start, there's a pergola hung with laurel wreaths on the roof, flanked by two winged Victories. The rest of the building, though, looks something like a giant safety-deposit box, its otherwise smooth facade studded with aluminium rivets, used to hold the thin

▲ Postsparkasse

grey marble slabs in place. Aluminium – a new and expensive material – is also used for the delicate glazed canopy over the entrance, and, most famously, for the heating cowls, which rise up into the main banking hall like giant curling tongs. It's worth exploring beyond counter 13 to the **museum** (€5), which allows you to see, among other things, Wagner's now defunct stripey Kleine Kassensaal (Small Banking Hall) and a model of the building.

As you leave, check out the emperor Franz-Josef's ceramic bust above the main staircase; moves by the Christian Socials to have the bust of the Postsparkasse's founder, government bureaucrat **Georg Coch** (1842–90), placed in here too were foiled, allegedly by high-placed Jewish opposition. The anti-Semitic mayor Karl Lueger (see p.105) stepped into the breach and got the square named after Coch, and – with Wagner's consent – placed Coch's bust on a plinth in the centre.

Archduke Franz Ferdinand remained unimpressed by Wagner's architecture, and made sure the competition for the **Kriegsministerium**, situated opposite the Postsparkasse, was won by Ludwig Baumann's conservative neo-Baroque entry. Completed in 1912, it's a thoroughly intimidating building, smacking of reactionary, bombastic militarism, personified by the equestrian figure of Marshal Josef Radetzky, scourge of the 1848 revolution in northern Italy, which stands in front of the main entrance. Grim busts of the empire's soldiers keep watch from the keystones above the ground-floor windows, while armed cherubs and a vast military panoply, guarded by a giant double-headed eagle with wings outstretched, look down from the pediment. The building now houses various governmental departments.

Stubenring ends at the Danube Canal, beside which stands Max Fabiani's **Urania** (Wwww.urania-sternwarte.at), built in the shape of an unorthodox ship in 1910. Conceived as an adult education centre, it remains a multi purpose institution, housing a cinema, puppet theatre, planetarium, observatory and canalside **café** (see p.267).

# Kunsthistorisches Museum

I n a city somewhat overloaded with museums, Vienna's **Kunsthistorisches Museum** (Art History Museum) stands head and shoulders above the rest. Thanks to the wealth and artistic pretensions of successive Habsburg rulers, it contains not only the fourth largest collection of paintings in the world, but also Egyptian, Greek and Roman antiquities, plus sundry more recent *objets d'art*. So numerous are the exhibits that several of the museum's departments are now housed in the Neue Burg wing of the Hofburg.

The vast majority of the art collection is comprised of sixteenth- and seventeenth-century masters. Most people come to see the collection of **Bruegels** – the largest in the world – which forms part of a superlative early Netherlandish and Flemish section. Due to the Habsburgs' territorial acquisitions, the museum is also loaded with **Venetian** works by the likes of **Tintoretto**, **Veronese** and **Titian**, and a goodly selection of **Velázquez** portraits. In addition, there are numerous paintings by **Rembrandt**, **Cranach** and **Dürer**, and whole rooms devoted to **Van Dyck** and **Rubens**. Lastly, don't miss the unrivalled collection of Mannerist works from the court of Rudolf II, especially the surrealist court painter, **Giuseppe Arcimboldo**.

One of the glories of the Kunsthistorisches Museum is, of course, the **building** itself, especially the main foyer and staircase, which is sumptuously decorated,

---

## Visiting the museum

The **Kunsthistorisches Museum** (ⓦ www.khm.at) is open Tuesday to Sunday 10am to 6pm; the picture gallery is also open on Thursdays until 9pm. The **admission fee** of €10 includes entry to the museum's temporary exhibitions and an audioguide to selected exhibits; the museum is free on public holidays. Even if you spend the whole day here, you'll be pushed to see everything, so it's best to concentrate on just one or two areas. If you're peckish, head for the *Gerstner* **café** in the upper foyer, which offers snacky meals and cakes for under €10. You are also allowed to nip out for a picnic (or a cigarette break), as long as you inform the museum staff. The painting titles are all in German; in our account they're given the English names by which they're usually known. **Guided tours** of the museum in English set off daily at 3pm and cost €3. If you come on Thursday evenings to the Gemäldegalerie, you should be treated to some live music too. The nearest **U-Bahn** is Museumsquartier.

from the monochrome marble floor to the richly stuccoed dome. Don't overlook Canova's *Theseus and the Minotaur*, which greets you on the main staircase, and note the lunettes, spandrel and intercolumnar murals on the first-floor balcony, which illustrate the history of art from ancient Egypt to Florence. Hans Makart was commissioned to undertake the work, but only managed to complete the lunettes before his death from syphilis in 1884. The spandrel and intercolumnar murals were completed, very much in Makart's classical style, by the youthful trio of Franz Matsch, Ernst Klimt and his more famous brother Gustav; diagrams point out which mural was painted by which artist.

# The Gemäldegalerie

The **Gemäldegalerie** (Picture Gallery), on the first floor, has around 800 paintings on display at any one time, a mere tenth of the museum's total catalogue. It's easy to become overwhelmed by the sheer volume of art, which dates mainly from the sixteenth and seventeenth centuries. Unlike most big galleries the Kunsthistorisches makes no attempt to cover a broad span of art history – the collection has changed very little since the Habsburgs bequeathed it. Consequently, British and French artists, and the early Italian Renaissance, are all under-represented, and the collection stops at the late eighteenth century.

The paintings are arranged in parallel rooms around two courtyards: the Italians, plus a few French and Spanish, lie to one side; the Germans, Dutch and Flemish to the other. The larger rooms that face onto the courtyards sport Roman numerals (I–XV), while the smaller outer rooms use the standard form (1–24), though the latter are often unmarked. It would be difficult to concoct a more confusing numerical system, but at least both wings are laid out (vaguely) chronologically. The account below starts, for want of a better place, with the Bruegels and continues in an anticlockwise direction to Vermeer; then it switches to Titian and heads off in a clockwise direction ending with Canaletto. However you plan your itinerary, be sure to avail yourself of one of the great assets of the Gemäldegalerie, the comfy sofas in the larger rooms.

# Bruegel and his contemporaries

Before you get to the Bruegel room you must pass through room IX, which contains works by the likes of **Pieter Aertsen** (c.1508–75), a contemporary of Bruegel's who also worked in the peasant genre. *Vanity – Still Life* is typical of his style: the detailed still life of the feast being prepared by Martha upstages her sister Mary at the feet of Jesus, portrayed in the background. **Frans Floris** (1516–70), a painter more famous in his day than Bruegel ever was, contributes a gruesome *Last Judgement*, while **Lucas van Valckenborch**'s (1535–97) months of the year (only five of them survive) are modelled on Bruegel's, which you'll see in the next room.

The great thing about the museum's works by **Pieter Bruegel the Elder** (c.1525–69), in room X, is the breadth and range of the collection, from innovative interpretations of religious stories to allegorical peasant scenes. Though well connected in court circles in Antwerp and, later, Brussels, Bruegel excelled in these country scenes, earning himself the soubriquet **"Peasant Bruegel"** – the story goes that he used to disguise himself in order to move freely among the peasantry. A classic example of the genre is his *Children's Games*, an incredibly detailed picture with more than 230 children playing 83 different games. Perhaps the most beguiling of all Bruegel's works within the peasant genre is the **cycle of seasons**, commissioned by a rich Flemish banker. Three (out of six) hang in this room: *The Gloomy Day*, *The Return of the Herd* and, the most famous of them all, *Hunters in the Snow*, in which Bruegel perfectly captures a wintry monochrome landscape.

Several of Bruegel's peasant works clearly have a somewhat high-handed **moral message**, too, as in the *Peasant Dance*, where the locals revel irreverently, oblivious to the image of the Madonna concealed in the top right-hand corner. Similarly, the *Peasant Wedding* comes over less as a religious occasion than as another excuse for gluttony. Others, such as *The Peasant and the Bird-Thief*, are more difficult to interpret, though it's thought to illustrate the inscrutable Flemish proverb: "He who knows where the nest is, has the knowledge; he who robs it, has the nest."

In *The Procession to Calvary*, we are confronted with a typically vigorous Bruegelian crowd, who seem utterly unmoved by the tragedy quietly and inconspicuously unfolding in their midst. Gruesome characters, revealing the influence of Bosch, inhabit *The Fight between Carnival and Lent*, a complex painting in which the orgy of Shrove Tuesday is contrasted with the piety of Ash Wednesday. *The Tower of Babel* (inspired, it's thought, by the Colosseum in Rome) is more straightforward, illustrating the vanity of King Nimrod – the detail on both the tower and the city below it is staggering, but get too near and you'll set off one of the alarms.

Bruegel lived through a particularly turbulent period in the history of the Netherlands, which was under Spanish Habsburg rule at the time, and many have tried to read veiled allusions to contemporary **political events** into his paintings (the Austrian troops accompanying Christ in *The Procession to Calvary*, for example). However, the most oft-quoted example, *The Massacre of the Innocents*, was, in fact, painted prior to the appointment of the Duke of Alba, and therefore cannot refer to the duke's Council of Blood, during which twelve thousand were executed, despite what some art historians might say.

# Early Netherlandish painting

Works by the generation of Flemish painters who preceded Bruegel are displayed in the adjoining rooms 14 and 15. **Jan van Eyck** (c.1390–1441), by far the most famous, is represented by two extremely precise portrait heads. There's a similar realism in **Hugo van der Goes**'s (1440–82) diptych, *The Fall of Man and the Lamentation of Christ*; the story here is given a misogynist twist by the portrayal of the serpent with a woman's head. The triptych by **Hans Memling** (1440–94) is altogether more Italian in form, with its carefully balanced symmetry and rich architectural framing.

The three panels that make up *Altarpiece with the Crucifixion and Two Donors* by Memling's teacher, **Rogier van der Weyden** (c.1400–64), are cleverly unified by the undulating landscape that continues across all three frames. Uniquely, the two donors, positioned to the right of the cross in the main scene, and the holy figures, are given almost equal importance. Meanwhile, **Gerhard David**'s (d.1523) *St Michael's Altar* features the very pretty saint serenely smothering seven very nasty apocalyptic beasties with his red velvet cloak. Also in this room is the museum's one and only work by **Hieronymus Bosch** (c.1450–1516), *Christ Carrying the Cross*, a canvas packed with a crowd of typically grotesque onlookers.

# Dürer, Cranach and Holbein

If you continue with the smaller rooms, you come to the excellent German collection, in particular the so-called "Danube School", a loose title used to group together various sixteenth-century German-speaking painters inspired by the landscape of the Danube. Room 16 shelters a colourful *Adoration of the Trinity* altarpiece by **Albrecht Dürer** (1471–1528). Amid his gilded throng are the donor, Matthäus Landauer (lower row, to the left), his son-in-law (lower row, to the right) and, with its feet firmly on the ground, Dürer himself (bottom right). The frame (a modern copy of the original) bears closer inspection, too, with those not heading for heaven being chained up and devoured by the devil. Dürer also appears, somewhat incongruously dressed in black, in the centre of his *Martyrdom of the Ten Thousand*; amid scenes of mass murder on Mount Ararat, he strolls, deep in conversation, with his recently deceased friend, the humanist Conrad Celtes.

Room 17 contains more Dürer, including his portrait of Emperor Maximilian I, from the year of the latter's death; the emperor holds a pomegranate, symbol of wealth and power. A small but prime example of the Danube School of painting is *The Crucifixion* by **Lucas Cranach the Elder** (1472–1553), one of his earliest works, with its gory depiction of Christ, spattered with, and vomiting up, blood, set against a rugged Danubian landscape. Cranach went on to become court painter to the Elector of Saxony, after which his style became more circumspect. In *Judith with the Head of Holofernes*, the Biblical heroine is depicted as an elegant Saxon lady, while his *Stag Hunt of Elector Frederick the Wise*, in which numerous stags are driven into the water so the royals can pick them off with crossbows, is almost playful, with little sense of the subsequent bloody slaughter. His son, Lucas Cranach the Younger (1515–86), contributes an equally jolly scene of slaughter in *Stag Hunt of the Elector John Frederick*, which hangs close by. Also in room 17 are several melodramatic religious paintings by **Albrecht Altdorfer** (c.1480–1538), another artist of the Danube School, who reveals his penchant for the pornographic in the incestuous *Lot and His Daughters*.

The large collection of works in room 18 by **Hans Holbein the Younger** (1497–1543), who was almost a generation younger than Cranach and Dürer, date from his period as court painter to the English king Henry VIII. One of his first royal commissions was a portrait of *Jane Seymour*, lady-in-waiting to Henry VIII's second wife, Anne Boleyn, who, after the latter's execution, became his third wife. (She died giving birth to Henry's one and only son, the future Edward VI.) The portrait of Emperor Karl V with his Ulm Mastiff, by Austrian artist **Jakob Seisenegger** (1505–67), helped popularize the full-length portrait among the European nobility, and was undoubtedly the model for Titian's more famous portrait of the emperor, which hangs in the Prado in Madrid.

## Brueghel, Arcimboldo and van Dyck

Room 19 contains several works by the son of "Peasant Bruegel", **Jan Brueghel the Elder** (1568–1625), whose detailed still lifes of flowers were highly prized, his luminous paintwork earning him the nickname "Velvet Brueghel". One of his most famous, non-flowery paintings is his reverential *Adoration of the Kings*, a beautifully detailed work that's a firm favourite on Christmas cards.

Also in room 19 are several works from the court of Rudolf II (1576–1612), the deeply melancholic emperor who shut himself up in Prague Castle surrounded by astrologers, alchemists and artists. It is Rudolf, whose portrait by **Hans von Aachen** (c.1551–1615) hangs in the room, we have to thank for the Bruegels and Dürers in the museum. Rudolf particularly enjoyed the works of Mannerist artists like **Bartholomäus Spranger** (1546–1611), who pandered to the emperor's penchant for depictions of erotic, mythological dreamworlds as in his *Venus and Adonis*. One of Rudolf's favourite court artists was **Giuseppe Arcimboldo** (1527–93), whose "composite heads" – surrealist, often disturbing, profile portraits created out of inanimate objects – so tickled the emperor that he had portraits made of every member of his entourage, right down to the cook. Among the four in the Kunsthistorisches, all of which are allegorical, are *Water*, in which the whole head is made of sea creatures, and *Fire*, where it's a hotchpotch of burning faggots, an oil lamp and various firearms.

**Anthony Van Dyck** (1599–1641) predominates in the adjacent room (XII): some pieces, like *Samson and Delilah*, date from the time when Van Dyck was working closely with Rubens, hence the characteristic, "ruffled" brushstrokes; others – mostly portraits – date from after Van Dyck's appointment as court painter to the English king Charles I.

## Rubens

Thanks to the Habsburgs' long-term control of the southern Netherlands, the Kunsthistorisches boasts one of the largest collections of paintings by **Peter Paul Rubens** (1577–1640) in existence, spread over three rooms (rooms 20, XIII & XIV). As is clear from his self-confident self-portrait at the age of 62, Rubens was a highly successful artist, who received so many commissions that he was able to set up a studio and employ a group of collaborators (among them Van Dyck and Jordaens). Rubens would supply the preliminary sketches – witness the sketches for giant high-altar paintings commissioned by the Jesuits in room XIV, and the end result, in the same room.

Perhaps the best-known of all the Rubens works is *The Fur*, in room XIII, a frank, erotic testament to the artist's second wife, Hélène Fourment, who was 37 years his junior. Rubens was clearly taken with his 16-year-old wife, who appears as an angel and as a saint (or possibly deity) in two other late works: the *Ildefonso Altar* and, looking directly at the viewer, in the *Meeting near Nördlingen*. The loose brushwork and painterly style in these two bear comparison with Titian's late work in room I, and Rubens pays tribute to the Italian in his *The Worship of Venus*, a veritable chubby cherub-fest set in a classical landscape.

## Rembrandt, Vermeer and the Brits

Rubens' Baroque excess is a million miles from the sparse, simple portraits by **Rembrandt van Rijn** (1606–69), several of which hang in room 21. There's a sympathetic early portrait of his mother (now thought to be a copy), the year before she died, depicted in all the fragility and dignity of old age, and a dream-like later study of his son, Titus, reading. There are also three self-portraits from the 1650s,

▲ Café at the Kunsthistorisches Museum

when, as the art critics love to point out, Rembrandt was beginning to experience financial difficulties. Whether you choose to read worry into Rembrandt's face or not, these are three superb studies of the human face.

Next door, in room 22, is the museum's one and only painting by **Jan Vermeer**, *Allegory of the Art of Painting*, considered by many to be one of his finest and thought to have been one of the artist's favourites. The bright light from the onlooker's left; the yellow, blue and grey; the simple poses, are all classic Vermeer trademarks, though the symbolic meaning, and even the title, of the work have provoked fierce debate. Close by, in room 24, are the museum's only **British paintings**: a gentle, honey-hued *Suffolk Landscape* by Thomas Gainsborough, a portrait of painstaking realism by Joseph Wright, an unfinished portrait of a young woman by Joshua Reynolds, and a portrait by Henry Raeburn.

## Titian and the Venetians

Over in the west wing, the museum boasts a superb selection of Venetian paintings, especially works by **Titian** (c.1488–1576), which span all sixty years of his artistic life. Very early works like *The Gypsy Madonna* in room I reveal Titian's debt to Giovanni Bellini, in whose studio he spent his apprenticeship. The colours are richer, the contours softer, but the essentially static composition is reminiscent of Bellini's own *Young Woman with a Mirror* (see below). The largest canvas in room I is Titian's *Ecce Homo*, a complex Mannerist painting from his middle period, in which, amid all the action and colour, Christ and Pontius Pilate are relegated to the top left-hand corner.

In *Girl in a Fur* and the portrait of the Elector John Frederick of Saxony, Titian shows himself equally capable of sparing use of colour, allowing the sitters' individual features maximum effect. By contrast, Titian's very last portrait, of the art dealer Jacopo Strada, whom the painter disliked, is full of incidental detail, colour and movement. Don't miss, too the portrait of Isabella d'Este, "First Lady of the World", depicted wearing a "borzo", a turban-like headgear that she was instrumental in popularizing. Towards the end of his life, Titian achieved a freedom of technique in his own personal works (as opposed to those produced for commission by his studio), in which "he used his fingers more than his brush", according to fellow painter Palma il Giovane. His masterpiece of this period is the *Nymph and Shepherd*, painted without a commission, using an autumnal palette and very loose brushwork.

A fragment of an altarpiece by Antonello da Messina, who is credited with introducing oil painting to northern Italy, hangs in the adjacent room 1, along with *Young Woman with a Mirror* and *Presentation of Christ in the Temple*, both by **Giovanni Bellini** (1460–1516), and a sculptural *St Sebastian* by Bellini's brother-in-law, **Andrea Mantegna** (c.1430–1506). Next door, in room 2, the subject matter of the *Three Philosophers* – in which the left-hand section of the painting appears to have gone missing – is almost as mysterious as its painter, **Giorgione**. All we know about him is that he was tall, handsome and died young (possibly of the plague); as for the painting, no one's sure if it depicts the Magi, the three stages of man's life or some other subject. Giorgione's sensuous portrait, *Laura* – fur and naked breasts are a recurring theme in the gallery – is one of his few works to be certified and dated on the back.

Colourful, carefully constructed, monumental Mannerist canvases by **Paolo Veronese** (1528–88) fill the walls of room II – his early *Anointing of David* is a classic example, with the subject matter subordinated to the overall effect. In room III, there are several impressive portraits by **Tintoretto** (1518–94), and a voluptuous *Susanna and the Elders*, full of contrasts of light and shade, old age and youthfulness, clothed and naked. However, it's also worth looking at the horizontal panels, depicting scenes from the Old and New Testaments and intended for use on furniture, not least for their refreshing immediacy and improvised brushstrokes.

## Raphael, Bronzino and Caravaggio

In room 3, the scene shifts across northern Italy to the Mannerist school of Emilia. **Antonio Correggio** (c.1489–1534) puts his bid in for the gallery's most erotic painting with *Jupiter and Io*, in which the latter is brought to the verge of ecstasy by Jupiter in the form of a lecherous cloud. *Self-portrait in a Convex Mirror* by **Parmigianino** (1503–40) was just the sort of tricksy art that appealed to Rudolf II, in whose collection it appeared in 1608. In room 4, the masterly *Madonna in the Meadow* is a study in Renaissance harmony and proportion, painted by **Raphael** (1483–1520) at the tender age of 22. Further on, in room 8, there's a typically icy *Holy Family* by **Agnolo Bronzino** (1503–72).

**Caravaggio** (1571–1610), several of whose works hang in room V, was nothing if not controversial. His chief artistic sin, in the eyes of the establishment, was his refusal to idealize his biblical characters, frequently using street urchins as his models, as in his *David with the Head of Goliath*; he also painted his self-portrait as the severed head of Goliath. He may have managed to outrage more than a few of his religious patrons, but his works had a profound effect on artists like Rubens and Bruegel, both of whom at one time or another owned the *Madonna of the Rosary*.

## Velázquez, Bellotto and Canaletto

If the Italians start to get you down – and there is a lot of less-than-fantastic seventeenth-century art out there – head for the Spanish in rooms 9 and 10. Here you can see Alonso Sánchez Coëllo's portrait of **Don Carlos**, Philip II's mentally and physically handicapped son, who was incarcerated by his father some four years later, and died shortly afterwards. Another portrait by Coëllo depicts Elisabeth of Valois, Philip II's third wife, whom he married despite the fact that she was already betrothed to Don Carlos – events familiar to those who know the plot of Verdi's opera *Don Carlos*.

The museum's smattering of works by **Diego Velázquez** (1599–1660), most of them gifts from the Spanish Habsburgs to the Austrian side of the family, include a portrait of Queen Maria-Anna of Spain, whose hairdo is twice the size of her face. Charles II of Spain looks utterly grotesque in the portrait by Juan Carreño de Miranda – it's scary to think that he probably looked even worse in real life. The most famous works are those of the Infanta Margarita Teresa, who was betrothed to her uncle, the future Emperor Leopold I, from the age of three.

Lastly, you might want to take a look at the large eighteenth-century views of Vienna in room VII, commissioned by the court from **Bernardo Bellotto**, to see how little the view from the Belvedere has changed over the centuries. The Viennese insisted on calling Bellotto "Canaletto", though he was in fact the latter's nephew and pupil. For real **Canalettos**, you must go next door, to room 13, where his much smaller, picture-postcard views of Venice hang alongside works by his compatriot, Francesco Guardi.

## Vermeyen and the Coin Cabinet

On the little-visited second floor a series of sixteenth-century cartoons and tapestries by **Jan Cornelisz Vermeyen** are displayed. Vermeyen accompanied

Emperor Karl V in 1535 during his crusade to recapture Tunis from the Ottoman Turks, at the head of a vast army of thirty thousand troops and over four hundred ships, and his detailed depictions of the maritime scenes, cityscapes, cavalry charges and hand-to-hand combat boast a remarkable topographical veracity and a skilful use of perspective.

The **Münzkabinett** (Coin Cabinet) also occupies several rooms on the second floor and includes a display of piggy banks from Roman times to the 1990s. Naturally enough, there are also coins, some dating as far back as 650 BC, others from more recent times: the Habsburg Empire, the Austro-fascist state, the Nazi period and even a few token euros. Also here, you'll find **Archduke Ferdinand II of Tyrol**'s remarkable collection of more than one thousand sixteenth-century postcard-sized portraits of popes, dukes, generals, poets and philosophers.

# The ground-floor galleries

The **ground floor** is laid out entirely chronologically using only Roman numerals: it kicks off with the Egyptian and Near Eastern Collection (I–VIII), passes through Greek and Roman Antiquities (IX–XVIII) and heads off into the Kunstkammer (XIX–XXXVII).

## Egyptian and Near Eastern Collection

Immediately to the right as you enter the museum are the purpose-built galleries of the **Egyptian and Near Eastern Collection**, which sport appropriately hieroglyphic decorations. Pink granite papyrus-stalk columns from around 1410 BC are even incorporated into the construction of Saal I, which is devoted to the **Egyptian death cult**. The entrance to the room is guarded by two statues of the fearsome, lion-headed goddess, Sekhmet; the museum owns just four out of the six hundred that once formed a colossal monument to the deity erected at Thebes by Amenophis III.

In the room itself, there's only one actual mummy, wrapped in papyrus leaves, but there are numerous wooden inner **coffins** in the shape of mummies, smothered with polychrome symbols and hieroglyphs. Below the mummy cases are the canopic jars, used for storing the entrails removed during mummification, with lids carved in· the shape of animal deities. In Saal III there are cabinets full of *shabti* figurines, in wood, stone and pottery, which were placed in the tomb in order to perform any task the gods might require (there had to be at least 365 in each tomb, plus 36 overseers). Notice, too, the cabinet of heart scarabs, which were placed upon the chests of mummies, bearing a spell that implored the deceased's heart not to bear witness against him or her during the Judgement of Osiris.

The Kunsthistorisches owns some superb examples of **Egyptian sculpture**, beginning in Saal VII with a rather wonderful duo of Horus, in his adult, falcon-headed form, seated alongside King Horemheb, who was the power behind the throne of Tutankhamun. En route to Saal IX, look out for a winsome **blue pottery hippo**, whose body is tatooed with papyrus leaves, lotus flowers and a bird, pictorial elements from its natural swamp habitat. Saal IX contains one of the collection's most prized possessions, the *Ersatz Kopf* or **Reserve Head** from around 2450 BC, a smooth, stylized head carved in limestone, which exudes

**Egyptian & Near Eastern Collection**
Rooms I–VIII
**Greek & Roman Antiquities**
Rooms IX–XVIII
**Sculpture & Decorative Arts**
Rooms XIX–XXXVII

N

KUNSTHISTORISCHES
MUSEUM: GROUND
FLOOR GALLERIES

Entrance
Maria-Theresien-Platz

an extraordinary serenity. Excavated by an Austrian archeological team at the beginning of the last century at Giza, it is thought to be a surrogate head for the immortal *ka*.

## Greek and Roman Antiquities

The **Greek and Roman Antiquities** begin in Saal X, with the vigorous high-relief **Amazonian Sarcophagus**, from the fourth century BC, depicting the struggle between the Greek heroes and the mythical female warriors.

At the centre of the large, arcaded Saal XI, which is packed with richly carved sarcophagi, is the magnificent fourth-century AD **Theseus Mosaic**, discovered in 1815 in a Roman villa near Salzburg. Theseus and the Minotaur are depicted in the middle of a complex geometric labyrinth, out of which the hero escapes with the help of the red thread given to him by Ariadne, who is pictured abandoned to the right.

Those in search of **Greek vases** need look no further than room XIV, which contains an excellent selection, from early Geometric vases from the eighth century BC to the sophisticated black-and-red-figure vases of the Classical period. Among the many onyx cameos in the adjoining room XV is one of the finest in the world, the first-century AD **Gemma Augustea**, which is surprisingly large at 19cm in height. The upper scene depicts the emperor Augustus in the guise of Jupiter, seated on a bench alongside Roma, with the emperor's star sign, Capricorn, floating between them; the lower scene shows the Romans' victory over the Dalmatians under Tiberius. Also in this room is the oldest Latin Edict of Senate in existence, dating from 186 BC, rather hopefully, forbidding Bacchic orgies.

The last three small rooms (XVI–XVIII) contain **gold work**, much of which, strictly speaking, postdates the collapse of the Roman Empire. The chain of honour with 52 pendants is an excellent example of early Germanic gold, its centrepiece a bead of smoky topaz, mounted with two tiny pouncing panthers. The most impressive haul is the treasure from Nagyszentmiklós (Sînicolaul Mare) in Romania, 23 pure gold vessels, weighing a total of 20kg, with runic inscriptions that continue to fox the experts.

Before you leave this section, admire one of the most famous classical statues here, the **Youth of Magdalensberg**. It is, in fact, a sixteenth-century bronze copy of the Roman original, something that was only discovered in 1983 when research was being conducted into the methods used in the casting.

## Kunstkammer
## (Sculpture and Decorative Arts)

The **Kunstkammer**, which occupies more than half of the ground floor galleries, has been closed since 2003, following the theft of its most famous exhibit, Benvenuto Cellini's **Saliera**. Though the *Saliera* – a slightly ludicrous sixteenth-century salt cellar upon which the gold figures of Neptune, holding a phallic trident, and Earth, squeezing her own nipple, appear to be engaged in some sort of erotic see-saw – was recovered in 2006, the galleries remain closed for refurbishment (and, presumably, the installation of a better security system). As a result the following account of the highlights excludes any mention of room numbers.

It's a patchy collection, with some real gems, and a lot of objects of great craftsmanship, but dubious artistic taste. *Kunstkammern* (Chambers of Marvels) became de rigueur among German-speaking rulers during the Renaissance and most of the exhibits were purchased or specially commissioned for such collections. The most avid collectors were Archduke Ferdinand II of Tyrol (died 1595) and Emperor Rudolf II (1576–1612). The latter took the whole thing very seriously indeed, even going so far as to incarcerate the Augsburg clockmaker, Georg Roll, when the celestial globe he made for him broke down, while the one supplied to his brother, the Archduke Ernst, continued to work.

To give you an idea of the tone of much of the collection – slightly vulgar, exquisitely executed kitsch – consider the gold vase holding tulips made from agate, jasper, chalcedony and rock crystal, or the gold chain, inset with rubies and made up of 49 portraits of the Habsburgs carved in shell. As with the majority of the exhibits, these pieces have no particular function; however, the rock-crystal dragon-lions were something of a party piece: liquid poured into their tails would gush into a shell through nozzles in the beast's breasts.

The museum owns many highly complex **ivory sculptures**, which became all the rage with royalty in the seventeenth century. It's difficult to look at ivory *objets d'art* without thinking of the unnecessary slaughter of elephants, and all the more so when the subject matter is also one of bloodshed, and the work itself so grotesquely cloying, as in the piece depicting Leopold I and Josef I gazing fondly into each other's eyes while the vanquished Turks make a muddled mess below. For a bit of variation, check out the elaborate ebony-and-ivory piggy bank, peppered with gilded figures, which belonged to the archduke Ferdinand II of Tyrol. Another typical *Kunstkammer* object is the ostrich led by a Moor, with its combination of exotic natural materials, such as coral, and human craftsmanship, exemplified by the silver-gilt ostrich.

The collection is a real hotchpotch, ranging from a striking six-winged sixteenth-century altarpiece, comprised of 156 panels, to a dubious trio of pearwood cherubs playing with one another's private parts, and a richly carved backgammon set featuring erotic scenes on each of the counters. Elsewhere, you'll find some remarkable miniature mining scenes carved out of tiny rocks, and some exquisitely beautiful astrological and scientific instruments, including one of the aforementioned celestial globes by Georg Roll. Unfortunately, the gold and silver automata in the collection can't be put through their paces, nor is there much ticking from the clocks and watches on display.

# The Vorstädte

Once the Turks were beaten back from the city gates in 1683, Vienna could, at last, spread itself safely beyond the confines of the medieval town walls. A horseshoe of districts, known as the **Vorstädte** (Inner Suburbs), quickly grew up and engulfed the villages around the old town, beyond the *glacis* (the sloping open ground outside the city walls). In 1704, the great military leader, Prince Eugène of Savoy, ordered the construction of a second, outer line of fortifications or *Linienwall*, to protect the new suburbs. Later, the *Linienwall* became the municipal boundary, where, in a Habsburg custom going back to the Middle Ages, every person entering the city had to undergo a thorough search, and pay a consumer's tax on goods purchased outside the city.

As the city spread still further out into the *Vororte* or rural parishes, the *Linienwall* was finally demolished in 1890, and became what's known today as the **Gürtel** – literally "belt" – a thunderous ring road, which has the added indignity of doubling as the city's red-light district. The seven districts of the Vorstädte – the third to the ninth – are neatly confined between the Ringstrasse and the Gürtel. They have remained residential for the most part, though each one is cut through with a busy commercial thoroughfare, the largest of which is the city's main shopping drag, **Mariahilferstrasse**, which divides the sixth and seventh districts. Sights in the Vorstädte are widely dispersed, so it pays to be selective – a *Netzkarte* and a grasp of the transport system are useful (see p.24). The following account goes round in a clockwise direction, beginning with the third district and finishing with the ninth. The second district, Leopoldstadt, east of the Danube Canal, is covered in Chapter Six.

The one sight in the Vorstädte that no visitor should miss is the **Belvedere**, in the third district, with its formal gardens and twin-set of Baroque palaces that house some superb works of art, including the city's finest collection of paintings by Gustav Klimt. Two other sights that positively heave with visitors in summer are the **Hundertwasserhaus**, also in the third district, and the **Freud-Museum** in the ninth. The former is a wacky piece of council housing designed by an old hippy, and, as such, is some kind of must, since opinion is so divided on the building. As for Freud's apartment, there's really not much to see, yet it remains the pilgrim's choice. The other reason to explore the Vorstädte is to

## The districts of the Vorstädte

Third – Landstrasse
Fourth – Wieden
Fifth – Margareten
Sixth – Mariahilf

Seventh – Neubau
Eighth – Josefstadt
Ninth – Alsergrund

wander round the shops, restaurants and bars in districts like Neubau (seventh) and Josefstadt (eighth).

# Landstrasse

**Landstrasse** – Vienna's third district – lies to the east and southeast of the Innere Stadt, framed by the Danube Canal (Donaukanal) to the east, and to the west by Prinz-Eugen-Strasse and Arsenalstrasse. By far the largest of the Vorstädte, it remains a predominantly working-class area, with a high immigrant population, mostly from Eastern Europe and the Balkans. The one exception is the diplomatic quarter around the **Belvedere**, where Prince Eugène of Savoy's summer palaces house a feast of fine art from medieval times to the early twentieth century. Just south of the Gürtel lies the city's **Arsenal**, home to the **Heeresgeschichtliches Museum**, built to glorify the Imperial Army in the nineteenth century and worth a stop for its fine quasi-Moorish architecture, even if you're not particularly keen on military paraphernalia.

Other sights are more widely dispersed. The **Hundertwasserhaus**, an idiosyncratic housing development in the nub of land to the north of the district, is now one of Vienna's top tourist attractions, something which cannot be said for the nearby modernist **Wittgensteinhaus**, designed by the famous philosopher. An incredible number of diehard fans make it out to the **St Marxer Friedhof**, where Mozart is thought to be buried – no one is quite sure where his bones actually lie. Finally, for tram-lovers, the **Strassenbahnmuseum** beckons in the far southeast of the district.

## Hundertwasserhaus and KunstHausWien

In 1983, the ageing hippy artist Friedensreich Hundertwasser (see box below) redesigned (for free) some council housing on the corner of Löwengasse and Kegelgasse,

---

### Friedensreich Hundertwasser (1928–2000)

Born in Vienna, under the name Friedrich Stowasser, **Friedensreich Hundertwasser** was brought up singlehandedly by his Jewish mother, who wisely had him baptized and enrolled him into the Hitler Youth shortly after the Anschluss, thus saving both their lives. Having spent just three months training as an artist at the Akademie der bildenden Künste, Hundertwasser left formal education for good in 1948 and shortly afterwards adopted his new *nom de plume*. He first made it as an artist in the 1950s, using distinctive coiling forms to produce "kaleidoscopic landscapes", reminiscent of Gustav Klimt, with a dash of Paul Klee. In the late 1960s, at the height of the hippy era, he achieved even greater notoriety for his speeches given in the nude, one of which was his architecture boycott manifesto *Los von Loos* (Down with Loos), in which he attacked the modernist establishment.

In many ways, Hundertwasser anticipated the current, widely accepted critique of modernism – that its emphasis on machine-like, undecorated flat surfaces was dehumanizing and alienating – stressing green issues and arguing for architectural variety. However, as an unrepentant hippy, experienced self-publicist and shrewd businessman, he also made no small number of enemies along the way, not least among contemporary Viennese architects, who felt his forays into their art form – his "painted boxes" – were crass, irreverent and populist. As one critic put it, his wavy lines and individually designed windows are akin to "a nineteenth-century quack flogging his bottles of coloured horsepiss as a miracle cure for all diseases".

**THE VORSTÄDTE**

N

Donaupark

Kaisermühlen-
VIC

Neue Donau

Donauinsel

River Danube

Vorgartenstrasse

BRIGITTENAU
20

Dresdner
Strasse

Jägerstrasse

Spittelau

Nussdorferstrasse

Michelbeuern

Franz-Josefs-
Bahnhof

Schuberts
Geburtshaus

Friedensbrücke

Liechtenstein
Museum

Freud-Museum

Universität

Allgemeines
Krankenhaus

Alser Strasse

Museum für
Volkskunde

Volksoper

Währingerstrasse-
Volksoper

Schottenring

Schottentor

ALSERGRUND
9

Rathaus

Piaristenkirche

Theater-in-
der-Josefstadt

JOSEFSTADT
8

Thaliastrasse

Josefstädter
Strasse

Praterstern

Wien Nord

Nestroyplatz

Taborstrasse

LEOPOLDSTADT
2

Messe
Prater

Kneau

Stadion

Ernst-
Happel-
Stadion

Prater

Danube Canal

Hundert-
wasserhaus

Wien-
Mitte

Landstrasse
Wien-Mitte

Schwedenplatz

INNERE STADT

Herrengasse

Hofburg

Volkstheater

Theater-in-
der-Josefstadt

in an unassuming residential area of Landstrasse (take tram #N to Hetzgasse). Following his philosophy that "the straight line is godless", he transformed the dour apartment block into **Hundertwasserhaus** (Ⓦwww.hundertwasserhaus.com), a higgledy-piggledy, kitsch, childlike jumble of brightly coloured textures that caught the popular imagination, while enraging the architectural establishment. It certainly runs the gamut of styles and consists of a frenzy of oriel windows, loggias, ceramic pillars, glass embellishments, a gilded onion dome, roof gardens and even a slice of the pre-1983 building.

Understandably, the residents were none too happy when hordes of pilgrims began ringing on their doorbells, asking to be shown round, so Hundertwasser obliged with an even tackier shopping arcade opposite, called **Kalke Village** (daily: Easter–Oct 9am–7pm; Oct–Easter 9am–5.30pm; free), providing a café (with a stream running along the bar) and information centre to draw the crowds away from the apartments (which are closed to the public), while simultaneously increasing the sales outlets for his artwork. Here, you can get the full Hundertwasser experience, the most disconcerting aspect of which is his penchant for uneven floors ("the uneven floor becomes a symphony, a melody to the feet").

### KunstHausWien

**KunstHausWien** (daily 10am–7pm; Mon €4.50, Tues–Sun €9; Ⓦwww .kunsthauswien.com), housed in a former Thonet furniture factory, four blocks north up Untere Weissgerberstrasse, is another of Hundertwasser's Gaudíesque conversions, though it has been less successful at attracting visitors; it features another shop and café, and a gallery devoted to Hundertwasser's own paintings. The gallery also hosts temporary exhibitions by other headline-grabbing contemporary artists. It's worth noting that admission is half-price on Mondays.

Two floors of the KunstHausWien are devoted to Hundertwasser's art and life, though devotees will be disappointed to discover the gallery floors are entirely flat. It's certainly easy to mock Hundertwasser's *bons mots*, which are scattered throughout the gallery, not to mention inventions such as his Water Purification Plant, and his colourful, childlike paintings are not everyone's cup of tea. The second-floor gallery offers more varied food for thought, from Hundertwasser's campaign to retain old-style Austrian number plates to his politically correct designs for various national flags. You can watch a video of Hundertwasser sailing his converted Sicilian salt trader, *Regentag*, painting in the nude and eating soup. Also displayed here are models of some of his architectural projects, such as the rubbish incineration plant in the north of Vienna, described on p.216.

# Wittgenstein-Haus to Portois & Fix

One sure way to lose the crowds is to head four blocks south to Kundmanngasse 19 and the **Wittgenstein-Haus** (Mon–Thurs 10am–noon & 3–4.30pm; €3), a grey, concrete-rendered house built in the modernist spirit of Adolf Loos, the very architect Hundertwasser spoke out against in 1968. The house was built in the late 1920s by Wittgenstein's sister, Gretl, herself a leading light among the Viennese intelligentsia and a personal friend of Freud's. She employed the architect Paul Engelmann, a pupil of Loos, but her brother, the philosopher Ludwig Wittgenstein, couldn't resist getting involved. As rigorous in his architecture as in his philosophical thinking, Wittgenstein advocated an austere functionalism, eschewing bourgeois trappings such as lampshades, carpets and curtains. Gretl no doubt saw the funny side of making Klimt's highly decorous

KunstHausWien ●1

RADETZKYSTRASSE

RADETZKYPLATZ ●2

WEISSGERBERLÄNDE

N

0    200 m

N

UNTERE VIADUKTGASSE

LÖWENGASSE

ADAMSGASSE

KRIEGLERGASSE

UNTERE WEISSGERBERSTRASSE

HINTERE ZOLLAMTSSTRASSE

KOLONITZ PLATZ

CUSTOZZAGASSE

BECHARDGASSE

HETZGASSE

Kalke Village

KOLLERGASSE

SEIDLGASSE

KEGELGASSE

Hundertwasserhaus

LÖWENGASSE

Danube Canal

●3

Wien-Mitte

MARXERGASSE

N

Ⓤ Landstrasse-
Wien-Mitte

GÄRTNERGASSE

SEIDLGASSE

LANDSTRASSE

HAUPTSTRASSE

●4

ERDBERGER LÄNDE

BEATRIXGASSE

UNGARGASSE

RASUMOFSKYGASSE

HÖRNESGASSE

KUNDMANNGASSE

PARKGASSE

GEUSAUGASSE

KUBECKGASSE

Wittgensteinhaus

SECHSKRÜGELGASSE

Ⓤ Rochusgasse

Karl-Borromäus-
Brunnen

ROCHUSGASSE

LANDSTRASSE

WASSERGASSE

ERDBERGSTRASSE

HINTZERSTRASSE

NEULINGGASSE

HAINBURGERSTRASSE

Arenberg Park

CAT

LINKE BAHNGASSE

DAPONTEGASSE

Flaktürme

HAUPTSTRASSE

Portois & Fix

BARICHGASSE

Russische
Kirche

CENTRAL LANDSTRASSE

| RESTAURANTS & CAFÉS | |
| --- | --- |
| Im KunstHaus | 1 |
| Stadtwirt | 3 |
| Wild | 2 |
| Zartl | 4 |

## Ludwig Wittgenstein (1889–1951)

*Whatever can be said can be said clearly, and that of which one cannot speak, one must remain silent about.*

*Tractatus Logico-Philosophicus*

With such pithy aphorisms, **Ludwig Wittgenstein** – who published just one complete text in his entire lifetime – made his name as one of the world's greatest philosophers. The youngest of a large, wealthy, cultured family in Vienna, Ludwig was raised a Catholic like his mother, though his father, a leading industrialist, was a Protestant convert of Jewish descent. Sceptical from an early age, Ludwig rejected his comfortable upbringing, reportedly never wearing a tie after the age of 23, and dispersing the fortune he inherited from his father to struggling writers such as Rainer Maria Rilke and Georg Trakl.

Like all the Wittgenstein children (three of whom committed suicide), Ludwig was educated at home, entering the Gymnasium in **Linz** at the age of 14 (Adolf Hitler, almost the same age as Wittgenstein, was a fellow pupil). From 1906 to 1908, he studied mechanical engineering in Berlin, completing his research in Manchester. From there, his interests shifted to mathematics and eventually to philosophy – in 1911 he arrived unannounced at the Cambridge college rooms of **Bertrand Russell**, who took a shine to the eccentric young Austrian, considering him a genius, "passionate, profound, intense and domineering". In 1913, Wittgenstein inherited the family fortune and went to live in a hut in Norway for two years, meditating and writing a series of notes on logic, which he put forward as his degree, only to be turned down when he refused to add a preface and references. During World War I, in between winning several medals for bravery, and being taken prisoner on the Italian front, he completed his *Tractatus Logico-Philosophicus*, seventy pages of musings on a wide range of subjects, including logic, ethics, religion, science, mathematics, mysticism and, of course, linguistics.

After the war, Wittgenstein gave away the rest of his father's fortune, this time handing it over to his brothers and sisters. He trained as a teacher, writing a spelling

portrait of her the focal point of the house's implacably minimalist interior. The building now belongs to the Bulgarian embassy – hence the bronze statues of the Slav saints, Cyril and Methodius, in the garden.

To the west, on the other side of Landstrasser Hauptstrasse, two blocks up Rochusgasse, is the little-known and rather unusual **Karl-Borromäus-Brunnen**, erected in 1909 by the sculptor Josef Engelhart, one of the founders of the Secession, and the Slovene architect, Josip Plečnik. Set within its own little sunken square, whose entrances are flanked by flowerpots sporting rams' and eagles' heads, the fountain is one of the hidden gems of Landstrasse. Centring on a plain triangular obelisk, it is shaped like a three-leaved clover, and covered with salamanders, bog-eyed frogs and reptiles of various kinds. Rings of cherubs holding hands dance beneath the leaves, while above, three groups of diminutive, free-standing figures tell the story of the saint, to whom the Karlskirche is also dedicated (see p.121).

Another arresting architectural sight in the vicinity is the **Portois & Fix** building, reached by going one block west of the fountain, and then south on Ungargasse to no. 59–61. Designed by Max Fabiani in 1900, this Jugendstil building copies Otto Wagner's innovative use of tiling for the facade of his Majolikahaus (see p.124). Instead of Wagner's more conventional floral pattern, however, Fabiani creates a strikingly modern, abstract, dappled effect with his tiles in various shades of lime green and brown, topped by a decorative, wrought-iron balustrade.

dictionary for schools, and working in several villages south of Vienna. Prone to pulling a pupil's hair if he or she failed to understand algebra, he wasn't greatly liked by the locals, and eventually returned to Vienna to design a house for his sister, Gretl (see p.148). During this time, he fell in love with a Swiss friend of his sister's called Marguerite, who refused his marriage proposal. In 1927, Wittgenstein came into contact with members of the **Vienna Circle**, a group of philosophers, scientists and mathematicians, including Karl Popper, Kurt Gödel, Rudolf Carnap and Moritz Schlick, who rejected traditional philosophy and espoused, instead, logical positivism. The Circle had chosen *Tractatus* as their working text, but their interpretation of it as an anti-metaphysical tract infuriated Wittgenstein, who preferred to dwell on its ethical and mystical aspects.

He was persuaded to return to Cambridge in 1929, putting forward *Tractatus* as his PhD, and consoling his examiners – among them Russell – with the remark, "Don't worry, I know you'll never understand it." He became a legend in his own lifetime: scruffily dressed, discussing philosophy with his chambermaid, devouring American pulp fiction, delivering lectures without notes, gesticulating violently and cursing himself at his own stupidity or maintaining long silences. Such was his ambivalence towards the smug, unnatural world of academia, and his conviction that philosophy precludes improvement, that he frequently tried to dissuade his students from continuing with the subject. He succeeded in persuading his lover, a promising young mathematician called **Francis Skinner**, to give up his studies and become a factory mechanic. In 1939, Wittgenstein acquired British citizenship and returned to Vienna (by now part of Nazi Germany) to secure the declassification of his family as Jewish. Wittgenstein considered it intolerable to be teaching philosophy in time of war, so he took a job as a porter at London's Guy's Hospital and as a lab assistant in Newcastle's Royal Victoria Infirmary researching wound shock. In 1946, he fell in love with another undergraduate, a medic forty years his junior called Ben Richards, with whom he stayed until his death from prostate cancer in 1951. He is buried in Cambridge.

# Along Rennweg

"East of Rennweg, the Orient begins" is one of Prince Metternich's much-quoted aphorisms, though he clearly meant a bit further along the road than his own house at no. 27 (now the Italian embassy), where he lived until forced to flee the city in 1848. **Rennweg** begins at Schwarzenbergplatz and runs for several kilometres through Landstrasse towards Hungary, but the section close to the Belvedere has always had a certain cachet. Nowadays, the streets immediately to the north are more desirable, dotted with embassies, among them the German, British and Russian legations. The last two are provided with their own churches, a red-brick Anglican one and an onion-domed Orthodox one, both on Jaurèsgasse.

Rennweg itself is now too busy with traffic to be truly fashionable, but when **Otto Wagner** built himself a "town house" here in 1891, at no. 3, it was clearly still des res. Now known as the Palais Hoyos and occupied by the Serbian embassy, this early Wagner work is very much in the Ringstrasse style, with its elaborate wrought-iron balconies, but you can discern hints of his later work in touches such as the projecting cornice and the very fine reliefwork in the upper floor. Wagner also designed the much less ornate houses on either side, including no. 5, where Gustav Mahler lived from 1898 to 1907 (see p.114).

Just up from Wagner's trio, towards Schwarzenbergplatz, is the **Gardekirche**, originally completed by Maria Theresia's court architect, Nicolo Pacassi, in 1763, but refaced in a rather dour, Neoclassical style just six years later. The Rococo interior, however, was left alone, and still retains its richly gilded stuccowork, ribbed dome, bull's-eye windows and lantern. Built as the chapel of the imperial hospital, it was handed over to the Polish Guards in 1782. The Gardekirche stands directly opposite the entrance to the Belvedere, but the great green dome that features so prominently in the view from the top of the Belvedere, is, in fact, the **Salesianerkirche**, further up on the south side of Rennweg. Along with its neighbouring convent, it was founded by Amelia Wilhelmina, widow of Josef I, in 1716, as her own private residence and as a college for daughters of the nobility (it's now the Botanisches Institut). Josef Emanuel Fischer von Erlach assisted in designing the exterior, which has more spatial interplay than the Gardekirche; the interior is less interesting, however.

## The Belvedere

Forget the Hofburg or even Schönbrunn – the **Belvedere**, to the south of Rennweg, is the finest palace complex in the whole of Vienna, at least from the outside. Two magnificent Baroque mansions, designed in the early eighteenth century by Lukas von Hildebrandt, face each other across a sloping formal garden, commanding a superb view over central Vienna. The man for whom all this was

▲ The Belvedere

built was **Prince Eugène of Savoy**, Austria's greatest military leader (see p.155), whose campaigns against the Turks enabled the city, at last, to expand beyond the walls of the old town. Today, the loftier of the two palaces, the Oberes Belvedere, houses one of the most popular art galleries in Vienna, with an unrivalled collection of paintings by Gustav Klimt plus a few choice works by contemporaries such as Egon Schiele and Oskar Kokoschka.

Prince Eugène himself was a great patron of the arts, but he left no direct heirs, and after his death in 1736, a distant cousin, Anna Victoria, inherited the estate and sold off the prince's possessions. The statues from Herculaneum were bought by the court of Dresden; nearly two hundred paintings were purchased by the

## Visiting the Belvedere

A ticket to the Oberes Belvedere costs €9.50, while entrance to the Unteres Belvedere is €7.50; to visit both, you can buy a Kombiticket for €12.50. Both galleries are open daily from 10am to 6pm (⑩www.belvedere.at). Entry to the Belvedere gardens is free. You'll find a very pleasant café on the ground floor in the east wing of Oberes Belvedere, and a pub called *Salm Bräu*, round the corner from the Unteres Belvedere, on Rennweg (see p.274). The easiest way to reach the Oberes Belvedere is to hop on tram #D; to reach the Unteres Belvedere, take tram #71 from the Ringstrasse.

king of Sardinia, head of the House of Savoy; the menagerie fell into disrepair; but the emperor Karl VI succeeded in buying the prince's personal library, which now resides in the Prunksaal of the Nationalbibliothek (see p.89). Finally, in 1752 the Belvedere itself was snapped up by Empress Maria Theresia, who decided to house the Habsburgs' own court art collection here, and who opened the palace gardens to the public in 1779.

The imperial art collection eventually moved into the purpose-built Kunsthistorisches Museum in the 1890s. In 1903, the Unteres Belvedere became home to the new Modernes Galerie (now the Österreichisches Galerie), while the Oberes Belvedere was taken over by **Archduke Franz Ferdinand** until his assassination in Sarajevo in 1914. He stayed here only occasionally, preferring to reside at his Bohemian castle of Konopiště, near Prague, since his wife was snubbed by the Habsburgs. Thanks to the patronage of Archduchess Valerie, Emperor Franz-Josef's daughter, the ailing composer, **Anton Bruckner**, was granted the ground-floor flat in the gatehouse of the Oberes Belvedere in July 1895 and spent the remaining sixteen months of his life here.

After World War I, both palaces were used as state art galleries (as they are today), though under the Austro-fascists (1934–38), Chancellor Kurt Schuschnigg also chose to reside here, before he was interned by the Nazis following the Anschluss. In 1955, the Austrian State Treaty, or Staatsvertrag, was formally signed by the Allied Powers, in the Marmorsaal of the Oberes Belvedere. Fifteen years later, the superpower Stategic Arms Limitation Talks (SALT) were officially opened in the same room by the then Foreign Minister, Kurt Waldheim.

### Unteres Belvedere

Completed in 1716 at the very bottom of the formal gardens, the **Unteres Belvedere** (Lower Belvedere) is a relatively simple garden palace, built for Prince Eugène's personal use, rather than for affairs of state or entertainment. Inside, however, it actually preserves more of its lavish original decor than the Oberes Belvedere, and is now used, along with the adjacent Orangerie, for temporary exhibitions.

The architectural highlight of the palace interior is the richly decorated **Marmorsaal** (Marble Hall), which extends over two floors at the central axis of the building. The whole hall is a hymn to Prince Eugène's military prowess, white stucco trophies and reliefs contrasting with the rich red marbling. Extra depth is given to the walls through trompe l'oeil niches and balconies, and to the ceiling by illusory moulding, leading up to Martino Altomonte's fresco featuring Prince Eugène himself enjoying his apotheosis in the guise of Apollo. At ground level, you can admire the original lead statues from the Donnerbrunnen on Neuer Markt (see p.49), sculpted by Georg Raphael Donner (1693–1741).

At the far end of the wing lies the **Groteskensaal**, with a "grotesque" decor of birds and beasts, and fanciful floral murals. The inspiration for this style of painting, very fashionable in its day, came from ancient Roman wall decoration, discovered during excavations of underground rooms. The rooms became known as "grottos" and the style of decor was dubbed "grotesque". Look out, too, for the bizarre, hyperrealist "character heads", carved by the eccentric sculptor Franz Xaver Messerschmidt (1732–83), which are usually displayed here. Next comes the **Marmorgalerie**, a richly stuccoed white-and-red reception room built by Prince Eugène to house his trio of classical statues from Herculaneum. These, now in Dresden, provided the inspiration for the Neoclassical sculptures by Domenico Parodi, which stand in niches along the walls.

By far the most mind-blowing room, though, is the adjacent **Goldkabinett**, a cabinet of mirrors, dating from Maria Theresa's reign, dotted with oriental vases

## Prince Eugène of Savoy (1663–1736)

The Austrians have never enjoyed the greatest of military reputations, so it comes as little surprise that their most revered military figure is, in fact, a Frenchman, **Prince Eugène of Savoy**. His first taste of military warfare came at the age of 20, when he offered his services to Emperor Leopold I, partly to avenge his brother, Louis Julius, who had recently died fighting the Turks. Eugène immediately fought in the front line against the 1683 Turkish siege of Vienna, earning himself a pair of golden spurs for his bravery. Subsequently, he was given command of a regiment by Leopold; by 30, he was a field marshal. His victory over the Turks at Zenta in 1697 helped win back Hungary for the Habsburgs, and he was made president of the Imperial War Council. His capture of Belgrade in 1718 was the single most important act in making Western Europe safe from the Ottomans. In between times, he even fought against his fellow countryman, Louis XIV, in the Spanish Wars of Succession (1701–14), assisting the Duke of Marlborough in the victories at Blenheim, Oudenarde and Malplaquet. Meanwhile, back in Vienna, he became one of the greatest patrons of the arts the city has ever known, building fabulous Baroque palaces, and amassing a huge library, art collection and menagerie.

If the prince's military achievements and artistic endeavours are well documented, very little is known about his childhood or his later personal life. There are no memoirs, and nothing written about him by anyone who was close to him. Born in Paris into a leading aristocratic family, Eugène was brought up in the most extraordinary circumstances. His mother, the Countess of Soissons, was not only one of Louis XIV's mistresses, but also a wild party animal, with a penchant for intrigue and black magic. She was eventually exiled from France in 1680, on suspicion of having poisoned her husband, and of plotting to kill the king himself. Whether the infant Eugène participated in the transvestite orgies conducted in his childhood home will never be known for sure. He remained unmarried all his life, and there is no mention of him ever having taken a mistress. Again, whether this was due to his own sexual preference, his troubled relationship with his mother, or his notoriously unprepossessing appearance, remains a mystery. Certainly, the Duchess of Orléans' description of him as a boy is far from flattering: "It is true that his eyes are not ugly, but his nose ruins his face; he has two large teeth which are visible all the time. He is always dirty and has lanky hair which he never curls . . . and an upper lip so narrow that he cannot close his mouth." As a result of the child's physical deficiencies, Louis XIV decided he should be brought up for the church rather than follow a military career. Given his mother's reputation, it's hardly surprising that Eugène was denied admission into the French army by the king in 1683, though Louis lived to rue his decision when the prince went on to humiliate him on the battlefield on several occasions.

and adorned with yet more "grotesques" painted onto a vast expanse of gaudy, 23-carat-gold panelling. Dominating this small room is *Apotheosis of Prince Eugène*, an explosion of marble by the Dresden court sculptor, Balthasar Permoser, in which a tangle of figures struggles to stay on the plinth. The prince is depicted in full armour, trampling on the enemy, while attempting modestly to muffle the horn of Fame.

## The gardens

The formal **gardens** (daily: April–Oct 6am to dusk; Nov–March 6.30am to dusk; free) of the Belvedere are laid out on a wide slope, punctuated with box hedges, fountains, waterfalls and statuary, and centred on a grand vista culminating in the magnificent Oberes Belvedere itself. Prince Eugène began buying up land for the gardens way back in 1693, employing Dominique Girard to use the skills he learnt at Versailles to create the perfect Baroque landscape. In the prince's day, the gardens would have been much more lavishly laid out, and the schematic arrangement of the sculptures far more complex: the lower section was put aside as the domain of the elements, while the upper section belonged to the gods. Today, this elaborate allegorical scheme only partially survives.

The central axis, flanked by statues of the Eight Muses, leads up to the **Lower Cascade**, a giant shell held up by tritons and sea nymphs. On either side of the central axis are sunken bosquets, or hedge gardens, two circular and two square, with statues of Pluto and Proserpina from the Underworld. The balustrades, which line the steps either side of the cascade, are peppered with putti representing the seasons and, beyond, the first of the sphinxes for which the Belvedere is famous. Fearsome beasts spurt water over the crest of the **Upper Cascade**, from where the water flows over a set of steps. The upper section of the garden was meant to represent Olympus, but the statues of the Greek gods were replaced in the nineteenth century by yet more sphinxes.

The main entrance actually lies to the south of the Oberes Belvedere, on busy Landstrasser Gürtel, its wonderful wrought-iron gateway flanked by standing lions clasping the Savoy coat of arms. The prince himself was a keen gardener, bringing rare and exotic plants and trees from all over the world to his garden. He also established a **menagerie**, situated to the east of the Oberes Belvedere (the ground plan of radial paths is all that survives), and an **aviary** (originally facing the orangery but now converted into apartments), where he kept numerous species of rare birds, and his favourite pet eagle which he himself fed by hand every day.

To the east of the main entrance on Landstrasser Gürtel is Europe's oldest **Alpengarten** (April–July daily 10am–6pm; €3.20), founded in 1803. It's a small, walled garden, packed with heathers, shrubs and hardy alpine flowers that stick close to the rockery to escape the chilling winds. To the north of the Alpengarten lies the university's **Botanischer Garten** (Easter–Oct daily 9am to 1hr before dusk; free), founded in 1754, and as large again as the formal gardens in the Belvedere. The overall layout is more like an English park, with a woodier section popular with red squirrels, sloping down to another pseudo-alpine shrubbery near the Mechelgasse entrance.

## Oberes Belvedere

Completed in 1724, the **Oberes Belvedere** (Upper Belvedere) is at least twice as big and twice as grand as the Unteres Belvedere. Its unusual roofline, like a succession of green tents, seems deliberately to echo the camps erected by the Turks during the siege of Vienna; others have even interpreted the domed octagonal pavilions as quasi-mosques. The whole building was purpose-built for the lavish masked balls, receptions and firework displays organized by the prince. Guests would pull up in their coaches underneath the central *sala terrena*, thickly adorned with white stucco, its four columns decorated with military trophies and held up by writhing Atlantes.

Originally an open arcade, the *sala terrena* was glassed in during the nineteenth century and now serves as the ticket office and entrance area of the museum. To the right is the trompe l'oeil frescoed **Gartensaal**, the first in a series of ground-floor rooms occasionally used for temporary exhibitions; to the left lies the bookshop and the café. The permanent galleries, displaying nineteenth- and twentieth-century art, are located on the first and second floors. The exact position of the paintings on the first floor changes from year to year, and you may find a handful of the paintings described below are on tour elsewhere.

If you're here for the Klimts and Schieles, then head straight upstairs to the **Marmorsaal**, a lighter and loftier concoction than the one in the Unteres Belvedere; it was here that the Austrian State Treaty of 1955 was signed, guaranteeing the withdrawal of foreign troops in return for Austria's neutrality. The permanent collection usually begins in the room to the right of the Marmorsaal with a sort of taster of works by Renoir, Manet and Monet, plus the *Plain at Auvers* painted by **Vincent van Gogh** a month before his suicide in 1890. Nearby hangs *Rack Railway on the Kahlenberg*, painted by fellow depressive Richard Gerstl in a similar, though slightly less intense, style; **Egon Schiele**'s *Interior 1907* also pays homage to the Dutch genius.

**Auguste Rodin**'s small terracotta study for the Victor Hugo Monument, in which the author is overwhelmed by allegorical figures from his own imagination, can be found in the second room, along with works by Klimt's lesser-known contemporaries, Kolo Moser, Carl Moll and Max Kurzweil.

## Gustav Klimt

The gallery's major works by **Gustav Klimt** (1862–1918) are displayed in the third room, including *The Kiss*, displayed behind a protective glass shield, and depicting Klimt himself embracing his long-term mistress, Emilie Flöge. Klimt's use of gilding – derived partly from his father, who was an engraver – proved extremely popular, and the painting was bought for the Austrian state during the Kunstschau of 1908 (see p.126), a rare seal of official approval for an artist whose work was mostly frowned upon by the establishment.

Klimt's ethereal, slightly aloof *Portrait of Sonja Knips*, from 1898, marked his breakthrough as an independent artist, and was the first of several **portrait commissions** of the wives of the city's wealthy Jewish businessmen. In a later example, the *Portrait of Fritza Riedler*, from 1906, Klimt's love of ornamentation comes to the fore, with the sitter engulfed in Egyptian eyes and sporting a Velázquez headdress.

Every summer Klimt spent his vacations at the Flöge family house on the Attersee in the Salzkammergut. As a way of relaxing, he liked to paint **landscapes** alfresco straight onto a square canvas, without preliminary sketches. Like Monet, he often used to row out into the middle of the lake and set up his easel on board, finishing the works off after the holidays in his Vienna studio. The gallery owns several of these landscapes and the results are rich, almost flat, one-dimensional tapestries of colour – some almost pointillist – which are easy on the eye and which sold extremely well in the salons (and still do).

The second Klimt room features one of his most famous works, *Judith I*, an early gold work from 1901, with the Jewish murderess depicted in sexual ecstasy having beheaded Holofernes. Also displayed here are several **unfinished canvases**, which were discovered in Klimt's studio following his death in 1918.

One such painting, *The Bride*, reveals how Klimt often painted his models in the nude before clothing them.

The gallery has recently been forced to relinquish five of its paintings by Klimt, including two portraits of Adele Bloch-Bauer, and three landscapes, which came into the gallery's hands via the Nazis. After a seven-year **legal battle**, the 90-year-old niece of Bloch-Bauer succeeded in winning back the paintings, and promptly sold the lot at auction for more than $327 million.

From one of the rooms dedicated to the artist's work, you can look down into the richly gilded, octagonal **Schlosskapelle**, designed by Hildebrandt to extend over two floors, looking pretty much today as it would have in Eugène's day.

## Egon Schiele and his contemporaries

Klimt actively supported younger artists like **Egon Schiele** (1890–1918), introducing them to his patrons, allowing them to exhibit in shows he organized, and even, in the case of Schiele, passing on his young models after he'd finished with them. Such was the case with the 17-year-old Wally Neuzil, with whom Schiele enjoyed a four-year affair. *Death and the Maiden* is a disturbingly dispassionate farewell portrait to Wally, painted in 1915, the year they split up. In it, Wally clings to Schiele, depicted in deathly, detached decay. The gallery also owns one of Schiele's most famous, erotic oil paintings, *The Embrace*, a double nude portrait of the artist and his model. (One artist who had a profound influence on both Schiele and Kokoschka was the Belgian sculptor **George Minne**, whose emaciated *Kneeling Boy*, sculpted in marble in the 1890s, is often displayed here.)

Schiele went on to marry **Edith Harms**, who came from a respectable middle-class family, in the same year. *The Artist's Wife* was bought directly from the artist by the gallery, though only after the director had got Schiele to repaint Edith's tartan skirt, which he felt was too "proletarian". Edith's pregnancy in spring 1918 was the inspiration for *The Family*, Schiele's last great painting, which remained unfinished at the time of his death from the influenza epidemic that had claimed Edith's life just three days earlier (and Klimt's eight months before that). Schiele is the father figure, the child is Schiele's nephew, Toni, but Edith had reservations about posing nude, and is clearly not the model for the mother. Though melancholic, the painting is positively upbeat compared with the harrowing *Mother with Two Children* from 1915, with its skeletal mother and two mannequin-like children.

Displayed alongside Schiele's works are a couple of Fauvist paintings by Edvard Munch, and **Richard Gerstl**'s manic *Laughing Self-Portrait* from 1908, a deeply disturbing image given that its subject was, in fact, in a deep depression at the time – his lover, Mathilde, whose portrait also hangs here, had gone back to her husband, the composer Arnold Schönberg. Gerstl committed suicide the very same year at the age of just 28.

## Oskar Kokoschka and others

The gallery's works by **Oskar Kokoschka** (1886–1980) mostly date from his first ten creative years, when he lived in Vienna. After 1915, Kokoschka only occasionally returned, usually staying with his mother, an affectionate portrait of whom hangs in the first room entirely devoted to his work, which comes straight after the Schiele rooms. Kokoschka's portraits contrast sharply with those of Schiele. "A person is not a *still* life," Kokoschka insisted, and he encouraged his sitters to move about and talk, so as to make his portrayals more animated. Among the portraits here is one of fellow artist Carl Moll, who was stepfather to Alma Mahler (widow of the composer) with whom Kokoschka had a brief, passionate affair. Moll committed suicide in 1945 when the Russians liberated Vienna, along with his daughter, Marie, and her husband.

Other works by Kokoschka, owned by the gallery, include his primeval *Tiger-Lion*, painted in London Zoo, and *Still Life with Lamb and Hyacinth* from 1910, painted in the kitchen of the art collector Dr Oskar Reichel, who had commissioned him to paint a portrait of his son. A smattering of other artists' works finishes off the early twentieth-century section, among them a Fauvist landscape by Kirchner, a characteristically dark, intense work by Emil Nolde, a Cubist offering from Fernand Léger and Max Oppenheimer's evocative *Klingier Quartet*.

## Historicism, Realism and Impressionism
The rooms in the west wing, on the other side of the Marmorsaal, are given over to more turn-of-the-century paintings. In the first room, it's difficult not to be somewhat taken aback by the gargantuan *Judgement of Paris* by Max Klinger, surrounded by an incredible 3D frame, within which a bored Paris is confronted by a boldly naked goddess, while the two others get ready to strip in the wings. Giovanni Segantini's *Evil Mothers* is a misogynist piece of anti-abortion propaganda, donated by the Secession to the gallery shortly after its foundation in 1903.

Less well known, and less well thought of now, is the Austrian artist **Hans Makart** (1840–84), to whom the westernmost room is devoted. Makart was a high-society favourite who was in great demand during his lifetime, but his work has suffered partly because of the materials he used, which have caused his paintings to lose much of their original vitality. He also had the posthumous misfortune of being one of Hitler's favourite artists. One wall is almost entirely taken up with Makart's gigantic, triumphant flesh-fest of *Bacchus and Ariadne*; on the opposite wall in long vertical panels are four of the *Five Senses*, featuring typically sensuous Makart nudes.

In the adjacent room, you can admire more work by Makart, whose fame eclipsed several of his more innovative contemporaries, among them **Anton Romako** (1832–89), so much so that the latter's death was rumoured to be a suicide. Compared with Makart's studied flattery, it's easy to see why Romako's uncomfortably perceptive psychological portraits were less popular – consider how far removed from official portraiture Romako's portrait of the Empress Elisabeth is, with its gloomy palette and its emphasis on Sisi's defensive body language. Look out, too, for Romako's most famous work, *Tegetthoff at the Naval Battle of Lissa*, which again reveals his unconventional approach; there's no hint of heroics, but simply manic fear and foreboding in the expressions of the crew.

## Classicism, Romanticism and Biedermeier
If you thought the previous section was patchy, then the top-floor galleries are positive deserts. Nevertheless, there are one or two fine works, such as **Angelika Kaufmann**'s relaxed *Portrait of Lord John Simpson*, executed during her lengthy sojourn in England. More rigidly Neoclassical is Gérard's portrait of the fabulously rich Fries family, who are deliberately posing like some sort of modern Holy Family. After wading through some uninspiring Italian and Italianate landscapes by minor Austrian artists, you should at least pause at Scheffer von Leonhardshoff's *The Dead Saint Cecilia*, a remarkable Raphaelite religious pastiche, which was a personal favourite of Franz I.

If you feel like you haven't quite got to grips with Biedermeier art, the final few rooms offer your big chance. There are copious genre paintings, portraits and landscapes by the chief exponent of Biedermeier, **Ferdinand Georg Waldmüller**, and a superrealist self-portrait by the bewhiskered Viennese artist Franz Eybl. Also worth seeking out is the gallery's superlative Romantic canvas, *Seashore in Mist* by Caspar David Friedrich.

# Südbahnhof and around

Vienna lost all its wonderful nineteenth-century railway stations in World War II, and the **Südbahnhof**, on the other side of the Landstrasser Gürtel from the Belvedere, is a typically grim postwar building. It is, in fact, two stations rolled into one: the old Ostbahnhof, now known as Südbahnhof (platforms 1–9), and Südbahnhof proper (platforms 11–19), each of which has separate arrivals and departures timetables. Trains from Eastern Europe tend to arrive here, a fact which has given the area something of a seedy reputation with the Viennese.

From the Südbahnhof, Prinz-Eugen-Strasse runs north along the side of the Belvedere to Schwarzenbergplatz. En route it passes the innocuous-looking Kammer für Arbeiter und Angestellte (Chamber of Workers and Employees), at no. 20–22. Before World War II, this was the site of the Palais Rothschild, where **Adolf Eichmann** set up the Nazis' euphemistically named "Central Office for Jewish Emigration", which oversaw forced expulsion of thousands of Jews from Austria and relieved them of their possessions. At his trial, Eichmann remembered his days there as "the happiest and most successful of my life". Round the corner, on Theresianumgasse 16–18, another former Rothschild palace served as the headquarters of the Nazi SD, the security service of the SS. Both palaces were destroyed in World War II.

West of Prinz-Eugen-Strasse lies **Wieden** – Vienna's fourth district – which is worth a mention for the **Bestattungsmuseum** (Undertakers' Museum), run by the state funeral company, at Goldeggasse 19. It's open by appointment (Mon–Fri noon–3pm; €4.50; ☎501 95-4227) for guided tours in German only, so this is really only for those who share the strong, morbid fascination with death for which the Viennese remain famous. The custom of magnificent funerals – known as having a "beautiful corpse" or *schöne Leiche* – is one to which many Viennese still aspire (only 18 percent opt for cremation). Inside the museum, you can admire the elaborate costumes of undertakers over the years, their banners, equipage and so on, and learn about some of the more bizarre rituals associated with Viennese funerals. Dead Habsburgs, for instance, used to have their faces smashed in, to make them appear more humble in the eyes of God, and it was common practice to install a bell inside the coffin, which the deceased could ring in case they came back to life. There are some wonderful examples of funereal merchandising: matches, photo albums, toy cars, and, best of all, undertakers' cigarettes, with the motto *Rauchen sichert Arbeitsplätze* ("Smoking guarantees work"). The *pièce de résistance*, though, is the reusable coffin instigated by Josef II (see p.87).

# Arsenal and the Heeresgeschichtliches Museum

A short distance south of the Südbahnhof, down Arsenalstrasse, lies the city's former **Arsenal**, a huge complex of barracks and munitions factories, built on strategic heights above the city in the wake of the 1848 revolution. At the same time, the emperor Franz-Josef I ordered the construction of the city's first purpose-built museum, the **Heeresgeschichtliches Museum** (daily except Fri 9am–5pm; €5.10; Ⓦwww.hgm.or.at), designed to glorify the Imperial Army. All Vienna's leading architects were invited to compete for the commission, and the winning design, a marvellous red-brick edifice, adorned with light-brick crosses and machiolated crenellations, was completed by the Ringstrasse architect Theophil Hansen, in neo-Byzantine style in 1856.

The ticket office and cloakroom of this vast museum are in the vaulted foyer or **Feldherrnhalle** (Hall of the Generals), which is crowded with life-sized marble statues of pre-1848 Austrian military leaders. Pick up the museum's excellent free audioguide (in English) and head upstairs to the **Ruhmshalle** (Hall of Fame), on the first floor, a huge domed hall of polished marble, decorated with worthy frescoes depicting Austrian military victories over the centuries. It's a heady mixture of architectural styles, gilded and arcaded rather like a Byzantine church or Moorish palace.

## From the Thirty Years' War to the Austro-Prussian War

The museum kicks off with the **Thirty Years' War** (1618–48), to the left as you reach the top of the stairs, and tells the story of the rise of the musketeer over the pikeman – there's an informative video showing how hellish it was to try and fire a musket. Beyond hang twelve huge battle paintings by the Dutch artist Pieter Snayers portraying the decisive encounters of the war.

The rich pickings to be had during the **Turkish Wars** proved a useful incentive to the imperial troops fighting the Ottomans, and a fine selection of trophies is displayed here. Among the most impressive is the Great Seal of Mustafa Pasha, which the Grand Vizier wore round his neck as a symbol of his absolute authority, and which fell into the hands of **Prince Eugène of Savoy** at the Battle of Zenta in 1697. Other bits and bobs relating to Prince Eugène include his minuscule vest, his marshal's baton, and the pall and cortège decorations from his magnificent state funeral. The end room contains the vast tent of the Grand Vizier, Damad Ali-Pasha, which Prince Eugène later used on hunting trips. The Grand Vizier was killed at the Battle of Peterwardein in 1716, in which Prince Eugène triumphed over an Ottoman army more than twice the size of his. Also displayed here is the "Mortar of Belgrade", a shot from which hit the Turkish powder magazine during the siege of 1717, killing three thousand Ottoman soldiers in one go and considerably aiding Prince Eugène's victory.

To continue chronologically, you need to head for the east wing. Most of the items displayed here relate to the **Napoleonic Wars**: Field-Marshal Radetzky's hat, map bag and sword, Prince Karl von Schwarzenberg's hat, sword and medals, and Napoleon's Russian greatcoat, thought to have been worn during his exile on Elba. The section concludes with paintings of the disastrous **Austro-Prussian War**, which ended in the Habsburgs' defeat at Könniggrätz in 1866.

## The road to World War I

A large area of the ground-floor west wing is taken up with the glorious **uniforms of the Imperial Army**, and those belonging to their opponents. At the beginning of the twentieth century, the Habsburgs could at least boast that they had the best-dressed army in Europe – while the other superpowers were donning various dull khakis as camouflage, their pristine white and cream won the prize for the most elegant uniform at the 1900 Paris Exhibition. The uniforms were at their most resplendent during the ball season, and certainly had the right effect on many female guests, as Anthony Trollope's mother, visiting in 1836, swooned:

I really know nothing at once so gorgeous and picturesque as the uniform of the Hungarian noble bodyguard, with their splendid silver accoutrements, their spotted furs, uncut, hanging at their backs, and their mustard-yellow Morocco boots. The rich and beautiful skins which they all carry, apparently in the very shape in which they came off the animal, give the most striking air of primitive and almost barbarous magnificence.

The Imperial Army also clung to other outdated practices, such as the code of honour, which meant that an officer's challenge to a duel had to be obliged (a practice only discontinued in 1911). Officers were automatically accepted at court and, like the aristocracy, used the familiar *du* with one another.

By far the most famous exhibits in this wing, though, relate to the **Archduke Franz Ferdinand**, in particular the splendid Gräf & Stift convertible in which the archduke and his wife, Sophie, were shot dead on June 28, 1914, by the Bosnian Serb terrorist, Gavrilo Princip. The car still has a bullet hole in it, but even more macabre is the archduke's reverentially preserved bloodstained light-blue tunic and unblemished, slightly comical hat with green feathers (the ceremonial uniform of an Austrian cavalry general), and the chaise longue on which he expired.

The final room of the wing is devoted to **World War I**, and includes video footage of the Habsburgs' various (mostly disastrous) campaigns. The room itself is dominated by a massive 38cm Howitzer, designed by Ferdinand Porsche, which had a range of 15km. Overlooking the gun is Albin Egger-Lienz's chilling *To the Unknown Soldier*, whose repetitive image of advancing infantry perfectly captures the mechanical slaughter of modern warfare.

## Republic and Dictatorship

Beyond the café in the east wing of the ground floor lies **Republic and Dictatorship**, an excellent section that takes you through the heady, violent interwar years that ended with the Anschluss in 1938. There are lots of period posters from both sides of the political spectrum, and plenty of fascinating interwar video footage. You can view the couch on which Dollfuss died during the abortive Nazi coup of 1934 (see p.61), a bust of his successor Kurt Schuschnigg, by Anna Mahler, the composer's daughter, who was a committed Austro-fascist. Amongst the Nazi memorabilia is the bust of Hitler that used to stand in the museum's Ruhmshalle during the Nazi period.

## Naval Power

The last room in the east wing is concerned with Austria's **Naval Power**, not something normally associated with a land-locked country, though, of course, under the Habsburgs, the empire had access to the Adriatic. Amid the model ships, figureheads and nauticalia, there's a model of the U-27 submarine commanded by Austria's most famous naval captain, Georg Ritter von Trapp of *Sound of Music* fame. Among the more surprising material is the video of the Austrian navy's involvement in the Boxer Rebellion, and the section on the Austrian Arctic expedition (1872–74), which discovered and named Franz Josef Land, an archipelago in the Barents Sea.

If you're keen on tanks, don't miss the **Panzergarten**, with its international parade of tanks from Soviet T34s to American Centurions.

# St Marxer Friedhof

In the 1780s, Emperor Josef II closed the inner-city cemeteries, and decreed that all burials, for health reasons, should take place outside the city walls. The first of these out-of-town graveyards was the **St Marxer Friedhof** (daily: April & Oct 7am–5pm; May & Sept 7am–6pm; June–Aug 7am–7pm; Nov–March 7am–dusk), founded in 1784 near the Landstrasser Gürtel, closed down in 1874, and also known as the Biedermeier cemetery since its corpses date mostly from that era. The main reason tourists trek out here is because it was at this place, on a rainy night in December 1791, that Mozart was given a pauper's burial in an unmarked mass grave with no one present but the gravediggers.

Though to contemporary minds the bare facts of Mozart's final journey seem a particularly cruel end for someone considered by many to have been the greatest composer ever, the reality is less tragic. In the immediate period after Josef II's reforms, mass burials were the rule; only the very wealthy could afford to have a family vault, and the tending of individual graves was virtually unknown. Funeral services took place in churches (Mozart's in the Stephansdom), and it was not customary for mourners to accompany the funeral cortège to cemeteries. In fact, bodies were only allowed to be taken to the cemetery after nightfall, where they were left in the mortuary overnight for burial the next day.

By the mid-nineteenth century, the Viennese had adopted the lavish tastes for funerals and monuments for which they remain famous to this day, and it was in this context that it became a scandal that no one knew where Mozart was buried. In 1844, his wife Constanze returned to try to locate the grave, but to little avail as graves were usually emptied every eight years and the bones removed to make way for more corpses. The most that Constanze discovered was that he had most likely been buried three or four rows down from the cemetery's central monumental cross. In 1859, the **Mozartgrab** was raised around this area, featuring a mourning angel and a pillar, broken in half to symbolize his untimely death.

Nowadays, the St Marxer Friedhof gives little indication of the bleak and forbidding place it must have been in Mozart's day, having been tidied up in the early part of the twentieth century and planted with a rather lovely selection of trees. The cemetery is four stops on tram #18 from Südbahnhof, or five stops from Schwarzenbergplatz on tram #71. To get to the Mozartgrab, head up the main avenue and bear left; you'll also find the graves of several other eighteenth-century artists here (a plan at the entrance to the cemetery locates the most famous graves).

## Strassenbahnmuseum (Tram Museum)

Occupying three brick-built sheds in the eastern corner of Landstrasse, the **Strassenbahnmuseum** (May–Sept Sat & Sun 9am–4pm; €3; Ⓦwww .wiener-tramwaymuseum.at), on Ludwig-Koessler-Platz, houses examples of just about every type of rolling stock that has trundled over the tramlines of Vienna, with a few buses thrown in for good measure. The vast majority of the trams

▲ Strassenbahnmuseum

## Gasometer

The city's earliest gasholders are four magnificently ornate, brick-built cylinders, originally built in the late 1890s and visible in the nether reaches of Erdberg, just over the border in Simmering. A hundred years later, having outlived their original function, the gasworks were expensively converted by four architectural teams into a housing, shopping and leisure complex, each one clad with a glass dome (Ⓦ www .wiener-gasometer.at). This being Vienna, there is of course a U-Bahn station – the wonderfully named **Gasometer** – so if you're into contemporary architecture, it's an easy and worthwhile visit.

The insides of the gasholders are all occupied by fairly ordinary shopping malls, but the cafés and bars within them are usually buzzing after work. From the U-Bahn, you immediately enter Gasometer A, designed by French architect Jean Nouvel, who has made much use of light-reflecting materials. It's from the outside you need to see Gasometer B, designed by Coop Himmelbau, Austria's famous deconstructivist architects, so as to take in the spectacular concave "shield" attached to one side; inside, it houses the 3000-seat music venue, BA Halle. By contrast, Manfred Wehdorn has done a much more low-key, straightforward job on Gasometer C, retaining the original entrance and simply filling the courtyard with cascading modernist terraced flats. Last, and probably the most happily inhabitable, is Gasometer D, in which Wilhelm Holzbauer has built a three-pointed housing complex around a central stairwell, each facing onto its own garden.

sport the familiar municipal red livery, with the exception of the wartime exhibits, the horse-drawn trams from the 1870s, and the wonderful steam tram (still working). Children will be disappointed not to be able to climb on any of the exhibits, although the model tram railway in the ticket office might just mollify them. You can also take an hour-long ride on a 1920s tram known as the **Oldtimer-Tramway** (May–Sept Sat 11.30am & 1.30pm, Sun 9.30am, 11.30am & 1.30pm; €15). Trams leave from beside the Otto Wagner pavilions on Karlsplatz; tickets are available from Karlsplatz U-Bahn.

# Mariahilf, Neubau and Josefstadt

**Mariahilf and Neubau** – Vienna's sixth and seventh districts – lie on either side of Mariahilferstrasse, the city's busy, mainstream shopping street, which stretches for more than 2km from the Kunsthistorisches Museum in the east to the Westbahnhof in the west. A few minor tourist sights are scattered across both districts, but the only area which actually merits a stroll is the narrow network of eighteenth- and early nineteenth-century streets in Neubau known as **Spittelberg**. You might also find yourself wandering up Burggasse or Neustiftgasse, further north, in search of some of the area's numerous restaurants, cafés and pubs. The eighth district, **Josefstadt**, to the north, is a slightly more homogenous residential area, created in the eighteenth century. It, too, has its sprinkling of sights; it's also popular with students, owing to its proximity to the university.

## On and off Mariahilferstrasse

Unlike most Western capitals, Vienna has relatively few big department stores, but those it does have are almost exclusively to be found on **Mariahilferstrasse**. As you

stroll along Mariahilferstrasse, you may well come across the Strasse der Sieger or "Avenue of Champions", which begins at the **Generali-Center**, at no. 77, one of Vienna's few indoor shopping malls. The Strasse der Sieger is a series of footprints, handprints and signatures in the pavement, belonging to the country's fifty most famous sports stars, and "as significant for sports fans as Hollywood's 'Walk of Fame' is for film enthusiasts", as the promotional blurb rather hopefully describes it. The first half – among them Arnold Schwarzenegger and Franz Klammer – are inside the shopping precinct; the next twenty-five – starring Thomas Muster, Niki Lauda and Gerhard Berger – punctuate the street as far as Webgasse.

Slightly more edifying is the little-known architectural work by Adolf Loos, located opposite the Generali-Center at no. 70, currently a branch of **Bank Austria**, but originally designed in 1914 for the Anglo-Austrian Bank. The typically imposing marble portal leads through to the central banking hall, which is largely unchanged, with lots more marble, a glass-tiled roof and some lovely brass lamps suspended from the ceiling.

The district of Mariahilf takes its name from the **Mariahilferkirche**, the big Baroque church set back from the street between nos. 55 and 57 and providing a welcome escape from the rampant consumerism outside. The miraculous *Mariahilf* (Mary's help) picture in the main altar is actually a seventeenth-century copy of the original Passau Madonna by Lucas Cranach. One of the most striking furnishings is the *Schutzengelgruppe*, opposite the pulpit, in which a gilded angel and child are set against an iridescent blue-and-gold-curtained baldachin. Before you leave, be sure to glance up and admire the ceiling frescoes by pupils of Paul Troger, and the Rococo organ, which features a gilded filigree clock suspended between the pipes.

### Esterházypark and Haus des Meeres

One block south of Mariahilferstrasse lies the diminutive **Esterházypark**, dominated by a Flakturm, or anti-aircraft tower, which is daubed around the rim with the gnomic "smashed into pieces (in the still of the night)". The hand- and

---

#### Flaktürme

Vienna's six unsightly **Flaktürme** (anti-aircraft towers), built during World War II, are some of the few visible legacies of the Nazi period. Positioned in three sets of two across the city, these tall, concrete monstrosities form a triangle with the Stephansdom at the centre: two in the Augarten in Leopoldstadt (see p.187), two in Arenbergpark in Landstrasse, one in the Stiftskaserne courtyard, behind MuseumsQuartier, and one close by in Esterházypark. The towers were used both as observation posts to light up the sky and as anti-aircraft gun posts – hence their name FLAK (Flieger Abwehr Kanone). In addition, they were capable of housing up to thirty thousand troops and could become completely self-sufficient in an emergency, with their own underground field hospital, munitions factory, water and power supply, and even air filters in case of a poison-gas attack. The Flaktürme were built to last for thousands of years, and after the war, the Nazis planned to clad the towers in marble and make them into victory monuments. Many Viennese view them with acute embarrassment; others argue that they serve as a useful and indelible reminder of that period. The real reason for their survival, though, is that, with walls of reinforced concrete up to 5m thick, they would be very costly and difficult to demolish. More recently the Flaktürme have begun to be put to good use: one of the towers in Arenbergpark has been rebranded as CAT (Contemporary Art Tower) by MAK and is used as exhibition space (May–Nov Sat & Sun 11am–6pm), while the one in Esterházypark houses an aviary and aquarium.

footholds of an artificial climbing wall now pepper the exterior, while a sloping green-glass aviary juts out on one side. The interior houses the **Haus des Meeres** (daily 9am–6pm, Thurs until 9pm; €10.30; ⓦwww.haus-des-meeres .at), a collection of reptiles, amphibians and fish – the crocs and snakes could do with larger tanks, but the tropical fish are spectacular. So too is the tropical aviary in whose dense foliage and flora you can spot tortoises, turtles, monkeys and vibrantly colourful birds.

The Flakturm's air-raid shelter contains the **Foltermuseum** (Torture Museum; daily 10am–6pm; €6; ⓦwww.folter.at). With various tableaux illustrating tortures through the ages, the museum treads a fine line between using torture as entertainment and putting across a serious message. The final Amnesty International video pulls no punches, however. Ask for the English information pack before you wander round.

## Hofmobiliendepot

Set back from Mariahilferstrasse itself, at Andreasgasse 7, is the Imperial Furniture Collection or **Hofmobiliendepot** (Tues–Sun 9am–6pm; €6.90; ⓦwww .hofmobiliendepot.at). Despite its uninviting title, this is a surprisingly interesting museum – like a cross between a junk warehouse and an applied arts study collection. Be warned, however, that it's vast – fascinating, but best taken at a canter.

Established by Maria Theresia in 1747, the Hofmobiliendepot basically supplied all the furniture needed by the Habsburgs for their various palaces, which, as a rule, were only furnished when members of the family stayed there. It was also a dumping ground for those items of furniture that had gone out of fashion. After 1918, the depot found itself with more than 650,000 items, and no imperial family to serve, so it became a museum. The first huge room, **Das Erbe** (The Heritage), gives you some idea of the sheer scale of the collection, with its forests of candelabra and coat stands, not to mention the bevy of Biedermeier spittoons.

The **Habsburgersaal** panders to imperial nostalgia with Winterhalter's classic portrait of Sisi, Crown Prince Rudolf's ebony highchair, scallop-shell cot, and, later on, funeral crown, while Maximilian of Mexico's serpent-wrapped walking stick and vastly oversized black sombrero have to be seen to be believed. What follows is a whole series of reconstructed **period interiors** ranging from one of Prince Eugène's wonderful chinoiserie rooms to the aforementioned Rudolf's Turkish boudoir, draped with carpets snapped up on his oriental version of the Grand Tour in 1881 – check out, too, Franz Ferdinand's monster walk-through wardrobe from the Belvedere. One of the most arresting interiors is that of Maria Ludovica d'Este, third wife of Franz I, who had very expensive (and outrageous) tastes. Here, you get to see her penchant for South American–themed murals, featuring genocidal acts by Spanish invaders; downstairs in the foyer, her vogueish Egyptian cabinet from the Hofburg is worth a peek.

The displays on the upper floors are patchier, though the special exhibitions can be fun. The highlight on the second floor is the **Hygienemöbel** (Sanitary Furniture), which displays imperial commodes, bedpans and spittoons through the ages. On the third floor, there are some Jugendstil pieces by the likes of Josef Hoffmann, original furniture from Adolf Loos's *Café Museum* (see p.265) and Mies van der Rohe's Tugendhat Haus, plus an entire reconstruction of Ernst Plischke's 1928 modernist design for potter Lucie Rie's bedroom in London. Before you head back down the stairs, however, make sure you take a look inside the **Wappensaal**, a library from a swanky villa in Mödling, its ceiling smothered in imperial coats-of-arms, originally designed in the 1880s to glorify the Habsburgs, but later modified to give it a more Pan-German character.

### Haydn-Memorial

The composer **Josef Haydn** (1732–1809) spent much of his life in the service of the Esterházy family at their seats in Eisenstadt (see p.232) and Esterháza (now in Hungary), but with the death of his chief patron, Prince Nikolaus Esterházy, in 1790, the composer was free at last to settle permanently in Vienna. In 1793, he bought a single-storey house at Haydngasse 19, two blocks south of Mariahilferstrasse, adding an extra floor in which he lived until his death in 1809 – this house is now the **Haydn-Memorial** (Wed & Thurs 10am–1pm & 2–6pm, Fri–Sun 10am–1pm; €2; Ⓦwww.wienmuseum.at). Here he wrote, among other works, his great oratorio, *Die Schöpfung* (The Creation), and spent the last few months of his life sitting at home, silently handing visitors a specially printed calling card, which began with a quote from one of his own texts, "Gone is all my strength..." At the time of his death, Vienna was occupied by Napoleonic troops, but such was his renown, that – so the story goes – Napoleon himself ordered a guard of honour to be stationed outside his house, and a French Hussars officer came and sang an aria from *Die Schöpfung* at his deathbed. Sadly, none of the original fittings survive from Haydn's day, and you'll learn little about the composer's life from this formulaic museum. The house also contains an equally unenlightening memorial room dedicated to the composer **Johannes Brahms** (1833–97), who lived near Karlsplatz.

## Spittelberg

Few areas in the Vorstädte have retained their original eighteenth- or early nineteenth-century appearance – the exception is the half-dozen parallel, narrow cobbled streets between Siebensterngasse and Burggasse known as **Spittelberg** (Ⓦwww.spittelberg.at). Traditionally a working-class and artisan quarter, it also doubled as the red-light district, conveniently backing onto two sets of barracks full of sex-starved soldiers. Bypassed by the late nineteenth century, the area was saved from demolition in the 1970s, its Baroque and Biedermeier houses carefully restored – and inevitably gentrified – and many of the streets pedestrianized.

It's a pleasant place to wander on any day of the week, but the small **craft market** on summer Saturdays along and around Spittelberggasse makes the stroll even more enjoyable. This functions daily during Easter and in the month leading up to Christmas, when the streets are heaving with folk drinking *Glühwein* and *Punsch*. Spittelberg also boasts one of the densest concentrations of bars, cafés and restaurants in the Vorstädte, not so much throbbing as gently swaying until the early hours. There's a sort of spill-over onto nearby Sankt-Ulrichs-Platz, a small, sloping square to the northwest, pedestrianized and dominated by the Baroque **Ulrichskirche**, where Christoph Wilibald Gluck was married, Schubert's requiem was celebrated and Strauss the Younger was christened.

Those with an interest in the work of Otto Wagner should stroll a couple of blocks west up Neustiftgasse to the **Otto Wagner-Wohnung** (Mon, Tues & Fri by appointment; ☏523 2233), on the first floor of Döblergasse 4. This was Wagner's town apartment and studio until his death in 1918. Both Döblergasse 4 and the next-door corner apartment block of Neustiftgasse 40 were designed by Wagner himself in 1912, and the only decoration on their austere facades are the bands of indigo-blue glass tiles and the sparing use of aluminium – it's the closest Wagner, better known for his Jugendstil works, ever came to the kind of austere functionalism later championed by the modernists. Inside, the blue patterning and aluminium theme are continued to great effect, while within the flat itself, though few of the original fittings have survived, there are plans to return the walls to their original colour, and re-create some feeling of how it was in Wagner's day.

One church worth seeking out in Neubau is the **Altlerchenfelder Kirche**, up Lerchenfelderstrasse. Begun in 1848, its neo-Romanesque exterior is a slightly sickly salmon colour; its vast interior, however, is pretty spectacular, thanks to Eduard van der Nüll, one of the architects of Vienna's opera house (see p.114). The walls and the saucer-domed ceiling are absolutely smothered in mid-nineteenth-century Romantic frescoes – where most churches have stained-glass windows, this one has murals and mosaics, ranging from the small saintly roundels in the nave to the richly gilded vision of the *Seven Sanctuaries* in the apse.

## Josefstadt

**Josefstadt** – Vienna's eighth district – was laid out in the early eighteenth century and named after Emperor Josef I (1705–11). Almost immediately, the Piarists were given a large slice of the land for their monastery, the Maria-Treu Kloster, which now forms a pleasant Baroque ensemble, centred on a cobbled square with its own Marian column, three-quarters of the way along Piaristengasse. Overlooking the square is the splendid convex Baroque facade, tall pediment and twin towers of the monastery church, better known as the **Piaristenkirche**, originally designed by Hildebrandt, but only completed in 1753. The light interior is a glorious slice of High Baroque, full of playful oval shapes and faded frescoes by the youthful Franz Anton Maultbertsch, though you can barely get a glimpse of it outside of services. It was on the church's still extant nineteenth-century organ that the young Anton Bruckner was examined, after which one of the judges exclaimed: "He should have been testing us!"

Close by the monastery, on the other side of Piaristengasse, facing Josefstädter Strasse, is the **Theater-in-der-Josefstadt** (ⓦwww.josefstadt.org), founded in 1788 as a variety theatre, but remodelled in Neoclasscial style by Josef Kornhäusel, and reopened in 1822 with a premiere of Beethoven's *Consecration of the House* overture, conducted by the composer himself. Between the wars, the theatre was under the direction of Max Reinhardt, the great theatrical innovator who helped found the Salzburg Festival, staged incredible large-scale productions, and eventually fled to Hollywood in the 1930s. Today, the theatre is one of the oldest in Vienna and has returned to its light-entertainment roots, staging comedies, melodramas and farce.

Three blocks north of the theatre, in Hildebrandt's Baroque Palais Schönborn on Laudongasse, is the **Österreichisches Museum für Volkskunde** (Tues–Sun 10am–5pm, Thurs until 8pm; €5; ⓦwww.volkskundemuseum.at), a folk art collection that seems out of place in such an urban setting. The museum, founded in 1894, has been sensitively modernized and there's enough variety to keep you entertained for an hour or so, with exhibits ranging from grass raincoats and magnificent Tyrolean wardrobes to an incredible limewood shrine to Emperor Karl I.

# Alsergrund

**Alsergrund** – Vienna's large, roughly triangular ninth district – is dominated by its medical institutions and associations. A vast swathe of land is taken up with the **Allgemeines Krankenhaus** or AKH (General Hospital), established by Josef II in 1784. The following year, Josef founded the **Josephinum**, an academy for training military surgeons, next door. Since then, various university science faculties have relocated here, and the area remains popular with doctors and medical students,

ALSERGRUND

RESTAURANTS
Flein            9
Kutschker        3
Stomach          7
Wickerl          8
Zum Reznicek     2

CAFÉS
Berg             11
Blaustern        1
Stadlmann        10
Statt-Beisl im WUK  6
Stein            5
Weimar           12
Weltcafé         13
Wilder Mann      4

0 — 200 m

as it has been since **Freud**'s day – his museum is now Alsergrund's chief tourist attraction. Alsergrund also boasts one of the few aristocratic summer palaces to survive into the modern era, now the **Liechtenstein Museum**, home to the prince's private art collection.

# Allgemeines Krankenhaus

The **Allgemeines Krankenhaus** (General Hospital) was one of the most modern medical institutions in the world when it was founded in 1784 to replace the Grossarmenhaus (Great Poor House). Vienna was the "medical Mecca" of the empire, and from its foundation, the overriding philosophy of the AKH was therapeutic nihilism. At its best, this meant letting nature take its course, rather than relying on the quack remedies popular at the time. At its worst, it meant neglecting patients while they were alive, and then concentrating on autopsy as a means of prognosis instead. By 1850, it was claimed that the only medicine used at the hospital was cherry brandy. Even at the beginning of the last century, conditions were dire, with nurses forced to work 24-hour shifts, and paid so badly they had to sell coffee and demand tips to make up their wages.

The original buildings, known as the Altes Allgemeines Krankenhaus, lie to the east of Spitalgasse and have been handed over to the university and converted into the new **Universitätscampus Wien**. The courtyards and various bars within the complex spill over with students, especially in the summer when the whole place becomes one enormous beer garden. The prime motive for exploring the old hospital's spacious courtyards, however, is to visit the **Museum of Pathological Anatomy** in the former lunatic asylum of the Narrenturm (see below). The modern **Neues Allgemeines Krankenhaus** lies to the west of Spitalgasse, and is one of the largest hospitals in Europe; its lengthy and expensive construction was accompanied by corruption at the highest level.

### Narrenturm

The circular **Narrenturm** (Wed 3–6pm, Thurs 8–11am & first Sat of the month 10am–1pm; €2; Ⓦwww.narrenturm.at) or "Fools' Tower" is an unprepossessing building, which looks something like a converted gasometer, situated in a scruffy, neglected courtyard of the Altes Allgemeines Krankenhaus. It was built in 1784 as a lunatic asylum with five floors, each housing 28 cells, which feed off a circular corridor; its nickname was the "Guglhupf", after the popular, ring-shaped cake. Despite its forbidding, prison-like design and slit windows, conditions were exceptionally humane for the period. It fell into disuse in 1866, and now houses the **Pathologisch-anatomisches Bundesmuseum** (Federal Museum of Pathological Anatomy). Locating the Narrenturm can be tricky, as there are several entrances to the Altes Allgemeines Krankenhaus – on Garnisongasse, Spitalgasse and, most conveniently, Alserstrasse – and whichever you choose, you'll need to consult the map inside each of the gateways in order to find your way to courtyard no. 13.

The museum is popular with medical students, and it certainly helps to have a strong stomach. The ground-floor cells contain a mock-up of Dr Robert Koch's 1882 discovery of the bacillus that causes tuberculosis, an apothecary from 1820, a section on artificial limbs, a mortuary slab, wax models of TB sufferers and the odd piece of anatomy preserved in formaldehyde. If you're already feeling queasy, don't, whatever you do, venture upstairs where the cells and corridors are filled with yet more examples of abnormalities and deformities preserved in formaldehyde from autopsies conducted around a hundred years ago.

# Josephinum

Founded in 1785 to the northeast of the Allgemeines Krankenhaus, the **Josephinum** (Mon–Fri 9am–3pm, first Sat of the month 10am–2pm; €2) is housed in an austere silver-grey palace, set back from Währingerstrasse behind a set of imposing wrought-iron railings. Having observed the primitive techniques used by army surgeons at first hand during his military campaigns, Emperor Josef II decided to set up an Institute for Military Surgery. The institute was closed in 1872, and the building now houses the Pharmacological Institute for Medicine and History of Medicine Institute instead – plus a museum run by the latter, known as the Museum für Geschichte der Medizin or Medizinhistorisches Museum.

Aside from the leech cups, amputation saws, dental instruments and the odd pickled stomach, the chief attraction of the institute's museum is its remarkable collection of anatomical **wax models**, or *Wachspräparate Sammlung*, commissioned by Josef II from a group of Florentine sculptors in 1780. The models are serene, life-sized human figures, for the most part, presented as if partially dissected, revealing the body's nerves, muscles and veins in full gory technicolour. Equally beautiful are the original display cases, fashioned from rosewood and fitted with huge, bobbly, hand-blown panes of Venetian glass. There's also a model of the Allgemeines Krankenhaus and the Narrenturm as they would have appeared in 1784, just for good measure.

# Sigmund-Freud-Museum

Sigmund Freud moved to the second floor of Berggasse 19 in 1891 and stayed here until June 3, 1938, when, unwillingly, he and his family fled to London. His apartment, now the **Sigmund-Freud-Museum** (daily 9am–5pm; €7; Ⓦwww.freud-museum.at), is a place of pilgrimage, though he himself took almost all his possessions – bar his library, which he sold – with him into exile (where they can still be seen in London's Freud Museum). His hat, coat and walking stick are still here, and there's home-movie footage from the 1930s, but the only room with any original decor – and consequently any atmosphere – is the waiting room, which contains the odd oriental rug, a cabinet of antiquities, and some burgundy-upholstered furniture, sent back from London by his daughter Anna after the war. The rest of the flat is taken up with a couple of rooms of photographs, a few rooms of Freud-inspired art, a library and a shop. There's a file available with English translations of the museum's captions, and an audioguide in English (for an extra €2).

# Servitenkirche and Friedhof Rossau

If you're heading from Freud's apartment to the Liechtenstein Museum, it's worth taking a slight detour to visit the **Servitenkirche**, an early Baroque gem of a church up Servitengasse, designed in the mid-seventeenth century by Carlo Carnevale, and the only church in the Vorstädte to survive the 1683 Turkish siege. Its oval-shaped nave, the first to be built in Vienna, was a powerful influence on the layout of the Peterskirche and Karlskirche. You can only peek through the exquisite wrought-iron railings, but that's enough to get a feel for the cherub-infested, stucco-encrusted interior, which features an exuberant gilded pulpit by Balthasar Moll. To the side of the entrance are two side-chapels worth noting, especially the one to the north, with its stucco relief of St John of Nepomuk taking confession from the Bohemian queen, and its very own grotto of the Virgin Mary.

A couple of blocks to the north, at Seegasse 9–11, is Vienna's oldest surviving Jewish cemetery, **Friedhof Rossau**, with gravestones dating back to 1540. In disuse now for two centuries, today it remains hidden from the street behind a supremely ugly, modern old-people's home, which occupies the site of the former Jewish Hospital and Old People's Home, demolished in 1972. It's possible to visit the cemetery at any reasonable time by simply walking through the foyer to the back of the building, where the graves that survived the Nazi desecration shelter under tall, mature trees. One of the most famous people to have been buried here was Samuel Oppenheimer (1630–1703), the first of the Court Jews to be allowed to settle in

▲ Sigmund-Freud-Museum

## Sigmund Freud (1856–1939)

Few people are so intimately associated with one place as **Sigmund Freud** is with Vienna. He may have been born to a Jewish wool merchant in Freiberg in Moravia in 1856, and died in 1939 in exile in London, but in the intervening 83 years, he spent most of his life in Vienna. The family moved to the capital when Freud was just four years old, and in 1873 he entered the university's medical faculty determined to be a scientist. He took three years longer than usual to complete his degree, and then decided to switch tack and train as a medic at the **Allgemeines Krankenhaus**. In 1887 Freud began practising as a neuropathologist, experimenting with cocaine, electrotherapy and hypnosis, before eventually coming up with the "pressure technique", using a couch for the first time and asking questions while pressing his hand on the patient's forehead. He later switched to the method of "free association", during which the patient says whatever comes into their mind. "The aim is modest," Freud said when describing his new science: "to turn neurotic misery into common unhappiness."

In 1896, Freud coined the term "**psychoanalysis**", and four years later published the book that established his originality, *The Interpretation of Dreams*. In it, Freud argued that "all dreams represent the fulfillment of wishes", and that these wishes are often (but not always) sexual. Freud's impact on modern thought has been profound, and several of his discoveries – the death wish, the Oedipus complex, transference, the Freudian slip, penis envy, the oral, anal and phallic stages of childhood, and so on – have become common parlance. Much of this popularization has come at the expense of Freud's original meaning – "Freudian symbols", for example, used exclusively by Freud for dream interpretation, are now widely used simply as a day-to-day form of sexual innuendo.

In 1902, Freud founded the **Psychoanalytical Society**, which met every Wednesday evening in his apartment, his wife serving *Guglhupf* and coffee, while academic papers were read and discussed. Freud ruled his disciples with an iron hand, ejecting anyone who disagreed with him, most famously Carl Jung, the Swiss psychoanalyst, in 1913.

Though Jung accused Freud of having slept with his wife's attractive younger sister, Minna, who lived with the family in Berggasse, Freud was in fact a disappointingly

Vienna after the 1670 expulsion (see p.66). He supplied the Habsburg army for its war with France, and organized the logistics of the defence of Vienna in 1683. When he died, however, the Habsburgs refused to honour their debts to his heirs, causing the family to go bankrupt, which in turn caused a major European financial crisis. His protégé, Samson Wertheimer (1658–1724), who became chief administrator of financial affairs to three successive Habsburg emperors, is also buried here.

## Liechtenstein Museum

At the turn of the seventeenth century, when the enormously wealthy Liechtenstein family commissioned Domenico Martinelli to build a summer palace, Alsergrund was still a rural idyll. Now hemmed in by nineteenth-century apartment blocks, the Baroque Palais Liechtenstein comes as something of a surprise, hidden away down the backstreet of Fürstengasse. Built on a giant scale, the palace now houses the **Liechtenstein Museum** (Fri–Mon 10am–5pm; €10; ⓦwww.liechtensteinmuseum.at), which provides a suitably grandiose setting for the family's private art collection, best known for its series of paintings by Rubens. The art collection was displayed here from Napoleonic times until World War II, but with the Red Army approaching, the works were smuggled back to Liechtenstein. The Austrian government claimed the collection had conventional Viennese paterfamilias. "What a terrible man! I am sure he has never been unfaithful to his wife. It is quite abnormal and scandalous," reported one of his fans, the French poet Countess Anna de Noailles, after meeting him. He was happily married all his life to **Martha Bernays**, a good Jewish *Hausfrau*, who gave birth to and brought up six healthy children. He saw patients without appointment daily from three to four in the afternoon, using the proceeds to buy the (occasionally erotic) antiquities that filled his study; afterwards he would write until as late as three in the morning. Every afternoon, he would walk the entire circuit of the Ringstrasse at a brisk pace; every Saturday evening he played the card game Tarock, and every Sunday in summer, the family would dress up in traditional Austrian peasant gear, right down to their Lederhosen, and go mushroom-picking in the Wienerwald.

In 1923, he was diagnosed as having **cancer of the jaw** (he was an inveterate cigar-smoker) and given just five years to live. A year later, aged 68, he was granted the freedom of Vienna, two years earlier than was the custom. As he joked to a friend, they clearly thought he was going to die. In the end, he lived another sixteen years in some considerable pain, taking only aspirin, undergoing 33 operations, and having his mouth scraped daily to accommodate an ill-fitting prosthesis.

Shortly after the Anschluss in March 1938, the SS raided Freud's flat. Martha, ever the accommodating host, asked them to put their rifles in the umbrella stand and to be seated. The Freuds' passports were subsequently confiscated and their money taken from the family safe. Freud dryly commented that *he'd* never been paid so much for a single visit. Before being allowed to leave the country, he was forced to sign a document to the effect that he had been treated with respect and allowed "to live and work in full freedom" after the Anschluss. This he did, but he asked to be allowed to add the following sentence: "I can heartily recommend the Gestapo to anyone."

Only through the efforts of his friends was Freud able to **escape to Britain** on June 3, 1938. Four of his sisters were not allowed to join him and died in the Holocaust. Finally, just over a year after having arrived in London, Freud's doctor fulfilled their eleven-year-old pact, and, when the pain became too much, gave him a lethal dose of morphine.

been illegally exported and only recently came to an agreement with the family, which paved the way for the paintings' return.

The **ticket office** is in the imposing *sala terrena*, which is flanked by two grandiose marble staircases and decorated with frescoes by the likes of Johann Michael Rottmayr and Andrea Pozzo. Originally open to the elements so that coaches could draw up here, the *sala terrena* now shelters the family's eighteenth-century gilded coach with its panels of celestial cherubs. The east wing of the ground floor is used for temporary exhibitions; the west wing is occupied by the family's gargantuan library with its green-brown marbling decoration and Rottmayr's trompe l'oeil frescoes. Heading up the east staircase, which retains its Rottmayr fresco, you come to the **Herkulessaal**, the largest secular Baroque hall in Vienna (and there's a fair bit of competition). Lined with red marble half-pillars topped by gilded composite capitals and interspersed with paintings and gilded reliefs, the hall's crowning glory is the Pozzo's ceiling fresco, which depicts the life of Hercules from the strangling of the snake in his cot to his final suicide. There are regular classical concerts in the hall on Sunday afternoons.

The galleries on the first floor are dominated by the paintings of **Pieter Paul Rubens** (1577–1640), with the largest room, Saal VII, taken up almost entirely with the Decius Mus Cycle, depicting the life of the Roman consul, who had to sacrifice his own life in order to secure victory for his army over the Latins.

The colours are fabulously strong, and the centrepiece of the cycle, *The Death of Decius Mus*, is a masterpiece of action-packed drama. In Saal VIII there's a lovely portrait by Rubens of his 5-year-old daughter, painted with a refreshing informality and intimacy, next to a more formal one of his two sons. *Mars and Rhea Silva*, in Saal IX, provides a striking contrast between the god's red cloak and the priestess's golden one. It's not all rippling flesh, however, as there are plenty of sober portraits to bring you down to earth, one by Frans Hals and a whole series by **Van Dyck**, including a superb portrait of the 19-year-old Maria de Tassis. Lastly, don't miss the surrealist head, *Terra*, by Rudolf II's court painter, Giuseppe Arcimboldo.

If you're in need of refreshment, you can pay a visit to the museum's *Rubens* café on the east side of the forecourt, or take a picnic into the landscaped **gardens** round the back of the palace.

## From the Strudlhofstiege to Schuberts Geburthaus

If you've just been to the Liechtenstein Museum, you might as well take a stroll up the **Strudlhofstiege**, an imaginative set of Jugendstil steps designed in 1910 by Theodor Jäger, which link Pasteurgasse with Strudlhofgasse above it. They may not have the fame nor the setting of Rome's Spanish Steps, but they are a beguiling vignette of fin-de-siècle Vienna, and provided the inspiration for a long

### Franz Schubert (1797–1828)

Of all the composers associated with Vienna, **Franz Schubert** fulfils more Romantic criteria than most. He died of syphilis at the age of just 31 (younger even than Mozart), he really was penniless (unlike Mozart, who was just careless with his money), and never lived to hear any of his symphonies performed (the first one wasn't published until fifty years after his death). The picture would be complete had he died while writing his eighth (unfinished) symphony – in fact, he abandoned it before he died, and went on, instead, to complete a ninth symphony.

Schubert was born the eleventh child (and fourth son) of an impoverished teacher. He was taught music from an early age and played viola in a string quartet with his older brothers. At the age of 9 or 10, he won a scholarship to go to boarding school, earning a place as a chorister at the Hofburgkapelle, and studying with the court organist at the local church on Marktgasse, where he had been baptized, and with Antonio Salieri, Mozart's famous court rival. He went on to become the church organist, and composed his first Mass for the church at the age of 17. After working as an assistant teacher at his father's school for three years, he became a freelance musician, thanks to financial help from his friends, and spent two summers as music tutor for the Esterházy family.

His intensely lyrical chamber music, fragile songs and melodic piano works were popular among the Viennese bourgeoisie, and he performed at numerous informal social gatherings, which became known as "Schubertiaden". In his personal life, he was fairly dissolute; a heavy drinker, who frequented "revolutionary" circles, he remained unmarried all his life, possibly gay, and eventually caught syphilis, most likely from a prostitute. Towards the end of his short life, he fulfilled a lifetime's ambition and met up with his hero Beethoven, though there are no reliable details of the encounter. He was one of the torchbearers at the great composer's funeral, and was buried, according to his wishes, three graves away from him in Währinger Friedhof the following year (he now lies with Beethoven in the Zentralfriedhof; see p.222).

novel of the same name written in 1951 by Heimito von Doderer, which is dear to the hearts of many Viennese.

## Schuberts Geburtshaus

Further north still, at Nussdorferstrasse 54, is **Schuberts Geburtshaus** (Tues–Sun 10am–1pm & 2–6pm; €2; Ⓦwww.wienmuseum.at), the unassuming, two-storey house where the composer was born in 1797. Inside, the charming courtyard has been lovingly restored, with wooden balconies festooned with geranium flower boxes. As so often with Vienna's musical memorials, however, there has been no attempt to reconstruct Schubert's family home, which would have consisted of just one room and a kitchen (the latter survives). In any case, Schubert would have had very little recollection of the place as the family moved down the road, to Säulengasse 3, when he was four years old. So, beyond admiring the composer's broken spectacles and his half-brother's piano, there's little to do here but listen to the excerpts from his music. However, fans of **Adalbert Stifter**, the writer and artist from the Böhmerwald who slit his throat in 1868 rather than suffer cancer of the liver, fare a little better than those on Schubert's trail. Although Stifter had nothing whatsoever to do with Schubert, several rooms in the museum have been given over to his idyllic Biedermeier landscapes.

Schubert's brother's house – 4, Kettenbrückengasse 6 (Tues–Sun 1.30–4.30pm; €2), near the Naschmarkt – the **Sterbewohnung** in which the composer died, has been made into a similarly unenthralling museum for the truly dedicated.

# Leopoldstadt and the east

eopoldstadt – the city's second district – is separated from the centre of Vienna by the Danube Canal, and (along with the twentieth district of Brigittenau) forms a misshapen island bordered to the east by the main arm of the Danube. For the most part, it's a drab residential suburb, only redeemed by the **Prater**, the vast city park, with its funfair, Ferris wheel, woods and numerous recreational facilities. However, Leopoldstadt also boasts a long history as the city's foremost Jewish quarter up until the Holocaust. The area has since been settled by a new wave of immigrants from Turkey, the Balkans and Africa, and few traces of the old community remain. It's also still something of a red-light district, with a sprinkling of strip joints and sex shops in the backstreets between Taborstrasse and Praterstrasse.

## Jewish Leopoldstadt

In Leopoldstadt, where the humbler Jews mostly congregate, there was suddenly an endless concourse of new, strange figures – men in long gabardines, tiny circular caps of silk or velvet on their heads, and corkscrew curls meandering down the sides of the face; women with wigs and ancient finery, blooming young Esthers and Susannahs ambling along with downcast eyes. Along the quays of the Danube Canal there was an endless procession of these – a new edition of Hebrew fugitives mourning by the waters. Rabbis in every costume and of every degree of holiness were scattered amongst them all.

Wolf von Schierbrand,
an American journalist stationed in Vienna in the late nineteenth century

It was probably Leopoldstadt's physical separateness that persuaded the emperor Ferdinand II to choose the area in 1624 as a site to establish a **walled Jewish ghetto**. For around fifty years the Jewish quarter flourished, the financial acumen and clout of its wealthiest burghers happily used by the Habsburgs to fund the Thirty Years' War. At the end of the 1660s the population peaked at around three or four thousand, but as the Counter-Reformation gathered pace, there were increasingly vociferous calls from devout Catholics – not least from the city council and the emperor's Spanish wife – to banish the community entirely. In 1670, Emperor Leopold I bowed to the zealots' pressure and expelled Jews from the city on the charges of spying for the Turks and blasphemy against the Virgin Mary.

# LEOPOLDSTADT AND THE EAST

0    1 km

N

**KAGRAN**

Ⓤ *Floridsdorf*

*Kagrener Platz* Ⓤ

26

31  33

*Angelibad*

*Alte Donau*

26

Ⓤ *Neue Donau*

🕌 **Islamisches Zentrum**

*Kagran* Ⓤ

Ⓤ *Handelskai*

**Donauturm**

*Alte Donau*

**Millennium Tower**

● Miniature Railway

Ⓤ *Dresdner Strasse*

**Austria-Center-Vienna**

*Donaupark*

WAGRAMER STRASSE

**UNO-City**

Ⓤ *Kaisermühlen-VIC*

**BRIGITTENAU**

*Donauinsel*

*Gänsehäufel*

*Augarten*

HEIDESTRASSE BRÜCKE

**DDSG Schiffahrtszentrum (Boat Launch)**

Ⓤ *Vorgarten-strasse*

31

**LEOPOLDSTADT**

Ⓤ *Taborstrasse*

Ⓤ *Praterstern*

AUSSTELLUNGSSTRASSE

**Wien-Nord**

21  *Nestroyplatz* Ⓤ

**VOLKSPRATER**

Ⓤ **Messe Prater**

HANDELSKAI

River Danube

DONAUINSEL

Neue Donau

**Riesenrad**

Ⓤ *Krieau*

*Messegelände*

21

Ⓤ *Schwedenplatz*

**Krieau Trabrennbahn (Racecourse)**

Ⓤ *Stadion*

*Landstrasse/ Wien-Mitte* Ⓤ

**Liliputbahn (Miniature Railway)**

**Ernst-Happel-Stadion**

*Rochusgasse* Ⓤ

HAUPT-ALLEE

Ⓤ *Kardinal-Nagl-Platz*

*Praterkai* Ⓢ

**Lusthaus**

*P r a t e r*

▶ Buddhist Pagoda

Ⓤ *Schlachthausgasse*

**Südbahnhof**

Ⓤ *Erdberg*

**Freudenau Rennbahn (Racecourse)**

*Danube Canal*

Ⓤ *Gasometer*

Ⓤ *Zippererstrasse*

Ⓢ *Haidestrasse*

Fortuitously, Leopoldstadt enjoyed a second period of Jewish settlement in the decades following the 1848 revolution, when official restrictions on Jews within the empire were finally abolished. Thousands took the opportunity to leave the *shtetls* of Bohemia, Moravia, Hungary and Galicia and migrated to the capital, the majority arriving by train at the Nordbahnhof (Wien-Nord) or the now defunct Nordwestbahn, and settling, initially at least, in the surrounding district of Leopoldstadt, where housing conditions were poor and rents cheap. The Strauss family, Sigmund Freud, Gustav Mahler, Arthur Schnitzler and Theodor Herzl all lived here at some point, before moving up in the world to the city's richer suburbs.

This time around, Leopoldstadt was only ever an unofficial Jewish quarter – at their peak, in 1923, the district's Jews comprised 38.5 percent of the population – though the area had the appearance of an old walled ghetto, partly owing to the high proportion of orthodox **Hasidic Jews**, with their distinctive dress. With the richer Jewish families moving out at the earliest opportunity, and poorer families constantly arriving to fill their place, the district remained trapped in a cycle of poverty, attracting the underprivileged ranks of Viennese society. By the beginning of the twentieth century the area was notorious as a hotbed of prostitution, much to the delight of the city's numerous anti-Semites.

During World War II, the Nazis turned Leopoldstadt back into the official ghetto, and forced the city's remaining Jews into its confines. The **deportations** to the camps began in earnest in 1941 and by the end of the following year the ghetto's Jewish population was reduced to a few thousand, most of whom were married to gentiles. A mere five hundred Jews returned to Vienna after the war, but with more recent Jewish immigration from the former eastern bloc, these numbers have increased to around seven thousand, many of whom have chosen to settle once more in Leopoldstadt. The pockets of kosher shops on Hollandstrasse and Tempelgasse, and the Jewish school on Castellezgasse, are evidence of the area's modest Jewish renaissance. The surviving wing of the district's largest synagogue, the neo-Byzantine **Leopoldstädter Tempel**, on Tempelgasse, gives a vague idea of the building's former glory; there's a mosaic from the missing central section on the facade of the Desider Friedmann building on the corner of Ferdinandstrasse and Tempelgasse. And throughout the district, there are now **Steine der Errinnerung** (commemorative stones) recording the locations of the old Jewish synagogues, cafés, schools and theatres, plus the assembly points, at Kleine Sperlgasse 2a and Malzgasse 7, used by the Nazis to round up the city's Jews for deportation to the camps.

# Prater

Of all the places in Leopoldstadt, it is the **Prater** – derived from the Spanish *prado* (plain) – which draws the biggest crowds. This large, flat tract of land, taking up almost half the island, includes vast acres of mixed woodland, sports stadiums, racecourses, a miniature railway, allotments, a trade-fair centre, a planetarium, an amusement park and, most famously of all, Vienna's giant Ferris wheel. Aside from the Wienerwald, the Prater is by far the most popular weekend destination for any Viennese searching for a breath of fresh air, a stroll in the woods, a jog in the park or a spot of rollerblading.

Traditionally a royal hunting preserve, the Prater was opened to the public in 1766 by Josef II, and soon became a popular spot for Viennese society. As the eighteenth-

## Visiting the Prater

The Prater is vast, and its backbone is the chestnut-lined **Hauptallee** which runs dead straight for 5km, from the Ferris wheel and tacky Volksprater in the northwest to the woodier section around the Lusthaus to the southeast.

Thanks to the new U-Bahn line to Stadion, there are several U-Bahn stations along the northern edge of the Prater. The park is also an easy stroll from Wien-Nord station (U-Bahn Praterstern), which is the terminus for **trams** #5 and #O, and a stop on tram #21, which terminates at S-Bahn Praterkai. Alternatively, tram #N from U-Bahn Schwedenplatz has its terminus right by the Hauptallee, a third of the way down from the Ferris wheel. Halfway down, **bus** #84A (every 10min) crosses the Hauptallee en route to and from U-Bahn Schlachthausgasse and Stadion. Finally, bus #77A (every 30min) from the same U-Bahn will take you all the way to or from the Lusthaus, even travelling some of the way down the Hauptallee itself.

**Getting around the Prater**, you can walk, jog, rollerblade, cycle, take a *Fiaker*, or rent one of the **pedal carriages**, which seat two adults (plus two kids if you wish). Another possibility is to buy a one-way ticket on the miniature railway or **Liliputbahn** (see p.183), which will get you almost halfway down the Hauptallee.

century Irish opera singer, Michael Kelly, noted: "There are innumerable cabarets, frequented by people of all ranks in the evening, who immediately after dinner proceed thither to regale themselves with their favourite dish, fried chicken, cold ham and sausages; white beer and Hoffner wines by way of dessert; and stay there until a late hour: dancing, music, and every description of merriment prevail; and every evening, when not professionally engaged, I was sure to be in the midst of it." In 1791, Mozart broke off work to go and watch François Blanchard go up in a hot-air balloon, with Archduke Franz himself cutting the rope.

Throughout the nineteenth century, the Prater continued to be *the* place to be seen, particularly on the long, central Hauptallee. On Sundays, the latter was the scene of the **Praterfahrt**, when, as one observer put it, "the newest shape in carriages, the last 'sweet thing in bonnets', the most correct cut of coat *à la Anglais*, is to be seen, walking, riding, or driving up and down." On Easter Sunday, May 1 and other special occasions, something like half the population of the city would turn up for the *Praterfahrt*. As one historian put it: "Everyone in Vienna joined in... if they could call a carriage their own or anything else on wheels with a nag to pull it. If not, they walked. Vienna had no more glamorous sight to offer, nor any which united all classes in this way."

In 1873, the Prater was the venue for the empire's *Weltausstellung* or **World Trade Fair**, which brought unprecedented numbers of tourists to Vienna. Some fifty thousand exhibitors from forty countries set up displays in the exhibition's rotunda, topped by a huge cupola 108m in diameter (the rotunda burned down in 1938). Unfortunately, just eight days after the emperor opened the fair on May 1, the Vienna stock exchange collapsed and what had been touted as a celebration of the empire's thriving liberal economy became a charade. In July, to further dampen the mood, a cholera epidemic broke out in the city, claiming three thousand victims. By November, seven million admissions were recorded – thirteen million fewer than expected – and the fair was forced to close.

In 1890, the First of May *Praterfahrt* was appropriated by the Socialist leader Viktor Adler, who helped organize the first **May Day Parade** of workers down the Hauptallee, though he himself was in prison on the day itself. There was panic among the ruling classes: "Soldiers are standing by, the doors of the houses are being closed, in people's apartments food supplies are prepared as though for an impending siege, the shops are deserted, women and children dare not go out into the street," reported the *Neue Freie Presse*. Even so, thousands took part, marching four abreast, carrying red flags and singing, and the demonstration passed off peacefully. The May Day Parade quickly became a permanent fixture in the city's calendar of celebrations.

# Volksprater

The easiest point of access from the city centre – and by far the busiest section of the Prater – is the northwest end, where you'll find the park's permanent funfair, known as the **Volksprater** (mid-March to Oct daily 10am–1am; free; Ⓦwww .prater.at). (It's also known as the *Wurstelprater*, not for the sausages sold in abundance here, but for the Punch-like character of Hanswurst, whose puppet booths were once a common sight.) Tourists may flock to the Volksprater for its famous Ferris wheel or Riesenrad, but the Viennese come here for the other **rides**, a strange mixture ranging from high-tech helter-skelters and white-knuckle affairs to more old-fashioned fairground rides like ghost trains, dodgems and strength contests that judge participants from *Weichling* (weakling), through *Fräulein* (girly) to *Weltmeister* (world champion). The fair has an impressive range of bad-taste attractions, too, including a tawdry "Sex-Museum" and a "Jack the Ripper" dark ride. For the kids, there are bouncy castles, horse rides and even a rather sad sleigh carousel pulled by real ponies.

The atmosphere is generally fairly relaxed during the day, though it can get a little more charged at night. If you get lost, you should be able to orientate yourself by one of the two open areas, Rondeau and Calafattiplatz, the latter named after the man who set up the first carousel in the Prater in 1840. The easiest point of reference of all is, of course, the Riesenrad. Sadly, there are no longer more than fifty restaurants and pubs to choose from as there were a hundred years ago, but if you're peckish, there's no shortage of *Würst* stands, plus a few more appetizing options, such as the famous *Schweizerhaus* (see p.276), whose roast pig is legendary.

## Riesenrad (Ferris Wheel)

Taking a ride on the **Riesenrad** (daily: Jan, Feb, Nov & Dec 10am–7.45pm; March, April & Oct 10am–9.45pm; May–Sept 9am–11.45pm; €8; Ⓦwww .wienerriesenrad.com) is one of those things you simply have to do if you go to Vienna; it's also a must for fans of the film *The Third Man*, as the place in front of which Orson Welles does his famous "cuckoo clock" speech. Built in 1898 for Emperor Franz-Josef I's golden jubilee celebrations, the Riesenrad was designed by the British military engineer Walter Basset, who had constructed similar Ferris wheels in Blackpool and Paris (both long since demolished). The cute little red gondolas were destroyed during World War II, and only half were replaced after 1945 in deference to the Riesenrad's old age. Acrophobes can reassure themselves with the fact that the gondolas, which hold up to twelve people standing, are entirely enclosed, though they do tend to wobble around a bit, and reach a height of over 65m. You should also be prepared for the fact that the wheel doesn't so much spin as stagger slowly round, as each gondola fills up with passengers; once you've done a complete circuit, you've had your twenty-minute ride.

## Prater Museum and Planetarium

If you've no interest in the amusements at the Volksprater, you're probably best off heading instead for the nearby **Prater Museum** (Tues–Thurs 10am–1pm, Fri–Sun 2–6pm; €2; Ⓦwww.wienmuseum.at), which records the golden age of the funfair. Old photographs of the likes of Semona, the fiery Amazonian snake-charmer, and

Liliputstadt, an entire miniature city inhabited by dwarves, give you something of the nineteenth-century flavour. Also displayed here are several of the characters from Hanswurst, various antique slot-machines (some of which you can play on) and a model of the 1873 *Weltausstellung*. The museum is housed in one room of the **Planetarium** (Tues–Sun; closed Aug to mid-Sept; €12; Ⓦwww.planetarium-wien .at), which was founded by the German optician Carl Zeiss in 1927, and puts on a varied programme, with commentary nearly always in German. Pick up a leaflet or visit the website to find out the latest listings.

### Kugelmugel

A little further down the Hauptallee from the Planetarium is the **Kugelmugel** (Ⓦwww.republik-kugelmugel.com), a spherical terracotta-coloured house belonging to the artist Edwin Lipburger. Following arguments over planning permission, Lipburger declared his house a self-governing republic or micro-nation, refused to pay taxes and began printing his own stamps. It was for this latter act that he received a prison sentence, though he was pardoned by the Austrian president. The republic's territory is marked out by a barbed-wire fence and its unofficial address is Antifaschismus-Platz.

## Beyond the Volksprater

The quirkiest method of escape from the Volksprater is by the miniature railway, known as the **Liliputbahn** (every 15–20min: April & Oct daily 10am–7pm; May–Sept Mon–Fri 9am–7pm, Sat & Sun 10am–7pm; €3.50; Ⓦwww.liliputbahn .com), which runs from near the Riesenrad over to the main stadium, a return trip of around 4km. The engines are mostly diesel, but some steam trains run in the summer. There are three stations: Praterstern by the Ferris wheel, the mid-point

▲ Liliputbahn

station Rotunde, named after the now-defunct exhibition hall of the 1873 *Weltausstellung*, and Stadion. En route, you pass the Hockey-Stadion and Bowling-Halle to the south, the ugly, expansive Messegelände (trade-fair grounds) and the Krieau Trabrennbahn (trotting-racecourse), to the north. **Trotting races** are held on Saturdays from September to June (ⓦwww.krieau.at).

### Ernst-Happel-Stadion

Beyond the Trabrennbahn lies the **Ernst-Happel-Stadion** (aka the Wiener or Prater Stadion). Opened in July 1931 with the International Workers' Olympics, the stadium's playing field was transformed into a giant stage, on which four thousand musicians, actors and gymnasts re-enacted the struggle of Labour over Capital from the Middle Ages to the present day. As a grand finale, the giant gilt idol representing capitalism was toppled, thousands of youths dressed in white marched forward carrying red flags and the crowd sang the *Internationale*. The show was repeated four times that year before a total audience of 260,000, and proved the cultural highpoint of interwar "Red Vienna" (see p.217).

Named after the Austrian football coach Ernst Happel (1925–1992), who won the European Cup twice (once with Feyenoord and once with Hamburg), the stadium itself is the largest in Austria, holding around fifty thousand spectators. It boasts a technically remarkable roof; invisible from the outside, it's a self-supporting light steel structure that hangs gracefully over the terraces. Despite staging the **Euro 2008 soccer final** and the odd European or international match, the stadium remains under-used.

### Beyond the Stadion

Notwithstanding the Autobahn and the railway line that cut across the south-eastern half of the Prater, the woods beyond the Stadion are among the most peaceful sections of the entire park, perfect for a picnic. If you've no provisions, walk to the far end of the Hauptallee where you'll find the **Lusthaus** restaurant (see p.276), a pretty octagonal building, remodelled from a hunting lodge into a pleasure palace by Isidor Canevale in 1783. Entirely surrounded by water in those days, it served as the centrepiece for a mass picnic laid on for twenty thousand soldiers on the first anniversary of the 1813 Battle of Leipzig, during the Congress of Vienna. It now forms the island of a roundabout, but preserves its original frescoed interior, and is still a popular spot for lunch, as is the more rustic *Altes Jägerhaus*, opposite.

To the southeast of the *Lusthaus* lies the **Freudenau Rennbahn**, a lovingly restored racecourse from the late nineteenth century. The racing season tradition-ally opens on Easter Sunday, with races taking place every other weekend from March to November. The season reaches its apogee during the annual Derby, organized by the Austrian Jockey Club since 1868, the year it was founded. Held on a Sunday in June, the Derby used to be attended almost unfailingly by the emperor himself, with various aristocrats often among the riders, and the wealthy young Viennese crowd dressed to the nines.

# Central Leopoldstadt

There's really very little to see in the rest of Leopoldstadt, beyond the **Johann-Strauss-Museum**, and the collection of sculptures in the **Gustinus-Ambrosi-**

**Museum** in the Augarten. And if Meissen porcelain is your thing, the Augarten **Porzellanmanufaktur** is worth a visit.

## The Danube Canal

The **Danube Canal** (Donaukanal), which separates Leopoldstadt from the old town, is the narrowest of the four arms of the River Danube. As the channel nearest to the city, this was the first section of the Danube to be regulated, as far back as 1598. Despite its human proportions, the canal's banks are by no means pretty, having been an easy target for bombs during World War II. The only building of note is Otto Wagner's dinky **Schützenhaus** (literally "defence tower"), on the embankment below Obere Donaustrasse, due to be turned into a café and museum to Otto Wagner in 2009. Clad in white marble, it features a playful wave pattern of cobalt-blue tiles, and is best viewed from the opposite embankment below Franz-Josefs-Kai.

Further downstream from the Schützenhaus, at no. 95, stands the IBM building, a typically unimaginative corporate office block, built on the site of the Diana Rooms, where, on February 15, 1867, **Johann Strauss the Younger** first performed the city's most famous signature tune, *An der schönen, blauen Donau*, known to the English-speaking world simply as *The Blue Danube*. A plaque by the building's entrance records the fact. What it doesn't tell you, however, is that the waltz was originally scored for male chorus, not orchestra, complete with ludicrous lyrics, and wasn't at all well received after its inept first performance. Only when Strauss took it to Paris, and performed it with an orchestra, did it become a stratospheric success.

## The Strauss family

Of all the many tunes associated with Vienna, perhaps the best known are the waltzes composed by the Strausses. Born in Vienna to a Jewish innkeeper in Leopoldstadt, **Johann Strauss the Elder** (1804–49) kept quiet about his origins, though it was the Nazis themselves who felt the need to falsify the parish register of Vienna's Stephansdom in order to make the Strauss family appear as true Aryans (a similar leniency was shown towards Hitler's much-loved composer Franz Léhar, whose wife was Jewish). Strauss began his career serenading diners in Viennese restaurants, along with the likes of Josef Lanner, who was to become his chief musical rival. However, it was in the dance hall of Zum Sperl in Leopoldstadt that Strauss the Elder made his name as a band leader, conducting a mixture of dances, orchestral phantasies and more serious music. His gypsy-like features, and wild, vigorous conducting style soon became very popular in Vienna. Later, he and his orchestra achieved a modicum of fame touring Europe, and he was eventually appointed k.k. Hofballmusikdirektor (Imperial-Royal Director of Music for Balls). Strauss's touring took its toll on domestic life, and he created a public scandal in 1842, when he left the family home and moved in with a young seamstress, who bore him several illegitimate children.

His eldest son, **Johann Strauss the Younger** (1825–99), followed in his father's footsteps, writing his first waltz at the age of six, though much against the latter's wishes (he wanted him to be a banker). It was, in fact, Johann's long-suffering mother, Anna, who directed her sons into musical careers. Father and son soon became rivals, both musically and politically. In 1848, while the Elder was busy conducting his famous *Radetzky March*, the signature tune of the *ancien régime*, the Younger was composing stirring tunes such as the *Revolution March* and the *Song of the Barricades*. Fourteen years after his father's death, Strauss the Younger was appointed k.k. Hofballmusikdirektor in 1863, rapidly surpassing even his father's enormous fame. He was one of the world's first international celebrities, feted on both sides of the Atlantic. On one memorable occasion in Boston in the US, he conducted *The Blue Danube* with twenty thousand singers, an orchestra of over a thousand, and twenty assistant conductors, to an audience of more than 100,000. Johann's operetta, *Die Fledermaus*, written to take Viennese minds off the economic crash of 1873, was another huge success – by the end of the decade, it was playing in some 170 theatres.

Despite his success, Johann, a difficult character like his father, was something of an outsider. He was also constantly irked by his lack of acclaim among serious musical critics, and his several attempts at straight opera flopped. Again like his father, he too caused a scandal, divorcing his second wife, Lili, in order to marry his mistress, Adele. As the Vatican would not annul his marriage, he was forced to convert to Lutheranism and become a citizen of Saxony, though he continued to live in Vienna until his death in 1899.

As for the remaining Strauss sons, Johann's two younger brothers, Josef – "the romantic-looking, chaotically pale" Strauss, as he was dubbed by one Viennese critic – and Eduard, were also musicians (again against their absent father's wishes). Josef was a successful composer in his own right, but died at the age of 43, while Eduard became k.k. Hofballmusikdirektor after Johann in 1872 and was left in charge of the Strauss orchestra.

# Praterstrasse: Johann-Strauss-Wohnung

Johann Strauss the Younger lived on nearby **Praterstrasse** – once a majestic boulevard, peppered with Yiddish theatres, that led to the Prater, it is now just a busy, wide street with little to recommend it. At the far end of Praterstrasse, nearest the Prater, stands the splendid **Tegetthoff Monument**, a tall rostral column, complete with frolicking sea-horses and topped by a statue of Wilhelm von Tegetthoff himself, celebrating the Austrian rear admiral's 1866 naval victory over the Italians at the Battle of Lissa.

Fans of the "Waltz King", however, should head for the **Johann-Strauss-Wohnung** (Tues–Thurs 2–6pm, Fri–Sun 10am–1pm; €2; @www.wienmuseum .at) on the first floor of no. 54, where the composer lived from 1863 until the death of his first wife, the singer Jetty Treffz, in 1878. In contrast to most of the city's musical museums, some attempt has been made here to re-create a period interior; one room, decorated with ceiling panels of cherubs, contains his grand piano, house organ and standing desk at which he used to compose. There's also a fascinating collection of ephemera from the balls of the day, with various gimmicky dance cards – one laid out in the form of a staircase – and quirky ball pendants, which were kept as a sort of memento of the evening.

# Kriminalmuseum

Leopoldstadt's most popular museum is the **Wiener Kriminalmuseum** (Tues–Sun 10am–5pm; €5; @www.kriminalmuseum.at), a prurient overview of Vienna's most gruesome crimes, at Grosse Sperlgasse 24. In between the voyeuristic photos of autopsies, there are some interesting sections on the city's social and political history, though with labelling in German only, these are lost on most foreign visitors. To cap it all, there's a fairly gratuitous section on flagellation, while the biggest criminals of the lot – the Nazis – get only the very briefest of mentions. All in all, it's worth giving this museum a wide berth. A more edifying museum on a similar subject is the Foltermuseum (Torture Museum), described on p.167.

# Augarten

The **Augarten**, in the north of Leopoldstadt, is one of Vienna's oldest parks, laid out in formal French style in 1650, and opened to the public in 1775 by Josef II. Sadly, it's come down in the world since its fashionable halcyon days when Mozart gave morning concerts here, and, a century later, Strauss the Younger championed Wagner's overtures. That said, the park does pull in the crowds in the summer, thanks to its open-air cinema, Kino unter Sternen (see p.289). The park has a slightly melancholic air due to the forbidding presence of not one, but two World War II Flaktürme (see p.166). These sinister concrete hulks put the dampeners on the formal section of the park; the only way to escape them is to head off into the woody network of chestnut-lined paths to the north, home to numerous, very tame, red squirrels and more elusive woodpeckers.

Hidden in this dense section of the park, by the eastern boundary, is the intriguing **Gustinus-Ambrosi-Museum** (Tues–Sun 10am–6pm; €5), a little-visited offshoot of the Österreichisches Galerie, which runs the Belvedere (the same ticket is valid for both). It's devoted to the prolific Austrian sculptor, Gustinus Ambrosi (1893–1975), whose larger works are clearly influenced by Auguste Rodin. However, Ambrosi is at his best with his bronze portrait heads, of which there are plenty here, his subjects drawn mainly from the artistic and political circles of the interwar period. Note the emaciated Otto Wagner the year before his death, a suitably overblown Nietzsche, and a youthful Mussolini (with hair). Your ticket also allows entry to the contemporary art shows staged at the adjacent **Atelier Augarten** (Ⓦwww.atelier-augarten.at), a purpose-built exhibition space, café with a summer terrace (open until midnight) and studio-home for the atelier's current artist-in-residence.

On the ruins of the Alte Favorita, Leopold I's summer palace, burnt to the ground by the Turks in 1683, Josef II erected a long, low-lying garden pavilion. From 1782, the pavilion's restaurant was the venue of the fashionable musical matinées conducted by the likes of Mozart and Beethoven; the building now serves as the headquarters of the **Wiener Porzellanmanufaktur** (Mon–Fri 9.30am–5pm; free; Ⓦwww.augarten.at), founded in 1718, eight years after Meissen. The factory's famous "flower and figure" porcelain is exhibited in the Silberkammer in the Hofburg (see p.82), though temporary exhibitions are also staged in the showroom foyer. The factory's current offerings – from gaudy Rococo to more subtle designs by the likes of Josef Hoffmann – are sold in the adjacent shop. Hour-long **guided tours** of the entire production process take place Monday to Friday at 9.30am (€6).

The **Augartenpalais**, to the east of the Porzellanmanufaktur, was designed by Johann Bernhard Fischer von Erlach at the end of the seventeenth century, and bought as a hunting lodge by Emperor Josef II in 1780. Unfortunately, you can't get a good look at the building, as it's now the boarding school of the Wiener Sängerknaben (Vienna Boys' Choir), for more on which see p.86. The choir's kindergarten and primary school are housed in the **Kaiser-Josef-Stöckl**, a pavilion hidden behind the palace, designed by Isidor Canevale in 1781 for Josef II, who preferred the Augarten above all his other residences.

# Donauinsel and Kaisermühlen

In the second half of the nineteenth century, the main course of the River Danube was straightened to allow larger vessels to dock. A parallel channel, the slow-flowing Neue Donau, was cut in the 1970s, thus creating a long, thin, artificial island, officially known as the **Donauinsel**, but dubbed variously Spaghetti Island or Copa Cagrana (after the end station on the nearby U-Bahn line). The original course of the Danube, known as the Alte Donau, to the east of the Neue Donau, was simultaneously dammed to create perhaps the most attractive stretch of water. The semicircular nub of land encompassed by the Neue and Alte Donau is known as **Kaisermühlen**, home to Vienna's UNO-City and the accompanying Donaupark. Neither deserves to top your itinerary, but each provides an interesting insight into modern Viennese life.

## Donauinsel

To be perfectly honest, the **Donauinsel** – measuring 20km by just 200m – is pretty bleak, a situation not helped by the views over to the unsightly east bank. Nevertheless, when the summer heat starts to kick in, the Viennese flock to the beaches here in droves, and the island's numerous bars, discos and food stalls, centred around the Donauinsel U-Bahn station, start to get busy. Joggers, skateboarders and cyclists also use the island, and every June it becomes the focus for the *Donauinselfest*, an open-air rock festival with fireworks organized by the

Social Democrat Party (SPÖ). To the north, there's a huge watersports complex, with a 200m-long water slide, boat rental, windsurfing and the like. To the south, there are fixed barbecue spots, and a nudist beach (FKK). Wherever you decide to go, in summer you should don some mosquito repellent.

# Vienna International Centre (UNO-City)

Since 1980, the **Vienna International Centre** (ⓦwww.unis.unvienna.org) – known as VIC to its inmates, and UNO-City to the mapmakers – has been the United Nations' number-three base (UNOV), after New York and Geneva. The idea for this was first mooted by the then UN secretary general, Kurt Waldheim, and its construction nearly bankrupted the country. The UN functionaries, until then housed in the Hofburg, were none too happy either. Today, the VIC is home to, among numerous other bureaucracies, the International Atomic Energy Authority, the Office for Outer Space Affairs, the Office on Drugs and Crime, and the ever-busy High Commission for Refugees (UNHCR).

Of the more than four thousand folk employed here, only a third are Austrians, but the place is clearly an important source of income for the city, and has ensured Vienna a bit part on the international stage. The adjacent conference-centre monstrosity – the imaginatively named Austria Center Vienna – has proved less of a money-spinner. Whatever the financial benefits, UNO-City is not a beautiful place to visit. Within earshot of a roaring autobahn, cordoned off with wire fencing, and bristling with armed police and CCTV cameras, the whole place is alienating and, essentially, ugly. The six Y-shaped, glass-fronted high-rise offices soar to a height of 110m, and radiate from a central block like a three-legged man on the run. **Guided tours** (Mon–Fri 11am & 2pm; €5) start from the UN visitors' centre at Gate One (remember to take your passport) – as well as telling you all about the UN they allow you to admire the contemporary Austrian art with which the interior is generously sprinkled.

# Donaupark and the Alte Donau

It's with a certain amount of relief that you descend from the VIC to the adjacent **Donaupark**, laid out on an old rubbish dump in 1964 as part of the Vienna International Garden Show. The most pleasant section is around the artificial lake, Irissee, and in the rose garden and walled Chinese garden beyond. An added incentive for kids is the miniature railway, the **Donauparkbahn**, which wends its way around the park (March–Oct daily 10am–7pm; round trip €5.50; ⓦwww.liliputbahn.com/donauparkbahn). Overlooking the park is the futuristic **Donauturm** (daily 10am–midnight; €5.20; ⓦwww.donauturm.at), which reaches a height of 252m. To enjoy the view, you can either simply take the lift to the viewing platform (at 155m), or eat in one of the tower's two revolving restaurants (at 160m and 170m). Clearly visible to the west, by Handelskai on the Danube, is Vienna's latest skyscraper – and Austria's second tallest building – the **Millennium Tower**, a shiny double cylinder designed by Peichl, Podrecca & Weber, that's 202m tall.

The Donaupark stretches from UNO-City to the **Alte Donau**, the old course of the Danube, and undoubtedly the most attractive and peaceful section of the river. There are numerous bathing areas south of Wagramerstrasse and on the **Gänsehäufel**, the large island in the middle of the Untere Alte Donau, which has its own beach area. Opposite the Gänsehäufel, you'll find numerous places to enjoy an alfresco drink along the eastern bank – again, mosquito repellent is a

▲ Donauturm

good idea. Probably the most accessible (and popular) public bathing area is the **Angelibad**, in the north near Neue Donau U-Bahn, with a popular *Schnitzel* place close by. Along the eastern bank there are also a number of sailing schools, which rent out boats and windsurfers and offer lessons too.

# Schönbrunn, the Wienerwald and the Zentralfriedhof

V ienna's outer suburbs or *Vororte*, which lie beyond the *Gürtel*, are predominantly residential and contain only a few top-drawer sights. Chief of these is **Schönbrunn**, the Habsburgs' former summer residence to the west of the city centre, which is one of Vienna's most popular tourist destinations after the Hofburg. The palace boasts some of the best Rococo interiors in central Europe, while the surrounding **Schlosspark** is home to the **Tiergarten**, Vienna's delightful zoo, and various other attractions. To the west of the neighbouring villa district of **Hietzing** is the much wilder parkland of the **Lainzer Tiergarten**, a former royal hunting-ground that's now a haven for wildlife.

The rest of the suburbs have a scattering of interesting museums and sights that call for a targeted approach, relying on the tram system to get you around. To the north, several wine-producing villages have been subsumed into the city and their **Heurigen** (wine taverns) pull in tourists by the bus load (see p.277). Vienna is very lucky to have the **Wienerwald** (Vienna Woods) on its doorstep, just beyond the *Heurigen*, and a trip up to one of its forested hills is rewarded with glorious views over the entire city.

Finally, in the southeast, there's the **Zentralfriedhof**, Vienna's truly awesome Central Cemetery, with a population almost twice that of the city itself, and featuring the graves of the likes of Beethoven, Schubert, Brahms, Schönberg and the Strauss family.

## Schönbrunn

Compared with the hotchpotch that is the Hofburg, the Habsburgs' summer residence of **Schönbrunn** (Ⓦwww.schoenbrunn.at) is everything an imperial palace should be: grandiose, symmetrical and thoroughly intimidating. Built over the course of the eighteenth century, it contains nearly 1500 rooms, and, in its day, would have housed more than a thousand servants. However, while the sheer scale of the place is undeniably impressive, the building itself is something of an acquired taste, its plain facade painted a rather sickly mustard yellow.

The riches are inside, with its superb array of Baroque and Rococo **Prunkräume** (State Rooms), dating from the time of the empress Maria Theresia, the first of the Habsburgs to make Schönbrunn the official imperial summer residence. There's also a fine collection of imperial carriages in the outbuilding of the **Wagenburg**, plus temporary exhibitions in the **Orangerie** and period-costume puppet performances in the **Marionettentheater**.

In the **Schlosspark**, you'll find the **Tiergarten** (Zoo), far more uplifting than most inner-city zoos, and close by, the tropical **Palmenhaus** and the desert-like **Wüstenhaus**. Last, but not least, there's the whole of the magnificent Schlosspark itself, and its **Irrgarten** (Maze) and follies, to explore.

## Schönbrunn in history

Compared with the Hofburg, Schönbrunn has a short Habsburg history. It only came into imperial ownership in 1569, when **Maximilian II** (1564–76) bought the property – then known as Katterburg – close to what is now the Meidlinger Tor, as a hunting retreat. His son **Matthias** (1612–19) had the place rebuilt after marauding Hungarians laid it to waste in 1605, and it was he who discovered the natural spring, from which the name Schönbrunn (Beautiful Spring) derives.

After the Habsburgs themselves had destroyed the place in anticipation of the Turks in 1683, **Leopold I** (1657–1705) commissioned a new summer palace for his son and heir from Johann Bernhard Fischer von Erlach. The latter's initial plans envisaged a structure to rival Versailles, perched on top of the hill and approached by a series of grandiose terraces. In the end, a much more modest building was agreed upon, and work began in 1696. Enough was built to allow **Josef I** (1705–11) to occupy the central section, but construction was stymied by the War of the Spanish Succession (1701–14).

Josef I's successor, Karl VI, was only interested in pheasant-shooting at Schönbrunn, and it was left to **Maria Theresia** (1740–80) to create the palace and gardens that we see today. Employing her court architect, Nicolo Pacassi, she added an extra floor to the main palace, to accommodate her ever increasing family, and had the interior transformed into a sumptuous Rococo residence. Her son, **Josef II** (1780–90), an enthusiastic gardener, rearranged the gardens in Classical style, adding the largest of the garden's monuments, the Gloriette triumphal arch, and growing his own tea, coffee and sugar, which he took great pleasure in serving to his guests. He did not, however, share his mother's love of Schönbrunn, and had much of the palace boarded up to save money.

**Napoleon** stayed at Schönbrunn in 1805 and 1809 – his eagles can still be seen on the main gates – and his son, the Duke of Reichstadt, lived out most of his brief life here, too (see p.201). However, it wasn't until the reign of

### Visiting Schönbrunn

Approaches to the palace suffer from the roar of traffic from the nearby Linke Wienzeile and Schönbrunner Schloss Strasse. Consequently, the best way to **get there** is to head straight for the Meidlinger Tor on Grünbergstrasse from U-Bahn Schönbrunn, rather than struggle along the multi-lane freeway to the main gates. You could also continue one stop further on the U-Bahn to Hietzing, and dive into the park via the Hietzinger Tor on Hietzinger Hauptstrasse. This enables you to peek at the nearby Hofpavillon Hietzing (see p.206) and brings you nearer to the Tiergarten, Palmenhaus and so on.

If you're thinking of visiting the palace, you should head for the **ticket office** first as queues can be lengthy. And if you're considering visiting any of the other attractions in Schönbrunn, it might be worth buying a **Gold Pass** (€36), which gets you into all nine. Equally, if you're not visiting the palace, but are going to visit the zoo, mazes and glasshouses, be sure to buy a **Kombi-Karte** (€16).

For **refreshments**, there's a reasonably priced *Beisl* near the Wagenburg, and a coffee shop beyond the ticket office in the palace itself. Whatever you do, don't be hoodwinked into going to the overpriced café-restaurant on the east side of the main courtyard. Tea and cakes are also on offer in the wonderful surroundings of the Gloriette, overlooking the Schlosspark, and there are usually a few food stalls in the main palace courtyard. The Tiergarten has still more eating options, from *Würst* stands to restaurants – you can even fix your own picnic from the shop in the zoo's Tirolerhaus. Nevertheless, by far the cheapest and most convenient option in fine weather is to bring your own supplies and find somewhere to relax in the park.

*Westbahnhof* ▲

Technisches Museum

LINZER STRASSE

GOLDSCHLAGSTRASSE

MARIAHILFERSTRASSE

HÜTTELGASSE

SCHLOSSALLEE

WINCKELMANNSTRASSE

SECHSHAUSER STRASSE

Auer-Welsbach-Park

Penzing

CUMBERLANDSTRASSE

REIZERGASSE

PENZINGER STRASSE

LINKE WIENZEILE

Schönbrunn

*River* *Wien*

HADIKGASSE

SCHLOSSSTRASSE

Schlosstheater **Schönbrunn**

Hofpavillon

SCHÖNBRUNNER

Orangerie **Meidlinger Tor**

HIETZINGER KAI

*Hietzing*

Wagenburg

GRÜNBERGSTRASSE

**Kaiserstöckl**

Kronprinzgarten

TIVOLIGASSE

**Hietzinger Tor**

Schlosspark

HIETZINGER HAUPTSTRASSE

**Palmenhaus**

**Irrgarten (Maze)**

**Schöner Brunnen**

LAINZER STRASSE

TRAUTMANNSDORFFGASSE

WATTMANNGASSE

**Obelisk**

MAXINGSTRASSE

BOTANISCHER GARTEN

Tiergarten

Neptunbrunnen

**Römische Ruine**

**Swimming Baths**

**Kleine Gloriette**

HOHENBERGSTRASSE

Tiroler Garten

Gloriette

**Villa Skywa-Primavesi**

GLORIETTEGASSE

WEISSENTHURNGASSE

*Werkbundsiedlung*

**Villa Schopp**

**HIETZING**

ALTMANNSDORFER STRASSE

MAXINGSTRASSE

SCHÖNBRUNNER SCHLOSSTRASSE

Friedhof Hietzing

SCHÖNBRUNNER ALLEE

GASSMANNSTRASSE

**N**

**Barracks**

WATTMANNGASSE

SCHÖNBERGGASSE

ELISABETHALLEE

EDELSINNSTRASSE

FASANGARTENGASSE

SCHLÖGLGASSE

HETZENDORFERSTRASSE

0          500 m

*Lainzer Tiergarten* ▼

**CAFÉS**
Dommayer  1
Gloriette  2

**SCHÖNBRUNN**

**Franz-Josef I** – who was born within the palace in 1830 and died here in 1916 – that Schönbrunnonce more occupied centre stage in court life. In November 1918, the last of the Habsburgs, **Karl I**, signed away all hopes of preserving the monarchy, in the palace's Blue Chinese Salon, and thereafter the entire place became state property. Badly damaged in World War II, Schönbrunn served first as the Soviet, and then the British, army headquarters before being handed back to the state in 1947.

# The palace

Compared to the sterility of the Hofburg's state apartments, Schönbrunn's **Prunkräume** (daily: April–June, Sept & Oct 8.30am–5pm; July & Aug 8.30am–6pm; Nov–March 8.30am–4.30pm) are a positive visual feast. That said, not every room is worthy of close attention, so don't feel bad about walking briskly through some of them. Visits to the Prunkräume are carefully choreographed. First, you must make your way to the ticket office on the ground floor of the east wing. Here, you'll be allocated a visiting time; if the palace is busy, you may well have to wait several hours, in which case you should head off into the gardens, or visit one of Schönbrunn's other sights.

There's a choice of two tickets: the "**Imperial Tour**" (€9.50), which takes in 22 state rooms, and the "**Grand Tour**" (€12.90), which includes all forty rooms open to the public. Even if you're no great fan of period interiors, it seems pointless to go on the first, since it skips some of the palace's most magnificent

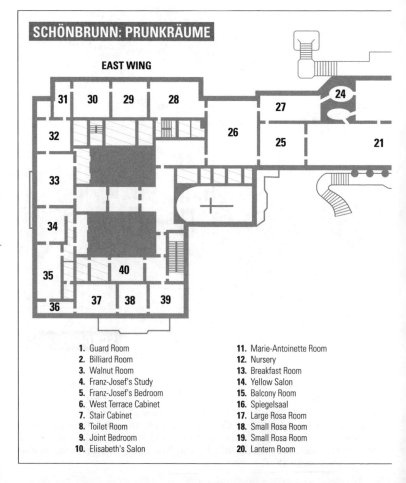

SCHÖNBRUNN: PRUNKRÄUME

EAST WING

| 1. | Guard Room | 11. | Marie-Antoinette Room |
| 2. | Billiard Room | 12. | Nursery |
| 3. | Walnut Room | 13. | Breakfast Room |
| 4. | Franz-Josef's Study | 14. | Yellow Salon |
| 5. | Franz-Josef's Bedroom | 15. | Balcony Room |
| 6. | West Terrace Cabinet | 16. | Spiegelsaal |
| 7. | Stair Cabinet | 17. | Large Rosa Room |
| 8. | Toilet Room | 18. | Small Rosa Room |
| 9. | Joint Bedroom | 19. | Small Rosa Room |
| 10. | Elisabeth's Salon | 20. | Lantern Room |

Rococo delights. For both tours, you are given a hand-held audioguide in English, lasting 35 and 50 minutes respectively; for the "Grand Tour", you also get the option of paying extra for an hour-long tour with a guide (€14.40). The disadvantage of following a tour guide is that they give you the same, short space of time in each room, whether it's worth pausing in or not.

## Emperor Franz-Josef I and Empress Elisabeth's apartments

Whichever tour you're on, you will enter via the **Blauerstiege** (Blue Staircase) on the ground floor of the west wing. If you're on the "Imperial Tour", you'll miss the nine private apartments of Franz-Josef – no great loss, as anyone who's been to the Hofburg will tell you – entering at Elisabeth's Salon, just after the couple's bedroom.

Visitors on the "Grand Tour", meanwhile, pass through the Guard Room into the **Billiard Room**, where, in Franz-Josef's day, those wishing for an audience with the emperor were made to wait. While kicking their heels, they could admire

Rooms Closed to the Public

0        20 m

**WEST WING**

21. Great Gallery
22. Small Gallery
23. Round Chinese Cabinet
24. Oval Chinese Cabinet
25. Carousel Room
26. Ceremonial Hall
27. Rössel Room
28. Blue Chinese Salon
29. Vieux-Laque Room
30. Napoleon Room
31. Porcelain Room
32. Millions Room
33. Gobelin Hall
34. Memorial Room
35. Red Salon
36. East Terrace Cabinet
37. Maria Theresia's Bedroom
38. Franz Karl's Study
39. Franz Karl's Corner Salon
40. Hunting Room

the paintings, but sadly weren't invited actually to play billiards. Audiences with the emperor were given in the **Walnut Room** next door, named after the wood used for the chairs and gilded Rococo panelling; even the chandelier is carved from wood (painted over with pure gold). A nasty brown hue lines the walls of the emperor's gloomy **Study**, where Franz-Josef spent much of the day stood over his desk, pedantically reading and signing thousands of official documents; on the wall is a portrait of the empress Elisabeth at 16, when she was betrothed to Franz-Josef. Next is the widower's **Bedroom**, with the simple iron bed on which the emperor died on November 21, 1916, at the age of 86; beside it stands Franz Matsch's reverential rendition of the scene. To one side is his imperial majesty's lavatory, installed in 1899 "according to the English system".

Passing through two tiny rooms, one of which the empress used as her study, while the other served as her dressing room, you come to the imperial couple's **Bedroom**, decorated in time for their nuptials in 1854 with matching blue Lyon silk upholstery, and twin rosewood beds. Elisabeth managed to avoid consummating the marriage for the first two nights. The story goes that at family breakfast on the first morning, Elisabeth's crabby mother-in-law, the formidable Archduchess Sophie, asked her how well her son had performed in bed, at which the young bride broke down and wept. Though the empress dutifully produced a son and heir (Rudolf, who later committed suicide; see p.231), within five years she had fled the marital bed entirely, apart from a brief reconciliation in 1867, so it's unlikely Elisabeth spent many nights here.

Empress Elisabeth's personal apartments smack even less of her personality than those in the Hofburg – hardly surprising since she spent so little time here. The decor, in fact, mostly dates from the time of Empress **Maria Theresia**, a century or so earlier, and the walls of three of the rooms – the Marie Antoinette Room, the Nursery and the Yellow Salon – are lined with portraits of the empress's numerous offspring. Her father, Karl VI, failed to produce a male heir, leaving Maria Theresia with an uphill struggle to convince the rest of Europe she was "man" enough for the job. She herself was determined to produce a good cropful of heirs – after the birth of her fourth child, she was heard to comment "I wish I were already in the sixth month of a new pregnancy." Out of her sixteen children, nine survived to adulthood.

Two of her sons went on to become emperors, Josef II and Leopold II, but the most famous of the lot was her youngest daughter, **Marie Antoinette**, who married Louis XVI and followed him to the guillotine in 1793. Under her portrait in the Nursery, to the right of the door to the empress Zita's private bathroom, is the only piece of furniture sent back to Vienna by the French after her execution. Off the Empire-style Yellow Salon lies the intimate **Breakfast Room**, a frothy Rococo concoction decorated with gilded cartouches containing floral silk embroidered by Maria Theresia and her daughters.

## The state apartments

The first of the more elaborate state apartments is the **Spiegelsaal** (Mirror Hall), where, in 1762, the precocious 7-year-old Mozart performed a duet with his older sister Nannerl, in the presence of the empress Maria Theresia and family, and famously "sprang on the lap of the empress, put his arms round her neck and vigorously kissed her", according to his father. From here you enter the **Large Rosa Room**, named for the idealized landscapes executed by the Polish court painter Josef Rosa in the 1760s, set into gilded frames on the walls.

The **Great Gallery** is, without doubt, the most splendid of all the rooms so far, a vast long hall, heavy with gilded stucco embellishments, lined with fluted pilasters sporting acanthus capitals and originally lit by over four thousand candles.

## Empress Maria Theresia (1740–80)

In 1740, Emperor Karl VI died suddenly, leaving no male heir. That the emperor's daughter, **Maria Theresia**, was able to ascend the throne was thanks to the Pragmatic Sanction of 1713, passed by her father, granting her the right of inheritance. But as she herself put it, "I found myself without money, without credit, without an army, without experience and knowledge, even without counsel, because all my ministers were wholly occupied in trying to discover which way the cat was going to jump." Despite this inauspicious beginning, she surprised her male entourage by surviving against the odds, no thanks to her husband, Franz Stephan, who was good at fencing, hunting, shooting and womanizing, but unfortunately not much else.

Throughout Europe she was known as the "Virgin Empress", though with sixteen children to her name, she clearly wasn't in the literal sense. She was, however, out of step with the promiscuity of the period. Jesuit-educated and deeply pious, she insisted, much to her husband's discomfort, that they share a marital bed (this was by no means the usual custom). It was partly her husband's extramarital activities that prompted her to set up the **Chastity Commission** in the autumn of 1747. Its commissioners were empowered to search houses, and to arrest any man found entertaining an opera singer, dancer or any other woman of presumed loose morals; offending ladies could be locked up in a convent or banished from the realm. Though in the end the commission fizzled out after just six months, it caused a certain amount of havoc – several acting troupes fell foul of the commission, as did Casanova himself, and one of the most celebrated sopranos of the day, Santini, who was escorted to the Venetian border.

Like her son, Josef II (see p.87), Maria Theresia was a keen reformer, establishing one of the best education systems in Europe at the time, with compulsory education for both sexes. However, she was no liberal, holding notoriously rabid anti-Semitic views. Though Vienna had barely five hundred Jews, the empress considered them to be an abomination, eventually expelling them all from the city in 1777, stating: "I know no worse public plague than this people, with their swindling, usury, and money-making, bringing people to beggary, practising all evil transactions which an honest man abhors; they are therefore to be kept away from here and avoided as far as possible." Normally, she would only communicate with them from behind a screen, though she happily used their money to help build Schönbrunn, and made an exception of the baptized Jew, Josef von Sonnenfels, who was one of her chief advisers.

Though Maria Theresia acquired a fun-loving reputation early in her reign, playing cards and dancing until all hours, her demeanour changed after the unexpected death of her husband on August 18, 1765. Thereafter she went into perpetual mourning, cutting her hair short, and wearing no jewellery or make-up. For the next fifteen years, she is supposed to have heard Mass every day in the Kaisergruft at the foot of the sepulchre containing her dead husband, spending every 18th of the month and the whole of August in silent prayer. On Franz Stephan's death, she immediately appointed Josef co-regent, and pretty much left him to take over the day-to-day running of the state. In her old age, she grew so large she found it hard to walk and rarely left Schönbrunn at all. She had difficulty breathing, and would keep the windows at the palace constantly open, though the wind and rain which came in gave her terrible rheumatism, and prevented her from writing the sackful of letters she usually winged off to her children.

Of the three ceiling frescoes by Guglielmo Guglielmi glorifying the Habsburgs, the last – depicting Austria's military prowess – was, ironically enough, destroyed by bomb damage in World War II, and is therefore a copy. Naturally, the hall was used for banquets during the Congress of Vienna in 1815, and it was here, in 1961, that J.F. Kennedy and Nikita Krushchev held their historic détente meeting.

It's worth venturing from here into the **Small Gallery**, which lies through the three arches to the south of the Great Gallery, to take a peek at the two chinoiserie rooms – one round, one oval – to either side. The parquet flooring is sublime, but it's the oriental lacquer panels set into the wainscoting, and the numerous pieces of blue-and-white Chinese porcelain, that give the rooms their names. Of the two, the **Round Chinese Cabinet** is the most renowned, as this was where Maria Theresia used to hold her secret meetings with, among others, her chief adviser, Prince Kaunitz, whose apartments were linked to the room by a spiral staircase hidden behind one of the doors in the panelling. Another quirky feature of the room was the table designed to rise up through the floor, laden with food and drink, allowing the empress to dine without the need of servants, who might otherwise eavesdrop on matters of state. Kaunitz himself was particularly fond of food, and his table manners were legendary; on one memorable occasion, he "treated the company with the cleaning of his gums, a nauseous operation which lasted a prodigious long time and was accompanied with all manner of noises".

At the far end of the Great Gallery, you must pass through the **Carousel Room**, which gets its name from the painting of the special ladies' tournament held in the Winter Reitschule in 1743 (the sleighs used can be viewed in the Wagenburg). The final room for those on the "Imperial Tour" is the **Ceremonial Hall**, displaying five large paintings by pupils of the court painter, Martin van Meytens. The majority are concerned with recording the elaborate festivities that accompanied the wedding of Maria Theresia's eldest son, Josef II, to Isabella of Parma, in 1760. The magnifying glass, over one section of the painting of the wedding's opera performance, helps you pick out Mozart and his father from the crowd, though the family didn't, in fact, arrive in Vienna until two years after the event.

It was in the beautiful surroundings of the **Blue Chinese Salon**, on November 11, 1918, that the last Habsburg emperor, Karl I, signed the document renouncing "all participation in the affairs of state". (He refused formally to abdicate or to renounce his claim to the throne, and made two unsuccessful attempts to regain the Hungarian half of his title in 1921, before dying in exile on Madeira the following year.) As the name suggests, the room is another chinoiserie affair – all the rage in the eighteenth century – lined with yellow wallpaper, hand-painted on rice paper, and inset with serene scenes of Chinese life on a deep-blue background.

## The audience rooms

The lightness of the Blue Chinese Room is in complete contrast to the oppressively opulent **Vieux-Laque Room**, with its black-and-gold lacquer panels, exquisite parquetry and walnut wainscoting. During his two sojourns at Schönbrunn, Napoleon is thought to have slept in the neighbouring walnut-panelled **Napoleon Room**, lined with Brussels tapestries depicting the Austrian army in Italy. It was also here that Maria Theresia is thought to have given birth to her brood, and where Napoleon's son by the archduchess Maria Louisa died in 1832, aged just 21. He had been kept a virtual prisoner in Schönbrunn, the stuffed skylark on the table among his few companions (see opposite).

Despite its name, only three items in the remarkable **Porcelain Room**, designed by Isabella of Parma, are actually genuine Meissen porcelain: the chandeliers, the clock and the wall bracket. The rest of the decor is carved from wood and painted over in blue and white to appear like porcelain. The delicate ink drawings set into the walls are signed works by Empress Maria Theresia's daughters, copied from French originals.

The most precious of all the rooms in Schönbrunn is the **Millions Room**, so called because it's estimated that Maria Theresia paid more than a million silver florins to have it decorated. Unfortunately the most priceless items in the room – the miniature seventeenth-century Persian watercolours of life in the Moghul court – are somewhat overwhelmed by the surrounding, richly gilded cartouches set into the Caribbean rosewood panelling. Just off the Millions Room is the handy little breakfast room, known as the **Miniatures Room**, containing more works by the talented archduchesses. Next door in the **Gobelin Hall** are yet more Brussels tapestries, not only decorating the walls but also upholstering the six chairs, which depict the twelve months. Tapestries were a status symbol, partly because they were so labour-intensive, and therefore very expensive; the central tapestry in this room took eight people twelve years to complete.

Passing quickly through the Archduchess Sophie's Study, the Red Salon and the East Terrace Cabinet, with its trompe l'oeil fresco of cherubs "in an azure firmament", as the brochure puts it, you reach **Maria Theresia's Bedroom**, also known as the Reiches Zimmer. The empress never actually slept in the red velvet and gold-embroidered four-poster bed, which was brought here from the Hofburg. Instead, the room was used exclusively for levées – a kind of official breakfast-in-bed – during her frequent pregnancies. This was also the modest little room in which Franz-Josef was born in 1830.

The last few rooms of the "Grand Tour" are those used by the **archduke Franz Karl** (Franz-Josef's epileptic father) and his wife, Archduchess Sophie, decked out in the usual red-damask and white panelling, and stuffed full of Habsburg portraits, including several by Martin van Meytens. The only items of note are the miniatures, in Franz Karl's Study by the window, by Maria Christina – Maria Theresia's favourite daughter, who was also the lover of Josef II's wife, Isabella of Parma. After Isabella's death from smallpox, Maria Christina went on to marry Albrecht of Saxony-Tetschen, with whom she helped found the Albertina (see p.93).

---

## L'Aiglon

When Napoleon's only son was born in 1811 to his second wife, Archduchess Maria Louisa, daughter of Franz I, he was destined to inherit a vast empire. Just four years later, in a futile gesture shortly after Waterloo, Napoleon abdicated and proclaimed his infant son Emperor of France in his place, saying: "I would rather my son were strangled than see him brought up as an Austrian prince in Vienna." It was, however, too late for Napoleon to have any say in the destiny of **L'Aiglon** or the "Little Eagle", as his son, Franz Karl Josef, was known. Maria Louisa had already returned to Vienna with Franz Karl during Napoleon's exile to Elba, and went on to marry a dashing cavalry officer called Count Neipperg, who was granted the Duchy of Parma.

Franz Karl, or "der kleine Napoleon", as the Viennese dubbed him, was left, orphaned, in Schönbrunn and given precisely the Habsburg aristocratic upbringing his father dreaded. Abandoned by his parents, the little boy enjoyed a privileged but lonely child-hood: his language of instruction was switched to German, all reminders of his past life, including toys, were removed. As Napoleon's son, he had been declared King of Rome, but under the Habsburgs, who had no use for him at all, he was given the title Duke of Reichstadt, a duchy that didn't in fact exist.

Franz Karl's health deteriorated badly from 1830 onwards, and by the winter of the following year he was seriously ill. He was prevented from moving to a drier climate, or even to the Habsburgs' favourite spa of Bad Ischl. He died at the age of 21 in the same room his father had slept in during his stay at Schönbrunn. Rumour had it that he had been poisoned by Prince Metternich, who saw him as a political embarrassment; others alleged that he had overindulged in sex; tuberculosis seems the most likely cause.

▲ Schönbrunn

### Kindermuseum and Berglzimmer

On the weekends and in the school holidays, the palace also organizes a **Kindermuseum** (school holidays & Sat & Sun 10am–5pm; €6.50) for kids aged between 4 and 12. The children get to dress up and learn about court life under the Habsburgs for everyone from the servants to the emperor and empress. The museum is laid out on the ground floor of the palace and also allows the kids access to the **Berglzimmer**: four relatively informal, though highly decorated, rooms dating from the reign of Maria Theresia, all of which look out onto the Schlosspark. The colourful floor-to-ceiling frescoes feature an abundance of exotic flora, fauna and trompe l'oeil trelliswork, and are the work of the Bohemian painter, Johann Wenzel Bergl. Make sure your kids check out the astonishing gilded Baroque stove in the shape of a tree trunk, with birds and animals frolicking on it.

## The outbuildings

With two exceptions (the Orangerie and the Wagenburg), the majority of the yellowy outbuildings that radiate from the main palace at Schönbrunn are closed to the public. A few, like the small Baroque **Schlosskapelle** in the ground floor east wing close to the ticket office, have limited opening hours (Sun 8–11am). The ornate **Schlosstheater**, built in 1747 by Pacassi on the west side of the main courtyard, is open only occasionally for summer performances by the Kammeroper (Wwww.wienerkammeroper.at) or the Marionettentheater (Wwww.marionettentheater.at); pick up a leaflet in the main ticket office.

The vast **Orangerie**, to the east of the palace, is used for temporary exhibitions, usually on an appropriately imperial theme, for which there is an additional charge. Nearby is the Privy Garden or **Kronprinzengarten** (daily: April–June, Sept & Oct 9am–5pm; July & Aug 9am–6pm; €2), a formal garden laid out in 1870 for the ill-fated Crown Prince Rudolf. Aside from this, by far the most rewarding of the outbuildings is the **Wagenburg**, housed in the former winter riding school to the west of the palace.

## Wagenburg

The main exhibition space of the **Wagenburg** (April–Oct daily 9am–6pm; Nov–March Tues–Sun 10am–4pm; €4.50; ⓦwww.khm.at) is crowded with nineteenth-century carriages, which are of limited interest to the nonspecialist. The best thing to do is pass quickly to the far end of the hall, where, below the gallery, there's an odd assortment of carriages and sleighs used to transport the imperial offspring. The most poignant is the phaeton designed for Napoleon's son, "L'Aiglon" (The Little Eagle; see p.201), with mudguards in the shape of eagles' wings; the bees that decorate the sides of the carriage were the Bonaparte family symbol.

The highlights of the collection, though, lie beyond the gallery, where you'll find the Baroque and Rococo carriages of the Habsburgs. The most outrageous is the enormously long **coronation carriage of Franz Stephan**, Maria Theresia's husband, dripping with gold plating, and fitted with windows of Venetian glass. The painted panels were added in time for the coronation of Josef II as Holy Roman Emperor in 1764. The whole thing weighs an incredible 4000kg, every kilo of it taken to pieces and transported on several occasions for coronations in Budapest, Frankfurt and Milan. Check out the wonderful horses' harnesses, too, embroidered in red velvet and gold, and the horses' plumes of ostrich feathers.

The equally ornate carriage opposite, painted entirely in black, was used during oath fealty ceremonies for the new emperor, which coincided with periods of official mourning for the previous incumbent. The relatively modest **red–leather litter**, which stands close by, studded with more than 11,000 gold-plated nails and buckles, is also worth a look. Originally built for long-distance travelling, to be carried by horses or mules, it was used, after 1705, solely for transporting the Archduke of Austria's hat from Klosterneuburg to Vienna and back for oath fealty ceremonies.

The richly carved, gold-plated carousel or **racing sleigh of Maria Theresia** is the sole survivor of a whole set built in the shape of giant scallops for the special ladies' tournament held in the Winter Reitschule in 1743; note the sleigh bells on the horses' mane decoration. Sleighs were frequently used during *Fasching* for rides in the parks and on the *glacis* outside the city walls. The wheels, on hand in case there was no snow, would be removed and the sleighs pulled by horses, steered by drivers who sat in the back seats and controlled the reins over the heads of the seated ladies.

The gallery is also the place to head if you've a yen to see the empress Elisabeth's horsewhip, with a photo of her husband set into the ivory handle, or the hoof of the horse used by the Emperor Franz-Josef I during his coronation as King of Hungary in 1867.

# Schlosspark

Even if you've no interest at all in visiting the interior of Schönbrunn, it's worth coming out here to enjoy the glorious **Schlosspark** (daily: April–Oct 6am–dusk; Nov–March 6.30am–dusk; free), concealed behind the palace. Like the Belvedere, the park is laid out across a sloping site ideal for the vistas and terraces beloved of Baroque landscape gardeners. Yet despite the formal French style of the gardens, originally executed in 1705 by Jean Trehet to Fischer von Erlach's design, there are also plenty of winding paths in the woods on the slopes to give a hint of wildness, the result of modifications made under Josef II's co-regency by Adriaen van Steckhoven and later Ferdinand Hetzendorf von Hohenberg. The latter was also responsible for the park's numerous architectural follies and features. Thanks to Josef II (see p.87), the Schlosspark was opened to the public as long ago as 1779.

## The lower park

The lower section of the Schlosspark is laid out in the formal French style, with closely cropped trees and yew hedges forming an intricate network of gravel paths. If you're approaching from the palace, however, the first thing that strikes you is the central axis of the **parterre**, decorated with carefully regimented flower-beds, leading to the Neptunbrunnen and, beyond, to the triumphal colonnaded arch of the Gloriette. Along the edges are just some of the park's tally of stone statues, more of which lie concealed in the lower section of the park.

The theatrical **Neptunbrunnen** (Neptune Fountain) itself, erected in 1781 at the foot of the hill rising up to the Gloriette, is by no means upstaged by its grand setting. In it, the eponymous sea god presides over a vast array of wild sea creatures and writhing Tritons and naiads attempting to break in their sea horses. Kneeling below Neptune, Thetis pleads with the sea god for calm seas to speed her son Achilles to Troy.

Hidden among the foliage to the east of the Neptunbrunnen are some of Hetzendorf's architectural follies. Particularly fine are the **Römische Ruine** (Roman Ruins), designed to tickle the imperial fancy of the Habsburgs and for use as a stage set for open-air concerts and theatre. The idea was that these were the remains of some Corinthian palace – they were, in fact, taken from the Schloss Neugebäude (see p.225) – whose fallen stones now provide a watery retreat for a couple of river gods. Close by the ruins is the outlet of the original **Schönerbrunnen**, a small grotto pavilion in which the nymph, Egeria, dispenses mineral water from a stone pitcher into a giant-scallop basin.

Further east still stands an **Obelisk**, smothered in hieroglyphs glorifying the Habsburgs, topped by an eagle and an orb, and supported at the base by four, originally gilded, long-suffering turtles. Below the obelisk is a giant cascade of grottos, and a pond inhabited by yet more river gods. Up the hill, past Schönbrunn's municipal swimming baths, stands the **Kleine Gloriette** hidden among the trees. The imperial family used to breakfast here in fine weather, but despite its name, it's nothing like its larger namesake, and not worth bothering with. The real reason to explore this heavily wooded part of the park is to feed the red squirrels, tits and nuthatches, which are all tame enough to eat out of your hand. Look out, too, for **woodpeckers**: Greater Spotted and Green woodpeckers are the most common, though you may be lucky and spot a Lesser Spotted, Middle Spotted or Grey-headed woodpecker.

## The Gloriette

If you do nothing else in the Schlosspark, you should make the effort to climb up the zigzag paths from the parterre to admire the triumphal **Gloriette**, and, of course, the view. Designed in Neoclassical style by Hetzendorf to celebrate the victory of the Habsburgs over the Prussians at the 1757 Battle of Kolín, the Gloriette stands at the focal point of the entire park, where Fischer von Erlach originally intended to build Schönbrunn itself. One eighteenth-century visitor found the whole thing a bit *de trop*, describing it as a "long portico kind of building, as ugly as possible". It's certainly an overblown affair, its central arch flanked by open colonnades of almost equal stature, and surmounted by trophies and an enormous eagle, wings outstretched; yet more colossal trophies, guarded by lions, stand at either end of the colonnades. The central trio of arches have been glazed to form a swanky **café**, from which – if you can get a window table – you can enjoy the view down to the palace. Alternatively, you can climb to the top of the colonnades to the **observation terrace** (daily: April–June & Sept 9am–6pm; July & Aug 9am–7pm; Oct 9am–5pm; €2) and take in the scene from there.

## Tiergarten (Zoo)

A substantial segment of the palace gardens is taken up by the **Tiergarten** (daily: Feb 9am–5pm; March & Oct 9am–5.30pm; April–Sept 9am–6.30pm; Nov–Jan 9am–4.30pm; €12; ⓦwww.zoovienna.at), which, originating in the royal menagerie founded by Franz Stephan back in 1752, is the world's oldest zoo. Here, the imperial couple would breakfast among the animals, in the octagonal pavilion designed for them by Jean-Nicholas Jadot, and decorated with frescoes by Guglielmi depicting Ovid's *Metamorphoses*. The pavilion has miraculously survived to this day – and is now a very pleasant café-restaurant – along with several of the original Baroque animal houses, making this one of the most aesthetically pleasing zoos any captive animal could hope for.

There are three **entrances** to the Tiergarten: the main entrance closest to Hietzing; the Neptunbrunnen entrance; and the Tirolergarten entrance up in the woods to the south. Once inside, you'll find all the usual attractions – elephants, tigers, lions, giraffes, zebras, penguins, camels, monkeys – plus a few less common inhabitants such as beavers, wolves, polar bears, otters and giant tortoises. A lot of money has been spent on the zoo, to great effect: the aquarium is state of the art with a wonderful walk-through tank, marmosets run round freely in the funky monkey-house and the rainforest glasshouse features tropical birds aplenty, plus fruit bats and terrapins. Those with small kids should head for the *Streichelzoo* (literally "stroking zoo"), where they can get a bit closer to the more benign animals.

The nicest feature of the zoo, by far, is the **Tirolergarten**, on whose woody slopes perches a large timber-framed farmhouse from the Tyrol. The original Tirolergarten was the dreamchild of the archduke Johann, younger brother of Franz II, who was fond of the Alps, and commissioned two Tyrolean houses and an alpine garden, in which the imperial family could dispense with the formalities of court life and "get back to nature". Sheep, cows and horses occupy the lower floors of the farm, while upstairs there's an exhibition on the history of the building. If you're short of provisions, or just a glutton, check out the traditional Tyrolese soup, bread, cheese and cold meats in the farmhouse kitchen/shop.

## Irrgarten and Labyrinth

Schönbrunn also boasts two mazes, known as the **Irrgarten and Labyrinth** (daily: April–Aug 9am–6pm; Sept & Oct 9am–5pm; Nov 10am–4pm; €2.90), situated adjacent to one another near the Neptunbrunnen. The **Irrgarten** – literally "Mad Garden" – is a conventional, head-height yew-hedge maze, based on the original that existed here from 1698 to 1892. While it's easy to get lost for some considerable time in the Irrgarten, the **Labyrinth** is only laid out with small knee-high yew and beech hedges. What the Labyrinth does have, however, are some fun stepping-stones, a glockenspiel grid, some zany mirrors and a mathematical teaser.

## Palmenhaus, Wüstenhaus and the Botanischer Garten

While its claim to be the largest greenhouse in the world, when it opened in 1882, may well be suspect, the Schönbrunn **Palmenhaus** (daily: May–Sept 9am–6pm; Oct–April 9.30am–5pm; €4) is certainly one of the most handsome, with its gracefully undulating wrought-iron frame. Inside, three climate-controlled rooms each have a glorious canopy of palm trees and lots of rhododendrons, lilies, hydrangeas and begonias to provide a splash of colour below. Next door, in the old Sonnenuhrhaus (Sundial House), completed in 1904, is the **Wüstenhaus** (daily: May–Sept 9am–6pm; Oct–April 9am–5pm; €4), a dry hothouse filled with cacti and inhabited by desert mammals, geckos, lizards and "peaceful doves". Schönbrunn also has a small **Botanischer Garten** of its own, established by Franz Stephan to the west of the Tiergarten, tucked away between the zoo and Maxing-strasse, and a beautiful place in which to escape the crowds.

# Hietzing

With the imperial family in residence at Schönbrunn for much of the summer, by the nineteenth century the neighbouring quarter of **Hietzing** – now Vienna's thirteenth district – had become a very fashionable suburb. Over the years, it has remained a favourite with Vienna's wealthier denizens, and today boasts some of the city's finest garden villas, ranging from the Biedermeier summer residences beloved of the nobility, to the Jugendstil and modernist villas favoured by the more successful artists and businessmen of late imperial Vienna. If you've a passing interest in architecture, you should check out the several villas within easy walking distance of Schönbrunn. The incumbents of the local cemetery also reflect the area's cachet, and include the likes of Gustav Klimt and Otto Wagner. In the far west of the district is the **Lainzer Tiergarten**, the former imperial hunting ground that is now a vast, woody retreat for the hoi polloi.

## Hofpavillon Hietzing

One sight in Hietzing which you should try to catch is the **Hofpavillon Hietzing** (Sun 10.30am–12.30pm; €2; Ⓦwww.wienmuseum.at), a one-off, Jugendstil pavilion built on the initiative of Otto Wagner in 1899 for the exclusive use of the imperial family and guests whenever they took the Stadtbahn (as the U-Bahn was then known). On the palace side of the gleaming white pavilion, Wagner provided a graceful wrought-iron canopy topped with miniature gilded crowns, underneath which the imperial carriage could shelter. At the centre of the building's rectangular ground-plan is an octagonal waiting-room, where, "in order to shorten the seconds spent waiting by the monarch with the sight of a work of art", Wagner commissioned a painting by Carl Moll, giving an eagle's-eye view of Vienna's Stadtbahn system. Wagner tried further to ingratiate himself with the emperor Franz-Josef by decorating the interior with patterns formed out of the Empress Elisabeth's favourite plant, the split-leaved philodendron. Despite all Wagner's best efforts, however, the pavilion was used precisely twice by the emperor, who had a pathological distrust of all things modern.

## Hietzinger Hauptstrasse

On the whole, Hietzing is just a sleepy little suburb now, with little to evoke the social whirl that was a feature of the place in the nineteenth century. The *Café Dommayer*, on the corner of **Hietzinger Hauptstrasse**, is one of the few social institutions of the period to have survived (see p.269). It was here that Johann Strauss the Younger gave his first public concert in 1844, with a programme that included six of his own waltzes and one of his father's. Round the corner from the café, the enormous *Parkhotel Schönbrunn*, built in 1907 for the emperor's personal guests, is another Hietzing landmark that's still going strong; the Kaiserstöckl, opposite, once the foreign minister's summer residence, is now the local post office.

# Friedhof Hietzing

The **Friedhof Hietzing** (daily: March, April, Sept & Oct 8am–5pm; May–Aug 8am–6pm; Nov–Feb 9am–4pm) can be a confusing place: not least because although it backs on to Schönbrunn's Schlosspark, the one and only entrance to the cemetery is on Maxingstrasse. And once you're inside, despite the map by the main gates, and the smallness of the graveyard, it's actually quite difficult to locate the tombs you want to see. Still, with perseverance, you should be able to find your way to Otto Wagner's rather pompous tomb from the early 1890s, designed by the architect himself, with some gloriously exuberant ironwork, but disappointingly devoid of even a hint of the Jugendstil motifs that became his later trademarks. Plans for a sarcophagus designed by Josef Hoffmann over Gustav Klimt's grave were never carried out, and a simple slab with gold lettering is all that marks the artist's resting place. Other notables buried here include Klimt's friend, the artist Kolo Moser; the Austro-fascist leader Engelbert Dollfuss, murdered by the Nazis in 1934; Franz Grillparzer, Austria's greatest nineteenth-century playwright; Katharina Schratt, Emperor Franz-Josef's mistress; and Alban Berg, the composer, who died in 1935 after an insect sting led to septicaemia.

# Hietzing's villas

A short stroll down Gloriettegasse immediately to the west of the Schlosspark gives a fair indication of the variety of architecture in Hietzing's villa-encrusted backstreets. Only fans of the international modern movement need continue their explorations further west to the Werkbundsiedlung; the rest can take tram #60 back to Hietzing U-Bahn, or continue west to the Lainzer Tiergarten.

## Gloriettegasse

Your first port of call should be the modest Biedermeier villa at Gloriettegasse 9, with its delicate window pediments of necking swans, where Franz-Josef's mistress, the Burgtheater actress **Katharina Schratt**, used to live. It was procured for Ms Schratt by the emperor himself, so that he could pop in for breakfast at around 7am, to enjoy a bit of intimacy before continuing with his paperwork. "Do not get up too early tomorrow morning, I beg of you," he would write to her, "Allow me to come and sit on your bed. You know that nothing gives me greater pleasure." Afterwards they would go for a stroll in Schönbrunn, where onlookers would applaud the happy couple, who would regularly feed the remains of their imperial breakfast to the bears in the Tiergarten.

Turning right down Wattmanngasse to no. 29 brings you to an interesting terraced apartment block embellished by Ernst Lichtblau in 1914 with bands of majolica between the windows, depicting various quasi-medieval figures holding fruits and flowers. Back on Gloriettegasse, at no. 21, stands the **Villa Schopp**, a wonderful Jugendstil house designed in 1902 by Friedrich Ohmann, set back from the street behind curvaceous wrought-iron railings, and flanked by hefty gateposts topped by big, black-capped lamps.

On the opposite side of the street, again set within its own grounds, is one of the most unusual of all Hietzing's villas, the **Villa Skywa-Primavesi**, at Gloriettegasse

14–16. Built in 1913–15 by Josef Hoffmann for the wealthy patrons of the Wiener Werkstätte, this is an almost obscenely large private house, designed in Neoclassical vein, with fluted pillars and huge triangular pediments. Nude miniatures perch on shelves at the tops of the pillars, while two larger figures recline in the pediments. Unfortunately, from the street, there's no way of seeing the bizarre, modern Teetempelchen (Little Tea Temple) Hoffmann built in the garden, complete with pergola and pond.

## Adolf Loos and the Werkbundsiedlung

"Loos swept clear the path before us. It was a Homeric cleansing: precise, philosophical, logical. He has influenced the architectural destiny of us all," Le Corbusier effused in the 1930s. The building authorities were less enthusiastic in 1912 when planning permission was sought for Adolf Loos's first Hietzing commission, **Haus Scheu**, at Larochegasse 3, on the other side of Lainzerstrasse from Gloriette-gasse. As with the infamous Loos Haus in the old town (see p.59), the architect's almost religious aversion to exterior ornament provoked a hostile reaction, as did the building's asymmetry, caused by the series of west-facing terraces that give the house its "stepped" look. Loos completed four other houses in Hietzing alone – Villa Strasser, Kupelwiesergasse 28; Villa Rufer, Schliessmanngasse 11; Haus Steiner, St-Veit-Gasse 10; and the "Wagonhaus" (covered-wagon house), Haus Horner, at Nothartgasse 7, with its barrel-shaped roof – though they're widely dispersed across the district. The main frustration, however, when visiting Loos's houses is that it was in his use of the open plan, and of in-built furniture, that Loos truly excelled – neither of which skills can be appreciated from his ornament-free exteriors.

A better bet for those in search of Bauhaus-style inspiration is to head for the **Werkbundsiedlung**, a model housing-estate of seventy houses, situated towards the west end of Veitingergasse, a short walk up Jagdschlossgasse from the terminus of tram #62. It was laid out between 1930 and 1932 by the Socialist city council for an exhibition of the Wiener Werkbund, an association for the advancement of industrial design, inspired by a similar housing-estate exhibition held at Stuttgart in 1927. Josef Frank was in overall control, inviting an international posse of modernists, including Adolf Loos and Josef Hoffmann, to take part. The emphasis was not on technical innovation, but on creating cheap, single-family houses using minimal space, Frank's "planned randomness" offering a more human alternative to the big housing projects of Red Vienna (see p.217). Fortunately, many of the houses are still owned by the council and were renovated in the 1980s, so the estate looks in pretty good shape. The most surprising thing about the whole project is how small the houses are, with miniature, winding roads to match. Within Werk-bundsiedlung, at Woinovichgasse 32 (designed by Frank himself), there's a small documentation centre with information on the estate.

## Egon Schiele in Hietzing

In 1912, the painter **Egon Schiele** rented a studio at Hietzinger Hauptstrasse 101, and, in between canvases, began flirting with the two respectable middle-class girls, Adele and Edith Harms, who lived opposite at no. 114. Edith and Schiele were ultimately married in 1915, and were expecting their first child when they were both killed in 1918 by the influenza that swept Europe following World War I, and which claimed more fatalities in Austria than had the war itself. Edith died first at their new studio flat at Wattmanngasse 6; Schiele succumbed three days later at his mother-in-law's house. Schiele is buried in the nearby **Friedhof Ober-St-Veit**, beneath a tombstone sculpted by the Hungarian Benjamin Ferenczy, commissioned by Schiele's friends on the tenth anniversary of his death.

# Lainzer Tiergarten

In the far west of Hietzing lies the former imperial hunting reserve of **Lainzer Tiergarten** (daily: April–Oct 8am–6.30pm or later; Oct–March 9am–5pm or later; free), enclosed within a 25km-long wall by Emperor Josef II. Since 1923, however, the reserve has been the wildest of Vienna's public parks. With virtually no traffic allowed within the park boundaries, and no formal gardens at all, this is the place to head for in the summer if you want to leave the urban sprawl far behind. It may not boast the views of Wienerwald, but you're more likely to spot wildlife here, including wild boar, mouflon, several species of woodpecker, and, most easily, red squirrels and deer; in addition, the famous Lipizzaner horses of the Spanische Reitschule spend their summer holidays in the park.

The main entrance is the **Lainzer Tor**, at the end of Hermesstrasse (tram #60 or #62 and bus #60B), where a **visitor centre** can help you get your bearings. The park's chief sight, the **Hermesvilla** (see below), is just ten minutes' walk from the Lainzer Tor. Those with more energy might aim for the **Hubertuswarte**, an 18m-high lookout tower at the top of Kaltbrundlberg (508m), beyond the Hermesvilla in the centre of the park. **Refreshments** are available in the Hermesvilla restaurant, and also from the *Rohrhaus* and the *Hirschgstemm*, both of which are signposted (with approximate walking times) from the Hermesvilla. Note that the St-Veiter Tor (tram #62 to terminus and then walk or hourly bus #55B), to the north of Lainzer Tor, is only open from mid-February to early November, and that in November and December, only the section of the park around the Hermesvilla is open to the public.

## Wien Museum Hermesvilla

In 1882, in an effort to ingratiate himself with his estranged wife, the emperor Franz-Josef decided to build Elisabeth an informal new residence, which she named **Hermesvilla** (Easter–Oct Tues–Sun 10am–6pm; Nov–Easter Fri–Sun 10am–4.30pm; €4; ⓦwww.wienmuseum.at) after her favourite Greek deity, the god of travel. Karl Hasenauer was employed to design the building, and Gustav Klimt and Hans Makart among those commissioned to decorate the interior; there was even a purpose-built exercise room in which the empress could indulge in her daily gymnastics. In the end, though, the villa failed to entice Elisabeth back to Vienna, and she stayed there only very occasionally. The house is now used to host exhibitions put on by the Wien Museum. Even if the particular show doesn't grab you, the well-preserved interior is rewarding in itself, though there's little general information on the Hermesvilla's imperial days, nor anything specific on Empress Elisabeth herself (for more on whom, see p.78).

Less of a villa and more of a mini-chateau, the Hermesvilla is a rather sickly mixture of Renaissance and Baroque, surrounded by outbuildings linked by a wonderful parade of wrought-iron colonnades. Inside, the decor has that heavy, slightly sterile, strangely unweathered look common to Historicist architecture. Downstairs, the **Dining Hall** serves up rich helpings of marble and stucco, but the best stuff is preserved upstairs. Elisabeth's **Gym** is suitably decorated in Pompeiian style, with muscle men and lusty satyrs engaging in feats of strength. The **Empress's Bedroom** is smothered floor-to-ceiling in one of Makart's sumptuous trompe l'oeil frescoes depicting Elisabeth's favourite Shakespearean text, *A Midsummer Night's Dream*, with Titania and Oberon in a chariot pulled by leopards. The four-poster bed, with its oppressive double-headed eagle over the headboard, would guarantee a disturbed night's sleep even in a more balanced individual than Elisabeth. The central chamber, the so-called **Kirchensaal**, is similarly overwrought, with gilded wood-panelling and a shallow oval dome.

# Further afield

The sights in this section are widely dispersed across the great swathe of suburbs that stretch away north of Hietzing to the Wienerwald. The first of the bunch, the **Technisches Museum**, is within easy walking distance of Schönbrunn, but the others require careful route-planning on the Viennese transport system. Of these, the most rewarding destination is the **Kirche am Steinhof**, Otto Wagner's Jugendstil masterpiece, high up on Baumgartner Höhe. Two more **Wagner villas** can be admired in the leafy surroundings of neighbouring Hütteldorf. There's a more brutalist piece of early modern architecture, the **Schmelzer Pfarrkirche**, by the spiritual godfather of postmodernism, Josep Plečnik, in the otherwise dour suburb of Ottakring. Further north still, in Pötzleinsdorf, the city's premier collection of Biedermeier furniture is housed in the peaceful **Geymüllerschlössel**.

## Technisches Museum

The **Technisches Museum** (Mon–Fri 9am–6pm, Sat & Sun 10am–6pm; €8.50; Ⓦwww.technischesmuseum.at), on the opposite side of Auer-Welsbach-Park from the main gates of Schönbrunn, was conceived in the last decade of Habsburg rule, and opened in 1918. The museum has since undergone a massive transformation and is now a truly innovative, hands-on place, with just about enough information to enable English speakers to enjoy the exhibits. With five floors to explore, you should leave yourself at least half a day to do the museum justice, and relax in the knowledge that the café on the ground floor is relatively good and inexpensive. Note that a few of the exhibits have timed showings, for which you must pay extra and book in advance.

The museum's main entrance is down in the basement, where you'll also find the **Nature and Knowledge** section. On the left, in Concepts and Consequences, you can learn about some basic scientific concepts from gravity to electromagnetics, while being entertained at the same time – don't miss the fog chamber at the far end. Also on this level is the interactive **Phenomena and Experiments** gallery, where, among other things, you can play at animation and doodle with a giant spirograph. Upstairs on the ground floor is the hangar-like Main Hall, with an early aeroplane and a satellite suspended above it. The **Heavy Industry** gallery, to one side, has a model of the giant steelworks set up by the Nazis in Linz, where the Basic Oxygen method of steel production first took place in 1952. The **Energy** gallery on the other side is a lot more fun, however, especially the giant, wind-up energy contraption by the entrance.

With the help of a Van de Graaff generator and a Tesla transformer, you can experience some hair-raising forms of energy in the **High Voltage Room**, one of the museum's highlights, on the first floor, for which you must book in advance (€2), as there is only one showing a day. When the museum was first built, a mock-up **Mine** was constructed in the basement; this has now been expanded to give an overview of mining over the last hundred years. Again, to visit the mine you need to book in advance (€2).

The special temporary exhibitions on the next floor up are always worth investigating. Also on this level is the **Musical Instruments** section – a good place to go for a breather, as you can sit down at one of the listening stations and hear some organ, piano or harpsichord music. Meanwhile, those with small kids should head for **das mini**, where 3-to-6-year-olds can romp around and have fun.

The **Transport** collection on the top floor is deservedly popular, boasting the oldest car in working order, dating back to 1875, plus other vintage vehicles by

Porsche, Benz, and Graf & Stift, and a whole load of old bicycles, motorbikes, model ships, trams and trains. Look out, too, for the Austrian lighthouse from the Dalmatian coast, and the small section from Sisi's (see p.78) personal railway carriage. Also on this floor is the **medien.welten** section, which concentrates on digital technology and its application in printing, photography and music – you can buy a **smart.card** (€2), which allows you to create your own "digital backpack", which you can then access via the Internet back at home. You can also book yourself into one of the twice-daily showings at the **Virtual Reality Theatre** (€2), where you don special glasses, brandish a lasar rod and enter a 3D wraparound virtual world.

# Kirche am Steinhof

Anyone with even a passing interest in Jugendstil architecture should make the effort to visit the **Kirche am Steinhof** (Sat 3–5pm; Mon–Fri by appointment ℡910 60-11 204; free), completed in 1907 by Otto Wagner as a chapel for the city's main psychiatric hospital. The church occupies a fantastic site on the commanding heights of the Baumgartner Höhe, looming over the hospital's grid-plan terraces below. In designing the building, Wagner clearly had the Karlskirche (see p.121) in the forefront of his mind: like the latter, the church is topped by a giant copper dome and lantern, both of which were originally gilded, and features two belfries capped with copper statues of seated saints; only Fischer von Erlach's columns are missing. Elements familiar from Wagner's other buildings are also evident, not least the marble veneer fixed onto the facade with copper bolts.

Inside, the church is deliberately organized on a north–south axis, rather than the usual east–west configuration, in order to allow more light to stream through the glorious mosaic windows, designed by Kolo Moser. Hygiene and safety were obviously a major concern: continuously running holy water in the fonts, no sharp edges to the pews, a raked floor to improve sightlines and facilitate cleaning, and special doors flanking the altar to allow hospital staff rapid access to the patients in emergencies. The interior decor is light and simple, focused very much on the main altar with its eye-catching, cage-like gilt baldachin, against a backdrop mosaic featuring Christ at the top of a Hollywood-style staircase crowded with sundry saints. Sadly, the church is little used nowadays; it's too cold for services during the winter, and even in summer there are few takers among the patients.

To get to the church, take bus #47A from Unter-St-Veit U-Bahn, but bear in mind that the bus runs only every fifteen minutes, and it's another good ten-minute hike up the hill through the hospital grounds to the church itself. Note that at 3pm, there's a **guided tour** – more of a dull monologue really – in German only (€4), but from 4pm you're free to wander around.

Close by, below the church in Pavillon V, a permanent exhibition commemorates those who suffered here during the war due to the hospital's shocking involvement in the **Nazi euthanasia** campaign (Wed–Fri 10am–noon & 1–5pm or by appointment ℡228 94 69-319; free; @www.gedenkstaettesteinhof.at). The museum tells the story of some of the thousands of patients who were put on transports to be gassed at Schloss Hartheim in Upper Austria, and the hundreds of (already ill) children who were experimented on at the hospital itself.

# Two Wagner villas

If you're fired with enthusiasm for Wagner's works, it's worth heading to the woody suburb of **Hütteldorf**, where two contrasting villas, built at either end of his career, stand side by side on Hüttelbergstrasse; to get there, take tram #49 to its terminus, after which it's a ten-minute walk beside the Halterbach stream.

**Villa Wagner I**, at no. 26, is an early work from 1888, designed in the style of a luxurious Palladian villa as the architect's very own out-of-town summer house. It's a grandiose building, typical of Wagner's Ringstrasse style, with a central Ionic portico flanked by two Doric pergolas. Badly damaged in World War II, the building was set to be destroyed by the council until, in 1968, a band of Austrian hippy artists, including Friedensreich Hundertwasser and Ernst Fuchs, protested by occupying the building. Fuchs, a purveyor of "fantasy-realism" from the *Judge Dredd* school of painting, eventually bought the property in 1972, and, since going into tax exile in Monaco, has turned it into the self-aggrandizing **Ernst-Fuchs Privatstiftung** (guided tours Mon–Fri 10am–4pm, Sat & Sun by appointment ☎914 8575; €11; ⓦwww.ernstfuchs-zentrum.com). Sadly, Wagner devotees come out of it worse than Fuchs fans. The latter can lap up his lurid nudes and admire the rock'n'roll decor; those hoping to see Wagner's work have to content themselves with the ceilings, and the north pergola, which retains its vegetal, Jugendstil windows added in 1900. The psychedelic touches on the exterior, such as the multicoloured cornice, are by Fuchs, though the wrought ironwork is original. Fuchs is, naturally, responsible for the huge fertility goddess with decorated mammaries that fronts the building, and has also added his very own Gaudí-, not to say gaudy, style Nymphaeum fountain-house in the garden.

Providing a perfect contrast to its neighbour is the cube-shaped **Villa Wagner II** (closed to the public), at no. 28, into which Wagner moved in 1913. It was to be his last work, and, with its austere, ornament-free facade, and its use of reinforced concrete and aluminium, conforms to his later conversion to rationalism and modernism. The exterior decoration is limited to a distinctive band of indigo-blue glass tiles alternating with aluminium bolts. Above the building's two entrances are the only other, gratuitous, decoration: the glass mosaic over the front door depicting Athene sporting her Gorgon's-head shield, and the series of colourful, mythological mosaics, which also feature under the side portico.

## Schmelzer Pfarrkirche

Don't be put off by the brutal, concrete classicism of its exterior: the **Schmelzer Pfarrkirche**, designed by the Slovene architect Josep Plečnik on Herbststrasse in 1913, is one of Vienna's hidden suburban gems. As the city's first-ever concrete church, it caused huge controversy, provoking Archduke Franz Ferdinand to pronounce it a ridiculous mixture "of a temple to Venus, a Russian bath, and a stable or hayloft". Despite such confusion, the main body of the church is surprisingly light and modern, while Otto Holub's Jugendstil high altar is simply outstanding. A dove flanked by two angels, all in aluminium low-relief, are framed against a semicircular golden sunburst, in turn set off against a "luxuriant gold and purple wall mosaic featuring the seven levitating attributes of the Holy Spirit, from *Frömigheit* (Piety) to *Gotesfurcht* (Fear of God)".

The church's *pièce de résistance*, however, is the concrete **crypt**, which you enter from stairs either side of the main altar; in order to see anything, you need to feed the light-meter. Several Jugendstil masterpieces brighten this gloomy underworld, with its low ceiling and trio of grottoes. On either side of the altar, murals feature Klimt-like celestial creatures: *Rachel Weeping for Her Dead Children* and *The Creation of Water*. Even more magical is the marble font, capped by a golden lid frothing with fish, out of which a heavenly figure rises up brandishing a cross.

# Geymüllerschlössel

In the first decade of the early nineteenth century, the wealthy banker Johann Heinrich von Geymüller had a luxury summer house – known today as the **Geymüllerschlössel** – built in the sleepy village (now city suburb) of Pötzleinsdorf. The Geymüllers were an archetypal wealthy Biedermeier family, *parvenu* business folk with bourgeois, artistic pretensions. Their house, so it was said, contained five grand pianos, one for each daughter; Franz Schubert and Franz Grillparzer were frequent visitors. It was at the Geymüllers' that Grillparzer fell in love with Katharina Fröhlich, a singer with "immense eyes, bottomless, really unfathomable"; they were engaged for a number of years, but in the end never married. Schubert, meanwhile, set one of Grillparzer's poems to music for a female quartet and alto solo, the serenade *Zögernd leise*, which was performed in the Geymüllers' garden one night as a surprise birthday treat for a friend of the family. Oddly, the house itself is no standard Biedermeier residence, but is, in fact, an exotic mixture of Gothic and Moorish elements executed by an unknown architect. It has the appeal of a garden folly, and the colour – white walls and green shutters – of an Italianate villa.

This building, so rich in Biedermeier associations, provides the best possible venue for the MAK's collection of **early nineteenth-century furniture**, and its temporary Biedermeier exhibitions, which are staged on the ground floor. Despite the limited opening hours (May–Nov Sun 11am–4pm; €7.90 includes admission to the MAK; Ⓦwww.mak.at), it's well worth the effort; to get there take tram #41 to its terminus. A beautiful cantilever staircase leads up to the suite of first-floor rooms, which house the **collection of clocks** bequeathed, along with the house in 1965, by Dr Franz Sobek, former director of the Austrian National Printing Works. The clocks – fascinating though they are – are a sideshow to the overall effect of the painstakingly restored **Biedermeier decor**. Though the term evokes a certain dull conventionality, the artistry of the period (1815–48) connects with contemporary tastes thanks to its subtle, almost minimalist, approach, and its emphasis on inlaid detail, sparing use of gilding, smooth, polished surfaces and trompe l'oeil. The most startling room is the **Salon mit Panoramatapete**, a drawing room equipped with period furniture made from ebony and gold and upholstered in deep blue, and dominated by the panoramic murals of idealized Oriental landscapes.

Given that the Geymüllerschlössel is something of a trek, it might be worth bringing a picnic to have in the house's extensive gardens; alternatively, you could pop across the road into the local *Heuriger*. Those with children might consider combining a trip out here with a visit to the nearby **Pötzleinsdorfer Schlosspark**, by the tram terminus, which has a big playground, red-squirrel-infested woods, and a small farm with hens, goats, sheep and guinea fowl.

# Döbling and the Wienerwald

Over the last century, **Döbling**, once a little village to the north of Vienna's *Linien-wall* or *Gürtel*, has gradually been subsumed into the city, and now gives its name to the vast nineteenth district which stretches right up into the **Wienerwald** or Vienna Woods. Though built-up in parts, the district is still peppered with vineyards and the remnants of several old villages, making it a unique mixture of city and countryside. Tourists and locals alike flock here in the summer to drink the local wine in one of the district's numerous *Heurigen*, or to get some fresh air during a walk in the hills.

Nearer town, there are a couple of places devoted to Beethoven, which draw a fair sprinkling of pilgrims, as does Vienna's most famous housing estate, which remains a symbol of both the success and failure of interwar "Red Vienna".

# Oberdöbling

Döbling itself used to be, in fact, two separate villages: Unterdöbling and **Oberdöbling**. These lay just outside the *Linienwall* (now the *Gürtel*), and were popular summer retreats for the wealthier denizens of Vienna in the days when they were surrounded by fields, gardens and vineyards. Nowadays, the two villages are mostly built up, and only dedicated Beethoven fans will get much out of the district's chief sight, the **Eroicahaus**. If you're here at the weekend, however, it's worth paying a visit to the nearby **Villa Wertheimstein**, a rambling, fin-de-siècle house that once attracted the city's literati to its door.

## Eroicahaus

In the summer of 1803, Beethoven took lodgings in a single-storey vintner's house – today's **Eroicahaus** (Fri 3–6pm and by appointment ☎505 87 47; €2; ⓦwww.wienmuseum.at), at Döblinger Hauptstrasse 92. Surrounded by gardens and vineyards, with a view across to Heiligenstadt, he grappled with the "heroic" concepts that would crystallize in his third symphony, the single most significant work of his entire life. Broadly speaking, until the emergence of this work, Beethoven was composing within the eighteenth-century tradition; with the third symphony, Beethoven entered the age of Romantic complexity.

The inspiration for the piece was clearly Napoleon, whom Beethoven hoped would liberate Europe from "bigotry, police control and Habsburg-worship", as one biographer put it. He intended to dedicate the work to Napoleon, but, shortly after completing it, received news that the former First Consul had crowned himself Emperor. Beethoven flew into a rage, tore up the dedication, and renamed the

## Theodor Herzl (1860–1904)

Along with fascism, psychoanalysis and atonal music, Vienna can also be said to be the birthplace of **Zionism**. The idea of a Jewish state in Palestine emerged slowly from the mid-nineteenth century onwards, and was eventually coined as a term in 1893 by Nathan Birnbaum. However, it wasn't until **Theodor Herzl** published his seminal *Der Judenstaat* (The Jewish State), in 1896, that the movement really took off. Herzl spent his childhood in Budapest, but lived in the Austrian capital on and off for much of his adult life. He was buried in the Jewish cemetery in Döbling until after World War II when he was disinterred and reburied in Jerusalem. Yet despite his beatification by the modern state of Israel, it's not at all clear what Herzl would have thought about his current place of rest.

His family, though Jewish residents of Budapest, were thoroughly assimilated, politically liberal and culturally German. While at Vienna's university studying law, Herzl himself was something of a dandy, "dark, slim, always elegantly clothed", according to one contemporary. His true ambition was to be a playwright, or at a push, "a member of the Prussian nobility". Having failed on both counts, he became, instead, Paris correspondent of the *Neue Freie Presse*. Herzl had experienced anti-Semitism in Vienna, but nothing prepared him for the bigotry aroused during the trial of the Jewish army officer, Alfred Dreyfus, in 1893–94. During this period, Herzl toyed with the idea of challenging Vienna's leading anti-Semites to a duel; his other, equally madcap scheme, was to lead the Jews of Vienna into the Stephansdom for a mass conversion to Roman Catholicism, with the approval of the pope.

Ironically enough, it was a performance of Wagner's *Tannhäuser* – in which the hero follows his heart rather than his head and returns to his spiritual homeland – that spurred Herzl into thinking about the creation of a new Jewish state, a utopian vision he later outlined in his most famous political pamphlet, *Der Judenstaat*. Yet Herzl's new state was more of a liberal utopia than a specifically Jewish one. The principal inducement for his fellow Jews was to be the new state's seven-hour day (one less than the Socialist International promised to deliver); to drive the point home the flag was to feature seven gold stars. Yet he was no revolutionary, decrying "That a highly conservative people, like the Jews, have always been driven into the ranks of revolutionaries, is the most lamentable feature in the tragedy of our race."

Initially, he proposed that the European powers grant the Jews sovereignty over a slice of their colonial territories. He tried, but failed to elicit the support of the likes of the Rothschilds; he even approached the tsar, the pope, the German kaiser and finally the Ottoman sultan, from whom he hoped to secure Palestine. Failing that, Herzl, unlike most of his followers, was prepared to accept a portion of Argentina or some central African colony. Despite his rejection by most wealthy, assimilated Jews, and by the Orthodox Jewry, Herzl's movement flourished, especially among the ghettos of Eastern Europe. At the first **World Zionist Congress** in Basel in 1897, Herzl was hailed "King of the Jews", and by the time of his death in 1904, the Zionist bank in London boasted 135,000 shareholders, the largest number financing any enterprise in the world.

symphony *Eroica*. In 1809, when Napoleon's artillery shelled Vienna, Beethoven hid under his kitchen table with a towel over his head, though this was probably less as a result of cowardice than in order to protect his poor hearing, which must have suffered terribly from the noise.

The rooms in which Beethoven lodged have been preserved, though the building's upper storey is a later addition. Despite the fact that the museum itself contains none of the composer's personal effects, you can get some idea of how the area looked in Beethoven's day from the contemporaneous maps and watercolours. All in all, notwithstanding the opportunity to listen to the *Eroica*, Beethoven fans would be better off visiting the composer's other memorial house in Heiligenstadt (see p.218).

## Villa Wertheimstein

Just up the street from the Eroicahaus, at the end of a driveway, is a much more enjoyable house-museum, the **Villa Wertheimstein** (Sat 3.30–6pm, Sun 10am–noon; closed July & Aug; free; ⓦwww.bezirksmuseum.at/doebling), which doubles as the local museum or Döblinger Bezirksmuseum. Built in the 1830s by the silk manufacturer and patron of the arts Rudolf Arthaber, it was bought in 1870 by the wealthy Jewish financier Leopold von Wertheimstein, who was manager of the Vienna branch of the Rothschild bank. While the latter spent most of his time in the family's town house, his young wife, Josephine, stayed at the Döbling villa, presiding over one of the most celebrated salons in Vienna, along with her only daughter, Franziska. The pianist Artur Rubinstein played there on more than one occasion, while more frequent visitors included the artist Hans Makart, the philosopher Franz Brentano, the poets Eduard Bauernfeld and Ferdinand Saar, and the writer Hugo Hoffmannsthal. When Franziska died in 1907, the villa and its contents were bequeathed to the city. The rooms given over to the local museum contain few surprises, but the three final rooms retain their hotchpotch decor from the salon's heyday, and contain, among other things, commemorative rooms for the two poets.

# Heiligenstadt

**Heiligenstadt** is typical of Vienna's outlying suburbs, a combination of barracks-like housing and remnants of the old wine-making village. It became a fashionable spa retreat for the Viennese from 1784 onwards, thanks to the discovery of a curative mineral spring. Nowadays, the easiest way to get there is on the U-Bahn, from which you get one of the best views there is of Friedensreich Hundertwasser's funky **Fernwärme Wien** (ⓦwww.fernwaermewien.at) in neighbouring Spittelau, his colourfully decorated paper-incineration plant from the late 1980s, which provides electricity for the surrounding district. Architecturally, it is, as one critic caustically dubbed it, merely "a painted shed", though it's certainly a lot more visually entertaining than most industrial plants, looking something like a psychedelic mosque. Guided tours – either technical or artistic – are possible by appointment on ⓣ313 26.

## Karl-Marx-Hof

If there is one housing complex that has come to symbolize the interwar municipal socialism of "Red Vienna", it is the **Karl-Marx-Hof**, the kilometre-long, peach-and-salmon-coloured "people's palace", whose distinctive giant archways greet you as you exit from Heiligenstadt U-Bahn. Though right-wing critics charged that these housing complexes were built as fortresses by the

## Red Vienna

The bloody history and colourful, monumental exterior of Karl-Marx-Hof have made it a potent symbol of **Red Vienna** (Rotes Wien), the city's Austro-marxist experiment in municipal socialism (1919–33). While other European socialist parties attempted piecemeal reforms, the Social Democratic Workers' Party (SDAP) developed a comprehensive **proletarian counterculture** which was intended to serve as an alternative to both bourgeois culture and the Bolshevik experiment in Russia. Cheap tickets to the theatre and opera were provided for the workers, and workers' symphony concerts were held under the baton of one of Schönberg's pupils, Anton Webern. Perhaps the most powerful display of working-class/SDAP power took place during the **International Worker Olympics** in 1931, when 100,000 people marched through the city to take part in a mass festival held in the Prater Stadion (see p.184), watched by countless more thousands.

Though one cannot but be impressed by the ambition and scope of the SDAP's social and cultural programme, a large section of the working class remained untouched by either initiative. Throughout, the SDAP remained controlled and led by an oligarchy of party elite, which held a patronizing and deeply paternalistic view of the rank and file, who, by and large, fulfilled a passive role in the whole process. The real achievements and failures of Red Vienna have become lost in the myths of time, but its legacy remains highly visible in the huge **housing complexes** that punctuate Vienna's outer suburbs. These workers' enclaves – purpose-built with communal laundries, bathhouses, kindergartens, libraries, meeting rooms, cooperative shops and health clinics – were designed to help create the "neue Menschen" of the Social-ist future. They may have failed in that lofty aim, but they continue to provide cheap and well-maintained housing for a populace who had, until then, been crowded into unsanitary tenements within the *Vorstädte*.

**Karl-Marx-Hof** may be the most famous of the Red Vienna housing complexes, but it is by no means the largest. Sandleiten-Hof and Friedrich-Engels-Hof are both larger; other biggies include Karl-Seitz-Hof and Raben-Hof. Though all are imposing, none are architecturally innovative, eschewing the modernist, avant-garde aesthetic of the interwar era for a more traditional, monumental architecture. If you're inter-ested, there are guided tours organized by the city council, or you can visit them off your own bat. After Karl-Marx-Hof, the most impressive architecturally are Reumann-Hof, 5, Margaretengürtel (tram #6 or #18), and Raben-Hof, 3, Rabengasse (Kardinal-Nagl-Platz U-Bahn).

socialists to protect their workers in case of civil war, their fragility was proved on February 12, 1934, when the World War I artillery of the Austro-fascist government reduced much of the Karl-Marx-Hof to rubble in a few hours. It took another four days for the government forces to flush the last defenders out, however. This is only the most famous of the battles of the civil war, which was fought just as keenly and bloodily in numerous other working-class housing estates in Vienna and other Austrian cities. Shortly after the battle, Edward VIII visited Vienna as Prince of Wales, and endeared himself to the Viennese socialists by asking to be taken to see the Karl-Marx-Hof – it would be difficult to think of a more unlikely political sympathizer.

### Hohe Warte

In the first decade of the twentieth century, the architect Josef Hoffmann built five houses in the fashionable **Hohe Warte**, the high ground above the village church of Heiligenstadt, at the terminus of tram #37. Hoffmann, a pupil of Otto Wagner, was one of the founders of the Secession and later of the Wiener

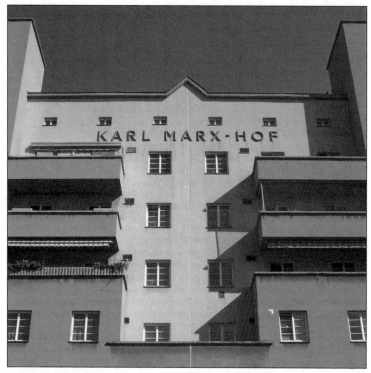

▲ Karl-Marx-Hof

Werkstätte (see p.129), but his architectural style, with its pared-down classicism and minimal decoration, is very much his own. The best-preserved of the houses is the ivy-strewn **Villa Spitzer**, Steinfeldgasse 4, an idiosyncratic mixture of the classical and the medieval, completed in 1902. The **Villa Ast** (now the Saudi Arabian embassy), at no. 2, completed nearly a decade later at the height of Hoffmann's classical period, provides an interesting contrast. Earliest of the villas, the **Villa Moser-Moll I**, a couple of semidetached houses built for his fellow Secession artists, Kolo Moser and Carl Moll, at no. 6 and no. 8 respectively, features decorative half-timbering similar to that of the Villa Spitzer. Carl Moll was, of course, the stepfather of Alma Mahler-Werfel (née Schindler), and it was to no. 8 that the composer Gustav Mahler went a-courting in the winter of 1901–02 (see box, p.114).

## Beethoven-Wohnung-Heiligenstadt

Beethoven moved out to the **Beethoven-Wohnung-Heiligenstadt** (Tues–Sun 10am–1pm & 2–6pm; €2; Ⓦwww.wienmuseum.at), Probusgasse 6, in 1802 on the advice of his doctor, who hoped the country air would improve his hearing. It was here he wrote his "Heiligenstadt Testament" – a facsimile of which is at the museum – addressed but never sent to his brothers. In it he apologizes for appearing "unfriendly, peevish, or even misanthropic", talks honestly about his deafness: "a sense which in me should be more perfectly developed than in other people", and the pain and embarrassment it brought him: "I was on the point of putting an end to my life – the only thing that held me back was my art." It reads like a will, though it was more of a confession, the cathartic soliloquy of someone who had reached rock bottom.

After the onset of his deafness, Beethoven kept a Conversation Book and a pencil with him at all times. He would offer the book and pencil to whomever he was trying to communicate with, though he himself rarely wrote in it, simply bellowing his replies to his companions. By the time of his death in 1827 there were four hundred "conversations", 136 of which have survived (and are kept in the Royal Library in Berlin). Despite his personal distress, while resident at Probusgasse Beethoven completed his joyful second symphony, "brought home right from the meadows of Heiligenstadt, so full is it of summer air and summer flowers" – a keen antidote to the simplistic theory of trying to fit the works to the composer's mood and life.

## Ludwig van Beethoven (1770–1827)

Born in 1770 in Bonn, **Ludwig van Beethoven** came to Vienna in 1787, but remained for just a few months owing to his mother's illness. Her death, and his father's subsequent death from alcoholism in 1792, freed Beethoven to return to the Austrian capital, where he lived until his own demise in 1827. Like Mozart, who was fourteen years his senior, he was taught by his father, a singer in the Hofkapelle, and played piano in public at a very early age (though his father used to pretend he was two years younger than he actually was). Again like Mozart, Beethoven was a virtuoso pianist, yet their techniques couldn't have been more different: Mozart gliding over the keys with smooth fluency, Beethoven raising his hands above his head, and smashing the keys with such force that he regularly broke the strings. Unlike both Haydn and Mozart, Beethoven was never a slave to the aristocracy, but an independent artist, whose patrons clubbed together to pay him an annuity just to keep him in Vienna, and prevent him having to take up the post of *Kapellmeister* at Westphalia which was offered him in 1809.

Though recognized as a genius by Viennese high society, he was also regarded as something of a freak: unprepossessing, scruffily dressed, reeking of body odour and swearing like a trooper. Despite such shortcomings, he was clearly attractive to women, and was, in his own words, "generally involved in one entanglement or the other". However, while the names of the women he was involved with are well known, no one can be sure that his love was ever consummated or even fully reciprocated. The objects of his affections were almost invariably young, beautiful, educated, aristocratic, and occasionally even married – in other words, unobtainable. One theory put forward as to why Beethoven never married is that he had syphilis, hence why he frequently changed doctors, and talked in his letters of "a malady which I cannot change and which brings me gradually nearer to death" – some suggest it may even have been the cause of his deafness.

In 1815, Beethoven's brother, Karl, died at the age of just 41. Beethoven then made the fateful decision to adopt his nephew, also named Karl, no doubt hoping that he would be the son the composer never had. After a long drawn-out custody battle with his sister-in-law, Beethoven succeeded in removing the boy from his mother in 1820, only to send him to boarding school. Beethoven proved totally unsuitable as a father, and Karl's misery reached such a pitch that in 1826, the 15-year-old tried unsuccessfully to shoot himself. He was immediately removed from Beethoven's care, at which the composer fell into despair, eventually dying of pneumonia in March 1827. His funeral, in contrast to Mozart's, attracted a crowd of twenty thousand to the Trinity Church of the Minorites on Alserstrasse, with Austria's chief poet, Franz Grillparzer, composing the funeral oration. Beethoven was buried in Währinger Friedhof, but now rests in the Zentralfriedhof (see p.222).

Beethoven changed addresses more times even than Mozart (see p.48), and spent a further four summers at various locations in Heiligenstadt. The house in Probusgasse is one of the best preserved of all Beethoven's many residences, and probably the most rewarding of the city's three memorial museums to the composer. The museum, on the far side of the shady, cobbled courtyard, occupies the rooms rented by Beethoven, and contains a lock of the composer's hair, his death mask, and the original doorhandle and lock from the Schwarzspanierhaus (now demolished), in which he died in 1827.

## Nussdorf and Grinzing

**Nussdorf** has less going for it than Heiligenstadt, though devotees of Otto Wagner might be persuaded to take a trip out here to see the architect's monumental **Nussdorfer Wehr- und Schleusenanlage** (weir and lock), completed in 1898 as part of Wagner's regulation of the Danube Canal. The most distinctive feature of the design are the pylons topped by a pair of fine bronze lions. Nussdorf's other claim to fame is that from 1932 the composer Franz Lehár lived in the small Baroque palace at Hackofergasse 18, previously home to the musical maestro Emanuel Schikaneder and now known as the **Lehár Schlössl**.

Further inland, up the slopes towards the Wienerwald, is the village of **Grinzing**, by far the most famous of the wine-making districts, whose *Heurigen* are mobbed by tour groups throughout the summer. To find a more authentic *Heuriger*, you're better off in any of the less-well-known neighbouring districts (see p.277), but fans of the composer Gustav Mahler (see p.114) might consider taking tram #38 to **Grinzinger Friedhof** (daily: May–Aug 7am–7pm; March, April, Sept & Oct 7am–6pm; Nov–Feb 8am–5pm). The composer was buried here in 1911, having converted to Catholicism earlier in his career in order to make himself more acceptable to the anti-Semitic Viennese establishment that ran the opera house. His modernist tombstone, designed by Josef Hoffmann, was commissioned by his widow, Alma Mahler-Werfel, who lies close by. Other notable corpses include the one-armed pianist Paul Wittgenstein (brother of philosopher Ludwig), and the writer Heimito von Doderer.

## Wienerwald

The forested hills of the **Wienerwald** (Vienna Woods) stretch from the northern tip of the city limits to the foothills of the Alps, away to the southwest. The peaks you can see to the north and west of Vienna are an uplifting sight – few other European capitals can boast such an impressive green belt on their doorstep. In the eighteenth century, the wealthier folk used to move out into the villages on the vine-clad slopes of the Wienerwald for the duration of the summer. With the arrival of public transport, even those without such means could just hop on a tram to the end of the line, and enjoy a day in the countryside. Even today, the Wienerwald remains a popular weekend jaunt, and throughout the summer, the wine gardens of the local *Heurigen* are filled not only with tour groups, pumped on the Wienerwald nostalgia industry, but also the Viennese themselves, who come here to sample the new wine.

### Kahlenberg, Leopoldsberg and around

One of the most popular places from which to admire the view over Vienna is **Kahlenberg** (484m), the higher of the two hills that rise to the north of Vienna, close by the Danube. There's a café, with a magnificent terrace and a viewing platform, but the whole place is literally mobbed at the weekend. According to

There are several ways of **approaching the Wienerwald**. Tram #38 deposits you in the centre of Grinzing. If you walk up Cobenzlgasse, turn right up Krapfenwaldgasse and then go straight on at the crossroads, up Mukenthalerweg, you'll find yourself on the right path to Kahlenberg. To avoid the worst of the crowds and the traffic, though, it's probably better to start walking from the terminus of tram #D in Nussdorf, following Beethovengang past the Beethoven memorial, then going up Kahlenberg- erstrasse. Either way, it's a good 3km uphill to Kahlenberg itself. The shortest, stiffest climb is from Kahlenbergerdorf S-Bahn station up Nasenweg, a kilometre-long path of tight switchbacks that takes you to the top of Leopoldsberg.

The lower reaches of the Wienerwald are no longer the rural idyll they once were, partly owing to the winding corniche, known as the Höhenstrasse, which was built in the 1930s, allowing traffic access to both Kahlenberg and Leopoldsberg. Bus #38A from Heiligenstadt U-Bahn will take you all the way to Kahlenberg, Cobenzl and (less frequently) Leopoldsberg. If you want to lose the traffic altogether, the best plan is to take the bus to one of the above places, and start walking from there. Although it is nice to bring your own picnic, all the above have several restaurants and cafés.

tradition, this was where the papal legate, Marco d'Aviano, and the Polish king, Jan Sobieski, celebrated Mass in 1683, before Sobieski led the Polish army down the mountain to relieve the city from the Turks. The Baroque **Josefskirche**, in which the event is supposed to have taken place, is now run by the Poles, and the church's Sobieski Chapel is a Polish national shrine. The most striking thing about the plain interior is the hundreds of rosaries, pendants, and lucky Madonna and Child talismans, which hang on the walls from floor to ceiling.

Tradition notwithstanding, it has been proved fairly conclusively that the aforementioned Mass actually took place on the neighbouring peak of **Leopoldsberg** (425m), just over 1km by road east of Kahlenberg. To confuse matters further, the two hills swapped names after the Leopoldskirche was built on what is now Leopoldsberg in 1693. This is certainly a more beguiling spot in which to relax and enjoy the view. There's a much more pleasant courtyard and café, shaded by pine trees, and a more dramatic view from the restored ramparts, originally built by the Babenbergs in 1135. The main lookout-point doubles as a memorial for the Austrian POWs who were finally allowed home from the Soviet Union in the 1950s. The church itself is also better looking than the one on Kahlenberg, and has a historical display of prints and documents relating to the Turkish siege.

If you're planning a longer walk in the woods, it probably makes more sense to get off bus #38A in the big car park at **Am Cobenzl**, which gives better access to some of the other peaks in this part of the Wienerwald. Cobenzl itself offers a variety of eating and drinking options, from the posh *Schlossrestaurant Cobenzl* to the more modest *Café Cobenzl*, both of which enjoy extensive views over Vienna. If you've got children with you, be sure to check out the wild boar penned up round the back of the *Schlossrestaurant*. A nicer spot for something to drink or eat is the *Oktogon*, a modern octagonal café, off the road, five minutes' walk to the west at Am Himmel. Behind the café is a musical tree-circle that's worth a quick look. From Cobenzl, it's around 3km via Bei der Kreuzeiche and Jägerkreuz to the lookout tower on **Hermannskogel** (542m). Alternatively, you can enjoy the view while walking downhill from Am Himmel or Am Cobenzl via the **Bellevuehöhe** (388m), where there's a plaque, erected in 1977 to commemorate Freud's discovery of the secret of dreams. At the bottom of the hill, you can catch bus #39A to Oberdöbling.

# Zentralfriedhof

In a city where some people still keep a separate savings account in order to ensure an appropriately lavish funeral, it comes as little surprise that the **Zentralfriedhof** (daily: March, April, Sept & Oct 7am–6pm; May–Aug 7am–7pm; Nov–Feb 8am–5pm) is one of the biggest cemeteries in Europe. Larger than the entire Innere Stadt, and with a much greater population – 2.5 million – than the whole city, it's so big it even has its own bus service to help mourners get about. It was opened in 1874, at the height of Viennese funereal fetishism, when having *eine schöne Leich* (a beautiful corpse) was something to aspire to. Today, it's still very much a working graveyard, and is particularly busy on Sundays and on religious holidays, most notably All Saints' Day (November 1), when thousands of Viennese make the trip out here and virtually every grave is left with a candle burning in remembrance.

## The Ehrengräber

Passing through the monumental Jugendstil **main gates** (2. Tor), designed by Max Hegele in 1905, you come to a semicircular sweep of red-brick arcades, which, though a little uncared for, contain some very elaborate tombs. The most extraordinary is in the first alcove on the left: a mock-up mine entrance guarded by lantern-wielding dwarves, commemorating the Austrian mining-magnate August Zang.

As you approach the central church, you pass through the main area of the so-called **Ehrengräber** (Tombs of Honour). In Gruppe 32A, to the left, facing the main avenue, you'll find the cemetery's most famous musicians. Centre stage is a memorial to Mozart, topped by a woman trying to stop a load of books from

## Visiting the cemetery

The quickest way to **reach the Zentralfriedhof** is on tram #6 or #71 from Simmering U-Bahn. Take note, however, that the cemetery has three separate tram stops on Simmeringer Hauptstrasse: the 1. Tor, the first stop, deposits you outside the old Jewish section; the second stop, the **2. Tor**, serves the main entrance; the third stop (and the terminus for tram #6) is the 3. Tor, close to the entrance to the Protestant section, and within easy walking distance of the new Jewish section. In addition to the tram stops on Simmeringer Hauptstrasse, there's an S-Bahn station, Zentralfriedhof, at the western edge of the cemetery, a short walk from the 11. Tor and 12. Tor; the station is on the S7 line to the airport, which calls at Wien-Nord, Wien-Mitte and Rennweg. The Rundkurs bus does a circuit of the graveyard every thirty minutes. There's an **information centre** (Mon–Fri 8am–2pm) in the building to the right of the 2. Tor, where you can buy a guide with a plan (in English) to the cemetery.

falling off. (He is, in fact, buried in St Marxer Friedhof; see p.162). Behind him, at a respectful distance, lie the graves of **Ludwig van Beethoven**, emblazoned with a busy gilded bee, and **Franz Schubert**, whose bust is about to receive the posthumous honour that eluded him during his lifetime in the shape of a garland. Beethoven and Schubert were disinterred from Währinger Friedhof in 1889, and reburied here – and fellow composer Anton Bruckner managed to get his hands on both composers' corpses during the operation, before being physically restrained by the officials present. Another composer reburied nearby is Maria Theresia's favourite, Christoph Willibald Gluck, who died in 1779 after refusing his doctor's orders that he drink no alcohol after dinner. Other composers to look out for include Johannes Brahms, Josef Lanner, Hugo Wolf, who died of syphilis in 1903, and the entire Strauss clan; Johann Jr's tomb, in particular, features a fine collection of musical cherubs.

The Ehrengräber on the opposite side of the main avenue, in Gruppe 14A, are the more eye-catching tombs of fin-de-siècle Vienna's wealthiest denizens. Few of the names mean much to non-Austrians, with the possible exception of Ringstrasse architect **Theophil Hansen** and artists Emil Jakob Schindler, father of Alma Mahler-Werfel, and **Hans Makart**, another victim of syphilis. Continuing towards the church, you come to a sort of sunken roundabout surrounded by shrubs; this is the illustrious **Präsidentergruft**, containing the remains of the presidents of the Second Republic, from **Dr Karl Renner**, the first postwar president to the former Nazi officer, Kurt Waldheim.

To the right of the presidents, in Gruppe 14C, are several other notable politicians, including the former chancellors Julius Raab and Leopold Figl; the architect **Josef Hoffmann** is also buried here. To the left of the presidents, in Gruppe 32C, you'll find more intriguing incumbents like the sculptor **Fritz Wotruba**, who lies under a self-designed tombstone. He also provided the highly appropriate cuboid tombstone for the atonal composer **Arnold Schönberg**, who died in Los Angeles in 1951. Adjacent to Schönberg, and more universally mourned by the Viennese, is **Bruno Kreisky**, the populist Austrian chancellor (1970–83). Nearby lie the graves of the writer **Franz Werfel**, the composer **Alexander Zemlinsky**, Schönberg's mentor, who died in exile in the USA in 1942, and the architect **Adolf Loos**, whose tomb is a typically ornament-free block of stone. Loos designed a similarly minimalist tombstone for his friend, the poet **Peter Altenberg**, who is buried in Gruppe O, by the wall to the left of the main gates. Those on the search for Austria's most famous pop star, Hans Hölzel – better known as "**Falco**", the man responsible for the hit *Rock Me Amadeus* – will find him buried in Gruppe 40.

## Dr Karl Lueger-Kirche and beyond

The focal point of the cemetery is the gargantuan Friedhofskirche or **Dr Karl Lueger-Kirche** (Mon–Sat 11am–3pm; free), completed by Max Hegele, a pupil of Otto Wagner, in 1910. Initially at least, this domed church resembles Wagner's Jugendstil Kirche am Steinhof (see p.211), but on closer inspection, it's clear that Hegele has taken a more austere Neoclassical approach. There are guided tours of the church on the first Sunday of the month after Mass (9.45am). The chief vault in the church is that of the anti-Semitic city mayor, Karl Lueger (see p.105).

Few tourists venture further than the Ehrengräber and the Friedhofskirche, but there are plenty of other points of interest, if you've got the legs for it. Directly behind the church a large **Soviet war cemetery** contains the graves of those who fell during the 1945 liberation of Vienna, centred on a statue of two Red Army soldiers, flags downcast, with patriotic quotes from Stalin around the plinth. Continuing down the central avenue, you come to Anton Hanak's despairing memorial to those who fell in **World War I**; behind it, in Gruppe 91, is a semicircular green field, its soft turf studded with small graves. To the southeast, in Gruppe 88, are the graves of Napoleonic troops who died during the 1809 French occupation of Vienna, the majority inscribed with the words "Français non identifié". More than seven thousand Austrians who died fighting in the Nazi Wehrmacht in **World War II** are commemorated by a field of black crosses to the southwest in Gruppe 97.

Those who died fighting for the freedom of their country from 1934 to 1945 have their own memorial – a big, heroic bronze man accompanied by two mourning women – at the giant intersection to the southeast of the Lueger-Kirche. Nearby are the uniform graves of those who died in the riot outside the Justitzpalast on July 15, 1927 (see p.109), and a memorial to war victims from the Czechoslovak section of the Austrian Communist Party. To the east, in Gruppe 28, the victims of the civil war of February 1934 (see p.315), those who died under the Austro-fascists, and martyrs of the Spanish Civil War, have their own memorial. Further east still, the **Social Democrats** have their own Ehrengräber featuring their early leaders, among them Otto Bauer, Viktor Adler, and the latter's brother, Friedrich Adler, who assassinated the prime minister Count Karl von Stürgkh in 1916 (see p.51). Opposite, the casualties of the 1848 revolution are commemorated by a simple obelisk.

Several non-Catholic denominations share the Zentralfriedhof: there's an **Evangelischer Friedhof** (Protestant Cemetery), accessible from 4. Tor, a growing Islamic section in Gruppe 26 and 36, and a small Russian Orthodox section around the onion-domed church in Gruppe 21, to the left of the main gates. In Gruppe 23, you'll also find the **Park der Ruhe und Kraft** (Park of Peace and Strength), a laudable attempt to address the spiritual needs of those who don't subscribe to an organized religion, with five symbolic areas to wander through, ranging from a stone circle to a labyrinth.

By far the largest non-Catholic sections, however, are the two Jewish cemeteries. The **Alter jüdischer Friedhof** (Old Jewish Cemetery), founded in 1863 and accessible from 1. Tor, was desecrated by the Nazis on *Kristallnacht*, though some 60,000 graves are still standing. Among those buried here are the Viennese branch of the Rothschild family and the playwright Arthur Schnitzler. The **Neuer jüdischer Friedhof** (New Jewish Cemetery), accessible from 5. Tor, on the other side of the Zentralfriedhof, was inaugurated in 1917, and, despite being damaged during *Kristallnacht*, still functions today. The sheer size of these two graveyards is a testament to the prewar magnitude of Vienna's Jewish community – testament also to the several generations systematically wiped out in the Holocaust.

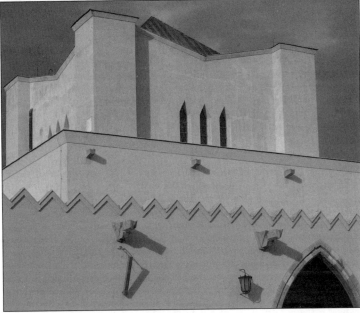
▲ The Krematorium

# The Krematorium and the Friedhof der Namenlosen

For the terminally obsessed, the city's **Krematorium** (hours as for Zentralfriedhof) is but a short stroll from the main gates (2. Tor) of the Zentralfriedhof; take the underpass to the other side of Simmeringer Hauptstrasse and walk in a northwesterly direction. The Roman Catholic Church forbids cremation, which was championed by the anticlerical Social Democrats between the wars as a secular alternative. The Viennese have never been entirely convinced by this ecologically sound form of burial, however, and less than twenty percent opt for it even today.

Nevertheless, the central complex of buildings is worth checking out, a startling work designed in the early 1920s by Clemens Holzmeister. The central courtyard, with its arcade of Gothic lancet arches, is the most impressive section, along with the zigzag roofline of the crematorium itself, all smothered in smooth, grey, rendered concrete. The crenellated perimeter walls of the crematorium date back to the **Schloss Neugebäude**, built as a magnificent Mannerist palace by the emperor Maximilian II. What remains of the palace can be seen at the far end of the Garden of Rest, behind the crematorium building.

Last, and probably least, is the **Friedhof der Namenlosen** (Cemetery of the Nameless Ones), to the east of the Zentralfriedhof at Alberner Hafen, containing the graves of the poor souls fished out of the Danube each year. Some of the corpses are later identified (and are therefore no longer "nameless"), but the majority are not, and the overriding feeling is one of melancholy. To get there, you have to study the timetable of bus #76A very carefully; it leaves from the terminus of tram #71, but only occasionally makes it as far as the cemetery – at other times, you'll have to alight at Sendnergasse and walk east down Mannswörtherstrasse.

# Out of the city

T
hanks to Austria's efficient public transport system, day-trips from Vienna are easy; the elegant spa town of **Baden** even has its own tram link with the capital. Though no longer the fashionable holiday retreat it once was, the town is still a good base from which to make a brief foray into the neighbouring Wienerwald (Vienna Woods; see p.220). Another possible day-trip is to **Eisenstadt**, a sleepy provincial town near the Hungarian border that's associated with the composer Josef Haydn, who worked for the Esterházy family most of his life, and is now buried in his very own mausoleum.

Heading up the River Danube is another popular way of day-tripping from the capital. The first place of interest is the glorious monastery of **Klosterneuburg**, barely beyond the northern limits of the city. Slightly further afield is the town of **Tulln**, birthplace of the artist Egon Schiele, and one of the stops for boats heading upriver from Vienna (see p.241). Of all Austrian towns on the Danube, though, there are few as beguiling as **Krems**, with its medieval counterpart, Stein. Beyond lies the **Wachau**, a tortuously winding stretch of the Danube where vine-bearing, ruin-encrusted hills roll down to the river on both sides. Marking the upstream end of the Wachau is **Melk**, arguably Austria's finest monastery, a stunning Baroque confection that towers over the town and river below.

# Baden bei Wien

Just 25km south of Vienna, the spa town of **BADEN** is an easy day-trip from the capital, accessible either by train or via its very own, much slower, tram link. This compact little town, peppered with attractive Neoclassical buildings, in varying shades of magnolia and ochre, comes across as deeply provincial, a haven of peace for its elderly spa patients. But back in the eighteenth and nineteenth centuries, Baden was *the* most fashionable spa town in the Habsburg Empire, the favourite summer holiday retreat of none other than the emperor Franz II (1792–1835). Baden's distinctive, uniform Biedermeier appearance is largely the result of a building frenzy – much of it under the direction of the architect Josef Kornhäusel – prompted by the devastating fire of 1812. A swim in Baden's **hot thermal baths** is still highly recommended and, as the town lies on the very edge of the Wienerwald, the walking and picnicking possibilities are a further enticement.

## The Town

The small, triangular **Hauptplatz**, at the centre of Baden's pedestrian zone, gives you an idea of the modest scale of the place. Almost dwarfing the surrounding buildings, including Kornhäusel's Neoclassical **Rathaus** from 1815, is the central plague column erected a hundred years earlier, and crowned with a gilded sunburst. Even the last of the Holy Roman emperors, Franz II, chose an unassuming three-storey building – now the **Kaiserhaus**, on the east side of the square – as his summer residence. The last of the Habsburgs, Emperor Karl I, also stayed here, during World War I, when Baden became the Austrian Army headquarters. (Baden later reached its nadir in the 1950s, when it was used as the Soviet Army headquarters.)

From 1804, Baden became a favourite retreat of Beethoven's, too; he made a total of fifteen visits, staying at various addresses, one of which, at nearby Rathausgasse 10, has been turned into the **Beethovenhaus** (Tues–Fri 4–6pm, Sat & Sun 10–noon & 4–6pm; €2). In the 1820s, the composer was well known around the spa as the local eccentric. As one friend recalls, "His hair was coarse and bristly … and when he put his hand through it, it remained standing in all directions which often looked comical." He even got himself arrested in the nearby town of Wiener Neustadt, after a local had been so frightened by his dishevelled appearance that she called the police. On being arrested, the composer said "I am Beethoven", to which the constable replied "You are a tramp, Beethoven doesn't look like that." Later that night the town's musical director was finally called out to identify him, and the mayor sent him back to Baden in the state coach.

Woefully, the three small rooms Beethoven rented contain no mementos of the composer's three sojourns here (there's even a section about later, lesser-known Badenites, including Katharina Schratt and Max Reinhardt, to pad things out). It was in these rooms that Beethoven wrote parts of his *Missa Solemnis* in 1821, and,

**BADEN BEI WIEN**

Lokalbahn

**RESTAURANTS & CAFÉS**

| | |
|---|---|
| Amterl | 2 |
| Central | 4 |
| Damals | 3 |
| Gasthaus zum Reichsapfel | 1 |

*Kaiser-Franz-Josef-Museum (500m)* ▲

▲ *Ruine Rauheneck (1km)*

0 — 400 m

N

Main Train Station

Beethoven-Tempel

Udinebrunnen

Stadttheater Pfarrkirche

Kaiserhaus

Kurhaus & Casino

Städtische Arena

Beethovenhaus Rathaus

Lokalbahn (Train Station)

Frauenbad

Römertherme

Sauerhof

Rollett-Museum

Schloss Weikersdorf

Thermalstrandbad

Doblhoffpark

Kurpark

Grüner Markt

## S&M in Baden

The staid spa town of Baden is the unlikely setting for *Venus im Pelze* (*Venus in Furs*), an account of sexual slavery written by **Count Leopold von Sacher-Masoch** (1836–95). The son of the chief of police in Lemberg (Lvov), the count was allegedly influenced by the brutality of the prisons he saw as a child. As an adult, he became professor of history at Graz University, and wrote several historical and folkloric novels. His renown today, however, rests on his affair in the 1860s with "Baroness Bogdanoff" (real name Fanny Pistor), to whom the count willingly signed away his freedom – becoming her manservant, taking the name of Gregor, and embarking upon "a liaison, marked materially by a prodigality in which furs and foreign travel were to be conspicuous". She agreed to wear furs "as often as possible, especially when in a cruel mood", while he agreed to "comply unreservedly with every one of her desires and commands". After six months of slavery, the two parted company, but the affair had inspired the count to write *Venus im Pelze*, which was published in 1870. In 1873, the count married Aurore Rümelin, who changed her name to Wanda in honour of the book's heroine. "Gregor" and Wanda became involved in a weird *ménage à trois* with a fake Polish countess, Anna von Kottowitz, who turned out to be a chemist's assistant.

We have the count to thank for the term **"sadomasochism"**, though he himself never coined the phrase. That was left to one of Freud's early mentors, Richard von Krafft-Ebing (1840–1902), who first used the term – with reference to Sacher-Masoch's numerous writings on the S&M theme – in his *Psychopathia Sexualis*, published in Latin in 1886 (and later translated into seven languages), about which the emperor Franz-Josef I once quipped, "It's about time someone brought out a decent book on Latin grammar." The same year, Sacher-Masoch split from Wanda, marrying his children's governess a year later. He died in 1895, depressed by the decline of his reputation and by Krafft-Ebing's use of his name to designate a sexual perversion.

two years later, finished his ninth symphony, though he had to get a friend to persuade the landlord to take him back on the promise of good conduct. The landlord agreed on condition that Beethoven pay for a set of new shutters (the previous set, on which the composer had made financial and musical calculations, had been sold by the landlord for a piece of gold).

### Kurpark

The focus of Baden the spa, as opposed to Baden the town, is the ochre-coloured *Kurhaus* (now a casino) and the *Sommerarena* (summer theatre) north of Hauptplatz by the **Kurpark**, which is laid out on the steep slopes of the Wienerwald. This is by far the nicest bit of Baden and the place to head for if you're intent on a spot of walking or picnicking, as the park's network of paths can quickly transport you high above the town. In its lowest reaches, closest to the town, the park is formally arranged around a bandstand and the **Udinebrunnen**, an eye-catching fountain featuring a gilded water-sprite emerging from a vast rockery replete with oversized frogs, serpents, fish and the sprite's giant stepfather. Higher up the park, various monuments emerge from the foliage: statues of Johann Strauss and his chief rival Josef Lanner, a temple to Mozart and, biggest of the bunch, the vine-garlanded **Beethoven-Tempel**, a Neoclassical rotunda from 1927, sporting some dubious underlit 1920s frescoes, but the best of all views across the spa.

For a more physically taxing walk, follow the signs to the offbeat **Kaiser Franz-Josef Museum** (April–Oct Tues–Sun 2–6pm; €2), roughly half an hour from the bandstand in a northwesterly direction. Although it advertises itself as a museum of folk art and craftwork, the collection is more eclectic than you might imagine. The reconstructed smithy is par for the course, but the

▲ Udinebrunnen, Baden bei Wien

mousetrap from the room in which Albrecht von Waldstein was murdered in 1634 is rather more unusual. In addition, there's a whole collection of arms and uniforms from the seventeenth to the twentieth centuries, banknotes, Habsburg memorabilia, a paper theatre, cake moulds, two penny farthings, and more.

## The Rollett-Museum and Doblhoffpark

An even more bizarre collection of exhibits fills the **Rollett-Museum** (daily except Tues 3–6pm; €2), ten minutes' walk southwest of Hauptplatz on Weikersdorferplatz. It's worth coming out here for the building alone, designed in extravagant neo-Renaissance style in 1905 as the town hall for Weikersdorf, only to become redundant seven years later when Weikersdorf was subsumed into Baden. The most fascinating section of the collection within is the array of skulls, busts, brains and death masks – plus a wax model of Marie Antoinette's hand, and a plaster cast of Goethe's – amassed by **Franz-Josef Gall** (1758–1828), the locally born founder of phrenology, a pseudoscience that claimed a person's talents or criminal traits could be traced to areas of the brain. The rest of the museum is a hotchpotch: some crystals, an Egyptian sarcophagus, and a cabinet of curios from the world tour of local nineteenth-century bigwig Josef von Doblhoff.

## The Mayerling tragedy

Mystery still surrounds the motives behind the suspected double suicide of **Crown Prince Rudolf** (1858–89), eldest son of the emperor Franz-Josef I and heir to the throne, and his half-Greek, 17-year-old mistress, Baroness **Maria Vetsera**. The tragedy took place in the early hours of the morning on January 29, 1889, at Rudolf's hunting lodge at Mayerling, 15km northwest of Baden. Subject of a ballet, several films and countless books, the event has captured the popular imagination for more than a hundred years. Even though Franz-Josef had the entire lodge demolished shortly after the incident, and a Carmelite nunnery erected in its place, folk still flock to the site, and as recently as 1988, an Austrian businessman confessed to having stolen Maria's coffin after becoming obsessed with Mayerling.

Numerous theories continue to be put forward as to why Rudolf chose to take his life. The Viennese, who love to sentimentalize the affair, tend to claim it was all for love, yet Rudolf was a notoriously fickle womanizer, and Maria Vetsera was just one in a long line of pretty mistresses. The plot thickens when we discover that the previous summer, Rudolf had proposed a suicide pact to another of his mistresses, **Mizzi Caspar**, who refused the offer. On the very night before his suicide, Rudolf spent the evening with Mizzi, before leaving to meet Maria at Mayerling. It's true that his marriage to **Princess Stephanie of Belgium** – arranged by his father for political reasons – was a dismal failure, but it wasn't enough to drive him to suicide, and certainly didn't prevent him from keeping bachelor digs at the Hofburg where he could receive his numerous mistresses. One plausible theory is that, at the beginning of 1887, he contracted a venereal disease which he believed to be incurable. Worse still, it's thought he had infected Stephanie, causing her to become infertile (having failed to provide a male heir to the throne).

Others contend that it was a **political** act, born of frustration with his lack of any part in the decision-making process of government. Franz-Josef allowed his son very little real power, and, in any case, disagreed with him on most issues. Rudolf, who was never close to his father, tended to mix with liberals opposed to his father's ministers' policies, and even wrote anonymous, critical articles for the liberal *Neues Wiener Tagblatt*. There were even rumours at the time that Rudolf had been assassinated by his political opponents, a version of events upheld by the empress Zita as recently as 1982. Another possible explanation is that Rudolf, having written to the pope to seek an annulment of his marriage, had been snubbed by the pontiff, who had returned the petition directly to Franz-Josef. We do know that on January 26, 1889, Rudolf and his father had a fierce argument – we shall never know what it was about.

Four days later, Rudolf's and Maria's bodies were discovered by Rudolf's hunting partner, Count Hoyos, who received no answer when he called in at **Mayerling**. The first official version of events was that Rudolf had died of apoplexy, but after the postmortem it was admitted that he had shot himself. As **suicides** were denied a Christian burial, the pathologists in charge were wise enough to suggest that "the act was committed in a moment of psychological unbalance", thus allowing the Catholic authorities an escape clause. Rudolf's request to be buried in the nearby village of Alland alongside his mistress was denied, and he was buried in the Kaisergruft amid much pomp and circumstance. Maria Vetsera's presence at Mayerling was never acknowledged by the Habsburgs, though rumours abounded. Some 36 hours after the incident, her fully clothed corpse, in the first stages of rigor mortis, was wedged upright in a carriage between her two uncles, transported to Heiligenkreuz and secretly buried in the cemetery there.

If you'd prefer something less mentally taxing, head for the vast, hot thermal **open-air swimming pool complex**, which hides behind the 1920s facade of the *Thermalstrandbad* on Helenenstrasse, or the ultramodern, stylish indoor pool, *Römertherme* (Ⓦwww.roemertherme.at), on Brusattiplatz, which is open daily until 10pm. After your dip, you can relax in the nearby **Doblhoffpark**, a lovely mix of formal gardens and English park, with a large rosarium, a pergola and a huge, bushy plane tree at the centre. To the north is the sixteenth-century **Schloss Weikersdorf**, seat of the Doblhoff family from 1741 until 1966 (it's now a hotel, but you should be able to sneak a look at the arcaded courtyard). Finally, if you've time to spare, check out the contemporary art in the low-slung, Neoclassical **Frauenbad** (Tues–Sun 10am–noon & 3–7pm) on Josefplatz.

## Practicalities

The quickest way to **get to Baden** is by train or S-Bahn from Vienna's Südbahnhof (every 30min; 20min) to Baden's main train station, ten minutes' walk southeast of the town centre. You could also jump on the special *Lokalbahn* trams – distinguishable from Vienna's other trams by their Prussian blue and cream livery – which run from the section of the Ringstrasse by the Staatsoper to Josefsplatz (every 15min; 1hr 10min). Baden's **tourist office** (May–Sept Mon–Sat 9am–6pm, Sun 9am–2pm; Oct–April Mon–Fri 9am–5pm; ☏02252/22600-600, Ⓦwww.baden.at) is attractively ensconced in the Leopoldsbad, a magnolia-coloured Biedermeier building on Brusattiplatz. The *Café Central*, on Hauptplatz (Ⓦwww.café-central.at; closed Mon), is a big, traditional *Kaffeehaus*, and a great place for watching life go by. For lunch, *Café Damals*, Rathausgasse 3 (closed Sat eve & Sun), offers reasonably priced **food**, but if the weather's fine, you're best off packing a picnic and heading into the woods. For something more substantial, the homely *Gasthaus zum Reichsapfel*, just east of the Pfarrkirche, down Spiegelgasse, offers a range of beers, traditional pub fare and good veggie options; the *Amterl*, at the top of Hauptplatz (Ⓦwww.amterl.at; closed Sun), serves nicely presented dishes, and has tables on the street.

# Eisenstadt

Some 50km southeast of Vienna, on the edge of a ridge of hills that slopes down gently to the Hungarian plain, **EISENSTADT** is known, above all, for its associations with the composer **Josef Haydn**, who was in the employ of the local bigwigs, the Esterházys, for most of his adult life. Haydn may be the main draw nowadays, but the town also has a well-preserved **Jewish ghetto** and an excellent Jewish museum. It also possesses a rather unusual history, having been Hungarian for much of its days, only becoming the capital of Burgenland by default in 1921, when the province changed hands from Hungary to Austria – all but for the old regional capital, Sopron (Ödenburg), which remained in Hungary.

## The Town

For a provincial capital – albeit of Austria's smallest *Land* – Eisenstadt is a tiny place, with a population of just twelve thousand and an old town made up of just three streets. **Domplatz**, the southernmost of the three, is open to traffic and used primarily as the local bus station; its fifteenth-century Domkirche was

**RESTAURANTS & CAFÉS**

| | |
|---|---|
| Esterházy Café | 1 |
| Haydnbräu | 3 |
| Silberfuchs | 2 |

**EISENSTADT**  0        200 m

only given cathedral status in 1960 and, apart from its gilded pulpit and organ, is nothing special. **Hauptstrasse**, the pedestrianized main street, is prettier, particularly the Rathaus, with its shapely Baroque gables, three oriel windows and lively folk paintings of the seven virtues, the Judgement of Solomon and several other biblical stories.

### Schloss Esterházy

Nothing about the town's modest little houses prepares you for the sheer scale of the **Schloss Esterházy** (April–Oct daily 8.30am–6pm; Nov–March Mon–Fri 9am–5pm; €6; Ⓦwww.schloss-esterhazy.at), which presides over Esterházyplatz, at the western end of Hauptstrasse. The Schloss was originally built as a medieval fortress with bulky corner towers, later received a Baroque conversion, and was finally redesigned in Neoclassical style (though you can't actually see the fancy, colonnaded north facade overlooking the gardens). The result is a strange, slightly heavy building, a sort of oversized French chateau, daubed in a fresh coat of imperial ochre-yellow paint with smart green shutters to match. Most of the rooms are now used as offices by the provincial government, but a few are open for guided tours; these are usually in German, so ask for the English notes from the ticket office.

There's a choice of guided tours, but the regular one (50min) will satiate most visitors. Whichever tour you take, you will get to see the only truly spectacular room, the **Haydnsaal**, its coved ceiling smothered with more than thirty colourful frescoes, its walls lined with painted roundels of Hungarian heroes. The acoustics are tremendous, and Haydn himself conducted numerous performances of his own music here. If you can catch a live **concert**, do (May–Oct weekly; Ⓦwww.haydnfestival .at) – it'll also save you having to endure the second half of the guided tour. This takes you round the **Esterházy-Ausstellung**, which contains Esterházy treasures, and traces the history of the family, who still own the Schloss, and who remain one of the wealthiest landowners in the country. At the end of this endurance test, you emerge in another fine concert hall, the **Empiresaal**, which takes its name from the Neoclassical, pastel green, blue and brown trompe l'oeil decor.

To get to the shady greenery of the **Schlosspark**, head down Glorietteallee; as well as the Neoclassical folly of the Leopoldinentempel, there's a vast Orangerie, now used as an exhibition space.

## Unterberg

A hundred metres or so west of the Schloss lies the old Jewish quarter of **Unterberg**, established as a walled ghetto back in medieval times, and for centuries home to a comparatively large Jewish population. All 446 of the town's Jews were deported to the camps shortly after the Anschluss in 1938, and today there are just two families left in Eisenstadt, though Unterberg has since been repopulated. The remarkable thing about the district, however, is that despite the human destruction that was wrought on the community, the ghetto itself – made up of five streets and two cemeteries to the north of Esterházystrasse – remains more or less physically intact. As you enter the ghetto's main street of Unterbergstrasse, you can even see one of the two stone piers, between which a chain was placed on the Jewish Sabbath (a practice continued right up until 1938).

## Österreichisches Jüdisches Museum

Further up Unterbergstrasse on the right, at no. 6, is the **Österreichisches Jüdisches Museum** (May–Oct Tues–Sun 10am–5pm; Nov–April Mon–Thurs 9am–4pm, Fri 9am–1pm; €3.70; ⓦwww.ojm.at), in the house that once belonged to Samson Wertheimer (1658–1724). Wertheimer was chief administrator of financial affairs to three successive Habsburg emperors, became the first rabbi of Eisenstadt, and was eventually appointed *Landesrabbiner* (Chief Rabbi) of the Hungarian Jewry in 1693 by Emperor Karl VI.

The museum stages temporary exhibitions on the ground floor, while the **permanent exhibition** on the first floor is a fairly standard rundown on Judaism, with a few models of Vienna's now-demolished synagogues and of Eisenstadt's old ghetto. Captions are in German, with the only English-language information in the museum's overpriced catalogue.

On the first floor is the **Wertheimer'sche Schul**, Wertheimer's private synagogue, built in the early eighteenth century, but whose current trompe l'oeil decor dates from the early nineteenth. It was one of the few in the Third Reich to survive *Kristallnacht*, perhaps because by then Eisenstadt had already been cleared of Jews, and was used in the decade after World War II by Jewish soldiers of the Red Army.

## Burgenländisches Landesmuseum

Another wealthy Jewish burgher's former home – the rather attractive house with the corner oriel at the junction of Unterbergstrasse and Museumgasse – has been converted into the **Landesmuseum** (Tues–Sat 9am–5pm, Sun 10am–5pm; €3; ⓦwww.burgenland.at/landesmuseum). As usual, there's no information in English, but the building itself is a lovely, rambling mansion, with a plant-filled rooftop loggia, and, in the cellar, a whole series of impressive Roman mosaics, the largest of which features Bellerophon killing the hybrid monster Chimera. The local history section on the first floor is particularly strong on the territorial dispute after World War I, with propaganda posters from the period depicting such subjects as Death in a Hungarian costume playing the fiddle over

Of the big three classical composers, **Josef Haydn** is seen as coming a poor third to Mozart and Beethoven, despite the fact that his music is in many ways just as radical as theirs. Part of the problem undoubtedly lies in the ordinariness of both Haydn's character and his life – during his lifetime he acquired the nickname "Papa Joe" for his generally amiable personality (notwithstanding his boorish behaviour towards his wife).

Haydn was born in 1732 to a master wheelwright in the Lower Austrian village of **Rohrau**. His father, who played the harp, recognized his son's musical talents, and at the age of 8, Josef joined the choir of the **Stephansdom** in Vienna, where he was a pupil for the next nine years. At this point, in 1749, Haydn's voice broke and he was kicked out of the choir, his little brother Michael becoming the new star pupil. Haydn then endured a difficult poverty-stricken decade as a freelance musician, which ended with his appointment in 1758 as music director for **Count von Morzin**, a rich Bohemian nobleman. Two years later Haydn made the biggest mistake of his life, as he later saw it, and married **Maria Keller**, the daughter of a hairdresser, with whom he could neither get on nor conceive children. She showed virtually no interest in his work, and is alleged to have used his manuscripts as pastry linings and curl papers.

More auspiciously, in 1761, Haydn was appointed assistant *Kapellmeister* to the **Esterházy family** at Eisenstadt. Haydn's patron, Prince Paul Anton Esterházy, was a keen music-lover – he even published his own songbook, *Harmonia Celestis* – but he died the following year. Luckily, he was succeeded by Prince Nikolaus (Miklós) "the Ostentatious", another music fan and a lavish entertainer. After a visit to Versailles in 1764, Prince Nikolaus decided to establish his own version of the French chateau on the other side of the Neusiedler See from Eisenstadt. Although equipped with a theatre, opera house and a marionette theatre, the palace – named **Esterháza** (Fertöd) – was intended only as a summer residence. In the end, however, it became a more or less permanent home for Prince Nikolaus and for Haydn, now the family's chief *Kapellmeister*, who was, in any case, glad of the chance to escape his wife and sleep with his mistress, the young Italian mezzo-soprano, Luigia Polzelli.

In 1790, Prince Nikolaus died; his successor, Anton, was less interested in music (and had less money). The family's court orchestra was disbanded, but as a sign of the family's respect for his loyalty, the Esterházys continued to pay Haydn's salary and allowed him to keep his title. He immediately moved to **Vienna**, embarked on two long tours of England, and enjoyed late but great acclaim, letting his hair down and earning himself a great deal of money at the same time. His final years were plagued by illness and he died during the second occupation of Vienna, in 1809 (see p.168).

Ödenburg. Finally, you shouldn't miss Franz Liszt's plushly furnished *Blauer Salon*, transferred here in its entirety from the Schottenhof in Vienna, where the Hungarian composer stayed on and off from 1869 to 1886.

### Haydn's Eisenstadt

The house Haydn bought in Eisenstadt, where he kept chickens, two horses and probably a cow, is now the **Haydnhaus** (Easter–Oct daily 9am–5pm; €3.50; ⓦwww.haydnhaus.at), on Josef-Haydn-Gasse. This was Haydn's home on and off from 1766 to 1788, though there's no attempt here to re-create his abode in any way. More evocative is the **Haydn-Kräutergarten** (May–Sept daily 9am–5pm; €3), the composer's "kitchen garden" complete with wooden summerhouse, situated east of the old town walls, on Bürgerspittalgasse.

A better way of paying your respects to Haydn is to head for the squat. Baroque **Bergkirche** (Palm Sunday to Oct daily 9am–noon & 1–5pm; also by appointment; €2.50; ☎02682/62638, ⓦwww.haydnkirche.at), which, as its name suggests, is located on raised ground 500m west of the Schloss, on the other side of Unterberg. The church interior is a trompe l'oeil fantasy in pinks and greys, but the reason most folk come is to visit the purpose-built **Haydn-Mausoleum**, erected by the Esterházys at the west end of the church in 1932 in order to receive Haydn's decapitated corpse. At the time, his head was still in Vienna's Gesellschaft der Musikfreunde, to which it had been bequeathed in 1895, having been stolen by one of Haydn's friends, a keen phrenologist, shortly after the composer's burial in 1809. Finally, in 1954, Haydn's head was reunited with his body, and the whole of Haydn now lies in the marble tomb mourned over by four lounging cherubs.

The Bergkirche's other star attraction (covered by the same ticket) is the **Kalvarienberg**, accessible from the eastern exterior of the church. Here, steps lead up to a small chapel, beside which a turnstile lets you into a labyrinth of mini-chapels begun in 1701, depicting the story of the Passion in theatrical tableaux of full-size statues. First, you enter a subterranean grotto, then you wind your way round the outside up to the Crucifixion tableau on top of the church (great views over Burgenland), and finally back down to the Entombment on the other side.

## Practicalities

You can catch a **train** to Eisenstadt from Vienna's Südbahnhof, though you'll have to change at some point; the journey takes just over an hour, with trains leaving every thirty minutes or so during the week, less frequently at weekends. Eisenstadt's **train station** is just ten minutes' walk southeast of the town centre, and you'll find the **tourist office** (April–Oct Mon–Fri 8am–5pm, Sat & Sun 9am–1pm; Nov–March Mon–Thurs 8am–4pm, Fri 8am–1pm; ☎02682/67390) in the east wing of the Schloss.

A nice place to **eat and drink** alfresco, and enjoy a view of the Schloss, is the smart, but reasonably priced *Esterházy Café* (ⓦwww.imesterhazy.at), directly opposite in the former stables and winter riding school, on Esterházy-Platz. Alternatively, *Silberfuchs*, near the Bergkirche on Kalvarienbergplatz, offers a good range of Austrian dishes and daily specials for around €6. Another good bet is the *Haydnbräu*, Pfarrgasse 22 (ⓦwww.haydnbraeu.at), a modern microbrewery where you can wash down your pub food with beer brewed on the premises.

# Klosterneuburg

Just north of the city limits, hidden from the capital by the hills of the Wiener-wald, the village of **KLOSTERNEUBURG** (ⓦwww.klosterneuburg.at) is one of the quickest and easiest day-trips from Vienna. Its chief attraction is its imposing Augustinian **monastery**, the oldest and richest in Austria, whose Baroque domes and neo-Gothic spires soar above the right bank of the Danube, but the village also has a private **modern art museum** hidden in its peripheral streets and filled with postwar Austrian art.

## The monastery

The **Stift Klosterneuburg** (daily 9am–6pm; ☎02243/411212, ⓦwww.stift-klosterneuburg.at) was founded in the twelfth century by the Babenberg duke Leopold III, who, so the story goes, vowed to build an abbey on the spot where he found his wife's veil, which had been carried off by the wind from a nearby castle. Leopold himself was canonized in 1485, and later became the patron saint of Austria, making Klosterneuburg a popular place of pilgrimage. Having withstood the Turkish siege of 1683, the monastery enjoyed a second golden age under Emperor Karl VI (1711–40), who planned a vast imperial palace here, along the lines of the Escorial in Spain. The project was never fully realized, but the one wing that was completed gives some idea of Karl's grandiose plans.

Of several tours on offer, the main two are the **Sacred Tour** (in German, daily hourly 10am–5pm; in English, Sat & Sun 2pm; €8), a guided tour that lets you see the Stiftskirche, the cloisters and the Verduner Altar, and the **Imperial Tour** (May–Oct wander-at-will daily 9am–6pm; Nov–April 30min guided tour, in German, by appointment, daily 12.15pm; €8), which allows visitors to explore the state rooms of the Residenztrakt. A **Kombiticket** for both costs €11.50.

The Sacred Tour starts with the **Stiftskirche**, which still hints at its origins as a Romanesque basilica, despite overzealous nineteenth-century restoration. Neo-Gothic finials and other details obscure the west front, but the south door, with its blind arcading, is still much as it would have been in the Babenbergs' day. Inside, the church is a riot of seventeenth-century early Baroque, replete with frescoes and mountains of stuccowork. The most impressive craftsmanship is in the chancel: the richly gilded choirstalls, exuberant high altar, and, above all, Johann Michael Rottmayr's *Assumption*, without doubt the pick of the frescoes.

To the north of the church are the **medieval cloisters**, built in the late thirteenth century. The central courtyard is encroached upon in the southwest corner by the little L-shaped Freisingerkapelle, containing the episcopal tomb of its namesake, who died in 1410. More intriguing is the polygonal wellhouse, which juts out into the courtyard from the eastern cloister, and boasts some fine tracery over the portal; the highlight is the magnificent, giant bronze candelabra, crafted in Verona in the twelfth century. The monastery's most outstanding treasure, however, is the **Verduner Altar**, in the Leopoldskapelle to the east of the cloisters. This stunning winged altar, completed in 1181 by Nikolaus of Verdun, is made up of more than fifty gilded enamel plaques, depicting biblical scenes from both testaments. Sadly, you can't get close enough to appreciate the detail, but the overall effect is dazzling. The top half of St Leopold is buried in the Wiener Werkstätte casket underneath the altar; his legs are beneath the nearby wrought-iron grille.

You can get some idea of the Spanish-bred Emperor Karl VI's big plans for Klosterneuburg on the **Imperial Tour** from the **Residenztrakt**, to the east of the medieval buildings. Plans were drawn up in 1730 for a vast imperial edifice, enclosing four inner courtyards, in deliberate imitation of El Escorial in Spain, which the Habsburgs had recently lost to the Bourbons. The building was to sprout numerous domes, which were to be capped by crowns, each one representing one of the Habsburg lands. In the end, the money ran out even before the completion of the first courtyard, and the roof sports just two domes, one capped with the imperial crown, the other with the archducal hat of Lower Austria. The showpiece of the Baroque wing is the **Marmorsaal** (Marble Hall), with its giant oval dome, supported by coupled composite columns, and decorated with frescoes by Daniel Gran glorifying the Habsburg dynasty.

It's also worth taking a stroll round the outlying monastic buildings, particularly those surrounding the **Leopoldhof**, a secluded little cobbled courtyard to the northwest of the monastery church, with an attractive, late-Gothic oriel window on one side. The main courtyard, Stiftsplatz, to the south of the church, centres on a lovely Gothic **Lichtssäule** (Lighted Column), once a common sight in Austrian towns, now a rare surviving example.

# Essl Museum

Klosterneuburg is also home to Austria's largest private art collection, the **Essl Museum** (Tues–Sun 10am–6pm, Wed until 9pm; €7, but free Wed 6–9pm; Ⓦsammlung-essl.at), a purpose-built gallery down by the Danube, to the south of the monastery. The collection features just about every renowned postwar Austrian artist, and has been accumulated over the last fifty years by Karlheinz and Agnes Essl, inheritors of the bauMax chain of DIY stores, which has its corporate headquarters in Klosterneuburg. Originally destined for the MuseumsQuartier in the heart of Vienna (see p.111), the collection found itself without a home after Ortner & Ortner's competition-winning entry for the complex ran into controversy and was eventually scaled down. The Essls responded by opening their own museum in a sort of concrete, modernist factory designed by Heinz Tesar.

The big white rooms on the first floor display a sort of overview of the collection, which is characterized by large abstract canvases, but ranges from Surrealist works by Maria Lassnig and "kaleidoscopic landscapes" by Friedrich Hundertwasser to works by the leading lights of Aktionismus, Vienna's very own, extremely violent version of 1960s performance art. In addition to the Austrian pieces, there are works by international contemporary artists such as Britain's Sean Scully and the American Nam June Paik. At least half the gallery space is given over to temporary exhibitions drawn from the collection. On the second floor, you'll find the **Grosser Saal**, with its distinctive floating, curved ceiling, and a café and bookshop.

A five-minute walk south beside the railway tracks from Essl Museum, the **Schömer-Haus** (Mon–Fri 10am–6pm, Sat & Sun 10am–1pm & 4–6pm; free) is another Tesar confection. Though primarily an office building, it doubles as an interesting space for events and installations. You're free to wander and appreciate the modern art dotted around the staircase that spirals through the atrium; a free audioguide is available at reception.

# Practicalities

The easiest way to get to Klosterneuburg is on **S-Bahn** line S40. If you already have a travelcard (see p.24), show it when buying your ticket. Trains depart from Franz-Josefs Bahnhof every half hour, taking just eight minutes to get to Klosterneuburg-Weidling (for the Essl Museum), and twelve minutes to

---

## Kafka in Kierling

While you're in the vicinity, you might be interested to know that the Prague-born writer **Franz Kafka** died of tuberculosis in Sanatorium Hoffmann (now converted into flats), in the nearby village of **Kierling** on June 3, 1924, at the age of 40. Devotees can catch bus #239 from outside the train station to Hauptstrasse 187, and visit the place in which he spent the last few weeks of his life, correcting proofs of his collection of short stories, later published as *The Hunger Artist*. The **Kafka-Gedenkraum** (by appointment ☎02243/444-323), on the second floor, is not, in fact, the very one in which he died, as that overlooked the garden and is currently occupied. To gain entry to the Gedenkraum, you must retrieve the key from Flat D along the corridor. Inside, there are photos of Dora Dyment, who nursed him in his sickness (along with Robert Klopstock, a Hungarian medical student), and whom he intended to marry, and of the old sanatorium, plus lots of books about (and by) Kafka.

get to Klosterneuburg-Kierling (for the monastery). To reach the Essl Museum, walk under the railway tracks and turn left, following the signs to the gallery. There's also a **free shuttle bus** to the museum (Tues–Sun every 2hr; 25min) that leaves from outside the Albertina. To get to the monastery from the train station, head up Hundskehle, and then take the steps to your left. To get to the monastery from the Essl Museum, cross back over the railway tracks and head up Leopoldstrasse.

If you're peckish, or have time to kill, it's worth checking out the *Stiftscafé* (daily 9am–6pm), on Rathausplatz, which offers reasonable **food**, and a chance to sample the local **wine**. The upper floor of the pricier *Stiftskeller* restaurant, next door, is open all day, though the *Keller* itself is only open in the evenings. A much more congenial place to have an evening meal, though, is the *Römerhof*, up the Stadtplatz, at the beginning of Kierlingerstrasse, which offers a range of beers on tap, all the usual pub snacks and a range of *Spätzle* dishes.

# Tulln

Another easy day-trip, slightly further up the river, is to the little town of **TULLN** (Ⓦwww.tulln.at), situated in the fertile Danube plain roughly 25km northwest of Vienna. The town has an ancient history, beginning its life as the Roman naval fort of Comagena, but its main claim to fame today is as the birthplace of the painter **Egon Schiele** (1890–1918), who was born above Tulln's main train station, where his father was stationmaster.

# The Town

On the hundredth anniversary of the artist's birth, Tulln finally honoured its most famous son by opening an **Egon Schiele-Museum** (April–Oct Tues–Sun 10am–noon & 1–5pm; €5; Ⓦegonschiele.museum.com) in the town's former prison by the banks of the River Danube. The ground floor is filled with reproductions of Schiele's works and photographs from his brief life. One of the original cells has been transformed to represent the Neulengbach prison cell in which the artist was incarcerated for 24 days in 1912. He was charged with displaying erotic drawings in a room open to children, and sentenced to three days in prison (by a judge who was himself a collector of pornography); since he had already served more than that in the course of his remand, he was immediately released. On the walls are reproductions of the watercolours he executed while imprisoned there, mostly angst-ridden self-portraits and interiors of his tiny cell.

The museum's modest collection of Schiele originals is displayed on the first floor. There's a goodly selection of pencil sketches, among them numerous nudes, a ghostly *Madonna and Child* in chalk and an early oil painting from 1908 of *Trieste Harbour*, a favourite destination of the artist, who, owing to his father's occupation, benefited from cheap train tickets. In the attic, you'll find one of the artist's sketchbooks and the energetic *Ruined Mill at Mühling*, painted in oil in 1916, when Schiele was employed as a clerk in a POW camp for Russian officers.

Despite its stylish modern premises, the **Tullner Museen** (March–Oct Tues–Sun 10am–6pm; €3), housed in the former Minorite (Franciscan) monastery, three blocks west down Albrechtsgasse, is a bit of a disappointment. You're better off taking a quick peek inside the adjacent Baroque **Minoritenkirche**, which has been lovingly restored and is positively gleaming with white Rococo stuccowork and colourful frescoes depicting, among other things, St John of Nepomuk being thrown to his death off Prague's Charles Bridge (also featured in gold relief on the pulpit). Be sure to peek through the glass door at the church's sacristry, with its cabinets of exquisite inlaid wood and Rococo ceiling decoration. At the west end of the church is the brick-built Loretokapelle, a mock-up of Mary's house in Nazareth, complete with obligatory Black Madonna and Child, surrounded by silver clouds, gold sunbeams and cherubs.

To the north, in the park by the banks of the Danube is the town's newest sight, the **Nibelungenbrunnen**, an enormous dancing fountain crowned with medieval figures acting out the meeting between Etzel (aka Attila the Hun) and Kriemhild (aka Gudrun), which took place in Tulln according to the epic poem, the *Nibelungenleid*. A short stroll east along the banks of the Danube, beyond the Schiele-Museum, stands the town's most impressive Roman remain, the bulky **Römerturm**. Built under the emperor Diocletian (284–305 AD), the old bastion was later used to store the town's precious salt supplies (and is sometimes still referred to as the Salzturm). If you're keen to learn more about Tulln's Roman history, head for the **Römermuseum** (April–Oct Tues–Sun 10am–noon & 1–5pm; €3), on Marc Aurel-Park, which houses the town's modest Roman finds, plus dioramas and a model of how Comagena might have looked.

Also worth a once-over is the **Pfarrkirche St Stephan**, two blocks east of the main square of Hauptplatz. Underneath this bulky Baroque church, the original Romanesque basilica can still be seen at ground level. Particularly fine is the west portal, which boasts thirteenth-century mug shots of the apostles. Best of all, though, is the old charnel house (*Karner*) to the east of the church, one of the best-preserved Romanesque buildings in Austria, dating back to 1250. The hexagonal rib vaulting looks clumsily restored, but the series of weird and

On most Sundays from mid-May to mid-September the DDSG or Donaudamfschif-fahrtsgesellschaft (Ⓦ www.ddsg-blue-danube.at) run a **boat trip** up the Danube from Vienna to Dürnstein. The boat leaves from Vienna's Reichsbrücke at 8.35am, calling at Tulln at 11.20am, Krems at 1.55pm. The DDSG boat back from Dürnstein calls in at Krems on the way back downstream at 5pm, reaching Tulln at 6.55pm, and arriving two hours later in Vienna. These times were correct when going to print; however, you should check with the local tourist office before setting out. Note that a boat launch in German is a *Schiffsstation*.

wonderful animals and beasts that decorate the walls, above the blind arcading, are fantastic, as are the devilish characters with outsized ears and noses that accompany them.

If you've time to kill while waiting for the train back to Vienna, you may as well visit **Egon Schieles Geburtszimmer** (by appointment ℡02272/64570; €1.45), occupying two rooms on the first floor of the main train station (Bahnhof Tulln), which has changed very little since Schiele's childhood. There's a reconstruction of the bedroom in which the artist was born in 1890, and a small model railway – understandably, trains were a major feature of Schiele's childhood, and a few of his early drawings of trains are reproduced here.

## Practicalities

Fast Regionalbahn **trains** run from Vienna's Franz-Josefs Bahnhof to Bahnhof Tulln, the main station, some fifteen minutes' walk southeast of the town centre (hourly; 25min). S40 S-Bahn trains take 45 minutes, but depart more frequently and terminate at Tulln-Stadt, less than five minutes' walk south of the centre. Tulln's **tourist office** (May–Sept Mon–Fri 9am–7pm, Sat & Sun 10am–7pm; Oct–April Mon–Fri 8am–3pm; ℡02272/67566), on the east side of Minoritenplatz, will furnish you with a free map and any other information you might need.

The best places for no-nonsense Austrian **food** are the *Albrechtsstuben*, Albrechts-gasse 24 (closed Sun eve & Mon), east of Minoritenplatz, and the down-to-earth *Ratsstüberl*, Hauptplatz 19 (closed Sun), with tables looking over the main square. If you're looking for food on a Sunday evening, the only place you're likely to find open is the *Lime* restaurant, Hauptplatz 5, which offers *crêpes* and baguettes as well as the usual fare.

# Krems an der Donau

Some 75km northwest of Vienna, **KREMS** (Ⓦ www.krems.info) sits prettily on the terraced, vine-clad slopes of the left bank of the Danube. Site of a twelfth-century Babenberg mint, Krems became a wealthy provincial wine-growing town during the thirteenth century. The architectural fruits of this boom period, which lasted until the seventeenth century, are clearly visible in the narrow streets of the Altstadt. Devastation in the Thirty Years' War, a shift in the trade routes, and a wane in traffic on the Danube led to a decline in building work during the Baroque period. Krems remains an important Danube port, but the

**KREMS AN DER DONAU**

STEIN

Filmgalerie

Donau-Universität

Grosser Passaurhof

STEINSPRENG

STEINER KELLERGASSE

STEINER KELLERGASSE

Frauenbergkirche

Mauthaus

HINTERE FAHR STRASSE

SCHÜRER-PLATZ

RATHAUS-PLATZ

Pfarrkirche

LUDWIG-V-KÖCHEL-PLATZ

Minoritenkirche

STEINER LANDSTRASSE

Salzstadl

Kremser Tor

Kunst-Halle-Krems

STEINER LÄNDSTRASSE

Karikaturmuseum

STEINER DONAULÄNDE

STEINER DONAULÄNDE

STEINER DONAULÄNDE

DR.-KARL-DORREK-STRASSE

KASERNSTRASSE

UNDSTRASSE

MEYERBECK STRASSE

REIFGASSE

N

Schiffsstation

TREPPELWEG

River Danube

**RESTAURANTS & CAFÉS**

| Jell | 2 |
|------|---|
| Stadtcafé | 1 |

foundation of a postgraduate university and the establishment of a thriving arts scene have added a much-needed dose of youthful culture to what is essentially a sedate, prosperous town.

## Krems Town

Present-day Krems is actually made up of three previously separate settlements: Krems, Und and Stein, giving rise to the side-splitting local joke, "Krems Und Stein sind drei Städte" ("Krems and Stein are three towns"). Most people tend to restrict their wandering to Krems proper, though it's worth taking the time to explore Stein too, since, in many ways, it's Stein that has most successfully retained its medieval character.

Krems' main thoroughfare, **Landstrasse**, three blocks north of the train station, is a busy, pedestrianized shopping street studded with old buildings. The finest of these is the **Bürgerspitalskirche**, originally built in 1470 on the site of the old Jewish ghetto as the town's hospital chapel. Over the doorway is the A.E.I.O.U. motto of Emperor Friedrich III (see p.45), while inside, the little church boasts some wonderful lierne vaulting. On the opposite side of the street stands the sixteenth-century **Rathaus**, whose Renaissance origins are only visible in the corner oriel window facing onto Kirchengasse. Further west along the main street, at Obere Landstrasse 10, it's worth peeping into the exquisite arcaded courtyard of **Fellnerhof**, which features Tuscan columns from 1618.

To the north of Landstrasse, the hilly cobbled streets and squares successfully preserve their late medieval character. The largest of the squares, Pfarrplatz, is dominated by the **Pfarrkirche**, originally a late Romanesque church, enlarged at the end of the seventeenth century – you can see this most clearly in the tower.

The interior is a perfect example of High Baroque drama, with trompe l'oeil masonry and gold covering just about everything, including the entire pulpit and the high altar: an explosion of gilded saints and cherubs set against the background of an enormous sunburst. The ceiling frescoes are by local-born Baroque artist Johann Martin Schmidt, known as "Kremser Schmidt", whose works can be found in churches and museums all over town.

A covered stairway known as the Piaristen Stiege, on the far side of Pfarrplatz, leads up to the imposing, late Gothic **Piaristenkirche**, whose tower doubled as the town's lookout post for many centuries. The church boasts some fine stellar vaulting, and several Baroque altarpieces by Kremser Schmidt, but it's worth the climb, above all, for the stupendous view across town. From here, you can descend via **Hoher Markt**, perhaps the prettiest of Krems' cobbled squares, which slopes down to the wonderfully scruffy-looking **Palais Gozzo**, a honey-coloured medieval palace with a ground-floor loggia. Round the corner, at Margarethenstrasse 5, the **Sgraffitohaus**, as its name suggests, is smothered in sixteenth-century sgraffito depicting medieval folk frolicking and feasting.

West of Pfarrplatz lies the town's **Weinstadt Museum** (March–Nov Tues 9am–6pm, Wed–Sun 1–6pm; €3), atmospherically located in the former Dominican monastery on Körnermarkt. Most of the museum amounts to little more than a mildly diverting trot through Krems' history and its viticulture. However, you do get the chance to look around the thirteenth-century monastery, whose cloisters feature unusual zigzag trefoil arcading, and whose church – now used for temporary exhibitions – is refreshingly free of Baroque clutter, and boasts the remnants of its original medieval frescoes. The museum also allows you the opportunity of a closer look at some of **Kremser Schmidt**'s artworks and sculptures. There's something dark and tortured about Schmidt's work that makes it compulsive viewing. Born in nearby Grafenwörth in 1718, he trained under local artisans and set up his own workshop in Krems, eschewing the cosmopolitan art scene of the capital. It's this attachment to provincial roots that sets his work apart from the more academic painters of the Austrian Baroque.

Landstrasse, and the old medieval town of Krems, officially terminate at the strangely hybrid **Steiner Tor**, a monstrously belfried fifteenth-century town gate, flanked by two cone-capped bastions. Appropriately enough, the district of **Und** links Krems, in the east, with Stein, to the west. There's no reason to pause in Und, unless you wish to visit the town's tourist office, housed in the former Capuchin monastery. And if you're keen to sample some of the region's **wines**, you can sign up for a wine-tasting tour of the monastery's cellars.

## Stein

It's the **Kremsor Tor**, ten minutes' walk west of the Steinertor, which, confusingly, signals the beginning of Stein. As you approach the gateway, it's difficult to miss the **Kunst-Halle-Krems** (Ⓦwww.kunsthalle.at), the town's vast new arts venue, which hosts major modern art exhibitions, stages shows in the nearby Minoritenkirche and puts on a whole series of events on Friday and Saturday evenings. It's also impossible to ignore the **Karikaturmuseum** (daily 10am–6pm; €9; Ⓦwww.karikaturmuseum.at), opposite, with its unruly zigzag roof. Designed by Gustav Peichl, an Austrian cartoonist whose alias is IRONIMUS, the museum puts on a rolling programme of exhibitions featuring caricatures, cartoons and other satirical visual media. A short distance north, up Dr Karl-Dorrek-Strasse, on the campus of Donau Univerisität, the **Filmgalerie** (Mon–Fri 2–6.30pm, Sat & Sun 11am–6.30pm; €8; Ⓦwww.filmgalerie.at) provides an interesting low-down on Austrian film. A combined ticket (€11) allows entrance to the Filmgalerie, Kunsthalle and Karikaturmuseum and is available at any of the three.

Stein itself is much quieter than Krems, and really does feel like a separate town, its narrow main street, **Steiner Landstrasse**, a sequence of crumbling old Renaissance facades with beautiful, often arcaded, courtyards, and every 100m or so, a small cobbled square that faces onto the Danube. The first church you come to is the impressive thirteenth-century shell of the **Minoritenkirche**, whose high-vaulted, late Romanesque interior was used as a tobacco warehouse, and which now stages exhibitions organized by the Kunst-Halle-Krems. At the southern end of Minoritenplatz the two sixteenth-century **Salzstädls** (salt barns) sport distinctive red-and-white quoins, characteristic of many of Stein's old buildings.

Further along Landstrasse, the Pfarrhof stands out owing to its rich Rococo stuccowork, followed shortly afterwards by the Gothic **Pfarrkirche**, which sports a classic Baroque onion dome and some finely carved choirstalls, but is otherwise fairly undistinguished. Steps round the east end of the church climb sharply to the fourteenth-century **Frauenbergkirche**, now a chapel to Austrian war dead. From here, you get a great view across Stein and the Danube to the onion domes of the hilltop monastery of Göttweig to the south. It's worth continuing a little further along Steiner Landstrasse to appreciate Stein's two other winsome squares, Rathausplatz and Schürerplatz, and its remarkable parade of Renaissance houses: in particular, the **Grosser Passauerhof**, with its half-moon battlements, and the **Mauthaus**, which boasts faded trompe l'oeil frescoes.

Kremser Schmidt lived in the prettily gabled Baroque house close by the squat **Linzer Tor**, which marks the western limit of the old town of Stein. If you're heading back to Krems, the backstreet of Hintere Fahrstrasse provides an alternative to Steiner Landstrasse.

## Practicalities

**Trains** to Krems leave from Vienna's Franz-Josefs Bahnhof (hourly; 1hr 5min). The town's **tourist office** is situated in the former Und monastery, halfway between Krems and Stein at Undstrasse 6 (May–Oct Mon–Fri 9am–6pm, Sat 11am–5pm, Sun 11am–4pm; Nov–April Mon–Fri 9am–5pm; ℡02732/82676). Without doubt, one of the best places to **eat** is at *Jell*, Hoher Markt 8–9 (closed Sat & Sun evenings & Mon), a seriously *gemütlich* rustic place, with imaginatively prepared food, and excellent wine from their own nearby vineyards. The *Stadtcafé*, on Südtirolerplatz, overlooking the Steiner Tor, is the town's most Viennese of cafés.

# Melk

Strategically situated at the western entrance to the Wachau, some 40km upstream from Krems, the town of **MELK** (ⓦwww.melk.gv.at) boasts by far the most spectacular Baroque **monastery** in Austria. Dramatically perched on a high granite bluff overlooking the Danube, the palatial mustard-yellow abbey dominates the landscape from whichever direction you approach, dwarfing the town into insignificance. Initially a Roman border-post and later a tenth-century Babenberg fortress, the site was handed to the Benedictines in 1089. Very little of the medieval structure survives, and what draws in a staggering half a million tourists a year is the flamboyant Baroque pile built in the first half of the eighteenth century.

# Stift Melk

Melk's early renown was based on its medieval scholarship (discussed in some detail in Umberto Eco's monastic detective story *The Name of the Rose*) and its possession of some very valuable relics, including the body of the Irish missionary St Koloman, who was revered for his powers of healing. The original **abbey** was gutted by fire during the Turkish invasion of 1683, and lay in ruins until Melk's ambitious abbot Bertold Dietmayr commissioned local architect Jakob Prandtauer to design a brand-new showpiece **monastery** (daily: mid-March to April & Oct daily 9am–4.30pm; May–Sept 9am–5.30pm; Nov to Easter guided tours only 11am & 2pm; €7.50; €1.70 extra with a guided tour; ⓦwww .stiftmelk.at). The project was so overblown that Dietmayr faced a rebellion by his own monks, dismayed by the affront to their asceticism, and the abbot had to prove that the monastery could afford the work before building could recommence. The abbey continues to function today, and its monastery school, containing some seven hundred boys and girls, remains one of Austria's most prestigious academic institutions.

Access to the monastery is via the main gates to the east. Tickets are available from the monastery's information point on the south side of the Torwartlhof (the first courtyard).

## The Kaisergang, Marmorsaal and Bibliothek

The **Kaisergang**, at the top of the Kaiserstiege, is a vast gallery – over 190m in length – designed to provide access to the 88 imperial chambers, some of which now house the abbey **museum**. Unfortunately, the abbey's most precious trio of artefacts is kept in the treasury, and they only come out on display on October 13 (St Koloman's Day): the Melker Kreuz, a fourteenth-century cross containing a piece of Christ's cross, studded with aquamarines, pearls and gems; the eleventh-century portable altar of Swanhild, portraying the life of Christ in walrus horn; and a thirteenth-century reliquary of the lower jaw and tooth of St Koloman. Nevertheless, the museum owns a good crop of medieval reliquaries on permanent display, including a striking example that once contained St Agnes's head. Another work of art you can be sure of seeing is the medieval monastery's winged altarpiece from around 1502 by Jörg Breu the Elder, one of the "Danube School" of artists, which included Lucas Cranach the Elder and Albrecht Dürer. The altar panels tell the story of Christ, employing the exaggerated facial expressions that were one of the hallmarks of the Danube School.

The rest of the abbey museum, which is basically a propaganda exercise by the monastery and its school, can be happily passed over in order to reach the two rooms by Prandtauer that make a visit to Melk worth the effort. The first is the red and grey **Marmorsaal** (Marble Hall), featuring Paul Troger's superb fresco depicting the Enlightenment. Troger specialized in fresco paintings, and his masterly handling of perspective makes the ceiling appear much higher than it really is. Despite its name, the only furnishings in the hall made from real marble are the doorframes. To get to Prandtauer's **Bibliothek** (Library), you must first take a stroll outside across the curvaceous terrace, from whose balcony you can admire the town below and the Danube in the distance. The library's ancient tomes – re-bound in matching eighteenth-century leather and gold leaf – are stacked up to the ceiling in beautifully carved shelves of aspen, walnut and oak. Despite having never been restored, Troger's colourful fresco – a cherub-infested allegory on Faith – has kept its original hue, thanks to the library's lack of lighting and heating. From the library, you descend a cantilevered spiral staircase to the Stiftskirche.

## Stiftskirche

The **Stiftskirche**, designed by Jakob Prandtauer in 1702 and completed in 1738 after his death, occupies centre stage at Melk, dominating the monastery complex with its fanciful symmetrical towers and octagonal dome. From the balconies above the side altars to the acanthus-leaf capitals of the church's fluted pilasters, the red stucco interior literally drips with gold paint. The Galli da Bibiena family of Italian theatrical designers are responsible for the stunning all-gold pulpit, and the design of the awesome high altar with its gilded papal crown suspended above the church's patron saints, Peter and Paul. The airy frescoes and side-altar paintings are mostly by Johann Michael Rottmayr, who, along with Troger, was responsible for importing High Baroque art to Austria from Italy.

It's impossible not to notice the grisly reliquaries in the church's side-altars, some of them featuring skeletons reposing in glittering garments. The most hallowed bones, those of St Koloman (presumably not including his jaw) are hidden away from the public gaze inside the sarcophagus in the north transept. Beyond this lies the entrance to the **Babenbergergruft**, where the remains of Babenberg rulers were traditionally thought to have been buried. In 1969, however, the remains were exhumed and examined, after which it was concluded that only Adalbert (1018–55), Ernst (1055–75) and possibly Heinrich I (994–1018) were actually interred here.

## Stiftspark

Tickets for the monastery also cover entry to the **Stiftspark** (May–Oct daily 9am–6pm; €3), which was laid out to the east of the abbey from 1750 onwards. The western section is more formal and open, and overlooked by the Baroque Gartenpavillon – now a café – built for the monks' recreation and decorated with frescoes of exotic bucolic scenes by Johann Wenzel Bergl. To the east lies the more wooded area, perfect for a picnic, and dotted with pavilions that play music, and talking stones that quote the Bible at you.

## The Altstadt

Melk's **Altstadt** is hardly much bigger than the monastery, and, inevitably, with such enormous numbers of tourists passing through, it does suffer from overcrowding in the summer. However, there are a few good-looking houses that repay a stroll around the town. Pretty painted shutters adorn the chemist's, next door to the Rathaus, and there are a couple of dinky turrets on the old bakery at the corner of Sterngasse, but the single most attractive building is the **Altes Posthaus**, built in 1792 at Linzerstrasse 3–5. The facade features stucco reliefs of horses' heads, agricultural tools, an eagle holding a post horn in its beak and so on, while the roof balustrade is peppered with urns spouting golden cacti, and, as its centrepiece, a double-headed crowned eagle. For a glimpse of old Melk that few tourists get to see, seek out the vine-covered **Haus am Stein**, set back in its own courtyard behind Kremserstrasse.

# Practicalities

The easiest way to reach Melk is by **train** from Vienna's Westbahnhof – there's a service every hour and the journey takes an hour and a quarter. Melk's **train station** is at the head of Bahnhofstrasse, which leads directly into the Altstadt. The **tourist office** is on Abbe-Stadler-Gasse (April & Oct Mon–Fri 9am–noon & 2–6pm, Sat 10am–noon; May–Sept Mon–Fri 9am–noon & 2–6pm, Sat & Sun 10am–noon & 4–6pm; ☎02752/5230 410). The plush *Hotel Stadt Melk*, Hauptplatz 1, has the town's finest **restaurant**; other places to eat include the family-run *Zum Fürsten*, next door at no. 3 (closed Wed), or the vast daytime *Stiftsrestaurant* (closed Feb) up near the abbey car park.

# Listings

# Listings

# Accommodation

As you might expect, Vienna has some of the most opulent, historic **hotels** in Europe, with mesospheric prices to match. However, reasonably priced, central accommodation can be found, especially in the numerous **pensions**. These are not necessarily inferior in quality or price to hotels – in fact some are a whole lot better. The distinction is purely technical: pensions occupy one or more floors, but not the whole, of a building; to be a hotel, the entire block must be occupied.

Vienna also has plenty of **hostels**, although these can be booked up months in advance, so try to ring ahead or email and make a reservation before you leave. **Private rooms** are another option, and inveterate **campers** have a wide choice of peripheral sites.

The **high season** for accommodation in Vienna is from April to October, and for the two weeks over Christmas and New Year (during which period there is sometimes a surcharge). Bear in mind also that it can be difficult to find a room on spec during the week running up to Lent, when *Fasching* reaches its climax (see p.29). That said, some hotels drop their rates in July and August, as the opera houses and theatres are all on vacation during this period. (The room price should, by law, be displayed in your room.) If you arrive without a booking, any of the **tourist offices** mentioned on p.36 can make a reservation for you, for which they charge a small fee.

## Hostels, student rooms and camping

Vienna's official **Hostelling International** *Jugendherbergen* or *Jugendgästehäuser* (youth hostels) are efficient, clean and, occasionally, even friendly. However, with just one exception, they are all a long way from the centre. Most of the beds are in segregated dorms, but the majority of places do now have bunk-bed doubles and many have en-suite facilities. Prices vary, but are usually around €15–20 a night

---

### Accommodation websites

You can book accommodation for free **online** at Ⓦ www.wien.info; payment is made directly to the hotel on checking out.

Other useful websites include Ⓦ www.lastminute.com, Ⓦ www.booking.com, Ⓦ www.eviennahotels.com and Ⓦ www.laterooms.com, which has great deals if you book right at the last moment. At Ⓦ www.hostelz.com you'll find reviews of Vienna **hostels** with star ratings, while Ⓦ www.couchsurfing.com puts travellers in touch with people to stay or hang out with.

# VIENNA ACCOMMODATION

0 — 500 m

① ② & ③   Schuberts Geburtshaus   ④

**ALSERGRUND**
9

Josephinum

Freud-museum

Rossauer Kaserne

Ringturm

Universität

Votivkirche

Börse

Schottentor

Universität

Schottenstift

**INNERE STADT**
1

CONCORDIA-PLATZ

⑬

FREYUNG

AM HOF

Rathaus

Rathaus

Burgtheater

Palais Ferstel

Kirche am Hof

Peterskirche

Minoriten-kirche

**JOSEFSTADT**
8

㉔

Michaeler-kirche

㉖

Herrengasse

⑯

Volksgarten

㉗

Parlament

Justizpalast

HELDEN-PLATZ

Hofburg

JOSEFS-PLATZ

Kaisergruft

㉜   ㉝

Lerchenfelder Strasse

NEUER MARKT

㉙

Naturhistorisches Museum

MARIA-THERESIEN-PLATZ

Volkstheater

Burggarten

ⓘ ㊴

Volkstheater

Burggarten

㊷

㊲

㊳

Kunsthistorisches Museum

Staatsoper

Museums-Quartier

OPERNRING

㊹

**SPITTELBERG**

Babenberger-strasse

Schillerplatz

Akademie der bildenden Künste

㊺

**NEUBAU**
7

㊼

Neubaugasse

㊽

Secession

Karlsplatz

㊾

**MARIAHIF**
6

Theater-an-der-Wien

Majolika-haus

Naschmarkt

㉒

Flackturm

Kettenbrücken-gasse

Third Man Museum

㊳

㊴

**WIEDEN**
4

⑤⑤

⑤⑦   ⑤⑤   ⑤⑨

N

⑥⑩ & Schönbrunn   Schönbrunn   ⑥①

**ACCOMMODATION**

| | | | | |
|---|---|---|---|---|
| Academia | 29 | Kolpingfamilie | | |
| Accordia | 8 | Jugendgästehaus | 60 |
| Altstadt Vienna | 38 | König von Ungarn | 28 |
| Am Schubertring | 46 | Kraml | 59 |
| Am Stephansplatz | 25 | Kugel | 45 |
| Anna | 49 | Landhaus Fuhrgassl-Huber | 3 |
| Art Hotel Vienna | 61 | Lerner | 14 |
| Astoria | 39 | Levante Parliament | 27 |
| Astra | 9 | Lindenhof | 47 |
| Atlanta | 1 | Mailbergerhof | 40 |
| Austria | 21 | Neuer Markt | 34 |
| Austria Classic | 7 | Nossek | 24 |
| Aviano | 36 | Orient | 13 |
| Bosch | 62 | Palais Coburg | 35 |
| Bristol | 44 | Pertschy | 26 |
| Carlton Opera | 54 | Post | 32 |
| City | 20 | Rathaus | 22 |
| Das Triest | 53 | Roomz Vienna | 51 |
| Das Tyrol | 48 | Ruthensteiner | 56 |
| Deutschmeister | 4 | Sacher | 42 |
| Domizil | 30 | Sacher Apartments | |
| Dr Geissler | 15 | am Stephansplatz | 23 |
| Etap | 50 | Schlossherberge | 31 |
| Gartenhotel Glanzing | 2 | Shermin | 52 |
| Hollmann Beletage | 17 | Starlight Suites | 12 |
| Im Palais | | Stephanie | 10 |
| Schwarzenberg | 55 | Strawbery | 58 |
| Imperial | 63 | Style | 18 |
| Jugendgästehaus | | Suzanne | 43 |
| Wien-Brigittenau | 5 | Wild | 33 |
| Jugendherbergen | 37 | Wilhelmshof | 6 |
| K & K Palais | 11 | Wombat's | 57 |
| Kärntnerhof | 19 | Zipser | 16 |
| | | Zur Wiener Staatsoper | 41 |

including a simple continental breakfast. You can join Hostelling International on the spot at any of the hostels listed below (if you're already a member of your national hostelling association, you're automatically in the HI). Last, but by no means least, you should make an **advance reservation by email or phone** as soon as you know when you might be arriving, as places often get booked up in advance; at the very least, you should ring before turning up on spec.

The biggest practical drawback to the official hostels is that they throw you out each day at the ungodly hour of 9am in order to clean, and won't let you back in until 3 or 4pm. Most hostels have 24hr receptions or they'll give you a night key on request. The lure of the **independent hostel**, then, is that while the prices are much the same as the HI hostels, the atmosphere is a bit less institutional, and there's either no lockout or a more generous one allowing a longer lie-in. However, the places are sometimes, though not always, a bit more run-down and ramshackle.

From July to September, you can stay in a room in one of the city's **student halls**, known as *Saisonhotels* (seasonal hotels). These can be booked directly or through the tourist office (see p.36). Finally, Vienna's **campsites** are all quite far out from the centre, on the perimeters of the city, and so for committed campers only. Pitches cost around €9, plus a fee of around €7 per person.

## Hostels

**Jugendgästehaus Wien-Brigittenau 20**, Friedrich-Engels-Platz 24 ☎332 82 94, ⓦwww.oejhv.or.at; tram #N from U-Bahn Schwedenplatz or U-Bahn Handelskai. Huge, clean, modern HI hostel in a dour working-class suburb; dorms and en-suite bunk-bed doubles.

**Jugendherbergen Wien-Myrthengasse 7**, Myrthengasse 7 ☎523 63 16, ⓦwww.oejhv.or.at; bus #48A or 10min walk from U-Bahn Volkstheater. The most central of all the HI hostels, with 200-plus dorm beds divided between two addresses around the corner from each other. Book well in advance.

**Kolpingfamilie Jugendgästehaus Wien-Meidling 12**, Bendlgasse 10–12 ☎813 54 87, ⓦwww.kolpinghaus-wien12.at; U-Bahn Niederhofstrasse. Modern HI hostel easily reached by U-Bahn from the centre, with single-sex and mixed dorms.

**Hostel Ruthensteiner 15**, Robert-Hamerling-Gasse 24 ☎893 42 02, ⓦwww.hostelruthensteiner.com; U-Bahn Westbahnhof. Excellent, quiet hostel with a nice courtyard to hang out in, within easy walking distance of the Westbahnhof, and with dorm beds, doubles and triples. Discounts for HI members.

**Hostel Schlossherberge 16**, Savoyenstrasse 2 ☎485 85 03-700, ⓦwww.hostel.at; bus #146B or #46B from U-Bahn Ottakring. Also known as the *Palace Hostel*, and beautifully located next to a Neoclassical mansion in the Wienerwald – this place is great as a quiet, bucolic base, but not one from which to sample Vienna's nightlife, despite the good transport links.

**Wombat's City Hostel "The Base" 15**, Grangasse 6 ☎897 23 36, ⓦwww.wombats.at; U-Bahn Westbahnhof. Friendly, laid-back place with clean en-suite dorms and bunk-bed doubles, and a party atmosphere. Within easy walking distance of Westbahnhof. 24hr reception. There's another great branch, with single-sex dorms, around the corner at Mariahilferstrasse 137.

## Student rooms

**Academia 8**, Pfeilgasse 3a ☎401 76-55, ⓦwww.academiahotels.at; tram #46 or #J. Large flagship *Saisonhotel* with small rooms in the studenty district of Josefstadt. Smaller branch next door at Pfeilgasse 4.

**Accordia 2**, Grosse Schiffgasse 12 ☎512 74 93; U-Bahn Schottenring or Schwedenplatz. Modern *Saisonhotel* with singles and doubles, a short walk from the city centre across the Danube Canal in Leopoldstadt.

**Strawberry 6**, Mittelgasse 18 ☎599 79 66-0, ⓦwww.strawberryhostels.com; U-Bahn Westbahnhof. Summer-only hostel a short walk from Westbahnhof; en-suite singles and doubles and no bunk beds. There's another branch round the corner at Bürgerspitalgasse 19.

## Campsites

**Camping Klosterneuburg Donaupark** An der Au ☎02243/258 77, ⓦwww.campingklosterneuburg

.at; S-Bahn Klosterneuburg-Kierling. Squeezed between the town centre and the Danube, just outside the city limits, this is a busy site, with very fast transport connections to Vienna. Open March–Oct.

**Camping Neue Donau** 22, Am Kleehäufl ☎ 202 40 10, ⓦ www.wiencamping.at; S-Bahn Lobau or bus #91A from U-Bahn Kaisermühlen-VIC. Not a first choice, as it's squeezed between the Autobahn and the railway lines on the east bank of the Danube. Open May to mid-Sept.

**Camping Rodaun** 23, An der Au 2 ☎ 888 41 54, ⓦ www.wiencamping.at; tram #60 from U-Bahn Hietzing to its terminus, then 5min walk. Nice rural location by a stream on the southwestern outskirts of Vienna, near the Wienerwald. Open mid-May to Oct.

**Wien West** 14, Hüttelbergstrasse 80 ☎ 914 23 14, ⓦ www.wiencamping.at; bus #152 from U-Bahn Hütteldorf or 15min walk from tram #49 terminus. Very popular site in the plush, far western suburbs of Vienna, close to the Wienerwald; with two- and four-person bungalows to rent between April and Oct (€29/45). Open March–Dec.

# Hotels and pensions

**Hotels and pensions** in Vienna tend to adhere to the standards of efficiency, modernity and cleanliness you'd expect in Austria. It's perfectly possible to stay right in the **Innere Stadt** without breaking the bank, although the cheapest places tend to be in the districts beyond the Ringstrasse. This is no bad thing, as areas like **Neubau** and **Josefstadt** have a wider choice of reasonably priced restaurants and trendy bars than the central tourist zone.

**Breakfast** is included in the price at most of the hotels and pensions, though what it actually amounts to can differ enormously. "Continental breakfast" means coffee and a couple of rolls; "full continental breakfast" means you should get a bit of choice, perhaps cold meats and cheeses, and if you're really lucky a hot egg-based snack; and "buffet" means you can gorge yourself on as much cereal, muesli, eggs, bread, rolls, cheese and meats as you can eat. It's always worthwhile having a look at a room before you commit yourself, as **natural light** is in short supply in some buildings in Vienna. Many old blocks of flats retain their beautiful antique **lifts**, some of which are so ancient they carry passengers up and not down, and can only be operated by placing a coin in the slot.

## Innere Stadt

The **Innere Stadt**, Vienna's old town and commercial centre, is where everyone wants to stay. Prices reflect this and there is a surfeit of bland upper-range hotels (many of which we haven't bothered listing below), and a corresponding

---

### Accommodation prices

All the hotels and pensions in this chapter are listed in alphabetical order under area headings. After each review you'll find a symbol that corresponds to one of nine price categories:

| | | |
|---|---|---|
| ❶ €50 and under | ❹ €71–80 | ❼ €126–150 |
| ❷ €51–60 | ❺ €81–100 | ❽ €151–200 |
| ❸ €61–70 | ❻ €101–125 | ❾ over €200 |

All prices are for the cheapest **double room** available in high season (April–Oct, Christmas & New Year). This may mean without a private bathroom or shower in the cheapest places. For a single room, expect to pay between half and two-thirds the price of a double.

## Vienna's Big Three

Vienna specializes in big **luxury hotels**, but three Ringstrasse piles stand head and shoulders above the others for their heavy, late nineteenth-century decor and their historical associations. During the occupation following the end of World War II, the Americans took over the *Bristol*, the Russians occupied the *Imperial*, while the British holed up in the *Sacher*.

**Hotel Bristol** 1, Kärntner Ring 1 ☎515 16-0, ⊛www.westin.com/bristol; U-Bahn Karlsplatz. The least remarkable of the three from the outside, but a feast of marble inside, with barley-sugar columns in the *Korso* restaurant, and opulent repro decor in all the rooms (doubles start at around €400; suites can cost up to eight times that). ❾

**Hotel Imperial** 1, Kärntner Ring 16 ☎501 10-0, ⊛www.luxurycollection.com/imperial; U-Bahn Karlsplatz. Incredibly lavish converted palace, built for the Duke of Würtemberg, and later the "favourite hostelry of crowned heads, their heirs-apparent, and ambassadors", according to one observer in 1877. Hitler stayed here on his return to the city in 1938, and it's still the first choice for visiting heads of government. Doubles can be had online for around €300; suites reach the stratospheric heights of €5000-plus. ❾

**Hotel Sacher** 1, Philharmonikerstrasse 4 ☎514 56-0, ⊛www.sacher.com; U-Bahn Karlsplatz. The most famous of the lot, not only because of its legendary *Sachertorte*, but also because this was where the aristocratic playboys used to hang out in the imperial days. The new rooms eschew the traditional heavy, wood-panelled, red velvet approach of the rest of the hotel, and opt for a more pared-down opulence. Double rooms range between €350 and €600. ❾

dearth of inexpensive places (most of which we *have* listed).

**Hotel am Schubertring** 1, Schubertring 11 ☎717 02-0, ⊛www.schubertring.at; U-Bahn Stadtpark. Solid choice on the Ring and one of the few not run by a hotel chain. The rooms (all on the fifth floor), are spacious and a/c; some have views over the Ringstrasse. ❼

**Hotel am Stephansplatz** 1, Stephansplatz 9 ☎534 05-0, ⊛www.hotelamstephansplatz.at; U-Bahn Stephansplatz. The decor is pretty dated, but the rooms are perfectly comfortable and spacious, and it's just about as central as you can get without actually being inside the Stephansdom. ❽

**Hotel Astoria** 1, Kärntnerstrasse 32–34 ☎515 77-0, ⊛www.austria-trend.at/asw; U-Bahn Karlsplatz. Grandiose, turn-of-the-century flagship of the *Austria Trend* hotel chain, and preferred pad of visiting opera stars owing to its proximity to the Staatsoper. The rooms are fully modernized and start at around €210. The entrance is on Fürichgasse. ❾

**Hotel Austria** 1, Fleischmarkt 20 ☎515 23, ⊛www.hotelaustria-wien.at; U-Bahn Schwedenplatz. Plush family-run hotel, pleasantly located in the quiet cul-de-sac of Wolfengasse, off Fleischmarkt, with some cheap rooms without en-suite facilities. ❺

**Pension Aviano** 1, Marco d'Avianogasse 1 ☎512 83 30, ⊛www.pertschy.com; U-Bahn Karlsplatz. Part of the *Pertschy* pension chain, squeezed onto the top floor of a building just off Kärntnerstrasse. Despite their low ceilings the rooms, all en suite, are spacious, with fluffy, floral decor and no a/c. ❻

**Pension City** 1, Bauernmarkt 10 ☎533 95 21, ⊛www.citypension.at; U-Bahn Stephansplatz. On the second floor of a wonderful late nineteenth-century building (birthplace of Franz Grillparzer) and run by a friendly female proprietor. Tastefully decorated rooms, all en suite. ❹

**Hotel Domizil** 1, Schulerstrasse 14 ☎513 31 99, ⊛www.hoteldomizil.at; U-Bahn Stephansplatz. Clean, bright pension with simple, smartly furnished en-suite rooms, just seconds from Stephansplatz. ❺

**Pension Dr Geissler** 1, Postgasse 14 ☎533 28 03, ⊛www.hotelpension.at; U-Bahn Schwedenplatz. On the eighth floor, this is an anonymous, modern place; the singles and doubles are clean, however, and those with shared facilities are among the cheapest in the Innere Stadt. ❷

**Hollmann Beletage** 1, Kollnerhofgasse 6 ☎961 19 60, ⊛www.hollmann-beletage.at; U-Bahn Karlsplatz/Stephansplatz. Small boutique hotel whose bright and cheery rooms are replete with contemporary furnishings. Service is pretty low-key, and there's no reception at night; breakfasts are excellent. **⑦**

**K & K Palais Hotel 1, Rudolfsplatz 11** ☏533 13 53, ⓦwww.kkhotels.com; U-Bahn Schwedenplatz. Built in 1890 and once the town house of Franz-Josef's mistress Katharina Schratt, the *K & K* retains an appropriately imperial ambience in the lobby. Breakfasts are king-sized and the a/c rooms kept in tip-top condition. Prices start at around €230. **⑨**

**Hotel Kärntnerhof 1, Grashofgasse 4** ☏512 19 23, ⓦwww.karntnerhof.com; U-Bahn Schwedenplatz/Stephansplatz. Located in a cul-de-sac off Köllnerhofgasse, with some very pleasant, characterful rooms, and others that are a little dingy. Make sure you see yours before checking in. **⑤**

**Hotel König von Ungarn 1, Schulerstrasse 10** ☏515 84-0, ⓦwww.kvu.at; U-Bahn Stephansplatz. Tastefully modernized hotel with a remarkable wooden-panelled, covered courtyard bar/lounge. Rooms are fair-sized, pleasantly decorated and a/c. Service is top notch and the location dead central. **⑨**

**Pension Lerner 1, Wipplingerstrasse 23** ☏533 52 19, ⓦwww.pensionlerner.com; U-Bahn Stephansplatz. Small, super-central, seven-room pension with friendly staff, Wi-Fi and super breakfasts. They also have a few apartments to let in Schulerstrasse. **④**

**Hotel Mailbergerhof 1, Annagasse 7** ☏512 06 41, ⓦwww.mailbergerhof.at; U-Bahn Karlsplatz/Stephansplatz. Converted Baroque palace on a delightfully discreet, narrow side-street off Kärntnerstrasse, with attractively furnished rooms for around €200. It's a smart place, but the ambience is relaxed, and the staff are supremely efficient and friendly. **⑨**

**Pension Neuer Markt 1, Seilergasse 9** ☏512 23 16, ⓦwww.hotelpension.at; U-Bahn Stephansplatz. Very popular, central pension on the second floor of a lovely old patrician building. Rooms are clean, comfortable and modern, and those without shower or en-suite toilet are a relative bargain – only a few have views over Neuermarkt. **⑨**

**Pension Nossek 1, Graben 17** ☏533 70 41, ⓦwww.pension-nossek.at; U-Bahn Stephansplatz. Old-fashioned, large family-run pension on three floors of an old building on the pedestrianized Graben, with en-suite doubles of varying sizes, and some real bargain singles with shared facilities. It's popular, so book in advance. **⑥**

**Hotel Orient 1, Tiefer Graben 30** ☏533 73 07, ⓦwww.hotelorient.at; U-Bahn Herrengasse. Vienna's equivalent of a Tokyo "love hotel", with rooms rented by the hour and per

▲ Lobby of Hotel Imperial

night. Couples come for the mind-boggling exotic decor, and the wide range of themed rooms. ❺

**Palais Coburg Residenz 1,** Coburgbastei 3 ☎518 18-0, Ⓦwww.palais-coburg.com; U-Bahn Stubentor. One of Vienna's seriously sumptuous palace hotels, a Neoclassical affair built for Duke Ferdinand of Saxe-Coburg & Gotha (Queen Victoria's uncle) in the 1840s. There's a stunning lobby and rooftop pool, while the suites themselves have all mod cons and a fully equipped kitchen. Prices start at around €450. ❾

🏃 **Pension Pertschy 1,** Habsburgergasse 5 ☎534 49-0, Ⓦwww.pertschy.com; U-Bahn Stephansplatz. Flagship of the *Pertschy* pension chain, with rooms off a series of plant-strewn balconies looking onto a lovely old courtyard. The characterful rooms have high ceilings, tasteful furnishings and TV. ❻

**Hotel Post 1,** Fleischmarkt 24 ☎515 83, Ⓦwww.hotel-post-wien.at; U-Bahn Schwedenplatz. Civilized, central hotel with more than a hundred mostly large, old rooms with modern furnishings. Those without shower and toilet are the real bargain. ❸

🏃 **Sacher Apartments am Stephansplatz 1,** Rotenturmstrasse 1 ☎533 32 38, Ⓦwww.pension-sacher.at; U-Bahn Stephansplatz. Incredible location on the seventh floor on the corner of Stephansplatz itself. There are just nine rooms, with lovely parquet flooring and pleasant furnishings. All have TV, shower, toilet, fridge and cooking facilities, and most have views out on to the Stephansdom. No breakfast. ❺

**Starlight Suites 1,** Salzgries 12 ☎535 92 22-0, Ⓦwww.starlighthotels.com; U-Bahn Schwedenplatz. Totally modernized apartments for around €180 and upwards, in a centrally located but quiet backstreet, not far from Schwedenplatz. Buffet breakfast is provided as there are no kitchen facilities. Two other branches exist at Renngasse 13 and Am Heumarkt 15, both a stone's throw from the Ring. ❽

**Style Hotel 1,** Herrengasse 12 ☎227 80-0, Ⓦwww.stylehotel.at; U-Bahn Herrengasse. Vienna's most central boutique hotel with a relentlessly minimalist, contemporary aesthetic, and rooms with all mod cons. Breakfast is not always included in the rates, which start at around €250. ❾

**Pension Suzanne 1,** Walfischgasse 4 _☎513 25 07, Ⓦwww.pension-suzanne.at; U-Bahn

Karlsplatz. Family-run pension just off Kärntnerstrasse, furnished in tasteful period style; rooms are spacious, and many have baths, balconies and even small kitchens (though breakfast is included). ❺

**Hotel zur Wiener Staatsoper 1,** Krugerstrasse 11 ☎513 12 74, Ⓦwww.zurwienerstaatsoper.at; U-Bahn Karlsplatz. Behind the flamboyant late nineteenth-century facade and foyer are small, clean rooms. The location, just off Kärntnerstrasse, is pretty good for the price. Closed Nov. ❻

## Landstrasse, Wieden and Margareten

Parts of **Landstrasse** (third district) are eminently avoidable, with the exception of the area around the Belvedere. **Wieden** (fourth district) and **Margareten** (fifth district) are quieter, residential areas, to the south of Karlsplatz and convenient for the Naschmarkt.

**Art Hotel Vienna (aka Golden Tulip Hotel) 5,** Brandmayergasse 7–9 ☎554 51 08, Ⓦwww.thearthotelvienna.at; tram #6 or #18 from U-Bahn Margaretengürtel. Margareten hotel with a penchant for wacky modern art and designer furnishings. All rooms are en suite. ❺

**Pension Bosch 3,** Keilgasse 13 ☎798 61 79, Ⓦwww.hotelpensionbosch.com; S-Bahn Rennweg or tram #0, or #71. Friendly pension in a quiet residential backstreet near the Südbahnhof, behind the Belvedere, an easy tram-ride into town. The thirteen rooms have lots of character; the cheapest have shared facilities. Closed Jan. ❸

**Carlton Opera 4,** Schikanedergasse 4 ☎587 53 02, Ⓦwww.carlton.at; U-Bahn Karlsplatz. Built in 1904, this grandiose hotel retains some appealing Art Deco touches and a faded charm – and staff are friendly. It's a short hop from Karlsplatz and the Naschmarkt, and they have apartments nearby, too. ❻

**Etap Hotel Wien St Marx 3,** Franzosengraben 15 ☎798 45 55, Ⓦwww.etaphotel.com; U-Bahn Gasometer. Totally modern, clean, budget chain hotel. The surroundings are far from attractive, though it's only a short walk from the new Gasometer development. ❷

**Hotel im Palais Schwarzenberg 3,** Schwarzenbergplatz 9 ☎798 45 15, Ⓦwww.palais-schwarzenberg.com; tram #D.

Hidden behind the Soviet War Memorial, this Baroque palace, with its own extensive gardens, was designed by Hildebrandt and Fischer von Erlach, with period furnishings courtesy of, among others, Rubens, Meissen and Gobelins. **⑨**

**Hotel-Pension Shermin 4, Rilkeplatz 7** ☎586 61 83, ⓦwww.hotel-pension-shermin.at; **U-Bahn Karlsplatz.** The lobby's a bit lugubrious, but the rooms are clean and spacious and the staff very friendly. Good location, just off Karlsplatz, and they have apartments nearby, too. **⑤**

**Das Triest 4, Wiedner Hauptstrasse 12** ☎589 18-0, ⓦwww.dastriest.at; **U-Bahn Karlsplatz.** Designer hotel hidden away in a nondescript building a short stroll from Karlsplatz. The super-smooth, minimalist interior comes courtesy of Terence Conran and the Italians, and is quirky in an understated way. Rooms, which start at around €265, are immaculate, and those on the top floor have great views across the city skyline. **⑨**

## Mariahilf, Neubau and Josefstadt

The sixth, seventh and eighth districts are home to some of Vienna's liveliest bars and choicest restaurants, and therefore ideal areas in which to be based. **Neubau** includes the lively Spittelberg area, while **Josefstadt** is more studenty.

**Altstadt Vienna 7, Kirchengasse 41** ☎522 66 66, ⓦwww.altstadt.at; **U-Bahn Volkstheater.** A cut above most other pensions, with laid-back, well-informed staff, a relaxing lounge and full-on buffet breakfast. Tastefully decorated en-suite rooms with high ceilings and a great location, near Spittelberg, and within easy walking distance of the U-Bahn and Ring. **⑦**

**Pension Anna 7, Zieglergasse 18** ☎523 01 60, ⓦwww.pension-anna.at; **U-Bahn Zieglergasse.** First-floor pension run by a friendly couple. The startling light-blue decor doesn't extend into the fourteen bedrooms, all of which have en-suite shower and toilet. Closed Christmas. **⑤**

**Pension Astra 8, Alserstrasse 32** ☎402 43 54, ⓦwww.hotelpensionastra.com; **U-Bahn Alserstrasse.** Mid-sized pension on the mezzanine of an old patrician building. Friendly staff and a range of modernized rooms, from simple doubles without toilet to roomy apartments. **③**

**Pension Kraml 6, Brauergasse 5** ☎587 85 88, ⓦwww.pensionkraml.at; **U-Bahn Zieglergasse/Neubaugasse.** Probably the friendliest and most reliable of the cheap pensions in the quiet streets off Mariahilferstrasse. Large, smart, clean, modern rooms, some with en-suite facilities. **①**

**Hotel Kugel 7, Siebensterngasse 43** ☎523 33 55, ⓦwww.hotelkugel.at; **U-Bahn Neubaugasse.** Long-established, family-run hotel within spitting distance of Spittelberg's numerous restaurants and bars. Bright, clean, en-suite rooms (some with modern four-posters), plus a few bargain singles with shared facilities. Closed Jan. **⑤**

**Levante Parliament 8, Auerspergstrasse 9** ☎228 28-0, ⓦwww.thelevante.com; **U-Bahn Volkstheater.** Vienna's latest designer hotel, a stone's throw from the Ring, with resolutely modernist decor throughout the rooms and, of course, all mod cons. Doubles start at around €275; they also have cheaper apartments deeper in Josefstadt. **⑨**

**Pension Lindenhof 7, Lindengasse 4** ☎523 04 98, ⓔpensionlindenhof@yahoo.com; **U-Bahn Neubaugasse.** On the first floor of a lugubrious turn-of-the-century building at the Spittelberg end of this long street. Lovely, up-only lift, a plant-strewn communal area and endearingly old-fashioned rooms (some of which are en suite), with high ceilings and creaky parquet flooring. **②**

**Hotel Rathaus 8, Lange Gasse 13** ☎400 11 22, ⓦwww.hotel-rathaus-wien.at; **U-Bahn Rathaus.** Discreet boutique hotel with bright, contemporary, wine-themed rooms in an old patrician building a few blocks west of the Rathaus. Breakfasts are superb, and you can opt (later) for some wine-tasting too. **⑧**

**Das Tyrol 6, Mariahilferstrasse 15** ☎587 54 15, ⓦwww.das-tyrol.at. Boutique hotel off Vienna's main shopping street. The rooms are quite small and the arty touches don't always work, but everything is spotlessly clean and smart and the staff are very helpful. **⑧**

**Pension Wild 8, Lange Gasse 10** ☎406 51 74, ⓦwww.pension-wild.com; **U-Bahn Volkstheater.** Friendly, laid-back pension, a short walk from the Ring in a student district behind the university, and especially popular with backpackers and gay travellers. Booking essential. **②**

**Hotel Zipser 8, Lange Gasse 49** ☎404 54-0, ⓦwww.zipser.at; **U-Bahn Rathaus.** Well-equipped, modern pension, offering a buffet breakfast – a reliable choice, just a short walk from the Ring behind the Rathaus. **④**

## Alsergrund

Separated from the rest of the Vorstädte by the giant city hospital, the ninth district, **Alsergrund**, has a life of its own, with a good selection of trendy cafés, bars and restaurants, and frequent tram connections to the centre.

**Hotel Atlanta** 9, Währinger Strasse 33 ⓣ405 12 39, ⓦwww.hotelatlanta.at; tram #37, #38, #40, #41 or #42. Plush Alsergrund hotel within easy walking distance of the district's best bars and restaurants. All rooms are en suite with cable TV. Prices drop significantly in low season. ❻

**Hotel Deutschmeister** 9, Grünentorgasse 30 ⓣ310 34 04, ⓦwww.city-hotels.at; U-Bahn Rossauer Lände or tram #D. Good, reliable hotel in the quiet backstreets of Alsergrund, and a pleasant 20min walk or a couple of tram/metro stops into town. ❻

## Leopoldstadt

Cut off from the Innere Stadt by the Danube Canal, **Leopoldstadt**, Vienna's second district, is quiet and seldom visited by tourists. Yet the area lies just a couple of tram stops from the central district and the greenery of the Prater. The backstreets near Wien-Nord train station double as a red-light district, but the atmosphere is rarely intimidating.

**Austria Classic Hotel Wien** 2, Praterstrasse 72 ⓣ211 30-0, ⓦwww.hotel-nordbahn.at; U-Bahn Nestroyplatz/Praterstern. If you want to stay in the second district, then the birthplace of Max Steiner, composer of film music for *Gone With the Wind* and *Casablanca*, is a

good choice. It's now a large, pleasantly modernized hotel with shower, toilet and TV in all rooms. ❻

**Hotel Stephanie** 2, Taborstrasse 12 ⓣ211 50-0, ⓦwww.schick-hotels.com; U-Bahn Schwedenplatz. A touch of well-worn splendour to the public areas, and some modern comforts in the rooms. Excellent breakfast, good restaurant, charming staff and a short stroll to the Innere Stadt. ❽

**Hotel Wilhelmshof** 2, Kleine Stadtgutgasse 4 ⓣ214 55 21, ⓦwww.wilhelmshof.at; U-Bahn Praterstern. Old patrician building a short stroll from Wien Nord and the Prater park, with simple, plain, modern furnishings and air conditioning in all the rooms. ❺

## The suburbs

**Gartenhotel Glanzing** 19, Glanzinggasse 23 ⓣ470 42 72-0, ⓦwww.gartenhotel-glanzing .at; tram #41. Classic interwar modernist villa in the northern suburbs. Some of the (all en suite) rooms have amazing views over Vienna, and there's a lovely shady garden. Sauna and solarium on site. ❻

**Landhaus Fuhrgassl-Huber** 19, Rathstrasse 24 ⓣ440 30 33, ⓦwww.fuhrgassl-huber.at; bus #35A from U-Bahn Nussdorferstrasse. A real *gemütlich* country hotel/wine producer right out in the vineyards at the foot of the Wienerwald. It takes a while to get into town by public transport. ❻

**Roomz Vienna** 11, Paragonstrasse 1 ⓣ743 17 17, ⓦwww.roomz-vienna.com; U-Bahn Gasometer. Designer functionalist budget hotel out by the awesome Gasometer development (see p.164). Clean and efficient, it has all mod cons, from air conditioning to Wi-Fi, and is just minutes from the U-Bahn. ❹

# Cafés

*You have troubles of one sort or another – to the COFFEEHOUSE!*
*She can't come to you for some reason no matter how plausible –*
*  to the COFFEEHOUSE!*
*You have holes in your shoes – the COFFEEHOUSE!*
*You have a salary of 400 crowns and spend 500 – THE COFFEEHOUSE!*
*You are frugal and permit yourself nothing – THE COFFEEHOUSE!*
*You find no woman who suits you – THE COFFEEHOUSE!*
*You are SPIRITUALLY on the threshold of suicide – THE COFFEEHOUSE!*
*You hate and disdain people and yet cannot do without them –*
*  THE COFFEEHOUSE!*
*Nobody extends you any more credit anywhere – THE COFFEEHOUSE!*

The Coffeehouse
Peter Altenberg (1859–1919)

More than a century on, the Viennese **Kaffeehaus** remains a haven of old-fashioned values. For the price of a small coffee, you can still sit for as long as you like without being asked to move on or buy another drink. Understandably, then, the price of this first drink is fairly steep and will set you back around €2.50–3.50.

*Kaffeehäuser* will always have at least a selection of **cakes**. Many will also offer a midday meal, and some will put aside a number of tables for those customers who wish to eat. The food is generally traditional Austrian fare, inexpensive and tasty. As well as the traditional *Kaffeehaus* there's also the **Kaffee-Konditorei**, where the coffee is a mere sideshow to the establishment's cakes and pastries (see colour section). Modern variants on the *Kaffeehaus* theme continue to evolve, particularly in the Vorstädte or inner suburbs. These places generally eschew the formality and heavy menu of the older *Kaffeehäuser* and consequently attract a younger crowd. For more on Vienna's coffee and cakes, see the colour section.

Lastly, some cafés have what is known as a *Schanigarten* – named after the assistant waiter or *Schani*, whose job it is to set out the tables and chairs – don't get too excited, however, as this is rarely much of a **garden**, simply a few tables alfresco.

All cafés detailed in this chapter are marked on the relevant **map** in the Guide – you'll find a page reference taking you there at each review. For a German food and drinks **glossary**, see p.341.

## Vegetarians

**Vegetarianism** has not caught on in a big way in Vienna – and there are remarkably few vegetarian restaurants. The key phrases are *Ich bin vegeterianisch(e)* ("I'm vegetarian") and *Ist das ohne Fleisch?* (literally "Is that without meat?"). There are usually a few traditional vegetarian dishes on most *Beisl* and *Kaffeehaus* menus: *Gebackener Emmenthaler* (or some other kind of cheese), which is breaded and deep-fried; *Knödel mit Ei* (dumplings with scrambled egg); *Spinatnockerl* (spinach pasta).

The following are the best of Vienna's small number of exclusively vegetarian eating places:

**Bio Bar**; see p.272

**Gesundes**; see p.263.

**Govinda**; see p.263.

**Nice Rice**; see p.274.

**St Josef**; see p.263.

**Vegi-Point**; see p.263.

**Wrenkh Natürlich**; see p.263.

## Cheap eats

This section lists **cheap eats** such as self-service chains and stand-up buffets, where you can snack on as much or as little as you like, more often than not on the hoof. The most obvious snack in Vienna is, of course, a *Wurst* or **hot dog** – *Hasse* in the local dialect – from one of the ubiquitous *Würstelstandln* around town. There are numerous varieties available: the *Bratwurst* (fried sausage) or *Burenwurst* (boiled sausage) are the most common, but you could also try a *Debreziner*, a spicy Hungarian sausage, a *Currywurst*, which speaks for itself, or a *Tirolerwurst*, a smoked variety. To accompany your sausage, you usually get a roll and some *Senf* (mustard), which can be either *scharf* (hot) or *süss* (sweet).

For something a bit healthier, there are a number of **takeaway stands** that sell grilled *Maiskolben* (corn on the cob), roasted *Maroni* (chestnuts), *Bratkartoffeln* (roast potatoes) and *Kartoffelpuffer* (potato puffs), depending on the season. Anker, the largest **bakery** chain in the country, with branches right across Vienna, produces excellent bread, rolls and pastries, and serves coffee too.

The best place to grab a quick bite and eat cheaply at the same time, however, is the **Naschmarkt** (see p.296), Vienna's premier fruit and vegetable market (Mon–Sat), where you can feast on seafood, kebabs, falafel, *burek*, noodles and much more besides, or, if you prefer, assemble a king-sized picnic.

As well as the student **Mensen** (see p.264), there are plenty of other **self-service** places, such as *Naschmarkt* – not to be confused with the aforementioned fruit and veg market – 1, Schottengasse 1 (U-Bahn Schottentor), with branches all over the city. More specialized, but equally reliable self-service chains include the fish and seafoody *Nordsee*, 1, Kärntnerstrasse 25 (U-Bahn Stephansplatz), the Middle Eastern *Levante*, 1, Wollzeile 19 (U-Bahn Stephansplatz), and the *Schnitzelhaus*, 1, Krugerstrasse 6 (U-Bahn Karlsplatz), again, each with numerous other branches. At all these places you'll get fast and efficient service and filling snacks for less than €10, but they are not places to idle away several hours.

**Bizi** 1, Rotenturmstrasse 4 ⓦ www.bizi.at; U-Bahn Stephansplatz; see map p.40. Branches include 7, Mariahilferstrasse 22–24; U-Bahn Museumsquartier. A reliable, functional filling station just off Stephansplatz. Devise your own pizza toppings, assemble your own salad, or choose one of the main dishes and/or roasted vegetables. Takeaway or sit down. Daily 10.30am–11.30pm.

**Breakfast Club** 4, Schleifmühlgasse 12–14; U-Bahn Karlsplatz; see map p.119. Small, plain café that specializes in early-hours breakfasts for less than €6, ranging from oriental style to ones with baked beans or sliced avocado. Mon–Fri 6am–2pm, Sat & Sun 6am–3pm.

**Deli 5, Naschmarkt Stand 421–436; U-Bahn Karlsplatz; see map p.119.** Small Turkish café in the Naschmarkt, whose famous breakfasts are super-popular. Mon–Sat 7am–10pm.

**Gesundes 2, Lilienbrunngasse 3 ⓦwww .gesundess.at; U-Bahn Schwedenplatz; see map p.185.** Organic health-food shop with just a few tables serving lunchtime-only veggie and vegan fare. Mon–Sat 9am–3pm.

**Govinda 7, Lindengasse 2a ⓦwww.govinda.at; U-Bahn Neubaugasse; see map p.165.** Hindu arts-and-crafts shop that serves a few simple vegetarian dishes at lunchtime. Mon–Fri 10am–6.30pm, Sat 10am–2pm.

**Meinl am Graben 1, Am Graben 19 ⓦwww .meinlamgraben.at; U-Bahn Stephansplatz; see map p.40.** The flagship store has an excellent seafood bar and a stand-up buffet on the ground floor, where you can eat traditional hot dishes and lighter snacks. Mon–Sat 8am–5pm.

**Rosenberger 1, Maysedergasse 2; U-Bahn Karlsplatz; see map p.119.** Budget, self-service restaurant serving grilled meats and fish dishes, with a big salad bar and lots of decent desserts. Daily 7.30am–11.30pm.

**Soho 1, Burggarten; U-Bahn Karlsplatz; see map p.74.** A cut above your average student canteen, this is the Nationalbibliothek's groovy café near the Palmenhaus, with a daily lunchtime menu for under €6; pay for the food at the bar and hand your counter in at the kitchen. Mon–Fri 9am–4pm, Sat 11am–4pm.

**St Josef 7, Mondscheingasse 10; tram #49; see map p.165.** Functional, friendly self-service canteen (with shop at back) serving tasty veggie dishes for under €10. No smoking. Mon–Fri 9am–6.30pm, Sat 9am–4pm.

**Trześniewski 1, Dorotheergasse 1 ⓦwww.trzesniewski.at; U-Bahn Stephansplatz; see map p.40. Branches at 6, Mariahilferstrasse 95; U-Bahn Neubaugasse, and elsewhere in the suburbs.** Minimalist sandwich bar that's a veritable Viennese institution, serving mouthwatering slices of rye bread (*Brötchen*) topped with fishy, eggy and meaty spreads – wash it all down with a *Pfiff*. Stand-up tables and a few seats. Mon–Fri 8.30am–7.30pm, Sat 9am–5pm.

**Vapiano 6, Theobaldgasse 19 ⓦwww.vapiano .at; U-Bahn Museumsquartier; see map p.165.** Bright, spacious, modern self-service place with an open kitchen, where they'll make your pizza or pasta dish in front of you. Daily 11am–1am.

**Vegi-Point 8, Florianigasse 18 ⓦwww .tunnel-vienna-live.at/vegipoint; U-Bahn Josef-städterstrasse; see map p.165.** Utilitarian, veggie fast-food: salads, soups, pasta dishes, and a veggie burger with French fries for €3. Mon–Sat 11am–8pm.

**Wrenkh Natürlich 1, Rauhensteingasse 12; U-Bahn Stephansplatz; see map p.40.** A small weekday-only snack bar around the back of the Steffl department store on Kärntner-strasse; soup or salad and a main course for €8. Mon–Fri 11am–7pm, Sat 10am–4pm.

**Zanoni & Zanoni 1, Lugeck 7 ⓦwww.zanoni .co.at; U-Bahn Stephansplatz; see map p.40.** Primarily an ice-cream parlour or *gelateria* – though also a *pasticceria* – and one of the few that's open all year round. Daily 7am–midnight.

**Zum schwarzen Kameel 1, Bognergasse 5 ⓦwww.kameel.at; U-Bahn Herrengasse; see map p.40.** A terribly smart, convivial deli that's not exactly cheap, but is a venerable Viennese institution, with stand-up tables and an excellent but expensive restaurant attached. Mon–Sat 8.30am–10.30pm.

# Cafés

## Innere Stadt (1st district)

The following places are marked on the map on p.40.

**Aera 1, Gonzagagasse 11 ⓦwww.aera.at; U-Bahn Schwedenplatz.** Relaxing, upstairs café serving tasty food to a mixed crowd – some smart, some trendy – live bands perform in the dimly lit cellar downstairs. Mon–Thurs & Sun 10am–1am, Fri & Sat 10am–2pm.

**Aida 1, Singerstrasse 1; 1, Bognergasse 3; 1, Rotenturmstrasse 24; all U-Bahn Stephansplatz. Many other branches; all ⓦwww.aida.at.** The largest Viennese *Konditorei* chain, serving a staggering selection of calorific cakes and coffee in dodgy 1960s and 1970s decor. Varied hours but usually Mon–Fri 7am–8pm, Sun 9am–8pm.

**Alt Wien 1, Bäckerstrasse 9; U-Bahn Stephansplatz.** Bohemian *Kaffeehaus* with *Beisl* decor, posters on nicotine-stained walls, and a dark, smoky atmosphere even on the sunniest day. Daily 10am–2am.

**Café Bräunerhof 1, Stallburggasse 2; U-Bahn Herrengasse.** Thomas Bernhard's favourite has a real *Kaffeehaus* atmosphere: nicotine-coloured walls, slightly snooty tuxedoed waiters and decent food, too. Live music Sat 3–6pm. Mon–Fri 8am–9pm, Sat 8am–7pm, Sun 10am–7pm.

**Café Central 1, Herrengasse 14 ⓦ www.ferstel .at; U-Bahn Herrengasse.** The most famous of all Viennese cafés, resurrected in the 1980s and still the most architecturally interesting (see p.61). Trotsky was once a regular. Piano music daily 5–10pm. Mon–Sat 7.30am–10pm, Sun 10am–10pm.

**Demel 1, Kohlmarkt 14 ⓦ www.demel.at; U-Bahn Herrengasse.** The king of the *Kaffee-Konditorei* – and one of the priciest. The cake display is a work of art, as is the interior. Daily 10am–7pm.

**Café Diglas 1, Wollzeile 10 ⓦ www.diglas.at; U-Bahn Stephansplatz.** Smoky old *Kaffeehaus*

– once Franz Lehár's favourite haunt – with burgundy upholstery and piles of cakes and papers to choose from. Piano music Tues, Wed, Fri & Sat 8.30–11.30pm. Daily 7am–midnight.

**Café Engländer 1, Postgasse 2 ⓦ www .café-englaender.com; U-Bahn Stubentor.** Great *Kaffeehaus* with a very long pedigree, currently sporting a smart modernist look and serving good food. Mon–Sat 8am–1am, Sun 10am–1am.

**Café Frauenhuber 1, Himmelpfortgasse 6; U-Bahn Stephansplatz.** The oldest *Kaffeehaus* in Vienna – Beethoven was a regular (as patron and pianist) – with vaulted ceiling, deep burgundy upholstery and an excellent menu. Mon–Sat 8am–11.30pm, Sun 10am–10pm.

**Café Griensteidl 1, Michaelerplatz 2; U-Bahn Herrengasse.** After nearly a hundred-year caesura, the literary *Griensteidl* was resurrected (at least in name) in 1990 – it's perfectly OK, but not what it was in 1897 (see p.69) and still needs the patina of age. Daily 8am–11.30pm.

**Café Hawelka 1, Dorotheergasse 6; U-Bahn Stephansplatz.** Small, smoky bohemian café run for sixty years by the same couple until

## Mensen

If you're on a tight budget, then it's worth considering using one of the city's numerous university canteens or **Mensen** (ⓦ www.mensen.at) – Mensa is the singular – which are open to the general public (you get an extra discount with student ID). It might not be cordon bleu, but the food is generally perfectly decent, traditional Viennese fare, and you usually get a couple of courses for around €5, about half what you'd pay in a café or restaurant.

**Afro-Asiatisches Institut (AAI)** 9, Türkenstrasse 3; U-Bahn Schottentor. Vienna's most multiethnic clientele, but not great for veggies; situated on the ground floor through the archway. Mon–Fri 11.30am–3.30pm.

**Biozentrum** 3, Dr Bohr-Gasse 9; tram #18 or #71. Lots of veggie choices amid the "brainfood" menu. Mon–Thurs 9am–4pm, Fri 9am–2pm.

**Musikakademie** 1, Johannesgasse 8; U-Bahn Karlsplatz. Small, central, musical Mensa with a pleasant summer courtyard; good for breakfast, but not great for veggies. Mon–Fri 7.30am–3pm.

**Neues Instituts Gebäude (NIG)** 1, Universitätsstrasse 7; U-Bahn Schottentor. This is the main university Mensa; take the dumbwaiter lift to floor 6 and then walk up another flight of stairs – you get a nice view over to the Votivkirche. Mon–Fri 11am–2pm.

**Technische Universität (TU)** 4, Wiedner Hauptstrasse 8–10; U-Bahn Karlsplatz. Big Mensa on the first floor (follow the yellow B signs) of the building behind the main university block on Karlsplatz, with regular veggie options. Mon–Fri 11am–2.30pm.

**Wirtschaftsuniversität (WU)** 9, Augasse 2–6; U-Bahn Spittelau. Unusually this Mensa is open for breakfast as well as lunch; some veggie options. Mon–Thurs 8am–7pm, Fri 8am–6pm. July & Aug closes 3pm.

Josefine Hawelka died in 2005; Leopold still works on and you may have to fight for a table. Mon & Wed–Sat 8am–2am, Sun 4pm–2am.

**Kleines Café 1, Franziskanerplatz 3; U-Bahn Stephansplatz.** Cosy little café, an early crossover between traditional *Kaffeehaus* and modern bar, designed by the Viennese architect Hermann Czech in the 1970s. Mon–Sat 10am–2am, Sun 1pm–2am.

**Café Korb 1, Brandstätte 9; U-Bahn Stephansplatz.** Traditional, endearingly worn 1950s formica-style *Kaffeehaus* tucked away in the backstreets of the Innere Stadt; rather surprisingly you can play skittles in the basement. Mon–Sat 8am–midnight, Sun 11am–9pm.

**Café Krugerhof 1, Krugerstrasse 8; U-Bahn Karlsplatz.** No-nonsense classic *Kaffeehaus* just off Kärntnerstrasse, with well-worn, flock beige upholstery, coat stands, newspapers, billiards, food and comfy booths. Mon–Fri 7am–5pm, Sat 7am–4pm.

**Café Markusplatz 1, Tuchlauben 16 ⓦwww .markusplatz.at; U-Bahn Stephansplatz.** Slip into one of the retro 1950s booths at the resurrected Café Tuchlauben and enjoy great coffee, patisserie, food and Wi-Fi. Mon–Fri 7.30am–7pm, Sat 8.30am–7pm.

**Café Tirolerhof 1, Tegetthoffstrasse/Fürichgasse; U-Bahn Karlsplatz.** A real, peaceful, old-fashioned *Kaffeehaus*, with classic decor and ambience, conveniently situated just behind the opera house. Mon–Fri 7am–9pm, Sat 7am–2am, Sun 9am–midnight.

## Ringstrasse & MuseumsQuartier

Unless otherwise specified, the following places are marked on the map on p.100.

**Am Heumarkt 1, Am Heumarkt 15; U-Bahn Stadtpark.** Venerable weekday *Kaffeehaus* with giant stone pillars, red booths, parquet floor and billards tables. Mon–Fri 9am–11pm.

**Café Bendl 1, Landesgerichtsstrasse 6; U-Bahn Rathaus.** Nicotine-stained favourite with the local student population for its cheap Austrian comfort food and late hours. Mon–Thurs 6am–2am, Fri 6am–4am, Sat 6pm–4am.

**Do & Co Albertina 1, Albertinaplatz 1 ⓦwww .doco.com; U-Bahn Karlsplatz.** Beautifully posh café with striking onyx interior and a raised terrace overlooking the Burggarten. Daily 9am–midnight.

**Café Eiles 8, Josefstädterstrasse 2; U-Bahn Rathaus.** Very traditional *Kaffeehaus* set back from the Ringstrasse, behind the Rathaus. The decor dates from the 1930s when the café was the meeting point for the Nazis who assassinated the Austro-fascist leader, Englebert Dollfuss. Mon–Fri 7am–10pm, Sat & Sun 8am–10pm.

**Halle 7, Museumsplatz 1; U-Bahn Museumsquartier.** The biggest and vibiest of the MuseumsQuartier cafés, the multilevel *Halle* throbs to funky music under a slice of Fischer von Erlach's old ceiling, and produces pricey Italian-fusion food. Daily 10am–2am.

**Café Imperial 1, Kärntner Ring 16; U-Bahn Karlsplatz.** Seriously intimidating, palatial café in the hotel of choice for visiting statesmen and business folk. Live piano Sat & Sun 3.30–7.30pm. Daily 7am–11pm.

**Kantina 7, Museumsplatz 1; U-Bahn Museumsquartier.** Simple, relaxed café near the MuseumsQuartier bookshop, with emerald green furniture, and a simple snacky menu of breakfasts, pitta sandwiches and salads. Mon–Wed & Sun 10am–midnight, Thurs–Sat 10am–2am.

**Café Landtmann 1, Dr-Karl-Lueger-Ring 4 ⓦwww.landtmann.at; U-Bahn Herrengasse/ Schottentor.** One of the poshest of the *Kaffeehäuser* – and a favourite with Freud – with impeccably attired waiters, and a high quota of politicians and Burgtheater actors. Live music Sun 8–11pm. Daily 7.30am–midnight.

**Café Leopold 7, Museumsplatz 1 ⓦwww .café-leopold.at; U-Bahn Museumsquartier.** Stylish modernist Leopold Museum café, with a summer terrace overlooking the courtyard. Sink into the beige-and-black leatherette armchairs inside and tuck into the tasty pasta and veggie dishes for less than €8. DJs after 10pm. Daily 10am–2am, Fri & Sat until 4am.

**Café Ministerium 1, Georg-Coch-Platz 4; U-Bahn Stubentor.** Not quite a classic *Kaffeehaus* – the streaked yellow paintwork puts paid to that – but the lunchtime cooking is excellent and it's popular with local civil servants. Mon–Fri 7am–11pm. Live piano Wed & Thurs 4–7pm.

**Café Museum 1, Friedrichstrasse 6 ⓦwww .cafe-museum.at; U-Bahn Karlsplatz.** L-shaped café that was once a favourite haunt of Klimt, Kokoschka and Schiele, among others. A recent refurbishment

▲ Café Palmenhaus

attempted to return the place to the original 1899 Adolf Loos colour scheme, but a lick of paint is really the last thing an old *Kaffeehaus* needs. Live music Tues–Fri 7.30–10pm. Mon–Sat 8am–midnight, Sun 10am–midnight.

**Österreicher im MAK** 1, Stubenring 5 ⓦ www .oesterreicherimmak.at; U-Bahn Stubentor. This museum café, with its wonderfully high nineteenth-century coffered ceiling, has been given a modernist redesign by Eichinger oder Knechtl, and, like the MAK itself (see p.127), is a trendy little spot. The delicious food comes courtesy of one of the city's top chefs. Daily 8.30am–1am.

**Café Palmenhaus** 1, Burggarten ⓦ www.palmenhaus.at; U-Bahn Karlsplatz. Stylish modern café set amid the palms of the greenhouse in the Burggarten. Breakfasts are great and the daily menu specializes in grilled fish and meats. A wonderful treat after visiting the Hofburg. DJs Fri from 9pm. Daily 10am–2am; Jan & Feb closed Mon & Tues.

**Café Prückel** 1, Stubenring 24 ⓦ www .prueckel.at; U-Bahn Stubentor. The *Prückel* has lost two-thirds of its original interior, but the retro 1950s refurbishment has given it a new lease of life, and draws in a great mix of young things, elderly shoppers and dog-owners from the nearby Stadtpark. Piano music Mon, Wed & Fri 7–10pm. Daily 8.30am–10pm.

**Café Sacher** 1, Philharmonikerstrasse 4; ⓦ www.sacher.com; U-Bahn Karlsplatz. For all its fame (see p.115), the *Sacher* is a bit of a let-down. The decor is imperial red and gold, but the *Sachertorte* overrated – practically the only folk who come here nowadays are tourists. Daily 8am–midnight.

**Café Schottenring** 1, Schottenring ⓦ www .café-schottenring.at; U-Bahn Schottentor/Schot-tenring. Situated on the corner of Börsegasse, this L-shaped 1879 *Kaffeehaus*, with its high stuccoed ceiling, is an oasis of calm on the Ringstrasse. Live piano daily 3–7pm. Mon–Fri 6.30am–11pm, Sat & Sun 8am–9pm.

**Café Schwarzenberg** 1, Kärntner Ring 17; U-Bahn Karlsplatz. Opulent café with rich marble, ceramic and wood-panelled decor, plus huge mirrors and a great cake cabinet. The super-snooty waiters can make it a bit of an ordeal. Live piano music Wed & Fri 7.30–11pm, Sat & Sun 5–7pm. Mon–Fri & Sun 7am–midnight, Sat 9am–midnight.

**Una** 7, Museumsplatz 1; U-Bahn Museumsquartier. The best of the MuseumsQuartier cafés, *Una* boasts a wonderful, vaulted floral ceramic ceiling, an imaginative menu and a friendly vibe. Mon–Fri 9am–midnight, Sat 10am–midnight, Sun 10am–6pm.

Urania 1, Uraniastrasse 1 ⓦ www.barurania
.com; U-Bahn Schwedenplatz. Grafted onto
the canalside of the Urania building is this
smart, modern café-bar, with a fabulous
terrace overlooking the Donaukanal.
Mon–Sat 9am–2am, Sun 9am–midnight.

## Landstrasse and Wieden
## (3rd & 4th districts)

Café Anzengruber 4, Schleifmühlgasse 19;
U-Bahn Karlsplatz; see map p.119. Classic
L-shaped Kaffeehaus with lino floor and
formica tables, last refurbished sometime
after World War II, and with some shock-
ingly bad art on the walls. The soupy pasta
fagioli is famous, filling and just €3.50. Mon
5pm–2am, Tues–Sat 11am–2am.

Café Goldegg 4, Argentinerstrasse 49; U-Bahn
Südtiroler Platz; see map p.153. Archetypal
no-nonsense Kaffeehaus a short stroll from
the Belvedere in the backstreets of Wieden.
Mon–Fri 8am–10pm, Sat 8am–1pm.

Im KunstHaus 3, Weissgerberlände 14
ⓦ www.kunsthauswien.com; tram #N;
map p.149. Around the corner from the
Hundertwasserhaus (see p.149), a wonky,
colourful, foliage-strewn café designed by
the man himself. Live music Sat & Sun
noon–5pm. Daily 10am–9pm.

Café Zartl 3, Rasumofskygasse 7; tram #N or
U-Bahn Rochusgasse; see map p.149. Local
corner Kaffeehaus – once Robert Musil's
local – with cream and green decor, billiards,
booths and lots of ice cream sundaes. Daily
8am–midnight; June–Aug Mon–Fri only.

## Mariahilf and around the Naschmarkt
## (4th, 5th & 6th districts)

Café Amacord 4, Rechte Wienzeile 15; U-Bahn
Karlsplatz; see map p.119. Fashionable smoky
Kaffeehaus by the Naschmarkt, with cool
(occasionally live) music, lots of newspapers
and inexpensive food on the menu. Daily
10am–2am.

Bar Italia 6, Mariahilferstrasse 19–21
ⓦ www.baritalia.net; U-Bahn Museumsquartier;
see map p.165. Very posey, sleek, modern
bar set in subterranean vaults not far from
the MuseumsQuartier; great coffee, pastries
and breakfasts and a cheap midday Italian
menu. Mon–Fri 8.30am–2am, Sat 9am–2am,
Sun 10am–2am.

Cuadro 5, Margaretenstrasse 77; U-Bahn
Pilgramgasse; see map p.119. Modern café
in the lovely Biedermeier courtyard of the

Schlossquadrat; defined by its vast backlit
glass wall, and well loved for its organic
breakfasts and square burgers. Mon–Sat
8am–midnight, Sun 9am–11pm.

Café Drechsler 6, Linke Wienzeile 22 ⓦ www
.cafedrechsler.at; U-Bahn Kettenbrückengasse;
see map p.119. Terence Conran has
given what was a scruffy Kaffeehaus by
the Naschmarkt a minimalist makeover,
and it's as popular as ever, especially with
clubbers attracted by the early opening
hours. Mon 8am–2am, Tues–Sat 3am–2am,
Sun 3am–midnight.

Café Jelinek 6, Otto-Bauer-Gasse 5; U-Bahn
Webgasse; see map p.165. Lovely, battered
old Kaffeehaus tucked away in the backstreets south of Mariahilferstrasse, this is a
rare survivor, still serving an exclusively local
clientele. Daily 9am–9pm.

Café Kafka 6, Capistrangasse 8; U-Bahn
Museumsquartier; see map p.165. Old, smokey
Kaffeehaus near the MuseumsQuartier that's
home (once a month) to Vienna's English
poetry group, and serves up veggie and
vegan dishes. Daily 8am–midnight.

Café Ritter 6, Mariahilferstrasse 73; U-Bahn
Neubaugasse; see map p.165. Vast, venerable,
high-ceilinged V-shaped café popular with
veteran card-players and shoppers.
Live piano Thurs–Sat 8–10pm. Daily
7.30am–11.30pm.

Café Rüdigerhof 5, Hamburger Strasse 20;
U-Bahn Kettenbrückengasse; see map p.165.
Wonderful Jugendstil building on the outside,
mishmash of 1950s kitsch on the inside. The
food is cheap and filling, but the riverside
terrace is marred by the nearby busy road.
Daily 9am–2am.

Café Savoy 6, Linke Wienzeile 36; U-Bahn
Kettenbrückengasse; see map p.101. A gay
café for most of the week, with wonderfully
louche, camp fin-de-siècle decor, and
packed with bohemian bargain-hunters
during the Saturday flea market. Mon–Fri
5pm–2am, Sat 9am–2am.

Servus 6, Mariahilferstrasse 57–59 ⓦ www
.servus-café.at; U-Bahn Neubaugasse; see map
p.165. Smart, traditional Kaffeehaus, with red
and white decor, that gets busy with shoppers at lunchtime. Mon–Sat 10am–midnight,
Tues, Thurs & Sat 8–11pm.

Sperl 6, Gumpendorfer Strasse 11
ⓦ www.cafesperl.at; U-Bahn Karlsplatz
/Babenbergerstrasse; see map p.165. One of
the classics of the Kaffeehaus scene, just
off Mariahilferstrasse: L-shaped, with billiard

tables and a hint of elegant, bohemian shabbiness. Mon–Sat 7am–11pm, Sun 11am–8pm (July & Aug closed Sun).

### Neubau (7th district)

Unless otherwise specified, the following places are marked on the map on p.165.

**Café Amadeus 15, Märzstrasse 4** ⓦwww .am.at; U-Bahn Burggasse/Westbahnhof. A genuine *Kaffeehaus*, just the other side of *Gürtel* from Neubau, with lovely old furnishings and a parquet floor. Open evenings only: Mon–Wed 5pm–1am, Thurs & Fri 5pm–2am, Sat 6pm–2am, Sun 6pm–1am.

**Europa 7, Zollergasse 8** ⓦwww.hinterzimmer .at; U-Bahn Neubaugasse. Lively, spacious café that attracts a trendy crowd, who love the posey window booths. The food is a tasty mixture of Viennese and Italian. DJ nights in the *Hinterzimmer* (back room) from 10pm. Daily 9am–4am.

**Lux 7, Schrankgasse 4/Spittelberggasse 3** ⓦwww.lux-restaurant.at; U-Bahn Volkstheater. Rambling modern Spittelberg *Kaffeehaus*, with a friendly bistro feel and an eclectic menu featuring tofu-based dishes, pizzas and pancakes. Mon–Fri 11am–2am, Sat & Sun 10am–2am.

**Das Möbel 7, Burggasse 10** ⓦwww.dasmoebel .at; U-Bahn Volkstheater. Café-bar on the edge of Spittelberg, packed with minimalist furniture (which you can buy), a youngish crowd, weird toilets and reasonable sustenance on offer. Daily 10am–1am.

**Café Weidinger 16, Lerchenfelder Gürtel; U-Bahn Berggasse.** One of the few surviving classic *Gürtel Kaffeehäuser*, with shabby upholstery, battered wood panelling and not a lick of paint for decades. Mon–Fri 7am–1am, Sat & Sun 8am–12.30am.

**Café Westend 7, Mariahilferstrasse 128; U-Bahn Westbahnhof.** Conveniently located directly opposite Westbahnhof, the faded grandeur of this traditional *Kaffeehaus* – once frequented by Hitler – is the best possible introduction to Vienna for those who've just arrived by train. Daily 7am–midnight.

### Josefstadt (8th district)

Unless otherwise specified, the following places are marked on the map on p.165.

**Café Florianihof 8, Florianigasse 45** ⓦwww.florianihof.at; U-Bahn Josefstädter Strasse. Pared-down, old neighbourhood *Kaffeehaus* that has retained one or two Jugendstil touches, and yet has a light and airy, modern feel. Mon–Fri 8am–midnight, Sat & Sun 10am–8pm.

**Café Hummel 8, Josefstädter Strasse 66** ⓦwww.cafehummel.at; U-Bahn Josefstädter Strasse. Big, bustling local *Kaffeehaus*, with formica fittings and tables looking out on the nearby square – they do a brisk lunchtime trade. Mon–Sat 7am–midnight, Sun 8am–midnight.

**Café der Provinz 8, Maria Treu Gasse 3** ⓦwww .cafederprovinz.at.tt; U-Bahn Rathaus or tram #J. Cute, cosy little neighbourhood café, with ad hoc wooden furnishings and delicious galettes, waffles and crêpes. Mon–Fri 8am–11pm, Sat 9am–11pm, Sun 10am–3pm.

**Tunnel 8, Florianigasse 39** ⓦwww .tunnel-vienna-live.at; U-Bahn Josefstädter Strasse. Popular, unpretentious, L-shaped student café with cheap food, big helpings, self-service breakfasts until 11am; live music in the basement from 8pm. Daily 9am–2am.

### Alsergrund (9th district)

The following places are marked on the map on p.170.

**Café Berg 9, Berggasse 8; U-Bahn Schottentor.** Relaxed, modern, mixed gay/straight café, attached to the city's chief gay bookshop, Löwenherz, with an attractive assortment of chairs and great breakfasts, light lunches and main meals. Daily 10am–1am.

**Blaustern 19, Döblinger Gürtel 2** ⓦwww .blaustern.at; U-Bahn Nussdorfer Strasse. Popular, long-established neighbourhood *Kaffeehaus*, in the middle of the *Gürtel*, that's been given a modernist makeover. Mon–Thurs 7am–1am, Fri 7am–2am, Sat 8am–2am, Sun 8am–1am.

**Café Stadlmann** 9, Währinger Strasse 26; U-Bahn Schottentor. Sepia-coloured *Kaffeehaus*, with unrenovated red-velvet alcoves, brass chandeliers and mirrors. Live music Tues & Thurs 7–10pm. Mon–Fri 8am–10pm; Oct–Feb also Sat & Sun 9am–4pm; closed mid-July to mid-Aug.

**Statt-Beisl im WUK** 9, Währingerstrasse 59 ⓦ www.wuk.at; tram #40, #41 or #42. Regular café-bar in the WUK cultural complex (to the left as you enter), offering lots of inexpensive veggie and vegan dishes. Mon–Fri 11am–2am, Sat & Sun 5pm–2am.

**Café Stein** 9, Währingerstrasse 6 ⓦ www .cafe-stein.com; U-Bahn Schottentor. Posey, studenty designer café, on the corner of Kolingasse, with minimalist decor, funky music, trendy loos, online facilities, baguettes, veggie food and breakfasts served until 8pm. Mon–Sat 7am–1am, Sun 9am–1am.

**Café Weimar** 9, Währingerstrasse 68 ⓦ www.cafeweimar.at; tram #40, #41 or #42. L-shaped 1900 *Kaffeehaus* with a high ceiling, chandeliers, tuxedoed waiters and snug booths. Good-value €8 lunchtime menu. Live piano daily 7.30–11.30pm. Mon–Thurs 7.30am–midnight, Fri & Sat 7.30am–2am, Sun 9am–midnight.

**Weltcafé** 9, Schwarzspanierstrasse 15 ⓦ www.weltcafe.at; U-Bahn Schottentor. Very popular fair-trade student café with shocking-red rag-rolled walls, poufs and sofas to collapse in, and cheap food. Daily 9am–2am.

**Café Wilder Mann** 18, Währingerstrasse 85; tram #40, #41 or #42. Established in 1897, this classic *Kaffeehaus* is characterized by its plain postwar decor – lino, booths and bentwood chairs. Mon–Fri 9am–9pm.

## Leopoldstadt (2nd district)

**Café Sperlhof** 2, Grosse Sperlgasse 41; U-Bahn Taborstrasse; see map p.185. Backstreet café that harbours hundreds of board games, playing cards, several billiard tables and other quirky artefacts. Mon–Sat 7.30am–midnight, Sun 8am–8pm.

## The suburbs

**Cobenzl** 19, Am Cobenzl 94 ⓦ www.cobenzl.at; bus #38A from U-Bahn Heiligenstadt; see map p.192. Kaisergelb hilltop pavilion from 1809, now a Wienerwald institution, with great views over the city from the summer terrace. Daily 10am–11pm.

**Café Dommayer** 13, Dommayergasse 1 ⓦ www.dommayer.at; U-Bahn Hietzing; see map p.195. Historic *Kaffeehaus* where Johann Strauss Junior made his premiere. Tuxedoed waiters, comfy alcoves, occasional live music and lots of coffee and cakes. A good rest stop after a hard day at Schönbrunn. Daily 7am–10pm. Live Strauss Sat 2–4pm.

**Gloriette** 13, Schönbrunn Schlosspark ⓦ www.gartenhotel.com; U-Bahn Hietzing/ Schönbrunn; see map p.195. Smart café in the dining hall of a grandiose monument with a spectacular view over Schönbrunn from the hill in the Schlosspark. A lovely 20min walk from the U-Bahn. Daily 9am to dusk.

**Oktogon** 19, Am Himmel ⓦ www.himmel.at; bus #38A from U-Bahn Heiligenstadt; see map p.192. Smart, modern, octagonal café-restaurant that makes a perfect lunch halt whilst out in the Wienerwald. April–Oct Mon–Fri noon–10pm, Sat & Sun 11am–10pm; Nov–March Wed–Sun only.

**CAFÉS** | Cafés

⑩

# Restaurants

Vienna's restaurant scene is dominated by the legacy of the **Beisl** (Yiddish for "little house"), the city's chief traditional eating and drinking establishment. Essentially, the *Beisl* is an unpretentious, muzak-free, wood-panelled inn or *Gasthaus*, where you're expected to share a table with other customers; a family-run place, where folk of all social classes and ages come to drink, socialize, and eat hearty Viennese home cooking. The *Beisl*, on its last legs a decade or so ago, has gained a new lease of life with the emergence of the neo-*Beisl*, a sort of pared-down, modern take on the old formula.

Most Viennese restaurants take great care over the preparation and presentation of their food, and nearly all offer highly **seasonal** fare: at Easter, you'll see dishes

---

## Viennese cuisine

**Viennese cuisine** (*Wiener Küche*) is more varied than in your average German-speaking city, reflecting the multiethnic origins of the old empire.

**Soup** (*Suppe*) is the starting point of most lunchtime menus. Be sure to ask for some of the delicious local **bread** (*Brot*) to go with it, and remember to count how many pieces you eat, as you'll be charged for each one at the end. The standard loaf or *Hausbrot* is a mixture of wheat and rye flour.

The capital's most famous **meat dish**, *Wiener Schnitzel*, is said to have originated from Milan. Traditionally deep-fried breaded veal, it can also be made from chicken or pork, and is normally accompanied by *Erdäpfelsalat*, a potato salad in a watery, sweet dill dressing. Emperor Franz-Josef's favourite dish (and that of many of his subjects) was *Tafelspitz*, thick slices of boiled beef, usually served with *G'röste* (grated fried potato or rosti). Another popular meat dish is *Backhendl*, a young chicken, breaded and deep-fried; and for the adventurous, there's the likes of *Beuschel* (veal-lung stew) to chew on.

The presence of **goulash** (*Gulasch*) on the menu is a Hungarian legacy, while the Italians are behind *Nockerl*, the Austrians' heavy version of pasta noodles; *Schinkenfleckerl*, flecks of ham baked in pasta, is especially popular. **Dumplings** (*Knödel*) are ubiquitous, and are more like English dumplings than the bread-like Czech version from which they derive. You'll also find **fish** on most menus, the most common being trout (*Forelle* or *Saibling*), pike (*Hecht*), carp (*Karpfen*) and pike-perch (*Fogosch*).

Obviously in a country with such a famously sweet tooth, there's no shortage of rich **desserts** (*Mehlspeisen*) on most menus. Apart from the ubiquitous *Apfelstrudel*, Bohemian *Palatschinken* (pancakes), filled with jam and/or curd cheese, are a regular feature. Look out, too, for *Marillenknödel*, sweet apricot dumplings, and the politically incorrect *Mohr im Hemd* – literally "Moor in a shirt" – a chocolate pudding with hot chocolate sauce and whipped cream.

For a German food and drinks **glossary**, see p.338.

## Restaurant prices

We've given each restaurant a price category (see below), which reflects the cost of the majority of **main course** dishes on the menu. These are only a guideline: obviously if you choose the most expensive item on the menu, you're going to exceed our estimate; equally, if you choose the cheapest item on the menu, you'll probably end up paying much less. Don't forget, however, that we have not included the price of starters or puddings, since the main dish alone is often filling enough, nor the price of any drinks:

**Inexpensive**: under €12
**Moderate**: €12–18
**Expensive**: over €18

seasoned with *Bärlauch* (wild garlic); in May, freshly harvested *Spargel* (asparagus) appears almost everywhere; in summer, the puddings will feature summer fruits like *Ribiseln* (redcurrants); in autumn, wild mushrooms such as *Steinpilze* (porcini) and *Eierschwammerl* (chanterelles) feature on menus; *Kürbis* (pumpkins) are put to good use in October; special game (*Wild*) menus appear in late October; and around St Martin's Day (Nov 11), you'll see *Gans* (roast goose) on just about every menu.

The other specifically Viennese institution to sample is the **Heuriger** or wine tavern, which you can find all over the city's wine-growing suburbs. These come into their own in the summer, when a night out at one is just about obligatory. *Heurigen* serve their own wine, and there's usually a traditional self-service cold buffet on offer too. In case you can't make it out to the suburbs, or arrive in the wrong season, there are even one or two *Stadtheurigen* in the city centre to sate yourself in.

The majority of our listings concentrate on typically Viennese establishments, although you can sample cuisines from all over the globe, from the Balkans to Japan. Note that while Vienna isn't a great city for **vegetarians**, it does have a few good veggie restaurants; see p.262 for details.

Remarkably, **prices** remain very reasonable compared to other European capitals, whether you eat in a traditional Viennese *Beisl*, a pizzeria or a posey minimalist restaurant. All restaurants are marked on the relevant map throughout this guide – you'll find a page reference taking you there at each review or section introduction.

**Advance reservations** are advisable in most places, and bringing **cash** is a good idea – plenty of places don't take credit cards. **Tipping** is usually done in a *Beisl* by simply rounding up to the nearest euro, so when the waiter gives you a bill for, say €7.50, you say €8 as you hand over the cash. In other restaurants, add fifteen percent to the bill unless it's already been done for you. To keep the price of meals to a minimum, look for the set **Tagesmenü** (predominantly at lunchtime and often known as a Mittagsmenü), which usually gives you two courses for less than €8. For really **cheap eats**, see p.262, and for **cafés**, which usually offer very good-value meals as well as coffee, cakes and snacks, see p.263.

### Innere Stadt (1st district)

The following places are marked on the map on p.40.

**Achilleus 1**, Köllnerhofgasse 3 ☏512 83 28; **U-Bahn Schwedenplatz**. Strangely Austrian-looking, but excellent, Greek restaurant. Mon–Sat 11am–midnight, Sun 11am–4pm. Inexpensive.

**Beim Czaak 1**, Postgasse 15 ☏513 72 15; **U-Bahn Schwedenplatz**. Lovely dark-green wood panelling and low lighting gives this well-established *Beisl* a cosy, but smart, feel. Mon–Sat 11am–midnight. Inexpensive.

**Bio Bar** 1, Drahtgasse 3 ☏ 968 93 51, ⓦ www .biobar.at; U-Bahn Stephansplatz. Sparse, modern veggie/vegan restaurant, with long benches and tables; the menu changes daily and features soya versions of classic meat dishes, plus risotto, vegetable paella, bruschetta and lots of salad. Mon–Fri 11.30am–3pm & 5.30–11pm, Sat & Sun noon–10.30pm. Inexpensive.

**Brezlg'wölb** 1, Ledererhof 9 ☏ 533 88 11; U-Bahn Herrengasse. Lovely candlelit cave-like restaurant with deliberately olde worlde decor. Hidden in a cobbled street off Draht-gasse, it serves the usual Austrian favourites at knock-down prices. Daily 11.30am–1am. Inexpensive.

**Culinarium Österreich** 1, Neuer Markt 10–11 ☏ 513 82 81, ⓦ www.culinarium.at; U-Bahn Stephansplatz. Very swanky deli, with an inexpensive midday menu for grabs on the ground floor and outside tables, plus a more formal first-floor restaurant specializing in Austrian cuisine. Mon–Sat 11.30am–midnight. Inexpensive–expensive.

**Do & Co** 1, Stephansplatz 12 ☏ 532 03 73, ⓦ www.doco.com; U-Bahn Stephansplatz. Large, loud, and extremely popular restaurant on the third floor of the Haas Haus, overlooking the Stephansdom, offering every type of cuisine from Wiener to sushi. Daily noon–3pm & 6pm–midnight. Expensive.

**Expedit** 1, Wiesingerstrasse 6; ☏ 512 33 13, ⓦ www.expedit.net; U-Bahn Stubentor. Bar, deli and cantina all rolled into one, this converted warehouse attracts a youthful crowd, who tuck into the antipasti and Ligurian speciali-ties with gusto. Don't forget to check out the indoor *boccia*, an Italian version of *boules* in the basement (€5 for half an hour). Mon–Fri noon–midnight, Sat 6pm–midnight. Moderate.

**Figlmüller** 1, Wollzeile 5 ☏ 512 61 77, ⓦ www.figlmueller.at; U-Bahn Stephansplatz. Branch nearby at 1, Bäckerstrasse 6 (closed July) and out at 19, Grinzingerstrasse 55 (tram #38). It's in every tourist guide to the city there is, but this is still *the* place to eat a giant *Wiener Schnitzel*, with a traditional potato salad, washed down with wine (there's no beer). Daily 11am–10.30pm. Closed Aug. Moderate.

**Gösser Bierklinik** 1, Steindlgasse 4 ☏ 533 75 98 12, ⓦ goesser-bierklinik.at; U-Bahn Stephans-platz. Ancient inn with wooden booths for drinking, and a more formal backroom restaurant serving traditional Austrian food. Mon–Sat 10am–11.30pm. Inexpensive.

**Griechenbeisl** 1, Fleischmarkt 11 ☏ 533 19 77, ⓦ www.griechenbeisl.at; U-Bahn Schwedenplatz. Possibly the most ancient of all Vienna's inns (see p.71), frequented by the likes of Beethoven, Schubert and Brahms, a fact that it predictably milks in order to draw in the tourists. Daily 11am–12.30am. Moderate.

**Gulaschmuseum** 1, Schulerstrasse 20 ☏ 512 10 17, ⓦ www.gulasch.at; U-Bahn Stubentor. Not a museum at all, just a *Beisl* specializing in some fifteen varieties of goulash for around €12. Mon–Fri 9am–midnight, Sat & Sun 10am–midnight. Inexpensive.

**Hollmann Salon** 1, Grashofgasse 3 ☏ 961 19 60 40, ⓦ www.hollmann-salon.at; U-Bahn Schwe-denplatz. A very classy (no-smoking) Viennese restaurant hidden away in the courtyard of the Heiligenkreuzhof, offering a good spread of immaculately presented meat, fish and veggie dishes. Mon–Sat 11am–10pm. Expensive.

**Hotel Riviera** 1, Schönlaterngasse 13 ☏ 907 61 49, ⓦ www.lametta.at; U-Bahn Schwedenplatz. Creamy white Italian restaurant, with a lovely summer terrace, that brings a slice of stylish Med cuisine to the backstreets of Vienna. Mon–Fri 11am–midnight. Inexpensive.

**Ilona-Stüberl** 1, Bräunerstrasse 2 ☏ 533 90 29, ⓦ www.ilonastueberl.at; U-Bahn Stephansplatz. Long-standing Gypsy-music-free Hungarian restaurant with lashings of goulash on offer. Daily noon–11pm; Oct–March closed Mon. Inexpensive.

**Immervoll** 1, Weihburggasse 17 ☏ 513 52 88; U-Bahn Stephansplatz. Small, but very popular lime- and pastel-green wood-panelled neo-*Beisl* designed by Hermann Czech, offering a small, but excellent Viennese menu. Daily noon–midnight. Inexpensive.

**Kornat** 1, Marc-Aurel-Strasse 8 ☏ 535 65 18, ⓦ www.kornat.at; U-Bahn Schwedenplatz. Small Croatian restaurant specializing in grilled saltwater fish and Dalmatian seafood dishes – go for the daily specials. Mon–Sat 11.30am–3pm & 6pm–midnight. Moderate.

**Limes** 1, Hoher Markt 10 ☏ 905 800, ⓦ www .restaurant-limes.at; U-Bahn Stephansplatz/ Schwedenplatz. Limes refers to the frontier of the Roman Empire, but this stark, minimal-ist eatery is indeed playfully decorated with a touch of lime; menu is a Med-influenced. Mon–Sat 10am–10.30pm. Moderate.

**Meinl am Graben** 1, Graben 19 ☏ 532 33 34, ⓦ www.meinlamgraben.com; U-Bahn Stephans-platz. Elegant first-floor restaurant at the flagship branch of the swanky Julius Meinl

# Coffee and cakes

Paris may have more of them, but Vienna is the spiritual home of the café or *Kaffeehaus*. Legend has it that coffee was first introduced to Vienna by a certain Georg Franz Kolschitzky, an Austrian spy who regularly penetrated the Turkish camp during the siege of 1683. When the siege was finally lifted, Kolschitzky was asked what he wanted in return for his services. He requested to be given the "camel fodder" – in actual fact sacks of coffee beans – left behind by the hastily departed Turks, and went on to open the first coffeehouse in Vienna the same year.

Kaffeehaus waiter ▲

Petits fours ▼

# A Viennese institution

By the late nineteenth century the *Kaffeehaus* had become Vienna's most important social institution. It was described by writer Stefan Zweig as "a sort of democratic club to which admission costs the small price of a cup of coffee. Upon payment of this mite, every guest can sit for hours on end, discuss, write, play cards, receive his mail, and above all, can go through an unlimited number of newspapers and magazines". The *Kaffeehaus* became an informal office for its *Stammgäste* or regulars, where they could work, relax and receive clients in warmth and comfort. At certain cafés, the head waiter or *Herr Ober* could direct each customer to a certain table or *Stammtisch* depending on what subject he (or less frequently she) wished to debate.

Even today, there is still something unique about the institution that makes a visit worthwhile. While the rest of the world queues up for fast food, the Viennese *Kaffeehaus* implores you to slow down, or, as the sign in one such café says, "Sorry, we do not cater for people in a hurry". In his own time, a tuxedoed waiter will ask for your order and, for the price of a small coffee, will allow you to sit for as long as you like without asking you to move on or buy another drink. At this point, you should admire your surroundings: the high ceiling, the marble table-tops, the velvety upholstery, the bentwood coat stands, perhaps a billiard table or two. Select yourself a newspaper and – thanks to the absence of piped music and the general censure on mobiles – appreciate the timeless tranquillity of the *Kaffeehaus*.

# Coffee

On average, the Austrians drink almost twice as much **coffee** as beer (more than a pint a day per head of the population). When ordering, few Viennese ever actually ask for a straight *Kaffee*, as the varieties are legion. However, whatever you order, it will come on a little silver tray, accompanied by a glass of water.

▲ Café society

**Brauner** Black coffee with a small amount of milk.

**Cappuccino** The Austrian version of a cappuccino comes with whipped cream (*Schlagobers*).

**Einspänner** Small black coffee, served in a tall glass and topped with whipped cream.

**Eiskaffee** Iced coffee with ice cream and whipped cream.

**Fiaker** A coffee with a shot of rum and whipped cream.

**Kaffee Crème** Coffee served with a little jug of milk.

**Konsul** Black coffee with a spot of cream.

**Kurz** Viennese version of an espresso.

**Mazagran** Coffee served with an ice cube and laced with rum, to be drunk in one gulp.

**Mélange** (pronounced like the French). Equal measures of frothed milk and coffee – more of a cappuccino than an Austrian *Cappuccino*.

**Milch Kaffee** Large hot, frothy, milky coffee.

**Pharisäer** Coffee in a glass topped with whipped cream, served with a small glass of rum on the side.

**Schwarzer** or **Mokka** Small or large black coffee.

**Türkische** Coffee grains and sugar boiled up together in individual copper pots to create a strong, sweet brew.

**Verlängerter Brauner** or **Schwarzer** Slightly weaker than normal coffee.

▲ Torten

▼ Billiards

Café Prückel ▲

Café Sperl ▼

Kaffeehaus newspaper rack ▼

# Cakes

Many *Kaffeehäuser* in Vienna will have *Torten* piled high in a display cabinet, in which case you can simply point to the one that takes your fancy.

The best cafés still bake their own cakes on site, and all can be served with a helping of *Schlagobers* (whipped cream).

The box below details some of the more common choices.

**Apfelstrudel** Apple and raisins wrapped in pastry and sprinkled with icing sugar.

**Biskuitroulade** The basic roulade is a jam roll, but it comes in various other creamier versions.

**Dobostorte** A rich Hungarian cake made up of alternate layers of biscuit sponge and chocolate cream.

**Esterházytorte** Several layers of cream and sponge coated in white icing with a feather design on top.

**Guglhupf** Sigmund Freud's favourite, at its most basic a simple sponge cake baked in a fluted ring mould and cut into slices.

**Linzertorte** Essentially a jam tart made with almond pastry.

**Mohnstrudel** A bread-like pudding rather like an *Apfelstrudel*, but with a poppy seed-and-raisin filling.

**Powidltascherl** This is basically a Danish pastry, filled with plum jam.

**Punschkrapfen** More of a *petit four* than a proper slice of cake, this is a mouthful of cake filled with jam, rum and chocolate and encased in icing.

**Sachertorte** The most famous of the Viennese cakes – and in some ways the least interesting – a chocolate sponge cake coated in chocolate, most often with a layer of apricot jam beneath the chocolate coating.

**Topfenstrudel** Like an *Apfelstrudel*, but with a sweet curd cheese filling.

**Zwetschgenkuchen** A spongy tart dotted with halved plums.

store, with a view straight down Graben. The cooking here is fairly flashy for Vienna, and very good, taking its inspiration from all over. Mon–Wed 8.30am–midnight, Thurs & Fri 8am–midnight, Sat 9am–midnight. Expensive.

**Ofenloch** 1, Kurrentgasse 8 ℡ 533 88 44, ⓦ www.ofenloch.at; U-Bahn Stephansplatz. Upmarket *Beisl*, just off Judenplatz, with wood-panelled booths and a cosy, *gemütlich* atmosphere. Mon–Sat 11am–midnight. Moderate.

▲ Ofenloch Beisl

**Palatschinkenkuchl** 1, Köllnerhofgasse 4 ℡ 512 31 05; U-Bahn Schwedenplatz. Informal restaurant popular with kids and adults alike for its savoury and sweet pancakes and milkshakes. Daily 10am–midnight. Inexpensive.

**Pfudl** 1, Bäckerstrasse 22 ⓦ www.gasthauspfudl .com. Old-fashioned, *gemütlich Gasthaus* with chequered tablecloths and classic Viennese dishes on the menu. Daily 10am–midnight. Moderate.

**Plachutta** 1, Wollzeile 38 ℡ 512 15 77, ⓦ www .plachutta.at; U-Bahn Stubentor. Branches in Nussdorf and Heitzing. Smart green decor adorns this traditional family-run Viennese restaurant, specializing in Emperor Franz-Josef's favourite dish, *Tafelspitz*. Daily 11.30am–midnight. Moderate.

**Regina Margherita** 1, Wallnerstrasse 4 ℡ 533 08 12, ⓦ www.barbaro.at; U-Bahn Herrengasse. Smart, bustling Neapolitan pizza-and-pasta joint in the inner court of the Palais Esterházy. Pizzas are cooked in a stupendous lava oven, and you can eat alfresco in the summer. Mon–Sat noon–3pm & 6pm–midnight. Moderate.

**Reinthaler** 1, Gluckgasse 5 ℡ 512 33 66; U-Bahn Karlsplatz. Dive down the steps to this genuine, no-nonsense Viennese *Beisl* that's busy with locals. No concessions to modern cooking (and none to veggies). Mon–Fri 9am–11pm. Inexpensive.

**Toko-Ri** 1, Salztorgasse 4 ℡ 533 77 77, ⓦ www.tokori.at; U-Bahn Schwedenplatz. Branches at the Naschmarkt and at 2, Franz Hochedlingergasse 2 (U-Bahn Schottenring). One of the city's better sushi outlets, with prices that are a relative bargain. Daily 10.30am–midnight. Moderate.

**Zum Finsteren Stern** 1, Schulhof 8 ℡ 535 21 00; U-Bahn Schwedenplatz. Vaulted wine bar in the side streets near Judenplatz with a lovely summer terrace and homemade pasta and other Italian delights on the menu. Mon–Sat 6pm–1am. Moderate.

## Ringstrasse

The following places are marked on the map on p.100.

**Glacisbeisl** 7, Museumsplatz 1 ℡ 526 56 60, ⓦ www.glacisbeisl.at; U-Bahn Volkstheater. Hidden in the entrails of the Museums-Quartier, *Glacisbeisl* has had a stark modern makeover; the food is even better than it used to be and the summer terrace as lovely as ever – be warned, though, it's very popular. Daily 11am–2am. Inexpensive.

**Gmoa Keller** 3, Am Heumarkt 25 ℡ 712 53 10, ⓦ www.gmoakeller.at; U-Bahn Stadtpark. Pared-down old *Beisl* with a lovely vaulted ceiling and parquet flooring, and good Viennese cuisine. Mon–Sat 11am–midnight. Inexpensive.

**Hansen** 1, Wipplingerstrasse 34 ℡ 532 05 42, ⓦ www.hansen.co.at; U-Bahn Schottentor. Attractive, smart restaurant located in the flower and gardening shop in the basement of the city's splendid former stock exchange. Mon–Fri 9am–9pm, Sat 9am–5pm. Moderate.

**Kervansaray** 1, Mahlerstrasse 9 ℡ 512 88 43, ⓦ www.kervansaray.at; U-Bahn Karlsplatz. This is the city's top fish and seafood restaurant: on the ground floor, Turkish waiters will tell

## Viennoiserie: origin of the pastries

According to some, Vienna is the home of the **bagel** and the **croissant**. The former is, of course, of Jewish origin, but is said to have been popularized here after a Jewish baker presented one to Jan Sobieski after the lifting of the 1683 siege of Vienna; its name is thought to come from *Bügel* (stirrup). The croissant also arose from this historical period, its shape said to represent the half-crescent moon on the Turkish flags. (Maria Theresia's daughter, Marie Antoinette, is responsible for exporting the croissant to France when she married the future Louis XVI.)

you what the specials are, while upstairs the *Hummerbar* specializes in lobster. Mon–Sat noon–midnight. Expensive.

**Steirereck 1, Stadtpark** ☏713 31 68, ⓦwww .steirereck.at; U-Bahn Stadtpark or Stubentor. Much hyped, pricey Styrian restaurant in the Stadtpark, which also runs the charming riverside *Meierei*, serving an incredible array of cheeses and less expensive meals from 9am. Mon–Fri 11.30am–3pm & 6.30–11pm. Moderate–expensive.

**Vestibül 1, Dr Karl-Lueger-Ring 2** ☏532 49 99, ⓦwww.vestibuel.at; U-Bahn Herrengasse. Buzzing restaurant in one of the ornate wings of the Burgtheater, serving up classy dishes to a moneyed crowd. Mon–Fri 11am–midnight, Sat 6pm–midnight; July & Aug closed Sat & Sun. Expensive.

**Zwillingswöbl 1, Universitätsstrasse 5;** U-Bahn Schottentor. Popular, unpretentious, smoky student *Beisl*, just down from the university. Mon–Fri 9am–1am, Sat 10am–1am. Inexpensive.

### Landstrasse (3rd district)

**Salm Bräu 3, Rennweg 8** ☏799 59 92, ⓦwww.salmbraeu.com; see map p.153. Conveniently located beer hall, which brews its own beer in an old monastic wine cellar, and serves filling pub food, right outside the Unteres Belvedere. Daily 11am–midnight. Inexpensive.

**Stadtwirt 3, Untere Viaduktgasse 45** ☏713 38 28, ⓦwww.stadtwirt.at; U-Bahn Landstrasse /Wien-Mitte; see map p.149. Large, classic, wood-panelled family-run *Beisl*; the food is traditional Viennese, the wine sourced from their own vineyard. Mon–Fri 10am–midnight, Sat 4pm–1am, Sun 11am–4pm. Moderate.

**Wild 3, Radetzkyplatz 1** ☏920 94 77; tram #N from U-Bahn Schwedenplatz; see map p.149. Stylish refurbished *Beisl* with lots of traditional dishes on the menu as well as more modern food. Daily 11.30am–11pm. Moderate.

### Wieden, Margareten and Mariahilf (4th, 5th & 6th districts)

**Aux Gazelles 6, Rahlgasse 5** ☏585 66 45, ⓦwww .auxgazelles.at; U-Bahn Museumsquartier; see map p.119. The full over-the-top North African monty, this converted brick factory houses a café and deli, caviar and oyster bar, *salon de thé*, club bar and even a small *hammam*. Mon–Sat 11am–2am. Moderate–expensive.

**Kiang Noodles 6, Joanelligasse 3** ☏586 87 96, ⓦwww.kiang.at; U-Bahn Kettenbrückengasse; see map p.165. Plus numerous branches. *Wagamama*-style designer noodle restaurant chain. All branches feature minimal, modernist decor, efficient service and freshly prepared dishes. Mon–Sat 6pm–midnight. Inexpensive–moderate.

**Nice Rice 6, Mariahilferstrasse 45** ☏586 28 39; U-Bahn Neubaugasse; see map p.165. Small vegetarian place, down a passageway off Mariahilferstrasse, serving a range of inexpensive Eastern rice dishes. Mon–Fri 11am–11pm, Sat 11am–6pm. Inexpensive.

**Ra'mien 6, Gumpendorferstrasse 9** ☏585 47 98, ⓦwww.ramien.at; U-Bahn Museumsquartier; see map p.119. Very popular, clubby, designer noodle restaurant with a late-night bar (open until the early hours) attached. Tues–Sun 11am–midnight. Inexpensive.

**Silberwirt 5, Schlossgasse 21** ☏544 49 07, ⓦwww.schlossquadr.at; tram #62 or #65 and bus #13A; see map p.119. Neo-rustic *Beisl* on a lovely courtyard just south of the Naschmarkt, serving traditional Viennese cuisine. Daily noon–midnight. Moderate.

**Tancredi 4, Grosse Neugasse 5/Rubensgasse 2** ☏941 00 48, ⓦwww.tancredi.at; U-Bahn Taubstummengasse or tram #62 or #65; see map p.119. Simple, bright, whitewashed restaurant with a lovely summer terrace that serves carefully prepared seasonal Viennese dishes. Tues–Fri 11.30am–2.30pm & 6pm–midnight, Sat 6pm–midnight. Moderate.

Umar 4, Naschmarkt Stand 76–79 ☎587 04
56; U-Bahn Karlsplatz; see map p.119. Fish
restaurant run by Naschmarkt fishmonger;
the stuff is as fresh as it gets in landlocked
Vienna, and it's simply prepared. Mon–Sat
11.30am–11pm. Inexpensive.

Wieden Bräu 4, Waaggasse 5 ☎586 03 00,
Ⓦwww.wieden-braeu.at; U-Bahn Taubstummengasse. Typical Austrian pub, with simple
decor, fine beers brewed on the premises,
and filling traditional food on the menu.
Mon–Sat 11.30am–1am, Sun 11.30am–
midnight; July & Aug closed Sat & Sun until
4pm. Inexpensive.

## Neubau (7th district)

The following places appear on the
map on p.165.

Centimeter II 7, Stiftgasse 4; U-Bahn
Volkstheater/Neubaugasse. Lively, popular
Spittelberg branch of this laid-back chain,
with a mixed crowd, very cheap, filling food,
and lots of beers on tap. Mon–Thurs
10am–1am, Fri & Sat 10am–2am, Sun
10am–1am. Inexpensive.

Grünauer 7, Hermanngasse 32 ☎526 40 80;
tram #49. Tiny local *Beisl*, in the backstreets
of Neubau, which takes its traditional Viennese cooking and wine cellar seriously. Mon
6pm–midnight, Tues–Fri 11.30am–2.30pm &
6pm–midnight. Inexpensive.

Plutzer Bräu 7, Schrankgasse 2 ☎526 12 15,
Ⓦwww.plutzerbraeu.at; U-Bahn Volkstheater.
Spacious designer beer bar in Spittelberg,
good for a quiet lunch or a much more bois-
terous evening drink. Regularly shows live
TV sports. Daily 10.30am–2am. Inexpensive.

Schilling 7, Burggasse 103 ☎524 17 75,
Ⓦwww.schilling-wirt.at; tram #5 or bus #48A.
A modish crowd frequents this nouveau,
stripped-down *Beisl* on the corner of
Halbgasse; the food is traditional but imaginatively presented and freshly prepared.
Daily 11am–1am. Inexpensive.

Schnitzelwirt 7, Neubaugasse 52 ☎523 37 71;
tram #49. Aside from *Figlmüller* (see p.165),
this is the place to eat *Wiener Schnitzel*
– here, they're just as huge, cheaper and
served with chips. Mon–Sat 11am–10pm.
Inexpensive.

Siebensternbräu 7, Siebensterngasse 19
☎523 86 97, Ⓦwww.7stern.at; tram #49.
Popular, modern microbrewery, serving solid
Viennese pub food, with lots of pan-fried
dishes served with dark rye bread. Daily
10am–midnight. Inexpensive.

Spatzennest 7, Ulrichsplatz 1 ☎526 16 59;
bus #13A or #48A. Much treasured,
down-to-earth local Viennese *Beisl*, just
off Burggasse. Daily except Fri & Sat
10am–midnight. Inexpensive.

Witwe Bolte 7, Gutenberggasse 13
☎523 14 50; U-Bahn Volkstheater. Long-
established *Wiener Beisl* in the charming
backstreets of Spittelberg, famous for
having been visited by Josef II incognito
in the eighteenth century. Lovely summer
garden. Daily 11.30am–11.30pm.
Inexpensive.

Zu den Zwei Lieseln 7, Burggasse 63 ☎523 32
82; tram #49 or bus #48A. Very old-fashioned
*Beisl*, with a nice summer garden, serving
cheap and succulent *Wiener schnitzel*. Daily
11am–10pm. Inexpensive.

## Beer

Most Austrian **beer** (*Bier*) is a high-quality brew of the light, continental-lager or
pilsner type. The most common are the local-brewed Gold Fassl from the suburb of Ottakring, and Gösser, from Styria. However, even the locals defer to the
Czechs when it comes to **beer,** and you should be able to find Bohemian Budvar
and Pilsner Urquell in quite a few bars and restaurants. Those with a keen interest
should check out the following microbreweries: *Salm Bräu* (see p.274), *Wieden
Bräu* (see p.275), *Plutzer Bräu* (see p.275), *Siebenstern Bräu* (see p.275) and
*Fischer Bräu* (see p.277).

Beer is generally drunk by the half litre or *Krügerl*, but you can also ask for a third
of a litre or *Seidl*, an eighth of a litre or *Pfiff*, and occasionally a *Mass* or litre jug.
Draught beer is *Bier vom Fass*, and you can occasionally get *dunkel* (dark) as
opposed to *hell* (light) beer, or ask for it *schnitt* (literally "cut"), half-dark-half-light.
Bottled *Weissbier* (wheat beer) is worth trying: note, however, that it's extremely fizzy,
and you must pour it very slowly to avoid creating a vast head.

## Josefstadt (8th district)

The following places are marked on the map on p.165.

**Il Sestante 8, Piaristengasse 50** ☎402 98 94, ⊛www.sestante.at; U-Bahn Rathaus. L-shaped Sicilian restaurant decked out in warm apricot colours, with modern furnishings and wood panelling, serving tasty pizzas, fresh pasta and risotto. Mon–Sat 11.30am–11.30pm. Inexpensive.

**¡Mas! 8, Laudongasse 36** ☎403 83 24, ⊛www .restaurante-mas.at; tram #5, #43 or #44. Stylish, modern Latino joint serving filling enchiladas and tacos, nicely washed down with a margarita. Mon–Sat 6pm–2am, Sun 10am–2am. Inexpensive.

**Schnattl 8, Lange Gasse 40** ☎405 34 00; U-Bahn Rathaus. Very formal restaurant serving local cuisine cooked with a Styrian bent by Herr Schnattl himself; call to reserve a table in the courtyard. Mon–Fri 11.30am–2.30pm & 6pm–midnight. Moderate.

**Die Wäscherei 8, Albertgasse 49/Laudongasse** ☎409 23 75-11, ⊛www.die-waescherei.at; U-Bahn Josefstädterstrasse. Funky, arty little bar with an imaginative menu, lots of veggie choices and great beers on offer. Mon–Fri 5pm–2am, Sat 10am–2am, Sun 10am–midnight. Inexpensive.

## Alsergrund (9th district)

The following places are marked on the map on p.170.

**Flein 9, Boltzmanngasse 2** ☎319 76 89; tram #37, #38, #40, #41 & #42. Lovely, inventive food served in a small informal setting. It's a perfect spot in fine weather, with a large terrace looking across Clam-Gallas Park. Mon–Fri 11am–midnight. Inexpensive.

**Kutschker 44 18, Kutschkergasse 44** ☎470 20 47, ⊛www.kutschker44.at; tram #40 or #41. One tram stop from Alsergrund, on the other side of the *Gürtel*, this is a very smart, modern neo-*Beisl* serving excellent Viennese food – try the duck breast. Tues–Sat 4pm–midnight. Moderate.

**Stomach 9, Seegasse 26** ☎310 20 99; tram #D. Informal Styrian *Beisl*, with a lovely cobbled courtyard, specializing in creative beef dishes, but also catering well for veggies. Wed–Sat 4pm–midnight, Sun 10am–10pm. Moderate.

**Wickerl 9, Porzellangasse 24a** ☎317 74 89, ⊛www.wickerl.at; tram #D. Unpretentious, popular neighbourhood *Beisl* serving cheap, classic Viennese fillers, plus live TV sports. Mon–Fri 9am–midnight, Sat 10am–midnight. Inexpensive.

**Zum Reznicek 9, Reznicekgasse 10** ☎317 91 40; tram #D. Popular local *Beisl*, a short walk from Franz-Josefs Bahnhof, serving superb offal specialities with loads of beers on tap. Daily noon–11pm. Inexpensive.

## Leopoldstadt (2nd district)

The following places are marked on the map on p.185.

**Altes Jägerhaus 2, Aspernallee, Prater** ☎728 95 77, ⊛www.altes-jagerhaus.com; bus #77A. Typical old-fashioned *Beisl*, at the far end of the Hauptallee, with a large summer terrace. A nice place to enjoy hearty fare and a Budvar beer. April–Sept daily 9am–11pm; Oct–Dec & March Wed–Sun 9am–11pm; Jan & Feb Wed–Sun 9am–6pm. Moderate.

**Gasthaus am Nordpol 3 2, Nordwestbahnstrasse 17/Nordpolstrasse** ☎333 58 54; tram #5 or #N. Ancient *Beisl* at the back of the Augarten, restored to new glory: lots of wood, friendly staff, and Bohemian bread, food and beer. Mon–Sat 5pm–midnight, Sun noon–midnight. Inexpensive.

**Leopold 2, Grosser Pfarrgasse 11** ☎218 22 81; U-Bahn Taborstrasse. Chic, modern neo-*Beisl*, with high ceiling, pine furniture, classic local dishes and great Sunday brunches. Daily Mon–Sat 6pm–midnight, Sun 10am–3pm. Inexpensive.

**Lusthaus 2, Freudenau 254, Prater** ☎728 95 65, ⊛www.lusthaus-wien.at; bus #77A. Eighteenth-century rotunda at the far end of Hauptallee that makes a perfect food halt while exploring the Prater. Jan–April daily noon–6pm; May–Sept Mon–Fri noon–11pm, Sat & Sun noon–6pm; Oct–April daily except Wed noon–6pm. Moderate.

**Schöne Perle 2, Leopoldsgasse/Grosser Pfarrgasse** ☎243 35 93, ⊛www.schoene-perle.at; U-Bahn Taborstrasse. Smart but relaxed L-shaped local neo-*Beisl* serving typical Viennese dishes made with organic produce. Daily noon–midnight. Inexpensive.

**Schuppich 2, Rotensterngasse 18** ☎212 43 40, ⊛www.schuppich.at; U-Bahn Taborstrasse. A taste of Trieste (once the Habsburgs' main sea port); à la carte or a four-course menu for €25. Wed–Sat 6pm–midnight, Sun noon–4pm & 6–10pm. Moderate.

**Schweizerhaus 2, Strasse des 1 Mai 116, Prater** ☎728 01 52, ⊛www.schweizerhaus.at;

U-Bahn Praterstern. **Massive** Czech-owned terrace restaurant in the Prater; known for its draught beer and Czech specialities such as tripe soup and grilled pigs' trotters (*Stelzen*). Mid-March to Oct Mon–Fri 11am–11pm, Sat & Sun 10am–11pm. Inexpensive.

**Skopik & Lohn** 2, Leopoldsgasse 17 ☎219 89 77, ⒲www.skopikundlohn.at; U-Bahn Taborstrasse. Mustard-coloured wood-panelled neighbourhood neo-*Beisl* with scribbly art on the ceiling, serving Med-influenced Viennese dishes; large and very nice summer terrace. Daily 5pm–1am. Moderate.

### The suburbs

**Fischer Bräu** 19, Billrothstrasse 17 ☎369 59 49, ⒲www.fischerbraeu.at; U-Bahn Nussdorferstrasse. Very civilized microbrewery pub, which produces a great, lemony, misty beer. Lots of tasty snacks and more substantial pub fare to be consumed in the bare-boards interior or the shady courtyard. Mon–Sat 4pm–1am, Sun 11am–1am. Inexpensive.

**Salettl** 19, Hartäckerstrasse 80 ☎479 22 22; bus #37A or #40A. Turn-of-the-century pavilion near the Döblinger Friedhof, with outdoor seating overlooking the Wienerwald. The breakfasts are varied and legendary. Daily 6.30am–1.30am. Inexpensive–moderate.

**Schloss Concordia** 11, Simmeringer Hauptstrasse 283 ☎769 88 88; tram #6 or #71. Popular destination for a post-funeral knees-up, the candlelit *Schloss Concordia* sits directly opposite the Central Cemetery and serves up a vast range of *Schnitzels* and other traditional food. Daily 10am–1am. Inexpensive.

**Strandcafé** 22, Florian-Berndl-Gasse 20 ☎203 67 47, ⒲www.strandcafe-wien.at; U-Bahn Alte Donau. This no-nonsense *Gasthaus* has a large riverside terrace overlooking the Alte Donau with UNO-City in the distance. Daily 10am–midnight. Inexpensive.

**Villa Aurora** 16, Wilhelminenstrasse 237 ☎489 33 33; bus #146B from U-Bahn Ottakring. Beautiful nineteenth-century villa serving traditional dishes out in the fields overlooking Vienna. Daily 10am–midnight. Inexpensive–moderate.

# Heurigen

**Heurigen** are the wine taverns found predominantly in the former villages of the city's outer suburbs, to the north and west of the centre on the slopes of the Wienerwald. The word *heurig* means "this year's": it was in these taverns that the vintner would encourage tastings in order to try and sell a few bottles of his (exclusively white) **wine**. As an institution they are as old as the city itself, but came into their own during the Biedermeier period (1815–48). In the good old days people used to bring their own picnics to consume, sat on wooden benches

### Wine

Austrians tend to drink a lot more beer than wine, though in Vienna it's **wine** (*Wein*) that holds a special place in the capital's history and geography. It's a spot literally surrounded by vineyards, many of which lie within the city boundaries – there are even suggestions that the city's name is itself derived from the word "wine".

The best place to try the local stuff is, of course, in a *Heuriger* or wine tavern. Wine is drunk by the *Viertel* (a 25cl mug) or the *Achterl* (a 12.5cl glass). The majority of wine produced in Austria is white, the dry, fruity *Grüner Veltliner* being the most popular. Most red wine hails from Burgenland, where *Blaufränkisch* is the ubiquitous grape type, producing a characteristically peppery wine with lots of blackcurrant flavour. Burgenland is also famous, of course, for the great antifreeze scandal of 1985, when several local wine growers were convicted of adulterating their wine.

It's common practice to water down your white wine with soda water by ordering a *Gespritzer*. Look out, too, for *Sturm*, the half-fermented young wine that hits the streets and bars in autumn, and be sure to try out a mug of *Glühwein* or mulled wine, available at Christmas markets all over the city in late November and December.

## Village Heurigen

**Grinzing** is the most famous of Vienna's *Heuriger* village-suburbs, and consequently the most touristy. There are numerous *Heurigen* on the main street of Sandgasse, but to avoid the worst of the crowds head further up Cobenzlgasse. Next most popular are the nearby areas of **Heiligenstadt** and **Nussdorf**. Less touristy alternatives include Sievering and Neustift am Walde. Another option is to cross over the Danube and head for the village of Stammersdorf, and its immediate neighbour Strebersdorf. The recommendations below are meant as starting points for each district.

### Grinzing

**Reinprecht** 19, Cobenzlgasse 22 ☏320 14 71, ⓦheuriger-reinprecht.at; tram #38 to the terminus. Huge, 300-year-old Heuriger housed in an old monastery, with live *Schrammelmusik*. Touristy but fun. March to mid-Dec daily 3.30pm–midnight.

**Zawodsky** 19, Reinischgasse 3 ☏320 79 78, ⓦwww.zawodsky.at; tram #38. Classic, simple *Heuriger*, with benches set out in a lovely apple orchard garden with fantastic views over Vienna. Mid-Feb–Dec Wed & Thurs 5pm–midnight, Fri, Sat & Sun 2pm–midnight.

### Heiligenstadt

**Mayer am Pfarrplatz** 19, Pfarrplatz 2 ☏370 33 61, ⓦwww.mayer.pfarrplatz.at; bus #38A from U-Bahn Heiligenstadt. One of Beethoven's many addresses in Vienna, now a cosy *Heuriger*, with live *Schrammelmusik* (daily from 7pm) and a large, shady patio garden out back. Mid-Jan to mid-Dec Mon–Sat 4pm–midnight, Sun 11am–midnight.

### Kahlenbergerdorf

**Hirt** 19, Eisernenhandgasse 165 ☏318 96 41; 15min walk from S-Bahn Kahlenbergerdorf. Lovely *Heuriger* tucked into the slopes below Leopoldsberg overlooking the Danube. April–Oct Wed–Fri 3–11pm, Sat & Sun noon–11pm; Nov–March Fri–Sun noon–11pm.

### Neustift am Walde

**Schreiberhaus** 19, Rathstrasse 54 ☏440 38 44, ⓦwww.dasschreiberhaus.at; bus #35A from U-Bahn Nussdorfer Strasse. Set in the midst of Neustift's sloping

in the vintner's garden while drinking the wine, but nowadays, most *Heurigen* provide a **self-service buffet** of traditional Viennese dishes.

According to Emperor Josef II's 1784 law, real *Heurigen* are only permitted to open for three hundred days in any one year (usually from March to November), and may only sell wine and food produced on the premises. If the *Heuriger* is open, the custom is to display a *Buschen* or bunch of evergreen boughs over the entrance and a sign telling you it's *ausg'stekt* (hung out). Those that still abide by the strict *Heurigen* laws generally have a sign saying *Buschenschank*, though it has to be said that some have now got themselves restaurant licences in order to open all year round.

Traditionally a visit to a *Heuriger* is accompanied by *Schrammelmusik*, sentimental fiddle, guitar and accordion **music**, though today this only features at the more touristy ventures – the Viennese tend to prefer the experience without accompaniment. *Heurigen* are especially popular with the locals in September and October when the new wine – *Sturm* or *Most* – is available. In addition to the *Heurigen* in the outer suburbs, there are a handful of wine taverns known as *Stadtheurigen* closer to the centre of town, usually in the cellars of the city's monasteries. These are not real *Heurigen* at all, but are still great places to drink wine and eat the local cuisine.

With the exception of the *Stadtheurigen*, the opening times of most *Heurigen* are unpredictable (most don't open until mid-afternoon except on the weekend), but part of the fun is to simply set off to one of the districts and take pot luck. A display board at the centre of each village lists those *Heurigen* that are open.

vineyards, this friendly *Heuriger* is popular with parties, but is big enough to absorb them. Daily 11am–1am.

### Nussdorf

**Schübel-Auer** 19, Kahlenbergerstrasse 22 ☎370 22 22, ⓦ www.schuebel-auer.at; tram #D to the terminus. Good, 100-year-old *Heuriger* right by the tram terminus, and a convenient staging post en route to *Sirbu* (below). Mid-Feb to mid-Nov Tues–Sat 4pm–midnight.

**Sirbu** 19, Kahlenbergerstrasse 210 ☎320 59 28; 15min walk from bus #38A terminus. Positioned in amongst the vineyards, with fabulous views from the hill above Nussdorf, and the usual self-service buffet and local wines. April to mid-Oct Mon–Sat 3pm–midnight.

### Sievering

**Haslinger** 19, Agnesgasse 3 ☎440 13 47, ⓦ www.buschenschank-haslinger.at; bus #39A from U-Bahn Heiligenstadt to the terminus. *Heuriger* overlooking the rooftops of Sievering, offering warm and cold buffets, and boasting a lovely, sloping orchard garden. Tues–Fri 2pm–midnight, Sat & Sun 11.30am–midnight.

### Stammersdorf

**Göbel** 21, Stammersdorfer Kellergasse 151/Breitenweg ☎294 84 20; tram #31, then bus ##228 or #233. Herr Göbel is an architect, so his *Heuriger* naturally has a modern feel to it, and a classy ambience, as well as prize-winning wines (red and white) and gourmet food. Phone to check opening times, which are usually Mon 3–10pm, Sat & Sun 11am–10pm.

**Wieninger** 21, Stammersdorfer Strasse 78 ☎292 41 06, ⓦ www.heuriger-wieninger .at; tram #31 to the terminus from U-Bahn Floridsdorf. Lots of fresh, light, pine inside, a courtyard garden outside, and above-average buffet and wine. Wed–Fri 3pm–midnight, Sat & Sun noon–midnight.

## Stadtheurigen

The following places are marked on the map on p.40.

**Augustinerkeller** 1, Augustinerstrasse 1 ☎533 10 26, ⓦ www.bitzinger.at; U-Bahn Karlsplatz. Vast array of green- and black-striped booths in the cellars underneath the Albertina. Fast service and hearty Viennese food; a tad touristy, but fun. *Schrammelmusik* from 6.30pm. Daily 11am–midnight. Inexpensive–moderate.

**Esterházykeller** 1, Haarhof 1 ☎533 34 82, ⓦ www.esterhazykeller.at; U-Bahn Herrengasse. Snug, brick-vaulted wine cellar with very cheap wine and a limited range of hot and cold snacks. Situated off Naglergasse. Mon–Fri 11am–11pm, Sat & Sun 4–11pm. Inexpensive.

**Gigerl** 1, Blumenstockgasse 2 ☎513 44 31; U-Bahn Stephansplatz. A kind of neo-*Stadtheuriger*, a modern, stylish take on an old theme. Daily 3pm–1am, Fri & Sat until 2am. Inexpensive.

**Göttweiger Stiftskeller** 1, Spiegelgasse 9 ☎512 78 17, ⓦ www.goettweiger-stiftskeller.at; U-Bahn Stephansplatz. Ground-floor monastic wine cellars that feel more like a family *Beisl*. Utterly traditional food and a mixed clientele – very popular, especially at lunchtime. Mon–Fri 8am–10pm. Inexpensive.

**Melker Stiftskeller** 1, Schottengasse 3 ☎533 55 30; U-Bahn Schottentor. Vast, high-ceilinged wine cellar owned by the famous Melk monks, serving traditional grub. Tues–Sat 5pm–midnight. Moderate.

**Zwölf-Apostelkeller** 1, Sonnenfelsgasse 3 ☎512 67 77, ⓦ www.zwoelf-apostelkeller.at; U-Bahn Stephansplatz. An attractive seventeenth-century building with bars housed in three levels of cellars. *The* place to drink wine, but it's often difficult to find a space; cold buffet only. Daily 4.30pm–midnight. Inexpensive–moderate.

# Bars, clubs and live venues

T he vast majority of the Viennese are safely tucked up in bed by as early as 10pm. Meanwhile, however, a hard core stay up until early in the morning – in fact it's quite possible to keep drinking round the clock.

Vienna's late-night **bars and clubs** are concentrated in two main areas. The most interesting is around the **Naschmarkt**, where late-night licences abound, and from where it's easy enough to wander over into Mariahilfer-strasse and Neubau to find further late-night distractions. The other main area is under the arches of the U6 U-Bahn, as it careers along the *Gürtel*, from Thaliastrasse northwards. In warmer weather, during term time, it's also worth checking out the courtyards of the **Universitätscampus**, off Alserstrasse – and of course, there are the outdoor bars on the Copa Cagrana on the **Donauinsel** (see p.188).

Vienna's **club scene** is small for a city of 1.5 million, but dance music, and in particular, techno and electronica, remain very popular. Nevertheless, the majority of Vienna's clubs are mostly tiny affairs, little more than late-night DJ bars, which might host live bands, or, more often than not, resident DJs spinning discs (both danceable and non-danceable), while punters simply chill out and drink. As such, it's often difficult to differentiate between a bar, a club and a live venue, so we've simply organized the listings by area.

To find out what's on at Vienna's clubs, check out the "Party" section in the weekly listings tabloid *Falter* (see p.28). The two big annual popular music events are the **Jazz Fest Wien** (Ⓦ www.viennajazz.org), an international jazz festival that takes place in various venues around the city in late June/early July, and the **Donauinselfest** (Ⓦ www.donauinselfest.at), the SPÖ-organized free summer pop festival on the Donauinsel.

Drink **prices** are pretty consistent – bars tend to charge either side of €5 for a *Krügerl* (half-litre) – except in a few of the clubs where there's an admission charge. As for how to get home in the wee hours, there are details on the city's **nightbuses** on p.26. Nightbuses leave from Schwedenplatz and usually do a circuit of the Ring before heading off to their destination – pick up a leaflet from the tourist office or one of the transport offices (see p.24).

# The Innere Stadt

**American Bar (Loos Bar) 1**, Kärntner Durchgang ⓦ www.loosbar.at; U-Bahn Stephensplatz. The "Loos Bar" is a small, dark late-night cocktail bar off Kärntnerstrasse with a wonderfully luscious glass, marble and onyx 1908 interior by Adolf Loos. Mon–Wed & Sun noon–4am, Thurs–Sat noon–5am.

**Badeschiff 1**, Donaukanal ⓦ www .badeschiff.at; U-Bahn Schwedenplatz. Boat moored on the canal, with an outdoor swimming pool, bar and club (below decks in the Laderaum). Laderaum: Tues–Sat 10pm–4am. Pool: May–Oct daily 8am–midnight.

**Club Habana 1**, Mahlerstrasse 11 ⓦ www .clubhabana.at; U-Bahn Karlsplatz. Nightly Latin American/Caribbean-themed mayhem for salsa, merengue and zumba fiends, just off Kärntnerstrasse. Mon–Thurs 7pm–4am, Fri 7pm–6am, Sat 7pm–6am.

**First Floor 1**, Seitenstettengasse 1; U-Bahn Schwedenplatz. A remake of a 1930s bar from Kärntnerstrasse, with a vast array of low-lit aquariums, courtesy of design team Eichinger oder Knechtl, packed with a sophisticated crowd. Mon–Sat 7pm–4am, Sun 8pm–3am.

**Flanagan's 1**, Schwarzenbergerstrasse 1–3 ⓦ www.flanagans.at; U-Bahn Karlsplatz. The most central, and probably the best of Vienna's rash of Irish pubs, with Guinness and Kilkenny, Irish/British food and big-screen sports. Mon–Thurs & Sun 10am–2am, Fri & Sat 10am–4am.

**Flex 1**, Donaukanal/Augartenbrücke ⓦ www.flex.at; U-Bahn Schottenring. The city's most serious dance-music club has a great sound system, and attracts the best DJs and a very young, enthusiastic crowd; it's situated at canal level, overlooking Wagner's Schützenhaus. Daily 8pm–4am.

**Jazzland 1**, Franz-Josefs-Kai 29 ⓦ www .jazzland.at; U-Bahn Schwedenplatz. Vienna's longest-running jazz venue is a cellar just below the Ruprechtskirche; music varies from trad and swing to blues and bebop; gigs start at around 9pm (no reservations taken). Mon–Sat 7pm–2am.

**Planters 1**, Zelinkagasse 4 ⓦ www .plantersclub.at; U-Bahn Schottenring. *Planters'* decadent, colonial cocktail bar decor, and the unbelievable array of drinks on offer, attracts a smart, dressed-up crowd. Daily 5pm–4am.

**Porgy & Bess 1**, Riemergasse 11 ⓦ www .porgy.or.at; U-Bahn Stubentor. This converted porn cinema is now the very stylish home of Vienna's top jazz venue, attracting top jazz and world music acts from all over the world; gigs start around 8.30pm. Daily 7.30pm–late.

**Strandbar Hermann 3**, Hermannpark 5 ⓦ www.strandbarhermann.at; U-Bahn Schwedenplatz. Another of Vienna's great summertime outdoor DJ venues: cocktails, deckchairs and sand by the confluence of the River Wien (Wien-Fluss) and the Donaukanal. May–Oct daily 6pm–2am.

# Ringstrasse

**Joe Zawinul's Birdland 3**, Landstrasser Hauptstrasse 2 ⓦ www.birdland.at; U-Bahn Landstrasse (Wien-Mitte). Jazz club near the Hilton, founded by the keyboardist from Weather Report, and veering more towards the easy listening/big band end of the jazz spectrum. Mon–Sat 6pm–2am.

**Ost 4**, Schwindgasse 1 ⓦ www.ost-klub.at; U-Bahn Karlsplatz or tram #D. As the name suggests, this place, off Schwarzenberg- platz, specializes in live acts from "east of Rennweg" – expect anything from Thracian clarinetists to women bands from St Peters- burg. Thurs–Sat 6pm–4am, plus other occasional nights.

**Passage 1**, Babenberger Passage, Burgring/ Babenbergerstrasse ⓦ www.sunshine.at; U-Bahn Museumsquartier/Volkstheater. This funky futurist conversion of a pedestrian underpass at the back of the Kunsthistor- isches Museum is the closest Vienna gets to a flashy, full-on club such as you'd find in Europe's bigger dance capitals. Daily 10pm–4am.

**Pavillon Volksgarten 1**, Burgring 1 ⓦ pavillon.volksgarten.at; U-Bahn Volk- stheater. The *Pavillon* is the relaxed garden café above the *Volksgarten* club; entry is usually free (apart from Tuesday's popular techno night), there's *boules* to play and usually live music or DJs later on. May to mid-Sept daily 11am–2am.

**Rotes Bar 7**, Neustiftgasse 1 ⓦwww .volkstheater.at; U-Bahn Volkstheater. The Volkstheater has opened up this grandiose fin-de-siècle space to a whole variety of live acts from cabaret and jazz to DJs and world music. Daily 10.30pm–1am.

**Volksgarten 1**, Burgring 1 ⓦwww .volksgarten.at; U-Bahn Volkstheater. Vienna's longest-running club is a firm favourite with the party crowd. The curvy *Banane* bar is groovy and the outdoor dance floor is a summertime treat. Daily 8pm–5am.

## Lesbian and gay nightlife

If Vienna's club scene is pretty small, the city's **lesbian and gay scene** is even smaller. There is only a handful of gay bars and clubs, scattered across the city, with a cluster in the "gay district" around the Naschmarkt. The social and political heart of the gay community is focused on the **Rosa-Lila Villa**, 6, Linke Wienzeile 102 (☎585 43 43, ⓦwww.villa.at; U-Bahn Pilgramgasse), the pink-and-purple HQ that proudly flies the rainbow flag and proclaims itself as a *Lesben und Schwulen Haus*. There's an annual pride event, **Regenbogenparade** (Rainbow Parade), held on the last Saturday in June, and an annual gay ball, Regenbogenball, in late January. For news (in German) on other events, visit ⓦwww.hosiwien.at. For listings, consult the "lesbisch/schwul" section in *Falter*, pick up the monthly freebie *Xtra* (ⓦwww.xtra-news.at), and check out the following places:

**Café Berg 9**, Berggasse 8; U-Bahn Schottentor (also reviewed on p.268). Cool café attached to the city's main gay bookshop with mixed gay/straight clientele, especially during the day. The food's good, and you can pick up flyers about up-and-coming gay events. Daily 10am–1am.

**Felixx 6**, Gumpendorferstrasse 5; ⓦwww.felixx-bar.at; U-Bahn Museumsquartier. Friendly, pink-and-purple late-night gay/lesbian bar-restaurant that hosts occasional events. Daily 7pm–3am.

**Frauencafé 8**, Lange Gasse 11; ⓦwww.frauencafe.com; U-Bahn Lerchenfelderstrasse. Vienna's only permanent women-only space is a small, friendly café next door to a feminist bookshop. Thurs 7pm–midnight, Fri & Sat 7pm–2am.

**🏃 Kaiserbründl 1**, Weihburggasse 18–20 ⓦwww.gaysauna.at; U-Bahn Stephansplatz. Wonderfully ornate nineteenth-century *hammam* with additional, more recent, camp-it-up frescoes, popular with gay men of all ages. Mon–Thurs 2pm–midnight, Fri 2pm–2am, Sat 1pm–2am, Sun 1pm–midnight.

**Mango Bar 6**, Laimgrubengasse 3; ⓦwww.mangobar.at; U-Bahn Kettenbrückengasse. Smart, stylish and pretty cruisey bar, packed with young guys. Daily 9pm–4am.

**Café Savoy 6**, Stiegengasse 8; ⓦwww.village-bar.at; U-Bahn Kettenbrückengasse. Apart from during the Saturday flea market, when a mixed crowd descends on the place, this high-camp fin-de-siècle café is predominantly populated with gay men. Mon–Fri 5pm–2am, Sat 9am–2am.

**Village 6**, Linke Wienzeile 36; U-Bahn Kettenbrückengasse. Swish, Americana-style cocktail bar that pulls in a crowd of smart young folk for its regular theme nights. Daily 8pm–3am.

**Why Not? 1**, Tiefergraben 22; ⓦwww.why-not.at; U-Bahn Herrengasse. Late-night gay/lesbian cellar bar and disco, popular with young gay men and women. Wed 9pm–3am men only, Fri & Sat 10pm–4am.

**Café Willendorf 6**, Linke Wienzeile 102 ⓦwww.cafe-willendorf.at; U-Bahn Pilgramgasse. Popular café-restaurant inside the Rosa-Lila Villa, with a nice leafy courtyard. Another good place to pick up information about events. Daily 6pm–2am.

## Mariahilf, Neubau & Josefstadt

**B72** 8, Stadtbahnbögen 72, Hernalser Gürtel ⓦwww.b72.at; U-Bahn Alserstrasse. Dark, industrial, edgy designer club underneath the U-Bahn arches – features a mixture of DJs and live indie bands. Daily 8pm–4am.

**Blue Box** 7, Richtergasse 8 ⓦwww.bluebox .at; U-Bahn Neubaugasse. Long-standing café with resident DJs and a good snack menu, including excellent brunch buffet. Live music from 8pm. Mon 6pm–2am, Tues–Sun 10am–2am.

**Camera** 8, Neubaugasse 2 ⓦwww.camera-club .at; U-Bahn Neubaugasse. Popular little dance club where the DJs keep the crowd happy with everything from Detroit Jazz to the local Icke Micke posse. Thurs–Sat 9.30pm–late.

**Chelsea** 8, U-Bahnbögen 29–31, Lerchenfelder Gürtel ⓦwww.chelsea.co.at; U-Bahn Thaliastrasse. Favourite anglophile venue with up-and-coming indie guitar bands, techno DJs and even Premiership matches screened live on a Sunday afternoon. Mon–Sat 6pm–4am, Sun 4pm–3am.

**Donau** 7, Karl Schweighofergasse 10 ⓦwww .donau.schraeg.org; U-Bahn Volkstheater. Chill-out sounds from the in-house techno DJs, and strange projections on the walls. Mon–Sat 9pm–4am, Sun 9pm–2am.

**futuregarden** 6, Schadekgasse 6; U-Bahn Neubau. Spartan, minimalist club-bar near the Esterházypark Flakturm, with DJs playing electro beats popular with the local art student crowd. Mon–Sat 9pm–2am, Sun 9pm–2am.

**rhiz** 8, Gürtelbögen 37–38, Lerchenfelder Gürtel ⓦrhiz.org; U-Bahn Lerchenfelder Strasse. A modish cross between a bar, a café and a techno club, with several DJs spinning everything from dance to trance from 9pm. Mon–Sat 6pm–4am, Sun 6pm–2am.

**Roxy** 6, Garbergasse 3 ⓦwww.roxyclub.at; U-Bahn Karlsplatz. Run by the slick Sunshine Enterprises posse who own *Passage* (see p.281), this place attracts an eclectic mix of local and international DJ talent. Mon–Sat 10pm–4am.

**Stadthalle** 15, Vogelweidplatz 14, ⓦwww .stadthalle.at; U-Bahn Burggasse. Vienna's chief large-scale venue, with two halls, attracting the usual roster of big-name acts. Gig times vary.

**Tanzcafé Jenseits** 6, Nelkengasse 3; U-Bahn Neubaugasse. Tiny, discreet bohemian bar with a plush fin-de-siècle feel, and retro dance tunes from every decade on the jukebox. Mon–Sat 9pm–4am.

**Tunnel** 8, Florianigasse 39 ⓦwww .tunnel-vienna-live.at; tram #5. Large, L-shaped student café-pub with daily live bands down in the cellar from 8pm. Daily 9am–2am.

## Alsergrund

**WUK** 9, Währingerstrasse 59 ⓦwww.wuk.at; tram #40, #41 or #42. Red-brick arts venue with a great café and a wide programme of events, including live music and DJ nights; check the *Falter* listings. Daily 11am–2am.

## Leopoldstadt

**Fluc** 2, Praterstern 5 ⓦwww.fluc.at; U-Bahn Praterstern. Anything (weird) goes at this industrial-style underground venue near the Prater, which features experimental live acts and DJs. Daily 6pm–2am.

## The suburbs

**Arena** 3, Baumgasse 80 ⓦwww.arena.co.at; U-Bahn Erdberg. It's a long trek out to this former slaughterhouse on the corner of Französengraben, but there's a real variety of stuff going on here – all-night raves, outdoor concerts, open-air cinema – so check the listings before setting out. Daily 4pm–2am.

**BA-CA Halle** 11, Guglgasse 12 ⓦwww
.gasometer.at; U-Bahn Gasometer. The best
medium-sized venue for catching imported
acts, located in the Gasometer complex.
Gig times vary.

**Reigen** 14, Hadikgasse 62 ⓦwww.reigen.at;
U-Bahn Heitzing. Unpretentious café, restaurant and live venue that's great for jazz,
blues, reggae, Latin and, in fact, music from
all over the world. Daily 6pm–4am.

**Szene Wien** 11, Hauffgasse 26 ⓦwww
.szenewien.com; U-Bahn Enkplatz. Regularly
good live music venue, with a café (and
garden) serving great food, run by a radical

bunch from Simmering. Doors open 8pm.
Closed mid-July to Aug.

**U4** 12, Schönbrunnerstrasse 222 ⓦwww
.clubnet.at; U-Bahn Meidling-Hauptstrasse.
Dark, cavernous disco, with frequent
and varied gigs and themed nights. Daily
10pm–late.

**Vorstadt** 16, Herbststrasse 37 ⓦwww
.vorstadt.at; U-Bahn Burggasse. Ottakring
*Beisl* just beyond the *Gürtel*, with a lovely
*Schanigarten* and a lively and varied
programme of live European folk and roots
music. Mon–Sat 5pm–2am, Sun 10am–2am.
Closed July & Aug.

# The arts

V ienna prides itself on its musical associations, and classical music and opera, in particular, are heavily subsidized by the Austrian state. The chief cultural festival – featuring opera, music and theatre – is the **Wiener Festwochen** (ⓦwww.festwochen.or.at), which lasts from early May until mid-June. At Easter, there's the **Osterklang** (ⓦwww .osterklang.at) festival of classical music, and in April and May, the **Frühlingsfestival**, a themed music festival held alternately at the Konzerthaus and Musikverein. The city's film festival, or **Viennale**, and the **Wien Modern** festival of contemporary classical music both take place towards the end of October, but by far the busiest time of the year is **Fasching**, Vienna's ball season. Last and least, there's the **International Accordion Festival** (ⓦwww .akkordeonfestival.at), held over the course of four weeks from late February to the middle of March.

To find out **what's on**, pick up the tourist board's free monthly listings booklet *Wien-Programm*, which gives the schedules of the big opera and concert houses and theatres, plus a day-by-day concert guide, ball calendar and details of current art exhibitions. The weekly listings tabloid *Falter* also has a pullout "Programm" section, which catalogues all theatre, dance, cabaret and classical music concerts (look for "Musik-E") as well as listing all films.

---

### Waltz and schmaltz

It's easy enough to hear a bit of classic Strauss or light Mozart at any time of the year in Vienna, though tickets don't come cheap: €35–50 is the average price range. The **Vienna Walzer Concerts** (☏512 57 90, ⓦwww.strauss-concerts.com) perform Strauss and the like decked out in Biedermeier costume every week, at the Kursalon in the Stadtpark (see p.126). The **Salonorchester Alt Wien** (☏512 57 90, ⓦstrauss-konzerte.at) also play there, and at other good-looking venues across the city. The **Wiener Residenzorchester** (☏817 21 78, ⓦwww .residenzorchester.at) perform Mozart and Strauss in period costume in the Palais Auersperg behind Parlament. The Mozart Ensemble put on chamber concert performances all year in the ornate *sala terrena* at Singerstrasse 7 (☏911 90 77, ⓦwww.mozarthaus.at). There are also regular **Schönbrunner Schlosskonzerte** (☏812 50 04, ⓦwww.imagevienna.com) of Mozart, Strauss and the like in parts of Schönbrunn. Finally, if you yearn to hear schmaltzy Viennese songs sung live in a more informal setting, check out **Café Schmid Hansl**, 18, Schulgasse 31 (☏406 36 58, ⓦwww.schmidhansl.at; tram #40 or #41 from U-Bahn Volksoper; Tues–Sat 8pm–4am).

Vienna may be an expensive place, but its top opera houses and concert halls are open to even the poorest music student thanks to the system of *Stehplätze* or **standing-room tickets**, which can cost as little as €2 each. *Stehplätze* are limited to one per person and usually go on sale one hour before the performance (for very popular concerts, you may find that tickets go on sale somewhat earlier, so check first). It's standard practice, once you've got into the auditorium, to tie a scarf to the railings to reserve your standing place. Bags and coats, though, should be put into the cloakroom.

## Tickets

Ticket **prices** vary enormously in Vienna: the Staatsoper is a case in point, with seats ranging from €10 to €250. For some events – most notably the Vienna Boys' Choir and the New Year's Day Concert – it's not so much price as availability that's a problem. However, the big state venues offer cheap *Stehplätze* on the day of the performance (see box above), and some offer unsold tickets at a discount to students, around an hour or thirty minutes before the show starts.

The cheapest way of **buying tickets** is to go to the venue's own box office. With the Staatsoper, Volksoper, Burgtheater, Akademietheater and Schauspielhaus, you can either buy direct or from their shared central box office, the Bundestheaterkassen, not far from the Staatsoper at 1, Goethegasse 1 (Mon–Fri 8am–6pm, Sat & Sun 9am–noon; ☎514 44-7880, ⓦwww .bundestheater.at; U-Bahn Karlsplatz). There's also a ticket booth, Wien-Ticket Pavillon, next to the Staatsoper (daily 10am–7pm), which sells tickets for all venues, and occasionally has half-price tickets for musicals and for other events.

## Opera and classical music

Vienna has a musical pedigree second to none. Josef Haydn, Wolfgang Mozart and Ludwig Beethoven spent much of their time in Vienna, as did local-born Franz Schubert. Johannes Brahms and Anton Bruckner followed in their wake, and coincided with the great waltz fever generated by the Strauss family and Josef Lanner. In the early twentieth century, the Vienna opera house was under the baton of Gustav Mahler, while its concert halls resounded to the atonal music of Arnold Schönberg, Anton Webern and Alban Berg.

Though Vienna hasn't produced any world-class composers for some time, it does still boast one of Europe's top opera houses in the **Staatsoper**, served by one of its finest orchestras, the **Wiener Philharmoniker** (ⓦwww .wienerphilharmoniker.at). The orchestra's New Year's Day Concert in the Musikverein is broadcast across the globe; to obtain tickets you must contact the box office on January 2 for the following year's concert (☎505 81 90, ⓦwww.musikverein.at). If you don't have a ticket, don't despair; not only is the concert broadcast live on Austrian TV, it's also relayed live on an enormous screen in front of the Rathaus at noon and again at 5pm. When the big state theatres are closed in July and August, opera and classical music concerts captured on film are also shown for free every evening outside the Rathaus.

The most famous musical institution in the city is, of course, the **Wiener Sängerknaben** (☎216 39 42, ⓦwww.wsk.at), or Vienna Boys' Choir, which performs Mass at the Hofburgkapelle in the Hofburg every Sunday at 9.15am

(Jan–June & mid-Sept to Dec). Tickets for the Mass (€5–30) are sold out weeks in advance, though some are held over each week and go on sale on Fridays (Fri 11am–1pm & 3–5pm). You can book in advance by fax or email (𝔽533 99 27-75, ℮hmk@aon.at), stating which Sunday Mass you wish to attend, and you will be sent back a reservation slip to take to the box office (along with cash to pay for the tickets) on arrival in Vienna. The other option is to settle for one of the free *Stehplätze*, which are distributed before Mass; get there for 8.15am to be sure of a place (although some people leave early having got bored). Be warned, however, that the choir remains out of sight up in the organ loft to all but the most expensive seats for the whole of Mass.

## Mostly opera and operetta

**Kammeroper** 1, Fleischmarkt 24 ☏512 01 00, ⓦwww.wienerkammeroper.at; U-Bahn Schwedenplatz. Vienna's smallest opera house is a Jugendstil theatre hidden in the backstreets of the Innere Stadt. Little-known works prevail – anything from Rossini to Britten – and the immediacy of the venue is a boon.

**Staatsoper** 1, Opernring 2 ☏513 15 13, ⓦwww.wiener-staatsoper.at; U-Bahn Karlsplatz. Vienna's largest opera house (see also p.114) stages a staggering forty operas a season played in rep. It's a conservative place, but attracts the top names, and has the benefit of the Wiener Philharmoniker in the pit. Ticket prices range from around €10 to €250, but with over 500 *Stehplätze* (€2–3.50) going on sale every night from the west side of the foyer, an hour before the curtain goes up, it is one of the most accessible opera houses in the world. Closed July & Aug.

**Theater-an-der-Wien** 6, Linke Wienzeile 6 ☏588 85, ⓦwww.theater-wien.at; U-Bahn Karlsplatz. Famous as the venue where Beethoven's *Fidelio* and Strauss's *Die Fledermaus* premièred (see p.124), this theatre has returned to its roots and now concentrates on opera; tickets range from around €10 to €150 with *Stehplätze* for €7.

**Volksoper** 9, Währingerstrasse 78 ☏514 44-30, ⓦwww.volksoper.at; U-Bahn Währingerstrasse-Volksoper or tram #40, #41 or #42. Vienna's number-two opera house is situated in the ninth district, near the *Gürtel*, and specializes in operetta, plus the occasional, more adventurous musical and opera production; tickets range from around €10 to €150 with seventy or so *Stehplätze* a night (€1.50–4).

▲ Volksoper

## Mostly classical music

**Bösendorfer-Saal** 4, Graf Starhemberggasse 14 ☎504 66 51-44, ⓦwww.boesendorfer.com; U-Bahn Taubstummengasse. Chamber music concerts performed using Bösendorfer pianos, and held in a hall with excellent acoustics, belonging to the famous Austrian piano-manufacturers.

**Konzerthaus** 3, Lothringerstrasse 20 ☎242 002, ⓦkonzerthaus.at; U-Bahn Karlsplatz. Early twentieth-century concert hall designed by Viennese duo Helmer & Fellner. Three main halls: the Grosser Saal, Mozart-Saal and Schubert-Saal, plus the (new) Neuer Saal, and three smaller rooms, the Schönberg Saal, Alban Berg Saal and the Wotruba Salon. The classical music programme here tends to be a bit more adventurous and varied than the Musikverein's, with the odd nod to world music, jazz and even pop.

**Musikverein** 1, Bösendorferstrasse 12 ☎505 81 90, ⓦwww.musikverein-wien.at; U-Bahn Karlsplatz. Two ornate concert halls in one building, gilded from top to bottom inside. The larger of the two, the Grosser Saal, has the best acoustics in the country, and is the unofficial home of the Wiener Philharmoniker, while the smaller hall, the Brahms Saal, is used mainly for chamber concerts; *Stehplätze* available for the Grosser Saal (€5–7).

# Theatre

Obviously, for the non-German-speaker, most of Vienna's **theatres** and satirical **cabarets** have limited appeal. However, there are a couple of English-speaking theatre groups, a few theatres that specialize in musicals, one dedicated dance venue, several puppet theatres, where language is less of a problem, and the Burgtheater, whose interior alone is worth the price of a ticket.

## Straight theatres

**Akademietheater** 3, Lisztstrasse 1 ☎514 44-41400, ⓦwww.burgtheater.at; U-Bahn Karlsplatz. Number two to the Burgtheater, using the same pool of actors, but specializing in more contemporary chamber works.

**Burgtheater** 1, Dr-Karl-Lueger-Ring 2 ☎514 44-4145, ⓦwww.burgtheater.at; U-Bahn Herrengasse. Vienna's most prestigious theatrical stage puts on innovative and serious drama in rep. The foyer and staircases are spectacular; the auditorium was modernized after bomb damage in 1945. Tickets cost from around €4 to €44, with 150 *Stehplätze* (€2) going on sale every night, an hour before the curtain goes up. Closed July & Aug.

**Theater-in-der-Josefstadt** 8, Josefstädterstrasse 24–26 ☎427 00, ⓦwww.josefstadt.org; U-Bahn Rathaus or tram #J. Beautiful, early nineteenth-century theatre that puts on a variety of serious popular German-language drama from classics to contemporary.

**Volkstheater** 7, Neustiftgasse 1 ☎523 27 76, ⓦwww.volkstheater.at; U-Bahn Volkstheater. Late nineteenth-century theatre designed by Helmer & Fellner, with the groovy *Rotes Bar* to hang out in (see p.282). Modern plays, foreign works and classics, plus even the odd operetta.

## Dance

**TanzQuartierWien (TQW)** 7, Museumsplatz 1 ☎581 35 91, ⓦwww.tqw.at; U-Bahn Museumsquartier. Experimental dance performance space, in the Kunsthalle building in the MuseumsQuartier complex.

## English-speaking theatres

**International Theatre** 9, Porzellangasse 8 ☎319 62 72, ⓦwww.internationaltheatre.at; tram #D. Local-based, expat (mostly American) company with a main venue on the corner of Müllnergasse and Porzellangasse, and a smaller stage, The Fundus, in the cellar of the nearby Servitenkirche (see p.172). Closed July & Aug.

**Vienna's English Theatre** 8, Josefsgasse 12 ☎402 12 60, ⓦwww.englishtheatre.at; U-Bahn Lerchenfelderstrasse. Larger, professionally run venue, with interesting productions flown in from abroad (mostly London and New York).

## Fasching

Though clearly analogous with Mardi Gras and Carnival, Vienna's **Fasching** lasts much longer, with the first balls taking place on November 11, and continuing – mostly on Saturdays and Sundays – until Ash Wednesday the following year and beyond.

Traditionally the most famous ball was the *Kaiserball*, held in the Hofburg on New Year's Eve and in days gone by presided over by the emperor himself. Its place at the top of the hierarchy is now challenged by the *Opernball*, held on the Thursday before Ash Wednesday in the Staatsoper, and pictured in many a tourist brochure, with the debutantes parading all in white. The other 300 or so balls are a hotchpotch held by various associations – everything from the gay and lesbian *Regenbogenball* to the *Ball der Burgenländischen Kroaten* – in Vienna's top hotels and palaces; those followed by the word *Gschnas* are masked. To find out what's on in *Fasching*, pick up a *Wiener Ballkalender* (ⓦwww.ballkalender.com) from the tourist office in the months leading up to and during the season. If you're worried about your dancing ability, there are numerous dance classes on offer; ask the tourist board for details.

### Miscellaneous

**RadioKulturhaus 4, Argentinierstrasse 30a** ☏501 70-377, ⓦradiokulturhaus.orf.at; U-Bahn Taubstummengasse. The Grosser Sendesaal is the main performance space of Austrian state radio, and home of the Vienna Radio Symphony Orchestra. However, it hosts a whole range of events and gigs from straight theatre to jazz concerts.

### Puppet theatre

**Figurentheater Lilarum 3, Göllnergasse 8** ☏710 26 66, ⓦwww.lilarum.at; U-Bahn Kardinal-Nagl-Platz. Puppet theatre out in Landstrasse, with several performances a day. Wed & Fri–Sun and during school holidays.

**Märchenbühne der Apfelbaum 7, Kirchengasse 41** ☏523 17 29-20, ⓦwww.maerchenbuehne .at; U-Bahn Volkstheater. Puppet theatre specializing in classic fairy tales, so even without any German you can at least follow the plot. Sat & Sun.

**Schönbrunner Schlossmarionettentheater 13, Schloss Schönbrunn, Hofratsktrakt** ☏817 32 47; ⓦwww.marionettentheater.at; U-Bahn Hietzing. String-puppet theatre in Schönbrunn specializing in over-long Mozart operas – try and catch a different show if you can. Performances Wed–Sun.

# Cinema

Austrian **cinema** is not really up there with the greats, and unless your German is up to scratch, you're best off sticking to British and American films. One film that's fun to see, and is shown every weekend at the Burg-Kino, is **The Third Man** (*Der Dritte Mann*), made in 1949, set amid the rubble of postwar Vienna and starring Orson Welles (see p.123).

The best place to check out the week's cinema **listings** is either *Der Standard* or *Falter*, the city's weekly listings tabloid, or on the website ⓦwww.film.at. *OF* means it's in the original without subtitles; *OmengU* means it's in the original with English subtitles; *OmU* means it's in the original with German subtitles, but should not be confused with *OmÜ*, which means it's in the original, but has a live voice-over German translation. And finally, *dF* means it's dubbed into German.

Cinema **tickets** cost €8 or less; Monday (*Kino-Montag*) is cheap-ticket day. Vienna's international film festival, the **Viennale**, takes place in the middle of October and is definitely worth catching. In July and August, you can watch **open-air films** in the Augarten (see p.187) and outside the Rathaus (see p.105).

**Artis International** 1, Schultergasse/Jordangasse ☎535 65 70; U-Bahn Stephansplatz. Central multiplex cinema showing films in English in six different salons.

**Bellaria** 7, Museumstrasse 3 ☎523 75 91; U-Bahn Volkstheater. Old Neubau cinema that specializes in German and Austrian black-and-white movies.

**Breitenseer Lichtspiele** 14, Breitenseerstrasse 21 ☎982 21 73, ⓦwww.nitschi.at/bsl; U-Bahn Hütteldorferstrasse. Vienna's oldest cinema, which opened in 1909, is still going strong, with much the same fittings.

**Burg** 1, Opernring 19 ☎587 84 06, ⓦwww .burgkino.at; U-Bahn Museumsquartier. Two-screen cinema on the Ringstrasse that shows films in the original, without subtitles. *The Third Man* has a regular spot (Fri 10.45pm & Sun 3.15pm).

**English Cinema Haydn** 6, Mariahilferstrasse 57 ☎587 22 62, ⓦwww.haydnkino.at; U-Bahn Neubaugasse. As the name suggests, this is a cinema that shows the latest films in English, without subtitles.

**Filmmuseum** 1, Augustinerstrasse 1 ☎533 70 54, ⓦwww.filmmuseum.at; U-Bahn Karlsplatz. Vienna's main art-house cinema, on the ground floor of the Albertina, with a very esoteric programme, all in the original, generally without subtitles.

**Gartenbaukino** 1, Parkring 12 ☎512 23 54, ⓦwww.gartenbaukino.at; U-Bahn Stubentor. 1960s Ringstrasse cinema – the largest in Vienna – owned by the Viennale, showing a mixture of classics and recent releases, usually in the original language.

**Kino unter Sternen** 2, Augarten ☎0800 664 040, ⓦwww.kinountersternen.at; tram #5. Open-air showings of classics in their original language "underneath the stars" in the Augarten. July to mid-Aug.

**Metro Kino** 1, Johannesgasse 4 ☎512 18 03, ⓦwww.filmarchiv.at; U-Bahn Stephansplatz. Amazing, ornate, centrally located cinema run by the Austrian Film Archives, showing classics and mini-festivals.

**Sommerkino Tribüne Krieau** 2, Nordportalstrasse 274 ☎722 17 43, ⓦwww.krieau .com; tram #N from U-Bahn Schwedenplatz. Open-air cinema in the Krieau racecourse in the Prater. July & Aug only.

**Stadtkino** 3, Schwarzenbergplatz 7 ☎712 62 76, ⓦwww.stadtkinowien.at; U-Bahn Karlsplatz. Art-house cinema with disabled access and just a short distance from the Innere Stadt. Closed Aug.

## Visual arts

In addition to its vast permanent collections of art (detailed in the main text of the Guide), Vienna has a large number of galleries that host temporary exhibitions. To check out the latest shows and opening times, consult the tourist board's free monthly booklet *Programm*.

**Architektur Zentrum Wien** 7, Museumsquartier, Museumsplatz 1; ⓦwww.azw.at; U-Bahn Volkstheater. In the courtyard of the MuseumsQuartier complex (see p.111), and specializing in contemporary architectural exhibitions. Daily 10am–7pm.

**BA-CA KunstForum** 1, Freyung 8 ⓦwww .ba-ca-kunstforum.at; U-Bahn Herrengasse. Major venue for visiting foreign exhibitions of big-name contemporary art exhibitions sponsored by one of Austria's high-street banks. Daily 10am–7pm, Fri until 9pm.

**BAWAG Foundation** 1, Tuchlauben 7a; ⓦwww.bawag-foundation.at; U-Bahn Herrengasse. Another great central venue, again sponsored by one of the country's leading banks, this time concentrating on film, video and photography. Mon–Sat 10am–6pm, Thurs 11am–8pm.

**Generali Foundation** 4, Wiedner Hauptstrasse 15; ⓦfoundation.generali.at; U-Bahn Karlsplatz. Funky modern space owned by the eponymous insurance company and hidden away a short stroll south of Karlsplatz, serving up interesting contemporary sculpture and mixed-media work. Tues–Sun 11am–6pm, Thurs 11am–8pm.

**Kunsthalle Wien** 7, Museumsplatz 1; ⓦwww .kunsthallewien.at; U-Bahn Volkstheater /Babenberger Strasse. The city's official space for big contemporary art exhibitions is a bit lost in the bowels of the old Winter Riding School in the MuseumsQuartier. Daily 10am–7pm, Thurs until 10pm.

**Kunsthalle Wien – project space** 4, Karlsplatz, Treitlstrasse 2; ⓦwww.kunsthallewien.at; U-Bahn Karlsplatz. Instead of the yellow Portakabin, there's now a glassy box used for international visiting exhibitions and frequented by Vienna's artiest crowd. Mon & Sun 1–7pm, Tues–Sat 4pm–midnight.

**Künstlerhaus** 1, Karlsplatz 5; Ⓦ www.k-haus.at; U-Bahn Karlsplatz. The Kunstverein (Artists' Society), next door to the Musikverein, puts on major retrospectives in painting, sculpture and photography. Daily 10am–6pm, Thurs until 9pm.

**Momentum** 7, Karl-Schweighofer-Gasse 12; Ⓦ www.momentum.co,at; U-Bahn Volkstheater. Photography gallery that promotes Austrian photography – from reportage to abstract – and has lots of prints for sale. Tues–Fri 11am–7pm, Sat 11am–5pm.

**Secession** 1, Friedrichstrasse 12; Ⓦ www .secession.at; U-Bahn Karlsplatz. The famous Jugendstil exhibition space, with Klimt's *Beethoven Frieze* in the basement (see p.119), continues to host provocative modern art shows and installations. Tues–Sun 10am–6pm, Thurs until 8pm.

**T-B A 21** 1, Himmelpfortgasse 13; Ⓦ www .tba21.org; U-Bahn Stephansplatz. Contemporary art gallery run by Francesca Habsburg, daughter of collector Thyssen-Bornemisza, who lives on the top floor. Tues–Fri noon–6pm, Sat & Sun noon–6pm.

**WestLicht** 7, Westbahnstrasse 40; Ⓦ www .westlicht.at; tram #5 or #49. The city's most innovative photography gallery. Tues, Wed & Fri 2–7pm, Thurs 2–9pm, Sat & Sun 11am–7pm.

# Shopping

ew people come to Vienna exclusively to shop, though, in fact, the city boasts quite a lot of quirky independent stores and prices belie the city's reputation as one of Europe's most expensive. Window shopping along **Graben** and **Kohlmarkt** can be fun, as, in among the international designers, you can still find shops sporting the "K. K." or "k.u.k." emblem – *kaiserlich und königlich* (Imperial and Royal) – of the last Empire. In the backstreets of the **Innere Stadt**, you'll also find numerous excellent bookstalls and some serious antique shops clustered around the Dorotheum (see opposite). The streets of **Neubau**, to the north of Mariahilferstrasse, are also good for browsing, and of course, the city boasts a great Saturday **Flohmarkt** (flea market) at the back end of the Naschmarkt.

For a capital, Vienna has very few large supermarkets, with just the small Billa and Julius Meinl stores scattered across the city. **Mariahilferstrasse** remains the main shopping drag for department stores and mainstream shops, along with **Kärntnerstrasse**.

## Arts, crafts and antiques

There's a whole cluster of **antique shops** (*Antiquitäten*) in the streets around the Dorotheum (see opposite), though there are few bargains to be had. Shops specializing in Art Nouveau and early twentieth-century gear can be found in Neubau, particularly around the Spittelberg area, off Siebensterngasse. For bric-a-brac, secondhand goods (*Altwaren*), and possibly a bargain or two, head for the streets around the Naschmarkt, and, of course, for the Naschmarkt flea market itself (see p.296), where you'll have to haggle.

### Opening times

**Shopping hours** in Vienna are strictly controlled by the state. Nowadays, shops are allowed to open Monday to Saturday 8am to 7pm, although most opt to open at 9 or 10am. Very few shops stay open any later on weekdays, or at all on Sundays, except those at the main railway stations. However, it wasn't very long ago that all shops had to close at noon on Saturdays – except on the first Saturday of the month (known as *Langersamstag*, or "long Saturday"), when shops were allowed to open until 5pm. Some shops outside the centre still stick to the old *Langersamstag* routine, and have weekday lunch-breaks or *Mittagssperre* usually between noon and 2pm.

**Adil Besim 1, Graben 30 ⓦ www.adil-besim
.co.at; U-Bahn Stephansplatz.** The king of
Vienna's carpet shops, in business since
1946, selling kilims, rugs and tapestries at
serious prices. Mon–Fri 9.30am–6pm, Sat
10am–5pm.
**Augarten 1, Stock-im-Eisen-Platz 3–4 ⓦ www
.augarten.at; U-Bahn Stephansplatz.** Vienna's
very own hand-painted china manufacturers
have an outlet here, though you can also
visit and buy direct (including some seconds) from the factory (see p.188). Mon–Fri
10am–6.30pm, Sat 10am–6pm.
**Backhausen 1, Schwarzenbergstrasse 10
ⓦ www.backhausen.at; U-Bahn Karlsplatz.**
Backhausen reproduce beautiful Wiener
Werkstätte textiles, ceramics and furniture, as well as housing a museum in the
basement. Mon–Fri 9.30am–6.30pm, Sat
9.30am–5pm.
**Bananas 5, Kettenbrückengasse 15 ⓦ www
.bananas.at; U-Bahn Kettenbrückengasse;
branch at 6, Gumpendorferstrasse 10–12.**
A stone's throw from the Naschmarkt (and
flea market), Bananas specializes in furniture
and accessories from the 1950s through to
the 1980s. Mon–Fri 1–6pm, Sat 11am–4pm.
**Dorotheum 1, Dorotheergasse 17 ⓦ www
.dorotheum.com; U-Bahn Stephansplatz.** "Aunt
Dorothy's", as it's known, is one of the
world's leading auction houses, with daily
sales and a fixed-price shop; there's even a
café for posing in. Mon–Fri 10am–6pm, Sat
9am–5pm.
**J. & L. Lobmeyr 1, Kärntnerstrasse 26; ⓦ www
.lobmeyr.at; U-Bahn Stephansplatz.** Famous

glass manufacturers, and a lovely shop,
with a museum on the top floor (see p.49).
You can buy glass designed by Adolf
Loos and Josef Hoffmann as well as more
modern pieces. Mon–Fri 10am–7pm, Sat
10am–6pm.
**Das Kunstwerk 4, Operngasse 20 & 6,
Laimgrubengasse 24 ⓦ www.daskunstwerk.at;
U-Bahn Karlsplatz & Museumsquartier.**
Jugendstil and Art Deco furniture, glassware
and lamps by the likes of Wagner, Lötz,
Loos and Thonet. Mon–Fri 11am–6pm,
Sat 10am–2pm.
**MAK-Shop 1, Weiskirchnerstrasse 3 ⓦ www
.mak.at; U-Bahn Stubentor.** Museum shop
selling wacky modern furniture and accou-
trements by the designers of the School
of Applied Arts. Tues 10am–midnight,
Wed–Sun 10am–6pm.
**Thonet 9, Berggasse 31 ⓦ www.thonet.com;
tram #D.** Furniture company, famed for its
bentwood chairs, and still producing Adolf
Loos and Wiener Werkstätte designs.
Mon–Fri 10am–6pm, Sat 9am–5pm.
**Wiener Silberschmiede Werkstätte 1, Spiegel-
gasse 14 ⓦ www.silberwerkstatt.at; U-Bahn
Stephansplatz.** Flagship store of revitalized
WW manufacturer that produces beautiful
vintage silverware. Mon–Fri 10am–6pm,
Sat 10am–5pm.
**Woka 1, Palais Breuner, Singerstrasse 16
ⓦ www.woka.com; U-Bahn Stephansplatz.**
Shop selling reproduction lamps and the
like, designed by Adolf Loos and other
Wiener Werkstätte artists. Mon–Fri
10am–6pm, Sat 10am–5pm.

# Bookshops

Though Vienna has a staggering number of **bookshops** (*Buchhandlungen*), most of
them in the Innere Stadt, only a handful are English-language. Nevertheless, many
of the stores below stock a wide choice of English-language volumes. Be warned,
however, that the Austrians slap tax on books and prices are consequently much
higher than elsewhere in Europe.

**Babette's 4, Schleifmühlgasse 17 ⓦ www
.babettes.at; U-Bahn Karlsplatz.** Smart little
cookery specialist, with lots of books (and
plenty in English) and even a daily lunchtime
menu to sample. Mon–Fri 10am–7pm, Sat
10am–5pm.
**British Bookshop 1, Weihburggasse 24–26
ⓦ www.britishbookshop.at; U-Bahn Stephansplatz; branch at 7, Mariahilferstrasse 4.** A fair

selection of novels and biographies
in English, with half the shop given over
to EFL teaching materials. Mon–Fri
9.30am–6.30pm, Sat 9.30am–6pm.
**Freytag & Berndt 1, Kohlmarkt 9 ⓦ www
.freytagberndt.at; U-Bahn Stephansplatz.** Flagship store of Austria's most prestigious
map-makers, with loads of maps, as well as
guides to Vienna and the rest of the world in

English, including a large selection of Rough Guides. Mon–Fri 9am–7pm, Sat 9am–6pm.

**Löwenherz 9, Berggasse 8** Ⓦ www.loewenherz.at; **U-Bahn Schottentor.** Gay bookstore attached to the wonderful *Café Berg* (see p.268). Mon–Thurs 10am–7pm, Fri 10am–8pm, Sat 10am–6pm.

**Morawa 1, Wollzeile 11** Ⓦ www.morawa.at; **U-Bahn Stubentor.** Huge bookshop stretching right back to Bäckerstrasse; the English section is on the first floor, guides and a vast range of English magazines and newspapers are at the back. Mon–Fri 9am–7pm, Sat 9am–6pm.

**Mord & Musik 7, Lindengasse 22** Ⓦ www.mordundmusik.at; **U-Bahn Neubaugasse.** Unusual shop specializing in crime fiction and experimental electronic music. Mon–Fri 2–7pm, Sat 11am–5pm.

**Prachner im MQ 7, Museumsplatz 1** Ⓦ www.prachner.at; **U-Bahn Volkstheater.** Vast bookshop piled high with coffee-table books on art, architecture and design. Mon–Sat 10am–7pm, Sun 1–7pm.

**Sallmayer'sche Buchhandlung 1, Neuer Markt 6; U-Bahn Stephansplatz.** Great art

and photography sections, lots on hobbies – anything from trains to Barbie dolls – plus a selection of Red Army watches. Mon–Fri 9am–6pm, Sat 9am–5pm.

**Satyr-Filmwelt 1, Marc-Aurel-Strasse 5; U-Bahn Schwedenplatz.** Loads of books in German, French and (mostly) English on movies and music. Good selection of art house videos and posters, and CD soundtracks, too. Entrance is at Vorlaufstrasse 2. Mon–Sat 10am–6pm.

**Shakespeare & Co 1, Sterngasse 2** Ⓦ www.shakespeare.co.at; **U-Bahn Schwedenplatz.** Floor-to-ceiling English-language bookstore, with friendly staff and a great selection of novels, art books and magazines. Mon–Sat 9am–7pm.

**Thalia 6, Mariahilferstrasse 99** Ⓦ www.thalia.at; **U-Bahn Neubaugasse; plus several other branches.** Vienna's biggest bookstore, with a well-stocked English section, lots of media on sale and a music department. Mon–Wed 9.30am–7pm, Thurs & Fri 9.30am–8pm, Sat 9.30am–6pm.

# Fashion

Vienna's Innere Stadt has branches of all the usual international **fashion** stores you'd find in most European capitals. The shops listed below concentrate on retro clothes and clubbing gear. There are also a few places listed where you can buy **Trachten**, the traditional Alpine costume of *Dirndl* dresses and blouses for women and *Walker* (jackets) or *Loden* (capes) for men, which is still alarmingly popular throughout the country.

**Derby Handschuhe 1, Plankengasse 5** Ⓦ www.derby-gloves-vienna.com; **U-Bahn Stephansplatz.** A veritable quality *Handschuh* (glove) fest in suede and leather. Mon–Fri 10am–6pm.

**Eselmist 7, Burggasse 89** Ⓦ www.eselmist.at; **U-Bahn Burggasse or bus #49A.** Eselmist (donkey shit) is a wonderful vintage clothing store in the backstreets of Neubau. Mon–Fri 10am–7pm, Sat 10am–5pm.

**EWA 7, Lindengasse 37; U-Bahn Neubaugasse.** Vast emporium of secondhand and retro gear with live DJs from 2pm daily and original fashions designed by the owners. Mon–Fri 10am–7pm, Sat 10am–5pm.

**Helford Jersey 1, Franz-Josefs-Kai 19; U-Bahn Schwedenplatz.** Model cars, baseball caps, Vienna T-shirts, and reasonably priced

*Trachten* clothes for the kids. Mon–Fri 10am–7pm, Sat 10am–5pm.

**Mühlbauer 1, Seilergasse 10; U-Bahn Stephansplatz.** *Hutmanufaktur* since 1903, this is the colourful hat company's white, minimalist showpiece; other branches sell clothes. Mon–Sat 10am–6.30pm, Sat 10am–6pm.

**Nachbarin 6, Gumpendorferstrasse 17; U-Bahn Museumsquartier.** Super-stylish women's clothing, shoes and jewellery from contemporary European designers. Mon noon–6pm, Tues–Fri 11am–6pm, Sat 11am–2pm.

**Rag 7, Mariahilferstrasse 20** Ⓦ www.rag.co.at; **U-Bahn Museumsquartier.** Baggy trousers and other slack accoutrements for the skateboarding posse. Mon–Fri 10am–7pm, Sat 10am–6pm.

**Tostmann** 1, Schottengasse 3a ⓦwww
.tostmann.at; U-Bahn Schottentor. *The* place
to fix yourself up head to toe in *Trachten*

– there's even a museum on the stuff in
the basement. Mon–Fri 10am–6pm, Sat
9.30am–6pm.

## Department stores

Vienna is still the land of the small shop, and has remarkably few **department
stores**. The main two are listed below.

**Gerngross** 7, Mariahilferstrasse 38–48
ⓦwww.gerngross.at; U-Bahn Neubaugasse.
Vienna's largest department store is
actually just several floors of franchises, but
it does sell everything from toys to clothes.
Good sushi bar on the top floor. Mon–Wed
& Fri 9.30am–7pm, Thurs 9.30am–8pm,
Sat 9.30am–6pm.

**Steffl** 1, Kärntnerstrasse 19 ⓦwww
.kaufhaus-steffl.at; U-Bahn Stephansplatz.
Classic department store – the only one in
the Innere Stadt – with perfume and jewellery
on the ground floor, free Internet access, a
café and bookstore on the fourth floor, and
the *Skybar*, with great views, on the top.
Mon–Fri 9.30am–7pm, Sat 9.30am–6pm.

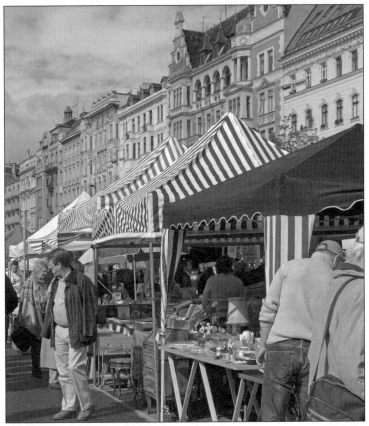

▲ Flea market

## Markets

**Bio-Bauernmarkt** 1, Freyung ⓦ www.biobauernmarkt-freyung.at; U-Bahn Schottentor/Herrengasse. Organic fruit, veg and other edibles from the neighbouring *Länder*, plus a fair few arts and crafts stalls. Fri & Sat 9am–6pm.

**Brunnenmarkt** 16, Brunnengasse; U-Bahn Thaliastrasse. Multicultural fruit and veg market in Ottakriung that stretches for something like a kilometre along Brunnengasse. Mon–Fri 6am–6.30pm, Sat 6am–2pm.

**Christkindlmarkt** 1, Rathausplatz ⓦ www.christkindlmarkt.at; U-Bahn Rathaus or tram #1 or #2. The Christmas market held in front of the Rathaus, selling gifts and food, is the biggest, though there are smaller ones in Spittelberg, Freyung and outside the Mariahilferkirche. Daily mid-Nov to Christmas Eve 9am–9pm.

**Flohmarkt** 6 & 7, Linke & Rechte Wienzeile; U-Bahn Kettenbrückengasse. Vienna's Saturday flea market is fascinating and worth checking out just for the vibe. East Europeans flock to it to sell off everything from old rags to old riches. Sat 6.30am–5pm.

**Flohmarkt im Autokino** Autokinostrasse 2, Gross Enzersdorf; bus #26A from U-Bahn Kagran; ⓦ www.autokino.at. A totally different experience from the Naschmarkt, and only really for the intrepid, this is a sprawling, chaotic fleamarket in the city's drive-in cinema. Sun 6am–1pm.

**Naschmarkt** 6 & 7, Linke & Rechte Wienzeile; U-Bahn Karlsplatz/Kettenbrückengasse. Vienna's most exotic fruit and veg market, with Turkish, Balkan, Chinese, Middle Eastern and Austrian produce, takeaway stalls plus clothes and sundries. On Saturday mornings, there's a *Flöhmarkt* (flea market) extension west of Kettenbrückengasse U-Bahn. Mon–Fri 6am–6.30pm, Sat 6am–5pm.

## Food and wine

For cheap fruit and veg, you really have to go to the **Naschmarkt** (see box above). With such small supermarkets, the gap is filled, in part, by the city's flash, quality **delis**.

**Anker** 15, Westbahnhof; U-Bahn Westbahnhof; hundreds of branches across Vienna. The largest bakery chain in the country, producing excellent bread, rolls and pastries; most branches also serve coffee. Mon–Fri 7am–6pm, Sat 7.30am–5pm, Sun 9am–5pm.

**Arthur Grimm** 1, Kurrentgasse 10 ⓦ www.grimm.at; U-Bahn Stephansplatz; branches at 2, Untere Augartenstrasse 39, & 4, Wiedner Haupstrasse 82. Most bakeries in Vienna are wonderful, but *Grimm's* is particularly wonderful, with a vast range of fresh bread and pastries. Serves coffee, too. Mon–Fri 6.30am–6.30pm, Sat 6.30am–noon.

**Billa** 1, Singerstrasse 6 ⓦ www.billa.at; U-Bahn Stephansplatz; branches all over the city. The most central of the ubiquitous supermarket chain, with a very groovy trolley escalator to take you into the basement. Handy for gathering picnic fodder – Ja! Natürlich is

their organic range. Mon–Thurs 8am–7pm, Fri 8am–7.30pm, Sat 7.30am–6pm.

**Biomaran** 7, Kaiserstrasse 57–59 ⓦ www.biomarkt.co.at; U-Bahn Burggasse or tram #5. The city's biggest organic supermarket with everything from fruit and veg to alcohol. Mon–Wed 7.30am–7pm, Sat 8am–5pm.

**Bobby's Food Store** 4, Schleifmühlgasse 8 ⓦ www.bobbys.at; U-Bahn Karlsplatz/Taubstummengasse. All those things from home you think you need, from Cadbury's chocolate and Weetabix to Colman's mustard and Marmite/Vegemite. Mon–Fri 10am–6.30pm, Sat 10am–6pm.

**Böhle** 1, Wollzeile 30 ⓦ www.boehle.at; U-Bahn Stubentor. Top-notch Austrian deli with a huge range of beer, wine, vinegar, fruit and salads, plus a daily takeaway menu. Mon–Fri 8.30am–7pm, Sat 8.30am–5pm.

**Culinarium Österreich** 1, Neuer Markt 10–11, ⓦ www.culinarium.at; U-Bahn Stephansplatz.

Very swanky deli, with an inexpensive midday menu for grabs on the ground floor and outside tables. Mon–Sat 8.30am– midnight.

**Demmer's Teehaus 1, Mölkerbastei 5 ⓦwww .demmer.at; U-Bahn Herrengasse.** Tea addicts' paradise, with Indian and Chinese teas sold loose, and a café upstairs. Mon–Fri 9am–6pm, Sat 9.30am–1.30pm.

**Gegenbauer 4, Stand 111–114 Naschmarkt; U-Bahn Karlsplatz.** Family-owned company selling a vast array of vinegar, flavoured oils and mustards in bottles, flagons and barrrels. Mon–Fri 9am–6pm, Sat 8am–5pm.

**Manner 1, Rotenturmstrasse 2 ⓦwww .manner.at; U-Bahn Stephansplatz.** Manner wafers have been going since 1890 and remain the country's most popular snack. This flagship store on the corner of Stephansplatz stocks a vast range. Daily 10am– 9pm.

**Meinl am Graben 1, Am Graben 19 ⓦwww .meinlamgraben.at; U-Bahn Stephansplatz.** The flagship Julius Meinl store has an incredible choice of luxury goodies to buy, eat and drink on two floors. Mon–Wed 8.30am–7.30pm, Thurs & Fri 8am–7.30pm, Sat 9am–6pm.

**Schönbichler 1, Wollzeile 4 ⓦwww.schoenbichler .at; U-Bahn Stephansplatz.** Amazing selection of more than 100 teas, plus china teapots, coffee, brandies, Kirsch and a staggering collection of malt whiskies. Mon–Fri 9am–6pm, Sat 9am–5pm.

**Unger & Klein 1, Gölsdorfgasse 2 ⓦwww .ungerundklein.at; U-Bahn Schwedeplatz /Schottenring.** Trendy Eichinger oder Knecht–designed wine shop where you can buy a glass to drink or a bottle to take away. Mon–Fri 3pm–midnight, Sat 5pm–midnight.

**Wein & Co 6, Getreidemarkt 1 ⓦwww.weinco .at; U-Bahn Karlsplatz.** Big wine emporium and deli, near the Naschmarkt, where you can eat, quaff or simply buy to take away. Mon–Fri 10am–midnight, Sat 9am–midnight, Sun 11am–midnight.

**Xocolat 1, Freyung 2 ⓦwww.xocolat.at; U-Bahn Karlsplatz.** Shop in the Freyung arcade selling bars, hot chocolate, chocolate spreads, Hülle mir Fülle and other choco delights from all over Europe. Mon–Fri 10am–6pm, Sat 10am–5pm, Sun noon–5pm.

**Zum schwarzen Kameel 1, Bognergasse 5; U-Bahn Herrengasse; ⓦwww.kameel.at.** Terribly smart deli that's yet another Viennese institution, eat-in or takeaway food and lots of very fancy wine too. Mon–Sat 8.30am–10pm.

**Zum süssen Eck 9, Währingerstrasse 65 ⓦwww.suesseseck.at; U-Bahn Währinger Strasse/Volksoper.** Retro candy store selling every type of boiled sweet from days of yore – worth a look just for the high-camp humour of the window display. Sun & Mon 2–7.30pm, Tues–Sat 10am–7.30pm.

# Music

**Arcadia 1, Kärntnerstrasse 40; U-Bahn Karlsplatz.** Bookshop beneath the arcades of the Staatsoper and full of things to do with opera. A great place to mug up on the plot before you go and see a show. Daily 10am–7pm.

**Audio Center 1, Judenplatz 9; U-Bahn Stephansplatz; ⓦwww.audiocenter.at.** The best selection of jazz CDs and records in the city (plus some world music), and lots of info on the local jazz scene. Mon–Fri 10am–7pm, Sat 10am–5pm.

**Black Market 1, Gonzagagasse 9 ⓦwww .soulseduction.com; U-Bahn Schwedenplatz.** Record store that's Vienna's unofficial dance music HQ – the bar is something of a clubbers' hangout. Mon–Fri noon–7pm, Sat 11am–6pm.

**Gramola 1, Graben 16 ⓦwww.gramola.at; U-Bahn Stephansplatz.** Excellent selection of cheap classical CDs in this tiny stuccoed store. Mon–Fri 9.30am–6.30pm, Sat 9.30am–6pm.

**Rave Up 6, Hofmühlgasse 1; U-Bahn Pilgramgasse; ⓦwww.rave-up.at.** Great record store with everything from indie music to hip hop, reggae and techno and lots of Viennese electronica, Mon–Fri 10am–6.30pm, Sat 10am–5pm.

**Teuchtler Alt & Neu 6, Windmühlgasse 10; U-Bahn Museumsquartier.** Secondhand CDs and records with a particularly good selection of jazz and classical, and low prices. Mon–Fri 1–6pm, Sat 10am–noon.

**Virgin Megastore 6, Mariahilferstrasse 37; U-Bahn Babenbergerstrasse.** Vienna's – and Austria's – biggest music store, with a vast collection of rock, pop, folk, soul, roots, rave and classical; plenty of listening posts too. Mon–Fri 10am–7pm, Sat 10am–5pm.

## Toys and accessories

**Hobby-Sommer** 7, Neubaugasse 26 Ⓦwww
.hobby-sommer-austria.at; U-Bahn Neubaugasse.
Model railways from around the world,
and models of the Airfix variety. Mon–Fri
9.30am–6pm, Sat 9am–5pm.

**Huber & Lerner** 1, Weihburggasse 4 Ⓦwww
.huber-lerner.at; U-Bahn Stephansplatz. This
former imperial stationers is the place to get
your bespoke headed notepaper (at a price).
Mon–Fri 9.30am–6pm, Sat 10am–5pm.

**Imaginarium** 1, Neuer Markt 8a Ⓦwww
.imaginarium.info; U-Bahn Karlsplatz. Brilliant
range of imaginative toys from this Catalan
toy chain, and a separate miniature
entrance for kids. Mon–Fri 10am–7pm,
Sat 10am–6pm.

**Lorenzi** 7, Siebensterngasse 41; tram #49;
Ⓦwww.lorenzi.co.at. Amazing selection of
*Stahlwaren* – pricey knives, scissors, daggers
and swords – by top manufacturers from a

shop that's been here since 1885. Mon–Sat
10am–6pm.

**Piatnik** 7, Kandlgasse/Kaiserstrasse Ⓦwww
.piatnik.com; U-Bahn Burggasse-Stadthalle.
Famous Austrian firm founded in 1824 that
makes playing cards and also sells Zippo
lighters, pipes, kids' toys and board games.
Mon–Fri 9.30am–6pm, Sat 9am–5pm.

**Rudolf Waniek** 1, Hoher Markt 5; U-Bahn
Schwedenplatz. Former court suppliers of
glassware and metalware, now peddling salt
cellars, decanters, coffee-making machines
and quality domestic utensils. Mon–Fri
9.30am–6pm, Sat 10am–5pm.

**Spielzeugschachtel** 1, Rauhensteingasse
5 Ⓦwww.spielzeugschachtel.com; U-Bahn
Stephansplatz. The "Toy Box" contains a
feast of jigsaws, games, wooden toys and
children's books. Mon–Fri 10am–6.30pm,
Sat 10am–5pm.

# Contexts

# Contexts

# A history of Vienna

## The Romans

People have lived in the area of modern-day Vienna for many thousands of years, due to its geographical position at the point where the ancient trade route or amber route crossed the Danube. Following on from early Bronze and Iron Age settlements, a Celtic tribe known as the Boii occupied the hills above Vienna, probably from as early as 500 BC, but were driven from the area in around 50 BC by the short-lived Dacian kingdom. Vienna was then swallowed up by the neighbouring Celtic kingdom of Noricum.

In 15 BC the **Romans**, under the emperor Augustus, advanced into Noricum as far as the Danube and the area was absorbed into the Roman province of Pannonia. For the next four centuries, the river was used as a natural military border or *limes* by the Romans, further strengthened by a series of forts along its banks. The main Roman camp along this stretch of the Danube was at Carnuntum, to the east, with Vienna – or **Vindobona** as it was then called – as a subsidiary fort.

The Roman Forum is thought to have been somewhere around the Hoher Markt (see p.68) in today's Innere Stadt. In the first century AD, Vindobona became the base for the 10th legion, whose job it was to fend off attacks from the neighbouring Germanic tribes to the north and east, particularly the Marcomanni and the Quadi. These two tribes crashed through the Danubian frontier in 169 AD only to be beaten back by the emperor Marcus Aurelius, who died in Vindobona in 180 AD.

## The Babenbergs

The Romans finally abandoned Vindobona to the **Huns** in 433 AD, and the city, like the rest of Europe, entered the **Dark Ages**. However, it's interesting to note that even at this early stage in its history, during the great migrations that followed the collapse of Roman power, the area of modern-day Vienna stood on one of the main ethnic crossroads of Europe: pressed from the east by first the Huns, later the Avars, from the north and south by the Slavs, and from the west by Germanic tribes.

The coronation of **Charlemagne** as Holy Roman Emperor in 800 marked the end of the Dark Ages in Europe. Parts of modern-day Austria, meanwhile, became a military colony – referred to by nineteenth-century historians as the "Ostmark" – of Charlemagne's Frankish Empire. With the collapse of the empire in 888, it was the Saxon king, Otto the Great, who succeeded in subduing the German lands. His successor, Otto II, went on to hand the "Ostmark" to the **Babenberg dynasty** in 976, whose job it was to protect the empire's eastern frontiers, once more formed by the Danube. The Babenberg dynasty ruled the territory for the next 270 years, first as margraves and later as dukes.

In their search for some kind of official birthday for their country, many Austrian scholars have latched on to the first known mention of the name

Ostarrîchi, which appears in a Latin parchment from around 996. However, throughout the Middle Ages, the region was mostly referred to either simply as *provincia orientalis* or else named after its first ruler, the **Margrave Leopold I** (976–94). To begin with, the Babenberg Margravate was confined to a small stretch of the Danube centred most probably on Melk, but gradually it expanded eastwards as far as the River Leitha and northwards as far as the River Thaya. Successive Babenbergs founded a number of monasteries in the region, in particular Leopold III (1095–1136), who was later canonized for his good works and became the country's patron saint.

In 1156, during the reign of **Heinrich II Jasomirgott** (1141–77), the Babenbergs' Margravate was at last elevated to a Duchy, with its new capital at Vienna and the ducal palace situated in Am Hof (see p.64). However, in 1246 the Babenberg male line came to an end with the death of Duke Friedrich II (1230–46) on the battlefield. The dispute over who should rule over the Duchy of Austria and Styria, as it was now known, dragged on for the next thirty years. In 1251, the future Bohemian king, **Otakar II**, took up residence in Vienna and claimed the duchy for himself, shoring up his claim by marrying Friedrich II's widow.

# The early Habsburgs

While Otakar was laying claim to the Babenbergs' inheritance, he was also putting himself forward as a candidate for the throne of the Holy Roman Empire. In the end, though, the throne was handed in 1273 to **Rudolf of Habsburg**, a little-known count whose ancestral home was the castle of Habichtsburg (hence Habsburg) above the River Reuss in modern-day Switzerland. In 1278 Otakar was defeated (and killed) by Rudolf's forces at the **Battle of Marchfeld**, to the east of Vienna, allowing Rudolf to lay claim to the Duchy of Austria. The Viennese, who had backed Otakar, were less than pleased about the outcome of the battle, and weren't easily placated by Rudolf's son, Albrecht, who had been given the duchy by his father.

The Habsburgs, though, were here to stay, their dynasty destined to rule over Austria for the next 640 years. Initially, however, Vienna only sporadically served as the dynastic capital. **Rudolf IV** (1356–65) was one of the few to treat it as such, founding the university and laying the foundation stone of what is now the Stephansdom, before dying at the age of just 26. Rudolf's endeavours earned him the nickname "The Founder", but he failed to secure a bishopric for Vienna.

For that the city had to wait until the reign of **Friedrich III** (1440–93). Despite numerous setbacks – he was besieged in the Hofburg by one of his own family in 1462 and briefly lost control of Vienna to the Hungarian king Matthias Corvinus in 1485 – it was Friedrich who was responsible for consolidating the Habsburgs' power base. In 1452, he became the last Holy Roman Emperor to be crowned in Rome, and the following year elevated the family's dukedom to an archdukedom. The Holy Roman Empire, famously dismissed by Matthias Corvinus as "neither holy, Roman, nor an empire", was something of a fantasy, whose emperor, theoretically at least, ruled over all the German-speaking lands. Though the reality was somewhat different, the Habsburgs persisted with their imperial pretensions, passing the title down the male line until its eventual dissolution in 1806 (see p.306).

In the meantime, the Habsburgs continued to add to their dynastic inheritance through a series of judicious marriages by **Maximilian I** (1493–1519) and his offspring, prompting the oft-quoted maxim, adapted from Ovid: "Let others wage war; you, happy Austria, marry." By the time the emperor Karl V came to the throne in 1519, the Habsburgs ruled over an empire on which, it was said, the sun never set, with lands stretching from its Spanish possessions in South America to Vienna itself – bolstered in 1526 by the addition of the kingdoms of Bohemia and Hungary. Vienna remained just one of several imperial residences, its development constantly hampered by the threat posed by the Ottoman army of Süleyman the Magnificent, who had been advancing steadily westwards across Europe.

# The Turkish sieges

In 1526, the Turks scored a decisive victory at the **Battle of Mohács** against the Hungarians, and began to advance into Habsburg territory. In the summer of 1529 they captured Budapest, and by September the Sultan's vast army were camped outside Vienna, the "city of the golden apple" as they called it. Although it is the later siege of 1683 (see below) that captured the imagination of historians, the **1529 siege** was a much closer-run thing. The Ottoman Empire was at its zenith and Vienna was defended only by a small garrison under Count Salm. However, having shelled the city and killed some 1500 Viennese, the Turks suddenly withdrew – whether because of bad weather or some other reason, no one knows – back to Hungary in October. It seems almost as if Vienna simply wasn't worth the effort, despite the fact that the city was there for the taking.

In a defiant gesture, **Ferdinand I** (1556–64) subsequently established Vienna as his permanent base, building the zigzag fortifications that were to surround the city for the next three hundred years or more. With the retreat of the Turks, Ferdinand's troubles were by no means over, however, for **Lutheranism** was spreading at an alarming rate among the German-speaking lands. By the middle of the century it's estimated that Vienna was eighty percent Protestant. To combat this new plague, Ferdinand called in the fiercely proselytizing Jesuits in 1556. Nevertheless, the new creed flourished under the relatively liberal reign of **Maximilian II** (1564–76), and it was only after Rudolf II (1576–1612) moved the capital to Prague, leaving the Archduke Ernst in charge of Vienna, that the tide began to turn due to the repressive measures introduced.

When the **Thirty Years' War** broke out in 1618, Vienna was well on the way to becoming a Catholic city again, thanks partly to the Jesuits' stranglehold on the education system. By the time of the Peace of Westphalia in 1648, the city, which had emerged from the war relatively unscathed, was firmly under the grip of the Counter-Reformation, and those Viennese who would not renounce their Protestantism were forced into exile.

## The siege of 1683

The fact that the city managed to survive the **1683 siege** was no thanks to its emperor, **Leopold I** (1657–1705), a profligate, bigoted man whose reign marked the beginning of the **Baroque era** in Vienna. Under Leopold, a whole new wing of the Hofburg was built, but the emperor is best known for his operatic extravaganzas – he himself was a keen composer – in particular the four-hour-long equestrian ballet he staged (see p.75), just one of some four hundred theatrical events put on during his reign.

While Leopold was busy working out ways to spend more of the state's coffers, the priest Abraham à Santa Clara was busy preaching against such indulgences, not to mention against the Protestant, the Jew and the Turk – "an Epicurean piece of excrement" as he put it in one of his fiery sermons. In 1679, a plague claimed the lives of an estimated 70,000 Viennese, and four years later, Vienna was to face the worst crisis in its history as the town was forced to endure its second siege by the Ottoman army. Naturally enough, at the approach of the Turks, Leopold, and anyone else who had the money, fled to the safety of Linz and Passau.

If anything, Vienna had more chance of surviving the siege of 1683 than it had in 1529. The Turks were no longer at the zenith of their power and the city was properly fortified this time – in addition, there was a relief force on its way, albeit rather slowly. Nevertheless, the city was still confronted with an army of more than 200,000, made up of 100,000 infantry, 50,000 cavalry, a harem of over 1500 concubines guarded by 700 black eunuchs, a contingent of clowns, and numerous poets trained in bawdy songs. The Viennese, protected by a garrison of just 10,000 men, were understandably ready to make peace with the grand vizier, **Kara Mustafa**.

The grand vizier's fatal flaw was overconfidence. Convinced that the city was his for the taking, and loath to share the booty among his army (which he would have to do if he took the city by force), he orchestrated a two-month siege of Vienna. By September, however, a relief force of Poles, under their king, **Jan Sobieski**, and sundry German troops under the Duke of Lorraine, finally came to the aid of the city. On September 12, the papal legate Marco d'Aviano conducted a Mass on the hills above the city and, though outnumbered, the imperial forces managed to rout the Turks, in the process capturing 20,000 buffaloes, bullocks, camels and mules, 10,000 sheep, corn and flour, sugar, oil and most famously, coffee. Diamonds, rubies, sapphires and pearls, silver and gold, and "the most beautiful sable furs in the world", belonging to Kara Mustafa, fell into the grateful hands of King Sobieski. The grand vizier was discovered to have decapitated his favourite wife and his pet ostrich, rather than have them fall into the hands of the infidels, and, as was the custom in humiliating cases of defeat, he effected his own execution by allowing an emissary to strangle him with a silken cord in Belgrade on Christmas Day later that year.

# The eighteenth century

Following the siege of 1683, Vienna could finally establish itself as the Habsburgs' permanent *Residenzstadt* or *Kaiserstadt*. Over the following years, Baroque art and architecture really took off, as extensive rebuilding of damaged churches, monasteries and palaces took place within the Innere Stadt. The Viennese aristocracy could also now at last build in the suburbs without fear of attack. Most famously the palace of Schönbrunn began to evolve, while Prince Eugène of Savoy (see p.155), who took command of the imperial forces and drove the Turks out of Hungary, built the Belvedere.

In keeping with the spirit of the age, **Emperor Karl VI** (1711–40) proved as spendthrift as his father Leopold, adding the magnificent Prunksaal library and the Winterreitschule to the Hofburg, and erecting Vienna's finest Baroque church, the Karlskirche (see p.121). The one area in which Karl VI singularly failed was in producing a male heir to the throne. In the end, the emperor had to accept the fact that his eldest daughter, Maria Theresia, was going to have to take over when he died. In an attempt to smooth her accession, Karl introduced the so-called Pragmatic Sanction in 1713, which allowed for female succession, and got all the states nominally within the Holy Roman Empire to promise to recognize his daughter's right to the Habsburgs' hereditary lands. Naturally enough, everyone agreed with the emperor while he was alive, and as soon as he died immediately went back on their word.

## Maria Theresia (1740–80)

So it was that **Maria Theresia** (see p.199) found herself forced to fight the **War of the Austrian Succession** (1740–48) as soon as she took over from her father. For a while, she was even forced to hand over the imperial title to Karl of Bavaria in an attempt to pacify him, though it was eventually regained and handed to her husband, Franz Stephan of Lorraine (she herself, as a woman, could not become Holy Roman Emperor). At the end of the war in 1748, Maria Theresia was forced to cede Silesia to Prussia, and despite an attempt to win it back during the **Seven Years' War** (1756–63), it remained, for the most part, in Prussian hands.

On the domestic front, Maria Theresia's reign signalled the beginning of the **era of reform**, influenced by the ideas of the Enlightenment. To push through her reforms the empress created a formidable centralized bureaucracy, taking power away from the provincial Diets. When the pope abolished the Jesuit order in 1773, Maria Theresia took the opportunity of introducing a state education system. In 1776 she abolished torture, and passed de facto abolition of the death penalty (though hard labour usually killed the convict within a year in any case). Despite her reforms, it would be wrong to get the impression that the empress was some free-thinking democrat. She believed wholeheartedly in absolutism, and, as a devout Catholic, ensured Catholic supremacy within the empire with yet more anti-Protestant edicts.

## Josef II (1780–90)

With the death of her husband in 1765, Maria Theresia appointed her eldest son, Josef, as co-regent. But it wasn't until after the empress's death in 1780 that Josef's reforming zeal could come into its own (see p.87). His most significant edict was the 1781 **Toleranzpatent**, which allowed freedom of worship to Lutherans, Calvinists and the Greek Orthodox. Like his mother, he was himself a devout Catholic, but was even more determined to curtail Church – and particularly papal – power. To this end, he dissolved four hundred contemplative or "idle" monasteries, and, as many saw it, was bent on "nationalizing" the Church.

Under Josef II all religious processions (previously a daily occurrence on the streets of Vienna) were banned except the annual Corpus Christi procession. Pope Pius VI was so concerned he came to Vienna in person in 1782 to try to change the emperor's mind, but to no avail. With the best of intentions, Josef interfered in every aspect of his citizens' lives, causing widespread resentment. For – again like his mother – despite his enlightened policies, Josef was still very much the despot. He was, above all, responsible for creating the Habsburgs' secret police force, which was to become so infamous in the nineteenth century.

# The Napoleonic era

Emperor Leopold II, who unenthusiastically succeeded Josef II in 1790, died suddenly of a stroke after a reign of less than two years. As a result, Leopold's eldest son became **Emperor Franz II** (1792–1835). No great military man – his troops had been fighting the French for two years before he bothered to show himself at the front line – Franz was an unlikely candidate to become one of Napoleon's great adversaries.

In 1797, during his first Italian campaign, **Napoleon** succeeded in humiliating the Habsburg forces at Mantua, and was within a hundred miles of Vienna when the Habsburg emperor sued for peace. It was a scenario that was repeated again in 1800 when Napoleon's forces were once more marching on Vienna. By 1803, the Habsburgs had lost the Netherlands plus several territories in northern Italy to the French. Napoleon then added insult to injury by declaring himself emperor the following year, with the clear intention of re-establishing the Holy Roman Empire under French hegemony. In retaliation, Franz declared himself Emperor Franz I of Austria (a hitherto nonexistent title), though the gesture looked more like an admission of defeat, since Franz was already Holy Roman Emperor.

## The 1805 occupation of Vienna

In 1805, in alliance with Russia and Britain, Austria decided to take on Napoleon again, only to suffer a crushing defeat at Ulm. Unable to stop the advance of the *Grande Armée*, the allies decided to regroup further east, leaving Napoleon free to march on Vienna, where he arrived on November 13, 1805. The imperial family had already taken flight to Hungary carrying the contents of the Hofburg with them. Though there was no fighting, having 34,000 French troops billeted in the city put an enormous strain on the place and supplies quickly ran short. The French stayed on until January 12, 1806, having exacted taxes, war reparations and appropriated many works of art, including four hundred paintings from the Belvedere. Four days later, Franz returned to Vienna amid much rejoicing, though in political terms there was little to rejoice about. During the French occupation, the Allies had lost the Battle of Austerlitz to Napoleon, and concluded the **Treaty of Pressburg**, leaving the Habsburgs without their Italian possessions, the Tyrol and the Vorarlberg. Further humiliation followed in 1806 when Napoleon established the Confederation of the Rhine and Franz was forced to call it a day by relinquishing his title of Holy Roman Emperor.

## The 1809 occupation of Vienna

For the next few years, there was no hope of the Austrians exacting any revenge. But in the spring of 1809, with Napoleon encountering problems fighting Wellington in Spain, the Austrians decided to seize the moment to reopen hostilities. Although they were once more defeated at Ratisbon, the Austrian forces under the emperor's brother, Archduke Karl, managed to regroup to the east of Vienna. Once more Napoleon was free to march on Vienna. As usual, the imperial family had taken flight to Hungary, but this time the city tried to defend itself. Napoleon reached the outskirts of the city on May 10, 1809, and sent two emissaries to negotiate. They were promptly lynched by the Viennese; the French bombardment started the following evening. It was an uneven battle – "Our batteries shot off a few shots; they were ineffective," as one eyewitness stated; the French, for their part, fired some 1600 shells, and killed 23 civilians. The next day the city capitulated, its 16,000-strong garrison no match for the 100,000 French troops.

Despite taking Vienna, Napoleon's *Grande Armée* went on to suffer its first major defeat ten days later at the **Battle of Aspern**, just east of Vienna, at the hands of Archduke Karl. However, Karl failed to press home his advantage, and Napoleon succeeded in holding on to Vienna, going on to defeat the Austrians decisively six weeks later at the **Battle of Wagram**, when the Austrians threw in the towel. The city was forced to celebrate the new emperor's birthday on August 13, and in the peace, signed on October 14, the Austrians were forced to give up Galicia and Croatia. Two days later Napoleon left Vienna, and on October 29, the French held a farewell ball. Towards the end of the following month, Emperor Franz crept back incognito into the Hofburg.

**Clemenz Metternich** became the chief minister of Austria, and began to pursue a policy of rapprochement. His greatest coup in this direction was getting Napoleon to marry Emperor Franz's 18-year-old daughter, Marie Louise, in March 1810 (see p.92). By 1813, with the tide turning against Napoleon, Metternich even managed to persuade his reluctant emperor to join the latest anti-French grand alliance.

## The 1815 Congress of Vienna

Vienna missed out on the rest of the Napoleonic wars, but it was centre stage when it came to the peace. Following the defeat of Napoleon at Leipzig and his exile to Elba, the victorious powers met for the **Congress of Vienna** in the autumn of 1814. If nothing else, the congress was a great social success (see p.307), or as one participant famously put it, *"Le congrès danse, mais il ne marche pas."* The most public celebration took place on the anniversary of the Battle of Leipzig, when some 20,000 war veterans were wined and dined alfresco in the Prater (see p.184). All of Vienna was agog at the spectacle, but by New Year, most of the foreigners had outstayed their welcome. The congress was costing the emperor a fortune that even he could not afford, forcing him to raise taxes, while many of the participants were living on credit notes. Nevertheless, it dragged on until after Napoleon escaped from Elba, finally winding itself up in May 1815, just twelve days before the Battle of Waterloo.

Despite the shenanigans, the congress did, in fact, manage fairly successfully to establish a status quo in Europe. Many of the borders agreed upon in Vienna were to endure for over a century. In the peace deal, Austria won back much of North Italy and Galicia, Croatia, Salzburg, the Tyrol and the Vorarlberg, but on Metternich's advice, claims over the Netherlands and other far-flung territories that would be hard to defend, were relinquished. The congress also pledged itself to further regular meetings between the heads of the victorious states – meetings at which it was agreed that in order to maintain international peace, they would combine to suppress any further revolutionary uprisings within Europe.

# Biedermeier Vienna

Following the congress, Vienna enjoyed more than thirty years of peace and stability, a period known retrospectively as the *Vormärz* – literally "pre-March", because it preceded the March 1848 revolution. The same stretch of time is also known throughout the German-speaking lands as the **Biedermeier era** (for more on the origin of the term, see p.343). In later years, the Viennese would look back on this period through rose-tinted spectacles as a time of introspective domesticity, played out to the tunes of Johann Strauss the Elder and the melodies of Franz Schubert.

As ever, there is more than a grain of truth in the myth, as there is in the counter-myth that this was one of the most oppressive regimes in the history of the Habsburgs. The man most closely associated with the conservative and reactionary politics of the Biedermeier era was **Metternich**. Under him, and his "poodle" – the chief of police Count Josef Sedlnitzky – the vast machinery of the Josephine civil service, which had been designed to help push through reforms, was now used to thwart any further change. Censorship and the activities of the secret police and its informers did so much to stifle intellectual life that by 1848 the playwright Franz Grillparzer reflected miserably, "Despotism has destroyed my life, at least my literary life."

With the death of the emperor Franz I in 1835, the Habsburgs faced something of a crisis, as the heir to the throne, **Ferdinand I** – a victim of Habsburg inbreeding – was, in the vocabulary of the day, an "imbecile", nicknamed *Nandl der Trottel* ("Ferdy the Dotty"). He was, in fact, nothing of the sort: he could be perfectly coherent, but suffered badly from epilepsy, which affected his short-term memory. To combat the latter's deficiencies, a Regency Council was established, with Ferdinand as chair – or in his absence his brother, Archduke Ludwig – and his brother Franz Karl, Count Kolowrat, and Metternich as permanent members. Within the council Metternich had to struggle to maintain his influence.

# The 1848 revolution

With the deposition of the French king and the outbreak of revolution in Paris in late February 1848, it was only a question of time before matters came to a head in the other European capitals. Vienna, now a city of 400,000, suffered from chronic overcrowding (though this was nothing new), and sporadic food shortages, yet it still came as some surprise when it became the first city to follow in the footsteps of the French. On **March 13**, the Estates of Lower Austria, consisting of nobles and senior clergy, were due to meet in the Landhaus on Herrengasse (see p.60). They were pressing for various reforms, including the freedom of the press, but top of the agenda was the removal of Metternich. In the morning a crowd gathered outside the Landhaus, and, after listening to a German translation of the inflammatory speech given recently by the Hungarian revolutionary Lajos Kossuth in the Hungarian Diet, forced their way into the building. At around 1pm, a detachment of Italian grenadiers fired into the crowd, killing around thirty unarmed protesters, mostly students, and sparking off a revolution.

That evening, after playing for time, Metternich finally resigned and fled from the capital (disguised as a washerwoman, according to popular legend). The emperor – who when told of the outbreak of revolution had apparently said "But do they have permission?" – immediately made a rapid retreat, declaring "Tell the people I agree to everything." A **National Guard** was formed – with Johann Strauss the Younger as *Kapellmeister* – augmented by an academic legion of armed students, with whom they were to man the city in place of the despised imperial troops. In addition, a constitution was promised, and a "Responsible Ministry" of bureaucrats formed to produce it. On April 25, a constitutional monarchy was proposed, with two chambers elected by limited franchise based on property. Not surprisingly, the idea was rejected and rioting, in favour of a single-chamber parliament elected by universal suffrage, ensued on May 15. Barricades were erected around the city, and the emperor and his entourage quickly fled to Innsbruck in a stagecoach.

Elections were duly held throughout the empire (with the exception of Italy and Hungary which were busy with their own revolutions) and the first **parliament** in Habsburg history met in the unlikely surroundings of the Hofburg's Winterreitschule (see p.88) on July 22. The deputies were by no means revolutionaries, the majority coming from the educated middle classes, with close to a third of peasant origin. Hampered throughout by disputes between the various nationalities, the assembly did manage to pass one lasting piece of legislation: the emancipation of the peasantry. By August, the court felt secure enough to return to Vienna, bolstered by General Radetzky's military victory over the rebels in Italy and the recapture of Prague by General Windischgrätz.

The spark that lit the final fuse of the Viennese revolution took place on **October 6**. A battalion, due to be sent to fight against Kossuth's Hungarian revolutionaries, mutinied and joined forces with radicals in the National Guard. Civil war then broke out as some within the National Guard fired on the radicals. In the confusion, the war minister, General Latour, was lynched by the mob (see p.64) and the imperial family removed themselves once more, this time to Olomouc in Moravia. As Windischgrätz marched his troops towards the capital, the radicals among the academic legion and the National Guard erected barricades and awaited the final showdown. Their only hope lay in the possibility of a Hungarian relief force, which in the event arrived too late. After several days' bombardment and around two thousand casualties, Windischgrätz flushed out the last of the rebels on October 31.

# The reign of Franz-Josef I

Meanwhile, back in Olomouc, the emperor Ferdinand (and his brother Franz Karl) was coerced by the imperial family into renouncing the throne in favour of the latter's 18-year-old nephew, **Franz-Josef** (see p.81). A new government was formed under the leadership of the arch-conservative Prince Felix Schwarzenberg, while the assembly continued to meet in the nearby Moravian town of Kremsier (Kroměříz) to try to thrash out a new constitution. Then, to the astonishment of the assembly, on February 28, 1849, Schwarzenberg announced that as the emperor had himself formulated a new constitution, their services were no longer required. Although the new constitution granted equal rights to all, it was anything but liberal, granting the emperor the power of veto over all legislation, the power to dissolve parliament and rule by decree, and the power to dismiss and appoint ministers as he saw fit. Meanwhile in Hungary, the Austrians were forced to swallow their pride and enlist the help of the Russians in order to defeat Kossuth's Hungarian revolutionaries once and for all.

In the immediate aftermath of the revolution, it was decided to strengthen the fortifications of the city. Eventually, though, the tide of opinion in the government shifted in favour of tearing down the walls, to prevent a repeat of October 1848 when the revolutionaries had managed to resist the forces of law and order. Finally, in 1857, the emperor decreed that the walls were to come down, and in their place a **Ringstrasse**, lined with noble institutions, was to be constructed (see p.99). This wide boulevard remains Franz-Josef's most significant architectural legacy, though it wasn't until the last decade of the emperor's reign that the final sections were completed.

# 1866 and all that

After some ten years of relative peace, Franz-Josef suffered his first of many embarrassing military setbacks at the Battle of Solferino in 1859. It was not so much the resultant loss of Lombardy that was the problem, but the opportunity it gave the Hungarians to demand their independence once more. In an attempt to placate them, Franz-Josef agreed in 1861 to establish a two-chamber parliament in Vienna. The Hungarians remained unimpressed and failed to send delegates to fill any of their 85 allotted seats in the lower house.

Five years later, the empire was rocked by an even greater crisis with its army's humiliating defeat at the **Battle of Königgrätz** in the Austro-Prussian War. Not only did the Habsburgs lose forever the battle for hegemony over the rest of Germany, but they were finally forced to strike a deal with the Hungarians (while studiously ignoring the demands of the empire's other nationalities).

With the 1867 **Ausgleich** or Compromise, the so-called Dual Monarchy of Austria-Hungary was established. According to this new arrangement, Franz-Josef was to be crowned king of Hungary (he was already emperor of Austria), and the Hungarians were to get their own parliament in Budapest, with autonomy over everything except defence, foreign affairs and the overall imperial budget. Everything within Hungary was to be prefaced with a "k." for *königlich*, everything in the rest of the empire was to be prefaced with the initials "k.k." or *kaiserlich-königlich* (imperial-royal), while everything Austro-Hungarian was prefaced with "k.u.k." or *kaiserlich-und-königlich*.

Meanwhile, delegates from the "Austrian" half of the empire met in Vienna's **parliament** (see p.107). Among the delegates were Czechs, Poles, Croats, Slovenes, Italians and German-speakers from every corner of the empire, who spent most of their time arguing over language issues and abusing each other both verbally and physically. The number of people eligible to vote increased gradually until universal male suffrage was finally introduced in 1907, but in reality, the emperor still ruled supreme since he and his ministers could pass any laws they wanted as "emergency measures", not to mention dissolve parliament and rule by decree (which they did on numerous occasions).

To make matters worse, the economy suffered its worst financial crisis ever in the crash of May 1873, shortly after the opening of Vienna's **Weltausstellung** or World Exhibition in the Prater (see p.180). The 72 banks in Vienna were reduced to eight in the decade following the crash; construction of the Ring was halted and the big projects – the Parliament, Rathaus, Burgtheater and Universität – were only completed in the 1880s. The empire's industrialization was also affected, with railway construction reaching an annual low of 75km of new track in 1880, which had a severe knock-on effect on the other heavy industries.

# Fin-de-siècle Vienna

From 1860 to the turn of the century, Vienna more than trebled in size, its population topping two million. Like most industrialized cities of the period, it was a city of enormous contrasts. Wealth and power were in the hands of the upper aristocracy, who alone had an entrée into court society, and exercised enormous influence over the careers of individuals through the sytem of *Protektion* or patronage. Meanwhile, the bulk of the population, many of them recently arrived immigrants from other parts of the empire, were packed like sardines in the *Mietkaserne* (rent barracks) of the newly built suburbs. At the bottom of the heap were the nocturnal *Bettgeher*, the five percent of the population who could afford only to rent someone else's bed from them during the day.

A significant proportion of the new immigrants were Jews from the empire's rural *shtetls* (small, predominantly Jewish towns). By the turn of the century they made up nearly ten percent of the population. In some walks of life, they comprised an even greater percentage: more than half of all the city's doctors and lawyers were Jews, as were most of its journalists and bankers. The Jew had long been a stock Viennese scapegoat (see p.66). Now with the 1873 crash – the fault, it was said, of Jewish financiers – and the continuing influx of Orthodox Jews into the city, **anti-Semitism** began to flourish. It found a spokesman in the figure of the pan-German nationalist **Georg von Schönerer**, whose fanatical followers used to wear the effigy of a hanged Jew on their watch chains. Schönerer's political career faltered, however, after 1888 when he was sent to prison for breaking into the offices of the Jewish-owned newspaper, the *Neues Wiener Tagblatt*.

Anti-Semitism was given a more respectable, populist twist by **Karl Lueger** (see p.105). This Vienna-born politician became leader of the Christian Social Party, whose combination of Catholicism, anti-Semitism and municipal social-ism went down alarmingly well with the Viennese electorate. In 1897, Lueger became mayor of Vienna, and the crowd that turned out for his funeral in 1910 was the largest the city had ever seen – among the mourners was the young **Adolf Hitler** (see p.117).

Most middle-class Jews, understandably, gravitated towards the other side of the political spectrum, dominating the upper echelons of the **Social Democratic Workers' Party** (SDAP), after it was founded in 1889. The party's chief ideo-logue before World War I was the Prague-born Jew Viktor Adler, whose peculiar ideology of **Austro-Marxism** was to dominate the party's thinking for the next half-century. As far as Adler was concerned capitalism was doomed to failure, so the party could afford to adopt a peaceful approach to politics until the time was right for revolution.

In among all the tensions between Right and Left, Jew and Gentile, rich and poor, **fin-de-siècle Vienna** also succeeded in nurturing intellectual and artistic creativity such as the city had never known, much of it inspired by the city's assimilated Jews. **Arnold Schönberg**, and his followers **Alban Berg** and **Anton Webern**, changed the face of classical music with their atonal – or as Schönberg preferred, "pantonal" – revolution (see p.120). **Gustav Mahler**, meanwhile, turned heads both as a composer and as boss of the Staatsoper. In medicine, **Sigmund Freud** (see p.174) coined the term "psychoanalysis", and expounded on the new discipline in his seminal *Interpretation of Dreams*. In 1897 **Gustav Klimt** led a revolt against the artistic establishment, known as the Secession; following in his footsteps were the likes of **Egon Schiele** and **Oskar Kokoschka**. Otto Wagner left the most visible legacy of this period, in the **Jugendstil** and early modernist buildings that can still be seen on the streets of Vienna today. For more on the Secession, see the colour insert in this book.

# World War I

On June 28, 1914, the heir to the throne, **Archduke Franz Ferdinand** and his wife, Sophie, were assassinated in Sarajevo by Bosnian Serbs, with weapons supplied by the chief of Serbia's army intelligence. There was little genuine sadness in court circles, for as Stefan Zweig bluntly put it, "The archduke Franz Ferdinand lacked everything that counts for real popularity in Austria: amiability, personal charm and easy-goingness." Even his uncle, Emperor Franz-Josef, was more relieved than anything else, as the two got on famously badly.

To begin with, there was also very little action by Austria on the diplomatic front, but eventually, on July 23, Franz-Josef and his ministers sent an ultimatum to Serbia, with an impossible set of conditions and a 48-hour time limit. As Serbia could not agree to all the conditions, Austria-Hungary declared war on her. The Russians immediately mobilized to defend their Slav brothers, with Britain and France, Russia's allies, following suit. By August 4, the major European powers were at war.

Perhaps surprisingly, the outbreak of war brought patriotic crowds on to the streets of Vienna, and other cities around the empire, with Left and Right alike rallying round the Habsburg cause. Of course, everyone thought the affair would be over by Christmas; it was only after years of military defeats, huge casualties and food shortages that the population began to turn against the war. On October 21, 1916, Viktor Adler's son Friedrich took matters into his own hands and assassinated the Austrian prime minister, **Count Karl Stürgkh** (see p.51). At his trial in May the following year, Friedrich Adler gave such a damning indictment of the war that his execution was postponed so as not to boost the antiwar cause further. On November 21, 1916, Franz-Josef finally died at the age of 86, leaving the throne to his 29-year-old great-nephew Karl.

**Emperor Karl I** is perhaps best known for his bungled attempt at negotiating a separate peace for his empire with the western allies in March 1917. The approach was rebuffed at the time and a year later became public knowledge, causing huge embarrassment to all concerned. Only victory on the battlefield could now save the dynasty, but it was not to come.

In October 1918, the empire began to crumble from within, with national committees taking over the regional capitals. In Vienna, the Social Democrats, who were in favour of self-determination for the empire's various nationalities, set up a provisional government under Karl Renner. On November 2, 1918, with the end of the war in sight, the Hungarian battalion guarding Schönbrunn upped and left, leaving the imperial family and their servants unguarded. The next day an armistice was signed, and eight days later, Emperor Karl I agreed to sign away his powers, withdrawing first to Eckartsau outside Vienna, and eventually, in 1919, going into exile in Switzerland.

# The First Republic

The Austrian Republic – or more correctly **Deutsch–Österreich** or "German Austria" – was proclaimed from the steps of Vienna's parliament on November 12, 1918 (see p.107); the colours chosen for the national flag – red, white, red – were those of the Babenbergs. At first, however, there was precious little enthusiasm for the new country among its people. The Christian Socials wanted a constitutional monarchy, the Pan-Germans wanted Anschluss with Germany, while the Socialists wanted Anschluss with a Socialist Germany. In the proclamation of November 12, the country was even described as "a constituent part of the German Republic". In the regions, both the Tyrol and Salzburg voted overwhelmingly in favour of Anschluss with Germany (requests which were denied by the international community), while the Vorarlberg voted to join the Swiss.

In February 1919, the first national elections took place, creating a coalition government of the SDAP and the Christian Socials under the chancellorship of Social Democrat **Karl Renner**. Nevertheless a political vacuum continued until the end of the year, with soldiers' and workers' councils threatening to follow the revolutionary soviet example of neighbouring Bavaria and Hungary. There were even two unsuccessful attempts by the newly formed Austrian Communist Party (KPÖ) to stage a putsch, in April and June 1919.

The new government's foremost task was to feed the population, particularly that of Vienna. Deprived of its former territories, and hampered by a bad harvest, they managed it only with the help of the Allied Famine Relief programme. The government's next most arduous job was to negotiate the **Treaty of St-Germain** with the victorious allies. Many in the delegation still hoped for Anschluss with Germany, but it was not to be. The Austrians (along with the Hungarians) were branded an "enemy state", while the rest of the so-called "successor states" like Czechoslovakia were not, and were expressly forbidden ever to undertake Anschluss with Germany. With his oft-quoted remark, Georges Clemenceau summed up the Austrians' lack of a bargaining position when he pointed to the map and said, "What's left is Austria."

## Red Vienna

Vienna began the war with an ethnically diverse population of 2.1 million, as imperial capital of a multinational empire of 52 million; by the end of the war, the city's population was down to 1.8 million, and it was head of a country of just 6.4 million. Only two significant minorities remained: Czechs and Jews, who together made up around twenty percent of the total population. The Czechs, who now had their own independent motherland, enjoyed the status of a protected minority, leaving the Jews to serve once more as chief scapegoat.

This situation was exacerbated by the very visible presence of around 25,000 Jewish refugees from Galicia, an army of poverty-stricken peddlers whose Orthodox garb made them all the more conspicuous. At the same time, the much larger assimilated Jewish population, who were prominent in the arts, the media and the SDAP, became the target of a vicious, anti-Semitic campaign led by the Christian Social and Pan-German parties. The cleric Ignaz Seipel, head of the Christian Socials, was one of the most vociferous anti-Semites, who flirted with the idea of re-ghettoizing the Jews. This sort of rhetoric was a permanent feature of the First Republic, and one that the SDAP consistently failed to tackle head-on.

In the municipal elections of May 1919, the Social Democrats won 54 percent of the vote, and Vienna got its first Socialist mayor, **Jakob Reumann**. The party held power in the capital for nearly fifteen years, a period which has gone down in history as **Rotes Wien** or "Red Vienna" (see p.217). Their social reforms have since become legendary, but their most visible legacy is the huge housing estates like the Karl-Marx-Hof (see p.216) that ring the city.

Meanwhile, in the national elections of June 1920, the SDAP–Christian Social coalition broke down, and in fresh elections in October that year, the latter came out as the biggest single party. The two parties remained at loggerheads throughout the 1920s, with the extremist Pan-German Greater German People's Party a further destabilizing element.

## Paramilitary politics

For most of the First Republic, then, the country remained split between the heavily industrialized Social Democrat capital of Vienna, where some thirty percent of the population lived, and the deeply conservative, Catholic, rural *Länder* where the Christian Socials dominated. What made this political polarization all the more dangerous was that by the mid-1920s both sides were backed up by paramilitary organizations, as if the country were at civil war.

On the one hand, the right-wing **Heimwehr** had their origins in armed groups that defended Austria's borders in the chaotic early days of the republic. Based on individual *Länder* and each with their own leader, the Heimwehr organizations didn't share a political platform but were united in their opposition to the Left. On the other hand, the Social Democrats had created the republic's first ad hoc army, the Volkswehr, in the last weeks of the war. They continued to dominate the Volkswehr until it was replaced by the establishment of the official Austrian army or Bundeswehr. As a result, the SDAP eventually formed its own armed division, the **Schutzbund**, in 1923. Throughout the 1920s the party mouthed the rhetoric of class war, while pursuing moderate, social democratic policies. In 1926, the party went even further and declared itself ready to use force if necessary to protect the interests of the workers. The bourgeois press interpreted this as a call for revolution, though the slogan coined by Otto Bauer was "Democratic as long as we can be; dictatorship only if we are forced to it, and insofar as we are forced." To the dismay of many on the left, the SDAP proved itself much less willing to resort to violence than its right-wing foes.

On July 14, 1927, three right-wing activists were acquitted of murdering a socialist man and boy. The following day several thousand workers spontaneously descended on the **Justizpalast** (see p.109) and set fire to it. Taken by surprise by the size of the demonstration, the mounted police panicked and fired point-blank into the crowd. In the ensuing chaos, 89 people were killed, and up to a thousand wounded, and the Justizpalast burned to the ground. The SDAP called an indefinite national strike, but refused to call out the Schutzbund. With the heavily armed Heimwehr acting as strike-breakers, the general strike was easily crushed and civil war was postponed for a few more years.

## Austro-fascism

The onset of the Great Depression further destabilized what was already a fragile democracy. In the elections of November 1930, the Heimwehr, under Prince Starhemberg, won its first parliamentary seats for its newly formed political wing, the Heimatblock. The Social Democrats, meanwhile, emerged for the first time since 1919 as the largest single party, with 41 percent of the vote, but once more it was the Christian Socials who went on to form a series of weak coalition governments. The last of these was formed in May 1932 under the chancellorship of **Engelbert Dollfuss**, with a parliamentary majority of just one.

On March 4, 1933, in an attempt to break a tied vote in parliament, the Social Democrat Karl Renner resigned as speaker in order to free himself to vote. When Renner's two deputy speakers from the Christian Social and Pan-German parties both followed suit, Dollfuss seized the opportunity to dissolve parliament, claiming it could no longer function properly. The same weekend, Adolf Hitler won an absolute majority in the German parliament. The onset of **Nazism** had a sobering effect on the majority of Austrians, particularly the SDAP, which immediately dropped their call for Anschluss.

On March 15, Dollfuss sent the police in to prevent parliament from reconvening. In response, the SDAP leadership procrastinated and held back from calling in the Schutzbund; two weeks later the latter was outlawed. Dollfuss was determined to combat the threat from Nazi Germany, but instead of agreeing to an anti-Nazi alliance with the SDAP, the chancellor threw in his lot with Mussolini, holding the first of many meetings with the Italian dictator in April. On May 21, no doubt prompted by Mussolini, Dollfuss established the Austro-fascist **Fatherland Front** (Vaterländische Front or VF), under the slogan "Austria Awake!"

In May the Communist Party was banned and in July the Austrian Nazi Party was outlawed. A violent showdown with the Social Democrats, who still controlled the Vienna city council, followed in February 1934. The first incident took place in Linz, where the local Schutzbund, on their own initiative, opened fire on the police. A three-day battle ensued, with the bloodiest set-to in Vienna's **Karl-Marx-Hof** housing estate, which Dollfuss eventually ordered the army to bomb into submission. The SDAP had stumbled into civil war and it was soundly beaten. The party was swiftly outlawed, and its leaders fled abroad or were imprisoned.

Just as it appeared he had successfully established an Austro-fascist state, Dollfuss was assassinated on July 25, 1934 (see p.61), during the **Juliputsch**, an abortive coup d'etat staged by Austrian Nazis, apparently without the knowledge of Hitler. His successor, **Kurt Schuschnigg**, was forced to rely ever more heavily on Mussolini for support. As a foreign policy this proved disastrous, for in 1935 Hitler and Mussolini began to patch up their differences, and suddenly Schuschnigg found himself being urged by Mussolini to come to an agreement with Hitler. Schuschnigg did just that in the Austro-German agreement of July 11, 1936. In return for Hitler's recognition of Austria's "full sovereignty", Schuschnigg agreed to an amnesty of all Nazi prisoners, and the appointment of various "prominent nationalists" – not Nazis, but fellow travellers – to his government.

In January 1938, the Austrian police raided the apartment of Leopold Tavs, one of Schuschnigg's deputies, and discovered a plan to overthrow the government with German help. As tension between the two countries mounted, the Nazi ambassador, Franz von Papen, suggested Schuschnigg should visit Hitler at his mountain retreat at Berchtesgaden near the Austrian border. At this meeting, Schuschnigg was given one of Hitler's command performances in which he ranted and raved and eventually demanded, among other things, that Schuschnigg hand over yet more key governmental posts to the Austrian Nazi Party. Schuschnigg acquiesced and agreed to appoint the Nazi **Dr Arthur Seyss-Inquart** interior minister.

As the Austrian Nazis increased their activities, Schuschnigg decided to chance his arm with a plebiscite to decide the country's future, reckoning (probably correctly) that the majority would vote against the Anschluss. Hitler was certainly not prepared to risk electoral defeat and swiftly demanded the resignation of Schuschnigg and his entire government. Schuschnigg announced his resignation over the radio, in order to avoid "spilling German blood", and Seyss-Inquart took over the chancellorship. President Wilhelm Miklas refused to agree to the latter's appointment and resigned, and Seyss-Inquart wasted no time in inviting the German army into the country on the pretext of preventing civil war.

# Anschluss and World War II

In the event, there was no bloodshed: German troops crossed the border into Austria on March 12, 1938, and encountered no resistance whatsoever. Hitler himself began his slow and triumphant journey to the capital in the wake of his troops. First he visited his birthplace of Braunau-am-Inn, then he moved on to his "home town" of Linz, where he was received with such enthusiasm by the locals that he decided there and then to immediately incorporate Austria into the Greater German Reich, rather than pursue the more conciliatory path of preserving Austrian autonomy. Eventually, on March 15, Hitler appeared on the balcony of the Hofburg before thousands of jubilant Viennese.

As a propaganda exercise, Hitler also decided to go ahead with Schuschnigg's plebiscite, which took place on April 10. The 99 percent "Yes" vote in favour of the **Anschluss** came as no surprise, with less than two thousand Viennese voting "No". To be fair, those known to be opposed to the Nazis, including Schuschnigg and his followers, had already been arrested – some 76,000 by the time Hitler arrived in Vienna – while Jews and other "undesirables" were barred from voting. On the other hand, many whom one would expect to have opposed the Anschluss publicly declared themselves in favour, including the archbishop of Vienna, Cardinal Theodor Innitzer, and the Social Democrat, Karl Renner.

Although the Treaty of St-Germain precluded any Anschluss with Germany, only the Soviet Union and Mexico lodged any formal international protest against the invasion. Meanwhile, the very name of Austria was wiped off the map, initially replaced by the term "**Ostmark**", but eventually simply divided into seven *Gaue* or districts, ruled by Nazi *Gauleiter*.

## The fate of Vienna's Jews

In the words of eyewitness George Clare, the Anschluss unleashed a "volcanic outburst of popular anti-Semitism". Jews were dragged out into the street, physically assaulted and humiliated, and then forced to scrub Schuschnigg slogans off the walls. In one instance in the well-to-do suburb of Währing, a group of Nazis urinated on local Jewish women as they forced them to scrub the streets in front of cheering onlookers. A large number of the city's most prominent Jews were arrested immediately, and either sent to concentration camps, or released with orders to leave the country.

In May, without warning, 2000 Jews were arrested and shipped off to Dachau, primarily to encourage still more Jews to emigrate. On the night of November 10–11 – dubbed **Kristallnacht** or "Crystal Night" – the majority of synagogues in the Reich were torched, and numerous Jewish premises ransacked. Another 7800 Jews were arrested that night, 4600 of whom were sent to Dachau. By the outbreak of World War II, more than half of Vienna's Jews had emigrated.

Once the Nazis had invaded Poland, their policy towards the Jews changed, with deportation to the death camps via ghettos favoured, over forced emigration. The deportations began in earnest in February 1941, while emigration came to a complete standstill in November 1941. Of the 57,000 Jews now left in Austria, more than half had been sent to the death camps by June 1942. By the end of the war, around 200 or so Austrian Jews had managed to survive in hiding, with just over 2000 returning from the camps after the war.

## Collaboration and resistance

Seyss-Inquart was initially appointed *Reichsstatthalter* (Governor) of Vienna, but was transferred to Poland after the outbreak of the war, and eventually ended up in control of the Netherlands, where as *Reichskommissar* he oversaw countless atrocities for which he was hanged at the Nuremberg war trials. Control of Vienna was eventually handed over to the dashing young German lieutenant, **Baldur von Schirach**, whose artistic pretensions – he wrote poetry – were considered highly suitable for Viennese sensibilities. Schirach made the most of his position, moving into the sumptuous governmental offices on Ballhausplatz, employing no fewer than seventeen chambermaids, and entertaining official visitors in lavish style in the Hofburg.

Although Hitler preferred to import German Nazis to fill many positions within the Austrian Nazi hierarchy, party membership was higher in Austria than in Germany, and Austrians themselves provided more than their ten percent population ratio of concentration-camp guards. The Linz-born Nazi **Adolf Eichmann**, who ran Vienna's "Central Office for Jewish Emigration" (see p.160) and was one of the architects of the "Final Solution", is probably the most infamous, though *Schindler's List* also increased the notoriety of the Vienna-born camp commandant Amon Goeth. Another Linz-born Nazi, Ernst Kaltenbrunner, rose to Heinrich Himmler's number two in the SS, while the Carinthian Odilo Globocnik – one-time *Gauleiter* of Vienna – with ninety other fellow Austrians on his staff, supervised the deaths of some two million Jews in the extermination camps of Sobibor, Treblinka and Belzec.

Organized **resistance** to Hitler was, it has to be said, extraordinarily difficult for anti-Nazi Austrians, given the level of collaboration among their fellow citizens, and the efficient way in which the Nazis had wiped out the potential leadership. Aside from individual acts of heroism, there was very little significant non-Communist resistance within Austria. Partisan activity was restricted to a few remote alpine areas, and it wasn't until the spring of 1944 that an organized home resistance, code-named **O5**, began to emerge.

Unlike every other Nazi-occupied country, however, the Austrians had no official government-in-exile. Exiled Austrian politicians spent their time bickering, split between an unlikely alliance between the son of the last emperor,

Otto von Habsburg, and the Communists, and the two mainstream political parties. The most significant diplomatic step took place in November 1943, when the Allied powers published the **Moscow Declaration** stating that Austria was a "victim" of Nazi aggression and that it should be re-established as a "free and democratic state".

## The liberation of Vienna

Vienna itself remained relatively free from direct contact with the war until 1944, when Allied bombing raids intensified. Over the next fourteen months, they were responsible for the deaths of some nine thousand Viennese civilians. Among the most important buildings hit were the Staatsoper, the Belvedere, the Burgtheater, Schönbrunn, the Rathaus, Parlament and the Universität; Stephansdom fell victim to Soviet artillery in the last few days of the city's liberation.

By April 5, 1945, the Red Army was nearing the outskirts of the city. The O5 leadership under Major Szokoll had planned to initiate an uprising against the Nazis the very next day, but were betrayed by a junior officer, Lieutenant Walter Hanslick. Several of the O5 leaders were arrested, tortured and publicly hung. The revolt had failed and it took the Russians another three days to reach the *Gürtel*, and another five days' street fighting to finally win control of the city.

The commander-in-chief of the Russian troops in Austria, **Marshal Tolbukhin**, gave his assurances that the Soviets would liberate the country, respect the social order and refrain from appropriating any territory. In reality, Soviet troops spent much of the next few months raping Austrian women and stealing anything they could find. The actions of the Red Army during this period gave rise to the grim Viennese joke that Austria could probably survive a third world war, but it could never endure a second liberation.

# Allied Occupation (1945–55)

On April 27, the Soviets sponsored the formation of a provisional government under the veteran Social Democrat **Karl Renner**, causing widespread alarm about Soviet intentions among the western Allies. Although Renner's cabinet was made up, for the most part, of Socialists and members of the newly founded right-wing People's Party or ÖVP, the Communists were given three posts, including the key positions of interior minister and education and information minister. As a form of protest at this unilateral action, the western Allies refused to recognize the Renner government.

Meanwhile, there was continuing confusion over the occupation zones. Although the Moscow Declaration had stated that Austria was a victim of Nazi aggression, the country was nevertheless to be divided just like Germany, with Vienna, as Berlin, lying deep within the Russian sector. However, controversy over the exact zoning of Vienna helped delay the arrival of western troops in the capital until late August. The Russians took the opportunity of fleecing the capital and eastern Austria of all they could. Vienna, it was agreed, was to be divided between the four Allies, with the Innere Stadt preserved as an international sector, patrolled by one representative of each of the occupying powers. This comical sight on the streets of Vienna became the hallmark of the so-called "four-in-a-jeep" period – and the setting for the famous film *The Third Man* – when, as Karl Renner put it, Vienna was like a small rowing boat in which four elephants sat at the oars pulling in various directions.

## Elections and de-Nazification

In October the western Allies finally recognized the Renner government, and the Russians, for their part, agreed to free elections. However, whatever hopes they might have had of the Communists gaining power in Austria were dashed by the results of the November 1945 elections. The Communists won a derisory 5.4 percent of the vote, up from their previous high of 1.9 percent in 1932, but earning them just four seats in the 165-seat parliament, and the consolation prize of the Ministry of Electrification. In an almost exact repeat of the election results of the 1920s, the country remained split down the middle between Left and Right. Although the ÖVP won almost fifty percent of the vote, it was Renner who headed the new coalition government of the Socialist Party (SPÖ) and the ÖVP.

One of the most pressing and controversial tasks of the postwar era was the **de-Nazification** process. Initially, this was the responsibility of the Allied powers: the Americans and the British busied themselves by handing out forms in which the respondents were invited to confess; the French, with collaborators of their own back home, were less keen to get involved; the Russians, predictably, were the most assiduous, though they were as concerned to remove political opponents as ex-Nazis. Of the half a million Austrians who were Nazi Party members, only a handful were executed at Nuremberg (for crimes committed outside of Austria); von Schirach was given twenty years. Back in

Austria itself, the government took over the de-Nazification process, condemning 38 Nazis to death, and depriving the rest of their civil rights for a brief period before an amnesty was agreed in 1948. Some attempt was made to rid the state bureaucracy of its ex-Nazis, but inevitably many slipped through the net, Eichmann among them, though he was later kidnapped, tried and executed in Israel in 1962.

## Communist agitation

When the Red Army liberated Vienna in April 1945, few people thought that the city and the country would remain under Allied occupation for ten years. However, the Soviets were keen to pay back the Austrians for their mass participation in the Nazi armed forces. At the postwar Potsdam conference, the Soviets were granted, instead of cash reparations for war damage, the right to all external German assets in eastern Austria. Over the next ten years, the Russians took this as a carte blanche to asset-strip the entire region of eastern Austria, transporting factories piece by piece back to the Soviet Union, and all in all reaping some half a billion dollars' worth of assets.

Soviet control of eastern Austria – the country's agricultural heartland – also gave them considerable political leverage. With the entire country suffering chronic food shortages, the Soviets deliberately hoarded supplies from their sector, supplying them direct to workers in Soviet-run industries. This won them considerable support in the eastern zone, and increased unrest in the western zones. For despite the Communists' electoral setback, the Russians still had hopes of taking control of Austria. The winter of 1946–47 was particularly harsh, and the Communists took advantage of this by fomenting food riots in May 1947. The rioters besieged the Austrian chancellery and called for a national strike. In the end the putsch failed, because the Socialist trade-union leaders refused to support the strike, and the Russians held back from using military force.

While **Marshall Plan** aid from the west helped ease conditions throughout Austria from the summer of 1947 onwards, the Communist coup in Czechoslovakia in February 1948 and the Berlin blockade (June 1948–May 1949) only increased political tensions. Despite their recent setbacks, the Communists had high hopes for the national elections of October 1949. However, though the ruling coalition lost ground, it wasn't to the Communists, who remained on a derisory five percent, but to the newly formed, extreme right-wing **Union of Independents** (VdU), who scored 11.6 percent of the vote, attracting the support of the majority of ex-Nazi Party members, who had recently been given back their voting rights.

In the autumn of 1950, Marshall Plan aid was cut back drastically. With the Austrian government forced to increase sharply the price of food, coal and electricity, strikes broke out among workers in cities across Austria. Seizing the moment, the Communists staged their second and most serious coup attempt. Once again, it began with a Communist-inspired mass demonstration outside the chancellery, after which barricades were erected, roads blocked, tram tracks cemented up and bus windows broken. The Russians stopped police reinforcements in their sector from being called up, and it was only with great difficulty that the situation was kept under control. In the end, however, the Socialist trade unions and the government took sufficient steps to stem the tide, and the general strike held on October 4, though heeded by large numbers of workers in the Russian sectors of the city and eastern Austria, was called off the following day.

## The Austrian State Treaty of 1955

The withdrawal of the four Allied powers from Austria in 1955 – or more specifically the Soviet withdrawal – was something of a unique event in the otherwise grim history of the Cold War. And something of a surprise, given the previously unscrupulous behaviour of the Soviets in Austria (and elsewhere in Europe).

For nearly ten years, negotiations over a peace treaty with Austria were at a stalemate, with the Soviets insisting that a German peace treaty be prerequisite to an Austrian treaty. The Soviet threat over the future of Austria was used by them to try and forestall German rearmament. However, with the establishment of the Federal Republic of Germany in 1949, it was clear that this policy had failed. A struggle within the Kremlin then ensued over Soviet policy towards Austria. Following the death of Stalin, this struggle intensified and was eventually won by Krushchev, who decided to use the **Austrian State Treaty** as a way of initiating a period of détente.

Other factors influenced Soviet policy. Hopes of creating a Communist Austria had died with the failure of the 1950 putsch. The Soviet sector meanwhile had been bled dry and was no longer of any great economic benefit. A neutral Austria, on the other hand, created a convenient buffer that split NATO's northern and southern flanks. And so on May 15, 1955, the Austrian State Treaty or Staatsvertrag was signed by the four powers in Vienna's Belvedere. The Austrian chancellor, Leopold Figl, waved the treaty triumphantly from the balcony and over half a million Austrians celebrated in the streets of the capital.

# 1955–83: consensus politics

With the popular vote split between Left and Right, the two main parties of the ÖVP and the SPÖ formed a succession of coalitions which lasted until 1966. To avoid repeating the mistakes of the past, and to placate the occupying powers, a system of **Proporz** was established, whereby each party shared equally every governmental and state post. In some ways institutionalized political corruption, this process began at the top among the ministries, and continued right down to the local post office. At the same time, various special bodies or chambers representing the various interest groups – the Chamber of Trade, the Chamber of Labour and so on – were established. Like *Proporz*, these new institutions ensured that the country enjoyed an unprecedented period of political and social stability, but left the parliament without an effective opposition and created a system open to widespread abuse. Like the Germans, though, the Austrians enjoyed a period of economic growth and prosperity, and there were few voices of complaint.

In the elections of 1966, the People's Party at last achieved an absolute majority and formed the first one-party government of the postwar era. Many Austrians feared a repeat of the 1920s, but in practice little changed. The system of *Proporz* and the institutions of the corporate state continued to hand out "jobs for the boys", and only at the very top level of government were the Socialists excluded from power. Their turn came, though, in 1970, when a slight economic downturn gave the SPÖ a narrow victory, followed by an outright majority in elections the following year. Under the chancellorship of **Bruno Kreisky**, the Socialists enjoyed thirteen years of power, during which Kreisky

## Simon Wiesenthal (1908–2005)

The Holocaust survivor and Nazi-hunter, **Simon Wiesenthal**, was one of the most controversial figures in Austria's postwar political scene.

Wiesenthal was born in Buczacz, a Yiddish-speaking *shtetl* in the Austro-Hungarian province of Galicia (later part of Poland and now Ukraine). His father was a well-to-do sugar merchant, who was killed fighting for the Habsburgs on the eastern front during World War I. As a young man, Wiesenthal studied architecture in Prague, since Polish architecture faculties were closed to Jews, and in 1936 returned home to marry Cyla Müller, an old schoolmate. The newlyweds moved to Lvov, where Wiesenthal worked as an architectural engineer until the Nazi–Soviet Pact of September 1939, when the Red Army marched into town and Wiesenthal was forced to forgo his "bourgeois" profession and work in a bedding factory.

The Nazi invasion of Soviet territory in June 1941 was celebrated with an anti-Semitic pogrom led by Ukrainian auxiliaries, during which Wiesenthal was lined up in front of a firing squad. He was saved by the timely ringing of the church bells calling the faithful (including the soldiers who were about to execute him) to Mass. That night a Ukrainian friend helped him by accusing him of being a Soviet spy – this meant he was beaten up and interrogated but not killed. He was then put to work in the OAW, a forced-labour railway-repair works, first as a sign-painter, and later as a draughtsman. He and his wife were comparatively well treated by the Nazi in charge, who even helped Cyla to escape, first to Lublin, and later to Warsaw. He also saved Wiesenthal from imminent execution in April 1943 – he was naked and lined up ready to be shot – and, in September of that year, encouraged him to go into hiding.

After concealing himself in an attic and hanging out with some partisans, Wiesenthal was eventually discovered hiding under the floorboards of a flat in June 1944. Transferred to the Gestapo headquarters in Lvov and fearing torture, he tried to commit suicide three times without success. As German troops fled from the advancing Soviets, he was sent westwards via Plaszow, Auschwitz, Gross-Rosen and Buchenwald, before ending up in **Mauthausen** in Austria, where he was left for dead in the "death block". On this occasion, he was saved by a Polish Kapo, who needed someone to design birthday cards for the guards. This meant that he was one of the lucky few still alive on May 5, 1945, when Mauthausen was liberated by the US Army.

carried the SPÖ further away from their radical Marxist past than ever before. The end came in the elections of 1983 when the SPÖ lost its overall majority and was forced into a coalition government with the far-right Freedom Party (FPÖ), successor to the postwar VdU (see p.320).

# The Waldheim affair

Having struggled to make the headlines of the international press in the 1960s and 1970s, Austria was catapulted onto the world media stage in 1986 during the campaign for the Austrian presidency. The candidate for the ÖVP was **Kurt Waldheim**, a figure of some international stature who had been UN Secretary-General for ten years (1972–82). However, during the campaign, Waldheim's war record was called into question. From the summer of 1942 until the end of the war, he had served as a lieutenant in the Balkans with the German Army. Waldheim was never a member of the Nazi Party

Just three weeks after the liberation of Mauthausen, Wiesenthal began to work for the US War Crimes Unit, helping them track down SS officers. He was soon transferred to the OSS, the American wartime intelligence group, in nearby Linz, where he was reunited with his wife, who had also, remarkably, survived, spending the last year of the war working as a slave labourer in Germany. In 1947, frustrated with the Allies' waning interest in Nazi-hunting, Wiesenthal eventually founded the **Dokumentationszentrum** (Documentation Centre), for which he is best known. It was during this period that he helped track down some two thousand former Nazis, including **Adolf Eichmann** and other leading figures. In 1953, he gave up his full-time pursuit of ex-Nazis and took a job helping with the rehabilitation and retraining of refugees. In 1961, Eichmann was kidnapped in Argentina by Mossad, the Israeli secret service, and spirited away to Israel to face prosecution. Wiesenthal was invited to attend the trial, and, with Mossad denying any involvement in the kidnapping, was only too happy to give press conferences on his early role in the pursuit of Eichmann. With the publication of *I Hunted Eichmann*, Wiesenthal's fame became widespread, and he decided to move to Vienna and reopen his Dokumentationszentrum to "work against Holocaust amnesia".

In Austria, Wiesenthal is probably best known for his public feud with Bruno Kreisky, the Austrian chancellor (1970–83) and fellow Jew, which began in 1970 when Wiesenthal exposed four of Kreisky's first cabinet as ex-Nazis. Kreisky called Wiesenthal a "Jewish fascist", and accused him of being a Nazi collaborator during his time at the OAW in Lvov. Legal battles between the two dragged on for years, and Wiesenthal was eventually awarded damages for slander, but Kreisky remained more popular with the public throughout the 1970s. Wiesenthal made even more enemies during the Waldheim affair, when he refused to back the line of the World Jewish Congress (WJC) and the US government, who together accused the Austrian president of being a war criminal. Wiesenthal maintained that there wasn't enough evidence to make such claims, and would only go so far as to brand Waldheim a liar and call for his resignation on those grounds.

The 1990s saw Wiesenthal's stature rise both globally and within Austria. Poland and Austria both bestowed their highest decorations on him, and shortly before his 87th birthday, the Vienna City Council voted to make him an *Ehrenbürger* (honorary citizen). The Simon Wiesenthal Center in Los Angeles (Ⓦ www.wiesenthal.com) continues his work to this day.

(one of the initial charges) and there was never any clear evidence that he was directly involved in the atrocities committed by the army in the Balkans, though he was formally charged with (but never tried for) war crimes by the Yugoslavs after the war. What was more difficult to believe, however, was his claim that he had no knowledge of the deportation of Greek Jews to the death camps, despite being an interpreter for the Italian Army in Greece for much of the war.

To the dismay of many around the world, these charges, albeit unproven, did Waldheim's candidacy no harm at all domestically, and he was duly elected to the Austrian presidency with 54 percent of the vote. The international campaign against Waldheim began with the boycott of his swearing-in ceremony by the US ambassador, and culminated in his being put on the US Department of Justice's "Watch List" of undesirable aliens. Waldheim – and by association Austria – became an international pariah, restricted in his state visits to Arab countries. At Waldheim's suggestion, a commission was set up to investigate the charges against him; however, far from exonerating him, the commission's report found him guilty of "proximity to legally incriminating acts and orders", a somewhat woolly phrase that could be applied to just about any Austrian who'd served in the German Army. The British government, meanwhile, followed up the Yugoslav charge that Waldheim had been involved in war crimes against British commandoes in the Balkans. The British enquiry concluded that Waldheim's rank was too junior to have had any influence over the fate of the commandoes, adding that "knowledge is not itself a crime".

# The rise and fall of the FPÖ

As if the Waldheim affair in the 1980s were not bad enough, the country had to contend with the rise of the FPÖ in the 1990s, under their charismatic leader **Jörg Haider**. A strange grouping of free-market liberals and ultraconservatives, the FPÖ was very much a fringe player in Austrian politics until 1983, when it became junior coalition partner with the SPÖ. In 1986, Haider became party chairman, causing the collapse of the SPÖ–FPÖ coalition and prompting elections. In his first stab at the polls, Haider won nearly ten percent of the vote, frightening the two main parties back into the grand SPÖ–ÖVP coalition of the postwar years. Unfortunately, this only served to play into Haider's hands, increasing popular resentment against the system of *Proporz* (from which the FPÖ is excluded) and thus boosting support for the FPÖ.

A dapper character with a sporty image, Haider presented himself as something new in national politics, free from the cynical power-sharing manoeuvres of the two main parties. Both of his parents were Nazi Party members who had felt sidelined by postwar Austrian society, and Haider himself deliberately courted far-right support in an attempt to gain notoriety. Elected provincial governor of Carinthia in 1990, Haider expressed enthusiasm for Nazi employment policy in a speech a year later – precipitating his fall from office, but not his fall from popularity.

Haider's main electoral plank was to exploit the fears shared by many Austrians over the country's new wave of **immigrants**, who arrived from the former eastern bloc and war-torn Yugoslavia in considerable numbers in the 1990s. Nationalist frustrations were compounded by the country's entry into the **European Union** in 1995. Although in a referendum sixty percent voted in favour of joining, the austerity measures the country needed to implement in order to meet the criteria necessary for joining a single European currency convinced many that it had been the wrong decision.

Haider's FPÖ gradually increased its share of the vote throughout the 1990s, taking 22 percent of the vote in the general elections of 1994 and 1995. The biggest shock, though, was in Vienna, in 1996, when the SPÖ lost its overall majority for the first time in the city's history, with the FPÖ receiving 28 percent of the vote and becoming the main opposition in the Rathaus, ahead of the ÖVP (with 15 percent).

## 1999: the ÖVP-FPÖ coalition

In **1999**, campaigning on an openly xenophobic platform – with posters reading "Stop der Überfremdung. Österreich zuerst" ("Stop the foreign tide. Put Austria first") setting the tone – the FPÖ surpassed even their own wildest dreams by getting 27 percent of the vote and squeezing into second place, beating the ÖVP into third by a margin of 415 votes (both the FPÖ and the ÖVP were awarded 52 seats in parliament). The SPÖ received 33 percent of the vote, their worst result since 1945, but most observers still assumed that the SPÖ and the ÖVP would once again close ranks to deny Haider a role in government. However, talks between the two parties broke down and President Klestil had no choice but to invite the ÖVP to enter talks with the FPÖ in the hope of forming a government.

Despite the fact that the FPÖ had got more votes, it was ÖVP leader **Wolfgang Schüssel** who fulfilled his dream of becoming chancellor, with several top posts going to the FPÖ. Haider refused to take part in the government, to the relief of many Austrians, preferring instead to remain in Carinthia. He quit the FPÖ leadership and was replaced by the less openly extremist Susanne Riess-Passer. The **ÖVP-FPÖ government** was sworn in by an unenthusiastic Klestil in February 2000. All other EU states immediately froze bilateral relations with Austria in protest at the FPÖ's inclusion in government. The new government's programme – centred on promises to cut government spending and pave the way for tax cuts – carefully avoided any reference to the FPÖ's pre-election rhetoric, and the EU withdrew their sanctions after six months. Those Austrians who had voted for the ÖVP or the FPÖ were resentful of the outside world's attempts to meddle in the nation's affairs. Others were deeply shamed by the FPÖ's accession to power, and launched the **Widerstand** (Resistance), a massive Heldenplatz demo followed by a rolling campaign of weekly demonstrations and cultural events designed to show that the liberal, tolerant values of centre-left Austria were still very much alive.

Paradoxically, the ÖVP profited more from the new situation than the cocksure FPÖ. Chancellor Schüssel, together with ÖVP foreign minister **Benita Ferrero-Waldner**, won popular support for the way in which they appeared to defend Austria's dignity against a hostile EU. The unpopular elements of government policy – public spending cuts and the introduction of university fees for students – tended to be blamed on their more radical coalition allies. Meanwhile, the FPÖ began to unravel, with Haider increasingly at odds with the rest of the party, eventually forcing the resignation of the FPÖ ministers and prompting new elections.

To the relief of many Austrians, the FPÖ vote collapsed in the **2002 elections**, dwindling to a mere 10 percent, while the ÖVP surged to 42 percent – the biggest swing in postwar Austrian politics – and the SPÖ a fairly respectable 37 percent. The FPÖ's internal divisions continued after the election with Haider finally throwing in the towel and forming his own party, the Alliance or BZÖ in 2005. The **2006 elections** simply confirmed the collapse of the far-right vote with the FPÖ taking 11 percent and the BZÖ a mere 4 percent. In many ways, these elections re-established the postwar status quo, with the SPÖ and ÖVP receiving 35 and 34 percent of the vote respectively and entering once more into a grand coalition.

The Waldheim affair and the rise of the FPÖ were a **PR disaster** for Austria, and there's a sense of bewilderment in the country that a nation that promoted itself so successfully as the home of Lipizzaner horses and happy alpine holidays should nowadays be internationally notorious for something entirely different. Despite this, Vienna continues to buck the trend, just as it did between the wars. The SPÖ won nearly half the votes in the 2005 municipal elections and thankfully they continue to run the city along solid social democratic principles, ploughing money into public services that make Vienna's education, health and public transport systems the envy of the world.

# Books

Books on the Habsburgs and the various artistic figures from Vienna's glorious past are easy to come by, but there's remarkably little written in English about the country in the twentieth century and not much fiction in translation – hence the rather uneven selection below.

## History and society

**Steven Beller** *Vienna and the Jews, 1867–1938*. Beller shows how the Jews played a central role in the vibrant cultural life of Vienna at the turn of the last century. Thorough, if rather dry.

**Gordon Brook-Shepherd** *The Austrians*. Readable, a little over-earnest, history that attempts to trace the Austrian-ness (or lack of it) in the country's history from the Babenbergs to entry into the EU in 1994. Brook-Shepherd draws on his experience as a *Telegraph* correspondent and as someone who worked in the Allied High Commission in Vienna after World War II.

**Frederic V. Grunfeld** *Prophets without Honour*. A useful insight into the intellectual figures of fin-de-siècle *Mitteleuropa*, including Freud, Kafka and Einstein.

**William M. Johnston** *The Austrian Mind: An Intellectual and Social History 1848–1938*. Johnston knows his stuff, and though this is a pretty academic approach, it's a fascinating insight into fin-de-siècle Vienna.

**Robert Knight** *Contemporary Austria and the Legacy of the Third Reich 1945–95*. Highlights the failure of de-Nazification and the subsequent rise of Haider's FPÖ, the consequences of which were partly obscured by the country's postwar prosperity.

**Elisabeth Lichtenberger** *Austria: Society and Regions*. A scholarly account of the awkward twentieth-century history of Austria, taking the reader up to the late 1990s.

**Frederic Morton** *A Nervous Splendor: Vienna 1888/1889*; *Thunder at Twilight: Vienna 1913–1914*; *The Forever Street: A Novel*. Morton (whose real name is Fritz Mandel-baum) has trawled through the newspapers of the time to produce two very readable dramatized accounts of two critical years in the city's history. The first centres on the Mayerling tragedy, the second on the Sarajevo assassination. *Forever Street* follows a Jewish family's fortunes from 1873 to the Holocaust.

**Robin Okey** *The Habsburg Monarchy c.1765–1918*. A comprehensive and up-to-date account of the empire.

**Hella Pick** *Guilty Victim: Austria from the Holocaust to Haider*. Probably the best book on postwar Austria, both as a political history and a meditation on the country's (often half-hearted) attempts to come to terms with the darker elements of its past.

**Carl E. Schorske** *Fin-de-Siècle Vienna*. Fascinating scholarly essays on, among other things, the impact of the building of the Ringstrasse, and of Freud, Klimt, Kokoschka and Schönberg on the city's culture.

**John Stoye** *The Siege of Vienna*. Account of the remarkable siege of 1683 when the Turks were only prevented from taking the city by the timely intervention of the Polish king, and during which the croissant was born.

**A. J. P. Taylor** *The Habsburg Monarchy 1809–1918*. Readable, forthright as ever and thought-provoking account of the demise of the Habsburgs.

**Andrew Wheatcroft** *The Habsburgs: Embodying Empire*. Wheatcroft's intriguing history traces the rise and fall of the Habsburgs from their modest origins in Switzerland to their demise at the head of the Austro-Hungarian empire, looking closely at individual family members, and the promotion of its dynastic image.

# Memoirs and travel

**Elias Canetti** *The Tongue Set Free*. The Bulgarian-born Nobel Prize-winning Canetti was a Sephardic Jew who lived in Vienna during the 1930s; his fragmentary memoirs of the period are superb.

**George Clare** *Last Waltz in Vienna: The Destruction of a Family 1842–1942*. Incredibly moving – and far from bitter – autobiographical account of a Jewish upbringing in interwar Vienna that ended with the Anschluss.

**Edward Crankshaw** *Vienna: The Image of a Culture in Decline*. Part travel journal, part history, and first published in 1938, this is a nostalgic, but by no means rose-tinted, look at the city. The same author's *Fall of the House of Habsburg* is an accessible popular history of the empire's last days.

**Helen Fremont** *After Long Silence*. Fremont was raised as a Roman Catholic in the US only to discover as an adult that her parents were Austrian Jews who survived the Holocaust, but kept silent about it for forty years.

**Patrick Leigh Fermor** *A Time of Gifts*. The first volume of Leigh Fermor's trilogy based on his epic walk along the Rhine and Danube rivers in 1933–34. Written forty years later in dense, luscious and highly crafted prose, it's an evocative and poignant insight into the culture of *Mitteleuropa* between the wars.

**Jakov Lind** *Counting My Steps*. In the first volume of his memoirs, Lind recounts his bookish Jewish childhood in Vienna in the 1930s, and his miraculous survival in wartime Berlin under a Dutch identity.

**Claudio Magris** *Danube*. In this highly readable travel journal from the 1980s, Magris, a wonderfully erudite Trieste-based academic, traces the Danube, passing through Austria along the way.

**Peter Singer** *Pushing Time Away*. A biography of the author's grandfather, David Oppenheim, giving insight into the wrangles in Freud's circle and Red Vienna, through the rise of fascism to the horrors of life and death in Theresienstadt.

**Reinhard Spitzy** *How We Squandered the Reich*. Chilling and frank autobiographical account of a young Austrian idealist who became a member of the SS.

**Simon Wiesenthal** *The Sunflower*. Wiesenthal relates an instance from his time at Mathausen when an ailing SS guard called him to his bedside and asked for forgiveness. In the second half of the book, Wiesenthal asks leading intellectuals to respond to the dilemma of forgiveness.

**Stefan Zweig** *The World of Yesterday*. Seminal account of fin-de-siècle Vienna written just before Zweig was forced by the Nazis into exile in South America, where he and his wife committed suicide.

# Biography

## The Habsburgs

**Steven Beller** *Franz Joseph*. Shortest and most portable of the books on Franz-Josef; more of a political than a biographical account, it's a bit lacking in personal history.

**T.C.W Blanning** *Joseph II*. Aimed at the general reader, this tells the story of Joseph and his attempts at reform against the background of the Austrian enlightenment.

**Jean Paul Bled** *Franz Joseph*. Well-rounded account of the old duffer, with a smattering of the sort of scurrilous gossip missing in some other biographies.

**Edward Crankshaw** *Maria Theresa*. Readable account of the "Virgin Empress", though disappointingly short on light touches.

**Charles Drazin** *In Search of The Third Man*. Background story full of anecdotes about the writing, filming and cult success of *The Third Man*.

✻ **Brigitte Hamann** *The Reluctant Empress; Hitler's Vienna*. The former is a surprisingly even-handed account of Empress Elisabeth's extraordinary life, warts and all. *Hitler's Vienna* is an account of Hitler's early youth in Vienna, which played an important part in

helping form the prejudices of the Nazi leader.

**Joan Haslip** *The Emperor and the Actress; The Lonely Empress: Elizabeth of Austria*. The first is a detailed, steamy account of Franz-Josef's relationship with his long-term mistress, the actress Katharina Schratt. Retreading some of the same material, *Lonely Empress* is a sympathetic portrayal of the Kaiser's unhappy spouse, Elisabeth.

**Alan Palmer** *The Twilight of the Habsburgs: The Life and Times of the Emperor Francis Joseph* and *Metternich*. The first is the latest scholarly and somewhat weighty tome on this much-biographied emperor; the latter a solid account of the arch-conservative who ruled the roost in the city from 1815 to 1848.

**Brigitte Timmerman** *The Third Man's Vienna*. A paperback coffee-table book full of stills of *The Third Man* and contemporary news archives, with text by the woman who started the city's *Third Man* tours.

**John Van der Kiste** *Emperor Francis Joseph*. If the Stephen Beller (see above) is too dry, then this slightly racier read about the bewhiskered ruler should do the trick.

## Music

**Peter Franklin** *The Life of Mahler*. A very accessible account of Mahler's life, in Cambridge UP's excellent "Musical Lives" series.

**Egon Gartenberg** *Johann Strauss, End of an Era*. The story of the waltz king and his world, creator

of the *Blue Danube*, as well as *Die Fledermaus*.

**Peter Gay** *Mozart*. A slim, easy-to-read volume which nevertheless includes a good deal of stimulating analysis. Easily the best compact Mozart biography you can get.

**Malcolm Hayes** *Anton von Webern*. Not as well known as Schönberg, or as successful as Berg, Webern is seen by some as a progressive, and accused by others of being a Nazi sympathizer. Hayes, understandably, sits on the fence.

🏃 **Alma Mahler-Werfel** *Diaries 1896–1902*. Gushingly frank diaries of a supremely attractive young woman, courted by the likes of Klimt and Zemlinsky. The period covered follows Alma until shortly after her marriage to the composer Gustav Mahler.

**Donald Mitchell** *Gustav Mahler*. Mitchell's three-volume life of Mahler is a benchmark biography, as dense and wide-ranging as one of its subject's colossal symphonies.

## Freud

**Frederick C. Crews** (ed) *Unauthorized Freud*. Crews is virulently anti-psychoanalysis and has gathered together a whole host of Freud critics to put forward the revisionist case.

**Sigmund Freud** (ed Peter Gay) *The Freud Reader*. A comprehensive selection of Freud's writings on art, literature and religion, as well as the more familiar musings on dreams and sexuality. Spans his entire career, and has a useful introduction.

## Wiesenthal

**Alan Levy** *Nazi-Hunter: The Wiesenthal File*. Thoroughly entertaining account of the controversial Vienna-based Nazi-hunter and the various Nazis he has helped to pursue, plus an account of the Waldheim affair.

🏃 **Hella Pick** *Simon Wiesenthal: A Life in Search of Justice*. Made

**Elizabeth Norman McKay** *Franz Schubert: A Biography*. Straightforward biography of Schubert, which does the best it can to unravel the composer's brief life from the limited source material available.

**David Nelson** *Vienna for the Music Lover: The Complete Guide to Vienna's Musical Sites and Performances Today*. Notwithstanding its cumbersome title, this is an interesting book that takes you in the footsteps of the composers, aided by maps and illustrations.

**H.C. Robbins Landon** *Mozart, the Golden Years 1781–1791*. Big, illustrated romp through the composer's mature, Vienna years; a mixture of biography and musicology.

**Peter Gay** *Freud*. Big tome, a healthy mixture of biography and philosophy, with a bit of spicy drama for good measure.

**Michael Jacobs** *Sigmund Freud*. Brief biography of the bearded one: a quick trot through his ideas and the subsequent criticisms thereof.

**Ernest Jones** *Life and Work of Sigmund Freud*. Abridged version of the definitive three-volume biography that Jones – one of Freud's disciples – published in the 1950s just before he died.

with the subject's cooperation shortly before his death, this biography tracks his wartime sufferings and catalogues his postwar activities. Pick is sympathetic yet objective, and gives a rare glimpse into the Nazi-hunter's personal life.

## Wittgenstein

**David Edmonds, John Eidinov** *Wittgenstein's Poker*. On October 25, 1946, Wittgenstein came face to face with Karl Popper in Cambridge. The ensuing ten minutes produced an argument that shook the western world. Lucid and readable.

**John Heaton and Judy Groves** *Wittgenstein for Beginners*. Even this accessible, irreverent series fails to shed much light on the great philosopher's complex thinking.

**Allan Janik** *Wittgenstein's Vienna*; *Wittgenstein's Vienna Revisited*. The first book (written with Stephen Toulmin) concentrates on the cultural life of the Habsburg capital in the years before World War I. The follow-up is a collection of essays on writers and thinkers who influenced Wittgenstein, among them composer Arnold Schönberg, philosopher Otto Weininger, poet Georg Trakl, and the logical positivists.

**Ray Monk** *Ludwig Wittgenstein: The Duty of Genius*. Exhaustive biography of the perplexing philosopher; a model of its kind, Monk's book interweaves Wittgenstein's life and thought into an inseparable entity.

# Austrian fiction

**Ingeborg Bachmann** *Songs in Flight*; *The Thirtieth Year*; *The Complete Poetry of Ingeborg Bachmann*. An acclaimed poet, novelist and short-story writer from the 1950s, Bachmann was fascinated by the impotence of language and developed a voice of her own. For a flavour of her work, try the bilingual edition of her poems, *Songs in Flight*.

**Thomas Bernhard** *Cutting Timber*; *An Irritation*; *Wittgenstein's Nephew*; *Extinction*; *Concrete*; *The Voice Imitator*. Dense, stream-of-consciousness ruminations from one of the leading critics of the hypocrisy and mediocrity of postwar Austria. Any of the above will prove to be a good introduction to his inimitable style.

**Hermann Broch** *The Death of Virgil*; *The Guiltless*. With the Anschluss, Broch, who was of Jewish parentage, was briefly interned in a camp, where he began *The Death of Virgil*, which focuses on the last hours of Virgil's life and his questioning of the role his art has given him in society. *The Guiltless* is a more direct and readable examination of the dark side of mid-twentieth-century German culture.

**Lilian Faschinger** *Vienna Passion*. A complex tale, whose black New Yorker heroine, researching into Anna Freud in Vienna, comes across the fascinating story of Rosa Havelka, servant to the empress and mistress to the heir to the throne at the end of the nineteenth century.

**Peter Handke** *Plays 1*; *A Sorrow Beyond Dreams*. Handke is Austria's most provocative contemporary playwright, whose partnership with filmmaker Wim Wenders has brought him international recognition. *Plays 1* gives you six of his best from the 1960s and 1970s, including *Kaspar* and *Offending the Audience*, Handke's favourite pastime. *A Sorrow Beyond Dreams* is a short, painful and moving prose elegy to his mother, following her suicide.

**Elfriede Jelinek** *Wonderful, Wonderful Times*; *The Piano Teacher*; *Lust*; *Greed*. The works of the Nobel Prize-winning Jelinek are often an uncomfortable read: *The Piano Teacher* delves into the world of masochism and voyeurism; *Wonderful, Wonderful*

*Times*, which takes place in the late 1950s, digs up the city's murky past.

**Mike Mitchell** *The Dedalus Book of Austrian Fantasy.* Everything from Kafka to modern surreal for those whose taste is on the wild side.

**Robert Musil** *The Man Without Qualities; Diaries 1899–1941.* Often compared with Joyce and Proust, Musil's 1000-page unfinished novel, *The Man Without Qualities*, takes place at the twilight of the Habsburg Empire. Those addicted to Musil's irony-drenched, essayistic prose should also dip into his diaries.

**Josef Roth** *Radetsky March.* Pitifully underrated, this is Roth's finest work – a nostalgic and melancholic portrait of the moribund Vienna of Franz-Josef. Check also the secondhand stores for Roth's masterful short novels *Job*, *The Emperor's Tomb* and – above all – *Flight Without End*, a heartbreaking tale of dislocation and world-weariness.

**Arthur Schnitzler** *Hands Around; Dream Story.* Schnitzler's play features ten seductions, each of which shares at least one character with the next one until the circle is complete. A classic portrayal of decadent Viennese fin-de-siècle society, it came back to prominence in the 1950s after being filmed as *La Ronde* by Max Ophüls, and enjoyed a comeback in the late 1990s on the stage in an adaptation called *The Blue Room* by David Hare. *Dream Story* was the inspiration for Stanley Kubrick's last film *Eyes Wide Shut*.

**Harold B. Segel** (ed) *The Vienna Coffeehouse Wits 1890–1938.* A rare opportunity to read translated snippets of work by *Kaffeehaus* regulars such as Karl Kraus, Peter Altenberg and Felix Salten (the little-known author of *Bambi* and *The Story of a Vienna Whore*, one of which was made into a Disney cartoon).

**Stefan Zweig** *The Burning Secret and Other Stories.* Exquisitely wrought tales from fin-de-siècle Vienna, including *Letter from an Unknown Woman*, best and most poignant of Zweig's tales, and another story adapted into a movie by Ophüls.

# Literature by foreign writers

**Phil Andrews** *Goodnight Vienna.* A light read for football fans as the English soccer coach is under threat, a key player is murdered and the trail leads beneath the streets of Vienna.

**Richard and John Lehmann Bassett** *Vienna, a travellers' companion.* Out of print, but, if you can get hold of a copy, it features some interesting travellers' impressions from over the centuries.

**Elias Canetti** *Auto-da-Fé; Crowds and Power.* The first novel of the Nobel Prize-winning Canetti, a Bulgarian-born Sephardic Jew who wrote in German, revolves around the life of a miserable scholar living in fin-de-siècle Vienna. *Crowds and Power* is a nonfiction work about mob mentality inspired by Canetti's participation in the torching of Vienna's Justizpalast in 1934.

**Graham Greene** *The Third Man.* Written by Greene as a film treatment, this differs quite a bit from the eventual celluloid version; it's printed along with *Fallen Idol*, a story set in London.

**Eva Ibbotson** *The Star of Kazan.* Any 9- to 12-year-old who has fallen in love with the Lipizzaner stallions will enjoy this old-fashioned adventure story.

**John Irving** *Setting Free the Bears.* Stream-of-verbiage novel centred (vaguely) on Vienna's zoo after the war.

**Philip Kerr** *A German Requiem*. Final volume of a gripping spy trilogy set in postwar Vienna.

**Robert Löhr** *The Chess Machine*. Enjoyable novel set in 1770 in Vienna, based around the true story of the world's first chess computer.

**Jody Shields** *The Fig Eater*. It's 1910 in Vienna and a young girl, a patient of Freud, is murdered. A flawed but intriguing mystery that conjures up a vivid picture of turn-of-the-century Viennese society.

**Mary Stewart** *Airs Above the Ground*. Murder mystery written in the 1960s and set in and around Vienna's Spanish Riding School.

**Frank Tallis** *Mortal Mischief*; *Vienna Blood*. Intriguing murder mysteries set in Vienna at the turn of the century starring a disciple of Freud. Strong on detail and atmosphere.

# Art and architecture

**Laurenc Bonet** *Otto Wagner / Gustav Klimt*. A good selection of coloured illustrations in this two-for-the-price-of-one book.

**Christian Brandstätter** *Wonderful Wiener Werkstätte 1903–1932*. You couldn't wish for a more exhaustively illustrated book on the early twentieth-century designers.

**Alessandra Comini** *Egon Schiele*; *Gustav Klimt*. The former contains a good selection of full-colour reproductions, as well as an account of Schiele's life set into its cultural context; the latter deals with all facets of Klimt's art and traces connections with the work of his contemporaries and the theories of Freud.

**Peter Haiko and Roberto Schezen** *Vienna 1850–1930 Architecture*. The ultimate coffee-table book on Vienna's most important works of architecture, beautifully photographed (by Schezen) and intelligently discussed.

**Ingrid Helsing Almaas** *Vienna: A Guide to Recent Architecture*. Dinky, illustrated pocket guide to Vienna's modern architecture of the last couple of decades, with forthright accompanying critiques and interviews.

**Erwin Mitsch** *Egon Schiele*. Nicely produced, with a short introduction, then eighty colour plates and eighty more black-and-white photos.

**Harry Rand** *Hundertwasser*. This illustrated account of his work is illuminated by conversations between author and artist.

**Aldo Rossi, B. Gravagnuolo** *Adolf Loos*. A wonderfully illustrated book for the general reader, covering the life and works of the "father of modernism".

**Rolf Toman** (ed) *Vienna Art and Architecture*. A huge coffee-table volume covering the city from the Middle Ages to the present day, with numerous colour illustrations, accompanied by lots of informative text.

**Peter Vergo** *Art in Vienna 1898–1918*. Deals with the major artists of the Secession, including Klimt, Kokoschka and Schiele, and the development of the Wiener Werkstätte.

**Alfred Weidinger** *Kokoschka and Alma Mahler: Testimony to a Passionate Relationship*. Detailed account of the artist's doomed relationship with Mahler's widow, illustrated with lots of Kokoschka's drawings and paintings from the period.

**Patrick Werkner** *Austrian Expressionism: The Formative Years*. Interesting articles on Schönberg, Schiele, Kokoschka, Gerstl and Kubin; black-and-white illustration only.

# Language

# Language

# German

lthough a high proportion of Austrians speak some English, any of
your attempts to converse in a few phrases of **German** will be heartily
appreciated. That said, German is a highly complex language that you
can't hope to master quickly. The biggest problem for English-speakers is
that German words can be one of three genders: masculine, feminine or neuter.
Each has its own ending and corresponding ending for attached adjectives,
plus its own definite article. If in doubt, it's safest to use either the neuter or
male forms.

Pronunciation (and spelling) is less of a problem, as individual syllables are
generally pronounced as they're printed – the trick is learning how to place
the stresses in the notoriously lengthy German words. Though Austrians speak
German with a distinct accent, and the Viennese have their own dialect, when
speaking to a foreigner most folk will switch to standard German.

The following is a rundown of the basics you'll need on a city break to
Vienna. For more detail, check out the *Rough Guide German Phrasebook*, set out
dictionary-style for easy access, with English–German and German–English
sections, cultural tips for tricky situations and a menu reader.

## Vowels and umlauts

a as in rather
e as in gay
i as in feet
o as in nose
u as in boot
ä is a combination of a and e, sometimes

pronounced like e in bet (eg Länder) and
sometimes like ai in paid (eg spät).
ö is a combination of o and e, which has no
real English equivalent, but is similar to the
French *eu*.
ü is a combination of u and e, like blue.

## Vowel combinations

ai as in why
au as in mouse
ie as in tree

ei as in trial
eu as in boil

## Consonants

Consonants are pronounced as they are written,
with no silent letters. The differences from
English are:
j pronounced similar to an English y
r is given a dry throaty sound, similar to
French
s pronounced similar to, but slightly softer
than an English z
v pronounced somewhere between f and v

w pronounced like an English v
z pronounced ts
The German letter ß usually replaces ss in a
word: pronunciation is identical.
ch is a strong back-of-the-throat sound as in
the Scottish loch.
sp (at the start of a word) pronounced shp
st (at the start of a word) pronounced sht

# German words and phrases

## Basics

| | |
|---|---|
| Ja, Nein | Yes, No |
| Bitte | Please/You're welcome |
| Bitte schön | A more polite form of Bitte |
| Danke, Danke schön | Thank you, Thank you very much |
| Wo, Wann, Warum? | Where, when, why? |
| Wieviel? | How much? |
| Hier, Da | Here, there |
| Geöffnet, Offen, Auf | All mean "open" |
| Geschlossen, Zu | Both mean "closed" |
| Da drüben | Over there |
| Dieses | This one |
| Jenes | That one |
| Gross, Klein | Large, small |
| Mehr, Weniger | More, less |
| Wenig | A little |
| Viel | A lot |
| Billig, Teuer | Cheap, expensive |
| Gut, Schlecht | Good, bad |
| Heiss, Kalt | Hot, cold |
| Mit, Ohne | With, without |
| Rechts | Right |
| Links | Left |
| Gerade aus | Straight ahead |
| Geh weg | Go away |

## Greetings and times

| | |
|---|---|
| Grüss Gott | Good day |
| Guten Morgen | Good morning |
| Guten Abend | Good evening |
| Gute Nacht | Good night |
| Auf Wiedersehen | Goodbye |
| Auf Wiederhören | Goodbye (on the telephone) |
| Tschüs | Goodbye (informal) |
| Servus | Hello/Goodbye |
| Wie geht es Ihnen? | How are you? (polite) |
| Wie geht es dir? | How are you? (informal) |
| Heute | Today |
| Gestern | Yesterday |
| Morgen | Tomorrow |
| Vorgestern | The day before yesterday |
| Übermorgen | The day after tomorrow |
| Tag | Day |
| Nacht | Night |
| Mittag | Midday |
| Mitternacht | Midnight |
| Woche | Week |
| Wochenende | Weekend |
| Monat | Month |
| Jahr | Year |
| Am Vormittag/ Vormittags | In the morning |
| Am Nachmittag/ Nachmittags | In the afternoon |
| Am Abend | In the evening |

## Days, months and dates

| | |
|---|---|
| Montag | Monday |
| Dienstag | Tuesday |
| Mittwoch | Wednesday |
| Donnerstag | Thursday |
| Freitag | Friday |
| Samstag | Saturday |
| Sonntag | Sunday |
| Jänner | January |
| Februar | February |
| März | March |
| April | April |
| Mai | May |
| Juni | June |
| Juli | July |

| August | August | Winter | Winter |
|---|---|---|---|
| September | September | Ferien | Holidays |
| Oktober | October | Feiertag | Bank holiday |
| November | November | Montag, der erste April | Monday, the first of April |
| Dezember | December | | |
| Frühling | Spring | Der zweite April | The second of April |
| Sommer | Summer | Der dritte April | The third of April |
| Herbst | Autumn | | |

## Some signs

| Damen/Frauen | Women's toilets | Notausgang | Emergency exit |
|---|---|---|---|
| Herren/Männer | Men's toilets | Krankenhaus | Hospital |
| Eingang | Entrance | Polizei | Police |
| Ausgang | Exit | Nicht rauchen | No smoking |
| Ankunft | Arrival | Kein Eingang | No entrance |
| Abfahrt | Departure | Drücken | Push |
| Ausstellung | Exhibition | Ziehen | Pull |
| Autobahn | Motorway | Frei | Vacant |
| Umleitung | Diversion | Besetzt | Occupied |
| Achtung! | Attention! | Verboten | Prohibited |
| Vorsicht! | Beware! | Kasse | Cash desk/ticket office |
| Not | Emergency | | |

## Questions and requests

All enquiries should start with the phrase *Entschuldigen Sie bitte* (Excuse me, please). Though strictly you should use *Sie*, the polite form of address, with everyone except close friends, young people often don't bother with it. However, the older generation and anyone official will certainly be offended if you address them with the familiar *Du*.

| Sprechen Sie Englisch? | Do you speak English? | Wieviel Uhr ist es? | What time is it? |
|---|---|---|---|
| Ich spreche kein Deutsch | I don't speak German | Sind die Plätze noch frei? | Are these seats taken? |
| Sprechen Sie bitte langsamer | Please speak more slowly | Die Rechnung bitte | The bill please |
| | | Ist der Tisch frei? | Is that table free? |
| Ich verstehe nicht | I don't understand | Die Speisekarte bitte | The menu please |
| Ich verstehe | I understand | Fräulein . . . ! | Waitress . . . ! (for attention) |
| Wie sagt mann das auf Deutsch? | How do you say that in German? | Herr Ober . . . ! | Waiter . . . ! (for attention) |
| Können Sie mir sagen wo . . . ist? | Can you tell me where . . . is? | Haben Sie etwas billigeres? | Have you got something cheaper? |
| Wo ist . . . ? | Where is . . . ? | Haben Sie Zimmer frei? | Are there rooms available? |
| Wieviel kostet das? | How much does that cost? | Wo sind die Toiletten bitte? | Where are the toilets please? |
| Wann fährt der nächste Zug? | When does the next train leave? | | |
| Um wieviel Uhr? | At what time? | Ich hätte gern dieses | I'd like that one |

| Ich hätte gern ein Zimmer für zwei | I'd like a room for two | Hat es Dusche, Bad, Toilette? | Does it have a shower, bath, toilet? |
| Ich hätte gern ein Einzelzimmer | I'd like a single room | | |

## Numbers

| | | | |
|---|---|---|---|
| null | 0 | neunzehn | 19 |
| eins | 1 | zwanzig | 20 |
| zwei | 2 | ein-und-zwanzig | 21 |
| drei | 3 | zwei-und-zwanzig | 22 |
| vier | 4 | dreissig | 30 |
| fünf | 5 | vierzig | 40 |
| sechs | 6 | fünfzig | 50 |
| sieben | 7 | sechzig | 60 |
| acht | 8 | siebzig | 70 |
| neun | 9 | achtzig | 80 |
| zehn | 10 | neunzig | 90 |
| elf | 11 | hundert | 100 |
| zwölf | 12 | tausend | 1000 |
| dreizehn | 13 | neunzehn-hundert-neun-und-neunzig | 1999 |
| vierzehn | 14 | | |
| fünfzehn | 15 | zweitausand | 2000 |
| sechszehn | 16 | zweitausand-und-fünf | 2005 |
| siebzehn | 17 | | |
| achtzehn | 18 | zweitausand-und-sechs | 2006 |

# Food and drink

## Basics

| | | | |
|---|---|---|---|
| Abendessen | supper/dinner | Mittagessen | lunch |
| Auflauf | omelette | Nachspeise | dessert |
| Beilagen | side dishes | Öl | oil |
| Brot | bread | Pfeffer | pepper |
| Butter | butter | Reis | rice |
| Ei | egg | Salat | salad |
| Frühstuck | breakfast | Salz | salt |
| Gabel | fork | Semmel | bread roll |
| Gebäck | pastries | Senf | mustard |
| Hauptgericht | main course | Spätzle/Nocker | pasta/noodles |
| Honig | honey | Speisekarte | menu |
| Käse | cheese | Suppe | soup |
| Knödel | dumplings | Tasse | cup |
| Kren | horseradish | Teller | plate |
| Löffel | spoon | Vorspeise | starter |
| Messer | knife | Zucker | sugar |

# Vegetables (Gemüse)

| | | | |
|---|---|---|---|
| Blaukraut | red cabbage | Kohlsprossen | Brussels sprouts |
| Bohnen | beans | Lauch | leek |
| Champignons | button mushrooms | Maiskolben | corn on the cob |
| Erbsen | peas | Paprika | green or red peppers |
| Erdäpfel | potatoes | | |
| Fisolen | green beans | Paradeiser | tomatoes |
| G'röste | fried grated potatoes | Pilze | mushrooms |
| | | Pommes Frites | chips/French fries |
| Gurke | gherkin/cucumber | Rote Rübe | beetroot |
| Karfiol | cauliflower | Sauerkraut | pickled cabbage |
| Karotten | carrots | Spargel | asparagus |
| Knoblauch | garlic | Spinat | spinach |
| Kohl | cabbage | Zwiebeln | onions |

# Meat (Fleisch) and poultry (Geflügel)

| | | | |
|---|---|---|---|
| Eisbein | pig's trotters | Kuttelfleck | tripe |
| Ente | duck | Lamm | lamb |
| Fasan | pheasant | Leber | liver |
| Gans | goose | Nieren | kidneys |
| Hackfleisch | mincemeat | Puter | turkey |
| Hammelfleisch | mutton | Rindfleisch | beef |
| Hase | hare | Schinken | ham |
| Hirn | brains | Schweinefleisch | pork |
| Hirsch | venison | Speck | bacon |
| Huhn | chicken | Taube | pigeon |
| Innereien | innards | Zunge | tongue |
| Kalbfleisch | veal | | |

# Fish (Fisch)

| | | | |
|---|---|---|---|
| Aal | eel | Matjes | herring |
| Forelle | trout | Meeresfrüchte | seafood |
| Hecht | pike | Muscheln | mussels |
| Hummer | lobster | Scholle | plaice |
| Karpfen | carp | Seezunge | sole |
| Krabben | prawns | Thunfisch | tuna |
| Krebs | crab | Tintenfisch | squid |
| Lachs | salmon | Zander | pike-perch |
| Makrele | mackerel | | |

# Common food terms

| | | | |
|---|---|---|---|
| Am Spiess | on the spit | Gebacken | fried in breadcrumbs |
| Blau | rare | Gebraten | roasted |
| Eingelegte | pickled | Gedämpft | steamed |
| Frisch | fresh | Gefüllt | stuffed |

| Gegrillt | grilled | Kalt | cold |
| Gekocht | cooked | Kümmelbraten | roasted with caraway |
| Geräucht | smoked | | seeds |
| Hausgemacht | home-made | Powidl | plum sauce |
| Heiss | hot | | |

## Fruit (Obst)

| Ananas | pineapple | Himbeeren | raspberries |
| Apfel | apple | Kirschen | cherries |
| Banane | banana | Marillen | apricots |
| Birne | pear | Pflaumen | plums |
| Brombeeren | blackberries | Ribisel | redcurrants |
| Erdbeeren | strawberries | Rosinen | raisins |
| Grapefruit | grapefruit | Trauben | grapes |
| Heidelbeeren | bilberries | Zwetschgen | plums |

## Desserts

See also the "Coffee and cakes" colour insert.

| Baiser | meringue | Käsekuchen | cheesecake |
| Bienenstich | honey and almond tart | Marillenknödel | sweet apricot dumplings |
| Buchteln | sweet dumplings | Mohr im Hemd | chocolate steamed pudding with cream |
| Kaiserschmarren | pancake and stewed fruit | Palatschinken | pancakes |

## Austrian specialities

| Backhendl | chicken fried in breadcrumbs | Schlipfkrapfen | ravioli-like pasta parcels with a meat and/or potato filling |
| Bauernschmaus | platter of cold sausage, pork and ham | Schweinshaxe | pork knuckle |
| | | Stelze | leg of veal or pork |
| Beuschel | chopped lung | Tafelspitz | boiled beef, potatoes and horseradish sauce |
| Brettljause | platter of cold meats and bread | | |
| Debreziner | paprika-spiced sausage | Tiroler Gröstl | potatoes, onions and flecks of meat fried in a pan |
| Grammelknödel | pork dumplings | | |
| Kärntner Käsnudl | large parcel of pasta dough filled with cheese | Tiroler Knödel | dumplings with pieces of ham, often eaten in a soup |
| Kasspätzln | pasta noodles with cheese | Wiener Schnitzel | breaded veal |
| Schinkenfleckern | ham with noodles | Zwiebelrostbraten | slices of roast beef topped with fried onions |

# Drinks (Getränke)

| | | | |
|---|---|---|---|
| **Apfelsaft** | apple juice | **Obstler** | fruit schnapps |
| **Bier** | beer | **Orangensaft** | orange juice |
| **Flasche** | bottle | **Roséwein** | rosé wine |
| **Gespritzer** | white wine with soda | **Rotwein** | red wine |
| **Glühwein** | mulled wine | **Sauermilch** | sour milk |
| **Grog** | hot water with rum and sugar | **Schnapps** | spirit |
| **Kaffee** | coffee | **Sekt** | sparkling wine |
| **Kakao** | cocoa | **Sturm** | new wine |
| **Kir** | white wine with blackcurrant | **Tee** | tea |
| | | **Traubensaft** | grape juice |
| **Korn** | rye spirit | **Trocken** | dry |
| **Kräutertee** | herbal tea | **Wasser** | water |
| **Milch** | milk | **Weisswein** | white wine |
| **Mineralwasser** | mineral water | **Zitronentee** | tea with lemon |

# Glossary

## German terms

**Ausstellung** Exhibition

**Bahnhof** Station

**Bau** Building

**Beisl** Pub

**Berg** Mountain, hill

**Bezirk** City district

**Brücke** Bridge

**Brünn** Brno, capital of Moravia (Czech Republic)

**Brunnen** Fountain

**Burg** Castle

**Denkmal** Memorial

**Dom** Cathedral

**Donau** River Danube

**Dorf** Village

**Durchgang** Passageway

**Durchhaus** Literally a "through-house" – a house whose ground floor is open, allowing access to a street or courtyard

**Einbahnstrasse** One-way street

**Erdgeschoss** Ground floor

**Erzherzog** Archduke

**Fasching** Carnival

**Feiertag** Holiday

**Flughafen** Airport

**Friedhof** Cemetery

**Fussgängerzone** Pedestrian zone

**Gasse** Alley

**Gemälde** Painting

**Gemütlich** Snug or cosy

**Grab** Grave

**Gürtel** The city's outer ring road

**Haltestelle** Bus/tram stop

**Haus** House

**Herzog** Duke

**Heuriger** Wine tavern

**Hof** Court, courtyard, mansion, housing complex

**Innere Stadt** Vienna's first district, the "Inner City"

**Jugendherberge** Youth hostel

**Kaffeehaus** Café

**Kaiser** Emperor

**Kapelle** Chapel

**Kärnten** Carinthia

**Kaserne** Barracks

**Kino** Cinema

**Kirche** Church

**Kloster** Monastery, convent

**König** King

**Kunst** Art

**Kunstkammer** Cabinet of curios

**Land** (pl. Länder) Name given to each of the nine federal provinces of Austria

**Niederösterreich** Lower Austria

**Not** Emergency

**Oberösterreich** Upper Austria

**Palast** Palace

**Platz** Square

**Pressburg** Bratislava, capital of Slovakia

**Prinz** Prince

**Rathaus** Town hall

**Reich** Empire

**Residenz** Palace

**Ring** The Ringstrasse, built on the old fortifications in 1857

**Ritter** Knight

**Saal** Hall

**Sammlung** Collection

**Säule** Column

Schanigarten Summer terrace/backyard

Schatzkammer Treasury

Schloss Castle

Stadt Town

Steiermark Styria

Stiege Steps

Stift Collegiate church

Stock Floor

Strasse Street

Tor Gate

Trakt Wing (of a building)

Turm Tower

Viertel Quarter, district

Volk People, folk

Vororte The outer suburbs which lie beyond the Gürtel: Vienna's tenth to twenty-second districts

Vorstädte The inner suburbs which lie between the Ring and the Gürtel: Vienna's third to ninth districts

Wald Forest

Wien Vienna

Zimmer Room

## Political terms and acronyms

Anschluss Literally a "joining together" or "union" – the euphemism coined by the Nazis for the invasion and annexation of Austria in March 1938.

Austro-fascism Term to describe the one-party state set up by Engelbert Dollfuss in 1934. Dollfuss headed the Fatherland Front, a non-Nazi clerical-fascist movement which lasted until the Anschluss in 1938.

Austro-Marxism Philosophy expounded by SDAP theorists such as Otto Bauer in the early twentieth century. While still adhering to the language of class war, its programme was essentially revisionist, arguing that the downfall of capitalism was inevitable, and didn't have to be brought about by violence.

Babenburg Dynasty who ruled over Austria from 976 to 1246.

Biedermeier The term (Bieder means "upright") derives from the satiric figure of Gottlieb Biedermeier, a Swabian schoolmaster created in 1850 by Ludwig Eichrocht, modelled on Eichrocht's own pious, law-abiding teacher in Baden-Baden, Samuel Sauter. It has come to be applied retrospectively to the period between 1815 and 1848 when Austria was under the sway of Prince Metternich. The era came to symbolize a safe, bourgeois, cosy lifestyle, and was applied to the history, art and culture of the period.

BZÖ (Bündis Zukunft Österreich). The rather ominous-sounding Alliance for the Future of Austria is a far-right party founded in 2005 by Jörg Haider and other

leading members of the FPÖ. In the 2006 parliamentary elections, the party gained seven seats.

CSP (Christlichsoziale Partei). The Christian Social Party was founded in the 1890s by Karl Lueger, who later became mayor of Vienna. The Christian Socials' combination of Catholicism, municipal socialism and anti-Semitism proved very popular with the Austrians. They were the main party of government in the 1920s and from their ranks rose Engelbert Dollfuss, who later introduced Austro-fascism in 1933.

FPÖ (Freiheitliche Partei Österreichs). The Austrian Freedom Party was the successor to the postwar VdU (see p.321). A far-right party which rose to prominence in the 1990s and scored spectacular electoral success under the charismatic and controversial leadership of Jörg Haider.

Habsburg Royal dynasty whose power base was Vienna from 1273 to 1918. They also held the office of Holy Roman Emperor from 1452 to 1806, and by marriage, war and diplomacy acquired territories all over Europe.

Heimwehr Right-wing militia whose origins lay in the local armed groups formed after the collapse of the empire in 1918. After 1927, these regional militias joined together and created a political wing, the Heimatblock, which supported the onset of Austro-fascism in 1933.

Holy Roman Empire Revived title of the Roman Empire first bestowed by the pope on Charlemagne in 800. The emperor was chosen by the seven electors and passed around between the Hohenstaufen, Luxembourg and Habsburg families until 1438, when the Habsburgs made the title hereditary. It was dissolved on the orders of Napoleon in 1806.

**Josephine** Of or pertaining to the reign of Emperor Josef II (1780–90).

**KPÖ** (Kommunistische Partei Österreichs). Austrian Communist Party.

**Kristallnacht** Literally "Crystal Night", after the broken glass which was strewn across the streets during the pogrom of November 9–10, 1938. On this one night the majority of Jewish shops and institutions in the Third Reich – and all but one of the synagogues in Vienna – were destroyed by the Nazis.

**k.u.k.** kaiserlich und königlich (Imperial and Royal) – a title used after 1867 to refer to everything in the Austro-Hungarian empire. Everything within Hungary was prefaced with a k for königlich, everything in the rest of the empire k. k. (kaiserlich-königlich; Imperial-Royal). For more details.

**NSDAP** (National Sozialistische Deutsche Arbeiterpartei). National Socialist German Workers' Party, the official name for the German Nazi Party.

**ÖVP** (Österreichische Volkspartei). Austrian People's Party, the postwar descendant of the Christian Socials, and the principal postwar centre-right party.

**Pan-German** This adjective covers a whole range of far-right political parties which advocated Anschluss with Germany, many of whom came together in the 1920s under the banner of the Greater German People's Party (Grossdeutsche Volkspartei, GDVP).

**Red Vienna** The period of Socialist municipal government in Vienna which lasted from 1919 to 1934.

**Schutzbund** SDAP militia founded in 1923.

**SDAP** (Sozial-Demokratische Arbeiterpartei). Social Democratic Workers' Party, the name given to the Socialist Party prior to World War II.

**SPÖ** (Sozialistische Partei Österreichs). The postwar Austrian Socialist Party, later changed to the Sozialdemokratische Partei Österreichs, but keeping the same acronym.

**Staatsvertrag** The Austrian State Treaty of 1955, which signalled the withdrawal of Allied troops – American, British, French and Soviet – from Austria, in return for Austrian neutrality.

**Toleranzpatent** The Patent of Tolerance decreed by Josef II in 1782, which allowed freedom of religious observance to Lutherans, Jews and, to a lesser extent, Protestants.

**VdU** (Verband der Unabhängigen). Union of Independents. Extreme nationalist party formed in 1949 and precursor of the FPÖ.

**VF** (Vaterländische Front). The Fatherland Front was founded in 1934 by Engelbert Dollfuss, the Christian Social Austrian chancellor who dissolved parliament and introduced Austro-fascism in 1933. The Front was a patriotic, clerical-fascist organization aimed at preventing the Nazis from seizing power.

## Architectural terms

**Ambulatory** Passage round the back of a church altar, in continuation of the aisles.

**Art Nouveau** Sinuous and stylized form of architecture and decorative arts, known as Secession or Jugendstil in Austria.

**Atlantes** Pillars in the shape of musclemen, named after the Greek god Atlas whose job it was to hold up the world.

**Baldachin** A canopy over an altar, tomb, throne or otherwise.

**Baroque** Expansive, exuberant architectural style of the seventeenth and eighteenth centuries, characterized by ornate decoration, complex spatial arrangement and grand vistas.

**Biedermeier** Simple, often Neoclassical, style of art and architecture popular from 1815 to 1848 and in part a reaction against the excesses of the Baroque period.

**Caryatid** Sculptured female figure used as a column. Similar to Atlantes (see above).

**Chancel** Part of the church where the main altar is placed, usually at the east end.

**Diapers** Ornamental patterning in brickwork.

**Empire** Neoclassical style of architecture and decorative arts practised in the first half of the nineteenth century.

**Filigree** Fanciful, delicate ornamental decoration in stone or metal.

**Fresco** Mural painting applied to wet plaster, so that the colours immediately soak into the wall.

**Glacis** Sloping ground between walls of Vienna's Innere Stadt and the suburbs prior to 1857.

**Gothic** Architectural style prevalent from the twelfth to the sixteenth centuries, characterized by pointed arches and ribbed vaulting.

**Historicism** Style of architecture which apes previous styles – ie neo-Baroque, neo-Renaissance, neo-Gothic – also known as Ringstrasse style.

**Jugendstil** German/Austrian version of Art Nouveau, literally "youthful style" – see also Secession, below.

**Loggia** Covered area on the side of a building, usually arcaded.

**Lunette** An oval or semicircular opening to admit light into a dome.

**Nave** Main body of a church, usually the western end.

**Neoclassicism** Late eighteenth- and early nineteenth-century style of architecture and design returning to classical Greek and Roman models as a reaction against the excesses of Baroque and Rococo.

**Oriel** A bay window, usually projecting from an upper floor.

**Quoins** External corner stones of a wall.

**Ringstrasse** Pompous historicist style of architecture which aped Gothic, Renaissance, Baroque and Classical architecture, and which was very popular during the construction of Vienna's Ringstrasse.

**Rococo** Highly florid style of architecture and design, forming the last phase of Baroque.

**Romanesque** Solid architectural style of the late tenth to thirteenth centuries, characterized by round-headed arches and geometrical precision.

**Secession** Movement of artists who split (seceded – hence the term) from the city's Academy of Arts in 1897. Also used more generally as a term synonymous with Jugendstil.

**Sgraffito** Monochrome plaster decoration effected by means of scraping back the first white layer to reveal the black underneath.

**Spandrel** The surface area between two adjacent arches.

**Stucco** Plaster used for decorative effects.

**Transepts** The wings of a cruciform church, placed at right angles to the nave and chancel.

**Trompe l'oeil** Painting designed to fool the onlooker into thinking that it is three-dimensional.

**Wiener Werkstätte** (Vienna Workshops). A group of Secession artists founded in 1903.

# Travel store

- **Read** Rough Guides' trusted travel info
- **Access** exclusive articles from Rough Guides authors
- **Update** yourself on new books, maps, CDs and other products
- **Enter** our competitions and win travel prizes
- **Share** ideas, journals, photos & travel advice with other users
- **Earn** points every time you contribute to the Rough Guide community and get rewards

## BROADEN YOUR HORIZONS

ROUGH GUIDES

**D**: Rough Guide
**DIRECTIONS** for
short breaks

Available from all good bookstores

**ROUGH** GUIDES Complete Listing

For more information go to www.roughguides.com

ROUGH
GUIDES

# Avoid Guilt Trips

Buy fair trade coffee + bananas ✓

Save energy – use low energy bulbs ✓
- don't leave tv on standby ✓

Offset carbon emissions from flight to Madrid

Send goat to Africa ✓

Join Tourism Concern today ✓

## Slowly, the world is changing.
### *Together we can, and will, make a difference.*

**Tourism Concern** is the only UK registered charity fighting exploitation in one of the largest industries on earth: people forced from their homes in order that holiday resorts can be built, sweatshop labour conditions in hotels and destruction of the environment are just some of the issues that we tackle.

Sending people on a guilt trip is not something we do. We know as well as anyone that holidays are precious. But you can help us to ensure that tourism always benefits the local communities involved.

### Call 020 7133 3330
or visit **tourismconcern.org.uk** to find out how.

*A year's membership of Tourism Concern costs just £20 (£12 unwaged) – that's 38 pence a week, less than the cost of a pint of milk, organic of course.*

Fighting Exploitation in Tourism

# TourismConcern

# Small print and
# Index

# A Rough Guide to Rough Guides

Published in 1982, the first Rough Guide – to Greece – was a student scheme that became a publishing phenomenon. Mark Ellingham, a recent graduate in English from Bristol University, had been travelling in Greece the previous summer and couldn't find the right guidebook. With a small group of friends he wrote his own guide, combining a highly contemporary, journalistic style with a thoroughly practical approach to travellers' needs.

The immediate success of the book spawned a series that rapidly covered dozens of destinations. And, in addition to impecunious backpackers, Rough Guides soon acquired a much broader and older readership that relished the guides' wit and inquisitiveness as much as their enthusiastic, critical approach and value-for-money ethos.

These days, Rough Guides include recommendations from shoestring to luxury and cover more than 200 destinations around the globe, including almost every country in the Americas and Europe, more than half of Africa and most of Asia and Australasia. Our ever-growing team of authors and photographers is spread all over the world, particularly in Europe, the USA and Australia.

In the early 1990s, Rough Guides branched out of travel, with the publication of Rough Guides to World Music, Classical Music and the Internet. All three have become benchmark titles in their fields, spearheading the publication of a wide range of books under the Rough Guide name.

Including the travel series, Rough Guides now number more than 350 titles, covering: phrasebooks, waterproof maps, music guides from Opera to Heavy Metal, reference works as diverse as Conspiracy Theories and Shakespeare, and popular culture books from iPods to Poker. Rough Guides also produce a series of more than 120 World Music CDs in partnership with World Music Network.

Visit www.roughguides.com to see our latest publications.

Rough Guide travel images are available for commercial licensing at www.roughguidespictures.com

# Rough Guide credits

**Text editor**: Samantha Cook
**Layout**: Nikhil Agarwal
**Cartography**: Katie Lloyd-Jones and The Map Studio
**Picture editor**: Sarah Cummins
**Production**: Rebecca Short
**Proofreader**: Diane Margolis
**Cover design**: Chloë Roberts
**Photographer**: Natascha Sturny
**Editorial**: **London** Ruth Blackmore, Alison Murchie, Karoline Thomas, Andy Turner, Keith Drew, Edward Aves, Alice Park, Lucy White, Jo Kirby, James Smart, Natasha Foges, Róisín Cameron, Emma Traynor, Emma Gibbs, James Rice, Kathryn Lane, Christina Valhouli, Monica Woods, Mani Ramaswamy, Joe Staines, Peter Buckley, Matthew Milton, Tracy Hopkins, Ruth Tidball; **New York** Andrew Rosenberg, Steven Horak, AnneLise Sorensen, April Isaacs, Ella Steim, Paula Nevderf, Courtney Miller, Anna Owens, Sean Mahoney; **Delhi** Madhavi Singh, Karen D'Souza
**Design & Pictures**: **London** Scott Stickland, Dan May, Diana Jarvis, Mark Thomas, Nicole Newman, Emily Taylor; **Delhi** Umesh Aggarwal,

Ajay Verma, Jessica Subramanian, Ankur Guha, Pradeep Thapliyal, Sachin Tanwar, Anita Singh
**Production**: Vicky Baldwin
**Cartography**: **London** Maxine Repath, Ed Wright; **Delhi** Jai Prakash Mishra, Rajesh Chhibber, Ashutosh Bharti, Rajesh Mishra, Animesh Pathak, Jasbir Sandhu, Karobi Gogoi, Amod Singh, Alakananda Bhattacharya, Swati Handoo
**Online**: Narender Kumar, Rakesh Kumar, Amit Verma, Rahul Kumar, Ganesh Sharma, Debojit Borah, Saurabh Sati, Ravi Yadav
**Marketing & Publicity**: **London** Liz Statham, Niki Hanmer, Louise Maher, Jess Carter, Vanessa Godden, Vivienne Watton, Anna Paynton, Rachel Sprackett, Libby Jellie; **New York** Geoff Colquitt, Katy Ball; **Delhi** Ragini Govind
**Manager India**: Punita Singh
**Reference Director**: Andrew Lockett
**Operations Manager**: Helen Phillips
**PA to Publishing Director**: Nicola Henderson
**Publishing Director**: Martin Dunford
**Commercial Manager**: Gino Magnotta
**Managing Director**: John Duhigg

# Publishing information

This fifth edition published July 2008 by
**Rough Guides Ltd**,
80 Strand, London WC2R 0RL
345 Hudson St, 4th Floor,
New York, NY 10014, USA
14 Local Shopping Centre, Panchsheel Park,
New Delhi 110017, India
**Distributed by the Penguin Group**
Penguin Books Ltd,
80 Strand, London WC2R 0RL
Penguin Group (USA)
375 Hudson Street, NY 10014, USA
Penguin Group (Australia)
250 Camberwell Road, Camberwell,
Victoria 3124, Australia
Penguin Books Canada Ltd,
10 Alcorn Avenue, Toronto, Ontario,
Canada M4V 1E4
Penguin Group (NZ)
67 Apollo Drive, Mairangi Bay, Auckland 1310,
New Zealand

Cover concept by Peter Dyer.
Typeset in Bembo and Helvetica to an original design by Henry Iles.
Printed and bound in China
© Rob Humphreys
No part of this book may be reproduced in any form without permission from the publisher except for the quotation of brief passages in reviews.
368pp includes index
A catalogue record for this book is available from the British Library
ISBN: 978-1-85828-620-4

1   3   5   7   9   8   6   4   2

# Help us update

We've gone to a lot of effort to ensure that the fifth edition of **The Rough Guide to Vienna** is accurate and up to date. However, things change – places get "discovered", opening hours are notoriously fickle, restaurants and rooms raise prices or lower standards. If you feel we've got it wrong or left something out, we'd like to know, and if you can remember the address, the price, the hours, the phone number, so much the better.

Please send your comments with the subject line "**Rough Guide Vienna Update**" to ©mail @roughguides.com. We'll credit all contributions and send a copy of the next edition (or any other Rough Guide if you prefer) for the very best emails.

Have your questions answered and tell others about your trip at ⊛community.roughguides.com

**ROUGH GUIDES**

**SMALL PRINT**

## Acknowledgements

Thanks to Kate for testing out the daybed, Val for the biblio and to Sam for sympathetic editing.

## Readers' letters

Thank you to all those readers who took the trouble to write in with their comments and suggestions (apologies for any misspellings or omissions):

Joan Allen, Muriel Cole, Ernst Genser, Dr John Kirkaldy, Roger & Andrea Mays, B W B Turner

## Photo credits

All photography by Natascha Sturny © Rough Guides except the following:

**Introduction**
View over Michaelerplatz © Aingolf Pompe/
  Getty Images
Strudel © Elan Fleisher/Getty Images
Majolikahaus © Jon Arnold Images/Alamy
Mozart Monument © Gary Cralle/Getty Images
Tram © Rob Humphreys

**Things not to miss**
**04** *The Third Man*
  © The Kobal Collection/London Films
**13** Schatzkammer © Corbis
**14** Belvedere (*Judith*, 1901, by Gustav Klimt )
  © Getty Images/Bridgeman Art Library

**The Secession colour section**
*Hygieia* (1900–7) Gustav Klimt, details from
  *Medicine* © Getty Images
Wiener Werkstätte vases and fabric
  © The Bachcausen Company
Beethoven Frieze by Gustav Klimt © Imagno/
  Gerhard Trumler
*Ver Sacrum* cover © Imagno/Austrian Archives/
  Getty Images
Kunstschau Poster, May–October 1908, by Oskar
  Kokoschka © The Bridgeman Art Library

**Black and whites**
**p.80** Elizabeth of Austria © Iconotec/Alamy

SMALL PRINT

*Selected images from our guidebooks are available for licensing from:*
**ROUGHGUIDESPICTURES.COM**

# Index

Map entries are in colour.

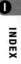

# C

INDEX

# M

# P

# R

# S

# Y

# Z

# Map symbols

maps are listed in the full index using coloured text

| | | | | |
|---|---|---|---|---|
| – – – | Chapter boundary | ▲ | Peak |
| – – –· | International boundary | ✈ | Airport |
| | Motorway | Ⓤ | U-Bahn |
| | Major road | Ⓢ | S-Bahn |
| | Minor road | ✡ | Synagogue |
| ⊞⊞⊞⊞⊞ | Steps | ⋈ | Mosque |
| )········( | Underpass tunnel | ⓘ | Information office |
| | Railway | ⊠ | Post office |
| | Tram line | | Park |
| | River/canal | | Building |
| ▪▪▪▪ | Wall | | Church |
| ⊠—⊠ | Gate | ⬭ | Stadium |
| ⊤ | Fountain | | Christian cemetery |
| ⚊ | Campsite | | Jewish cemetery |

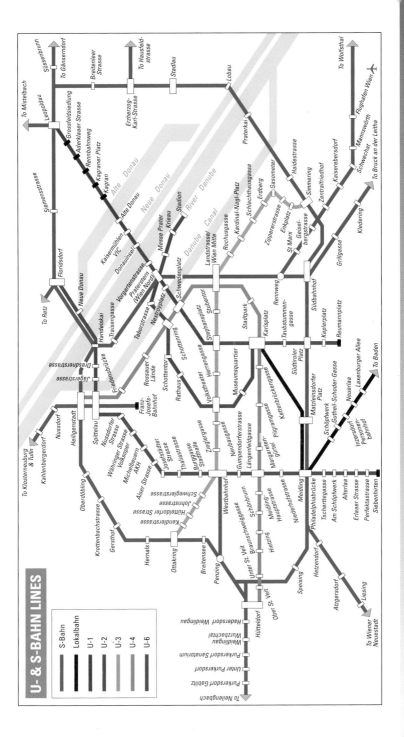

# U- & S-BAHN LINES

S-Bahn
Lokalbahn
U-1
U-2
U-3
U-4
U-6

**TRAM, BUS AND U-BAHN ROUTES**

Legend:
- Bus Route
- Tram routes
- U-1
- U-2
- U-3
- U-4
- U-6

0 — 500 m

Handelskai · River Danube · Dresdnerstrasse · STROMSTRASSE · Jägerstrasse · DRESDNERSTRASSE · UNO-City · Praterstern · Taborstrasse · Wien-Nord · Nestroyplatz · Schwedenplatz · Wien-Mitte · Landstrasse/Wien-Mitte · Stubentor · Stadtpark · Rochusgasse · RENNWEG · Südbahnhof · Südtiroler Platz · WIEDNER GÜRTEL

Spittelau · HEILIGENSTÄDTER STRASSE · DÖBLINGER HAUPTSTRASSE · Nussdorferstrasse · KLOSTERNEUBURGER STRASSE · Franz-Josefs-bahnhof · Friedensbrücke · OBERE AUGARTENSTRASSE · Danube Canal · Währinger Strasse Volksoper · NUSSDORFERSTRASSE · WÄHRINGER GÜRTEL · Michelbeuern AKH · Alser Strasse · SPITALGASSE · WÄHRINGERSTRASSE · Schottenring · Schottentor · FRANZ-JOSEFS-KAI · SCHOTTENRING · DR-KARL-LUEGER-RING · Herrengasse · Stephansplatz · STUBENRING · Rathaus · Volkstheater · BURGRING · OPERNRING · Stubentor · Museumsquartier · Karlsplatz · Herrengasse

Josefstädter Strasse · ALSERSTRASSE · JOSEFSTÄDTER STRASSE · Thalia strasse · LERCHENFELDER STRASSE · Burggasse Stadthalle · Volkstheater · Neubaugasse · MARIAHILFERSTR. · Zieglergasse · West-bahnhof · Westbahnhof · GUMPENDORFER STRASSE · Gumpendorfer Strasse · MARGARETENGÜRTEL · Margaretengürtel · Pilgramgasse · Kettenbrücken-gasse · WIEDNER HAUPTSTRASSE · Taubstummen-gasse · PRINZ-EUGEN-STRASSE · UNGARGASSE · Längenfeldgasse · Schönbrunn

35A · 10A · 37A, 40A · 37 · D · 38 · 40, 41 · 42 · 43 · 44 · 5, 23 · 46 · 48A · 49 · 5 · 13A · 14A · 12A · 62 · 6, 18, 62 · 10A · 57A · 6, 18 · 57A · 12A · 62, 65 · 59A · 13A · 18 · 71 · 35A · 35A · 31, 33 · 5A, 35A · DRESDNERSTRASSE · 5 · 21, N · 21 · 5A · 40A · 37, 38, 40, 41, 42 · 1, 2, D · 1, 2, N · 1, 2 · 6, 33 · J · D

N